AMERICAN FOREIGN RELATIONS
1974
A DOCUMENTARY RECORD

COUNCIL ON FOREIGN RELATIONS BOOKS

AMERICAN FOREIGN RELATIONS 1974

A DOCUMENTARY RECORD

Continuing the Series
DOCUMENTS ON AMERICAN FOREIGN RELATIONS
THE UNITED STATES IN WORLD AFFAIRS

Edited by RICHARD P. STEBBINS and ELAINE P. ADAM

A Council on Foreign Relations Book
Published by
New York University Press • New York • 1977

PREFACE

This volume combines a narrative account of America's foreign relations during 1974 with a selection of the important documents reflecting the national experience in that critical year. On the narrative side, it continues the series of annual foreign policy surveys initiated by the Council on Foreign Relations in 1931 and issued with some regularity, under the title *The United States in World Affairs*, until the inception of the present series in 1971. In addition, the volume's documentary content continues the service provided for more than three decades by the *Documents on American Foreign Relations* series, initiated by the World Peace Foundation in 1939 and carried forward by the Council on Foreign Relations from 1952 through 1970. The fusion of narrative and documentation, commenced on a trial basis on the inauguration of the present series in 1971, is designed to provide a single, comprehensive, and authoritative nongovernmental record of American foreign policy as it develops through the bicentennial decade and beyond.

The interests of orderly presentation have appeared best served by the inclusion of an introductory essay followed by a series of broadly chronological chapters, each focused on one or two outstanding developments in a particular area of foreign policy concern. Within each chapter, the story is told in part by the editors (whose contributions are invariably enclosed within square brackets) and in part by the documents themselves, which are presented in authoritative texts with whatever editorial apparatus seemed necessary for independent reference use. Footnote citations of the relevant source materials are presented in condensed form, and publications referred to by abbreviated titles are fully identified in the Appendix, which lists the principal documentary and secondary works found useful in preparing the volume. All dates refer to the year 1974 unless a different year is specifically indicated.

The editorial procedure adopted in this series admittedly involves considerable exercise of individual judgment and demands all possible objectivity in the handling of controversial events and data. While hopeful that the volume will not be found wanting in these respects, the editors wish to emphasize that the editorial viewpoint is of necessity a personal one and in no way reflects the outlook of the Council on Foreign Relations or any of its officers and directors, members, or staff.

Among their immediate associates, the editors would note their special indebtedness to John Temple Swing, Vice-President and

v

Secretary; Grace Darling Griffin, Publications Manager; and Janet Rigney, Librarian, of the Council on Foreign Relations; and to Robert L. Bull, Managing Editor; Despina Papazoglou, Associate Managing Editor; and other friends at NYU Press. They are indebted also to various official agencies which have provided documentary material, and to *The New York Times* for permission to reprint texts or excerpts of documents appearing in its pages. The maps were executed by Howard Sperber. The editors themselves are of course responsible for the choice and presentation of the documents as well as the form and content of the editorial matter.

R.P.S.
E.P.A.

December 30, 1976

CONTENTS

MAPS

INTRODUCING 1974

NINETEEN SEVENTY-FOUR will be remembered as a year of accelerating change in world affairs and heightened anxiety for the future of a human community that had begun to seem incapable of coping successfully with the demands of global interdependence. "The world is unhappy," President Valéry Giscard d'Estaing of France acknowledged in the course of a celebrated news conference on October 24, 1974. "It is unhappy because it does not know where it is going and because it guesses that if it did know, it would discover that it is advancing toward catastrophe."

"The crisis of the contemporary world is a lasting one," the new French leader elaborated. "What it involves is not the passage of a temporary disturbance but . . . the recognition of a permanent change." Mankind, Giscard intimated, was entering a new era, one whose destinies might be decided less by the rivalries and apprehensions of the superpowers than by the relationships between developed and developing countries—by such factors as global population growth, shortages of raw materials and energy, the growing scarcity of food, and the huge financial deficits already being incurred by countries that were obliged to meet their oil requirements by imports from abroad.

That the world had in fact involved itself in a crisis that was both unprecedented in scope and largely indecipherable in its long-run implications would have been disputed by few if any of Giscard's contemporaries on either side of the Atlantic. For years it had been evident that the unregulated progress of industrial civilization was creating conditions inimical to human welfare and even, in the final analysis, to life itself. The end of the postwar era and the dawning of a new age of global relationships, so often foretold by presidents and pundits in the past dozen years, had by 1974 been unmistakably made manifest by the wrenching of familiar associations and the emergence of imperious new preoccupations that dwarfed the hopes and fears of earlier times. The Arab-Israeli war of October 1973, with its sharp though transitory threat of Soviet-

1

American nuclear confrontation, had been perhaps the final act of an expiring drama shaped largely by the inherited concerns of the East-West "cold war." The accompanying intensification of the international energy crisis, precipitated by the oil-exporting countries through sudden price increases accompanied by drastic manipulations of supply, signaled a new era that might in the end be dominated merely by the universal struggle to stay alive.

To judge by the record of its earliest months, this new era that was now dawning might represent no great improvement over its predecessors. Human nature, in all its varied aspects, continued to manifest itself in ways that ranged from the breathtaking to the banal. Attesting the persistence of man's higher aspirations was the successful completion of the Skylab 3 space mission and the safe return of its three-man crew on February 8, 1974, after a record-breaking 84 days in orbit. Symbolic of other, less salubrious elements in the human makeup were such episodes as the expulsion from the Soviet Union of Aleksandr I. Solzhenitsyn, Russia's most illustrious contemporary writer and a leading critic of the Soviet system, on February 13; the murder by Arab terrorists of 20 Israeli children, and the wounding of some 70 others, in a predawn raid on the town of Maalot on May 15; the massacre by bombing of 30 people (with over 150 injured) in the Irish Republic on May 17, in an apparent extension of the carnage that had long since become habitual in adjacent, British-ruled Northern Ireland; and the fatal shooting of Rodger P. Davies, U.S. Ambassador to Cyprus, on August 19 in the course of an anti-American protest demonstration following the Turkish invasion and occupation of a substantial portion of that island republic.

More directly symptomatic of a world in transformation was the emergence of new political leadership in several of the leading nations, under circumstances that in some cases were less than edifying from the standpoint of accepted value systems. The people of the United States, still incompletely recovered from the stresses of the recent war in Indochina, were compelled to traverse the period of national shame that culminated in the resignation of Richard M. Nixon, their 37th President, in order to avoid impeachment and almost certain conviction in connection with the Watergate scandals and other well-documented abuses of his administration. This unprecedented action, which would exert profound effects upon America's self-awareness and international standing, would also leave to other hands the elaboration of that "structure of peace" which had been viewed by the departed President as the central concern of his administration. Former Vice-President Gerald R. Ford, in taking the oath as President Nixon's successor on August 9, emphatically pledged "an uninterrupted and sincere search for peace"; and guarantees of continuity were added by the retention of Dr. Henry A. Kissinger, a principal luminary of the Nixon years, in the posts of Secretary of State and Assistant to the President for National Security Affairs. Yet the change of incumbency in the White House could only accentuate the prevalent feeling, both in America and elsewhere, that a chapter of postwar history had closed and that a new one was commencing under rather ominous circumstances.

Elsewhere in the democratic world, the people of the United Kingdom had already determined, in an election held in the midst of a national fuel emergency and three-day working week, to dismiss the Conservative leadership of Prime Minister Edward Heath and call the Labour Party under Harold Wilson to a new term of office, later ratified and extended by the outcome of a second election in October. In France, the death of President Georges Pompidou on April 2 occasioned a two-stage election in May in which M. Giscard d'Estaing, as leader of the Independent Republicans, began by decisively outpolling the Gaullist Jacques Chaban-Delmas and then went on to secure a hair's-breadth victory over François Mitterrand, the candidate of the combined leftist parties. Scandal, meanwhile, had rocked the Federal Republic of Germany as Chancellor Willy Brandt, the leader of the federal government since 1969, admitted carelessness in regard to a personal assistant who had turned out to be an East German spy. Retaining leadership of the governing Social Democratic Party, Brandt resigned the chancellorship to Helmut Schmidt, a fellow Social Democrat and a strong personality in his own right. Other noteworthy governmental changes occurred in Israel, where the recriminations that followed the 1973 October War occasioned the resignation of Prime Minister Golda Meir and other familiar figures and the installation of a younger leadership headed by Yitzhak Rabin. In Japan, disclosure of shady real estate and financial dealings resulted late in the year, soon after a visit from President Ford, in the resignation of Prime Minister Kakuei Tanaka and his replacement by Takeo Miki, the leader of a minor faction of the ruling Liberal Democratic Party.

Although a certain number of the year's political changes involved the demise of repressive and unpopular regimes, the gains in political and personal freedom were not in every instance immediate or unequivocal. The conservative Portuguese government of Prime Minister Marcelo Caetano was overthrown on April 25 by a group of military officers who differed widely among themselves but were at one in acknowledging the inevitability of far-reaching changes both in Portugal and in its overseas territories in Africa and elsewhere. In Greece, an ill-judged attempt to foment revolution in Cyprus led in August to the resignation of the incumbent military junta and a long-delayed return to democratic methods under the guidance of ex-Premier Constantine Caramanlis. Another military junta, this one in Ethiopia, deposed the 82-year-old Emperor Haile Selassie, whose record as a domestic reformer had increasingly lagged behind his international prestige as a patriotic symbol. In Argentina, a rather precarious experiment with civilian government was fatally undermined by the death of President Juan D. Perón on July 1 and the accession of his widow, Isabel Martínez de Perón, to the presidency. In Chile, the repressive military dictatorship installed on the death of President Salvador Allende in 1973 continued to incur a volume of international criticism proportionate to its inflexibly authoritarian style of government.

Taxed by an unusual variety of domestic ills, the rich and powerful nations of Europe, North America, and the Pacific also confronted novel difficulties in their relations with one another and with the members of other international groupings. Especially problematical in many ways was the relationship between the United States, as long-time leader of the Western world, and its major partners and friends. The year 1973, envisaged by the Nixon administration as a "Year of Europe" that would be largely devoted to strengthening and reaffirming the indissoluble bonds between the Western European nations, the United States, and Japan, had in fact been marked by unexampled divisiveness, culminating late in the year in a virtual *sauve qui peut* as allied countries scrambled to dissociate themselves from the United States' support of Israel and to protect their oil supplies by declarations favoring the Arab position on the matters at issue in the Middle East. The bitterness engendered by these events would persist through much of 1974, a year when growing uncertainty about the future of the world economy caused fresh delays in the ongoing effort to revamp the international monetary system and revise the international trade rules administered under the General Agreement on Tariffs and Trade (GATT).

The processes of East-West détente, which had been so sensational a feature of the earlier 1970s, were also destined to experience a slowdown in 1974 as the American and Soviet governments attempted to grapple with their respective internal difficulties as well as the contradictions inherent in their developing relationship. President Nixon's second visit to the U.S.S.R., which took place barely a month before his resignation in August 1974, proved insufficient to ensure the hoped-for completion of a treaty on the limitation of strategic offensive arms, although the broad outlines of such a treaty were subsequently agreed upon by President Ford and General Secretary Leonid I. Brezhnev at their

November meeting in Vladivostok. Also continued without much evidence of significant progress were the multilateral negotiations begun in 1973 on reduction of military forces in Central Europe and questions of European security and cooperation. Plans for a major expansion of bilateral economic relations between the United States and the U.S.S.R. foundered on Moscow's unwillingness to relax its restrictions on Jewish emigration in order to obtain American trade concessions under the conditions set by the U.S. Congress.

Détente with the People's Republic of China also failed to advance significantly at a time when the United States remained hesitant to modify its historic relationship with the Republic of China on Taiwan and when the mainland regime, in addition to Watergate-related anxieties, was probably preoccupied with matters relating to the succession to the 80-year-old Chairman Mao Tse-tung and the 75-year-old Premier Chou En-lai. Nor was there any essential change with respect to the other Communist regimes of the Asian mainland. The struggle over Indochina still continued, despite the nominal settlements achieved in 1973; but the United States no longer played any direct role in the operations of the opposing military forces, which remained at a comparatively indecisive level during this transitional year that preceded the definitive Communist takeovers in South Vietnam, Cambodia, and Laos in 1975. In Korea, the North-South dialogue that had seemed to begin so promisingly a year or two earlier had by this time degenerated into a sterile propaganda exchange, diversified by occasional armistice violations on land and sea but with no decisive change in the relationship of the opposing regimes.

To an increasing number of intelligent observers, it seemed by 1974 that these familiar "cold war" situations had lost much of their importance and that the truly significant movements in world affairs concerned that much more numerous group of Asian, African, and Latin American nations alternatively referred to as the "third world," the "nonaligned" or "less developed" countries, or, in a United Nations context, as the "Group of 77" (actually totaling over 100) which had originally been formed at the First U.N. Conference on Trade and Development (UNCTAD) in 1964. If there is any one magnetic center around which the events of 1974 may tend to group themselves, it will unquestionably be found in the increasing prominence of these third world countries, their growing weight in the scales of international action, and their growing tendency to avenge their own often abysmal misery by the energy of their verbal and parliamentary assaults on the advanced, industrial nations whose dominance of the world scene had till lately been taken almost for granted.

It is true that the majority of these nations still lingered near the threshold of material development and remained deficient in many of the elements of national power. Aside from the human sympathy their plight could scarcely fail to evoke, the world had rung for years with warnings of catastrophe as the seemingly inexorable growth of their populations continued to outstrip the slower expansion of the world's available food supplies. International conferences on the twin subjects of population and food would in fact take rank among the notable events of 1974, a year when the plight of many developing countries was significantly worsening thanks to the precipitous increases in the prices they were compelled to pay for the petroleum and related products they imported from other, more fortunately situated developing countries.

Despite these built-in handicaps, however, the ongoing transformation of the international scene appeared to be creating an increasing number of situations in which the third world countries could pursue their special aims with considerable hope of success, often in direct defiance of the "developed," industrial countries. While the actual line-up differs from case to case, examination of the events of 1974 will disclose an underlying pattern in which countries of the third world group (1) endeavored, not without success, to seize the initiative, set the pace, and establish the ground rules of world affairs; and (2) were frequently found at opposite poles from the United States—and often from other industrial countries—in their approach to specific international questions. Variants of this underlying pattern, which obviously reflects a difference in value systems as well as specific interests, can be found in the record of most of the central international issues of 1974. A number of these may be listed here by way of introduction to the documentary chapters that follow.

Energy. A classic exercise of third world power had been the fourfold increase in crude petroleum prices during 1973 which had been imposed by the Organization of Petroleum Exporting Countries (OPEC), to the accompaniment of production cutbacks in most of the Arab oil-producing states and an outright embargo on shipments to the United States and the Netherlands on the grounds of their alleged partiality to Israel. (Shipments to Portugal, Rhodesia, and South Africa were also embargoed as a mark of sympathy with African liberation movements.) Although this politically motivated embargo against the affected Western countries was lifted in the course of 1974, the price increases were maintained throughout that year in spite of falling worldwide consumption and a consequent decline in output. The resultant global intensification of inflationary pressures, balance-of-payments dislocations, and recessionary tendencies was among the principal causes of the sense of bewilderment and apprehension that gripped the world through most of 1974. Attempts by the United States to promote the adoption of a common strategy by the principal oil-consuming countries encountered considerable resistance, particularly from France, and tended, at least initially, to widen existing rifts among developed countries as well as between the latter and members of the third world group.

Atomic weapons. India's successful underground nuclear test of May 18, 1974, though assertedly carried out exclusively for peaceful purposes and with no intention of developing nuclear weapons, afforded dramatic evidence that third world status no longer precluded the achievement of a nuclear military capability. By expanding the membership of the so-called "nuclear club" from five to six (China, France, India, the U.S.S.R., the United Kingdom, and the United States), the Indian action accentuated existing doubts about the adequacy of the system of restraints embodied in the 1968 Treaty on the Nonproliferation of Nuclear Weapons, to which India, in common with China, France, and various other countries, had never become a party. From a technical point of view, it would be a comparatively easy matter for other nonnuclear weapon states to duplicate India's achievement, thus superseding the already obsolescent arrangement whereby such capabilities had originally been limited to so-called "great" powers.

The Middle East. Hopes for a just and lasting settlement of the conflict between Israel and its Arab neighbors, though temporarily revived with the opening of the Geneva Conference on the Middle East in December 1973, receded once again in 1974 as positions hardened on all sides and even the non-Arab nations of the third world increasingly rallied to the support of Israel's foes. Secretary Kissinger's diplomatic success in bringing about a disengagement of the opposing military forces at the Suez Canal and on the Golan Heights was largely offset by the increasing political rigidity of the states concerned, the serious acts of terrorism that continued to be perpetrated in the name of the displaced Arab people of Palestine, and the growing international acceptance of the Palestine Liberation Organization (PLO), a political entity whose claims to speak for the Palestinian Arabs were strenuously opposed by Israel and the United States but were increasingly accepted both in third world quarters and in the United Nations General Assembly.

Cyprus. The most important interstate military conflict of 1974 actually took place in the territory of a third world country— Cyprus—and involved two neighboring nations, Turkey and Greece, which likewise boasted numerous third world affinities notwithstanding their political and military alignment with the Western group. Among the effects of this tragic conflict, in which

Turkey intervened with military force on behalf of the Turkish Cypriot minority while Greece looked on in impotent rage and dismay, was a weakening of both nations' Western ties and, in Turkey's case, a reinforcement of its links with the Asian-Islamic world. While Greece withdrew from military cooperation under the North Atlantic Treaty Organization (NATO) and canceled previous arrangements looking toward the "homeporting" of American naval vessels, Turkey threatened to close American bases in its territory in retaliation for a threatened cutoff of American military aid at the behest of the U.S. Congress.

Africa. The remaining bastions of Western colonialism in Africa began to crumble visibly in 1974 as Portugal's new government, acknowledging the futility of further resistance to the local liberation movements in the Portuguese African territories, conceded the independence of former Portuguese Guinea (Guinea-Bissau) and prepared for similar transfers of power to the insurgent liberation forces in Cape Verde, Mozambique, and Angola. In turn, the impending dissolution of the Portuguese African empire increased the pressure on the part of third world governments and indigenous forces for decisive action against the white minority regimes in Southern Rhodesia, Namibia (South West Africa), and South Africa. Continued opposition by the United States and other Western governments to violent, illegal, or otherwise potentially counterproductive measures in Southern Africa occasioned a number of clashes with third world elements in the United Nations. Although a Western veto cut short an attempt to order South Africa's expulsion from the United Nations, third world and associated elements achieved one notable success in obtaining a suspension of the South African delegation from participation in the 29th Regular Session of the General Assembly in the fall of 1974.

Economic development. The distressed material condition of the developing countries, once seen as a potential field for fruitful and harmonious cooperation with the industrial powers, had by 1974 become a subject of recrimination and anger as vehement as the political grievances that were being voiced by many of the same countries. The increased prices of imported petroleum products had struck a new and crippling blow at many developing nations, and the attempts to ease their plight were not made easier by the atmosphere of confrontation and complaint that now pervaded international discussion of development questions. The most significant developing-country achievement of 1974 was the adoption at separate sessions of the U.N. General Assembly of two grandiose rhetorical statements, a declaration and program of action on "The Establishment of a New International Economic Order" and a "Charter of Economic Rights and Duties of States." Both statements forfeited American support by what was viewed in U.S. official circles as their ideologically unbalanced character. American authorities did not hide their doubt that such one-sided articulations of developing country demands could promote the satisfaction of legitimate developing country needs.

The United Nations. The growing prominence of third world issues and the growing vehemence of their protagonists exerted a measurable impact upon the functioning of the United Nations and its related agencies. Particularly shocking to the United States were such aspects of the United Nations record in 1974 as the exclusion of South Africa from the General Assembly session, the special honors accorded PLO leader Yasir Arafat on the occasion of his November 13 address to the Assembly, and the Assembly's later adoption of resolutions recognizing the PLO as the representative of the Palestinian people and granting it permanent observer status at the General Assembly and at U.N.-sponsored international conferences. Further adverse comment was elicited, both in the United States and elsewhere, by the actions of the General Conference of the U.N. Educational, Scientific and Cultural Organization (UNESCO) in Paris, which undertook to exclude Israel from various UNESCO activities ostensibly because of its actions affecting architectural interests in East Jerusalem. The reaction of some U.N. delegates to a mild reproof from Ambassador John Scali regarding the penchant for adopting "unenforceable, one-sided resolutions" showed how wide had become the gulf between the United States and the emerging U.N. majority.

Dismaying as was the news that reached them from many international fronts, however, Americans by and large continued to find still greater cause for uneasiness in developments nearer home. President Ford, it was soon evident, had been not a little overoptimistic when he declared on taking office that "our long national nightmare is over." Inflation, for one thing, continued to rage with unabated fury, in spite of a flurry of high-level economic conferences and a presidential anti-inflation campaign built around the letters WIN (Whip Inflation Now). Economic activity, meanwhile, had been declining since the beginning of the year. Unemployment was up, stocks were down, and by November 12 the White House itself was admitting (what others had been saying for many weeks) that the United States appeared to be "moving into a recession." Given the unusual conditions prevailing in the world economy, no one could state with certainty whether this recession would prove as short-lived as its predecessors or whether it might not deepen into a world depression comparable to that of the 1930s.

A sense of moral unease was almost equally prevalent as Americans began to realize that the departure and pardon of President Nixon and the bringing to trial of many of his associates had not resolved all doubts about the conduct of their government, past or present. Even within the foreign policy-national security area, there remained a residue of uncertainty about such Nixon-era questions as Dr. Kissinger's role in instigating the FBI wiretapping of officials and newsmen in 1969-71, a subject on which the recollections of those concerned appeared to differ and which had remained to a large extent unclarified despite the Senate Foreign Relations Committee's manifest disinclination to reopen the matter.[1]

Of potentially graver import were the new disclosures that were now beginning to occur with reference to the operations of the government's intelligence agencies abroad and at home. On September 8, 1974, a *New York Times* story by Seymour M. Hersh disclosed that contrary to the impressions hitherto created by official spokesmen, the so-called "40 Committee" headed by Dr. Kissinger had authorized the expenditure in Chile of over $8 million during the period 1969-73 for what were loosely called "political destabilization" activities in support of opponents of the late President Allende. Still another Hersh story, in the *New York Times* of December 22, offered a first public intimation that the Central Intelligence Agency, in addition to its authorized intelligence duties abroad, had conducted "a massive, illegal domestic intelligence operation during the Nixon Administration against the antiwar movement and other dissident groups in the United States"—and, furthermore, that the agency's files contained evidence of "dozens of other illegal activities by members of the C.I.A. inside the United States, beginning in the nineteen-fifties, including break-ins, wiretapping and the surreptitious inspection of mail."

Inundated from every direction by the fallout of old illusions, compelled as seldom in the past to fight the odors of decay arising from within and without, how could thoughtful Americans escape a sense of proximate doom as the clock ticked onward toward a bicentennial celebration now less than two years away? Had Nikita S. Khrushchev been right in declaring that "We will bury you"? Even Secretary Kissinger, the nation's closest approach to an official philosopher, admitted that in his activity as a statesman he had to try to transcend a sense of pessimism that might have been more suited to his earlier academic status.

"I think of myself as a historian more than as a statesman," he told James Reston of the *New York Times* in October. "As a historian, you have to be conscious of the fact that every civilization that has ever existed has ultimately collapsed.

---

[1]For further discussion see Chapter 12 at notes 1-2.

"History is a tale of efforts that failed, of aspirations that weren't realized, of wishes that were fulfilled and then turned out to be different from what one expected. So, as a historian, one has to live with a sense of the inevitability of tragedy; as a statesman, one has to act on the assumption that problems must be solved."[2]

Great as the problems of the time undoubtedly were, however, Secretary Kissinger professed to feel no doubt that they could in fact be brought to a solution. Americans, he suggested, might even be thought to possess a special aptitude in this regard:

" . . . There is a strain in America which is, curiously, extremely relevant to this world. We are challenged by the huge problems—peace and war, energy, food—and we have a real belief in interdependence; it is not just a slogan.

"The solution of these problems really comes quite naturally to Americans; first, because they believe that every problem is soluble; secondly, because they are at ease with re-doing the world, and the old frontier mentality really does find an expression, and even the old idealism finds a way to express itself.

"In what other country could a leader say, 'We are going to solve energy; we're going to solve food; we're going to solve the problem of nuclear war,' and be taken seriously? So I think it is true that there are strains in our domestic debate; I think it is also true that there are many positive aspects in our domestic debate that can help us reach these larger goals."[3]

President Giscard d'Estaing, at the October 24 news conference already referred to, displayed a similar confidence in his country's ability to meet the problems he himself had outlined in such Cassandra-like tones. The human mind is not at ease with too much pessimism, and no political leader could seem to despair if he expected to retain the support of his constituents. By the end of 1974, there would be signs that while the problems remained largely unsolved and in some cases had not even been properly defined, public confidence was already beginning to revive as the world emerged from the trough of the waves and moved onward toward another crest. How many such experiences it could survive and still remain afloat might nevertheless depend on how it used the interval before the next wave.

[2]*Bulletin*, 71: 629.
[3]Same: 630.

1. DISENGAGEMENT AT SUEZ

(January 18, 1974)

[Three questions weighed with special urgency upon the United States as 1974 began, intruding with sinister persistence upon the contentment of the holiday season. The first concerned the dangerous situation that still existed in the Middle East in the wake of the 1973 "October War" between the Arab states and Israel, a conflict that had almost produced a military confrontation between the United States and the Soviet Union and had left the area in a state of confusion in which a renewal of hostilities remained an ever-present possibility. A second problem centered in the international energy crisis precipitated by recent increases in the export price of crude petroleum and the simultaneous cutbacks in production by Arab oil exporting countries, accompanied by an out-and-out embargo on shipments to the United States and other countries friendly to Israel. The third and possibly even more fundamental issue had to do with the ability of the United States itself to play a constructive role in world affairs at a time when its internal processes had been distorted and the viability of its constitutional arrangements was being increasingly called in question by the unfolding of the Watergate scandals and a growing threat to the survival of the Nixon administration.

Although the initiative in Watergate matters had long since slipped from President Nixon's hands, the interrelated problems of energy and the Middle East continued to afford broad scope for executive action. It was on January 9 that the President, then sojourning at San Clemente, California, invited the heads of government of the "major industrial consumer nations" to send their Foreign Ministers to Washington in February in order to seek a coordinated approach to the global energy crisis and prepare for a later meeting with producer representatives.[1] Approaching the matter from a somewhat different angle, Secretary of State Kissinger left Washington the following evening for Aswan to meet with

[1]See Chapter 3 at note 3.

President Anwar al-Sadat of Egypt in a continuation of his efforts to promote a disengagement and separation of the dangerously tangled Israeli and Egyptian armies.

The military operations of the October War, in which Egyptian forces had initially crossed the Suez Canal from west to east and Israeli forces had later crossed from east to west, had created a tensely explosive situation that clearly needed to be straightened out before there could be any prospect of the wider peace negotiations to which the parties were committed under the relevant U.N. cease-fire resolutions.[2] At the recent opening of the Geneva Conference on the Middle East, convened ostensibly to promote negotiations aimed at a "just and durable peace," it had been acknowledged even by the Soviet Union that an "effective disengagement of forces" was "the urgent and top priority task" and must take precedence over such longer-range, highly controversial questions as the future of Israeli-occupied territories and the rights of Palestinian Arabs. Although the Geneva Conference had set up a "military working group" to deal with the disengagement problem, it had been recognized on all sides that Dr. Kissinger, having gained the confidence of both the Arab and the Israeli governments, would spearhead the disengagement effort as he had in fact been doing ever since the recent conflict. Apart from lessening the danger of new armed clashes, such an effort might if successful speed the lifting of the embargo on oil shipments to the United States which had been decreed by the Arab exporting countries on October 17, 1973, and was still in force long after the guns had been formally silenced.

Thanks largely to the positive attitude displayed by President Sadat, it had been evident that a disengagement of Egyptian and Israeli forces would be easier to arrange than a similar separation involving Syria or Jordan, Israel's other close-quarter antagonists. But even Secretary Kissinger seems not to have anticipated that an agreement covering the points of greatest immediate interest could be worked out in a single week of intensive "shuttle diplomacy" between Aswan and Jerusalem, the seat of the Israeli Government still headed at that time by Prime Minister Golda Meir. By January 17, nevertheless, President Nixon was able to announce in Washington that a military disengagement agreement between Egypt and Israel would be signed the very next day in the presence of Lieutenant General Ensio P. H. Siilasvuo, Commander of the United Nations Emergency Force (UNEF) set up to act as a buffer between the two armies.]

---

[2]Especially Security Council Resolution 338 (1973), Oct. 22, 1973, in *AFR, 1973*: 459. The October war and its aftermath are briefly outlined in same: 443-79, 529-39, and 603-13.

*(1)   Egyptian-Israeli Agreement on Disengagement and Separation
of Military Forces, signed January 18, 1974.*

*(a)   Radio-television announcement by President Nixon,
January 17, 1974.*[3]

Ladies and gentlemen, I have an announcement that I am sure
will be welcome news, not only to all Americans, but to people all
over the world. The announcement has to do with the Mideast, and
it is being made simultaneously at 3 o'clock Washington time in
Cairo and in Jerusalem, as well as in Washington.

The announcement is as follows: "In accordance with the decision of the Geneva Conference, the Governments of Egypt and
Israel, with the assistance of the Government of the United States,
have reached agreement on the disengagement and separation of
their military forces. The agreement is scheduled to be signed by the
Chiefs of Staff of Egypt and Israel at noon Egypt-Israel time, Friday, January 18, at Kilometer 101 on the Cairo-Suez Road. The
Commander of the United Nations Emergency Force, General
Siilasvuo, has been asked by the parties to witness the signing."

A brief statement with regard to this announcement, I think, is in
order.

First, congratulations should go to President Sadat, to Prime
Minister Meir, and their colleagues, for the very constructive spirit
they have shown in reaching an agreement on the very difficult
issues involved which made this announcement possible.

Also, we in the United States can be proud of the role that our
Government has played, and particularly the role that has been
played by Secretary Kissinger and his colleagues, in working to
bring the parties together so that an agreement could be reached,
which we have just read.

The other point that I would make is with regard to the
significance of the agreement. In the past generation there have
been, as we know, four wars in the Mideast, followed by uneasy
truces. This, I would say, is the first significant step toward a permanent peace in the Mideast. I do not understate, by making the
statement that I have just made, the difficulties that lie ahead in settling the differences that must be settled before a permanent peace
is reached, not only here but between the other countries involved.
But this is a very significant step reached directly as a result of
negotiations between the two parties and, therefore, has, it seems
to me, a great deal of meaning to all of us here in this country and
around the world who recognize the importance of having peace in
this part of the world.

[3]Text from *Presidential Documents*, 10: 61-2.

The other point that I would make is with regard to the role of the United States. Our role has been one of being of assistance to both parties to bring them together, to help to narrow differences, working toward a fair and just settlement for all parties concerned where every nation in that area will be able to live in peace and also to be secure insofar as its defense is concerned.

Looking to the situation in the world generally, I think that we could probably say that the area of the world that potentially is the one in which the great powers can be brought into confrontation is the Mideast, that that area more than any other is in that category, as recent events have indicated.

Now the announcement we have made today is only a first step, but it is a very significant step. It paves the way for more steps which can lead to a permanent peace. And I personally shall see that all negotiations, any efforts which could lead to that permanent peace, not only between Egypt and Israel, but between the other countries involved, have the full and complete support of the Government of the United States.

Thank you.

[The arrangement announced by President Nixon comprised a number of elements, not all of which were included in the formal agreement to be signed on January 18. Israel, in effect, had agreed to yield a part of the military advantage gained in October and to withdraw its military forces to a line some fifteen miles east of the Suez Canal. Egyptian forces, under this arrangement, would be deployed along the Canal's eastern bank for the first time since 1967. A "zone of disengagement," to be patrolled by the United Nations, would separate the two armies; and a limitation of armament and forces would prevail in the adjacent areas controlled respectively by Egypt and by Israel. In addition, the "package deal" negotiated by Dr. Kissinger (and reflecting, to a considerable extent, the ideas of Israeli Defense Minister Moshe Dayan) included certain unpublished understandings and commitments, most of which had been insisted upon by Israel as compensation for its military pullback.[4]

As President Nixon had announced, the agreement on disengagement of forces was signed on January 18 at 12:25 P.M. local time (1025 hours GMT) at Kilometer 101 on the Cairo-Suez road, the signers being the Chiefs of Staff of the Egyptian and Israeli armed forces with General Siilasvuo as witness.]

---

[4]For the detailed negotiating history see Kalb, *Kissinger*: 529-49; Golan, *The Secret Conversations of Henry Kissinger*: 156-78; Sheehan, *The Arabs, Israelis, and Kissinger*: 108-12.

(b) Text of the Agreement, signed January 18, 1974 at Kilometer 101 on the Cairo-Suez Road.[5]

Egyptian-Israeli Agreement on disengagement of forces in pursuance of the Geneva Peace Conference

A. Egypt and Israel will scrupulously observe the cease-fire on land, sea and air called for by the United Nations Security Council[6] and will refrain from the time of the signing of this document from all military or paramilitary actions against each other.

B. The military forces of Egypt and Israel will be separated in accordance with the following principles:

1. All Egyptian forces on the east side of the canal will be deployed west of the line designated as Line A on the attached map.[7] All Israeli forces, including those west of the Suez Canal and the Bitter Lakes, will be deployed east of the line designated as Line B on the attached map.

2. The area between the Egyptian and Israeli lines will be a zone of disengagement in which the United Nations Emergency Force (UNEF) will be stationed. UNEF will continue to consist of units from countries that are not permanent members of the Security Council.

3. The area between the Egyptian line and the Suez Canal will be limited in armament and forces.

4. The area between the Israeli line (B on the attached map) and the line designated as Line C on the attached map, which runs along the western base of the mountains where the Gidi and Mitla Passes are located, will be limited in armament and forces.

5. The limitations referred to in paragraphs 3 and 4 will be inspected by UNEF. Existing procedures of UNEF, including the attaching of Egyptian and Israeli liaison officers to UNEF, will be continued.

6. Air forces of the two sides will be permitted to operate up to their respective lines without interference from the other side.

C. The detailed implementation of the disengagement of forces will be worked out by military representatives of Egypt and Israel,

---

[5]U.N. Document S/11198, Jan. 18; text from U.N. Security Council, *Official Records: 29th Year, Supplement for Jan., Feb. and Mar. 1974*: 84-5.
[6]Security Council Resolutions 338, 339, and 340 (1973), in *AFR, 1973*: 459-60 and 469-70.
[7]The official map is appended to U.N. document S/11198/Add.1, Jan. 23, 1973 (*Official Records, loc. cit.*, p. 86).

who will agree on the stages of this process. These representatives will meet no later than 48 hours after the signature of this Agreement at Kilometre 101 under the aegis of the United Nations for this purpose. They will complete this task within five days. Disengagement will begin within 48 hours after the completion of the work of the military representatives and in no event later than seven days after the signature of this Agreement. The process of disengagement will be completed not later than 40 days after it begins.

D.   This Agreement is not regarded by Egypt and Israel as a final peace agreement. It constitutes a first step toward a final, just and durable peace according to the provisions of Security Council resolution 338 (1973) and within the framework of the Geneva Conference.

For Egypt:
Mohammad Abdel Ghani EL-GAMASY

Major-General
Chief of Staff of the Egyptian
Armed Forces

For Israel:
David ELAZAR

Lieutenant-General
Chief of Staff of the Israel
Defence Forces

Witness:
Ensio P. H. SIILASVUO

Lieutenant-General
Commander of the United Nations
Emergency Force

[As noted earlier, the text of the accord as signed and made public on January 18 reflected only a part of the agreements and understandings reached. Other elements too sensitive to be included in the formal agreement were embodied in various unpublished documents drawn up with American assistance and reliably described in press accounts at the time.

Whereas the published agreement provided only that the forward areas bordering the zone of disengagement would be "limited in armament and forces," the actual limitations were set forth in some detail in a separate document, known as the "United States proposal," which was signed on January 18 by Prime Minister Meir in Jerusalem and by President Sadat in Aswan, Secretary Kissinger being present on both occasions. Letters from President Nixon to

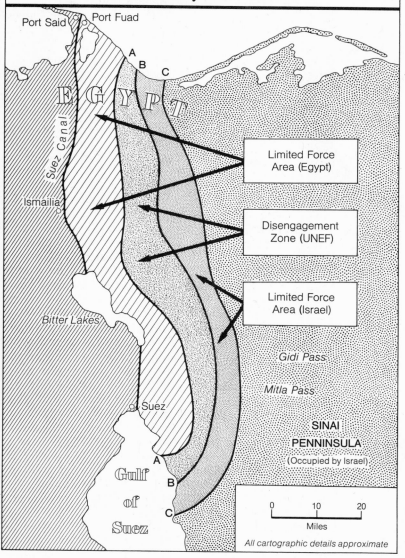

EGYPT - ISRAEL DISENGAGEMENT AGREEMENT
January 18, 1974

Port Said Port Fuad

A
B
C

E G Y P T

Suez Canal

Ismailia

Limited Force Area (Egypt)

Disengagement Zone (UNEF)

Limited Force Area (Israel)

Bitter Lakes

Gidi Pass

Mitla Pass

Suez

SINAI

PENNINSULA

(Occupied by Israel)

A

Gulf

B

of

C

Suez

0   10   20
Miles

All cartographic details approximate

the Israeli and Egyptian leaders are said to have accompanied this document.

In addition, Secretary Kissinger is said to have furnished the Israelis with a secret "Memorandum of Understanding" setting forth certain commitments by both Egypt and the United States. Though Israel failed in its main hope of winning an Egyptian promise of nonbelligerency, it apparently did obtain (1) an Egyptian commitment to the United States—though without any precise timetable—to clear the Suez Canal, rebuild the cities in the Canal area, and permit transit of the Canal by Israeli cargoes carried in non-Israeli vessels; (2) a mutual agreement to U.S. aerial reconnaissance of the disengagement area; and (3) an American assurance that the United States would make every effort to be fully responsive to Israel's continuing and long-term military equipment needs.[8] The Israelis also cited certain further understandings to the effect that the U.N. Emergency Force would not include countries with which Israel did not have diplomatic relations, and that there would be no interference with Israeli shipping through the Straits of Bab-el-Mandeb at the entrance to the Red Sea.

Disengagement of forces in accordance with the Kilometer 101 agreement actually began on January 25 and was completed on schedule on March 5. Admittedly, however, this limited Israeli withdrawal fell far short of meeting Egypt's hopes for the recovery of the entire Sinai Peninsula, not to mention the standard Arab demand for Israeli withdrawal from all the territories occupied in 1967. The Arab oil exporting countries, while generally approving the American performance, were not as yet sufficiently impressed to relax the embargo on petroleum shipments, which was to remain in effect until March 18, 1974.

Dr. Kissinger's negotiations had, however, served to defuse the single most explosive situation left over from the 1973 conflict, and to set a possible precedent for the application of a comparable "step-by-step" approach in other sectors. Among the presumed advantages of the technique was the fact that it created no new openings for the expansion of Moscow's already considerable influence in the area. With President Sadat's encouragement, the Secretary of State stopped over in Damascus on his way back to Washington in order to explore with President Hafez al-Assad the possibility of working out a similar disengagement of Israeli and Syrian forces on the Israeli-occupied Golan Heights. But both the physical and the political conditions in this area were much more difficult than on the southern front, and more than four months were to elapse before an Israeli-Syrian disengagement agreement was in fact negotiated and President Nixon was able to undertake his subsequent precedent-shattering visit to the Middle East.[9]]

[8]Sheehan: 111-12.
[9]Cf. Chapters 11 and 12.

2. THE STATE OF THE UNION

(January 30, 1974)

[Dr. Kissinger's successful negotiations in the Middle East cast a ray of cheer across a scene that in other respects was perhaps as bleak as at any time since the onset of World War II. Gone was the euphoria that had accompanied President Nixon's triumphant return to office the year before, infecting even Nixon opponents with a sense of confident expectancy as the nation moved toward its bicentennial observance in 1976. Of the leading bugbears of the 1960s and early 1970s—Vietnam, crime, and inflation—the first at least had been scotched, if not killed, in 1973; but both the others appeared to most people to be raging virtually unchecked. The energy emergency which had suddenly developed in the last quarter of 1973 had become a source not merely of current inconvenience but of profound misgivings about the future, all the more so because American power and wealth were being set at naught by countries which, according to American standards, had thus far not ranked high in the scale of greatness. Adding to the sense of humiliation was the spectacle of a President who, in recent months, had seemed less concerned with pursuing his plans for a "generation of peace" than with secreting the evidence that could entail his own removal from office.

Already facing a lively possibility of impeachment as the result of studies undertaken by the House Judiciary Committee, Mr. Nixon continued nevertheless to maintain an air of outward confidence as he performed the routine functions of his office. The State of the Union address which he delivered to a Joint Session of the Congress on January 30 offered the usual well-balanced, if somewhat overoptimistic, appraisal of the nation's domestic and foreign affairs at this critical passage of its history. In tone as well as content, the President's statement offers an essential point of departure to any who would understand the national experience in the troubled months to follow.]

*(2)   The State of the Union: Address delivered by President Nixon
before a Joint Session of the Congress, January 30, 1974.* [1]

(Excerpts)

Mr. Speaker, Mr. President, [2] *my colleagues in the Congress, our
distinguished guests, my fellow Americans:*

We meet here tonight at a time of great challenge and great opportunities for America. We meet at a time when we face great
problems at home and abroad that will test the strength of our fiber
as a Nation. But we also meet at a time when that fiber has been
tested and it has proved strong.

America is a great and good land, and we are a great and good
land because we are a strong, free, creative people and because
America is the single greatest force for peace anywhere in the
world. Today, as always in our history, we can base our confidence
in what the American people will achieve in the future on the record
of what the American people have achieved in the past.

Tonight, for the first time in 12 years, a President of the United
States can report to the Congress on the state of a Union at peace
with every nation of the world. Because of this, in the 22,000-word
message on the state of the Union that I have just handed to the
Speaker of the House and the President of the Senate, [3] I have been
able to deal primarily with the problems of peace—with what we
can do here at home in America for the American people—rather
than with the problems of war.

The measures I have outlined in this message set an agenda for
truly significant progress for this Nation and the world in 1974.
Before we chart where we are going, let us see how far we have
come.

It was 5 years ago on the steps of this Capitol that I took the oath
of office as your President. In those 5 years, because of the initiatives undertaken by this Administration, the world has changed.
America has changed. As a result of those changes, America is
safer today, more prosperous today, with greater opportunity for
more of its people than ever before in our history.

Five years ago America was at war in Southeast Asia. We were
locked in confrontation with the Soviet Union. We were in hostile
isolation from a quarter of the world's people who lived in
Mainland China.

[1]Text from *Presidential Documents*, 10: 113-22.
[2]Speaker of the House Carl Albert and President of the Senate Gerald R. Ford.
[3]Text in *Presidential Documents, loc. cit.*, pp. 122-48; excerpt in *Bulletin*, 70: 161-9.

Five years ago our cities were burning and besieged.

Five years ago our college campuses were a battleground.

Five years ago crime was increasing at a rate that struck fear across the Nation.

Five years ago the spiraling rise in drug addiction was threatening human and social tragedy of massive proportion, and there was no program to deal with it.

Five years ago—as young Americans had done for a generation before that—America's youth still lived under the shadow of the military draft.

Five years ago there was no national program to preserve our environment. Day by day our air was getting dirtier, our water was getting more foul.

And 5 years ago American agriculture was practically a depressed industry with 100,000 farm families abandoning the farm every year.

As we look at America today we find ourselves challenged by new problems. But we also find a record of progress to confound the professional criers of doom and prophets of despair. We met the challenges we faced 5 years ago, and we will be equally confident of meeting those that we face today.

Let us see for a moment how we have met them. After more than 10 years of military involvement, all of our troops have returned from Southeast Asia and they have returned with honor. And we can be proud of the fact that our courageous prisoners of war, for whom a dinner was held in Washington tonight, that they came home with their heads high, on their feet and not on their knees.

In our relations with the Soviet Union, we have turned away from a policy of confrontation to one of negotiation. For the first time since World War II, the world's two strongest powers are working together toward peace in the world. With the People's Republic of China after a generation of hostile isolation, we have begun a period of peaceful exchange and expanding trade.

Peace has returned to our cities, to our campuses. The 17-year rise in crime has been stopped. We can confidently say today that we are finally beginning to win the war against crime. Right here in this Nation's Capital—which a few years ago was threatening to become the crime capital of the world—the rate in crime has been cut in half. A massive campaign against drug abuse has been organized. And the rate of new heroin addiction, the most vicious threat of all, is decreasing rather than increasing.

For the first time in a generation no young Americans are being drafted into the Armed Services of the United States. And for the first time ever we have organized a massive national effort to protect the environment. Our air is getting cleaner. Our water is getting purer, and our agriculture, which was depressed, is prospering.

Farm income is up 70 percent, farm production is setting alltime records, and the billions of dollars the taxpayers were paying in subsidies has been cut to nearly zero.

Overall, Americans are living more abundantly than ever before today. More than 2½ million new jobs were created in the past year alone. That is the biggest percentage increase in nearly 20 years. People are earning more. What they earn buys more, more than ever before in history. In the past 5 years the average American's real spendable income—that is what you really can buy with your income, even after allowing for taxes and inflation—has increased by 16 percent.

Despite this record of achievement, as we turn to the year ahead we hear once again the familiar voice of the perennial prophets of gloom telling us now that because of the need to fight inflation, because of the energy shortage, America may be headed for a recession.

Let me speak to that issue head on. There will be no recession in the United States of America. Primarily due to our energy crisis, our economy is passing through a difficult period. But I pledge to you tonight that the full powers of this Government will be used to keep America's economy producing and to protect the jobs of America's workers.

We are engaged in a long and hard fight against inflation. There have been, and there will be in the future, ups and downs in that fight. But if this Congress cooperates in our efforts to hold down the cost of government, we shall win our fight to hold down the cost of living for the American people.

As we look back over our history, the years that stand out as the ones of signal achievement are those in which the Administration and the Congress, whether one party or the other, working together, had the wisdom and the foresight to select those particular initiatives for which the Nation was ready and the moment was right—and in which they seized the moment and acted.

Looking at the year 1974 which lies before us, there are 10 key areas in which landmark accomplishments are possible this year in America. If we make these our national agenda, this is what we will achieve in 1974:

We will break the back of the energy crisis; we will lay the foundation for our future capacity to meet America's energy needs from America's own resources.

And we will take another giant stride toward lasting peace in the world—not only by continuing our policy of negotiation rather than confrontation where the great powers are concerned but also by helping toward the achievement of a just and lasting settlement in the Middle East.

We will check the rise in prices, without administering the harsh medicine of recession, and we will move the economy into a steady period of growth at a sustainable level.

We will establish a new system that makes high-quality health care available to every American in a dignified manner and at a price he can afford.

We will make our States and localities more responsive to the needs of their own citizens.

We will make a crucial breakthrough toward better transportation in our towns and in our cities across America.

We will reform our system of Federal aid to education, to provide it when it is needed, where it is needed, so that it will do the most for those who need it the most.

We will make an historic beginning on the task of defining and protecting the right of personal privacy for every American.

And we will start on a new road toward reform of a welfare system that bleeds the taxpayer, corrodes the community, and demeans those it is intended to assist.

And together with the other nations of the world, we will establish the economic framework within which Americans will share more fully in an expanding worldwide trade and prosperity in the years ahead, with more open access to both markets and supplies.

In all of the 186 State of the Union messages delivered from this place in our history, this is the first in which the one priority, the first priority, is energy. Let me begin by reporting a new development which I know will be welcome news to every American. As you know, we have committed ourselves to an active role in helping to achieve a just and durable peace in the Middle East, on the basis of full implementation of Security Council Resolutions 242 and 338.[4] The first step in the process is the disengagement of Egyptian and Israeli forces which is now taking place.

Because of this hopeful development I can announce tonight that I have been assured, through my personal contacts with friendly leaders in the Middle Eastern area, that an urgent meeting will be called in the immediate future to discuss the lifting of the oil embargo.[5]

This is an encouraging sign. However, it should be clearly understood by our friends in the Middle East that the United States will not be coerced on this issue.

Regardless of the outcome of this meeting, the cooperation of

---

[4]Resolution 242 (1967), Nov. 22, 1967, in *Documents, 1967*: 169-70; 338 (1973), Oct. 22, 1973, in *AFR, 1973*: 459.

[5]A meeting of ministerial representatives of the Organization of Arab Petroleum Exporting Countries (OAPEC), originally scheduled to take place in Tripoli, Libya, on Feb. 14, was postponed but eventually took place on Mar. 13-18.

the American people in our energy conservation program has already gone a long way toward achieving a goal to which I am deeply dedicated. Let us do everything we can to avoid gasoline rationing in the United Staes of America.

Last week I sent to the Congress a comprehensive special message[6] setting forth our energy situation, recommending the legislative measures which are necessary to a program for meeting our needs. If the embargo is lifted, this will ease the crisis, but it will not mean an end to the energy shortage in America. Voluntary conservation will continue to be necessary. And let me take this occasion to pay tribute once again to the splendid spirit of cooperation the American people have shown which has made possible our success in meeting this emergency up to this time.

The new legislation I have requested will also remain necessary. Therefore, I urge again that the energy measures that I have proposed be made the first priority of this session of the Congress. These measures will require the oil companies and other energy producers to provide the public with the necessary information on their supplies. They will prevent the injustice of windfall profits for a few as a result of the sacrifices of the millions of Americans. And they will give us the organization, the incentives, the authorities needed to deal with the short-term emergency and to move toward meeting our long-term needs.

Just as 1970 was the year in which we began a full-scale effort to protect the environment, 1974 must be the year in which we organize a full-scale effort to provide for our energy needs not only in this decade, but through the 21st century.

As we move toward the celebration 2 years from now of the 200th anniversary of this Nation's independence, let us press vigorously on toward the goal I announced last November for Project Independence.[7] Let this be our national goal. At the end of this decade in the year 1980, the United States will not be dependent on any other country for the energy we need to provide our jobs, to heat our homes, and to keep our transportation moving.

To indicate the size of the Government commitment, to spur energy research and development, we plan to spend $10 billion in Federal funds over the next 5 years. That is an enormous amount. But during the same 5 years, private enterprise will be investing as much as $200 billion—and in 10 years, $500 billion—to develop the new resources, the new technology, the new capacity America will require for its energy needs in the 1980's. That is just a measure of the magnitude of the project we are undertaking.

But America performs best when called to its biggest tasks. It can

---

[6]Message on the energy crisis, Jan. 23, in *Presidential Documents*, 10: 72-87.
[7]Cf. radio-television address, Nov. 7, 1973, in *AFR, 1973*: 520-28.

truly be said that only in America could a task so tremendous be achieved so quickly, and achieved not by regimentation, but through the effort and ingenuity of a free people, working in a free system.

* * *

America's own prosperity in the years ahead depends on our sharing fully and equitably in an expanding world prosperity. Historic negotiations will take place this year that will enable us to ensure fair treatment in international markets for American workers, American farmers, American investors, and American consumers.

It is vital that the authorities contained in the trade bill I submitted to the Congress[8] be enacted so that the United States can negotiate flexibly and vigorously on behalf of American interests. These negotiations can usher in a new era of international trade that not only increases the prosperity of all nations but also strengthens the peace among all nations.

In the past 5 years, we have made more progress toward a lasting structure of peace in the world than in any comparable time in the Nation's history. We could not have made that progress if we had not maintained the military strength of America. Thomas Jefferson once observed that the price of liberty is eternal vigilance. By the same token, and for the same reason, in today's world, the price of peace is a strong defense as far as the United States is concerned.

In the past 5 years, we have steadily reduced the burden of national defense as a share of the budget, bringing it down from 44 percent in 1969 to 29 percent in the current year. We have cut our military manpower over the past 5 years by more than a third, from 3½ million to 2.2 million.

In the coming year, however, increased expenditures will be needed. They will be needed to assure the continued readiness of our military forces, to preserve present force levels in the face of rising costs, and to give us the military strength we must have if our security is to be maintained and if our initiatives for peace are to succeed.

The question is not whether we can afford to maintain the necessary strength of our defense, the question is whether we can afford not to maintain it, and the answer to that question is no. We must never allow America to become the second strongest nation in the world.

I do not say this with any sense of belligerence, because I recognize the fact that is recognized around the world. America's

[8]Message on trade reform, Apr. 10, 1973, in *AFR, 1973*: 99-115.

military strength has always been maintained to keep the peace, never to break it. It has always been used to defend freedom, never to destroy it. The world's peace, as well as our own, depends on our remaining as strong as we need to be as long as we need to be.

In this year 1974 we will be negotiating with the Soviet Union to place further limits on strategic nuclear arms. Together with our allies, we will be negotiating with the nations of the Warsaw Pact on mutual and balanced reduction of forces in Europe. And we will continue our efforts to promote peaceful economic development in Latin America, in Africa, in Asia. We will press for full compliance with the peace accords that brought an end to American fighting in Indochina,[9] including particularly a provision that promised the fullest possible accounting for those Americans who are missing in action.

And having in mind the energy crisis to which I have referred to earlier, we will be working with the other nations of the world toward agreement on means by which oil supplies can be assured at reasonable prices on a stable basis in a fair way to the consuming and producing nations alike.

All of these are steps toward a future in which the world's peace and prosperity, and ours as well as a result, are made more secure.

Throughout the 5 years that I have served as your President, I have had one overriding aim, and that was to establish a new structure of peace in the world that can free future generations of the scourge of war. I can understand that others may have different priorities. This has been and this will remain my first priority and the chief legacy I hope to leave from the 8 years of my Presidency.

This does not mean that we shall not have other priorities, because as we strengthen the peace we must also continue each year a steady strengthening of our society here at home. Our conscience requires it, our interests require it, and we must insist upon it.

As we create more jobs, as we build a better health care system, as we improve our education, as we develop new sources of energy, as we provide more abundantly for the elderly and the poor, as we strengthen the system of private enterprise that produces our prosperity, as we do all of this and even more, we solidify those essential bonds that hold us together as a nation.

Even more importantly, we advance what in the final analysis government in America is all about.

What it is all about is more freedom, more security, a better life for each one of the 211 million people that live in this land.

We cannot afford to neglect progress at home while pursuing peace abroad. But neither can we afford to neglect peace abroad

---

[9]Agreement on Ending the War and Restoring Peace in Vietnam, Jan. 27, 1973, in same: 39-52.

while pursuing progress at home. With a stable peace, all is possible, but without peace, nothing is possible.

In the written message that I have just delivered to the Speaker and to the President of the Senate, I commented that one of the continuing challenges facing us in the legislative process is that of the timing and pacing of our initiatives, selecting each year among many worthy projects those that are ripe for action at that time.

What is true in terms of our domestic initiatives is true also in the world. This period we now are in in the world—and I say this as one who has seen so much of the world, not only in these past 5 years, but going back over many years—we are in a period which presents a juncture of historic forces unique in this century. They provide an opportunity we may never have again to create a structure of peace solid enough to last a lifetime and more, not just peace in our time, but peace in our children's time as well. It is on the way we respond to this opportunity, more than anything else, that history will judge whether we in America have met our responsibility. And I am confident we will meet that great historic responsibility which is ours today.

It was 27 years ago that John F. Kennedy and I sat in this Chamber, as freshmen Congressmen, hearing our first State of the Union address delivered by Harry Truman.[10] I know from my talks with him as members of the Labor Committee, on which we both served, that neither of us then even dreamed that either one or both might eventually be standing in this place that I now stand in now and that he once stood in before me. It may well be that one of the freshmen Members of the 93d Congress, one of you out there, will deliver his own State of the Union message 27 years from now, in the year 2001.

Well, whichever one it is, I want you to be able to look back with pride and to say that your first years here were great years and recall that you were here in this 93d Congress when America ended its longest war and began its longest peace.

Mr. Speaker, and Mr. President and my distinguished colleagues and our guests:

I would like to add a personal word with regard to an issue that has been of great concern to all Americans over the past year. I refer, of course, to the investigations of the so-called Watergate affair.

As you know, I have provided to the Special Prosecutor voluntarily a great deal of material. I believe that I have provided all the

[10]Message of Jan. 6, 1947; excerpts in *Documents, 1947*: 1-2.

material that he needs to conclude his investigations and to proceed to prosecute the guilty and to clear the innocent.

I believe the time has come to bring that investigation and the other investigations of this matter to an end. One year of Watergate is enough.

And the time has come, my colleagues, for not only the executive, the President, but the Members of Congress, for all of us to join together in devoting our full energies to these great issues that I have discussed tonight which involve the welfare of all of the American people in so many different ways as well as the peace of the world.

I recognize that the House Judiciary Committee has a special responsibility in this area, and I want to indicate on this occasion that I will cooperate with the Judiciary Committee in its investigation. I will cooperate so that it can conclude its investigation, make its decision, and I will cooperate in any way that I consider consistent with my responsibilities to the Office of the Presidency of the United States.

There is only one limitation. I will follow the precedent that has been followed by and defended by every President from George Washington to Lyndon B. Johnson of never doing anything that weakens the Office of the President of the United States or impairs the ability of the Presidents of the future to make the great decisions that are so essential to this Nation and to the world.

Another point I should like to make very briefly. Like every Member of the House and Senate assembled here tonight, I was elected to the office that I hold. And like every Member of the House and Senate, when I was elected to that office, I knew that I was elected for the purpose of doing a job and doing it as well as I possibly can. And I want you to know that I have no intention whatever of ever walking away from the job that the people elected me to do for the people of the United States.

Now, needless to say, it would be understatement if I were not to admit that the year 1973 was not a very easy year for me personally or for my family. And as I have already indicated, the year 1974 presents very great and serious problems as very great and serious opportunities are also presented.

But my colleagues, this I believe: With the help of God, who has blessed this land so richly, with the cooperation of the Congress, and with the support of the American people, we can and we will make the year 1974 a year of unprecedented progress toward our goal of building a structure of lasting peace in the world and a new prosperity without war in the United States of America.

[President Nixon's hopes for an early termination of the Watergate investigations were doomed to bitter disappointment as the process of indictment, trial, and conviction (or acquittal) of his erstwhile associates gained momentum in the following months. Already two of the President's one-time cabinet officers, former Attorney-General John N. Mitchell and former Secretary of Commerce Maurice H. Stans, were under indictment on eighteen counts of conspiracy, obstruction of justice, and perjury in connection with the affairs of fugitive financier and campaign contributor Robert L. Vesco. By the time of their acquittal in New York on April 28, 1974, Mitchell had been indicted a second time—this time with H. R. Haldeman, John D. Ehrlichman, and other former presidential aides—in the Watergate cover-up case,[11] while Ehrlichman and others had also been indicted in a separate case that stemmed from the burglarizing by the White House "plumbers" of the Beverly Hills office of Dr. Daniel Ellsberg's psychiatrist in 1971.[12]

Other casualties of the season included former White House staffers Dwight C. Chapin and Jeb Stuart Magruder, sentenced in May on diverse charges growing out of the Watergate inquiry; former Attorney-General Richard G. Kleindienst, who pleaded guilty to a lack of candor in testifying about the affairs of the International Telephone and Telegraph Corporation; Herbert W. Kalmbach, President Nixon's former personal lawyer, whose fund-raising activities confessedly had included the promise of an ambassadorial appointment in exchange for a $100,000 campaign contribution; and former presidential aide Charles W. Colson, found guilty of attempting to obstruct justice by spreading derogatory information—assertedly at President Nixon's urging—concerning Dr. Ellsberg and his counsel in the "Pentagon Papers" trial. Still to come was the indictment on July 29 (and subsequent acquittal) of yet another Nixon cabinet officer, former Secretary of the Treasury John B. Connally, on charges of accepting payments from representatives of the dairy industry in connection with the fixing

[11]Brought to trial in U.S. District Court in Washington on Oct. 1, 1974, Ehrlichman, Haldeman, and Mitchell were found guilty on Jan. 1, 1975 of conspiracy to obstruct justice, obstruction of justice, and/or false declarations to grand juries; former Assistant Attorney General Robert Mardian was found guilty of conspiracy to obstruct justice; Kenneth Parkinson, a lawyer retained by the Committee for the Reelection of the President, was acquitted. The conviction of Ehrlichman, Haldeman, and Mitchell was upheld, and that of Mardian was reversed, by the U.S. Court of Appeals on Oct. 12, 1976.

[12]The U.S. District Court in Washington on July 12, 1974 found Ehrlichman, G. Gordon Liddy, Bernard Barker, and Eugenio R. Martinez guilty of conspiring to violate the civil rights of psychiatrist Dr. Lewis Fielding; Ehrlichman was also found guilty on three of four counts of making false statements to the Federal Bureau of Investigation and to grand juries. The conviction of Ehrlichman and Liddy was confirmed by the U.S. Court of Appeals on May 17, 1976.

of milk support prices in 1971. Also awaiting sentence was former presidential counsel John W. Dean 3rd, who had long since pleaded guilty in the Watergate cover-up and was expected to bear witness against various past associates, including the President himself, during the coming months.

These actions affecting his subordinates were, of course, merely incidental to the question of President Nixon's personal fate and his ability to withstand the mounting pressure for his resignation or impeachment. No one, except the President himself—and possibly Mr. Haldeman—was in possession of the full facts about his role in the "cover-up" effort that had followed the disclosure of the "bugging" of the Democratic National Committee headquarters on June 17, 1972. Not until late spring would it be known that the grand jury which indicted Haldeman, Ehrlichman, *et al*. in the cover-up on March 1 had also branded the President himself as an "unindicted co-conspirator," one whose guilt supposedly was demonstrated by the contents of a bulging briefcase turned over to District Court Judge John J. Sirica by the Watergate prosecuting force. But even without knowledge of this crucial fact, there would be indications enough in these months that Mr. Nixon's credibility and position were being further undermined with each successive effort to prevent the full facts from coming to light.

Right up to his final capitulation on August 8, the man responsible for leading the American Republic in peace or war would bear the burden of this lonely, unremitting, and increasingly desperate struggle for political and personal survival. This dualism within the leadership confers an oddly schizophrenic quality upon the history of the period. At a superficial level, the presidency and the government continued to function more or less normally, as though nothing much were amiss; yet there were occasional glimpses beneath the surface that half revealed the existence of a seething caldron of doubt, suspicion, and anxiety, of alternating hope and despair, of calculations a thousand times renewed. To measure the interaction of public and private concerns in such a situation is obviously beyond the scope of a documentary narrative; yet any attempt to reconstruct the events of this troubled period must obviously take due account of this only partially hidden dimension.]

3. THE WASHINGTON ENERGY CONFERENCE

(February 11-13, 1974)

[Energy, as President Nixon pointed out in his State of the Union address, had emerged in 1974 as the nation's top priority concern, a status never previously accorded it in all the 186 years of the American presidency. True, the international energy crisis that had developed with such stunning abruptness in the fall of 1973 had not been unforeseen by responsible U.S. authorities. For years, American spokesmen from the President down had been urging coordinated steps to meet a situation in which the energy requirements of the industrial nations were rapidly outstripping the supplies expected to become available under existing economic conditions. President Nixon, once the crisis had struck, had proposed in a speech of November 7, 1973, that the United States commit itself to a "Project Independence" effort aimed at nothing less than energy self-sufficiency by 1980.[1] As to the industrial nations as a group, few if any of which were blessed with undeveloped energy sources comparable to those of the United States, Secretary Kissinger in a London address of December 12, 1973, had proposed the formation of an Energy Action Group of "senior and prestigious officials" to develop within three months "an initial action program for collaboration in all areas of the energy problem."[2]

Such had been the origin of the Washington Energy Conference, to which, as already noted, the President had issued formal invitations on January 9, 1974. Even while it endeavored through diplomatic means to persuade the Arab oil exporting countries to raise the current embargo, the United States proposed to mobilize its friends of the industrial world with a view to preventing the

[1]*AFR, 1973*: 520-28. For background cf. same: 498-501.
[2]Same: 573.

development of similar crises in the future. Limited initially to eight major consuming countries plus the United States, the list of participants was later extended to include ministerial representatives of the nine member states of the European Community, together with West German Foreign Minister Walter Scheel, as President of the Council of the Communities, and François-Xavier Ortoli, the President of the Commission; representatives of Canada, Japan, and Norway; and Emile van Lennep, the Secretary-General of the Organization for Economic Cooperation and Development (OECD). In an attempt to assuage any hurt feelings among the oil-producing countries, President Nixon wrote the heads of government of the thirteen-member Organization of Petroleum Exporting Countries (OPEC) that he hoped there would be a joint conference of consumer and producer nations once a consensus had been established within the former group.[3]

In taking this initiative, the President and Secretary Kissinger had surely recognized that the convening of a meeting of consumer countries was calculated to bring to a head some of the more controversial issues that had divided the industrial powers (including Japan as well as the Atlantic nations) in the recent past. Far more dependent than the United States on a continuing flow of Arab oil, most of these countries had differed sharply with U.S. policy in the Arab-Israeli conflict and remained decidedly wary of anything that could be viewed as "confrontation" of the oil-producing nations. French Foreign Minister Michel Jobert, one of the most articulate European critics of American policy, maintained that rather than a separate meeting of consumer countries as proposed by Washington, the United Nations should sponsor a world energy conference at which *all* interested parties could have their say. "Our attitude is very simple," said Jobert's boss, President Georges Pompidou, on January 24. "We must talk; producers and consumers must understand one another. Therefore, they must meet, and we are ready to meet bilaterally at the European level with a group of Arab producers, for example, and at a global level between rich and poor consumers—for there are important consumers which are poor and are already suffering severely from the situation. . . ."[4]

---

[3]Full texts in *Bulletin*, 70: 123-4; partial texts in *Presidential Documents*, 10: 32-3. See also *Keesing's*: 26357-8.
[4]Quoted in Daniel Colard, "De la Crise de l'énergie au dialogue 'Nord-Sud'," *Studia Diplomatica* (Brussels), 28: 637 (1975).

(3)   The Washington Energy Conference, February 11-13, 1974.

[Although France did not, in the end, refuse to attend the Washington conference, M. Jobert provided an openly unsympathetic audience for Secretary Kissinger's exposition of American views on the ramifications of the energy crisis and the obligations of the nations involved. The Secretary's opening statement nevertheless provided a useful checklist of the endeavors to be set on foot by the United States and other nations over the next several months.]

(a)   Views of the United States: Statement to the conference by Secretary of State Kissinger, February 11, 1974.[5]

On behalf of the President of the United States, I welcome you to this conference.

My great predecessor Dean Acheson once observed that sometimes there is nothing man can do to avert disaster but more often our failure lies "in meeting big, bold, demanding problems with half measures, timorous and cramped." The nations gathered in this room are confronted with an unprecedented challenge to our prosperity and to the entire structure of international cooperation so laboriously constructed over the last generation. The impact of the energy crisis reaches around the world, raising fundamental questions about the future of the developing countries, the prospects for economic growth of all nations, and the hopes for global stability.

The dimensions of the problems were recognizable at least a year ago; indeed, we addressed them as part of our original proposal for a new relationship with Europe and Japan.[6] The challenge will be with us for at least the rest of this decade and perhaps beyond. The seriousness of the problem, its pervasiveness, and the impossibility of national solutions all compel international cooperation—among major consumer nations, among developed and developing nations, and among producer and consumer nations.

The United States has called this conference for one central purpose: to move urgently to resolve the energy problem on the basis of cooperation among *all* nations. Failure to do so would threaten the world with a vicious cycle of competition, autarky, rivalry, and depression such as led to the collapse of world order in the thirties. Fortunately, the problem is still manageable multilaterally: National policies are still evolving, practical solutions to the energy

[5]Department of State Press Release 46, Feb. 11; text and subtitles from *Bulletin*, 70: 201-6.
[6]*AFR, 1973*: 181-9.

problem are technically achievable, and cooperation with the producing countries is still politically open to us.

Let me summarize the U.S. views on the major issues confronting us:

First, the energy situation poses severe economic and political problems for *all* nations. Isolated solutions are impossible. Even those countries, like Canada and the United States, capable of solving the energy problem by largely national means would still suffer because of the impact on them of a world economic crisis. Consumer or producer, affluent or poor, mighty or weak—all have a stake in the prosperity and stability of the international economic system.

Second, this challenge can be met successfully only through concerted international action. Its impact is controllable if we work together; it is unmanageable if we do not.

Third, the developing countries must quickly be drawn into consultation and collaboration. Their futures are the most profoundly affected of all. Unable to meet present prices for oil and fertilizer, they face the threat of starvation and the tragedy of abandoned hopes for further economic development. In the name both of humanity and common sense we cannot permit this.

Fourth, cooperation *not* confrontation must mark our relationships with the producers. We each have legitimate interests. We each face looming dangers. We need each other. If we move rapidly and cooperatively toward collective action, all will benefit.

Fifth, the United States recognizes its own national responsibility to contribute significantly to a collective solution. While we are less immediately affected than others, we see it as a matter of enlightened self-interest—and moral responsibility—to collaborate in the survival and restoration of the world economic system. Project Independence, which will reduce the American demand for world supplies, can be a way station on the road to a new Project Interdependence. We are willing to share American advances in energy technology, to develop jointly new sources of supply, and to establish a system of emergency sharing. We are prepared to make specific proposals in these areas in the follow-on work of this conference.

The Energy Problem

The energy crisis has three dimensions; first, the oil embargo; second, the shortage of supply; and finally, the quantum increase in prices.

The embargo now is directed largely at the United States. We will deal with this issue and ask for no assistance. But while the embargo's immediate economic impact may be selective, its political dimension should be of more general concern. For it carries profound implications for the world community—the manipulation of raw material supplies in order to prescribe the foreign policies of importing countries.

The basic economic problem goes deeper, however. The explosion of demand has outstripped the incentives of producers to increase production. Inflationary pressures in the consumer countries have tended to create incentives to withhold production. This is especially true in a sellers' market, where the producing countries can increase their income by raising prices rather than output.

But there are hopeful signs. World demand has been reduced in recent weeks—partly because of rising prices—and may well remain below last September's level. Thus we may be at the beginning of a dramatic change in the long-term outlook for the world petroleum market. Determined conservation efforts in the consuming countries and vigorous pursuit of alternative energy sources can further reduce the rate of growth in demand for oil.

The most immediate and critical problem concerns price. Current price levels[7] are simply not sustainable. At these levels, the industrial countries alone will incur a current account deficit of \$36–\$40 billion in 1974. Such large increases in costs would seriously magnify both unemployment and inflation in the importing countries, while the effect on domestic production would be deflationary. Pressures for import quotas will become irresistible; a general decline in world trade will follow inevitably.

The threat to the world's poorer nations is even more profound. At present prices the less developed nations will face a current account deficit of \$25–\$30 billion in 1974, of which more than \$10 billion is caused by the increase in oil prices. This deficit is three times the total aid flow of the entire world in recent years. Neither the developing nations nor traditional aid donors can finance such a sum. Even the attempt would destroy two decades of hard-won progress, leaving in its wake a legacy of political tension, social turmoil, and human despair.

Moreover, as a direct result of the oil price hikes the poorer nations' supply of crucial fertilizer has been severely reduced in recent months. Fertilizer prices have at least doubled, raising the specter of famine. We cannot permit this to happen.

The producing countries themselves will not be spared these consequences. Their unprecedented opportunity for dramatic and rapid economic progress cannot escape the effect of global inflation, mounting restrictions in the world's trading and monetary

---

[7]At a meeting of OPEC member countries in Tehran on Dec. 22-23, 1973, the posted price of Saudi Arabian light crude petroleum had been set at \$11.651 per barrel as from Jan. 1, 1974. This compared with a posted price of \$2.591 a year earlier.

system, and the political tensions of unbridled competition. A major task before this conference is to begin creating a framework of cooperation that will fulfill both the hopes of the producing and the needs of the consuming nations.

These global dilemmas cannot be avoided through exclusive bilateral arrangements. We do not dispute the right of sovereign nations to make individual arrangements. But we believe that it is essential that these arrangements follow agreed rules of conduct. In their absence, unrestrained bilateralism is certain to produce disastrous political and economic consequences.

No conceivable increase in bilateral trade with the producing nations can cover the massive payments deficits that each nation faces. The only result of unmanaged bilateralism will be to bid up prices, perhaps even beyond present levels, and to stabilize them at levels that will ruin the countries making the bilateral arrangements before they ruin everyone else.

Thus the ultimate challenge is to the fragile fabric of international principles and institutions. If we fail to achieve a cooperative solution, each of us will be tempted to transfer the problem onto others. This was the approach the industrial world followed during the "beggar-thy-neighbor" policies of the 1930's. We all know the consequences.

A Seven-Point Approach to Cooperation

The great goal of American policy for the past quarter century has been to try to achieve a more cooperative world, to put permanently behind us the narrowly competitive approach which has traditionally ended in conflict—economic or military or both. We maintain our faith in the validity of this goal. In pursuit of the common interest, the United States is willing to make a major contribution, in effort, in science, in technology, and in resources, to a common solution to the energy problem.

The United States is prepared to join with the nations assembled here, and later with the producers and other consumers, to make a truly massive effort toward this major goal: the assurance of abundant energy at reasonable costs to meet the entire world's requirements for economic growth and human needs.

To this end, we suggest that this conference consider seven areas for cooperative exploration: conservation, alternative energy sources, research and development, emergency sharing, international financial cooperation, the less developed countries, consumer-producer relations.

1. *Conservation:* The development of a new energy ethic designed to promote the conservation and most efficient use of ex-

isting energy supplies is crucial. We need a basic commitment to share the sacrifices and costs of conservation and thus reduce pressures on world supply. The United States recognizes that it is the world's most profligate energy consumer. Yet our own national program has, within the past four months, reduced government energy use by 20 percent, industrial consumption by more than 10 percent, gasoline consumption by 9 percent, and natural gas and electricity consumed in residential and commercial buildings by 6 and 10 percent respectively. We shall continue to expand this program. We are prepared as well to join other consumers in pledging a sustained conservation effort. The United States is willing to collaborate in a review of the national programs of each consumer country, in an appraisal of their effectiveness, and in recommendations to governments for additional measures.

2. *Alternative Energy Sources:* The demands of this decade cannot be met unless we expand available supplies through vigorous development of alternative energy sources.

To produce quick results, we must concentrate on known fuel resources. Coal is in abundant supply, but we need to develop the technology neglected during the period of low-cost oil. Continental shelves and nonconventional deposits—coal, shale, and similar resources—need to be developed rapidly.

The United States is prepared to explore the following possibilities for consumer cooperation:

—A collective commitment to develop the fossil fuel resources that are available within our respective borders.

—Coordinated policies to encourage the flow of private capital into the new higher cost energy industries, such as synthetic oils and gas from coal and shale.

—Governmental arrangements to accelerate the global search for new energy sources such as offshore oil.

—International programs to reduce the vulnerability of the major industrial countries to the interruption and manipulation of supply, such as the orderly conversion of key sectors away from petroleum.

3. *Research and Development:* New technologies, and not only new explorations, can provide us with additional sources of energy. Many of our countries are launching large new programs. Our own national program contemplates the expenditure of more than $11 billion in government funds over the next five years and an expected investment of $12.5 billion in private funds in the same period. But we have no monopoly on the most advanced and promising approaches. It is to our mutual benefit to coordinate and com-

bine our efforts. Thus the United States is prepared to make a major contribution of its most advanced energy research and development to a broad program of international cooperation in energy.

Without a doubt, a significant portion of new energy will be supplied from nuclear reactors, for which increased quantities of enriched uranium will be needed. Within a framework of broad cooperation in energy, the United States is prepared to examine the sharing of enrichment technology—diffusion and centrifuge. Such a multilateral enrichment effort could be undertaken in a framework of assured supply, geographic dispersion, and controls against further proliferation. We shall submit principles to guide such a cooperative enterprise for the follow-on work which we are proposing.

4. *Emergency Sharing:*   The allocation of available supplies in time of emergencies and prolonged shortages is essential.

None of us can be certain how the world balance of supply and demand for petroleum will develop or what political contingencies may arise. But we cannot leave our security or our national economies to forces outside our control.

The United States declares its willingness to share available energy in times of emergency or prolonged shortages. We would be prepared to allocate an agreed portion of our total petroleum supply provided other consuming countries with indigenous production do likewise. As we move toward self-sufficiency, our ability for sharing would of course increase.

Building on the earlier work done in the OECD, definite recommendations should be submitted to governments including:

—A sharing formula;
—Criteria to determine when a supply shortage exists;
—A mechanism which would implement and terminate the sharing arrangement; and
—Complementary programs such as stockpiling and standby rationing schemes.

5. *International Financial Cooperation:*   The structure and strength of the world's trading and monetary system must be restored and strengthened. If there is no way for the industrial countries collectively to eliminate the trade deficits created by their higher oil import bills, they can attempt to do so individually only at the cost of enlarging someone else's problems. In addition, the producing nations are accumulating financial claims against the consuming nations at a rate unprecedented in history.

In the past, the various national and international money markets have efficiently recycled oil revenue funds back into the economies of the consuming countries. At least for industrial countries, these markets can in large part continue to perform that function. The removal of our capital controls and the easing of controls in other countries should help. But the magnitude of the new flows could put serious strains on the operations of these markets. The funds flowing to particular consumer countries may not reflect their needs for balance of payments financing; severe instability could result if these funds were repeatedly shifted across currency boundaries without adequate financial cooperation among the industrialized countries. Here again there is a crucial congruent interest between the producers and consumers and an urgent need for cooperative solutions.

Measures to deal with the economic effects of high oil prices must be adopted on a broad front. Recommendations should include:

—New mechanisms to facilitate the distribution of international capital flows from oil revenue surpluses.

—Means for producers and consumers to cooperate in building confidence in investment policies and the integrity of investments.

—Steps to facilitate the fuller participation of producing nations in existing international institutions and to contribute to the urgent needs of the developing consumer countries.

6. *The Less Developed Countries:* The needs of the developing countries are a particularly urgent dimension of the energy crisis. Massive increases in oil import costs are occurring at a time when the export prospects of many less developed countries have sharply diminished as a result of the slowdown in world economic activity. Even at lower oil prices, the balance of payments problems of the less developed countries would require sustained attention.

Our approach to this human and economic challenge should be based on several principles:

—The developing consumer countries should be invited to join the next stage of our deliberations.

—Developed countries should avoid cutting their concessional aid programs in response to balance of payments problems. In this regard, the United States will urge the Congress to restore our contribution to the International Development Association (IDA).[8]

—The wealth of the producer nations opens up a potential new source of large-scale capital assistance for development.

[8]Cf. Chapter 24 at notes 2 and 8.

The producer nations should have a special understanding for the problems facing the poorer nations. We should encourage and facilitate their participation in international and regional institutions.

—Urgent measures must be taken to assure sufficient fertilizer supplies for the coming year. The immediate problem is to provide oil at a price that will allow existing fertilizer production capacity to be fully utilized. The longer term problem is to create sufficient capacity to meet the world's rapidly growing needs. The United States would be prepared to contribute its technological skills to such a joint enterprise.

7. *Consumer-Producer Relations:*   Our ultimate goal must be to create a cooperative framework within which producers and consumers will be able to accommodate their differences and reconcile their needs and aspirations. Only in this way can we assure the evolution and growth of the world economy and the stability of international relations. We must work toward the objective of preventing coercion of the weak by the strong as of the strong by the weak; the producing nations must be given a secure stake in an expanding world economy and the consuming nations a secure source of supply.

It seems clear that enlightened self-interest of consumers and producers need not and should not be in conflict. Future generations may not enjoy a permanent source of petroleum. Excessively high prices are already calling forth massive investments in alternative energy sources, which raises the prospect of lower prices and shrunken export markets for the producers in the future. But stable oil earnings, at just prices, wisely invested and increasing by the principle of compound interest, will be available as a long-term source of income.

Thus the producers must have an interest in a "just" price and in stable long-term political and economic relations. Therefore, at the consumer-producer conference for which we are heading, let us discuss what constitutes a just price and how to assure long-term investments. A well-conceived producer-consumer meeting, in which the consumers do not seek selfish advantages either as a group or individually, far from leading to confrontation, could instead lay the basis of a new cooperative relationship. But it will do so only if it is well prepared—and if the consumers have first constructed a solid basis of cooperation among themselves.

The Next Steps

The United States is not interested in establishing new institutions for their own sake. We are solely concerned with practical results. Some of the tasks I have suggested can be carried out by existing international mechanisms; others will break new ground. The essential requirement is to see that concrete recommendations are submitted to the next conference. In order to carry our work forward, we believe a coordinating group should be established with the following responsibilities:

—To relate the tasks that are assigned to existing bodies to our future work.

—To undertake those tasks for which there are presently no suitable bodies.

—To prepare for the next meeting.

Another conference of consumers should then be called at the foreign minister level to assess the work in all seven areas. This conference could include representatives of the less developed countries.

This meeting would lead to a third conference of consumers and producers.

We are open to suggestions about the locale of these next conferences. We should aim to complete the entire process by May 1.

The approach to global cooperation outlined here has prompted the President's invitations to you to join us here today. This conception is ambitious, but the need is great. Therefore let us resolve:

—To meet the special challenges and opportunities facing the major consuming nations with a program of cooperation.

—To bring the developing nations into immediate consultation and collaboration with us.

—To prepare for a positive and productive dialogue with the producing nations.

As we look toward the end of this century, we know that the energy crisis indicates the birth pains of global interdependence. Our response could well determine our capacity to deal with the international agenda of the future.

We confront a fundamental decision. Will we consume ourselves in nationalistic rivalry which the realities of interdependence make suicidal? Or will we acknowledge our interdependence and shape cooperative solutions?

Our choice is clear, our responsibility compelling: We must demonstrate to future generations that our vision was equal to our challenge.

[Buttressed by more technical statements by Federal Energy Administrator William E. Simon and Secretary of the Treasury George P. Shultz,[9] the American action program won broad approval from all participants save France, whose philosophical and practical objections occasioned some dissension among the European delegations and prolonged the conference for an extra day. The main conclusions of the meeting were set forth in a final communiqué in which the negative position of France was duly noted.]

(b) Final communiqué of the conference, February 13, 1974.[10]

Summary Statement

1. Foreign Ministers of Belgium, Canada, Denmark, France, the Federal Republic of Germany, Ireland, Italy, Japan, Luxembourg, The Netherlands, Norway, the United Kingdom, the United States met in Washington from February 11 to 13, 1974. The European Community was represented as such by the President of the Council and the President of the Commission. Finance Ministers, Ministers with responsibility for Energy Affairs, Economic Affairs and Science and Technology Affairs also took part in the meeting. The Secretary General of the OECD also participated in the meeting. The Ministers examined the international energy situation and its implications and charted a course of actions to meet this challenge which requires constructive and comprehensive solutions. To this end they agreed on specific steps to provide for effective international cooperation. The Ministers affirmed that solutions to the world's energy problem should be sought in consultation with producer countries and other consumers.

Analysis of the Situation

2. They noted that during the past three decades progress in improving productivity and standards of living was greatly facilitated by the ready availability of increasing supplies of energy at fairly stable prices. They recognized that the problem of meeting growing demand existed before the current situation and that the needs of the world economy for increased energy supplies require positive long-term solutions.

3. They concluded that the current energy situation results from

[9]*Bulletin*, 70: 207-20.
[10]Washington Energy Conference Document 17 (rev. 2); text from *Bulletin*, 70: 220-22.

an intensification of these underlying factors and from political developments.

4. They reviewed the problems created by the large rise in oil prices and agreed with the serious concern expressed by the International Monetary Fund's Committee of Twenty at its recent Rome meeting[11] over the abrupt and significant changes in prospect for the world balance of payments structure.

5. They agreed that present petroleum prices presented the structure of world trade and finance with an unprecedented situation. They recognized that none of the consuming countries could hope to insulate itself from these developments, or expect to deal with the payments impact of oil prices by the adoption of monetary or trade measures alone. In their view, the present situation, if continued, could lead to a serious deterioration in income and employment, intensify inflationary pressures, and endanger the welfare of nations. They believed that financial measures by themselves will not be able to deal with the strains of the current situation.

6. They expressed their particular concern about the consequences of the situation for the developing countries and recognized the need for efforts by the entire international community to resolve this problem. At current oil prices the additional energy costs for developing countries will cause a serious setback to the prospect for economic development of these countries.

7. *General Conclusions.* They affirmed, that, in the pursuit of national policies, whether in trade, monetary or energy fields, efforts should be made to harmonize the interests of each country on the one hand and the maintenance of the world economic system on the other. Concerted international cooperation between all the countries concerned including oil producing countries could help to accelerate an improvement in the supply and demand situation, ameliorate the adverse economic consequences of the existing situation and lay the groundwork for a more equitable and stable international energy relationship.

8. They felt that these considerations taken as a whole made it essential that there should be a substantial increase of international cooperation in all fields. Each participant in the Conference stated its firm intention to do its utmost to contribute to such an aim, in close cooperation both with the other consumer countries and with the producer countries.

9. They concurred in the need for a comprehensive action program to deal with all facets of the world energy situation by cooperative measures. In so doing they will build on the work of the OECD. They recognized that they may wish to invite, as ap-

[11] Jan. 17-18. 1974: cf. Chapter 10 at note 1.

propriate, other countries to join with them in these efforts. Such an action program of international cooperation would include, as appropriate, the sharing of means and efforts, while concerting national policies, in such areas as:

—The conservation of energy and restraint of demand.
—A system of allocating oil supplies in times of emergency and severe shortages.
—The acceleration of development of additional energy sources so as to diversify energy supplies.
—The acceleration of energy research and development programs through international cooperative efforts.[12]

10. With respect to monetary and economic questions, they decided to intensify their cooperation and to give impetus to the work being undertaken in the IMF [International Monetary Fund], the World Bank and the OECD on the economic and monetary consequences of the current energy situation, in particular to deal with balance of payments disequilibria. They agreed that:

—In dealing with the balance of payments impact of oil prices they stressed the importance of avoiding competitive depreciation and the escalation of restrictions on trade and payments or disruptive actions in external borrowing.*[13]
—While financial cooperation can only partially alleviate the problems which have recently arisen for the international economic system, they will intensify work on short-term financial measures and possible long-term mechanisms to reinforce existing official and market credit facilities.*
—They will pursue domestic economic policies which will reduce as much as possible the difficulties resulting from the current energy cost levels.*[14]
—They will make strenuous efforts to maintain and enlarge the flow of development aid bilaterally and through multilateral institutions, on the basis of international solidarity embracing all countries with appropriate resources.

11. Further, they have agreed to accelerate wherever practicable their own national programs of new energy sources and technology which will help the overall world-wide supply and demand situation.

---

[12]France does not accept point 9. [Footnote in original.]
[13]In point 10, France does not accept paragraphs cited with asterisks. [Footnote in original.]
[14]In point 10, Frances does not accept paragraphs cited with asterisks. [Footnote in original.]

12. They agreed to examine in detail the role of international oil companies.

13. They stressed the continued importance of maintaining and improving the natural environment as part of developing energy sources and agreed to make this an important goal of their activity.

14. They further agreed that there was need to develop a cooperative multilateral relationship with producing countries, and other consuming countries that takes into account the long-term interests of all. They are ready to exchange technical information with these countries on the problem of stabilizing energy supplies with regard to quantity and prices.

15. They welcomed the initiatives in the UN to deal with the larger issues of energy and primary products at a world-wide level and in particular for a special session of the UN General Assembly.[15]

Establishment of Follow-on Machinery

16. They agreed to establish a coordinating group headed by senior officials to direct and to coordinate the development of the actions referred to above. The coordinating group shall decide how best to organize its work. It should:

—Monitor and give focus to the tasks that might be addressed in existing organizations;

—Establish such *ad hoc* working groups as may be necessary to undertake tasks for which there are presently no suitable bodies;

—Direct preparations of a conference of consumer and producer countries which will be held at the earliest possible opportunity and which, if necessary, will be preceded by a further meeting of consumer countries.[16]

17. They agreed that the preparations for such meetings should involve consultations with developing countries and other consumer and producer countries.[17]

[The coordinating group provided for in paragraph 16 of the communiqué was duly constituted later in February, and held a working session at Brussels on March 13-14 at which it referred some topics to the OECD for further study and assigned others to working parties drawn from its own membership. The ultimate

---

[15]Cf. Chapter 7.
[16]France does not accept points 16 and 17. [Footnote in original.]
[17]France does not accept points 16 and 17. [Footnote in original.]

result would be the International Energy Program and International Energy Agency established in November.[18]

The plan for a world energy conference or a conference of producer and consumer nations, meanwhile, was at least temporarily thrust aside by the demand of many developing countries for a special session of the U.N. General Assembly that would address itself not merely to energy problems but to the whole question of raw materials and development. That meeting, to be held in New York April 9-May 2, would mark a further intensification of the general "North-South" dialogue between developing and industrial countries.[19]]

[18]Cf. Chapter 29.
[19]Cf. Chapter 7.

4. AN AMERICAN DIALOGUE: PANAMA AND TLATELOLCO

(February 7-23, 1974)

[In Latin America as elsewhere, the events of 1973 had introduced what could be readily identified as the beginning of a fundamentally "new era" in international relations. Quite early in that year, the deepening dissatisfaction of most Latin American countries with the workings and achievements of the "inter-American system" had led the General Assembly of the Organization of American States (OAS) to set up a special study committee, known by its Spanish initials as CEESI, to conduct a thoroughgoing reexamination of the inter-American association and propose appropriate measures for its restructuring. Armed with this mandate, CEESI had lost little time in initiating a complete rewriting of the basic Inter-American Treaty of Reciprocal Assistance (Rio Pact) of 1947[1] as well as the OAS Charter which had been adopted in 1948 and extensively revised in the late 1960s.[2]

Criticism of U.S. policy in the hemisphere, fed by lively dissatisfaction with the U.S. position on a host of economic and political issues of interest to Latin American and Caribbean countries, had meanwhile reached an explosive climax at the time of the military coup of September 11, 1973, against the Chilean administration led by President Salvador Allende Gossens. Although U.S. authorities were categorical in their disclaimers of responsibility for the events in Chile, the death of Allende and the resultant wave of anti-U.S. sentiment could only reinforce the conviction that the time had come to try to cultivate a more satisfactory rela-

[1]Opened for signature at Rio de Janeiro Sept. 24, 1947 and entered into force Dec. 3, 1948 (TIAS 1838); text in *Documents, 1947*: 534-40.
[2]Charter of the Organization of American States, signed at Bogotá Apr. 30, 1948 and entered into force Dec. 13, 1951 (TIAS 2361; text in *Documents, 1948*: 484-502); Protocol of Amendment to the Charter of the Organization of American States, signed at Buenos Aires Feb. 27, 1967 and entered into force Feb. 27, 1970 (TIAS 6847; 21 UST 607; summary in *Documents, 1968-69*: 399-401).

tionship with the nations to the south. One of Dr. Kissinger's first acts after becoming Secretary of State on September 22, 1973, had been a proposal to the Latin American countries to enter into a "new dialogue" with the United States in a concerted effort to find solutions to hemispheric problems.[3] Responding to what was hailed as an unusual mark of U.S. interest, the Latin American Foreign Ministers had met in Bogotá, Colombia, in November 1973 to draw up an agenda for the proposed dialogue and to prepare for an early meeting with the U.S. Secretary of State.[4]]

(4)   Accord with Panama, February 7, 1974.

[Even before his projected meeting with the Latin American Foreign Ministers, Secretary Kissinger had moved to ease one hemisphere problem whose solution was widely thought to be long overdue. This was the long-pending matter of a renegotiation of the treaties governing the status of the Panama Canal and the Canal Zone, an undertaking to which the United States and Panama had committed themselves as far back as 1964 without, however, arriving as yet at any satisfactory conclusion. Aware of Panama's increasing impatience and of the widespread tendency to view the issue as a test of U.S. intentions, Secretary Kissinger had sent Ambassador at Large Ellsworth Bunker to Panama in November 1973 with instructions to develop a "new approach" to agreement on a "modernized" Canal treaty.[5] By February 1974, the results of this "new approach" impressed the Secretary of State as being sufficiently promising to warrant a personal visit to the Panamanian capital, where he was joined by Panamanian Foreign Minister Juan Antonio Tack in a statement setting forth the fundamental principles on which they both agreed that the eventual treaty should be based.]

(a)   Agreement on Principles for Negotiation of a New Panama Canal Treaty: Joint statement initialed by Secretary of State Kissinger and Juan Antonio Tack, Minister of Foreign Affairs of the Republic of Panama, at Panama City, February 7, 1974.[6]

---

[3]Toast at New York, Oct. 5, in *AFR, 1973*: 415-17.

[4]Documents of the Conference of Bogotá (Nov. 14-16, 1973) are collected in U.S. Senate, 93d Cong., 2d sess., Committee on Foreign Relations, *The Inter-American Conference of Tlatelolco in Mexico City: Report of Senator Mike Mansfield* (Committee print; Washington: GPO, Mar. 1974): 8-11.

[5]For background see *AFR, 1971*: 486-93; same, *1973*: 119-10, 126-39, and 412.

[6]Text from *Bulletin*, 70: 184-5.

JOINT STATEMENT BY THE HONORABLE HENRY A. KISSINGER,
SECRETARY OF STATE OF THE UNITED STATES OF AMERICA,
AND HIS EXCELLENCY JUAN ANTONIO TACK,
MINISTER OF FOREIGN AFFAIRS OF THE REPUBLIC OF PANAMA,
ON FEBRUARY 7, 1974 AT PANAMA

The United States of America and the Republic of Panama have been engaged in negotiations to conclude an entirely new treaty respecting the Panama Canal, negotiations which were made possible by the Joint Declaration between the two countries of April 3, 1964, agreed to under the auspices of the Permanent Council of the Organization of American States acting provisionally as the Organ of Consultation.[7] The new treaty would abrogate the treaty existing since 1903 and its subsequent amendments,[8] establishing the necessary conditions for a modern relationship between the two countries based on the most profound mutual respect.

Since the end of last November, the authorized representatives of the two governments have been holding important conversations which have permitted agreement to be reached on a set of fundamental principles which will serve to guide the negotiators in the effort to conclude a just and equitable treaty eliminating, once and for all, the causes of conflict between the two countries.

The principles to which we have agreed, on behalf of our respective governments, are as follows:

1. The treaty of 1903 and its amendments will be abrogated by the conclusion of an entirely new interoceanic canal treaty.

2. The concept of perpetuity will be eliminated. The new treaty concerning the lock canal shall have a fixed termination date.

3. Termination of United States jurisdiction over Panamanian territory shall take place promptly in accordance with terms specified in the treaty.

4. The Panamanian territory in which the canal is situated shall be returned to the jurisdiction of the Republic of Panama. The Republic of Panama, in its capacity as territorial sovereign, shall grant to the United States of America, for the duration of the new interoceanic canal treaty and in accordance with what that treaty states, the right to use the lands, waters and airspace which may be necessary for the operation, maintenance, protection and defense of the canal and the transit of ships.

5. The Republic of Panama shall have a just and equitable share of the benefits derived from the operation of the canal in its territory. It is recognized that the geographic position of its ter-

[7]*Documents, 1964*: 311-12.
[8]Listed in *AFR, 1973*: 132 n. 23 and 24.

ritory constitutes the principal resource of the Republic of Panama.

6. The Republic of Panama shall participate in the administration of the canal, in accordance with a procedure to be agreed upon in the treaty. The treaty shall also provide that Panama will assume total responsibility for the operation of the canal upon the termination of the treaty. The Republic of Panama shall grant to the United States of America the rights necessary to regulate the transit of ships through the canal and operate, maintain, protect and defend the canal, and to undertake any other specific activity related to those ends, as may be agreed upon in the treaty.

7. The Republic of Panama shall participate with the United States of America in the protection and defense of the canal in accordance with what is agreed upon in the new treaty.

8. The United States of America and the Republic of Panama, recognizing the important services rendered by the interoceanic Panama Canal to international maritime traffic, and bearing in mind the possibility that the present canal could become inadequate for said traffic, shall agree bilaterally on provisions for new projects which will enlarge canal capacity. Such provisions will be incorporated in the new treaty in accord with the concepts established in principle 2.

[Although these principles would obviously require careful spelling out in the future treaty, their acceptance even in this preliminary form appeared to mark the first significant advance in the negotiations in several years. Particularly noted was the abandonment by the United States of its previous insistence on perpetual control of the Canal and related facilities and areas. Some of the broader implications for U.S.-Latin American relations were brought out by Secretary Kissinger in an address at the initialing ceremony.]

(b) Address by Secretary of State Kissinger at the initialing ceremony, Panama City, February 7, 1974. [9]

We meet here today to embark upon a new adventure together. Our purpose is to begin replacing an old treaty and to move toward a new relationship. What we sign today, hopefully, marks as well the advent of a new era in the history of our hemisphere and thus makes a major contribution to the structure of world peace.

Meeting as we do on this isthmus which links North and South and Atlantic with Pacific, we cannot but be conscious of history—a history which has profoundly changed the course of human affairs. Four centuries ago the conquistadors landed here bringing faith

---

[9]Department of State Press Release 42, Feb. 7; text from *Bulletin*, 70: 181-4.

and taking booty. They were representatives of the traditional style and use of power. Seventy years ago, when the Panama Canal was begun, strength and influence remained the foundations of world order.

Today we live in a profoundly transformed environment. Among the many revolutions of our time none is more significant than the change in the nature of world order. Power has grown so monstrous that it defies calculation; the quest for justice has become universal. A stable world cannot be imposed by force; it must derive from consensus. Mankind can achieve community only on the basis of shared aspirations.

This is why the meeting today between representatives of the most powerful nation of the Western Hemisphere and one of the smallest holds great significance. In the past our negotiation would have been determined by relative strength. Today we have come together in an act of conciliation. We recognize that no agreement can endure unless the parties to it want to maintain it. Participation in partnership is far preferable to reluctant acquiescence.

What we do here today contains a message, as well, for our colleagues in the Western Hemisphere who, in their recent meeting in Bogotá, gave impetus to this negotiation. The method of solution and the spirit of partnership between Panama and the United States as embodied in this agreement are an example of what we mean by the spirit of community in the Western Hemisphere; it can be the first step toward a new era which we believe will be given fresh hope and purpose when we meet again with the Foreign Ministers of all the hemisphere in two weeks' time.

The United States and Panama

The relationship between Panama and the United States is rooted in extraordinary human accomplishment—the Panama Canal, a monument to man's energy and creative genius. But as is so often the case, man's technological triumph outstripped his political imagination:

—For 60 years the safe, efficient, and equitable operation of the canal has given to Panama, to the United States, and to all nations benefits beyond calculation.

—Yet the canal still operates under the terms of a treaty signed in 1903, when the realities of international affairs were still shaped by traditional precepts of power.

—The tensions generated by these contradictions, the endless debates over the costs and benefits of the convention of 1903, have jeopardized the ability of our two countries not only to work together to meet future demands upon the canal but also to develop a constructive relationship as friends.

We must assess the document we have just signed against this background. Above all, we must judge it in the context of what it means for the peoples of the United States and Panama and what it can mean for the people of the Western Hemisphere.

The eight principles in this agreement constitute, as General Torrijos [Brig. Gen. Omar Torrijos, Head of Government of Panama] has said, a "philosophy of understanding." Sacrificing neither interest nor self-respect, Panama and the United States have made a choice for partnership. Meeting in dignity and negotiating with fairness, we have acknowledged that cooperation is imposed on us by our mutual need and by our mutual recognition of the necessity for a cooperative world order. Foreign Minister Tack and Ambassador Bunker have shown that Panama's sovereignty and the vital interests of the United States in the Panama Canal can be made compatible. They have engaged in an act of statesmanship impelled by the conviction that we are part of a larger community in the Americas and in the world.

In that spirit of partnership the United States and Panama have met as equals and have determined that a just solution must recognize:

—First, that Panama and the United States have a mutual stake in the isthmus: Panama in its greatest natural resource, and the United States in the use and defense of the canal.

—Second, that the arrangement which may have been suitable 70 years ago to both the United States and Panama must be adjusted to meet the realities of the contemporary world.

—Third, that a new treaty is required which will strengthen the relationship between us while protecting what is essential to each. A new agreement must restore Panama's territorial sovereignty while preserving the interests of the United States and its participation in what is for us an indispensable international waterway.

While we have taken a great stride forward, we must still travel a difficult distance to our goal. There is opposition in both our countries to a reasonable resolution of our differences. Old slogans are often more comforting than changes that reflect new realities. It is the essence of revolutions that to their contemporaries they appear as irritating interruptions in the course of a comfortable normalcy. But it is equally true that those who fail to understand new currents are inevitably engulfed by them.

We are determined to shape our own destiny. Our negotiators will require wisdom, purposefulness, tenacity. They will meet obstacles and disagreements. Yet they will succeed—for our relations and our commitments to a new community among us and in this hemisphere demand it.

In the President's name, I hereby commit the United States to complete this negotiation successfully and as quickly as possible.

The Western Hemisphere Community

We are here today not just as two sovereign nations, but as representatives of our hemisphere. We meet at the place where Simón Bolívar enunciated the concept of an inter-American system. We meet at a point of time between meetings of Foreign Ministers in Bogotá and Mexico City which can mark a historic turning point in making Bolívar's vision come true.

I know that many of my country's southern neighbors believe they have been the subject of too many surveys and too few policies. The United States is accused of being better at finding slogans for its Latin American policy than at finding answers to the problems that face us all.

Some of these criticisms are justified. At times rhetoric has exceeded performance. But the United States has been torn by many problems; only from afar does it appear as if all choices are equally open to us. We have not been willfully neglectful. And in any case, we have recognized that the time for a new approach is overdue.

I have come here today to tell you on behalf of our President that we are fully committed to a major effort to build a vital Western Hemisphere community. We understand our own needs:

—To live in a hemisphere lifted by progress, not torn by hatreds;

—To insure that the millions of people south of us will lead lives of fulfillment not embittered by frustration and despair; and

—Above all, to recognize that in the great dialogue between the developed and the less developed nations, we cannot find answers anywhere if we do not find them here in the Western Hemisphere.

It is in this spirit that I shall meet my colleagues in Mexico City later this month to deal with the issues posed by them in their Bogotá meeting. We attached particular significance to the fact that the meeting in Mexico City—its substance and its impetus—is the product of Latin American initiative. It is a response to the necessities of the times such as the United States had hoped to achieve with partners elsewhere in the world.

The United States will not come to Mexico City with a program that presumes to have all the answers. Nor will we pretend that our lost opportunities can be remedied by yet another freshly packaged program labeled "Made in the U.S.A." But we shall come with an open mind and, perhaps more importantly, with an open heart. We are at a moment of truth, and we shall speak the truth.

We know that our neighbors are worried about the blackmail of the strong. We want them to know that we are sympathetic to this concern. At the same time, blackmail is no more acceptable from any other source. We need each other. So let us all seek solutions free of pressure and confrontation, based on reciprocity and mutual respect. In Mexico City we can but lay the foundations for the future. But building upon what we achieve in Mexico City we can, over the months and years ahead, erect an edifice of true partnership, real trust, and fruitful collaboration.

Thus we approach the meeting in Mexico with but one prejudice: a profound belief that the Americas, too, have arrived at a moment of basic choice, a time of decision between fulfillment together and frustration apart. Our choice will be found in the answers we give to these critical questions:

—Can we make our diversity a source of strength, drawing on the richness of our material and moral heritage?

—In short, can the countries of Latin America, the Caribbean, and the United States, each conscious of its own identity, fashion a common vision of the world and of this hemisphere—not just as they are, but as they are becoming and as we feel they should be—so that we can move together toward the achievement of common goals?

We will conduct the broader dialogue we have all set for ourselves in Mexico City with the same commitment to reciprocity, the same consideration of each other's interests, that marked the negotiations between the United States and Panama.

For centuries men everywhere have seen this hemisphere as offering mankind the chance to break with their eternal tragedies and to achieve their eternal hopes. That was what was new about the New World. It was the drama of men choosing their own destinies.

An American poet [T. S. Eliot] has written:

> We shall not cease from exploration
> And the end of all our exploring
> Will be to arrive where we started
> And know the place for the first time.

Panama and the United States have now begun this exploration. Our sister republics can make the same choice. Our creativity, our energy, and our sense of community will be on trial. But if we are equal to the opportunity, we will indeed arrive where we started—a hemisphere which again inspires the world with hope by its example. Then we shall indeed know the place for the first time, because for the first time we shall truly have fulfilled its promise.

(5) The Conference of Tlatelolco (Mexico City), February 18-23, 1974.

[Dr. Kissinger's repeated references to the forthcoming meeting in Mexico City reflected the importance attached by the United States as well as the Latin American countries to this new hemispheric dialogue which was to begin within a few days of the conclusion of the Washington Energy Conference. For the first time in memory, the Secretary of State was to be accompanied by a delegation that would include the leadership of both houses of Congress as well as other legislators experienced in inter-American affairs.[10]

Attended by the Foreign Ministers of 24 Latin American and Caribbean countries and with only Cuba conspicuous by its absence, the "Conference of Tlatelolco" (a suburb of Mexico City) was held in two successive phases, the Latin American and Caribbean representatives meeting alone on February 18-20 before being joined by Secretary Kissinger and the U.S. delegation for the second and final phase on February 21-23.

Addressing the conference soon after his arrival on the 21st, the Secretary of State provided some fresh details about the way the United States proposed to implement the evolving relationship with its southern partners.]

(a) Statement to the conference by Secretary of State Kissinger, February 21, 1974.[11]

We owe our host country and its leaders a profound debt of gratitude for sponsoring this meeting. Personally, I have spent many happy days in this great country. And I have had the privilege of the advice, wisdom, and on occasion the tenacious opposition of your President and Foreign Minister.[12] I look forward to an equally frank, friendly, intense, but constructive dialogue at this conference.

[10]Secretary Kissinger was accompanied by Senators Mike Mansfield (Majority Leader), Hugh Scott (Minority Leader), and Gale W. McGee (Chairman, Foreign Relations Subcommittee on Western Hemisphere Affairs), and by Representatives Carl Albert (Speaker), Dante B. Fascell, and William S. Mailliard, who soon afterward succeeded Ambassador Joseph J. Jova as U.S. Representative to the OAS.

[11]Department of State Press Release 62, Feb. 21; text and subtitles from Bulletin, 70: 257-62.

[12]Emilio O. Rabasa, Mexican Secretary of Foreign Relations, was President of the conference.

On a plaque in Mexico's imposing Museum of Anthropology are etched phrases which carry special meaning for this occasion:

Nations find courage and confidence to face the future looking to the greatness of their past. Mexican, seek yourself in the mirror of this greatness. Stranger, confirm here the unity of human destiny. Civilizations pass; but we will always reflect the glory of the struggle to build them.

We assemble in the splendid shadows of history's monuments. They remind us of what can be achieved by inspiration and of what can be lost when peoples miss their opportunity. We in the Americas now have a great opportunity to vindicate our old dream of building a new world of justice and peace, to assure the well-being of our peoples, and to leave what we achieve as a monument to our striving.

Our common impulse in meeting here is to fulfill the promise of America as the continent which beckoned men to fulfill what was best in them. Our common reality is the recognition of our diversity. Our common determination is to derive strength from that diversity. Our common task is to forge our historical and geographical links into shared purpose and endeavor.

In this spirit the United States offered a new dialogue last October. In this spirit the countries of the Americas responded in Bogotá last November.

We meet here as equals—representatives of our individual modes of life, but united by one aspiration: to build a new community.

We have a historic foundation on which to build. We live in a world that gives our enterprise a special meaning and urgency.

On behalf of President Nixon, I commit the United States to undertake this venture with dedication and energy.

The U.S. Commitment

One concern has dominated all others as I have met privately with some of my colleagues in this room. Does the United States really care? Is this another exercise of high-sounding declarations followed by long periods of neglect? What is new in this dialogue?

These questions—not unrelated to historical experience—define our task. On behalf of my colleagues and myself, let me stress that we are here to give effect to a new attitude and to help shape a new policy. The presence of so many distinguished leaders from the U.S. Congress underlines the depth of the U.S. concern for its neighbors and the determination of our government to implement our agreements through a partnership between the executive and legislative branches.

The time has come to infuse the Western Hemisphere relationships with a new spirit. In the 19th and early 20th centuries, the United States declared what those outside this hemisphere should not do within it. In the 1930's we stipulated what the United States would not do. Later we were prone to set standards for the political, economic, and social structures of our sister republics.

Today we meet on the basis of your agenda and our common needs. We agree with one of my distinguished colleagues who said on arrival that the time had come to meet as brothers, not as sons. Today, together, we can begin giving expression to our common aspirations and start shaping our common future.

In my view, our fundamental task at this meeting, more important even than the specifics of our agenda, is to set a common direction and infuse our efforts with new purpose. Let us therefore avoid both condescension and confrontation. If the United States is not to presume to supply all the answers, neither should it be asked to bear all the responsibilities. Let us together bring about a new commitment to the inter-American community. Let us use the specific issues we discuss here as a roadmap for the future.

Let us not be satisfied with proclamations but chart a program of work worthy of the challenge before us.

Let us create a new spirit in our relations—the spirit of Tlatelolco.

An Interdependent World

A century ago a U.S. President [Grover Cleveland] described to the Congress the difficulties facing the country: "It is a condition which confronts us—not a theory." The condition we confront today is a world where interdependence is a fact, not a choice.

The products of man's technical genius—weapons of incalculable power, a global economic system, instantaneous communications, a technology that consumes finite resources at an ever-expanding rate—have compressed this planet and multiplied our mutual dependence. The problems of peace, of justice, of human dignity, of hunger and inflation and pollution, of the scarcity of physical materials and the surplus of spiritual despair, cannot be resolved on a national basis. All are now caught up in the tides of world events—consumers and producers, the affluent and the poor, the free and the oppressed, the mighty and the weak.

The world and this hemisphere can respond in one of two ways:

There is the path of autarky. Each nation can try to exploit its particular advantages in resources and skills and bargain bilaterally for what it needs. Each nation can try to look after itself and shrug its shoulders at the plight of those less well endowed. But history tells us that this leads to ever more vicious competition, the waste of resources, the stunting of technological advance, and most fundamentally, growing political tensions which unravel the fabric of global stability. If we take this route, we and our children will pay a terrible price.

Or we can take the path of collaboration. Nations can recognize that only in working with others can they most effectively work for themselves. A cooperative world reflects the imperatives of technical and economic necessity but, above all, the sweep of human aspirations.

The United States is pledged to this second course. We believe that we of the Americas should undertake it together.

This hemisphere is a reflection of mankind. Its diversity reflects the diversity of the globe. It knows the afflictions and frustrations of the impoverished. At the same time many of its members are leaders among modernizing societies. Much has been done to overcome high mortality rates, widespread illiteracy, and grinding poverty. This hemisphere uniquely includes the perceptions of the postindustrial societies, of those who are only beginning to sample the benefits of modernization, and of those who are in midpassage.

The Americas reach out to other constellations as well. The nations of Latin America and the Caribbean share much of the stirrings of the Third World. The United States is engaged in the maintenance of peace on a global basis. Pursuing our separate ways narrowly, we could drift apart toward different poles. Working together, we can reinforce our well-being and strengthen the prospects for global cooperation.

So let us begin here in this hemisphere. If we here in this room fail to grasp the consequences of interdependence, if we cannot make the multiplicity of our ties a source of unity and strength, then the prospects for success elsewhere are dim indeed. The world community which we seek to build should have a Western Hemisphere community as one of its central pillars.

President [Luis] Echeverría [Alvarez] foresaw the gathering force of interdependence in 1972 when he set forth his Charter of the Economic Rights and Duties of States as a guide for the conduct of relations among countries at different levels of economic development.[13] Last September before the U.N. General Assembly I endorsed that concept. At first, some were concerned because they saw the charter as a set of unilateral demands; it has since become clear that it is a farsighted concept of mutual obligations. In the emerging world of interdependence, the weak as well as the strong

[13]Proposed at the Third U.N. Conference on Trade and Development (UNCTAD III), held in Santiago, Chile, Apr. 13-May 21, 1972; cf. Chapter 32 at note 17.

have responsibilities, and the world's interest is each nation's interest.

We can start by making the concept of the charter a reality in the Western Hemisphere.

The U.S. View of the American Community

The United States will do its full part to see that our enterprise succeeds. We can make a major contribution, but it would be in nobody's interest if we raised impossible expectations, leaving our peoples frustrated and our community empty. We will promise only what we can deliver. We will make what we can deliver count.

I have carefully studied the agenda for this meeting you prepared in Bogotá. I will respond in detail to its specifics in our private sessions. But I will say here that I have come to a greater understanding of the deeply felt motivations behind the phrases. You are concerned:

—That the United States has put aside its special commitment to the hemisphere.

—That we will allow old issues to go unresolved while new ones are created.

—That we seek not community but dominance.

—That our relationship does not adequately contribute to human welfare in the hemisphere, that it is often irrelevant to your needs and an obstacle to their fulfillment.

In response let me outline the direction the United States proposes to its friends in rededicating itself to a new era of Western Hemisphere relationships. I look forward to hearing your own views so that together we can make the Western Hemisphere community a reality.

The United States will do its utmost to settle outstanding differences. During the past year, the United States and Mexico solved the longstanding Colorado River salinity dispute.[14] Two weeks ago Panama and the United States, taking account of the advice of their partners at Bogotá, signed a document that foreshadows a new relationship.[15] And just 48 hours ago, Peru and the United States settled a dispute over compensation for the exercise of Peru's sovereign right to nationalize property for public purposes.[16]

The United States is prepared to work with the other nations of

[14]By exchange of notes of Aug. 30, 1973; cf. *Bulletin*, 69: 393-6 (1973).
[15]Document 4a.
[16]On Feb. 19; text of Nixon statement and White House Fact Sheet in *Presidential Documents*, 10: 223 and *Bulletin*, 70: 272-3.

this hemisphere on methods to eliminate new disputes or to mitigate their effect.

Some of our most troublesome problems have arisen over differences concerning the respective rights and obligations of private U.S. firms operating in foreign countries and the countries which host them. These differences are based largely on differing conceptions of state sovereignty and state responsibility.

On the one hand, in keeping with the Calvo doctrine, most nations of this hemisphere affirm that a foreign investor has no right to invoke the protection of his home government. On the other hand, the United States has held that nations have the right to espouse the cause of their investors if they believe they have been unfairly treated. This conviction is reflected in the legislative provisions of the Gonzalez and Hickenlooper amendments.[17]

Realistically, we must admit that these two elements cannot be easily or quickly reconciled. But the United States is prepared to begin a process to this end and to mitigate their effects. Even before a final resolution of the philosophical and legal issues, we are ready to explore means by which disputes can be removed from the forefront of our intergovernmental relations.

In our private meetings I shall make specific proposals to establish agreed machinery which might narrow the scope of disputes. For example, we might consider the establishment of a working group to examine various procedures for factfinding, conciliation, or the settlement of disputes. Other approaches are possible, and I shall welcome the views of my colleagues. Let me affirm here that a procedure acceptable to all the parties would remove these disputes as factors in U.S. Government decisions respecting assistance relationships with host countries. We would be prepared to discuss with our Congress appropriate modifications of our legislation.

But we cannot achieve our goals simply by remedying specific grievances or even by creating mechanisms that will eliminate the sources of disputes. A special community can only emerge if we infuse it with life and substance.

We must renew our political commitment to a Western Hemisphere system. Thomas Macaulay once observed, "It is not the machinery we employ but the spirit we are of that binds men together." We are here because we recognize the need for cooperation. Yet we can only cooperate if our people truly believe that we are united by common purposes and a sense of common destiny.

[17] The Calvo Doctrine, named for the nineteenth-century Argentine publicist Carlos Calvo, stresses the obligation of foreign nationals to seek redress of grievances from local authorities rather than their home governments. On the Gonzalez and Hickenlooper amendments cf. *Digest of United States Practice in International Law, 1974*: 418, and see further note 12 to Chapter 35.

The United States will be guided by these principles:

—We will not impose our political preferences.
—We will not intervene in the domestic affairs of others.
—We will seek a free association of proud peoples.

In this way, the Western Hemisphere community can make its voice and interests felt in the world.

We realize that U.S. global interests sometimes lead to actions that have a major effect on our sister republics. We understand, too, that there is no wholly satisfactory solution to this problem.

However, to contribute to the sense of community we all seek, the United States commits itself to close and constant consultation with its hemispheric associates on political and economic issues of common interest, particularly when these issues vitally affect the interests of our partners in the Western Hemisphere.

In my view, the best way to coordinate policies is to make a systematic attempt to shape the future. I therefore recommend that today's meeting be considered the first of a series. The Foreign Ministers assembled here should meet periodically for an informal review of the international situation and of common hemispheric problems. In the interval between our meetings, the heads of our planning staffs or senior officials with similar responsibilities should meet on a regular basis to assess progress on a common agenda. The principle of consultation on matters affecting each other's interests should be applied to the fullest extent possible. Specifically:

—The United States is prepared to consult and adjust its positions on the basis of reciprocity, in the multilateral trade negotiations.

—The United States also recognizes a fundamental congruity of interests among the countries of the hemisphere in global monetary matters. We favor a strong voice for Latin America in the management of a new monetary system, just as we favor its effective participation in the reform of this system.

—The United States is ready to undertake prior consultation in other international negotiations such as the Law of the Sea Conference, the World Food Conference, and the World Population Conference.

The Western Hemisphere community should promote a decent life for all its citizens. No community is worthy of its name that does not actively foster the dignity and prosperity of its peoples. The United States as the richest and most powerful country in the hemisphere recognizes a special obligation in this regard.

Let me sketch here the program which President Nixon has authorized and which I shall discuss in greater detail with my colleagues this afternoon:

—*First, in trade.* During the period of great economic uncertainty arising from the energy situation, it is essential that nations behave cooperatively and not take protective or restrictive action. I pledge to you today that the United States will do its utmost to avoid placing any new limitations on access by Latin America to its domestic market.

In the same spirit we renew our commitment to the system of generalized tariff preferences. We shall strongly support this legislation. Once it is enacted, we will consult closely with you on how it can be most beneficial to your needs.

—*Second, in science and technology.* We want to improve our private and governmental efforts to make available needed technology, suited to varying stages of development in such vital areas as education, housing, and agriculture. Private enterprise is the most effective carrier of technology across national borders. But government, while not a substitute, can usefully appraise the overall needs and spur progress. The United States therefore recommends that we establish an inter-American commission on technology. It should be composed of leading scientists and experts from all the Americas and report to governments on the basis of regular meetings.

—*Third, in energy.* This hemisphere, linking oil-producing and oil-consuming countries, is uniquely situated for cooperative solutions of this problem. The United States is prepared to share research for the development of energy sources. We will encourage the Inter-American Development Bank to adapt its lending and fundraising activities to cushion the current strains. We are also prepared to explore ways of financing oil deficits, including the removal of remaining institutional impediments to your access to U.S. capital markets.

—*Fourth, in development assistance.* The U.S. Government in its executive branch is committed to maintain our aid levels, despite rising energy costs. On the other hand, the development problem can no longer be resolved simply by accelerating official assistance. We need a comprehensive review and recommendations on how all flows of capital and technology—whether from concessional assistance, world capital markets, or export credits—can contribute most effectively to hemispheric needs. I recommend charging the inter-American body with these tasks.

—*Fifth, in reshaping the inter-American system.* We must identify and preserve those aspects of the Rio Treaty and the Organization of American States [OAS] which have shielded the hemisphere from outside conflict and helped preserve regional peace.

Some form of institutional structure for peace and cooperation is clearly necessary. However, we must reinforce the formal structure of the OAS by modernizing its institutions and agreeing on the principles of inter-American relations. The United States is prepared to cooperate in creative adjustments to meet new conditions.

A Spanish poet once wrote: "Traveler, there is no path; paths are made by walking." This is our most immediate need. We are not here to write a communique, but to chart a course. Our success will be measured by whether we in fact start a journey. I suggest we move ahead in three ways:

—First, let us make clear to our peoples that we do have a common destiny and a modern framework for effective cooperation.

—Second, let us agree on an agenda for the Americas, a course of actions that will give substance to our consensus and inspiration to our peoples.

—Third, let us define a program to bring that agenda to life.

Mr. President, my distinguished colleagues, four centuries ago totally alien cultures met for the first time near here. We are moving toward a world whose demands upon us are nearly as alien to our experience as were the Spaniards and the Aztecs to each other.

Today, if we are to meet the unprecedented challenge of an interdependent world, we will also have to summon courage, faith, and dedication. The United States believes we can build a world worthy of the best in us in concert with our friends and neighbors. We want future generations to say that in 1974, in Mexico, the nations of the Western Hemisphere took a new road and proclaimed that in the Americas and the world they have a common destiny.

[The task of agreeing on an agenda and defining a program for the coming dialogue was initiated in the so-called "Declaration of Tlatelolco," a voluminous statement which noted among other things that the dialogue would be continued in the United States in April, when the General Assembly of the OAS was due to hold its Fourth Regular Session in Atlanta.]

(b) The "Declaration of Tlatelolco," adopted by the conference and made public February 24, 1974.[18]

[18]Department of State Press Release 67, Feb. 24; text from *Bulletin*, 70: 262-4.

I

At the request of President Nixon, Secretary of State Kissinger invited the Foreign Ministers and other representatives of Latin America and the Caribbean attending the 28th Session of the United Nations General Assembly to meet with him on October 5, 1973. At that time the Secretary of State suggested the initiation of a new dialogue to deal with matters of concern to the Americas.

Mindful of this important initiative, the Government of Colombia extended an invitation to Dr. Kissinger to participate actively and personally in such a dialogue at an opportune time. Dr. Kissinger immediately accepted this invitation. Thereafter, the Government of Colombia convoked the "Conference of Foreign Ministers of Latin America for Continental Cooperation," held in Bogotá from November 14-16, 1973. On that occasion the Foreign Ministers of Latin America and the Caribbean agreed it would be advantageous to initiate a dialogue on the following topics:

Cooperation for Development
Coercive Measures of an Economic Nature
Restructuring of the Inter-American System
Solution of the Panama Canal Question
Structure of International Trade and the Monetary System
Transnational Enterprises
Transfer of Technology
General Panorama of the Relations between Latin America and
the United States of America

In accordance with the agreement reached at the "Conference of Foreign Ministers of Latin America for Continental Cooperation," and with the concurrence of the Government of the United States of America, the Government of the United Mexican States convoked the Conference of Tlatelolco. This Conference took place in Mexico City from February 18-23, 1974.

The agenda of the Conference of Tlatelolco comprised the eight items listed above, with the addition of two others suggested by the Secretary of State in accordance with the agreement reached in Bogotá regarding "the willingness of the participating countries to discuss any other matters the United States of America wishes to propose." The topics suggested by the Government of the United States were "Review of the International Situation" and "The Energy Crisis."

Attending the Conference of Tlatelolco were the Foreign Ministers of Argentina, Bahamas, Barbados, Bolivia, Brazil, Chile, Colombia, Costa Rica, the Dominican Republic, Ecuador, El Salvador, Guatemala, Guyana, Haiti, Honduras, Jamaica, Mexico, Nicaragua, Panama, Paraguay, Peru, Trinidad and Tobago, the United States of America, Uruguay and Venezuela.

The Conference was held in two parts, one with exclusively Latin American and Caribbean participation from February 18-20 and the other from February 21-23, with the participation of Secretary of State Kissinger. In the first phase of the Conference of Tlatelolco, the Latin American and Caribbean Foreign Ministers agreed on procedures for the initiation of the new dialogue, which Secretary Kissinger had proposed be founded on "friendship based on equality and respect for the dignity of all," and upon methods for delineating the "bases for a new dialogue between Latin America and the United States." The Secretary of State agreed to these procedures.

II

The Conference took place in an atmosphere of cordiality, free from the old rigidities which have so often obstructed our dialogues in more traditional forums. The participants met as equals, conscious that the policy initiated here may be of deep historical significance. But for it to be so we must recognize that we are at a turning point and be prepared to dedicate ourselves to new horizons of understanding and cooperation.

The Foreign Ministers agreed that the Americas have arrived at an historic moment—a time of unprecedented opportunity for achieving the goals of justice, peace and human dignity which have for so long been the essential promise of the new world.

They recognized that in the modern age the demands of technology and the drive of human aspirations make impossible the narrow pursuit of purely national interests.

They agreed, as well, that interdependence has become a physical and moral imperative, and that a new, vigorous spirit of inter-American solidarity is therefore essential.

Relations between the countries of the Americas must be placed in the context of today's world; a world characterized by interdependence, the emergence onto the world stage of the developing countries, and the need to overcome inequalities. The existence of a modern inter-American system, the affirmation of the reality of Latin American unity, and the similarity of the problems of Latin America and those of other developing countries are the foundation for a dialogue and a frank and realistic relationship with the United States.

Inter-American relations should be based on an effective equality between states, on non-intervention, on the renunciation of the use of force and coercion, and on the respect for the right of countries to choose their own political, economic and social systems. Inter-American relationships, thus redefined by an authentic political will, would create the necessary conditions for living together in harmony and working cooperatively for expanded and self-sustaining economic development.

The Foreign Ministers reaffirmed the principle that every State has the right to choose its own political, economic and social system without foreign interference and that it is the duty of every State to refrain from intervening in the affairs of another.

The new opportunities for cooperative development call for a revision of the concept of regional security, which cannot, and should not, be based solely on political-military criteria, but must also encompass a practical commitment to peaceful relations, cooperation and solidarity among states.

To this end, inter-American cooperation should be supplemented by the establishment of a system of collective economic security that protects the essential requirements of integral development; that is to say, parallel progress in the social, economic and cultural fields.

By mandate of the United Nations General Assembly, a group of countries representing diverse economic systems is engaged in examining the possibilities of restructuring international economic relations, through the preparation of a draft charter on the economic rights and duties of states.[19] This charter can create the general framework for facing specific problems through practical and fair regulations and mechanisms.

The Conference of Tlatelolco agreed that a just application of the principles of the charter can foster the internal and external conditions necessary for the American nations to satisfy their own needs and ensure their full development on an equitable basis. The Conference also recognized that peace and progress, in order to be solid and enduring, must always be based on respect for the rights of others, and the recognition of reciprocal responsibilities and obligations among developed and developing countries.

III

In the course of permanent dialogue that has been successfully initiated at the Conference of Tlatelolco, a continuing effort should be made to reach, as soon as possible, joint solutions to the pending questions included in the Bogotá document, which served as the basis for this Conference.

[19]Cf. above at note 13.

IV

The Conference goes on record as follows:

(1)   The Foreign Ministers recognized that the success of the Conference of Tlatelolco emphasizes the value of the new dialogue of the Americas. Mindful of the growing interaction between themselves and the rest of the world and that their countries have different needs and different approaches on foreign policy, the Foreign Ministers were nevertheless agreed that the relations between their countries, which history, geography and sentiment have produced and continued to sustain, call for an expansion of the processes of consultation between their governments.

As an initial step in this continuing process of consultation, they agreed to continue on April 17, 1974, at Atlanta, Georgia, in the United States of America, the dialogue initiated in Mexico.[20] In the same spirit they agreed to consult with the view to seeking, as far as possible, common positions in appropriate international consultations, including multilateral trade negotiations.

(2)   The Conference welcomes the agreement reached in Panama City on February 7, 1974, by the Governments of Panama and the United States of America, by which they established the guiding principles for their current negotiations leading to a new Canal treaty.[21] The Conference holds that this agreement is a significant step forward on the road to a definitive solution of that question.

(3)   The Foreign Ministers agreed that, if progress toward a new inter-American solidarity is to be made, solutions must be found not only to existing differences, but means must also be provided for the solution of problems that may arise.

(4)   In this spirit, the Foreign Ministers of Latin America have taken due note and will continue to examine the suggestion advanced by the Secretary of State of the United States of America with respect to the controversies that may arise from matters involving private foreign investment.

The Secretary of State of the United States proposed the establishment of a fact-finding or conciliation procedure that would limit the scope of such controversies by separating the issues of fact from those of law. This could provide an objective basis for the solution of disputes without detriment to sovereignty.

He further proposed the creation of an inter-American working group to study the appropriate procedures that might be adopted.

(5)   With regard to the problems of transnational corporations,

---

[20]The next meeting of Foreign Ministers was actually held in Washington on Apr. 17-18, 1974; cf. Chapter 8, Document 9.

[21]Document 4a.

the Foreign Ministers discussed the different aspects of their operation in Latin America and have agreed to continue the examination of the matter at a later meeting.

(6) The Foreign Ministers agreed on the need for intensifying work on the restructuring of the inter-American system.

(7) The Foreign Ministers agreed that one of the principal objectives is the accelerated development of the countries of the Americas and the promotion of the welfare of all their peoples. In this regard, the United States accepts a special responsibility; and the more developed countries of the Americas recognize that special attention should be paid to the needs of the lesser developed.

They further agreed that development should be integral, covering the economic, social and cultural life of their nations.

(8) The United States offered to promote the integral development of the region in the following fields:

Trade

(A) Make maximum efforts to secure passage of the legislation on the system of generalized preferences during the present session of Congress,[22] and then work with the other countries of the hemisphere to apply these preferences in the most beneficial manner.

(B) Avoid, as far as possible, the implementation of any new measures that would restrict access to the United States market.

Loans for Development

(A) Maintain, as a minimum, present aid levels despite growing costs.

(B) Cooperate throughout the region and in international institutions to facilitate the flow of new concessional and conventional resources toward those countries most affected by growing energy costs.

(C) Examine with others in the Committee of Twenty and the Inter-American Development Bank all restrictions on the entry of hemispheric countries to capital markets in the United States and other industrialized countries.

(9) The Foreign Ministers further declare:

(A) They reaffirm the need of Latin American and Caribbean countries for an effective participation of their countries in an international monetary reform.

[22]Cf. Chapter 35 at note 19.

It was acknowledged that the net transfer of real resources is basic, and that ways to institutionalize transfers through adequate mechanisms should be considered.

It was reaffirmed that external financial cooperation should preferably be channeled through multilateral agencies and respect the priorities established for each country, without political ties or conditions.

(B) With respect to "transfers of technology," the Foreign Ministers agreed to promote policies facilitating transfers of both patented and unpatented technical knowledge among the respective countries in the field of industry as well as education, housing and agriculture, taking into account conditions prevailing in each country and in particular the needs of the Latin American and Caribbean countries for introduction of new manufactures, for greater utilization of the human and material resources available in each country, for increased local technical development and for creation of products for export. It was further agreed that transfers of technology should be on fair and equitable terms without restraint upon the recipient country. Particular emphasis is to be placed upon sharing knowledge and technology for development of new sources of energy and possible alternatives.

(10)   The Foreign Ministers agreed that it would be desirable to establish an inter-American Commission of Science and Technology. They left over for later decision whether this Commission should be adapted from existing institutions or whether a new body should be formed.

V

In adopting this document, the Foreign Ministers expressed their confidence that the spirit of Tlatelolco will inspire a new creative effort in their relations. They recognized that they are at the beginning of a road that will acquire greater significance through regular meetings and constant attention to the matters under study.

The Conference expresses its satisfaction over the fact that the mutual understanding which has prevailed throughout encourages the hope that future conferences of a similar nature, within a permanent framework devoid of all rigid formality, will produce fruitful results for the benefit of the peoples of the Americas.

TLATELOLCO DF, *February 24, 1974.*

5. MEETING OF THE ANZUS COUNCIL

(Wellington, February 26-27, 1974)

[While Secretary Kissinger exchanged opinions with his Latin American colleagues at Tlatelolco, his second in command, Deputy Secretary of State Kenneth Rush, was en route to Wellington, New Zealand, for a not dissimilar discussion with leaders of the allied governments of Australia and New Zealand. Linked with the United States through the ANZUS Pact of 1951[1] as well as the Southeast Asia Collective Defense Treaty (Manila Pact) of 1954,[2] these governments had also been engaged in a far-reaching reappraisal of their external relationships that had intensified with the advent to power of Labor Party ministries in both Canberra and Wellington toward the close of 1972.

With détente in the air and the war in Vietnam approaching its end, both the new Australian government under E. Gough Whitlam and the New Zealand cabinet headed by Norman E. Kirk had appeared less than totally enthusiastic about the continuance of the broader regional security arrangements that centered in the South-East Asia Treaty Organization (SEATO), the political and military superstructure erected upon the Manila Pact of 1954. But even while arguing for a restriction of SEATO's role, both governments had stressed their firm intention to maintain their ANZUS ties with the United States; and both had also continued their participation in the Five-Power Defense Arrangements set up in 1971 in cooperation with Malaysia, Singapore, and the United Kingdom.

A confirmation of the importance each of the ANZUS partners attached to their common ties was the principal accomplishment of the ANZUS Council at its 23rd meeting—the first to be held since the changes of government in Australia and New Zealand—which

[1]Tripartite Security Treaty between the Governments of Australia, New Zealand, and the United States, signed in San Francisco Sept. 1, 1951 and entered into force Apr. 29, 1952 (TIAS 2493; 3 UST 3420); text in *Documents, 1951*: 263-5.
[2]See note 2 to Chapter 23.

took place in Wellington on February 26-27. "This is the first ANZUS Council Meeting that the three of us have attended," D. R. Willesee, Australia's Minister for Foreign Affairs and leader of his country's delegation, observed at a parliamentary luncheon held in connection with the meeting. "In the case of Australia it is the first time that a Labor Government has had the opportunity to attend. But it is business as usual as far as we are concerned. There has been no difference between the previous Governments, and our own Government in attitudes towards ANZUS. The pressures will be different, the opportunities different, but the will to make ANZUS work is continuing."[3]

Comparable sentiments were expressed both on and off the record by Prime Minister Kirk of New Zealand, who personally held the Foreign Affairs portfolio, and by Deputy Secretary Rush. The scope of their official discussions, in which they touched on most of the salient aspects of the international scene, was suggested in a final communiqué that further emphasized the central role of this tripartite association in the foreign policies of all three powers.]

(6) 23rd Meeting of the ANZUS Council, Wellington, New Zealand, February 26-27, 1974: Communiqué issued at the conclusion of the meeting.[4]

The ANZUS Council held its 23rd Meeting in Wellington on 26 and 27 February 1974. Senator the Hon. D. R. Willesee, Minister for Foreign Affairs represented Australia, the Hon. Kenneth Rush, Deputy Secretary for State, represented the United States, and the Rt Hon. Norman Kirk, Prime Minister and Minister of Foreign Affairs, represented New Zealand.

The Ministers, recalling that this was the first meeting of the Council since the changes of Government in Australia and New Zealand, exchanged views on a wide range of subjects of political and economic as well as strategic concern to the ANZUS partners. They noted that the relationship among the three countries, based as it is on a substantial community of interest and a shared heritage of representative democracy, individual freedom and respect for the rule of law, is among the most enduring features of their foreign policies. The ANZUS Treaty and the regular consultations for which it provides are a natural expression of this relationship.

The Ministers welcomed the progress towards detente among the major countries. They noted that policies of detente gave other countries the opportunity to develop and strengthen relationships among themselves. The Council welcomed efforts to bring about

[3]*Australian Foreign Affairs Record* (Canberra), Feb. 1974: 123-4.
[4]Text from same, 125-6.

peace in South-East Asia, and more recently in the Middle East, and the improving relationships within the Asia-Pacific Region. The Ministers took note of the continued growth of regional co-operation and self-reliance in South-East Asia as exemplified in particular by the increasing stature of the Association of South-East Asian Nations. The Ministers indicated the desire of their countries to assist this co-operation.

The Ministers agreed that the Five Power Defence Arrangements contributed to the climate of confidence in the area and provided a useful framework for practical co-operation in the defence field. The Ministers agreed that as a result of a major review in 1973,[5] the structure and role of the South-East Asia Treaty Organization was now better suited to today's conditions, and that the commitment represented in the treaty remains important to the region.

The Ministers reviewed the situation in Indochina one year after the signing of the Paris Agreement on Viet-Nam.[6] They welcomed the encouraging progress towards political settlement in Laos. While gratified that the scale of fighting in South Viet-Nam has greatly diminished, they regretted the continuing loss of life and expressed the desire that all parties would strictly observe the ceasefire. They reiterated the hope that the right to self-determination of the South Vietnamese people would be respected. The Council deplored the continuing tragic fighting and destruction in Cambodia and called on all Cambodian parties to negotiate a peaceful solution to the conflict.

Consideration was given to the world economic situation and trade and to the possible effects of recent events upon the economic stability of the Asia-Pacific region. The Ministers consulted on the implications of the energy crisis, and agreed on the need for co-operation between producing and consuming States to mitigate the serious effects of the world's continuing energy shortage, and on the longer-term need for more rational use of the world's energy and other irreplaceable resources. They further noted that a major effort in constructive international co-operation would be required within the United Nations and other appropriate international bodies to counter disruptions occurring in the world economy, including trade and payments, and minimise the adverse effects on the economies of the region. They saw the need for a special effort to ensure that these difficulties should not be allowed to diminish the flow of real resources to the developing countries of Asia and the Pacific. The Ministers underlined the great value they attached to the United Nations Conference on Food to be held in Rome in

---

[5]Cf. *AFR, 1973*: 373-4 and 376-7.
[6]For details cf. the following chapter.

November,[7] stressing the need for the Conference to formulate arrangements that would increase supplies of food and fertilisers to the developing countries.

Noting the continued atmospheric testing of nuclear weapons in Asia and the Pacific, the Council once again called for universal adherence to the Partial Nuclear Test Ban Treaty of 1963,[8] to which all three ANZUS partners were parties. It also affirmed support for the early achievement of an effective Comprehensive Test Ban Treaty. The Council agreed that further measures of arms control are a necessary concomitant of the present trend towards detente and the establishment of a just and stable international order. It expressed satisfaction at the progress made in the Strategic Arms Limitation Talks between the United States and the Soviet Union and hoped that despite the complexities of the situation further progress will not be delayed. The Council supported the current negotiations, in the context of European security, to achieve mutual and balanced force reductions as an important stage in the effort to bring about genuine limitation of conventional arms. It welcomed as a reflection of the international community's wishes the attention being given to arms control within the United Nations system, and expressed the hope that all nations would co-operate in these endeavours.

The Ministers welcomed the development of a community of independent and self-governing states in the South Pacific. The representatives of Australia and New Zealand outlined the role of the South Pacific Forum, emphasising its importance as a catalyst in the development of a common approach to the problems of the area. Representatives of the three countries noted with approval the work of the South Pacific Commission in promoting development and co-operation within the area. They were pleased that a meeting of participating Governments would be held at Wellington from 5 to 7 March, 1974, and would consider proposals for a merger of the Commission and the South Pacific Conference.[9]

In conclusion, the ANZUS partners reaffirmed the great value each placed on the alliance. They stated that in a period of great change, both within the ANZUS area and throughout the world, the continuity symbolised by the ANZUS Treaty was important. The three partners would continue to consult closely, united as they were by shared interests and experience, and by a common concern for the peaceful development of the Asia-Pacific region.

[7]Cf. Chapter 27.

[8]*Documents, 1963*: 130-32; cf. Chapter 33 at notes 6-7.

[9]A reorganization of the South Pacific Commission, which would be known thereafter as the South Pacific Conference, was effected by a memorandum of understanding signed at Raratonga, Cook Islands, on Oct. 2, 1974.

6. INDOCHINA: THE BITTER DRAUGHT

(March 25, 1974)

[Second only to its diplomatic successes with the Soviet Union and the People's Republic of China, the Nixon administration had taken pride in the Indochina peace agreement signed in 1973 as the culmination of a military and diplomatic effort whose beginnings long antedated President Nixon's election to office. Admittedly, the document signed in Paris on January 27, 1973[1] had fallen rather short of Mr. Nixon's 1968 pledge to the New Hampshire voters to "end the war and win the peace in the Pacific."[2] Although the last American troops had been brought home and all American prisoners of war in enemy hands had been released, the Communist North Vietnamese had proved most uncooperative in carrying out those provisions of the agreement that called upon them to assist in locating the 1,300 Americans listed as missing in action, and in locating and caring for the graves of the dead in preparation for their exhumation and repatriation. The United States, on its side, had responded to North Vietnam's noncompliance with these and other obligations by shelving any plans to aid the latter in its postwar reconstruction as envisaged by a separate article of the peace agreement.

Potentially even more serious was the fact that the Paris agreement had not, in any real sense, brought peace either to South Vietnam or to the neighboring states of Laos and Cambodia, whose anti-Communist governments had been and still were threatened by a combination of indigenous insurgents and North Vietnamese forces. Neither the military nor the political provisions of the agreement regarding South Vietnam had been carried out in a consistent manner. Far from joining hands to implement the political clauses of the peace agreement, both the anti-Communist Saigon govern-

[1]*AFR, 1973*: 39-52.
[2]*New York Times*, Mar. 6, 1968; cf. *AFR, 1972*: 264 n. 67.

ment of the Republic of Vietnam, headed by President Nguyen Van Thieu, and the Communist-directed "Provisional Revolutionary Government (PRG) of the Republic of South Vietnam," nominally led by Huynh Tan Phat, appeared to be concentrating their major efforts on preparations for an eventual military showdown. Still seemingly committed to unifying the whole of Vietnam under Communist rule, the northern government in Hanoi had also continued to reinforce and resupply its military forces in the South despite the restrictions of the Paris agreement and the repeated complaints of the United States. Actual military clashes during the first year of nominal peace, according to the Saigon government, had claimed the lives of no fewer than 57,835 Vietnamese fighting men, three-fourths of them on the Communist side.

In Laos, the situation appeared somewhat less discouraging. After concluding their own cease-fire and political agreement in February 1973, the contending forces in that Mekong River kingdom had subsequently drawn up detailed plans for a tripartite, coalition-type "Provisional Government of National Union" in which Prince Souvanna Phouma, the head of the existing Royal Laotian Government, would be Prime Minister while his half brother, the leftist Prince Souphanouvong, would serve as one of his deputies.[3] In Cambodia, on the other hand, hopes for a cessation of fighting between the incumbent "Khmer Republic" government under President Lon Nol and the Communist-led insurgent forces had been bitterly disappointed. Particularly since August 1973, when the United States had discontinued its air support of the Phnom Penh forces as directed by Congress, the military situation had gone from bad to worse. By late 1973, when Congress refused to heed an appeal from President Nixon to vote an extra $200 million to buy ammunition for the beleaguered republicans, their full collapse was widely regarded as only a matter of time.[4]

"We must guard against the tendency to express relief at our military extrication from Southeast Asia by 'washing our hands' of the whole affair," President Nixon had cautioned in transmitting to Congress his formal message on the State of the Union on January 30, 1974. "Men and women are still dying there. We still have a responsibility there. We must provide those ravaged lands with the economic assistance needed to stabilize the structures of their societies and make future peace more likely. We must provide, as well, the continued military aid grants required to maintain strong, self-reliant defense forces. And we will continue to insist on full compliance with the terms of the agreements reached in Paris, including

---

[3]Agreement signed Sept. 14, 1973; cf. *AFR, 1973*: 374-6.
[4]Same: 542-3 and 545-50.

a full accounting of all our men missing in Southeast Asia."[5]

But despite the President's resolute words, affairs in Indochina no longer possessed great interest for most Americans at a time when U.S. forces had been withdrawn from that part of the world and were barred from further combat by Act of Congress.[6] Thus the published records of 1974 are largely devoid of the lengthy policy exposés so frequent during the earlier years of the American involvement. One of the few comprehensive statements of official views on Indochina during 1974 is found in Secretary Kissinger's response of March 25 to an inquiry put forward by Democratic Senator Edward M. Kennedy of Massachusetts in his capacity as Chairman of the Subcommittee on Refugees of the Senate Judiciary Committee.

This exchange, it should be noted, took place at a time of rising uncertainty about the administration's intentions in light of the apparent breakdown of the Paris agreement, the increasingly bellicose demeanor of the opposing sides in Vietnam, and the President's apparent determination to secure substantially increased allotments for economic and military aid for Vietnam in the new fiscal year beginning July 1, 1974. Compounding the uncertainty were the repercussions of an article published in the *New York Times* of February 25, 1974, in which correspondent David K. Shipler of the paper's Saigon bureau had intimated that the United States itself was hampering the restoration of peaceful conditions through its support of President Thieu's regime.

According to this account, a "vast program of American military aid to the Saigon government" had continued "to set the course of the war more than a year after the signing of the Paris peace agreements and the final withdrawal of American troops." Even if the United States itself was adhering to the letter of the agreements, Shipler wrote, "the aid directly supports South Vietnamese violations and so breaks the spirit of the accords." Noting that both U.S. Ambassador Graham A. Martin and the U.S. Defense Attaché, Major General John E. Murray, had refused requests for interviews, and that Ambassador Martin had also silenced local officials of the U.S. Agency for International Development (AID), Shipler added: "The Ambassador has reportedly told several non-Government visitors recently that South Vietnam is in a crucial period and that he sees his role as unyielding support to build up and preserve a non-Communist regime."

Responding to these observations in a cablegram to the State Department—which would, in its turn, be partially made public in the *New York Times* of March 9—Ambassador Martin complained

[5]*Presidential Documents*, 10: 146.
[6]*AFR, 1973*: 335-47.

of "numerous inaccuracies and half-truths" in the Shipler dispatch, asserted that it "deliberately omits or treats skeptically the flagrant Communist violations of the Paris accords," and intimated that the "slanted impression" the article allegedly sought to convey was directly related to what the Ambassador described as Hanoi's plan to wage an all-out campaign aimed at persuading Congress to reduce aid to Saigon. The reason he and General Murray had refused to meet with the author while the article was in preparation, Ambassador Martin added, was because "to do so would permit their own reputations for integrity to be used as a platform for promoting a campaign to grossly deceive the American Congress and the American people."

These allegations lay in the immediate background of the inquiries to which the Secretary of State responded in the following document.]

(7)   United States Policy Toward Indochina: Letter from Secretary of State Kissinger to Senator Edward M. Kennedy, Chairman of the Subcommittee on Refugees of the Senate Committee on the Judiciary, March 25, 1974.[7]

MARCH 25, 1974.

DEAR MR. CHAIRMAN: In response to your letter of March 13 on various aspects of United States policy toward Indochina, I am enclosing our comment on the nine specific items you have outlined. I hope this information will be useful to you. As to the recommendations of the Subcommittee's Study Mission to Indochina last year, which were enclosed with your letter, I have asked Governor Holton [Linwood Holton, Assistant Secretary for Congressional Relations] to review these and to prepare our comments for submission to you as soon as possible.

Your letter also expresses concern over a March 6 cable by Ambassador Martin commenting on a recent press article on the United States role in Viet-Nam. I do not believe the Ambassador is suggesting a cause-and-effect relationship between decisions in Hanoi and the views of any individual Members of Congress or their staffs. What he is describing is a very real and sophisticated propaganda effort by North Viet-Nam to bring to bear on a wide spectrum of Americans its own special view of the situation in Indochina. The Ambassador believes, and in this he has our full confidence and support, that we must counter these distortions emanating from Hanoi and continue to provide the best answers to the concerned questions many Americans have about our Indochina policy.

Warm regards,

HENRY A. KISSINGER.

Enclosure:
Comment on Indochina Policy Issues.

The Honorable EDWARD M. KENNEDY,
Chairman, Subcommittee on Refugees, Committee on the Judiciary, United States Senate.

ENCLOSURE

1) "The general character and objectives of American policy towards Indochina as a whole and towards each government or political authority in the area;"

There are two basic themes in our policy toward Indochina. The first is our belief that a secure peace in Indochina is an important element in our efforts to achieve a worldwide structure of peace. Conversely, we believe that an evolution toward peace in other troubled areas helps bring about the stability for which we strive in Indochina. Consequently, our Indochina policy has been geared to bring about the conditions which will enable the contending parties to find a peaceful resolution of their differences.

A resolution of differences can, of course, be achieved by other than peaceful means. For example, North Viet-Nam might seek to conquer South Viet-Nam by force of arms. Such a resolution, however, would almost certainly be a temporary one and would not produce the long-term and stable peace which is essential. Therefore, a corollary to our search for peace, and the second theme of our policy, is to discourage the takeover of the various parts of Indochina by force. Forcible conquest is not only repugnant to American traditions but also has serious destabilizing effects which are not limited to the area under immediate threat.

We would stress the point that the United States has no desire to see any particular form of government or social system in the Indochina countries. What we do hope to see is a free choice by the people of Indochina as to the governments and systems under which they will live. To that end we have devoted immense human and material resources to assist them in protecting this right of choice.

Our objective with regard to the Government of Viet-Nam, the

Government of the Khmer Republic and the Royal Lao Government is to provide them with the material assistance and political encouragement which they need in determining their own futures and in helping to create conditions which will permit free decisions. In Laos, happily, real progress has been made, partly because of our assistance. The Vientiane Agreement and Protocols give clear evidence of the possibility for the peaceful settlement our policies are designed to foster. We have supported the Royal Lao Government and, when it is formed, we will look with great sympathy on the Government of National Union. We welcome a peaceful and neutral Laos and, where appropriate, we will continue to encourage the parties to work out their remaining problems.

In Cambodia we are convinced that long-term prospects for stability would be enhanced by a cease-fire and a negotiated settlement among the Khmer elements to the conflict. Because such stability is in our interests we are providing diplomatic and material support to the legitimate government of the Khmer Republic, both in its self-defense efforts and in its search for a political solution to the war.

Our objective in Viet-Nam continues to be to help strengthen the conditions which made possible the Paris Agreement on Ending the War and Restoring Peace in Viet-Nam. With this in mind we have supported the Republic of Viet-Nam with both military and economic assistance. We believe that by providing the Vietnamese Government the necessary means to defend itself and to develop a viable economy, the government in Hanoi will conclude that political solutions are much preferable to renewed use of major military force. The presence of large numbers of North Vietnamese troops in the South demonstrates that the military threat from Hanoi is still very much in evidence. Because of that threat we must still ensure that the Republic of Viet-Nam has the means to protect its independence. We note, however, that the level of violence is markedly less than it was prior to the cease-fire and believe that our policy of support for South Viet-Nam has been instrumental in deterring major North Vietnamese offensives.

Our objective with regard to the Democratic Republic of Viet-Nam, and its southern arm, the Provisional Revolutionary Government, is to encourage full compliance with the Paris Agreement. We have been disappointed by North Viet-Nam's serious violations of important provisions of the Agreement. However, we still believe that the Agreement provides a workable framework for a peaceful and lasting settlement, and we will continue to use all means available to us to support the cease-fire and to encourage closer observance of it. Our future relations with Hanoi obviously depend in large part on how faithfully North Viet-Nam complies with the Agreement.

2) "The general content and nature of existing obligations and commitments to the governments in Saigon, Phnom Penh and Vientiane;"

The U.S. has no bilateral written commitment to the Government of the Republic of Viet-Nam. However, as a signator [*sic*] of the Paris Agreement on Ending the War and Restoring Peace in Viet-Nam, the United States committed itself to strengthening the conditions which made the cease-fire possible and to the goal of the South Vietnamese people's right to self-determination. With these commitments in mind, we continue to provide to the Republic of Viet-Nam the means necessary for its self-defense and for its economic viability.

We also recognize that we have derived a certain obligation from our long and deep involvement in Viet-Nam. Perceiving our own interest in a stable Viet-Nam free to make its own political choices, we have encouraged the Vietnamese people in their struggle for independence. We have invested great human and material resources to support them in protecting their own as well as broader interests. We have thus committed ourselves very substantially, both politically and morally. While the South Vietnamese Government and people are demonstrating increasing self-reliance, we believe it is important that we continue our support as long as it is needed.

Our relations with the Government of the Khmer Republic also do not stem from a formal commitment but are based on our own national interests. Recognizing that events in Cambodia relate directly to the bitter hostilities in other parts of Indochina, we have sought to help create stability in that country as a part of our effort to encourage the development of peace in the entire region. We, therefore, support the legitimate government of Cambodia, in the hope that its increasing strength will encourage the Khmer Communists toward a political settlement rather than continued conflict.

We have also undertaken our assistance to Laos and support for the Royal Lao Government because of our own broad national interests, not because of any formal commitment to that country. The most important and visible of our interests is our desire for a just settlement of the tragic war in Indochina. Laos plays a key role in this effort to achieve the peace. Indeed, Laos is the bright spot in Indochina where the fruits of our efforts to assist and support the Royal Lao Government are most clearly seen. A cease-fire based on an agreement worked out by the two Lao parties has endured for more than a year. The two parties have together organized joint security forces in the two capital cities of Vientiane and Luang Prabang and a coalition government may not be far away. We feel that these large steps toward a lasting peace in Laos would probably not have succeeded but for our steadfast support for the efforts of the Royal Lao Government.

3)   "The kinds, categories and levels of support and assistance given or projected to the governments in Saigon, Phnom Penh and Vientiane for fiscal year 1973 through 1975—including (a) a breakdown of the number, distribution, activities and agency/departmental association of official American personnel, as well as those associated with private business and other organizations under contract to the United States government; and (b) a breakdown from all sources of humanitarian assistance, police and public safety oriented assistance, general supporting and economic development assistance, and military assistance;"

(a)   *U.S. Economic Assistance*

Our annual Congressional Presentation books provide the data requested here in considerable detail. These Congressional Presentation books for FY 1975 will shortly be delivered to the Congress. We provide these first, as a matter of course, to the authorizing and appropriations Committees of the Senate and the House and then routinely make them available to all Members as well as the interested public. We will be happy to provide your Subcommittee on Refugees with copies as soon as available.

The Congressional Presentation books focus, of course, on our proposals for the coming year, FY 1975, but also contain data on both the current fiscal year, FY 1974, and the preceding, FY 1973. This year, as last, we are preparing a separate book providing the details of our economic assistance programs for the Indochina countries.

These Congressional Presentation books form a partial basis, of course, for extensive Hearings held each year by the authorizing committees in the Senate and House, and then by the appropriations committees. We would expect the question you pose, as well as many others, to be further explored in considerable depth during the course of these hearings.[8]

(b)   *U.S. Military Assistance*

Our military assistance to South Viet-Nam and Laos is provided under MASF [military assistance service funded]. The breakdown of this assistance for the period you requested is as follows:

<hr>

[8]For details see *Bulletin*, 70: 528 and 712-13; same, 71: 51-2, 287-8, and 291-4.

		New Obligational
Year	Ceiling	Authority
FY 1973	$2.735 Billion	$2.563 Billion
FY 1974	1.126 Billion	907.5 Million
FY 1975	1.6 Billion	1.450 Billion[a]
	(Requested)	

[a] Viet-Nam only; Laos will be included under MAP for FY-75.

The level of official U.S. military/civilian personnel in South Viet-Nam during the same period is as follows:

Year	Military	Civilian
January, 1973	23,516 (Assigned)	730
January, 1974	221 (Authorized)	1200
June, 1974	221 (Authorized)	936

The number of U.S. civilian contractors has declined from 5,737 in January, 1973, to 2,736 in January, 1974. This number is expected to decrease further to 2,130 by June, 1974. We do not yet have a projected level of U.S. civilian contractors for FY 1975.

Our military assistance to Cambodia is furnished under MAP [military assistance program]. This assistance totalled $148.6 million in FY 1973 and $325 million in FY 1974. The level of our military assistance for FY 1975 is now under review. The amount to be proposed will be included in the Congressional presentation documents on military assistance which we expect to submit to Congress shortly.

U.S. military and civilian personnel in Cambodia during the period you requested is as follows:

Year	Military	Civilian
December, 1972	112	53
December, 1973	113	55
December, 1974	113	DNA*

*Data Not Available.

U.S. military and civilian personnel in Laos during the period you requested is as follows:

Year	Military	Civilian
December, 1972	185	457
December, 1973	180	424
December, 1974	30**	DNA*

**Based on the assumption that a coalition government will be formed in Laos before the end of this year.

4) *"The current status and problems of reported efforts to establish an international consortium for general reconstruction assistance to the area."*

In April 1973, President Thieu asked the International Bank for Reconstruction and Development (IBRD) to help form an aid group for the Republic of Viet-Nam. The IBRD agreed to make the effort, provided that this would be acceptable to the Bank membership and that the group could be organized in association with both the IBRD and the Asian Development Bank. In May the World Bank sent a study mission to Viet-Nam to review the situation. In August, Japan suggested that the Bank arrange a preliminary meeting to exchange views on aid to the countries of Indochina. The Japanese also proposed that the member countries discuss the formation of a loose Indochina consultative group for the areawide coordination, with sub-groups for any of the four countries concerned which might request such a group and where conditions were satisfactory.

An initial meeting was held at the Bank's Paris office in October. The United States supported the Bank's efforts as well as the Japanese proposal. The Bank sent a second mission to Viet-Nam in November and subsequently proposed that a follow-on meeting be held in February of this year to discuss the formation of the Indochina consultative group. However, the reactions of participating countries to the energy crisis and to the Congressional decision on IDA [International Development Association] replenishment[9] led the Bank to postpone the meeting, tentatively until late Spring. In February, at the request of the Lao Government, a World Bank team also visited Laos to assess the situation and to discuss a possible consultative group for that country.

The United States continues to support efforts to form an Indochina consultative group. We also favor the proposal that there be sub-groups for each recipient country to which donors may contribute as they wish. The sub-groups would be formed when considered appropriate by donors and at the request of the recipient. We remain in close consultation with the World Bank and other in-

---

[9]Cf. Chapter 24 at note 2.

terested parties on this matter. We are hopeful that a second meeting of participants might be held in the near future and that such a meeting might lead to the establishment of the groups in question. A reversal of the negative Congressional action on IDA replenishment would clearly enhance the possibility of success in this regard.

5) "The current status and problems of the Administration's stated intention to encourage internationalizing humanitarian assistance to the area;"

In addition to U.S. bilateral humanitarian assistance to the Indochina countries which totals $111.4 million for FY 1974, the Department and the Agency for International Development (AID) continue to encourage other donors, including international organizations, to provide such assistance. AID made a grant of $2 million on November 1, 1973, to the Indochina Operations Group of the International Committee of the Red Cross and discussions are continuing about an additional grant to that organization. UNICEF [United Nations Children's Fund] has recently completed its study of the problems in the Indochina countries and has just submitted its proposed program to possible donor countries. We have encouraged UNICEF in its study and are pleased that it is now prepared to expand its activities in all three countries.

The World Health Organization has had meaningful programs in Laos, Cambodia, and Viet-Nam which supplement and do not overlap with activities supported by the United States. We have encouraged that organization to play an even more important role, particularly in the malaria control program, and we at the same time would phase out of our activities in that field.

Our discussions with Indochina countries have stressed the desirability of establishing plans and priorities for programs and projects which require assistance so that other donor countries and organizations can fit their assistance efforts into the host country requirements.

6) "The current status of negotiations between Washington and Hanoi on American reconstruction assistance to North Viet-Nam."

Following the conclusion of the Peace Agreement last year, preliminary discussions of post-war reconstruction were held in Paris between U.S. and North Vietnamese members of the Joint Economic Commission. These talks have been suspended since last July. The Administration's position, which we believe is shared by the great majority of members of Congress, is that the U.S. cannot at this time move forward with an assistance program for North

Viet-Nam. To date, North Viet-Nam has failed substantially to live up to a number of the essential terms of the Agreement, including those relating to the introduction of troops and war materiel into South Viet-Nam, the cessation of military activities in Cambodia and Laos, and the accounting for our missing-in-action. Should Hanoi turn away from a military solution and demonstrate a serious compliance with the Agreement, then we would be prepared, with the approval of Congress, to proceed with our undertaking regarding reconstruction assistance to North Viet- Nam.

7)   *"The Department's assessment on the implementation of the ceasefire agreements for both Viet-Nam and Laos;"*

The cease-fire in Viet-Nam has resulted in a substantial decrease in the level of hostilities; for example, military casualties since the cease-fire have been about one-third the level of casualties suffered in the years preceding the Paris Agreement. Nonetheless, it is unfortunately evident that significant violence continues to occur and that the cease-fire is far from scrupulously observed. The fundamental problem is that the North Vietnamese are still determined to seize political power in the South, using military means if necessary. To this end they have maintained unrelenting military pressure against the South Vietnamese Government and have continued widespread terrorism against the population. In particularly flagrant violation of the Agreement North Viet-Nam has persisted in its infiltration of men and materiel into the South, bringing in more than one hundred thousand troops and large quantities of heavy equipment since the cease-fire began. South Vietnamese forces have reacted against these attacks by North Vietnamese forces and several sizable engagements have taken place.

Despite these serious violations, we continue to believe that the Paris Agreement has already brought substantial benefits and continues to provide a workable framework for peace. After more than a quarter century of fighting it would have been unrealistic to expect that the Agreement would bring an instant and complete end to the conflict. What it has done, however, is to reduce the level of violence significantly and provide mechanisms for discussion. The two Vietnamese parties are talking to each other and are achieving some results, even if these results are much less than we would like to see. The final exchange of prisoners which was completed on March 7 is illustrative.

We assess the cease-fire agreement in Laos as being so far largely successful. The level of combat was reduced substantially immediately following the cease-fire and has since fallen to a handful of incidents per week. There is hope that if developments continue as they have, the Laos cease-fire will work and the Lao, through their own efforts, will be able to establish a coalition government and a stable peace in their country.

   8)   "The Department's assessment of the overall situation in Cambodia and the possibility for a ceasefire agreement."

Despite continued pressure by the Khmer insurgents, now generally under the control of the Khmer Communist Party, the Khmer armed forces have successfully repulsed two major insurgent operations, one against Kompong Cham and, more recently, against Phnom Penh, with no U.S. combat support. Serious military problems remain, and continued hard fighting during the next few months is expected, both in the provinces and around the capital.

A broadened political base, a new Prime Minister and a more effective cabinet[10] offer signs of improvements in the civil administration. The enormous dislocation of war, destroying production, producing over a million refugees and encouraging spiralling inflation, face the leaders of the Khmer Republic with serious problems.

Nonetheless, we are convinced that with U.S. material and diplomatic support the Khmer Republic's demonstration of military and economic viability will persuade their now intransigent opponents to move to a political solution of the Cambodian conflict. The Khmer Republic's Foreign Minister on March 21 reiterated his government's position that a solution for Cambodia should be peaceful and not forced by arms or capitulation. Instead, his government will continue to seek talks with the other side. His government hopes their efforts for peace will achieve some results after the current insurgent offensive.

   9)   "Recent diplomatic initiatives, involving the United States, aimed at a reduction of violence in Indochina and a greater measure of normalization in the area."

Since the signing of the Viet-Nam cease-fire agreement, the United States has been in constant liaison with the interested parties, including those outside of the Indochina area. While it would not be useful to provide details of all of these contacts, we can assure the Congress that we have used every means at our disposal to encourage a reduction in the level of violence and an orderly resolution of the conflict. We believe these measures have had some success. The level of fighting is down substantially from 1972 and

[10]Long Boret succeeded In Tam on Dec. 26, 1973 as head of a reorganized government in which Keuk Ky Lim became Minister of Foreign Affairs.

the Vietnamese parties have taken at least beginning steps toward a satisfactory accommodation. Further, the interested outside parties remain basically committed to building on the framework of the cease-fire agreement.

When Hanoi established a pattern of serious violations of the Agreement shortly after its conclusion, Dr. Kissinger met with Special Adviser Le Duc Tho and negotiated the Paris communique of June 13, 1973,[11] with a view to stabilizing the situation. Secretary Kissinger returned to Paris in December, 1973, to again discuss with Special Adviser Tho the status of the implementation of the Agreement.[12] We will continue to maintain such contacts with Vietnamese and other parties in the hope that Hanoi will eventually be persuaded that its interests lie in peaceful development rather than in conflict.

In Laos, we have offered every encouragement to an evolution toward peace. At this time the Laotian parties are making great progress in the formation of a government of national union. We can help in this regard with our sympathy and encouragement while properly leaving the issue in the hands of those most interested, the Lao people.

The Government of the Khmer Republic, with our complete endorsement, has made notable efforts to terminate the hostilities in that country. Following the cease-fire in Viet-Nam, the Cambodian Government unilaterally ceased hostile activity by its forces in the hope that the other side would respond. Unfortunately that striking gesture was rebuffed. On frequent occasions thereafter the Khmer Republic made proposals designed to move the conflict from the battlefield to political fora, with our strong support in each instance. Although all of those proposals have been ignored by the Khmer Communists, we continue to hope that the current relative military balance will make apparent to the other side what the Khmer Republic has already perceived, that peace is a far more hopeful prospect for Cambodia than incessant conflict.

[Secretary Kissinger's hopes for a gradual improvement of conditions in the Indochinese countries were to be very imperfectly realized. In Laos, the situation was at least temporarily stabilized with the formal installation on April 5 of the Provisional Government of National Union, followed by an exchange of prisoners and a withdrawal of U.S. and Thai military forces—though even here it was generally understood that large numbers of North Vietnamese military personnel remained in the country in contravention of the Paris agreement. In Cambodia, a military stalemate that persisted

[11]*AFR, 1973*: 239-46.
[12]Cf. Kissinger news conference, Jan. 3, in *Bulletin*: 70: 78.

through most of the year left the Khmer Republic in precarious control of the capital and the principal towns but unable either to better its military position or to engage its adversaries in peace negotiations.

The most serious military and political deterioration, however, occurred in South Vietnam itself, where the cease-fire machinery set up under the Paris agreement became virtually inoperative during the spring as enemy forces increasingly resorted to sizable military offensives in various parts of the country, apparently aimed at depriving the Saigon administration of important tracts of territory together with their inhabitants. The U.S. Congress, meanwhile, refused to heed administration pleas for increased military assistance to the Saigon government, going so far as to reduce the proposed allotment for military aid in the fiscal year 1975 from $1.4 billion to $700 million.[13] (Similarly, military aid for Cambodia was limited to $200 million, in a total authorization of $377 million in all forms of aid to that country.)[14]

The difficult plight of President Thieu's regime was observed with understandable satisfaction in Hanoi, where it was evidently assumed that the United States would be in no position to reenter the conflict even if offensive operations were further stepped up. According to subsequent disclosures from the North Vietnamese side, the closing weeks of 1974 were in fact devoted to drawing up a two-year strategic plan for 1975-76 that called for "widespread, large surprise attacks" in 1975 in order to create conditions for a "general offensive and uprising to completely liberate the South" in the following year.[15] What even North Vietnam's leaders apparently did not realize was that the offensive to be launched in the spring of 1975 would suffice in itself to destroy the South Vietnamese army as a fighting force, precipitate the final collapse of President Thieu's regime, and ensure the extension of Communist rule to Cambodia and Laos as well.]

---

[13]Title VII, Department of Defense Appropriation Act, 1975 (Public Law 93-437, Oct. 8, 1974).

[14]Sec. 39, Foreign Assistance Act of 1974 (Public Law 93-559, Dec. 30, 1974); cf. Chapter 35 at note 26.

[15]Van Tien Dung (North Vietnamese Chief of Staff), "Great Spring Victory: A Summation of Senior General Van Tien Dung of the Combat Situation in the Spring of 1975," excerpted in *New York Times*, Apr. 26, 1976.

7. ENCOUNTER WITH THE THIRD WORLD

(New York, April 9-May 2, 1974)

[If there was room for doubt about the permanence of the settlement in Indochina, there could be no uncertainty at all about the imperious challenge being posed by the underdeveloped, third world countries that represented roughly 70 percent of the earth's 3.89 billion inhabitants, and had been making no secret of their demand for a "new deal" in their relationship with the other, more favored 30 percent. The onset of the global energy crisis had heightened the determination expressed by many third world governments to press for a far-reaching redress of old grievances and a significant redistribution of resources and economic power.

President Houari Boumediene of Algeria, who had already enunciated a startling theory of "rich-poor" antagonism at the Algiers conference of nonaligned nations in September 1973,[1] continued to act as spearhead of this movement in his capacity as chairman of the nonaligned group, currently numbering 76 nations. Reacting to France's January 1974 proposal looking toward a U.N.-sponsored world energy conference,[2] the Algerian leader had called on January 31 for a broader discussion that would take place in the framework of a special session of the U.N. General Assembly, would concern itself with the overall problems of raw materials and development, and would try to devise a new system of international economic relations based on the equality and common interest of all states. Following prompt endorsement by the requisite majority of the U.N. membership, the Assembly's Sixth Special Session accordingly took place at U.N. Headquarters in New York from April 9 to May 2, 1974.

Elected by acclamation as President of the Special Session, Ambassador Leopoldo Benites of Ecuador (who had previously served

---

[1]Cf. *AFR, 1973*: 495-6.
[2]Cf. Chapter 3 at note 4.

as President of the 28th Regular Session in 1973) declared that the meeting would surely represent a milestone in the history of the United Nations. This was true, he asserted, not so much because of the concrete accomplishments that might be possible in so short a space of time as "because, from today onwards, it will be necessary to devise a completely new approach to international economic problems, a critical reformulation of the guiding principles and a restructuring of co-operation among States."[3] President Boumediene, delivering the keynote address on April 10, elaborated upon his previous statements about the need for "profound reorganization of economic relations between rich and poor countries." It was high time, the Algerian leader declared, to do away with an economic order which, "in the eyes of the vast majority of humanity," was "as unjust and as outdated as the colonial order to which it owed its origin and substance."[4]

Secretary Kissinger, speaking on April 15 in the course of the Assembly's general debate, undertook to warn against the confrontationist approach that had seemed to dominate the opening days of the session. While stressing the U.S. commitment to rational development efforts, the Secretary of State implied that nothing was to be gained by substituting hostility for cooperation or confusing rhetoric with purposive action.]

(8) *Sixth Special Session of the United Nations General Assembly, New York, April 9-May 2, 1974.*

(a) *"The Challenge of Interdependence": Statement to the Assembly by Secretary of State Kissinger, April 15, 1974.*[5]

We are gathered here in a continuing venture to realize mankind's hopes for a more prosperous, humane, just, and cooperative world.

As members of this organization, we are pledged not only to free the world from the scourge of war but to free mankind from the fear of hunger, poverty, and disease. The quest for justice and dignity—which finds expression in the economic and social articles of the United Nations Charter—has global meaning in an age of instantaneous communication. Improving the quality of human life has become a universal political demand, a technical possibility, and a moral imperative.

[3] *UN Monthly Chronicle*, May 1974: 34.
[4] Same: 36.
[5] As-delivered text and subtitles from *Bulletin*, 70: 477-83.

We meet here at a moment when the world economy is under severe stress. The energy crisis first dramatized its fragility. But the issues transcend that particular crisis. Each of the problems we face—of combating inflation and stimulating growth, of feeding the hungry and lifting the impoverished, of the scarcity of physical resources and the surplus of despair—is part of an interrelated global problem.

Let us begin by discarding outdated generalities and sterile slogans we have—all of us—lived with for so long. The great issues of development can no longer realistically be perceived in terms of confrontation between the "haves" and "have-nots" or as a struggle over the distribution of static wealth. Whatever our ideological belief or social structure, we are part of a single international economic system on which all of our national economic objectives depend. No nation or bloc of nations can unilaterally determine the shape of the future.

If the strong attempt to impose their views, they will do so at the cost of justice and thus provoke upheaval. If the weak resort to pressure, they will do so at the risk of world prosperity and thus provoke despair.

The organization of one group of countries as a bloc will, sooner or later, produce the organization of potential victims into a counterbloc. The transfer of resources from the developed to the developing nations—essential to all hopes for progress—can only take place with the support of the technologically advanced countries. Politics of pressure and threats will undermine the domestic base of this support. The danger of economic stagnation stimulates new barriers to trade and to the transfer of resources.

We in this Assembly must come to grips with the fact of our interdependence.

The contemporary world can no longer be encompassed in traditional stereotypes. The notion of the northern rich and the southern poor has been shattered. The world is composed not of two sets of interests but many: developed nations which are energy suppliers and developing nations which are energy consumers, market economies and nonmarket economies, capital providers and capital recipients.

The world economy is a sensitive set of relationships in which actions can easily set off a vicious spiral of counteractions deeply affecting all countries, developing as well as technologically advanced. Global inflation erodes the capacity to import. A reduction in the rate of world growth reduces export prospects. Exorbitantly high prices lower consumption, spur alternative production, and foster development of substitutes.

We are all engaged in a common enterprise. No nation or group of nations can gain by pushing its claims beyond the limits that sustain world economic growth. No one benefits from basing progress on tests of strength.

For the first time in history, mankind has the technical possibility to escape the scourges that used to be considered inevitable. Global communication insures that the thrust of human aspirations becomes universal. Mankind insistently identifies justice with the betterment of the human condition. Thus economics, technology, and the sweep of human values impose a recognition of our interdependence and of the necessity of our collaboration.

Let us therefore resolve to act with both realism and compassion to reach a new understanding of the human condition. On that understanding, let us base a new relationship which evokes the commitment of all nations because it serves the interests of all peoples. We can build a just world only if we work together.

The Global Agenda

The fundamental challenge before this session is to translate the acknowledgment of our common destiny into a commitment to common action, to inspire developed and developing nations alike to perceive and pursue their national interest by contributing to the global interest. The developing nations can meet the aspirations of their peoples only in an open, expanding world economy where they can expect to find larger markets, capital resources, and support for official assistance. The developed nations can convince their people to contribute to that goal only in an environment of political cooperation.

On behalf of President Nixon, I pledge the United States to a major effort in support of development. My country dedicates itself to this enterprise because our children—yours and ours—must not live in a world of brutal inequality, because peace cannot be maintained unless all share in its benefits, and because America has never believed that the values of justice, well-being, and human dignity could be realized by one nation alone.

We begin with the imperative of peace. The hopes of development will be mocked if resources continue to be consumed by an ever-increasing spiral of armaments. The relaxation of tensions is thus in the world interest. No nation can profit from confrontations that could culminate in nuclear war. At the same time, the United States will never seek stability at the expense of others. It strives for the peace of cooperation, not the illusory tranquility of condominium.

But peace is more than the absence of war. It is ennobled by making possible the realization of humane aspirations. To this purpose this Assembly is dedicated.

Our goal cannot be reached by resolutions alone. It must remain the subject of constant, unremitting efforts over the years and decades ahead.

In this spirit of describing the world as it is, I would like to identify for this Assembly six problem areas which, in the view of the U.S. delegation, must be solved to spur both the world economy and world development. I do so not with the attitude of presenting blueprints but of defining common tasks to whose solution the United States herewith offers its wholehearted cooperation.

Expanding the Supply of Energy

First, a global economy requires an expanding supply of energy at an equitable price.

No subject illustrates global interdependence more emphatically than the field of energy. No nation has an interest in prices that can set off an inflationary spiral which in time reduces income for all. For example, the price of fertilizer has risen in direct proportion to the price of oil, putting it beyond the reach of many of the poorest nations and thus contributing to worldwide food shortages. A comprehension by both producers and consumers of each other's needs is therefore essential:

—Consumers must understand the desires of the producers for higher levels of income over the long-term future.

—Producers must understand that the recent rise in energy prices has placed a great burden on all consumers, one virtually impossible for some to bear.

All nations share an interest in agreeing on a level of prices which contributes to an expanding world economy and which can be sustained over the long term.

The United States called the Washington Energy Conference[6] for one central purpose—to move urgently to resolve the energy problem on the basis of cooperation among all nations. The tasks we defined there can become a global agenda:

—Nations, particularly developed nations, waste vast amounts of existing energy supplies. We need a new commitment to global conservation and to more efficient use of existing supplies.

—The oil producers themselves have noted that the demands of this decade cannot be met unless we expand available supplies. We need a massive and cooperative effort to develop alternative sources of fuels.

—The needs of future generations require that we develop new and renewable sources of supply. In this field, the developed nations can make a particularly valuable contribution to our common goal of abundant energy at reasonable cost.

Such a program cannot be achieved by any one group of countries. It must draw on the strength and meet the needs of all nations in a new dialogue among producers and consumers.

In such a dialogue, the United States will take account of—and take seriously—the concern of the producing countries that the future of their peoples not depend on oil alone. The United States is willing to help broaden the base of their economies and to develop secure and diversified sources of income. We are prepared to facilitate the transfer of technology and to assist industrialization. We will accept substantial investment of the capital of oil-producing countries in the United States. We will support a greater role for oil producers in international financial organizations as well as an increase in their voting power.

Avoiding Imbalances in Raw Materials

Second, a healthy global economy requires that both consumers and producers escape from the cycle of raw material surplus and shortage which threatens all our economies.

The principles which apply to energy apply as well to the general problem of raw materials. It is tempting to think of cartels of raw material producers to negotiate for higher prices. But such a course could have serious consequences for all countries. Large price increases coupled with production restrictions involve potential disaster: global inflation followed by global recession from which no nation could escape.

Moreover, resources are spread unevenly across the globe. Some of the poorest nations have few natural resources to export, and some of the richest nations are major commodity producers.

Commodity producers will discover that they are by no means insulated from the consequences of restrictions on supply or the escalation of prices. A recession in the industrial countries sharply reduces demand. Uneconomical prices for raw materials accelerate the transition to alternatives. And as they pursue industrialization, raw material producers will ultimately pay for exorbitant commodity prices by the increased costs of the goods they must import.

Thus the optimum price is one that can be maintained over the longest period at the level that assures the highest real income. Only through cooperation between consumers and producers can such a price be determined. Such a cooperative effort must include urgent international consideration of restrictions on incentives for the trade in commodities. This issue—dealing with access to supply as well as access to markets—must receive high priority in GATT [General Agreement on Tariffs and Trade] as we seek to revise and modernize the rules and conditions of international trade.

In the long term, our hopes for world prosperity will depend on our ability to discern the long-range patterns of supply and demand and to forecast future imbalances so as to avert dangerous cycles of surplus and shortage.

For the first time in history, it is technically within our grasp to relate the resources of this planet to man's needs. The United States therefore urges that an international group of experts, working closely with the United Nations Division on Resources, be asked to undertake immediately a comprehensive survey of the earth's non-renewable and renewable resources. This should include the development of a global early warning system to foreshadow impending surpluses and scarcities.

Crisis in Food Production

Third, the global economy must achieve a balance between food production and population growth and must restore the capacity to meet food emergencies. A condition in which 1 billion people suffer from malnutrition is consistent with no concept of justice.

Since 1969, global production of cereals has not kept pace with world demand. As a result, current reserves are at their lowest level in 20 years. A significant crop failure today is likely to produce a major disaster. A protracted imbalance in food and population growth will guarantee massive starvation—a moral catastrophe the world community cannot tolerate.

No nation can deal with this problem alone. The developed nations must commit themselves to significant assistance for food and population programs. The developed nations must reduce the imbalance between population and food which could jeopardize not only their own progress but the stability of the world.

The United States recognizes the responsibility of leadership it bears by virtue of its extraordinary agricultural productivity. We strongly support a global cooperative effort to increase food production. This is why we proposed a World Food Conference at last year's session of the General Assembly.[7]

Looking toward that conference, we have removed all domestic restrictions on production. Our farmers have vastly increased the acreage under cultivation and gathered record harvests in 1973.

[7]*AFR, 1973*: 364-5; see further Chapter 27.

1974 promises to be even better. If all nations make a similar effort, we believe the recent rise in food prices will abate this year, as it has in recent weeks.

The United States is determined to take additional steps. Specifically:

—We are prepared to join with other governments in a major worldwide effort to rebuild food reserves. A central objective of the World Food Conference must be to restore the world's capacity to deal with famine.

—We shall assign priority in our aid program to help developing nations substantially raise their agricultural production. We hope to increase our assistance to such programs from $258 million to $675 million this year.

—We shall make a major effort to increase the quantity of food aid over the level we provided last year.

For countries living near the margin of starvation, even a small reduction in yields can produce intolerable consequences. Thus, the shortage of fertilizer and the steep rise in its price is a problem of particular urgency—above all for countries dependent on the new high-yield varieties of grain. The first critical step is for all nations to utilize fully existing capabilities. The United States is now operating its fertilizer industry at near capacity. The United States is ready to provide assistance to other nations in improving the operation of plants and to make more effective use of fertilizers.

But this will not be enough. Existing worldwide capacity is clearly inadequate. The United States would be prepared to offer its technological skills to developing a new fertilizer industry in developing countries and especially in oil-producing countries, using the raw materials and capital they uniquely possess.

We also urge the establishment of an international fertilizer institute as part of a larger effort to focus international action on two specific areas of research: improving the effectiveness of chemical fertilizers, especially in tropical agriculture, and new methods to produce fertilizers from non-petroleum resources. The United States will contribute facilities, technology, and expertise to such an undertaking.

Nations at the Margin of Existence

Fourth, a global economy under stress cannot allow the poorest nations to be overwhelmed.

The debate between raw material producers and consumers must not overlook that substantial part of humanity which does not produce raw materials, grows insufficient food for its needs, and has not adequately industrialized. This group of nations, already at the margin of existence, has no recourse to pay the higher prices for the fuel, food, and fertilizer imports on which their survival depends.

Thus, the people least able to afford it—a third of mankind—are the most profoundly threatened by an inflationary world economy. They face the despair of abandoned hopes for development and the threat of starvation. Their needs require our most urgent attention. The nations assembled here in the name of justice cannot stand idly by in the face of tragic consequences for which many of them are partially responsible.

We welcome the steps the oil producers have already taken toward applying their new surplus revenues to these needs. The magnitude of the problem requires, and the magnitude of their resources permits, a truly massive effort.

The developed nations, too, have an obligation to help. Despite the prospect of unprecedented payment difficulties, they must maintain their traditional programs of assistance and expand them if possible. Failure to do so would penalize the lower income countries twice. The United States is committed to continue its program and pledges its support for an early replenishment of the International Development Association.[8] In addition, we are prepared to consider with others what additional measures are required to mitigate the effects of commodity price rises on low-income countries least able to bear the burden.

Applying Science to the World's Problems

Fifth, in a global economy of physical scarcity, science and technology are becoming our most precious resource.

No human activity is less national in character than the field of science. No development effort offers more hope than joint technical and scientific cooperation.

Man's technical genius has given us labor-saving technology, healthier populations, and the Green Revolution. But it has also produced a technology that consumes resources at an ever-expanding rate, a population explosion which presses against the earth's finite living space, and an agriculture increasingly dependent on the products of industry. Let us now apply science to the problems which science has helped to create:

—To meet the developing nations' two most fundamental problems, unemployment and hunger, there is an urgent need for farming technologies that are both productive and labor in-

⁸Cf. Chapter 24 at notes 2 and 8.

tensive. The United States is prepared to contribute to international programs to develop and apply this technology.

—The technology of birth control should be improved.

—At current rates of growth, the world's need for energy will more than triple by the end of this century. To meet this challenge, the U.S. Government is allocating $12 billion for energy research and development over the next five years, and American private industry will spend over $200 billion to increase energy supplies. We are prepared to apply the results of our massive effort to the massive needs of other nations.

—The poorest nations, already beset by manmade disasters, have been threatened by a natural one: the possibility of climatic changes in the monsoon belt and perhaps throughout the world. The implications for global food and population policies are ominous. The United States proposes that the International Council of Scientific Unions and the World Meteorological Organization urgently investigate this problem and offer guidelines for immediate international action.

An Open Trade and Finance System

Sixth, the global economy requires a trade, monetary, and investment system that sustains industrial civilization and stimulates growth.

Not since the 1930's has the economic system of the world faced such a test. The disruption of the oil price rises, the threat of global inflation, the cycle of contraction of exports and protectionist restrictions, the massive shift in the world's financial flows, and the likely concentration of invested surplus oil revenue in a few countries—all threaten to smother the dreams of universal progress with stagnation and despair.

A new commitment is required by both developed and developing countries to an open trading system, a flexible but stable monetary system, and a positive climate for the free flow of resources, both public and private.

To this end the United States proposes that all nations here pledge themselves to avoid trade and payment restrictions in an effort to adjust to higher commodity prices.

The United States is prepared to keep open its capital markets so that capital can be recycled to developing countries hardest hit by the current crisis.

In the essential struggle to regain control over global inflation, the United States is willing to join in an international commitment to pursue responsible fiscal and monetary policies.

To foster an open trading world the United States, already the largest importer of the manufacturers [*sic*] of developing nations, is prepared to open its markets further to these products. We shall work in the multilateral trade negotiations to reduce tariff and non-tariff barriers on as wide a front as possible. In line with this approach we are urging our Congress to authorize the generalized tariff preferences which are of such significance to developing countries.[9]

Matching Physical Needs With Political Vision

All too often, international gatherings end with speeches filed away and with resolutions passed and forgotten. We must not let this happen to the problem of development. The complex and urgent issues at hand will not yield to rhetorical flourishes. Their resolution requires a sustained and determined pursuit in the great family of United Nations and other international organizations that have the broad competence to deal with them.

As President Nixon stated to this Assembly in 1969:[10]

Surely if one lesson above all rings resoundingly among the many shattered hopes in this world, it is that good words are not a substitute for hard deeds and noble rhetoric is no guarantee of noble results.

This Assembly should strengthen our commitment to find cooperative solutions within the appropriate forums such as the World Bank, the International Monetary Fund, the GATT, and the World Food and Population Conferences.[11] The United States commits itself to a wide-ranging multilateral effort.

Mr. President, Mr. Secretary General [Kurt Waldheim], we gather here today because our economic and moral challenges have become political challenges. Our unprecedented agenda for global consultations in 1974 already implies a collective decision to elevate our concern for man's elementary well-being to the highest political level. Our presence implies our recognition that a challenge of this magnitude cannot be solved by a world fragmented into self-contained states or competing blocs.

Our task now is to match our physical needs with our political vision.

President Boumediene cited the Marshall plan of a quarter century ago as an example of the possibility of mobilizing resources for development ends. But then the driving force was a shared sense of purpose, of values, and of destination. As yet, we lack a com-

[9]Cf. Chapter 35 at note 19.
[10]*Documents, 1968-69*: 467.
[11]Cf. Chapters 20 (population) and 27 (food).

parable sense of purpose with respect to development. This is our first requirement. Development requires, above all, a spirit of cooperation, a belief that with all our differences we are part of a larger community in which wealth is an obligation, resources are a trust, and joint action is a necessity.

We need mutual respect for the aspirations of the developing as well as the concerns of the developed nations. This is why the United States has supported the concept of a Charter of Economic Rights and Duties of States put forward by President Echeverría of Mexico.[12]

The late President [Sarvepalli] Radhakrishnan of India once wrote:

> We are not the helpless tools of determinism. Though humanity renews itself from its past, it is also developing something new and unforeseen. Today we have to make a new start with our minds and hearts.

The effort we make in the years to come is thus a test of the freedom of the human spirit.

Let us affirm today that we are faced with a common challenge and can only meet it jointly. Let us candidly acknowledge our different perspectives and then proceed to build on what unites us. Let us transform the concept of world community from a slogan into an attitude.

In this spirit let us be the masters of our common fate so that history will record that this was the year that mankind at last began to conquer its noblest and most humane challenge.

[Secretary Kissinger's warning against undue reliance on "rhetorical flourishes" was hardly designed to win applause in a gathering whose orientation had from the first impressed observers as being more rhetorical than practical. From early in the session, it was apparent that its chief result would be the adoption of a more or less apocalyptic declaration setting forth majority views about the "new international economic order" desired by so many of the participating countries. In a belated attempt to infuse some solid content into the Assembly's deliberations, the United States on April 30 put forward a surprise proposal involving a $4 billion program of emergency assistance to the most distressed countries over the next eighteen months in the form of grants, loans, commodity aid, and debt renegotiation, to which the United States itself would contribute an unspecified "fair share." Supposedly delayed by disagreements between the State Department and the Treasury, the proposal came too late to be seriously considered, and was with-drawn next day as the Assembly proceeded—without a formal vote —to adopt the resolutions already pending.[13]

The results of the Assembly's three-week debate were therefore embodied in a "Declaration on the Establishment of a New International Economic Order," nominally adopted "by consensus," together with a "Programme of Action" designed to ensure its realization.]

(b) "Declaration on the Establishment of a New International Economic Order," adopted by the General Assembly as Resolution 3201 (S-VI), May 1, 1974.[14]

THE GENERAL ASSEMBLY

Adopts the following Declaration:

Declaration on the Establishment of a New International Economic Order

We, the Members of the United Nations,

Having convened a special session of the General Assembly to study for the first time the problems of raw materials and development, devoted to the consideration of the most important economic problems facing the world community,

Bearing in mind the spirit, purposes and principles of the Charter of the United Nations to promote the economic advancement and social progress of all peoples,

Solemnly proclaim our united determination to work urgently for

The Establishment of a New International Economic Order

based on equity, sovereign equality, interdependence, common interest and co-operation among all States, irrespective of their economic and social systems which shall correct inequalities and redress existing injustices, make it possible to eliminate the widen-

---

[13]*New York Times*, May 1 and 2, 1974; *U.S. Participation, 1974*: 149.
[14]Unofficial text from *UN Monthly Chronicle*, May 1974: 66-9; adopted without vote.

ing gap between the developed and the developing countries and ensure steadily accelerating economic and social development in peace and justice for present and future generations.

1. The greatest and most significant achievement during the last decades has been the independence from colonial and alien domination of a large number of peoples and nations which has enabled them to become members of the community of free peoples. Technological progress has also been made in all spheres of economic activities in the last three decades, thus providing a solid potential for improving the well-being of all peoples. However, the remaining vestiges of alien and colonial domination, foreign occupation, racial discrimination, *apartheid* and neo-colonialism in all its forms continue to be among the greatest obstacles to the full emancipation and progress of the developing countries and all the peoples involved. The benefits of technological progress are not shared equitably by all members of the international community. The developing countries, which constitute 70 per cent of the world population, account for only 30 per cent of the world's income. It has proved impossible to achieve an even and balanced development of the international community under the existing international economic order. The gap between the developed and the developing countries continues to widen in a system which was established at a time when most of the developing countries did not even exist as independent States and which perpetuates inequality.

2. The present international economic order is in direct conflict with current developments in international political and economic relations. Since 1970, the world economy has experienced a series of grave crises which have had severe repercussions, especially on the developing countries because of their generally greater vulnerability to external economic impulses. The developing world has become a powerful factor that makes its influence felt in all fields of international activity. These irreversible changes in the relationship of forces in the world necessitate the active, full and equal participation of the developing countries in the formulation and application of all decisions that concern the international community.

3. All these changes have thrust into prominence the reality of interdependence of all the members of the world community. Current events have brought into sharp focus the realization that the interests of the developed countries and the interests of the developing countries can no longer be isolated from each other; that there is close interrelationship between the prosperity of the developed countries and the growth and development of the developing countries, and that the prosperity of the international community as a whole depends upon the prosperity of its constituent parts. Interna-

tional co-operation for development is the shared goal and common duty of all countries. Thus the political, economic and social well-being of present and future generations depends more than ever on co-operation between all members of the international community on the basis of sovereign equality and the removal of the disequilibrium that exists between them.

4. The new international economic order should be founded on full respect for the following principles:

(a) Sovereign equality of States, self-determination of all peoples, inadmissibility of the acquisition of territories by force, territorial integrity and non-interference in the internal affairs of other States;

(b) Broadest co-operation of all the member States of the international community, based on equity, whereby the prevailing disparities in the world may be banished and prosperity secured for all;

(c) Full and effective participation on the basis of equality of all countries in the solving of world economic problems in the common interest of all countries, bearing in mind the necessity to ensure the accelerated development of all the developing countries, while devoting particular attention to the adoption of special measures in favour of the least developed, land-locked and island developing countries as well as those developing countries most seriously affected by economic crises and natural calamities, without losing sight of the interests of other developing countries;

(d) Every country has the right to adopt the economic and social system that it deems to be the most appropriate for its own development and not to be subjected to discrimination of any kind as a result;

(e) Full permanent sovereignty of every State over its natural resources and all economic activities. In order to safeguard these resources, each State is entitled to exercise effective control over them and their exploitation with means suitable to its own situation, including the right to nationalization or transfer of ownership to its nationals, this right being an expression of the full permanent sovereignty of the State. No State may be subjected to economic, political or any other type of coercion to prevent the free and full exercise of this inalienable right;

(f) All States, territories and peoples under foreign occupation, alien and colonial domination or *apartheid* have the right to restitution and full compensation for the exploitation and depletion of, and damages to, the natural and all other resources of those States, territories and peoples;

(g) Regulation and supervision of the activities of transnational corporations by taking measures in the interest of the national economies of the countries where such transnational corporations operate on the basis of the full sovereignty of those countries;

(h) Right of the developing countries and the peoples of territories under colonial and racial domination and foreign occupation to achieve their liberation and to regain effective control over their natural resources and economic activities;

(i) Extending of assistance to developing countries, peoples and territories under colonial and alien domination, foreign occupation, racial discrimination or *apartheid* or which are subjected to economic, political or any other type of measures to coerce them in order to obtain from them the subordination of the exercise of their sovereign rights and to secure from them advantages of any kind, and to neo-colonialism in all its forms and which have established or are endeavouring to establish effective control over their natural resources and economic activities that have been or are still under foreign control;

(j) Just and equitable relationship between the prices of raw materials, primary products, manufactured and semi-manufactured goods exported by developing countries and the prices of raw materials, primary commodities, manufactures, capital goods and equipment imported by them with the aim of bringing about sustained improvement in their unsatisfactory terms of trade and the expansion of the world economy;

(k) Extension of active assistance to developing countries by the whole international community, free of any political or military conditions;

(l) Ensuring that one of the main aims of the reformed international monetary system shall be the promotion of the development of the developing countries and the adequate flow of real resources to them;

(m) Improving the competitiveness of natural materials facing competition from synthetic substitutes;

(n) Preferential and non-reciprocal treatment for developing countries wherever feasible, in all fields of international economic co-operation, wherever feasible;

(o) Securing favourable conditions for the transfer of financial resources to developing countries;

(p) To give to the developing countries access to the achievements of modern science and technology, to promote the transfer of technology and the creation of indigenous technology for the benefit of the developing countries in forms and in accordance with procedures which are suited to their economies;

(q) Necessity for all States to put an end to the waste of natural resources, including food products;

(r)   The need for developing countries to concentrate all their resources for the cause of development;

(s)   Strengthening—through individual and collective actions—of mutual economic, trade, financial and technical co-operation among the developing countries mainly on a preferential basis;

(t)   Facilitating the role which producers associations may play, within the framework of international co-operation, and in pursuance of their aims, *inter alia*, assisting in promotion of sustained growth of world economy and accelerating development of developing countries.

5.   The unanimous adoption of the International Development Strategy for the Second Development Decade[15] was an important step in the promotion of international economic co-operation on a just and equitable basis. The accelerated implementation of obligations and commitments assumed by the international community within the framework of the Strategy, particularly those concerning imperative development needs of developing countries, would contribute significantly to the fulfilment of the aims and objectives of the present Declaration.

6.   The United Nations as a universal organization should be capable of dealing with problems of international economic co-operation in a comprehensive manner and ensuring equally the interests of all countries. It must have an even greater role in the establishment of a new international economic order. The Charter of Economic Rights and Duties of States, for the preparation of which this Declaration will provide an additional source of inspiration, will constitute a significant contribution in this respect.[16] All the States Members of the United Nations are therefore called upon to exert maximum efforts with a view to securing the implementation of this Declaration, which is one of the principal guarantees for the creation of better conditions for all peoples to reach a life worthy of human dignity.

7.   This Declaration on the Establishment of a New International Economic Order shall be one of the most important bases of economic relations between all peoples and all nations.

[Developing country demands were set forth in even greater detail in the "Programme of Action on the Establishment of a New International Economic Order" that accompanied the foregoing Declaration.[17] Among the specific demands were such highly con-

[15]General Assembly Resolution 2626 (XXV), Oct. 24, 1970; excerpts in *Documents, 1970*: 324-31.

[16]Cf. Chapter 32 at note 17.

[17]General Assembly Resolution 3202 (S-VI), May 1, 1974.

troversial items as the linking of prices of raw materials and manufactures (indexation); the right to determine unilaterally the compensation to be paid for nationalized foreign enterprises; the use of
IMF Special Drawing Rights (SDRs) as an instrument of development financing; and control over the activities of multinational or
transnational corporations. Also included was a request to
Secretary-General Kurt Waldheim to draw up a special program of
emergency measures for the benefit of the most seriously affected
countries, now becoming known as MSAs. Still other proposals
which had been put forward by the United States and other governments were referred to the Economic and Social Council
(ECOSOC) for subsequent consideration.

Though nominally adopted "by consensus," these actions were
taken in face of the known dissatisfaction not only of the United
States but of most of the other major industrial powers. American
views with regard to what was obviously a widening rift with many
of the third world countries were indicated by Ambassador John
Scali, the U.S. Representative to the United Nations, in one of the
numerous statements of position that were placed in the Assembly's records before its adjournment on May 2.]

(c) United States Reservations: Statement to the Assembly by Ambassador John Scali, United States Representative to the United Nations, May 1, 1974.[18]

As this Assembly draws to a close, it is time to take stock. Much
good has been done. The world community, represented by its leading statesmen, has devoted several weeks of intensive attention to
the critical situation which has arisen in the international economic
arena. We believe this was right, proper, and useful.

Many constructive suggestions were made on how to cope with
the range of problems in this field. We are, I must confess, disappointed that it was not possible to emerge from our deliberations
with unanimous agreement on how these problems can best be
solved.

Over the years we have negotiated out our differences on complicated economic and development questions in various other appropriate fora. We seriously question what value there is in adopting
statements on difficult and controversial questions that represent
the views of only one faction.

Some have referred to the procedure by which these documents
have been formulated as that of "consensus." My delegation
believes the word "consensus" cannot be applied in this case. The

document which will be printed as the written product of this special General Assembly does not in fact—whatever it is called—represent a consensus in the accepted meaning of that term.

My delegation, Mr. President, did not choose to voice objection to the resolution presented to us this evening even though at the last moment it was presented without mention of the word "consensus." The intent, however, was clear. This was intended as a consensus procedure. But our objecting at the last second would only have served to exacerbate the divisions that we have worked to the best of our ability to bridge during the past weeks.

The document in question contains elements which many members of the United Nations, large and small, and on every continent, do not endorse. The U.S. delegation, like many others, strongly disapproves of some provisions in the document and has in no sense endorsed them. The document we have produced is a significant political document, but it does not represent unanimity of opinion in this Assembly. To label some of these highly controversial conclusions as "agreed" is not only idle, it is self-deceiving. In this house, the steamroller is not the vehicle for solving vital, complex problems.

The major concern of my own government has been to assure some immediate and effective relief to those developing countries which have been most adversely affected by recent changes in the world economy. While a program of action has been adopted, we are, frankly, not convinced that it will respond to these immediate needs. I would draw your attention to the fact that just yesterday my own delegation advanced a number of ideas which were addressed primarily to this area of most critical need. We regret that the shortage of time made it impossible to obtain agreement. I wish to assure the Assembly, however, that my own government is examining carefully what additional measures it can take to provide assistance to those countries which have suffered most.

The United States remains deeply concerned about the need for a cooperative effort to resolve the difficulties which face the international community on a whole range of issues, including commodity prices, aid, trade, energy, food, and monetary stability. We remain committed to seeking solutions to these issues on a cooperative basis and through true consensus rather than confrontation.

The sixth special session of the United Nations General Assembly has acknowledged mankind's common destiny. Our nations met in a global forum to come to grips with what once were considered national problems: inflation, economic growth, feeding the hungry, and uplifting the impoverished.

The challenge has been to accept our mutual dependence and to agree on an agenda for common action to improve the quality of life across the globe. Success cannot be determined by one nation or by one group of nations seeking to impose its will. Nor will it result from one session of the General Assembly.

Too often in the past this organization has been the forum for unrealistic promises and unfulfilled commitments. The ideal has been substituted too often for the attainable, and the results have often been no more than increased frustration and disappointment. Historically, the United States has not made commitments that we did not intend to fulfill. Thus, as Secretary of State Kissinger recently told the Foreign Ministers of Latin America and the Caribbean,[19] the United States will promise only what it can deliver. And we will make what we can deliver count.

In this spirit, on behalf of President Nixon, Secretary Kissinger in his address to this Assembly two weeks ago[20] pledged the United States to a major effort in support of development. He stated that the United States would make a substantial contribution to the special needs of the poorest nations.

We have set forth our specific proposals and commitments to help assure an abundant supply of energy at an equitable price, to achieve a more stable balance between raw material supply and demand, to narrow the gap between food and population growth, to build a trade, monetary, and investment system that encourages economic growth rather than economic warfare, and to bring the best minds of all nations to apply science to meet the problems that science has helped create.

It is easy to agree to yet another set of principles, to another program of action, to more steps that other nations should take. But each nation must ask itself what can it do, what contribution can it make. The needs of the poor will not be met by empty promises; the needs of an expanding global economy will not be met by new restrictions on supply and demand; the growing interdependence of all nations cannot be managed on the basis of confrontation.

There are provisions in the declaration and the special program to which the U.S. Government cannot lend its support. I will deal here only with our most important reservations.

Perhaps the most difficult subject which the declaration of principles addresses is that of permanent sovereignty over natural resources. It will be recalled that this problem was successfully dealt with by the General Assembly in 1962 when, in a meeting of minds of developing and developed countries, widespread agreement was achieved on the terms of Resolution 1803 (XVII).[21] The U.S. delegation regrets that the compromise solution which Resolution 1803 (XVII) embodies was not reproduced in this declaration.

---

[19]Chapter 4, Document 5a.
[20]Document 8a.
[21]Adopted Dec. 14, 1962; cf. *Documents, 1962*: 435.

If it were, on this count the United States would gladly lend its support. Resolution 1803 (XVII) provides among other things that, where foreign property is nationalized, appropriate compensation shall be paid in accordance with national and international law; it also provides that foreign investment agreements by and between states shall be observed in good faith. By way of contrast, the present declaration does not couple the assertion of the right to nationalize with the duty to pay compensation in accordance with international law. For this reason, we do not find this formulation complete or acceptable. The governing international law cannot be and is not prejudiced by the passage of this resolution.

The United States does not support the provisions of the declaration which refer only to the exertion of economic pressure for some ends, but which do not condemn generally the exercise of economic pressure. In this respect, the declaration contrasts unfavorably with that of this Assembly on principles of international law concerning friendly relations and cooperation among states.[22] Nor does the United States support the provisions of the resolution that refer to restitution and full compensation for exploitation of and damage to certain resources and peoples.

Neither can the United States accept the idea of producer associations as a viable means of promoting development nor of fixing a relationship between import and export prices. Artificial attempts to manage markets which ignore economic realities and the legitimate interests of consumers as well as producers run the risk of political confrontation on the one hand and economic failure on the other.

I also wish to make mention of that part of the declaration dealing with the regulation and supervision of the activities of multinational corporations. The United States is of the view that multinational corporations must act as good corporate citizens of the states in which they operate, and that multinational corporations are subject to the regulation and supervision of the countries in which they operate, but such regulation and supervision must be non-discriminatory and otherwise conform to the norms of international law.

The program of action has too many objectionable features, from our point of view, to permit a detailed listing and explanation in a brief statement. Among these features are the emphasis on marketing arrangements for primary products which exclude the interests of consumers and the impractical proposals to establish artificial and fixed price relationships between prices of exports and imports of developing countries. Our skepticism about commodity agreements is well known, but we are prepared to consider them on

[22]Resolution 2625 (XXV), Oct. 24, 1970.

a case-by-case basis. The current GATT negotiations and other actions we support can increase the trade of developing countries, but it is out of the question for us to allocate a specified share of our market for the developing countries. We object to the Assembly's making recommendations now on the provisions related to the link between SDR's and development finance, the provisions to reform the international financial institutions, and subsidization of interest payments and other involved questions that should be left to the IMF.

As this special session of the General Assembly nears its close, there is one central concern in the minds of all of us. Many of the less developed nations of the world are afflicted with the most serious and debilitating economic ills of their lifetime. There are parallel economic dislocations in the industrialized world, but it is better prepared to recover.

Before the special session began, the U.S. delegation said it would negotiate in a spirit of compromise and conciliation. This is still our attitude. It will continue to be as the United Nations and its individual states seek ways to lighten the burdens of the less developed countries.

Unfortunately, the time to consider programs for the neediest countries has been short. We nevertheless regret that ways were not found, even though the hour was late, to explore varying proposals of substance.

I wish to point out an obvious truth. Despite scores of public speeches, hundreds of hours of detailed discussions, and thousands of hours of consultations, we have not yet agreed on the kind of coordinated action which will provide the immediate emergency relief that is indispensable in the present crisis.

Words cannot feed the starving nor help the impoverished. The sudden increased cost of life is still being borne by the poor. This moment demands more of us than words—more of us than promises which may materialize many months from now, if ever. Have we measured up to the challenge?

While this Assembly has not been without accomplishment, we must not go home in the belief that we have already met the central task before us. Let us go home, each nation determined to do its part to meet the immediate crisis that challenges our interdependent world community. I can assure this Assembly that the United States will do its share.

8. AN AMERICAN DIALOGUE (CONTINUED): WASHINGTON AND ATLANTA

(April 17-May 1, 1974)

[The special session of the U.N. Assembly overlapped a pair of meetings, held at other points in the United States, at which the Foreign Ministers of most of the American nations attempted to carry forward the regional discussion initiated at Secretary Kissinger's invitation earlier in the year.[1] Though limited essentially to Western Hemisphere matters, these inter-American talks could also be regarded as a component of the broader, ongoing discussion between developed and developing, "third world" countries. Until fairly recently, most Latin American countries had not participated actively in the so-called nonaligned movement. They were, however, anything but strangers to the various economic issues by which the third world countries now appeared to be chiefly motivated. They themselves had been agitating for years about such questions as the relative prices of raw materials and manufactured goods, the nationalization of foreign-owned enterprises, and the multinational corporation—issues which, as we have just seen, were now assigned a prominent place in the emerging concept of a "New International Economic Order."[2]

Neither in the United Nations nor among its neighbors of the Americas had the United States felt able to agree with the majority view concerning these sensitive issues, and it had been widely anticipated that the U.S.-Latin American dialogue proposed by Secretary Kissinger would become more acrimonious in proportion as it came to grips with these deep-rooted ideological and practical differences. That stage had not been reached at the February meeting in Mexico City, at which the assembled ministers had confined

[1]Cf. Chapter 4, Document 50.
[2]Cf. Chapter 7, Document 8b.

113

themselves to drawing up a list of general principles and desirable objectives. More surprising was the degree of harmony that still prevailed at the second meeting, which took place in Washington on April 17-18 in what had been planned as a kind of curtain-raiser to the annual session of the OAS General Assembly. (In a departure from the usual pattern, the latter event was to take place this year in Atlanta, Georgia, a choice designed to emphasize the United States' position as not merely the site of the meeting but its official host.)

The main results of the Washington meeting of Foreign Ministers were summarized in the official communiqué released on April 18.]

(9)   Meeting of Western Hemisphere Foreign Ministers, Washington, April 17-18, 1974.

(a)   Final communiqué of the meeting, April 18, 1974.[3]

1. Accepting the invitation of the United States Secretary of State, the Foreign Ministers of Latin America met April 17-18 in Washington to resume the dialogue begun at the Conference of Tlatelolco in Mexico eight weeks ago.[4] Attending this meeting were the Foreign Ministers of Argentina, the Bahamas, Barbados, Bolivia, Brazil, Chile, Colombia, Costa Rica, the Dominican Republic, Ecuador, El Salvador, Guyana, Haiti, Honduras, Jamaica, Mexico, Nicaragua, Panama, Paraguay, Peru, Trinidad and Tobago, the United States of America, Uruguay and Venezuela, and the representative of the Foreign Minister of Guatemala.

2. The meeting of Foreign Ministers continued in the atmosphere of cordiality and openness which characterized the Conference of Tlatelolco. The Foreign Ministers reiterated their conviction that these meetings contribute to greater inter-American cooperation and solidarity. The topics discussed were: Structure of International Trade and the Monetary System; Cooperation for Development; Transnational Enterprises; Solution of the Question of the Panama Canal; Coercive Measures of an Economic Nature; and Transfers of Technology.

3. The Foreign Ministers of the Latin American countries presented their views and positions on the several topics covered by the agenda. The Secretary of State of the United States responded, stating United States policy on the respective subjects and express-

---

[3]Department of State Press Release 149, Apr. 18; text from *Bulletin*, 70: 517-19.
[4]Chapter 4, Document 5.

ing the intention and desire of the United States to cooperate effectively in the integral development of the Latin American countries.

4. On the subject of trade, the Foreign Ministers of Latin America attached special importance to the standstill commitment made by the United States in Caracas in February 1970[5] and reaffirmed by Secretary Kissinger at Tlatelolco, and to the urgency of eliminating restrictions on access to the United States market for products of special interest to Latin America. They stressed that, in order to improve trade relations and promote new flows of trade from Latin America to the United States, as a minimum, no new import restrictions should be applied and existing import restrictions should not be expanded.

5. The Secretary of State recognized the importance of the United States market for the economies of Latin America. In the new spirit growing out of the Conference of Tlatelolco, he expressed his support of Latin America's aspirations in the trade field. In particular, he stressed the intention of his Government to refrain to the extent possible from establishing new trade restrictions. He reiterated the interest of his Government in achieving enactment of the proposed Trade Reform Act which would authorize generalized preferences, including in them the products of interest to Latin America, and in further liberalizing the access of Latin American products to the United States market. Similarly, he reaffirmed the commitments of his Government under resolution REM 1/70,[6] and especially stated his agreement to hold consultations with Latin America on the inclusion in the GSP [Generalized System of Preferences] of products of special interest for the area before making final decisions. Secretary Kissinger also expressed his Government's intention to support the effective participation of Latin America in reform of the international monetary system.

6. The Secretary of State of the United States considered favorably the views held by Latin America in the matter of Multilateral Trade Negotiations as regards nonreciprocity, differentiated and most favored treatment of the Generalized System of Preferences toward the developing countries [sic] and indicated his agreement to hold consultations with a view to the harmonization of positions on this subject.

The Foreign Ministers of the Latin American countries noted with satisfaction the fact that the Special Representative of the President of the United States for Trade Negotiations [William D. Eberle] is initiating extensive bilateral consultations with the coun-

---

[5]At the Eighth Special Meeting of the Inter-American Economic and Social Council (IA-ECOSOC), held Feb. 3-6, 1970; cf. *Documents, 1970*: 276.
[6]Adopted at the meeting referred to in note 5.

tries of Latin America to promote the achievement of these objectives.

7. The Foreign Ministers emphasized the importance of hemispheric cooperation in the field of economic development and the establishment of an international system of collective economic security for development. They stressed the importance of increasing the volume of real resource transfers to Latin America. The Ministers of Foreign Affairs recognize the importance of the policy of export diversification for the developing countries of the region and believe that this policy should be supported as an essential aspect of the progress of Latin America.

8. The Foreign Ministers stressed the need to provide preferential attention to the less developed countries of the region, especially the land-locked countries and those of insufficient internal market. They expressed their conviction concerning the importance of concessionary loans for the financing of enterprises and projects that are fundamental to the economic and social development process in those countries. They furthermore agreed on the usefulness of multilateral financial mechanisms to provide help in cases of emergency with which they are unable to cope by themselves.

9. The Foreign Ministers discussed the problem of economic coercion and the desirability of their [*sic*] elimination from relations among the countries of the Americas which would contribute in a positive manner to a more authentic spirit of cooperation. The Foreign Ministers of Latin America also expressed concern over proposals that would tend to restrict the access of products of developing countries to the United States market.

10. The Foreign Ministers of Latin America reiterated in its entirety the Declaration adopted in Bogotá at the "Conference of Chancellors of Latin America for Continental Cooperation"[7] as regards the solution of the Panama Canal question and reaffirmed it without change during the course of the new dialogue begun at the Conference of Tlatelolco.

The Foreign Ministers reiterated their confidence that the bilateral negotiations presently in progress between the governments of Panama and the United States would continue in a positive tone and conclude as soon as possible with satisfactory results in conformity with the spirit of the new dialogue.

11. The Foreign Ministers decided to establish a Working Group, consisting of governmental representatives from all of the participating states, with the mandate to prepare for submission to the consideration of the next meeting, a document that would contain principles to be applicable to transnational enterprises. The Work-

[7] Cf. Chapter 4, preamble to Document 5b.

ing Group will meet at least two months prior to the date on which the Conference of Buenos Aires will convene.[8] In the preparation of the document, the Working Group should bear in mind the Report that the United Nations Organization has prepared on the subject, as well as those that are emanating from other international forums.

12. The Foreign Ministers, recognizing the importance of technology in social and economic development, agreed to convene a Working Group of Governmental representatives to study the possibility of creating a Committee on Science and the Transfer of Technology, that would have as its objective matching scientific capability with practical needs, and overcoming obstacles to the flow and use of technology in the industrialization process. For this purpose, and at the earliest possible moment, the members of that Working Group will be designated and requested to submit their report within a period of not more than six months. Without prejudice to the foregoing, the United States and Latin America will continue supporting and encouraging the existing technological development programs, especially the OAS Inter-American Committee on Science and Technology. Their efforts must be coordinated in order to avoid duplication of programs.

13. In approving this communique, the Foreign Ministers reaffirmed the value and promise of the new dialogue in inter-American relations. They believe that their meeting just concluded in Washington has given additional impulse to achievement of progress on matters of common concern.

14. The Foreign Ministers agreed to meet again in Buenos Aires in March 1975.[9]

[A more informal appraisal of the Washington meeting was offered at a news conference held the same day by Assistant Secretary of State Jack B. Kubisch.]

(b) Appraisal of the meeting: News conference statement by Jack B. Kubisch, Assistant Secretary of State for Inter-American Affairs, April 18, 1974.[10]

(Excerpt)

Ladies and gentlemen: I understand you do have a copy of the communique that was approved by the Foreign Ministers this after-

[8]Cf. par. 14.
[9]The Buenos Aires meeting was later postponed; cf. Chapter 35 at notes 19-20.
[10]Text from *Bulletin*, 70: 516-17.

noon.[11] I would just like to say a few words about this meeting that has taken place here in Washington yesterday and today, discuss a few of the highlights and the main points covered in the communique, and make an announcement or two, following which I would be glad to take your questions.

First, as you know, this meeting here in Washington, which began yesterday and took place among the 25 Foreign Ministers, including Secretary of State Kissinger, was really the second phase of the new dialogue and the new fresh approach to multilateral diplomacy in this hemisphere that began with Secretary Kissinger's invitation to the Foreign Ministers to a new dialogue last October shortly after he became Secretary of State.[12] They accepted his invitation to this new dialogue. They established an agenda. They met with him just eight weeks ago in Mexico City for their first consideration of the topics on that agenda, which was followed by the Declaration of Tlatelolco,[13] the suburb of Mexico City where the conference took place.

It was decided as that conference was concluded in Mexico City that it would be worthwhile for them to meet again soon, to continue their discussions in a frank and cordial and open manner, to address problems of great interest to all of them.

It was decided, since of the 25, 23 would be coming to the United States in any case in April to attend the annual General Assembly of the Organization of American States, Secretary Kissinger would have them come here and they would have these meetings.

They continued to address the agenda items that were agreed upon before—those are set forth in the communique. And as you will note from the communique, the Ministers reaffirmed the atmosphere and constructive spirit which characterized these discussions.

The meetings were private. There will not be, by me at least, any identification of who said what at the meetings. There was complete freedom for all Foreign Ministers to speak on any topic as they saw fit and to make any observations they wanted to make. They presented their views on some very important questions in the economic, trade, commercial, financial fields, and other aspects of inter-American relationships. Secretary Kissinger responded stating the U.S. policy. He expressed the intention and desire of the United States to cooperate effectively with the countries of Latin America in an effort to revitalize our relationships in this region.

They considered a number of specific topics, which are sum-

---

[11]Document 8a.
[12]*AFR, 1973*: 415-17.
[13]Chapter 4, Document 5b.

marized in the communique, and it was decided that they would meet again. They considered just when the next meeting should take place and decided that since the Foreign Ministers would be returning to the United States this fall for a meeting of the General Assembly of the United Nations, Secretary Kissinger extended an invitation to them to meet with him in New York for a luncheon of the type they had last October when they were present in New York.[14]

They agreed that it was not possible in the short time available to them really to analyze in depth and reach important decisions on some of the very complex issues that they were addressing, and therefore they decided to set up several working groups and study groups and preparatory groups to prepare for their next meeting, and those are summarized in the communique as well. They specifically wished to have a working group study the question of multinational corporations and to develop recommendations as to principles applicable to the operations of those companies.

There also was considerable interest in the whole question of science and the transfer of technology, and they decided to set up a working group also of governmental representatives to study this subject and to make recommendations to them.

And finally, they concluded that it would be desirable for them to have their next meeting, to continue this in this framework, in Buenos Aires in March 1975 and to make the preparations between now and then for that meeting.[15]

Most of the Foreign Ministers, not all—the Foreign Ministers of Guyana and Bahamas, two of the 25 who were present in Washington, are not members of the Organization of American States—but the other 23, including Secretary Kissinger, are proceeding now to Atlanta—Secretary Kissinger will go tomorrow—which will be the site this year of the annual General Assembly of the Organization of American States. And they will continue there their formal discussions and consideration of some of these topics.[16]

I would just say that Secretary Kissinger, I believe, was particularly gratified at the manner in which he and his colleagues were able to meet here in Washington and to continue in the open, candid, and useful kinds of exchanges that they first had in Mexico just eight weeks ago. From his point of view, and I think from the standpoint of the other Ministers as well, although of course they will speak for themselves, it was a meeting of great value for all concerned. And they do want to continue.

[14]Cf. note 12. Secretary Kissinger hosted a second luncheon in New York on Oct. 2, 1974; cf. *Bulletin*, 71: 583-6.
[15]See note 9 above.
[16]Cf. Document 10.

* * *

[The Atlanta session of the OAS General Assembly had a broader focus, consistent with the prerogatives and functions assigned that body as the supreme policy organ of the inter-American system. Such a meeting, Secretary Kissinger stated in his welcoming speech on April 19, should prove well suited to discuss not only "the elements of our common progress" but the institutional arrangements required to give effect to American aspirations.]

(10) Fourth Regular Session of the General Assembly of the Organization of American States (OAS), Atlanta, April 19- May 1, 1974.

(a) Welcoming statement by Secretary of State Kissinger, April 19, 1974.[17]

This meeting is the first General Assembly of the OAS to be held in the United States outside Washington. It is no accident that we are meeting in the southern part of our country, a region renowned for its warmth, its spaciousness, and its hospitality.

On behalf of all my colleagues I want to thank Governor [Jimmy] Carter and Mayor [Maynard] Jackson and all the people of Atlanta for the warmth of their reception to me and all of my colleagues. The arrangements could not have been done more beautifully and more warmly.

To our friends from Latin America and the Caribbean, I offer the welcome of President Nixon and of the people of the United States.

As we meet here outside the governmental atmosphere of Washington, the Americas can broaden their understanding of each other and of each other's people.

Governor Carter and those of you who have not attended our meetings previously, you will hear a great deal at these meetings about something called the spirit of Tlatelolco, and it is important that we say a few words about this.

Last year some of my friends, the Foreign Ministers from Latin America, suggested that there had been too many proclamations and too few policies, that the peoples of the Western Hemisphere needed a new approach to their relationship. Picking up this idea, very insistently urged upon me by the distinguished Foreign Minister from Mexico [Emilio O. Rabasa], I invited the Foreign

[17]Department of State Press Release 150, Apr. 19; text from *Bulletin*, 70: 509-10.

Ministers from Latin America who were at the General Assembly in New York to a lunch. I proposed to them a new dialogue among equals. This led the distinguished Foreign Minister of Colombia [Alfredo Vázquez Carrizosa] to call a meeting in Bogotá which outlined an agenda for common action. And this in turn led to a meeting in Mexico at the Foreign Ministry, located in Tlatelolco—a part of Mexico City—in which the nations assembled here and two others that are not part of the OAS dedicated themselves to a new dialogue among equals.[18]

This dialogue has been continued this week in Washington,[19] and we can say with confidence that we are making progress in understanding, progress in dedication, and above all, progress in concrete programs that will realize the aspirations of the Americas. In our meeting in Atlanta we can discuss the institutions that can give effect to these aspirations, and we can discuss the elements of our common progress.

At Tlatelolco all our countries agreed to dedicate ourselves to new horizons of understanding and cooperation. We saw that we had reached a time of unprecedented opportunity for achieving the goals of justice, peace, and human dignity which have for so long been the essential promise of the New World. In the spring of Atlanta let us take new, confident steps toward these new horizons.

I also have the great honor of reading to you a message from President Nixon:

> On behalf of the people of the United States I send greetings to the Foreign Ministers of the Americas on the occasion of the annual General Assembly of the Organization of American States.
>
> The Organization of American States has long been a symbol and expression of our Hemispheric cooperation and partnership, and it is indeed a profound pleasure and honor for the United States to host this distinguished gathering. It is my sincere hope that this meeting will result in further contributions to the improving atmosphere of relations in the Americas.
>
> RICHARD NIXON.

[Secretary Kissinger recurred to the same themes in his formal presentation to the Assembly, in which he also alluded briefly to the restructuring of the OAS that was already under study by the special committee set up in 1973.]

[18]Chapter 4, Document 5.
[19]Document 9.

*(b) Views of the United States: Statement to the Assembly by '
Secretary of State Kissinger, April 20, 1974.*[20]

As this General Assembly of the Organization of American
States convenes, a special session of the General Assembly of the
United Nations is underway in New York.[21] This is more than a coincidence. In this continent as in the world,
our nations face together a broad agenda of interdependence. In-
stantaneous communcations, global economics, and weapons of
vast destructiveness have thrust mankind into a proximity which
transforms world community from a slogan into a necessity. Our
problems are unprecedented in type and scale. But our purpose is
age-old: to realize man's eternal aspiration for a life of peace, well-
being, dignity, and justice.

The challenge before the Americas is to define our place in this
global quest. What should be this hemisphere's purposes in the
modern world? How can the distinctive and special bonds that have
united us, and that are reflected in this organization, foster cooperation among the nations assembled here and among all of the nations of the world?

Montaigne once wrote:

The archer must first know what he is aiming at and then set
his hand, his bow, his strength, his arrow and his movements for
that goal. Our plans go astray because they have no direction.

The Americas have identified their target: to make our mutual
dependence define a program for effective cooperation.

We have come a long way together in the past six months. When
we began our dialogue in New York last October, many feared that
we might repeat the familiar cycle of new slogans followed by renewed neglect. We asked of each other: Could we make our diversity a source of strength, drawing on the richness of our material and
spiritual heritage? Could we define together a concrete and realistic
role for the United States to support the development efforts of our
Latin American neighbors? Could the nations of the hemisphere
fashion a vision of the world as it is so that we could move together
toward the achievement of common goals while retaining individual dignity and uniqueness?

In Bogotá last November, the nations of Latin America took the
initiative in providing an answer and proposed an agenda for action. In Mexico City in February, we came together again and

[20]As-delivered text and subtitles from *Bulletin*, 70: 510-15.
[21]Cf. Chapter 7.

launched a new process of collaboration based on this agenda and inspired by a new attitude—the spirit of Tlatelolco.[22] This week in Washington, we reaffirmed our mutual commitment and moved toward concrete achievements.[23]

What is the spirit of Tlatelolco that has given such impetus to our current efforts?

On one level, it is the enduring recognition that our nations are joined by unique and special bonds—of geography, tradition, self-interest, and common values. For all our differences, the nations of the Americas share a common origin, a history of mutual support, and a common devotion to national independence, social progress, and human dignity. For centuries we have seen ourselves as a beacon to the world, offering mankind the hope of leaving behind its eternal tragedies and achieving its enduring dreams. For decades we have been linked in an inter-American system that has been a vehicle for joint action. But on a deeper level, the spirit of Tlatelolco defines something new and vital, of importance not only in the hemisphere but across the oceans. For most of our shared history, the United States alone determined the pattern and set the pace of our cooperation. We were often tempted to do for others what we thought was best for them. That attitude no longer shapes our relationships.

New Dialogue a Necessity For All

We in the United States have come to recognize that a revolution has taken place in Latin America. Industrialization and modern communications have transformed economic and social life. A new generation is molding strengthened institutions. A sense of regional and national identity has acquired new force. The commitment to modernization has become fundamental. Brazil's gross national product approaches that of Japan less than two decades ago. The countries of the Andean Group have begun a major collaborative effort to hasten development. Argentina and Mexico are industrializing rapidly. And the newly independent countries of the English-speaking Caribbean have brought different perspectives and traditions, a fresh vitality, and if I may say so, a new charm to hemispheric relations.

The United States, too, has changed enormously in the last decade. We have learned that peace cannot be achieved by our efforts alone and that development is far more than simply an economic problem. Through years of anguish and trial, we have found that the United States cannot remake the world and that neither

---

[22]Chapter 4, Document 5.
[23]Document 9.

peace nor development is achievable unless it engages the effort and the commitment of other nations. This is why our new dialogue is not a concession by the United States, but a necessity for us all. We convene as equals, on the basis of mutual respect—each recognizing that our special relationship can be preserved only if we transform it to meet the new conditions of our time and the new aspirations of our peoples.

In the 19th century, the United States declared what those outside the hemisphere should not do within it. In the 1930's, the United States proclaimed what would no longer do within it— the policy of the Good Neighbor. In 1974 in Mexico City, in Washington, and now in Atlanta, we of the Americas jointly proclaim our cooperative actions—the policy of the Good Partner.

Our new dialogue has already been marked by substantial progress:

—We have committed ourselves to a cooperative development effort and to the creation of a system of collective economic security.

—We have agreed to devote special attention to the needs of the poorest countries of the hemisphere.

—We have agreed to consult in order to develop common positions, so far as possible, in major international negotiations, especially on economic issues.

—We have established a working group to develop principles for the conduct of transnational enterprises.

—We have set up a Working Group on Science and the Transfer of Technology to strengthen our cooperation in the process of industrialization.

—We have decided on multilateral financial institutions to deal with those natural disasters and economic crises that our countries cannot deal with alone.

—Above all, we agreed in the Declaration of Tlatelolco[24] that "interdependence has become a physical and moral imperative, and that a new, vigorous spirit of inter-American solidarity is therefore essential."

For its part, the United States knows that if the answers to the great dialogue between the developed and the developing countries cannot be found in the Western Hemisphere they may not be found at all. We seek a hemisphere lifted by progress, not torn by divisions. We are committed to shaping our action to accelerate Latin America's efforts to fulfill the aspirations of its peoples.

[24]Chapter 4, Document 5b.

We will do our utmost to expand Latin American access to U.S. markets, to maintain our assistance levels, and to consult on political and economic issues of common concern. We have moved to resolve old disputes with Peru, Panama and Mexico[25] that have blocked progress along our common road.

Together, we must now ask ourselves: What are our ultimate goals? We in the Americas have always believed that our efforts and our achievements had relevance beyond our shores. Thus it is clear that our special relationship cannot mean the formation of an exclusive bloc. The world has already seen enough of pressure groups, exclusive spheres, and discriminatory arrangements.

A bloc implies a rigidity that would deny our different perspectives and constrain our reach in different directions. Some of us have global responsibilities; some of us feel affinities with the Third World; developing ties with many regions attract us all. We seek not a common front against others but, rather, a common effort with others toward the global cooperation which is dictated by political and economic realities.

A healthy special relationship is not a bloc. Working together, the Western Hemisphere can lead the world toward solutions to those basic problems of the contemporary period that are now being discussed in New York. Rejecting autarky, respecting diversity, but in a spirit of solidarity, we in the Americas can both promote our common objectives and strengthen the fabric of global cooperation.

The Inter-American Agenda

In this context of our wider purposes, let me outline for your consideration some principles and tasks to guide our common efforts.

Inter-American solidarity must be rooted in a free association of independent peoples. The spirit of dialogue, of give-and-take, that has so enriched our meetings in Mexico and Washington must be perpetuated. For its part, the United States pledges that it will not seek to impose its political preferences and that it will not intervene in the domestic affairs of its Western Hemisphere neighbors.

Effective collaboration requires continuing and close consultation. The United States understands that its global policies and actions can have a major impact upon the other nations of this hemisphere. Therefore we have pledged ourselves to a constant and intimate process of consultation.

We look forward to periodic meetings of America's Foreign Ministers to discuss issues of mutual concern in the Americas and

[25]Cf. Chapter 4 at notes 14-16.

in the world. We will consult closely in the global monetary and trade talks and in other international negotiations. We do not expect an identity of views. We do believe that better comprehension and sensitivity to one another's positions will benefit us all.

Our relationship must assure progress and a decent life for all our peoples. The ultimate test of our relations will be to translate our aspirations into concrete programs, especially in the decisive field of development.

Earlier this week, before the special session of the United Nations,[26] I listed six principles which economic reality and our common humanity dictate should be the guiding principles for international action to spur development:

—We need to expand the supply of energy at an equitable price.

—We need to free the world from the cycle of raw material shortages and surpluses.

—We need to achieve a balance between food production and food demand.

—We need to extend special consideration to the poorest nations.

—We need to accelerate the transfer of science and technology from developed to developing nations.

—We need to preserve and enlarge a global trade, monetary, and investment system which will sustain industrial civilization and stimulate its growth.

This hemisphere has a vital stake in the world community's response to these challenges. Some of these problems, such as the inventory of raw material resources in relation to needs, are best carried out on a global basis. But on many of the items of this agenda the nations of this hemisphere can provide leadership and inspiration and advance the welfare of their peoples through joint actions.

In the field of *energy*, the hemisphere uniquely encompasses both producers and consumers. The United States is ready to collaborate with its hemisphere partners in a major way both bilaterally and multilaterally.

The Working Group on Science and the Transfer of Technology established by the Foreign Ministers two days ago in Washington can be charged with setting up programs for sharing information on energy conservation and for pooling our efforts to expand available supplies, to develop alternative sources of conventional fuels, and to encourage the discovery of new and renewable energy sources. The Latin American Energy Organization and the United

---

[26]Chapter 7, Document 8a.

Nations Economic Commission for Latin America provide additional mechanisms for cooperation.

The United States is prepared to link its technology with the resources and capital of the hemisphere's oil producers to help them expand their production and diversify their economies.

The Western Hemisphere has a special role to play in overcoming the *world food shortage*. This continent, even as it is scarred by malnutrition and hunger, has a vast agricultural potential. President Nixon is asking the Congress to raise our assistance to food production programs in the Americas by 50 percent. We have, as well, lifted our own domestic production restrictions.

The shortage of fertilizer and the steep rise in its price are a problem of particular urgency. The United States will give high priority to linking our technological skills with the raw material and capital of oil-producing countries to encourage the development of new fertilizer capacity.

In a collective effort, I propose that we cooperate in a program to increase food production in this hemisphere substantially by the end of this decade. This program should encompass research, the application of science and technology, and the intensified application of foreign and domestic resources:

—As an initial step, we should ask the Inter-American Economic and Social Council to help focus our efforts to increase production and productivity. The Working Group on Science and the Transfer of Technology should explore new ways to increase agricultural productivity, especially in the continent's vast tropical zones.

—A comprehensive hemispheric agricultural survey would be an important contribution to the success of the World Food Conference.

—Food processing is another high-priority field for cooperation and innovation.

Only this week, the Foreign Ministers of the Americas pledged to give special attention to the problems of the *least developed* among us. To this end, the Inter-American Development Bank should adapt its lending policies to ease the shock of rising energy prices on the poorest nations in the hemisphere. We welcome the decision of Venezuela to assist the Bank in this task, including concessional lending assistance to those who require it most.

The United States, as the hemisphere's richest nation, has a particular obligation. We will urge our Congress to maintain our assistance levels to the hemisphere. It is an expression of our special relationship that U.S. bilateral and multilateral aid to the hemisphere is larger, on a per capita basis, than to any other region of the globe. In accordance with the recommendations of the recent Washington Conference, we are now urgently examining whether Latin America's share can be further increased.

The *transfer of science and technology* may be an even more important bottleneck in the development effort than capital. The United States, as a technologically advanced nation, recognizes a special responsibility in this regard. We believe that normally private investment is the most efficient vehicle for the transfer of these resources, but governments can facilitate the transfer of advanced technology to stimulate balanced development.

The Working Group on Science and the Transfer of Technology can seek to overcome obstacles to the flow and use of productive technology. In addition to those I have already mentioned relating to energy and agriculture, its tasks should encompass:

—Improving the dissemination of information on available technologies, including managerial and engineering skills;
—Spurring the search for new technologies in such areas as marine sciences and labor-intensive industry; and
—Identifying how to adapt technology most effectively to different national circumstances and industries.

In addition to these projects, all of which require improved cooperation among governments, current OAS programs aimed at strengthening university and basic research and training institutions in Latin America should continue to receive the wholehearted support of this Assembly.

The Americas are in a position to participate effectively and to make an important contribution to the reform of the international systems that govern *trade, monetary, and investment* relations. The United States will support such efforts.

Trade is critical in the development process. The United States is strongly committed to a system of generalized tariff preferences, and once this legislation is enacted, we will consult closely with our partners in this hemisphere on how it can be made most beneficial to your needs. Despite the uncertainties arising from the energy crisis, we will do our utmost to avoid new restrictions on Latin America's access to our markets.

The United States recognizes that trade within this hemisphere depends significantly on global patterns. Trade expansion worldwide is one of our longstanding objectives. Mutual support in the forthcoming multilateral trade negotiations [under the General Agreement on Tariffs and Trade (GATT)][27] can help us overcome many bilateral trade problems within the hemisphere.

In the spirit of Tlatelolco, the United States is prepared to adjust its position on specific issues in these negotiations to take account

[27]Cf. Chapter 10 at note 2.

of Latin American objectives. As a first step, the President's Special Trade Representative, Ambassador Eberle, departs today to begin bilateral consultations with many of your governments. Similar efforts are planned through organs of the OAS and in Geneva.

Private investment is crucial to development. At times, it has also been a source of friction. At the Washington Foreign Ministers Conference, we agreed to join with you in a study commission which would prepare guidelines applicable to the conduct of transnational corporations. We cannot afford to let our political relations and our economic cooperation be distorted by commercial quarrels.

A modern inter-American system requires that the Treaty of Rio and the OAS be adjusted to new conditions.[28] The inter-American system is the oldest major association of nation-states. It has pioneered the concept of international organization and collective security. It has been in the forefront of the development of international law. It has championed the principles of self-determination and nonintervention. It has functioned productively for more than 70 years because it has been adaptable. Today, as we contemplate past experience and future needs, we see that further modification is necessary.

First, development is impossible without security. The Rio Treaty has helped keep this hemisphere largely free of turmoil and conflict. We should modernize it, in keeping with our times, but we should preserve its essentials.

Second, we need to reform the OAS so that it becomes a more effective instrument for hemispheric cooperation. It is overly rigid in its structures, unnecessarily formal in its procedures, and insufficiently broad in its membership. To remedy these weaknesses:

—All major OAS meetings, including the General Assembly, should be made less formal.

—The Permanent Council should be recognized as the central executive body of the OAS.

—OAS membership should be open to all the nations who have attended the recent Foreign Ministers conferences.

—The OAS should be restructured to become a more effective instrument for our economic consultations.

One of our principal tasks should be to create institutions to implement the decisions of the new dialogue.

Broadening the Dialogue

Our dialogue will remain formal if confined to diplomats or offi-

[28]Cf. Chapter 4 at notes 1-2.

cials. It must involve our peoples, catching their imagination and liberating their abilities. The efforts on which we are embarked require all the human and intellectual resources of our continent. To this end, the United States will see to it that its cultural and educational exchange programs make a more important contribution to cooperation as well as to mutual understanding. We will:

—Increase our emphasis on professional exchanges designed to link comparable institutions in the United States and Latin America;
—Encourage seminars and joint research on such topics as urbanization, protection of the environment, and other problems common to all our countries; and
—Stimulate awareness of the extraordinary cultural richness of the Americas by promoting tourism, exhibitions, and other activities to expand our awareness of each other and our appreciation of our common humanity.

Distinguished Ministers and friends, delegates, Mr. Secretary General:[29] The warmth of the welcome you have received here testifies to the friendship of the American people for our neighbors to the south. The ultimate hemispheric solidarity comes from the heart, not from the mind. It is rooted in history and inspired by common traditions.

As our Mexican colleague[30] said at Tlatelolco, we of the Americas have advanced from political speeches to political dialogue and now to political consultation. This must be the design for our new purpose, for great challenges lie before us. We hear the demand of our peoples for justice and dignity; we know their yearning for security and progress; we cannot give them less, for it is their birthright.

In 1900 José Enrique Rodó wrote his classic "Ariel." He viewed the two Americas at the turn of the century as in fundamental opposition. Yet he foresaw that another kind of relationship could eventually emerge. He wrote:

To the extent that we can already distinguish a higher form of cooperation as the basis of a distant future, we can see that it will come not as a result of unilateral formulas, but through the reciprocal influence and skillful harmonization of those attributes which give our different peoples their glory.

Let us here choose such a future now, and not in the distance. Let us realize the glory of our peoples by working together for a

---

[29]Galo Plaza Lasso (Ecuador).
[30]Emilio O. Rabasa.

better life for our children. In so doing, we shall realize the final glory and common destiny of the New World.

[A noticeable feature of Secretary Kissinger's presentation was his omission of any reference to the two political issues that were currently of greatest interest to the Latin American countries and, from many points of view, to the United States as well. In initiating the new inter-American dialogue, the Secretary of State had made important preliminary moves to reduce existing tensions with regard to the Panama Canal, and had even journeyed to Panama City to initial the relevant statement of negotiating principles.[31] Thus far, however, there had been no comparable adjustment in the U.S. stance with respect to the Castro regime in Cuba, now in its sixteenth year of power and still formally ostracized by the OAS in accordance with decisions taken at a period in the early 1960s when Cuba's Soviet ties and revolutionary activities in the Americas had been causing widespread concern.

A movement favoring Cuba's readmission to the American family had, however, been developing for a number of years, and still appeared to be gaining ground despite the recent overthrow and death of President Allende of Chile, one of its foremost proponents. Mexican Foreign Minister Rabasa, who had lately visited Havana, told his OAS colleagues at the April meetings that he believed Cuba might even accept an invitation to take part in the new Foreign Ministers' meeting that was to be held in Buenos Aires in 1975. The Foreign Minister of Argentina, speaking for the populist administration of President Perón, loudly inveighed against the existing barriers to trade with Cuba. Peru and Colombia also seemed to feel that a change was overdue, though Chile, under its new right-wing regime, insisted that Castroism had by no means ceased to threaten the peace and security of the continent.

Secretary Kissinger, as representative of an administration not hitherto known for any pro-Castro leanings, seems not to have taken an active part in the discussion. Some of those present nevertheless gained an impression that while the United States itself had no intention of according diplomatic recognition to the Havana regime, it would not oppose the lifting of sanctions imposed by the OAS if a decision to that effect were to be taken at a subsequent Foreign Ministers' meeting. Some of the Latin American representatives were thus encouraged to move ahead with the diplomatic preparations that would ultimately lead to the holding of a special Meeting of Consultation of American Foreign Ministers at Quito, Ecuador, in November.[32]]

[31]Cf. Chapter 4, Document 4.
[32]Cf. Chapter 28. The formal decisions of the OAS General Assembly will be found in OAS document OEA/Ser.P/IV-0.2, May 7, 1974, vol. 1.

9. MEETING OF THE CENTO COUNCIL

(Washington, May 21-22, 1974)

[Despite the prevalent talk of East-West détente and North-South polarization, the United States had been in no haste to abandon its longstanding commitment to the system of regional security pacts concluded during the first postwar decade, among them the North Atlantic Treaty Organization (NATO), the Central Treaty Organization (CENTO), and the Southeast Asia Treaty Organization (SEATO) as well as the ANZUS Pact, whose Council meeting was noted in an earlier chapter. In each of these organizations, the emphasis in recent years had shifted to some extent from the military area toward heightened concern with economic and social matters; but each of them was still regarded by the member countries as retaining important security responsibilities as well.

In the case of CENTO, the concern with regional security had been accentuated of late years by Britain's military withdrawal from the Persian (Arabian) Gulf and the emergence of an important Soviet military presence in the Mediterranean, the Gulf, and the Indian Ocean. The United States, which had been reluctant to increase its direct responsibilities in the area (apart from the acquisition of a minor foothold on the British Indian Ocean island of Diego Garcia), had undertaken instead to assist in building up the peacekeeping potential of the most important regional powers on the two sides of the Gulf—Iran, which was already a virtual ally and a founding member of CENTO, and Saudi Arabia, which, though not formally allied with the United States, had long been regarded as one of its most trustworthy friends in the Arab world.

This type of proxy guardianship seemed well attuned to the desires of the Iranian and Saudi governments, both of which were ambitious to enlarge and modernize their military establishments and, with oil prices climbing to unprecedented levels, saw little reason to quail at the expense involved. Iran, in addition to its his-

132

toric mistrust of the Soviet Union, was also engaged in a running quarrel with its neighbor Iraq, a fact that redoubled the eagerness of its ruler, Mohammad Reza Shah Pahlavi, to place his country in an unassailable military position. President Nixon, stopping over in Tehran on his way home from the Soviet Union in May 1972, is said to have offered the Shah a virtually unrestricted choice among American-built conventional weapon systems, including the opportunity to purchase 80 of the sophisticated F-14 aircraft at a cost of $2.2 billion. To this visit has been traced a large-scale U.S. arms sales effort in Iran that is said to have aggregated some $10 billion over the next four years.[1]

As an additional accommodation to the Iranian monarch, the United States apparently began at roughly this same period to provide clandestine assistance for the Kurdish insurgent forces, led by Mullah Mustafa Barzani, that were resisting the central government of Iraq and thus weakening that country in its confrontation with Iran. The object of this assistance, to judge from a 1974 document of the Central Intelligence Agency (CIA) as published in an unofficial and unauthorized version some two years later, was not actually to promote a Kurdish victory, but rather to produce "a stalemate situation" in which the Kurds would serve as "a uniquely useful tool for weakening [Iraq's] potential for international adventurism."[2]

Conditions in this part of Western Asia still presented a decidedly unpeaceful appearance in the early months of 1974. A larger than usual frontier clash between Iraqi and Iranian forces took place on February 10, occasioning an urgent meeting of the U.N. Security Council and the appointment by Secretary-General Waldheim of a special representative, Ambassador Luis Weckmann-Muñoz of Mexico, to investigate on his behalf. By May 21, however, Mr. Waldheim was able to inform the Council that the two sides had been persuaded to withdraw their troops from the border and resume their efforts to settle outstanding issues. Further clashes were nevertheless to occur in the following months; and meanwhile Iraq's internal war against the Kurds had entered an acute phase with the breakdown of negotiations on Kurdish autonomy and the opening in mid-March of an all-out Iraqi offensive,

---

[1] U.S. Senate, 94th Cong., Committee on Foreign Relations, *U.S. Military Sales to Iran*, by Robert Mantel and Geoffrey Kemp (Committee print; Washington: GPO, 1976), as described by Leslie H. Gelb in *New York Times*, Aug. 2, 1976; additional details in same, Sept. 18 and 28, 1976.

[2] U.S. House of Representatives, 94th Cong., Select Committee on Intelligence, report completed Jan. 1976 as excerpted in *Village Voice* (New York), Feb. 16, 1976: 85 and 87.

vigorously resisted by Barzani's forces with Iranian and clandestine U.S. support. (Kurdish resistance against increasingly heavy odds was to continue until the spring of 1975, when outside aid was abruptly terminated following a resolution of differences between Iran and Iraq.)

Pakistan and Turkey, CENTO's two other "regional" members, were also having problems as the time approached for the annual meeting of CENTO's Ministerial Council, which was to be held in Washington on May 21-22. Turkey, long at odds with Greece over conflicting interests and ambitions in Cyprus, now faced a wider range of differences with its Aegean neighbor centering on the delimitation of the continental shelf and the search for offshore oil deposits. Pakistan, not yet fully recovered from its 1971 war with India, had only recently reached agreement with that country and with Bangladesh over the repatriation of the many thousands of prisoners of war and internees left over from that conflict. None of the world's political leaders seemed more disturbed than Pakistani President Zulfiqar Ali Bhutto at the news of India's "peaceful" underground nuclear explosion on May 18. "Now that India has begun to brandish its nuclear sword," said Bhutto, Pakistan must lose no time in alerting CENTO, the United Nations, and the major powers to the necessity of providing it with a "nuclear umbrella" to protect it against "nuclear blackmail."[3]

New faces were in the majority as the CENTO Council began its 21st session in Washington on May 21. The United Kingdom was now represented by James Callaghan, Secretary of State for Foreign and Commonwealth Affairs in the new Labor government headed by Harold Wilson. Secretary Kissinger, also a relative newcomer to his present responsibilities, was unable to be present because of urgent business in the Middle East, where he was now endeavoring to work out a military disengagement between the Israeli and Syrian forces on the Golan Heights.[4] Thus it fell to Deputy Secretary of State Rush, presiding in his capacity as Acting Secretary of State and head of the U.S. "observer" delegation, to extend a formal welcome to his colleagues from the four allied governments.]

(11)   21st Session of the Council of Ministers of the Central Treaty Organization (CENTO), Washington, May 21-22, 1974.

(a)   Welcoming statement by Acting Secretary of State Kenneth Rush, head of the United States observer delegation, May 21, 1974.[5]

[3]*Keesing's*: 26585.
[4]Cf. Chapter 11.
[5]Department of State Press Release 210, May 21; text from *Bulletin*, 70: 637.

On behalf of the President of the United States, I welcome you to the 21st ministerial conference of the Central Treaty Organization. I particularly welcome the opportunity this meeting provides for a review of the international situation with our good friends and colleagues from Iran, Pakistan, Turkey, and the United Kingdom.

The President of the United States has asked me to read the following message:

It is with great pleasure that I welcome each of you to the United States. I consider it a distinct honor that the CENTO Council of Ministers is meeting in Washington for the second time during my administration.[6]

I should like on this occasion to reaffirm once again the support of the United States for CENTO. I believe the fundamental purposes of CENTO remain unchanged—a partnership of friends brought together to safeguard the peace and a vehicle for constructive cooperation. I note with pride that both within CENTO and in our bilateral relations with each other, we have been able to develop increasingly close ties among our countries. The pattern of cooperation that has evolved is a fruitful one. It is my earnest hope and expectation that it will continue to be.

The world community has much unfinished business in the effort to achieve lasting peace. I am confident that your discussions here will further strengthen our cooperation as friends and partners and will help to advance the cause of peace.

I look forward to meeting with the Council while you are in Washington[7] and to what I am confident will be a rewarding discussion.

[American views on the current role of the alliance were set forth more fully in a formal statement by the U.S. delegation head.]

(b) Opening statement by Acting Secretary Rush, May 21, 1974.[8]

I have the pleasure of reading to you the following message from Secretary Kissinger:

As my CENTO colleagues know, the demands of the present Middle East negotiations prevent me from attending this important conference of the Council of Ministers. I particularly regret

---

[6]The Council had met previously in Washington on May 14-15, 1970; cf. *Documents, 1970*: 149-50.

[7]See Document 11c, par. 19.

[8]Department of State Press Release 211, May 21; text from *Bulletin*, 70: 637-9.

my inability to be with you since this would have been my first opportunity to participate personally in a meeting of the Council, but you can be sure that my absence in no way diminishes my country's strong and longstanding support for CENTO. Quite the contrary, for the same commitment to peace which CENTO embodies also dictates that I continue my current efforts in the Middle East.

The discussions which you are now undertaking provide an ideal opportunity:

—To renew our common dedication to the ideals for which CENTO stands;
—To strengthen the bonds of friendship among our nations; and
—To replenish our commitment to peace and security in the CENTO region and throughout the world.

As well, let this be the occasion for a thorough examination of the challenges and opportunities—economic, technological and social—that confront us in this rapidly changing global environment. We must, for example, give careful attention to the problem of translating the growing resource wealth of the CENTO area into wide-ranging and steady economic development.

In my absence, Acting Secretary Rush has complete authority to represent President Nixon's firm commitment to maintaining the strength and vitality of CENTO. I will follow reports of your discussions with great interest, and upon my return I intend to review in detail the proceedings and results of the conference.

I look forward to the next opportunity to meet with my friends and colleagues from Iran, Pakistan, Turkey, and the United Kingdom. For now, you have my very best wishes for a fruitful conference and a memorable visit.

A generation has passed since our partnership was born. A region burdened by the threat of outside intervention, chronic conflicts, and grinding poverty now holds forth the promise of fundamental transformation. What once seemed unrealistic dreams are now compelling opportunities.

But just as our opportunities have grown, so have the potential consequences of failure to achieve them.

The products of man's technical genius have compressed this planet and multiplied our mutual dependence. No nation can escape the results of attempts to achieve narrow national advantage in an interdependent world. Nuclear war, massive starvation, rampant inflation followed by global recession respect no national boundaries.

A world which urgently requires a new level of international cooperation makes our sense of common purpose more essential than ever before.

So let us at this meeting bring a new spirit to our relationship and initiate a dialogue about its future.

Two decades ago the United Kingdom and the United States were expected to provide the principal leadership and the bulk of the resources to sustain our partnership.

Such a relationship is no longer acceptable to any of us, and it is no longer required. The ability of each to contribute to the resolution of our common concerns has substantially changed:

—The great courage and vision of Prime Minister Bhutto and the Government of Pakistan are helping to establish the foundation for stable and peaceful relations with India and Bangladesh, for a new era in South Asia.

—The Shah of Iran and his government are working with the states of the Persian Gulf to insure that region does not become a new area of conflict.

—President [Fahri] Koruturk, Prime Minister [Bulent] Eçevit, and the Government of Turkey are making an essential contribution to the security of both the CENTO and NATO regions.

The role of the United States, too, has changed enormously in the last decade. We have learned that the United States cannot act alone, that neither peace nor development is achievable unless they engage the effort and the commitment of other nations.

In a relationship of shared leadership and shared responsibility the United States will do its part. We will be guided by these three principles:

—First, the pursuit of détente must not undermine the alliances which make détente possible. Each of us is in the process of broadening our relations with the Soviet Union. The United States pledges that it will never do so at the expense of its allies.

—Second, economic development is a moral imperative and a political necessity. Within the CENTO region, the demands of development remain urgent. But the needs of development can now be met increasingly from resources within the region.

—Third, effective collaboration requires continuing and close consultation. I particularly look forward to the discussions we will be having over the next two days to share more fully our impressions of the Middle East and to obtain your views on the eve of President Nixon's meeting in Moscow with General Secretary Brezhnev.[9]

[9]Cf. Chapter 15.

Our traditional cooperation takes many forms and it must continue:

—The independence and integrity of Pakistan are a central concern of American foreign policy. We will continue to make a major contribution to Pakistan's own efforts for social justice and self-sustaining growth.

—We share with Turkey a profound interest in the security of the volatile eastern Mediterranean. As the Turkish economy has grown in strength, Turkey is increasingly meeting with its own resources the requirements for defense and development.

—As an emerging industrial power, Iran's ties with the United States have taken on a global dimension. The necessity and the potential for a new level of mutually beneficial cooperation have clearly grown.

But beyond the bilateral dimension to our partnership, there is the question of the Central Treaty Organization itself.

CENTO has made a modest but worthwhile contribution to regional economic development. It has provided a symbol of our common concern for regional defense and brought us together for periodic political consultations. Indeed, events of the past year have emphasized the importance of our partnership.

At the same time we must recognize that our perspectives are not always identical, our interests not always in common. While seeking to perpetuate our tradition of broad cooperation, we must also seek what we can do with others toward the global cooperation which is dictated by political, economic, and strategic realities.

In an environment of new hope and new opportunities, new problems and new challenges, it is fitting for each of us to take a fresh look at CENTO—at its place in our national policy and at its place in our relations with each other over the coming decade. In this endeavor we would particularly value the regional members' conception of the future.

Our partnership will enter its third decade next year. Let us seize this moment to demonstrate that nations united in one era can find a new sense of purpose, a new commitment, in a radically transformed world.

Let us demonstrate that nations can be motivated by vision as well as fear. As Dag Hammarskjold wrote, "He who keeps his eye fixed on the far horizon will find his right road."

The United States pledges today to join in finding the path of renewed purpose and common destiny for our nations over the decade ahead.

[The main accomplishments of the meeting were summarized in the usual press communiqué.]

(c) Final press communiqué issued at the conclusion of the meeting, May 22, 1974.[10]

WASHINGTON, D.C., May 22, 1974—The Council of Ministers of the Central Treaty Organization (CENTO) held its 21st session in Washington on May 21 and 22, 1974.
The delegations were led by:

1. H.E. Mr. Abbas Ali Khalatbary, Minister for Foreign Affairs	Iran
2. H.E. Mr. Aziz Ahmed, Minister of State for Defence and Foreign Affairs	Pakistan
3. H.E. Mr. Melih Esenbel, Ambassador of Turkey to the United States	Turkey
4. The Rt. Hon. James Callaghan, Secretary of State for Foreign and Commonwealth Affairs	United Kingdom
5. The Hon. Kenneth Rush, Acting Secretary of State	United States

2. The meeting opened with a message of welcome from the President of the United States, reaffirming the support of the United States for CENTO and expressing the earnest hope that the pattern of co-operation that has evolved among the partners in the Organization will continue to be fruitful. This was followed by opening statements by the leaders of the delegations and the Secretary General of CENTO.[11] Appreciation was expressed for the President's message and the warm hospitality of the host government.

3. The Honourable Kenneth Rush, the Acting Secretary of State of the United States, presided at the session in the absence of Secretary of State Kissinger. Secretary Kissinger sent a message to the Council of Ministers expressing his support for CENTO and his regret at being unable to attend the session because of his need to remain in the Middle East in connection with efforts to bring peace to that region.

4. The Ministers had a thorough and constructive exchange of views on recent international developments, giving special attention to matters of interest in the CENTO region and reviewed intensive-

[10]Text from *Bulletin,* 70: 639-41.
[11]Nassir Assar (Iran).

ly the prospects for further promoting cooperation within the Alliance in all possible fields.

5. The Ministers reiterated their firm resolution for the respect of the principles and the purposes of the United Nations and stressed the necessity of strengthening its role in the service of mankind and world peace.

6. Having reviewed the situation in the Middle East, the Ministers agreed that the prolonged conflict in the area has constituted a grave threat to world peace. They welcomed the steps taken so far towards attainment of a just, honourable and durable peace in the area and expressed the hope that all parties concerned would persevere in these efforts. They expressed their appreciation for the efforts of the Secretary of State Kissinger. The Ministers reaffirmed their support for the Security Council Resolution 242, of 22 November 1967.[12]

7. The Council of Ministers exchanged views on the developments in Europe, especially with reference to the Conference on European Security and Co-operation (CESC) and the Mutual and Balanced Force Reduction (MBFR). They expressed the hope for a successful conclusion of the further stages leading to the establishment of genuine peace and security in Europe and that the détente attained in Europe will lead to a relaxation of tension in other regions of the world. In this context, the Ministers stressed that security in the CENTO region constitutes an important element of European security.

8. The Ministers noted with satisfaction the progress made during the past year towards normalisation of the situation in the South Asian Sub-continent. They agreed that the recognition of Bangladesh by Pakistan had made a significant contribution to the promotion of reconciliation between the two countries and that the successful outcome of the tripartite meeting between Pakistan, India and Bangladesh, which resulted in a satisfactory settlement of the outstanding humanitarian problems, had paved the way for further progress toward the establishment of durable peace in the region.

9. The Ministers noted that the Indian nuclear test of May 18 had introduced a new factor with world and regional implications which will require further study. They expressed their opposition to nuclear proliferation.

10. The Ministers reaffirmed the vital importance they attach to the preservation of the independence and territorial integrity of each of the member states in this region.

11. The Ministers also noted Pakistan's steady economic progress made during the past year, a progress which was all the more

remarkable because it was achieved despite wide-spread floods which caused a devastating loss of life and livelihood.

12. The Ministers noted the impressive socio-economic development programme conducted by Iran under the direction of His Imperial Majesty including the provision of free educational and essential health services for all citizens.

13. The Ministers also noted the substantial measures taken by the Government of Turkey to speed its industrial growth, increase its agricultural production and expedite the improvement of its communications and transport systems.

14. The Ministers, reviewing the report of the Economic Committee, expressed their pleasure at the continuing progress in the improvement of transportation and communications facilities in the region. They welcomed the decision of the Iranian Government to complete the last (Kerman-Zahedan) link in the railway linking Pakistan with Iran and Europe. They also noted Iran's decision to build a road which will link the rapidly developing port of Chahbahar with Pakistan and also Pakistan's projections for future arrangements to develop the Mekran coast. The Ministers also noted that plans are being made for studies to be made of the railroad ferry system across Lake Van and the improvement of roads connecting Turkish ports with Iran. The Ministers expressed their hope that this progress would continue. They approved the recommendation of the Economic Committee that there be a meeting of high level officials to discuss the matters of common interest and expressed their wish that this group study carefully how the Organization can best contribute to the economic strength of its members.

15. The Ministers noted the report of the Military Committee and expressed satisfaction with the progress made during the past year in the improvement of co-operation among the partners in the military field.

16. The Ministers noted with concern the continuing subversive threat against the region, and reaffirmed their resolve to eliminate this threat. They noted that the past year had seen substantial advances in the political and economic life of the people of the region and expressed their confidence that these subversive efforts are farther from success than ever. They expressed the determination of their governments to continue their progressive political and economic programmes to further strengthen their countries.

17. Concluding their review, the Ministers noted with appreciation the annual report of the Secretary General. They reaffirmed their desire that the alliance continues to contribute to the peace, security and stability of the region and to promote the social and economic welfare of its people.

18. The Council, noting that this is the last meeting at which the

current Secretary General would be present, expressed its deep appreciation for the distinguished services he has rendered during his tenure as well as the way he has directed the work of the alliance. The Ministers invited the Government of Turkey to provide a candidate to be the next Secretary General.[13]

19. Following the conclusion of the discussion, the Ministers were received at the White House by the President of the United States.

20. The Ministers accepted the invitation of the Government of Turkey to host the next session of the Council in May 1975, in Ankara.[14]

[13]Umit Bayülken (Turkey) began a three-year term as Secretary-General on Jan. 1, 1975.
[14]The 22nd session of the Council took place in Ankara on May 22-23, 1975; for the communiqué see *Bulletin*, 72: 818-19.

10. MEETING OF THE OECD COUNCIL

(Paris, May 29-30, 1974)

[While Secretary Kissinger labored to promote a military disengagement on the Golan Heights, others were hastening to the aid of a world economy that by now was teetering on the brink of potential disaster. The heady third world talk about a "New International Economic Order" would have tragically little meaning if even the existing economic order, such as it was, were to fall to pieces under the lash of recent events. The four-fold increase in international petroleum prices, though regarded by some of its sponsors as nothing worse than a belated application of the laws of supply and demand, had already heaped fresh fuel upon the existing worldwide inflation, prepared the groundwork for a globe-girdling recession, brought virtual desperation to many of the poorer developing countries that depended on imported oil and fertilizer, and complicated beyond measure the reformist efforts already under way in the areas of international trade and monetary affairs.

The much-discussed reconstruction of the international monetary system, entrusted twenty months earlier to a special committee of the International Monetary Fund (IMF) which had hoped to complete its work by the summer of 1974, had already had to be rescheduled in light of the abrupt and significant changes occurring in the world balance-of- payments structure. At a meeting in Rome on January 17-18, the IMF "Committee of Twenty"—officially, the "Committee on Reform of the International Monetary System and Related Issues"—had come out for an "evolutionary" approach that would give priority to the most urgent issues while frankly recognizing that some aspects of the proposed reform would have to be postponed to an indefinite date. In thus bowing to the inevitable, the committee had taken the advice of Secretary of the Treasury Shultz in warning against a "beggar-my-neighbor" approach to the current crisis. Deprecating "policies which would merely aggravate the problems of other countries," the committee had particularly stressed "the importance of avoiding competitive depreciation and the escalation of restrictions on trade and payments."[1]

A comparable sense of dislocation had been present in Geneva at meetings of the Trade Negotiations Committee which had been set up under the General Agreement on Tariffs and Trade (GATT) to guide the "Tokyo Round" of multilateral trade negotiations initiated in the Japanese capital in September 1973. The uncertainty of the current economic picture had already dimmed the hope that this complex venture, "the most comprehensive ever attempted," could be completed as early as 1975. In a report released in April 1974, the Secretariat of the GATT organization warned that the crucial stage of active negotiations would not be reached for another several months, and that it would be unwise to expect rapid concrete results even when negotiations were actually started.[2] Among other factors that made it unlikely the original schedule could be met was a serious disagreement between the Nixon administration and the Congress about some features of the legislation that would be needed before the United States could enter into new trade agreements.[3]

Some other elements of the world economic situation had already come up for piecemeal examination during the early months of 1974. Problems of the energy consuming countries had been discussed at the Washington conference in February, and the plight of the developing countries had been the main concern of the special U.N. Assembly session.[4] On another front, IMF Managing Director H. Johannes Witteveen was exploring the possibility of setting up a special "oil facility" to cushion the impact of recent price rises and help recycle the estimated $65 billion in excess "petrodollars" that the OPEC countries seemed likely to accumulate in the course of the calendar year.[5] A more broadly focused discussion of the world economy and its problems was expected to develop at the annual ministerial-level meeting of the Organization for Economic Cooperation and Development (OECD), the 24-nation group of (mostly) advanced industrial nations whose leading economic spokesmen were scheduled to convene at the organization's

[1]*IMF Survey*, 3: 17; for background cf. *AFR, 1973*: 381-2 and 394-6.
[2]*IMF Survey*, 3: 129-31; for background cf. *AFR, 1973*: 379-81 and 383-94.
[3]Cf. same: 421-2 and 617, and see further Chapter 24 at note 17.
[4]Chapters 3 and 7.
[5]*IMF Survey*, 3: 129 and 133-6.

Paris headquarters for a two-day session on May 29-30.

The moment was not in all respects well chosen for what would amount to the year's first full-dress assemblage of the principal non-Communist powers. Far from abating with the start of a new year, the strains that had racked the Western association at the time of the Arab-Israeli war in October 1973 had persisted and in some respects had actually grown worse. The mutual irritations that had become almost the daily bread of the Western nations in recent months had reached what might prove to have been an all-time climax with President Nixon's blunt assertion, at a Chicago question-and-answer session on March 15, 1974, that "the day of the one-way street is gone" and that "the Europeans . . . cannot have the United States participation and cooperation on the security front and then proceed to have confrontation and even hostility on the economic and political front."[6] Among the recent consequences of this mutual ill feeling, by no means personal to the President, had been the shelving at least for the time being of the United States' long-contemplated plans for mutual declarations of Atlantic solidarity with the members of NATO and/or the European Communities.[7]

Nor was the prevalent uneasiness confined to European-American relationships. Persistent uncertainty cloaked the intentions of the Wilson government in Great Britain, which had come to office in March with a commitment to renegotiate the terms of British entry into the European Communities, particularly as regards such matters as the common agricultural policy and the methods of financing the Community budget. The resultant apprehensions had been only partially assuaged by Foreign Secretary Callaghan's detailed description of the British desiderata at a meeting of the Community's Council of Ministers on April 1.

By May, however, the political atmosphere in the Atlantic world had undergone some further improvement. President Pompidou of France had died on April 2, and President Nixon, attending the memorial services in Paris the following weekend, had used the opportunity to calm the waters and, perhaps, refurbish his own image in a vigorous round of conferences with Western, Japanese, and Soviet representatives. One not unhappy result of the events in France was the withdrawal of Foreign Minister Jobert, never the most pro-American of French civil servants, and—after an electoral campaign that was to occupy most of the next six weeks—the introduction of the more conciliatory style of foreign policy associated with President Giscard d'Estaing.

---

[6] *Presidential Documents*, 10: 327.
[7] Cf. *AFR, 1973*: 177-89 and 353-4, and see further Chapter 14.

Another effect of the governmental changes that occurred in Germany as well as France at this period was the development of something like a temporary hiatus in foreign economic policy just at the time of the OECD meeting. Though President Giscard d'Estaing had personally won his spurs as France's Minister of Economy and Finance, his new cabinet team, in which Jacques Chirac was to serve as Prime Minister, Jean Sauvagnargues as Minister of Foreign Affairs, and Jean-Pierre Fourcade as Minister of Economy and Finance, was not completed until the very eve of the OECD session. Helmut Schmidt, who succeeded Willy Brandt as West German Chancellor on May 16, was also an ex-Finance Minister and a man of strong economic views but one who, for the moment, was still obliged to feel his way. The United States, too, had lately undergone a change of economic leadership with the resignation of Secretary of the Treasury Shultz and his replacement by William E. Simon, the former Deputy Secretary of the Treasury and Administrator of the Federal Energy Office. Still new to a position he had occupied for only three weeks, Secretary Simon did not attend the OECD meeting, at which the U.S. representation was headed by Ambassador William D. Eberle, the President's Special Representative for Trade Negotiations, and Herbert Stein, the Chairman of the Council of Economic Advisers.

The fact that they were meeting at a time of rapid transition did not prevent the OECD participants from issuing a workmanlike communiqué which, like that of the IMF Committee of Twenty, emphasized the importance of avoiding unilateral measures designed to protect one nation's interests at the expense of its neighbors.]

(12) The Organization for Economic Cooperation and Development (OECD): Meeting of the Council at Ministerial Level, Paris, May 29-30, 1974.

(a) Communiqué issued at the conclusion of the meeting, May 30, 1974.[8]

The Council of the OECD met at Ministerial level in Paris on 29th and 30th May, 1974, under the Chairmanship of Mr. Antonio Giolitti, Minister for the Budget and Economic Planning of Italy. Ministers welcomed this opportunity to have an exchange of views in the light of the present international economic problems and underlined the constructive role which co-operation in the OECD can play in helping to solve these problems.

[8]Text from *OECD Observer*, June 1974: 3-5 and 41. Statements by U.S. delegation members are printed in *Bulletin*, 71: 25-31.

The Problems

Ministers identified three main outstanding problems which need further international co-ordination of national policies if they are to be solved:

—The widespread problem of inflation, already of serious proportions, has been aggravated by the sharp increase in the price of oil; anti-inflationary policies must be carefully chosen so as to avoid serious unemployment problems.

—For most OECD countries the international payments situation, radically altered by the oil price increase, has moved into substantial deficit on current account.

—Certain developing countries, including some of the poorest nations in the world, are facing a grievously worsened economic and financial situation.

The Response

Governments are resolved to approach all these problems jointly and concurrently, and Ministers emphasized their determination to develop a coherent set of measures to this end. In particular, they recognise that no acceptable solution to individual countries' problems of internal and external balance can be found in action which only shifts those problems across frontiers.

Inflation and Employment. Ministers recognise that, in all OECD countries, the present rates of inflation constitute a threat to economic and social progress. Their Governments therefore accord high priority to reducing the rate of price increases. They will seek to maintain economic activity at satisfactory levels and avoid policies that would transfer employment problems from one country to another. But Ministers agreed that great care is at present needed to avoid the emergence of excess demand in the OECD area, and that fiscal and monetary policies have to be shaped to this end. They also emphasized the need to use, where feasible, other, more selective, measures to increase supply and reduce inflationary expectations. And they agreed that OECD, taking account of work in other international bodies, should seek to identify policies conducive to better market stability of primary products with adequate supplies at prices equitable both for producing and for consuming countries.

Trade and Payments Policy. The need for OECD countries to adapt to the new balance of payments situation is a problem that, particularly, has to be tackled on an international basis. Governments are determined to take all appropriate action to limit the size and duration of the weakening of their current account positions.

But they recognise that, in the years immediately ahead, a deterioration has to be accepted because of the oil price-rise. Ministers have also recognised that the financing of external deficits persisting despite the implementation of appropriate adjustment policies will constitute a difficult problem for some Member countries.

In these circumstances, Ministers are conscious of the special danger of mutually conflicting policies to improve national competitive positions and agreed on the need to prevent new unilateral action which may have a detrimental impact on international economic relations. They have, as part of an overall response to the current situation, issued the attached Declaration,[9] stating the determination of their Governments, for a period of a year, to avoid recourse to new restrictions on trade or other current account transactions and the artificial stimulation of visible and current invisible exports, which would be contrary to the objectives of the Declaration.

The Declaration, at the same time, also expresses the agreement of Governments to co-operate fully to facilitate the financing of the deficits described above, and their readiness to consider appropriate arrangements which may prove necessary in this respect.

In addition, Ministers reaffirmed their support for the multilateral trade negotiations in the framework of the GATT and urged that these negotiations be regarded as a matter of priority. They stressed the importance in the present situation of these new efforts to liberalise trade.

Ministers welcomed the intensification of the Organisation's work on the issues related to international investment and to multinational enterprises, with a view to improving co-operation on these issues.

Development Co-operation. Ministers noted that Members of the Development Assistance Committee (DAC) and some other Member countries of the OECD will make strenuous efforts to maintain and enlarge the flow of their official development assistance with a view to promoting further economic and social progress of developing countries.

Ministers expressed particular concern at the acute economic problems of those developing countries with low income which are most seriously affected by the increase in the prices of oil and other essential imports. Although there is as yet no generally agreed estimate as to the amount of special assistance required by these countries, they noted the preliminary studies made by certain inter-

[9]Document 10b.

national organisations indicating that these requirements might amount, as an order of magnitude, to some $3-$4 billion up to the end of 1975.

Ministers of the countries which are Members of the DAC and some other OECD Members, recognising the need to contribute constructively to the follow-up of the Sixth Special Session of the General Assembly of the United Nations on Raw Materials and Development,[10] agreed to make every effort to contribute in an appropriate manner to the special relief needed by the most seriously affected developing countries, bilaterally and within the framework of the appropriate international institutions. The DAC will review the progress of its Members' relief efforts under way and any further steps which may be appropriate. Ministers reiterated the view that all countries throughout the world in a position to do so should share the responsibility to contribute to the special relief of the most seriously affected developing countries.

Ministers agreed that all possible efforts should be made to ensure that shipments of fertilizers to developing countries with urgent needs are maintained at their previous level and that, through financial and technical assistance, encouragement should be given to increased production of fertilizers in developing countries.

Energy. Ministers discussed the consequences of recent developments in the world energy market. They agreed that a strong co-operative effort is needed if serious damage to the economic and social welfare of the OECD community as well as to the world economy is to be avoided. Ministers underlined their will to intensify international co-operation on energy problems and to strengthen OECD capability in this field.

Ministers noted that the work on the Long-Term Assessment of energy and related policies being prepared by the OECD has been accelerated and that the assessment will be at the disposal of Governments in October 1974 at the latest. They underlined the necessity to ensure energy supplies without undue, adverse impact on environmental conditions.

Ministers stressed the importance of OECD's work, already under way, in the fields of energy conservation and demand restraint, accelerated development of conventional energy sources, allocation of oil supplies in times of emergency and severe shortages, and energy research and development. The work on these subjects has been speeded up in order to permit early policy decisions.[11]

[10]Cf. Chapter 7.
[11]Cf. Chapter 29 at note 15.

[By all odds the most remarkable product of the OECD meeting was the formal declaration of a one-year moratorium on new trade and current account restrictions, an idea previously mooted by Secretary Kissinger as well as former Treasury Secretary Shultz.[12]]

(b) Declaration on the avoidance of new trade restrictions, adopted May 30, 1974.[13]

DECLARATION

Adopted by Governments of OECD Member countries on 30th May, 1974

GOVERNMENTS OF OECD MEMBER COUNTRIES[14]

Considering that, among other factors, the rise in oil prices is aggravating the economic problems confronting Member countries, and notably the problem of inflation, as well as causing additional structural problems, and that it is creating an unprecedented change in the structure of the balance of payments and, in particular, a deterioration of current accounts of Member countries as a whole;

Considering that all Member countries are affected by these developments though in varying degrees;

AGREE:

that the nature and size of the above-mentioned problems facing Member countries as well as a number of developing countries call for wide co-operative action in the fields of economic, trade, financial, monetary, investment and development policies;

that the financing of international payments deficits will constitute a difficult problem for certain Member countries and that, accordingly, Member countries will co-operate fully to facilitate such financing and are ready to consider appropriate arrangements which may prove necessary in this respect;

that unilateral trade or other current account measures by one or more Member countries to deal with this situation would aggravate the problems of other countries and, if generalised, would be self-defeating and have a depressing effect on the world economy;

---

[12]Cf. Shultz in *Bulletin*, 70: 254-5; Kissinger in Document 8a above.
[13]Text from *OECD Observer*, June 1974: 31.
[14]Including the European Communities. [Footnote in original.]

that countries have responsibilities both as importers and exporters to avoid disruption of regular trade flows;

that, as a matter of urgency and without prejudice to the outcome of the monetary and trade negotiations, there is therefore a need for a joint undertaking having as its objective to prevent new unilateral action which may have a detrimental impact on international economic relations;

DECLARE THEIR DETERMINATION, in the light of the foregoing and for a period of one year,

(a) to avoid having recourse to unilateral measures, of either a general or a specific nature, to restrict imports or having recourse to similar measures on the other current accounts transactions, which would be contrary to the objectives of the present Declaration;

(b) to avoid measures to stimulate exports or other current account transactions artificially; and, inter alia, abstain from destructive competition in official support of export credit and aim at taking appropriate co-operative actions to this effect in the immediate future;

(c) to avoid export restrictions which would be contrary to the objectives of the present Declaration;

(d) to consult with each other, making full use of the general procedures of consultation within OECD, in order to assure that the present Declaration is properly implemented;

(e) to implement the present Declaration in accordance with their international obligations and with due regard to the special needs of developing countries.

[The significance of the foregoing declaration from an American point of view was emphasized by a special statement of the Department of State in Washington.]

(c) Comment by the Department of State, May 30, 1974.[15]

Today the member countries of the Organization for Economic Cooperation and Development in Paris declared their determination over the next 12 months to avoid unilateral measures which would shift the burden of current account deficits to their trading partners.[16] Attempts by the major trading nations to deal with the consequences of the current international economic situation, par-

---

[15]Department of State Press Release 228, May 30; text from *Bulletin*, 71: 26.
[16]Document 12b.

ticularly the rise in energy costs, by such unilateral actions would present a potentially serious threat to the stability of the international economic structure. The declaration helps meet that threat.

Major problems still confront the world's trade and monetary systems. Progress in the multilateral trade negotiations and toward reforming the international monetary and trade systems is more essential than ever. But with this declaration the member countries of the OECD have renewed their commitment to a cooperative multilateral approach to resolving the problems of our ever more interdependent world.

Moreover, they have helped assure stability in international economic relations while the governments of their nations proceed with more fundamental reform of the world economic system. Secretary of State Kissinger and former Treasury Secretary Shultz had called for this type of action, and the U.S. Government now warmly welcomes the successful achievement of this declaration and pledges its full support to its objectives.

11. DISENGAGEMENT ON THE GOLAN HEIGHTS

(Geneva and New York, May 31, 1974)

[The negotiation of an agreement for the disengagement of
Israeli and Syrian military forces on the Israeli-held Golan Heights
was a far more difficult enterprise than that of the Egyptian-Israeli
disengagement agreement completed in January.[1] The Soviet-sup-
ported Syrian Government of President Hafez al-Assad was less
favorably inclined toward the United States, and less prepared for
even temporary compromise with Israel, than the Egyptian regime
of President Sadat had proved to be. Unlike the Sinai desert,
moreover, the Golan Heights was settled, cultivated territory, at
once too limited in extent and too important to those concerned to
be conveniently divided or shared on even a provisional basis.
Syria, as an uncompromising adherent of the Arab view that Israel
must unequivocally withdraw from all the territories it had occupied in 1967, was wholly disinclined to settle for anything less
than full restitution of the entire Golan Heights area, as well as the
additional territory east of Golan that Israel had occupied in 1973.
Israel, on its side, was at least equally averse to surrendering any of
its territorial assets, especially at a time when artillery duels along
the cease-fire line had remained an almost daily occurrence, punctuated by occasional air battles and, from mid-April onward, by a
recurrence of ground fighting in what amounted to a continuing
war of attrition.

At the same time, it could be argued that both Israel and Syria
would have something to gain from an arrangement that would put
a stop to the present fighting and reduce the likelihood of a renewal
of full-scale hostilities. For Syria, the recovery of even a part of the
Golan would be an achievement of some value, especially if it could
be made to look like a step toward total recovery. President Assad
is said to have intimated at a comparatively early stage of his

[1]Cf. Chapter 1.

discussions with Secretary Kissinger that he might settle, initially, for the recovery of *half* the Golan Heights territory, including the ruined regional capital of El Quneitra. But Israel, already immersed in the cabinet crisis that preceded Prime Minister Meir's formal resignation on April 11 and her actual departure from office at the beginning of June, gave Dr. Kissinger to understand that while it might be persuaded to surrender half the salient east of the Golan that it had captured the previous October, it did not intend to give up any of the Golan proper.[2]

Persevering in the face of even the most unfavorable auguries, the American Secretary of State devoted slightly over a month, from late April to late May, to a painfully arduous but ultimately successful effort to persuade the two parties to whittle down their demands to the point where an agreement might be reached. This airborne diplomatic feat, involving multiple trips between Jerusalem, Damascus, and other Middle Eastern capitals, was made even more difficult by a series of particularly gruesome terrorist actions in northern Israel, succeeded in each case by Israeli retaliatory strikes against guerrilla bases or suspected guerrilla locations in southern Lebanon.

A pattern for such activity was established by the killing of eighteen Israelis, including five women and eight children, by infiltrators at the northern town of Qiryat Shemona on April 11, an action that provoked an Israeli raid on six Lebanese villages, a debate in the U.N. Security Council, and the adoption on April 24 of a resolution that condemned Israel by name and also, though more diffusely, voiced Security Council disapprobation of acts of violence in general.[3] A still graver incident occurred at Maalot in northern Galilee on May 15 when terrorist infiltrators, in what the Beirut-based "Popular Democratic Front for the Liberation of Palestine" described as a deliberate attempt to sabotage the Kissinger mission, seized a school in an operation that resulted in the death of twenty children and the wounding of about 70. Again there were heavy Israeli reprisals by air and sea against Palestinian sites in southern Lebanon, although the Security Council did not take action in this instance.

In spite of pressures and near-breakdowns, the Kissinger negotiations moved gradually closer to a conclusion which, like the earlier Egyptian-Israeli agreement, would involve a reaffirmation of the 1973 cease-fire, a partial withdrawal of Israeli military forces, the

[2]For the detailed negotiating history see especially Sheehan, *The Arabs, Israelis, and Kissinger*: 116-28, and Golan, *The Secret Conversations of Henry Kissinger*: 151-212.
[3]Security Council Resolution 347 (1974), adopted Apr. 24 by a vote of 13 (U.S.)-0 with China and Iraq not participating.

establishment of a U.N.-patrolled buffer zone, and a limitation of armaments and forces in the forward areas of the two sides. Broadly, Israel undertook to relinquish not only its 1973 conquests but a portion of the Golan territory occupied in 1967. The problem of El Quneitra was solved by returning it to Syrian administration but leaving it within the U.N. buffer zone, while the Israelis retained possession of three hills to the west of the town—where, however, they were forbidden to install heavy weapons. A six-month time limit was placed upon the whole arrangement, subject to possible extension by mutual agreement.

A notable feature of the arrangement was the fact that it was brought to completion entirely under American auspices and with only the most nominal participation on the part of the Soviet Union, whose contact with the negotiations was limited to a pair of meetings between Secretary Kissinger and Foreign Minister Andrei A. Gromyko in Geneva on April 28 and in Nicosia, Cyprus, on May 7. The U.S.S.R. appears, however, to have made no special effort to discourage the agreement, and did not refuse its cooperation in providing suitable facilities for its completion. Like the Egyptian-Israeli disengagement agreement, the Israeli-Syrian arrangement was prepared for signature under the nominal auspices of the Geneva Conference on the Middle East, which had met briefly under joint American and Soviet sponsorship—though without Syrian participation—in December 1973. In contrast to the Israeli-Egyptian agreement, which had been signed in the field, the agreement between Israeli and Syrian military representatives was actually to be signed at the conference seat in Geneva.

President Nixon announced the completion of Dr. Kissinger's mission in a special broadcast on May 29, two days before the scheduled signature.]

(13) Israeli-Syrian Agreement on Disengagement of Forces, May 31, 1974.

(a) Announcement of the Agreement: Remarks by President Nixon on radio and television, May 29, 1974.[4]

Ladies and gentlemen, I have an announcement that will also be made today in Jerusalem and in Damascus. The announcement reads as follows:

The discussions conducted by United States Secretary of State

[4]Text from *Presidential Documents*, 10: 561-2.

Dr. Henry Kissinger with Syria and Israel have led to an agreement on the disengagement of Syrian and Israeli forces. The agreement will be signed by Syrian and Israeli military representatives in the Egyptian-Israeli Military Working Group of the Geneva Conference on Friday—this Friday—May 31.

Just a word about the significance of this development. It is obviously a major diplomatic achievement, and Secretary Kissinger deserves enormous credit for the work that he has done, along with members of his team, in keeping this negotiation going and finally reaching an agreement when at many times over the past few weeks it seemed that the negotiations would break down.

Also, credit goes to the governments concerned who had great differences which had to be resolved. I have sent messages of congratulations to Prime Minister Meir of Israel and also to President Asad of Syria, congratulating them with regard to the statesmanship that they have shown in resolving differences that seemed totally without any prospect of resolution a month or so ago and even, as a matter of fact, several times over the past month.

This particular agreement, together with the agreement that was reached earlier on disengagement of Egyptian and Israeli forces,[5] now paves the way for progress in Geneva and, of course, with the various governments involved, toward our objective and, we trust, their objective as well, of achieving a permanent peace settlement for the entire Mideast area.

However, we should have in mind that despite the fact that these two agreements have now been signed, or have been reached, that there are many difficulties ahead before a permanent settlement is reached. However, what was a major roadblock to any permanent settlement has now been removed and, I think, the most difficult roadblock, the roadblock being the differences that had long existed between Israel and Syria.

As far as the United States is concerned, we shall continue with our diplomatic initiatives, working with all governments in the area toward working toward achieving the goal of a permanent settlement, a permanent peace. And I can only say that based on the success in reaching this agreement in which the differences were so great that the prospects for reaching agreement on a permanent basis, I think, now are better than they have been at any time over the past 25 years.

Thank you.

[The heart of the arrangement worked out with Dr. Kissinger's aid was an "Agreement on Disengagement between Israeli and

[5]Chapter 1, Document 1b.

Syrian Forces," which, with an accompanying Protocol and an official map, was to be signed at Geneva on May 31 within the framework of the Egyptian-Israeli Military Working Group of the Geneva Conference. Signatures were duly affixed at about noon on May 31 by Major General Herzl Shafir of Israel and Lieutenant General Adnan Wajih Tayara of Syria, with Lieutenant General Ensio Siilasvuo of Finland, Commander of the U.N. Emergency Force (UNEF) in the Sinai, presiding and witnessing the signatures on behalf of the United Nations. Also present, in addition to an Egyptian military representative, were Ambassadors Ellsworth Bunker of the United States and Vladimir M. Vinogradov of the U.S.S.R., representing the governments co-sponsoring the Geneva Conference.]

(b) Agreement on Disengagement Between Israeli and Syrian Forces and Accompanying Protocol, as prepared for signature and signed at Geneva May 31, 1974. [6]

Agreement on Disengagement between Israeli and Syrian Forces

A. Israel and Syria will scrupulously observe the cease-fire on land, sea and air and will refrain from all military actions against each other, from the time of the signing of this document, in implementation of United Nations Security Council resolution 338 (1973) dated 22 October 1973. [7]

B. The military forces of Israel and Syria will be separated in accordance with the following principles:

1. All Israeli military forces will be west of the line designated as Line A on the map attached hereto, [8] except in the Quneitra area, where they will be west of Line A-1.
2. All territory east of Line A will be under Syrian administration, and Syrian civilians will return to this territory.
3. The area between Line A and the line designated as Line B on the attached map will be an area of separation. In this area will be stationed the United Nations Disengagement Observer Force established in accordance with the accompanying protocol.
4. All Syrian military forces will be east of the line designated as Line B on the attached map.

[6] U.N. document S/11302/Add.1, May 30, 1974, in Security Council, *Official Records: 29th Year, Supplement for Apr., May and June 1974*: 145.
[7] Text in *AFR, 1973*: 459.
[8] The official map was subsequently issued in U.N. document S/11302/Add.3, in Security Council, *Official Records: 29th Year, Supplement for July, Aug. and Sept. 1974*: 14-15.

5. There will be two equal areas of limitation in armament and forces, one west of Line A and one east of Line B as agreed upon.
6. Air forces of the two sides will be permitted to operate up to their respective lines without interference from the other side.

C. In the area between Line A and Line A-1 on the attached map there shall be no military forces.

D. This Agreement and the attached map will be signed by the military representatives of Israel and Syria in Geneva not later than 31 May 1974, in the Egyptian-Israeli Military Working Group of the Geneva Peace Conference under the aegis of the United Nations, after that group has been joined by a Syrian military representative, and with the participation of representatives of the United States of America and the Soviet Union. The precise delineation of a detailed map and a plan for the implementation of the disengagement of forces will be worked out by military representatives of Israel and Syria in the Egyptian-Israeli Military Working Group who will agree on the stages of this process. The Military Working Group described above will start their work for this purpose in Geneva under the aegis of the United Nations within 24 hours after the signing of this Agreement. They will complete this task within five days. Disengagement will begin within 24 hours after the completion of the task of the Military Working Group. The process of disengagement will be completed not later than 20 days after it begins.

E. The provisions of paragraphs A, B and C shall be inspected by personnel of the United Nations comprising the United Nations Disengagement Observer Force under this Agreement.

F. Within 24 hours after the signing of this Agreement in Geneva all wounded prisoners-of-war which each side holds of the other as certified by the International Committee of the Red Cross will be repatriated. The morning after the completion of the task of the Military Working Group, all remaining prisoners-of-war will be repatriated.

G. The bodies of all dead soldiers held by either side will be returned for burial in their respective countries within 10 days after the signing of this Agreement.

H. This Agreement is not a peace agreement. It is a step towards a just and durable peace on the basis of Security Council resolution 338 (1973) dated 22 October 1973.

For Israel: *For Syria:*

Witness for the United Nations:

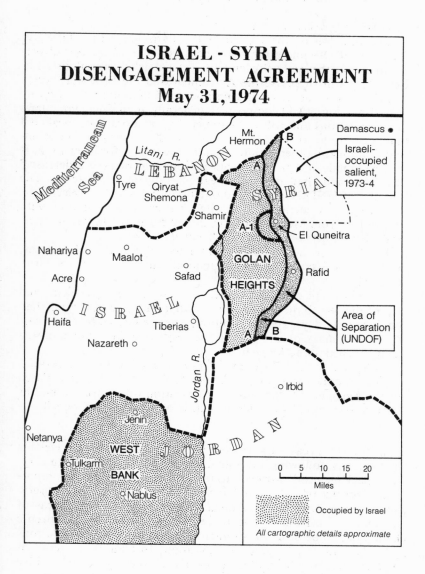

ISRAEL - SYRIA DISENGAGEMENT AGREEMENT
May 31, 1974

Mediterranean Sea

Litani R.

LEBANON

Mt. Hermon

Tyre

Qiryat Shemona

Shamir

SYRIA

Damascus

Israeli-occupied salient, 1973-4

El Quneitra

Nahariya

Maalot

Safad

GOLAN

Rafid

Acre

HEIGHTS

ISRAEL

Haifa

Tiberias

Area of Separation (UNDOF)

Nazareth

A

B

Jordan R.

Irbid

JORDAN

Netanya

Jenin

WEST

Tulkarm

BANK

Nablus

| 0 | 5 | 10 | 15 | 20 |

Miles

Occupied by Israel

All cartographic details approximate

Protocol to the Agreement on Disengagement between Israeli and Syrian Forces concerning the United Nations Disengagement Observer Force

Israel and Syria agree that:

The function of the United Nations Disengagement Observer Force (UNDOF) under the Agreement will be to use its best efforts to maintain the cease-fire and to see that it is scrupulously observed. It will supervise the Agreement and the Protocol thereto with regard to the areas of separation and limitation. In carrying out its mission, it will comply with generally applicable Syrian laws and regulations and will not hamper the functioning of local civil administration. It will enjoy freedom of movement and communication and other facilities that are necessary for its mission. It will be mobile and provided with personal weapons of a defensive character and shall use such weapons only in self-defence. The number of UNDOF shall be about 1,250, who will be selected by the Secretary-General of the United Nations in consultation with the parties from Members of the United Nations who are not permanent members of the Security Council.

UNDOF will be under the command of the United Nations, vested in the Secretary-General, under the authority of the Security Council.

UNDOF shall carry out inspections under the Agreement, and report thereon to the parties, on a regular basis, not less often than once every 15 days, and, in addition, when requested by either party. It shall mark on the ground the respective lines shown on the map attached to the Agreement.

Israel and Syria will support a resolution of the United Nations Security Council which will provide for the UNDOF contemplated by the Agreement.[9] The initial authorization will be for six months subject to renewal by further resolution of the Security Council.

[Although a cease-fire was put into effect on the Golan Heights immediately following the signature of the foregoing document, the "package deal" worked out by Dr. Kissinger had other important elements that did not figure directly in the Geneva observances. Among them was a detailed agreement on the "areas of limitation in armament and forces" that spelled out the specific limitations to be observed by each side in a fifteen-mile-wide zone on either side of the area of separation. In addition, a series of political propositions and tacit agreements that were too sensitive to be formalized in the normal manner were embodied in what were

---

[9]Cf. Document 14.

described as "American memoranda . . . conveyed to both sides."
The most important of these tacit understandings, dealing with the question of any future terrorist raids against Israel, was outlined by Prime Minister Meir in a statement to the Israeli Knesset (Parliament) on May 30. It was the view of the United States, Mrs. Meir stated, that raids by armed groups or individuals across the demarcation line were contrary to the cease-fire; that Israel, in the exercise of its right of self-defense, could act to prevent such actions by all available means; and that the United States would not regard such actions by Israel as violations of the cease-fire but would "support them politically"—presumably meaning that it would veto any condemnatory resolution that might be brought forward in the Security Council. Referring to other matters discussed with Secretary Kissinger, Mrs. Meir further stated: ". . . I can say with more assurance that the consistent aid of the United States to Israel has been assured for the future by the President of the United States."[10]

Another critical element in the disengagement package was the proposed U.N. Disengagement Observer Force (UNDOF) that was to supervise the implementation of the cease-fire and disengagement agreement. The task of establishing such a force and approving guidelines for its operation was taken up by the Security Council in New York within hours of the signature ceremony at Geneva. Secretary-General Kurt Waldheim, in anticipation of this development, had already advised the Security Council that in organizing UNDOF he planned to act in accordance with the general principles already approved by the Security Council in setting up the U.N. Emergency Force (UNEF) in the Sinai region.[11] At the meeting on May 31, the Secretary-General's plans were endorsed by U.S. Representative John Scali in a statement that also hailed the cooperation of the Soviet Union in bringing matters to their hoped-for conclusion.]

(14) Establishment of the United Nations Disengagement Observer Force (UNDOF), May 31, 1974.

(a) Statement by Ambassador Scali to the Security Council, May 31, 1974.[12]

I hope I speak for all members of the Security Council when I express the great satisfaction with which my government welcomes

[10]*New York Times*, May 31, 1974; cf. also Sheehan: 243-4.
[11]Cf. *AFR, 1973*: 472-5.
[12]USUN Press Release 58, May 31; text from *Bulletin*, 70: 698-9.

the agreement announced Wednesday [May 29] between Syria and Israel. As you all know, this agreement[13] provides for the disengagement of Syrian and Israeli forces. It was signed today by Syrian and Israeli military representatives in the Egyptian-Israeli Military Working Group of the Geneva Conference.

The Israeli-Syrian disengagement agreement, together with the agreement reached earlier on disengagement of Egyptian-Israeli forces, in our view, will open the way for progress in Geneva toward the achievement of an enduring settlement in the Middle East. As President Nixon said Wednesday,[14] the prospects for such a peace now are better than at any time in the past 25 years. President Nixon also pledged that the United States would continue working with all governments in the area toward that goal.

We congratulate the Governments of Israel and Syria. Our President has commended Prime Minister Meir and President Asad for the vision and statesmanship with which they have resolved the great differences that seemed insurmountable only a short time ago. We are pleased that the United States, through the efforts of Secretary Kissinger, was privileged to help bring about this agreement. We express our appreciation also for the cooperation of the Soviet Union, as reflected in the three conversations which the Secretary of State and the Foreign Minister have held in recent weeks.[15]

Israel and Syria have recognized that the United Nations should play a crucial role in the execution of this agreement. A protocol to the disengagement agreement provides for the establishment of a United Nations Disengagement Observer Force. This Force will play a key and indispensable role in maintaining a cease-fire and seeing that it is scrupulously observed. I ask, therefore, that the Council authorize the creation of the United Nations Disengagement Observer Force.

In approving the resolution which you have before you,[16] the Council will be taking the next critical step in what we hope will be a quickening movement toward a permanent peace in the Middle East. It is another important step on the long road before us.

The resolution is simple and straightforward. It is grounded in the recent successful actions of this Council and the statement we heard yesterday from the Secretary General. The Secretary General's statement of yesterday on the applicability of the general

[13]Document 13b.
[14]Document 13a.
[15]In addition to the meetings referred to in the text, Secretary Kissinger and Foreign Minister Gromyko had conferred in Washington on Feb. 3-5 and in Moscow on Mar. 24-28.
[16]U.N. document S/11305/Rev.1, May 30, identical to Document 14b below.

principles which guided the United Nations Emergency Force clearly applies to all aspects of the United Nations Disengagement Observer Force, including the assurances of its continued effective functioning for the duration of the mandate established by the resolution. I urge this resolution's speedy adoption.

Today we are considering not merely abstract issues of military units and borders. We are, rather, grappling with the most important and yet the most human of issues—war or peace.

We have indeed come a long way in the past few months. The peoples of the Middle East have started on a new course which offers the promise of greater security and greater prosperity for *all* the peoples of this historic region. It is within our power to ease and assist that process. I am confident that with the aid of the United Nations, and of this Council in particular, steady progress can continue to be made until we attain our long-sought goal—lasting peace in the Middle East.

[Even the Soviet Government "assessed the [disengagement] agreement favorably," according to Ambassador Yakov A. Malik, and the Soviet Union was listed with the United States as one of the two co-sponsors of the Security Council resolution by which the new Disengagement Observer Force was formally established. Thirteen of the Security Council's fifteen members voted in favor of this resolution, and none opposed it, though China and Iraq refrained from voting in conformity with their usual stand on such questions.]

(b) Security Council Resolution 350 (1974), adopted May 31, 1974.[17]

The Security Council,

Having considered the report of the Secretary-General contained in documents S/11302 and Add.1,[18] and having heard his statement made at the 1773rd meeting of the Security Council [on May 30],

1. *Welcomes* the Agreement on Disengagement between Israeli and Syrian Forces,[19] negotiated in implementation of Security Council resolution 338 (1973) of 22 October 1973;[20]

2. *Takes note* of the Secretary-General's report and the annexes thereto and his statement;

---

[17]Text from Security Council, *Official Records: 29th Year, Resolutions and Decisions*: 4.

[18]Cf. above at note 6.

[19]Document 13b.

[20]*AFR, 1973*: 459.

3. *Decides* to set up immediately under its authority a United Nations Disengagement Observer Force, and requests the Secretary-General to take the necessary steps to this effect in accordance with his above-mentioned report and the annexes thereto; the Force shall be established for an initial period of six months, subject to renewal by further resolution of the Security Council;

4. *Requests* the Secretary-General to keep the Security Council fully informed of further developments.

[In conformity with this mandate, contingents from Austria, Peru, Canada, and Poland were promptly transferred from UNEF to UNDOF, together with other personnel that soon swelled the ranks of the new force to approximately 1,200. Under the overall supervision of Brigadier General Gonzalo Briceño Zevallos of Peru, UNDOF's interim Commander, disengagement operations were commenced without delay and completed on schedule, with the full cooperation of the parties, on June 25. An exchange of wounded and other prisoners of war was meanwhile carried out under the aegis of the International Red Cross, a total of 68 Israelis being exchanged for 392 Syrians and 16 prisoners of other Arab nationalities.

In the midst of these arrangements there took place the formal retirement of Mrs. Meir's government and the installation on June 3 of the new Israeli cabinet headed by Yitzhak Rabin, in which Yigal Allon was Deputy Premier and Minister of Foreign Affairs (succeeding Abba Eban) while Shimon Peres succeeded Moshe Dayan as Minister of Defense. Among the new government's first tasks would be the completion of arrangements for a visit by President Nixon, who had eagerly awaited the opportunity to undertake a personal tour of the Middle East.]

12. PRESIDENT NIXON VISITS THE MIDEAST

(June 10-19, 1974)

[To President Nixon and his remaining supporters, the Golan disengagement agreement was doubly welcome because it cleared the way for still another spectacular exercise of presidential diplomacy, this one a precedent-breaking visit to countries situated on both sides of the Israeli-Arab battle lines. Ostensibly designed to signalize a renascence of American influence throughout the Middle East, the trip was also calculated to portray the President in his favorite role of world statesman and refurbish the personal prestige that had been so badly tarnished by developments in the Watergate case.

Particularly damaging to the presidential image had been the effects of Mr. Nixon's release on April 30 of a mass of tape-recorded, Watergate-related conversations, in an expurgated text that placed the President and his associates in a highly unflattering light yet failed to meet the demand for original tapes put forward by Special Prosecutor Leon Jaworski. Upholding the Jaworski subpoena, Judge Sirica ruled on May 20 that the original tapes of 64 specified conversations must be made available by the end of the month—a deadline the administration contrived to evade only by taking what ultimately proved to be the even more dangerous course of a direct appeal to the Supreme Court. The House Judiciary Committee, meanwhile, continued to press its separate demand for evidence pertinent to the impeachment inquiry, despite the President's refusal, on both constitutional and practical grounds, to provide it with further data.

The effectiveness of the Middle East journey as an antidote to these difficulties was lessened by the reopening just at this period of the supposedly long-settled question of Dr. Kissinger's role in the national security wiretapping of certain officials and newsmen that had been instituted in the spring of 1969. Annoyed by the reiterated suggestion that he might have understated the extent of his responsibility for this activity, the Secretary of State had explained his views in a series of public declarations that culminated in a sensational news conference at Salzburg, Austria, on June 11—the first morning of the presidential trip—at which he intimated that he was determined to resign unless his "public honor" was vindicated by the Senate Foreign Relations Committee, the body that had originally recommended his confirmation as Secretary.[1] (Following further executive hearings held at Dr. Kissinger's request, the Foreign Relations Committee would conclude on August 6 that there were no significant discrepancies between the new information and his previous testimony. Accordingly, it reaffirmed its original conclusion that ". . . Mr. Kissinger's role in the wiretapping of 17 government officials and newsmen did not constitute grounds to bar his confirmation as Secretary of State.")[2]

A dangerous and painful attack of phlebitis was added to President Nixon's problems as he began the Middle Eastern phase of his journey[3] on June 12 with an apparently euphoric entry into Cairo and a spectacularly friendly meeting with President Sadat, followed next day by the still more emotional welcome accorded Mr. Nixon in Alexandria. Diplomatic relations between the United States and Egypt had already been restored within weeks of the Sinai disengagement agreement, and the time now seemed ripe for launching a more intimate relationship. The decisions of the two Presidents, which included not only the inauguration of a binational Joint Commission on Cooperation but also, and more surprisingly, an American commitment to supply the Egyptians with nuclear reactors and fuel, were summarized in a joint declaration that was issued on June 14 as Mr. Nixon prepared to fly on to Jidda, Saudi Arabia.]

[1]News conference, June 6, in *Bulletin*, 70: 701 and 704-5; news conference, Salzburg, June 11, in *New York Times*, June 12, 1974. For background cf. *AFR, 1973*: 195-6 and 351-2.

[2]*Senate Foreign Relations Committee History, 1973-4*: 182-3. That Dr. Kissinger had played only an "inactive role" in the wiretapping of former National Security Council aide Morton H. Halperin was confirmed in a finding by the U.S. District Court for the District of Columbia on Dec. 16, 1976 (*New York Times*, Dec. 17, 1976).

[3]For detailed documentation see *Presidential Documents*, 10: 611-50 or (more fully) *Bulletin*, 71: 77-127. Narrative highlights will be found in Bernstein and Woodward, *The Final Days*: 208-20.

(15) "Principles of Relations and Cooperation Between Egypt and the United States," signed in Cairo June 14, 1974 by President Nixon and President Muhammad Anwar al-Sadat of the Arab Republic of Egypt.[4]

The President of the Arab Republic of Egypt, Muhammed Anwar el-Sadat, and the President of the United States of America, Richard Nixon,

—Having held wide-ranging discussions on matters of mutual interest to their two countries,

—Being acutely aware of the continuing need to build a structure of peace in the world and to that end and to promote a just and durable peace in the Middle East, and,

—Being guided by a desire to seize the historic opportunity before them to strengthen relations between their countries on the broadest basis in ways that will contribute to the well-being of the area as a whole and will not be directed against any of its states or peoples or against any other state.

Have agreed that the following principles should govern relations between Egypt and the United States.

I. GENERAL PRINCIPLES OF BILATERAL RELATIONS

Relations between nations, whatever their economic or political systems, should be based on the purposes and principles of the United Nations Charter, including the right of each state to existence, independence and sovereignty; the right of each state freely to choose and develop its political, social economic and cultural systems; non-intervention in each other's internal affairs; and respect for territorial integrity and political independence.

Nations should approach each other in the spirit of equality respecting their national life and the pursuit of happiness.

The United States and Egypt consider that their relationship reflects these convictions.

Peace and progress in the Middle East are essential if global peace is to be assured. A just and durable peace based on full implementation of U.N. Security Council Resolution 242 of November 22, 1967,[5] should take into due account the legitimate interest of all the peoples in the Mid East, including the Palestinian people, and the right to existence of all states in the area. Peace can

---

[4]Text from *Presidential Documents*, 10: 622-5. The spelling of Arabic names follows the official text.

[5]*Documents, 1967*: 169-70.

be achieved only through a process of continuing negotiation as called for by United Nations Security Council Resolution 338 of October 22, 1973,[6] within the framework of the Geneva Middle East Peace Conference.

In recognition of these principles, the Governments of the Arab Republic of Egypt and the United States of America set themselves to these tasks:

They will intensify consultations at all levels, including further consultations between their Presidents, and they will strengthen their bilateral cooperation whenever a common or parallel effort will enhance the cause of peace in the world.

They will continue their active cooperation and their energetic pursuit of peace in the Middle East.

They will encourage increased contacts between members of all branches of their two governments—executive, legislative and judicial—for the purpose of promoting better mutual understanding of each other's institutions, purposes and objectives.

They are determined to develop their bilateral relations in a spirit of esteem, respect and mutual advantage. In the past year, they have moved from estrangement to a constructive working relationship. This year, from that base, they are moving to a relationship of friendship and broad cooperation.

They view economic development and commercial relations as an essential element in the strengthening of their bilateral relations and will actively promote them. To this end, they will facilitate cooperative and joint ventures among appropriate governmental and private institutions and will encourage increased trade between the two countries.

They consider encouragement of exchanges and joint research in the scientific and technical field as an important aim and will take appropriate concrete steps for this purpose.

They will deepen cultural ties through exchanges of scholars, students, and other representatives of the cultures of both countries.

They will make special efforts to increase tourism in both directions, and to amplify person-to-person contact among their citizens.

They will take measures to improve air and maritime communications between them.

They will seek to establish a broad range of working relationships and will look particularly to their respective Foreign Ministers and Ambassadors and to the Joint Commission on Cooperation,[7]

---

[6]*AFR, 1973*: 459.

[7]Agreement on the formation of a joint cooperation commission had been announced on May 31; cf. *Presidential Documents*, 10: 566-7, or *Bulletin*, 70: 698.

as well as to other officials and organizations, and private individuals and groups as appropriate, to implement the various aspects of the above principles.

II. JOINT COOPERATION COMMISSION

The two governments have agreed that the intensive review of the areas of economic cooperation held by President El-Sadat and President Nixon on June 12 constituted the first meeting of the Joint Cooperation Commission, announced May 31, 1974. This Commission will be headed by the Secretary of State of the United States and the Minister of Foreign Affairs of Egypt. To this end, they have decided to move ahead rapidly on consultations and coordination to identify and implement programs agreed to be mutually beneficial in the economic, scientific and cultural fields.

The United States has agreed to help strengthen the financial structure of Egypt. To initiate this process, United States Secretary of the Treasury William Simon will visit Egypt in the near future for high level discussions.

III. NUCLEAR ENERGY

Since the atomic age began, nuclear energy has been viewed by all nations as a double-edged sword—offering opportunities for peaceful applications, but raising the risk of nuclear destruction. In its international programs of cooperation, the United States Government has made its nuclear technology available to other nations under safeguard conditions. In this context, the two governments will begin negotiation of an Agreement for Cooperation in the field of nuclear energy under agreed safeguards. Upon conclusion of such an agreement,[8] the United States is prepared to sell nuclear reactors and fuel to Egypt, which will make it possible for Egypt by the early 1980s to generate substantial additional quantities of electric power to support its rapidly growing development needs. Pending conclusion of this Agreement, the United States Atomic Energy Commission and the Egyptian Ministry of Electricity will this month conclude a provisional agreement for the sale of nuclear fuel to Egypt.

IV. WORKING GROUPS

The two governments have agreed to set up Joint Working

[8]A joint statement setting forth principles for the proposed agreement was initialed in Washington on Nov. 5, 1975; text in *Bulletin*, 73: 732 (1975).

Groups to meet in the near future to prepare concrete projects and proposals for review by the Joint Commission at a meeting to be held later this year in Washington, D.C.[9] These Joint Working Groups will be composed of governmental representatives from each country and will include the following:

(1) A Joint Working Group on Suez Canal Reconstruction and Development to consider and review plans for reopening the Suez Canal and reconstruction of the cities along the Canal, and the United States role in this endeavor.

(2) A Joint Working Group to investigate and recommend measures designed to open the way for United States private investment in joint ventures in Egypt and to promote trade between the two countries. Investment opportunities would be guided by Egypt's needs for financial, technical, and material support to increase Egypt's economic growth. The United States regards with favor and supports the ventures of American enterprises in Egypt. It is noted that such ventures, currently being negotiated, are in the fields of petrochemicals, transportation, food and agricultural machinery, land development, power, tourism, banking, and a host of other economic sectors. The estimated value of projects under serious consideration exceeds two billion dollars. American technology and capital combined with Egypt's absorptive capacity, skilled manpower and productive investment opportunities can contribute effectively to the strengthening and development of the Egyptian economy. The United States and Egypt will therefore negotiate immediately a new Investment Guarantee Agreement between them.

(3) A Joint Working Group on Agriculture to study and recommend actions designed to increase Egypt's agricultural production through the use of the latest agricultural technology.

(4) A Joint Working Group on Technology, Research and Development in scientific fields, including space, with special emphasis on exchanges of scientists.

(5) A Joint Working Group on Medical Cooperation to assist the Government of Egypt to develop and strengthen its medical research, treatment and training facilities. These efforts will supplement cooperation in certain forms of medical research already conducted through the Naval Medical Research Unit (NAMRU), whose mutually beneficial work will continue.

(6) A Joint Working Group on Cultural Exchanges to encourage and facilitate exhibitions, visits, and other cultural endeavors to en-

---

[9]The Joint Commission held its second meeting in Washington in conjunction with a visit by Egyptian Foreign Minister Ismail Fahmy on Aug. 12-19; cf. *Bulletin*, 71: 381-3.

courage a better understanding of both cultures on the part of the peoples of the United States and Egypt.

The two governments have agreed to encourage the formation of a Joint Economic Council to include representatives from the private economic sector of both countries to coordinate and promote mutually beneficial cooperative economic arrangements.

In support of their economic cooperation, the United States will make the maximum feasible contribution, in accordance with Congressional authorization, to Egypt's economic development, including clearing the Suez Canal, reconstruction projects, and restoring Egyptian trade. In addition, the United States is prepared to give special priority attention to Egypt's needs for agricultural commodities.

Consistent with the spirit of cultural cooperation, the United States Government has agreed to consider how it might assist the Egyptian Government in the reconstruction of Cairo's Opera House. The Egyptian Government for its part intends to place the "Treasures of Tutankhamen" on exhibit in the United States.

Both governments, in conclusion, reiterate their intention to do everything possible to broaden the ties of friendship and cooperation consistent with their mutual interests in peace and security and with the principles set forth in this statement.

In thanking President El-Sadat for the hospitality shown to him and the members of his party, President Nixon extended an invitation to President El-Sadat, which President El-Sadat has accepted, to visit the United States during 1974.[10]

MUHAMMED ANWAR-EL-SADAT   RICHARD NIXON
Cairo, Egypt,
June 14, 1974.

[With Saudi Arabia, the United States had already established a structure of institutional relationships that paralleled and in some respects went beyond those now contemplated with Egypt. On June 8, immediately before his departure from Washington with the President, Secretary Kissinger had joined with Prince Fahd bin Abd al-Aziz Al Saud—a half-brother of the King, and Saudi Arabia's Second Deputy Prime Minister and Minister of the Interior—in an agreement that provided for the establishment of a

---

[10]President Sadat visited the U.S. Oct. 26-Nov. 5, 1975. Agreements signed during the visit included, in addition to the statement of principles referred to in note 8, an income tax treaty and agreements on agricultural commodities, health cooperation, and the "Treasures of Tutankhamun" exhibition. For documentation see *Presidential Documents*, 11: 1195-1200 and 1232-3 (1975), or (more fully) *Bulletin*, 73: 721-31 and 754-6 (1975).

Joint Commission on Economic Cooperation as well as a second Joint Commission to review programs already under way in connection with the modernization of the Saudi armed forces.[11] As with Iran, the developing military relationship between the United States and Saudi Arabia was a potent counterweight to any strains associated with the continuing difficulties over Middle East petroleum exports and price policies. With most of the relevant technicalities already disposed of, President Nixon and King Faisal were left free to concentrate during the President's stopover on June 14-15 on the ceremonial aspects of an association that had developed over more than three decades. The spirit of the meeting, which produced among other things an unusually forthright declaration of political support for President Nixon, was well reflected in the concluding remarks of the two heads of state as the American visitor prepared to fly on to Damascus early on June 15.]

(16)   Remarks of President Nixon and King Faisal of Saudi Arabia at Riasa Palace, Jidda, June 15, 1974.[12]

THE PRESIDENT. *Your Majesty, Your Royal Highnesses, Your Excellencies, ladies and gentlemen:*

Once again, it has been my great privilege and pleasure to meet with Your Majesty, as well as with Crown Prince Khalid[13] and other members of the Saudi Arabian Government.

Our talks have been constructive and far-reaching, covering problems on the whole world. We have particularly directed our attention to, and have reviewed in detail, the momentous changes that are occurring in this area of the world, the Middle East.

While we both recognize that important steps have already been taken on the long road to permanent peace in this area, there is much that remains to be done in reaching our goal.

And the United States intends to persevere in its active efforts to achieve this difficult but great goal of a permanent and equitable and just peace in this area, and essential elements in the search for peace are the fundamental developments that we are witnessing in American relations with Saudi Arabia and with other nations in the Arab world.

The American and Arab nations are rapidly moving into an era

---

[11]Text of joint statement in *Bulletin*, 71: 10-11.

[12]Text from *Presidential Documents*, 10: 627-8. King Faisal's remarks are a translation from the Arabic. The spelling of Arabic names follows the official text.

[13]Crown Prince Khalid bin Abd al-Aziz Al Saud, brother of the King and First Deputy Prime Minister; became King following the assassination of King Faisal on Mar. 28, 1975.

of close cooperation and interdependence, an era unprecedented in the long history of our relationships. It is entirely fitting that one of the first manifestations of this new era should come in the relationships between Saudi Arabia and the United States, the two nations that have been closely bound by ties of friendship for more than three decades.

In exploring avenues of cooperation, His Majesty and I have focused in particular on the work of the joint commissions which were agreed to a week ago during the visit of His Royal Highness Prince Fahd and other senior Saudi Ministers to Washington. These commissions and the goals they represent hold rich promise for the future of Saudi Arabia and for the future of the entire Mideast.

And, Your Majesty, the United States intends to be Saudi Arabia's active and constructive partner in insuring the success of these goals.

His Majesty and I have also reviewed the efforts by the United States to assist Saudi Arabia in maintaining its defense forces. Our two nations are totally dedicated to peace. But to achieve that goal in this area, Saudi Arabia must have a level of security that is consistent with its role as a leader in this part of the world. If Saudi Arabia is strong and secure as it will be, we will enhance the prospects for peace and stability throughout the Middle East and in turn throughout the world.

As we conclude these talks after having met on several occasions before, I would say that today American ties with Saudi Arabia have never been stronger and have never more solidly been based than they are now. We have long been good friends, and our friendship which now develops into an active partnership will be further strengthened through active cooperation between us in the areas that I have described.

And, Your Majesty, on behalf of all the Americans traveling with me, I would like to express our grateful appreciation to you for the very generous hospitality you have extended to us and also to express appreciation to you for the gestures of hospitality and the counsel you have provided for Secretary Kissinger during his visit to your nation.[14]

And personally, I look forward to meeting you again when you next can plan a trip to the United States. I can assure you of a warm and friendly reception.

KING FAISAL. *Mr. President, Excellencies, distinguished guests:* It is a source of great appreciation to meet with you again, Mr.

[14]Secretary Kissinger had last visited Riyadh on May 9; cf. *Bulletin*, 70: 683-6.

President, only this time in our country, and to receive you so warmly as you may have seen, so genuinely, on the part of the people and the Government of Saudi Arabia.

We greatly appreciate, Mr. President, your genuine expressions of friendship and solidarity and cooperation between our two countries. We have no doubt whatsoever that everybody who is genuine and who knows us well, both sides of us, is absolutely assured of our agreeing with you fully about the strengthening and deepening of our relations.

And as I have mentioned to you, Mr. President, I have the conviction that all our Arab brethren are desirous of and are seriously looking forward to improve the relations that bind them to the United States of America in ties of friendship and respect.

It is our sincere hope that all the problems and the blemishes that seem to mar the relationship between the United States of America and some Arab countries will be removed so that the clear waters will go back to their natural course.

We are fully confident in the efficacy of Your Excellency's endeavors to remove all these problems and blemishes so that we can once again, the Arab world and the United States of America, be very close and deep friends.

But what is very important is that our friends in the United States of America be themselves wise enough to stand behind you, to rally around you, Mr. President, in your noble efforts, almost unprecedented in the history of mankind, the efforts aiming at securing peace and justice in the world.

It goes without saying that in addition to our professions, genuine professions of friendship between us, and our desires to strengthen the ties, there is no doubt that our ultimate objectives, both you and us, are in the same direction, namely aiming at securing peace, justice, stability, and prosperity to the whole world.

And anybody who stands against you, Mr. President, in the United States of America or outside the United States of America, or stands against us, your friends in this part of the world, obviously has one aim in mind, namely that of causing the splintering of the world, the wrong polarization of the world, the bringing about of mischief, which would not be conducive to tranquillity and peace in the world.

Therefore, we beseech Almighty God to lend his help to us and to you so that we both can go hand in hand, shoulder to shoulder in pursuance of the noble aims that we both share, namely those of peace, justice, and prosperity in the world.

And we sincerely hope that God will grant us success to our joint efforts in reaching those noble aims for all peoples of the world.

I would like to assure you, Mr. President, that for our part, we will pursue, realize, and carry out every item that we have agreed upon, both sides, between Dr. Kissinger, and his Royal Highness Prince Fahd, between the American side and the Saudi side in the fields of cooperation.

And I would like to reiterate my thanks and gratification at your having taken the trouble to grace us with this very kind and most welcome visit and certainly beseech Almighty God to grant you continued success in your noble endeavors.

Thank you.

[A more temperate reception awaited the presidential party in Syria, where President Assad had only recently overcome his objections to American policy sufficiently to agree to a temporary disengagement on the Golan Heights. Apart from its "get-acquainted" aspect, the most definite result of the visit was an agreement on the immediate resumption of diplomatic relations, which had been broken off by Syria in 1967. Other matters of mutual interest were lightly touched upon in remarks by the two Presidents preceding Mr. Nixon's departure for Tel Aviv on June 16.]

(17)   Remarks of President Nixon and President Hafez al-Assad of the Syrian Arab Republic at the Presidential Palace, Damascus, June 16, 1974.[15]

PRESIDENT ASAD. It was a good opportunity to receive in Damascus Mr. Richard Nixon, the President of the United States of America, since his visit afforded us the opportunity to exchange views on matters concerning our bilateral relations and the Middle East issue. Many values of civilization and humanity link the American people and the Syrian-Arab people. It is natural that the American citizens of Syrian descent form one of the bridges of understanding that would pave the way for a new phase in relations between our two peoples, relations based on the mutual interests and the respect of each side for the independence and sovereignty of the other side.

We welcome the participation of the United States of America in the Damascus International Fair this year. We declare our readiness for conducting a dialog to consolidate friendship between the peoples of both countries and to establish ties of cooperation in the educational and economic fields so as to serve the interests of both sides.

[15]Text from *Presidential Documents*, 10: 681-2. President Assad's remarks are a translation from the Arabic. The spelling of Arabic names follows the official text.

The Syrian Arab Republic extends thanks to President Nixon for the constructive efforts which the United States of America exerted for reaching an agreement on the disengagement of forces on the Golan Heights. The Syrian Arab Republic declares its readiness to pursue its sincere and constructive cooperation with the Government of the United States of America for laying down the firm basis for a just and lasting peace in the Middle East region.

The agreement of the disengagement of forces and our understanding constitutes a first step towards and an integral part of the comprehensive just settlement of the issue. Such a settlement cannot be reached without Israel's withdrawal from all the occupied Arab territories and the securing of the national rights of the Palestinian people in conformity with our understanding of Security Council Resolution Number 338 of October 22, 1973, this understanding which we communicated to the United Nations in due time.

We are dedicating our utmost efforts for achieving a just and lasting peace in our region. We consider this peace an essential condition for the stability of international peace and security. We believe that peace in any region cannot be consolidated if the people of that region is robbed of his basic rights that are recognized under the Charter of the United Nations and its resolutions.

President Nixon and I have agreed to consolidate dialog and cooperation between our two countries for achieving a just and lasting peace in our region and in the world.

We also agreed to enhance the relations between our countries in all fields.

Finally, we have agreed that diplomatic relations between our two countries be restored as of today at the Ambassadorial level.

Thank you.

PRESIDENT NIXON. *President Asad, distinguished guests:*

I join President Asad in expressing my pleasure that our two Governments are today reestablishing diplomatic relations. The American and the Syrian peoples have a long history of friendly relations, and we in America are proud to count on many persons of Syrian descent among our citizens.

We look forward now to an expansion in contacts and cooperation between the United States and Syria. President Asad and I have agreed that Ambassadors will be named within 2 weeks.[16]

In the many contacts which have taken place in recent weeks between the United States and Syrian Governments, in the course of

---

[16]Richard W. Murphy was nominated as U.S. Ambassador to Syria on July 30 and confirmed by the Senate on Aug. 7. Ambassador Sabah Kabbani of the Syrian Arab Republic presented his credentials to President Ford on Aug. 19.

the negotiations on disengagement, each side has made clear its respect for the independence and for the sovereignty of the other. I want to reaffirm that relations between our two countries shall be based on this principle of international law. I also want to take this opportunity to express my admiration for the efforts of President Asad and his colleagues, the efforts they have undertaken in the interest of peace. The United States will work closely with Syria for the achievement of a just and lasting peace in implementation of United Nations Security Council Resolution 338—a peace which will bring a new era of growth, and prosperity, and progress in the Middle East.

The renewed contacts between our Governments, and especially the intensive discussions leading to the agreement on the disengagement of the Israeli and Syrian military forces, have contributed markedly to a deeper understanding and improvement in the overall relationship between the United States and Syria and between our two peoples. President Asad and I consider this agreement a first step toward a just and lasting peace in this area.

President Asad and I have agreed our Governments will review and develop further concrete ways in which the United States and Syria can work more closely together for their mutual benefit. A senior Syrian official will visit Washington in the near future to discuss specific plans to achieve this goal.[17] In the general context of strengthening our bilateral relations, I have affirmed that the United States is prepared to resume educational and cultural exchanges. President Asad extended an invitation to the United States to participate in the Damascus International Trade Fair next month, and I have accepted this invitation with great pleasure on behalf of the United States.

I have extended an invitation to President Asad to visit the United States at a time to be agreed, and I am delighted to announce that he has accepted this invitation.

[Speaking that same evening at a state dinner in Jerusalem, President Nixon attempted to allay whatever misgivings his Israeli hosts might have felt about his enthusiastic visits to Arab lands, his promise of nuclear aid to Egypt, and the known belief of his aides—and presumably the President himself—that Israel should by now be thinking of military withdrawals on the Jordanian as well as the Egyptian and Syrian fronts. "Under no circumstances," Mr. Nixon emphasized, "does the fact that the United States is seeking bet-

---

[17]Deputy Prime Minister and Foreign Minister Abd al-Halim Khaddam met with Secretary Kissinger in Washington on Aug. 22-25; cf. *Bulletin*, 71: 362-5.

ter relations with some of Israel's neighbors mean that the friendship of the United States and the support for Israel is any less."[18] Affirming "the continuing and long-term nature of the military supply relationship between the two countries," the President also pledged continued, long-range economic assistance and promised an agreement on the sale of nuclear reactors and fuel on much the same basis already contemplated with Egypt. These and other commitments were set forth in a joint statement issued in the names of the President and Prime Minister Rabin as the visit concluded on June 17.]

(18)   Joint Statement released at Jerusalem by President Nixon and Prime Minister Yitzhak Rabin of Israel at the conclusion of the President's visit, June 17, 1974.[19]

The President of the United States, Richard Nixon, visited Israel June 16-17, 1974. This is the first visit ever to have been paid by an American President to the State of Israel. It symbolizes the unique relationship, the common heritage and the close and historic ties that have long existed between the United States and Israel.

President Nixon and Prime Minister Rabin held extensive and cordial talks on matters of mutual interest to the United States and Israel and reviewed the excellent relations between their two countries. They discussed in a spirit of mutual understanding the efforts of both countries to achieve a just and lasting peace which will provide security for all States in the area and the need to build a structure of peace in the world. United States Secretary of State Henry Kissinger and members of the Israeli Cabinet participated in these talks.

Prime Minister Rabin expressed Israel's appreciation for the outstanding and effective role of the United States in the quest for peace under the leadership of President Nixon assisted by the tireless efforts of Secretary Kissinger and indicated Israel's intention to participate in further negotiations with a view to achieving peace treaties with its neighbors which will permit each State to pursue its legitimate rights in dignity and security.

President Nixon and Prime Minister Rabin agreed that peace and progress in the Middle East are essential if global peace is to be

[18]*Presidential Documents*, 10: 637. During his visits to Arab countries the President is said to have offered strong though unpublicized assurances that the United States would favor Israeli withdrawal to the frontiers of 1967 (Sheehan, *The Arabs, Israelis, and Kissinger*, pp. 132-3).

[19]Text from *Presidential Documents*, 10: 638-41.

assured. Peace will be achieved through a process of continuing negotiations between the parties concerned as called for by U.N. Security Council Resolution 338 of October 22, 1973.

The President and the Prime Minister agreed on the necessity to work energetically to promote peace between Israel and the Arab States. They agreed that States living in peace should conduct their relationship in accordance with the purposes and principles of the United Nations Charter, and the U.N. Declaration on Principles of International Law concerning Friendly Relations and Co-operation among States[20] which provides that every State has the duty to refrain from organizing or encouraging the organization of irregular forces or armed bands including mercenaries for incursion into the territory of another State. They condemned acts of violence and terror causing the loss of innocent human lives.[21]

The President and the Prime Minister expressed their great pleasure in the intimate cooperation which characterizes the warm relationship between their two countries and peoples. They agreed to do everything possible to broaden and deepen still further that relationship in order to serve the interests of both countries and to further the cause of peace.

President Nixon reiterated the commitment of the United States to the long-term security of Israel and to the principle that each State has the right to exist within secure borders and to pursue its own legitimate interests in peace.

Prime Minister Rabin expressed his appreciation for the U.S. military supplies to Israel during the October War and thereafter. The President affirmed the continuing and long-term nature of the military supply relationship between the two countries, and reiterated his view that the strengthening of Israel's ability to defend itself is essential in order to prevent further hostilities and to maintain conditions conducive to progress towards peace. An Israeli Defense Ministry delegation will soon come to Washington in order to work out the concrete details relating to long-term military supplies.

President Nixon affirmed the strong continuing support of the United States for Israel's economic development. Prime Minister Rabin expressed the gratitude of Israel for the substantial help which the United States has provided, particularly in recent years.

---

[20]General Assembly Resolution 2625 (XXV), Oct. 24, 1970.

[21]Three women had been killed on June 13 in a new terrorist incursion at Shamir, in northern Israel, which was followed by a series of retaliatory Israeli air strikes in southern Lebanon that began within hours of President Nixon's departure from Israel on June 17. A further terrorist attack on the seaside town of Nahariya on June 24-25 caused three additional Israeli deaths.

The President and Prime Minister agreed that future economic assistance from the United States would continue and would be the subject of long-range planning between their governments. The President affirmed that the United States, in accordance with Congressional authorization, will continue to provide substantial economic assistance for Israel at levels needed to assist Israel to offset the heavy additional costs inherent in assuring Israel's military capability for the maintenance of peace.

In the economic field, the President and the Prime Minister noted with satisfaction the effective working relationship between their governments at all levels and the depth of the relationship between the economies of the two nations. They agreed to strengthen and develop the framework of their bilateral relations. The primary goal will be to establish a firmer and more clearly defined structure of consultation and cooperation. Where appropriate, they will set up special bi-national committees. Both sides recognize the importance of investments in Israel by American companies, the transmission of general know-how and marketing assistance, and cooperation of American companies with Israeli counterparts on research and development. The United States Government will encourage ventures by American enterprises and private investment in Israel designed to increase Israel's economic growth, including in the fields of industry, power, and tourism. They agreed to begin immediately negotiations for concrete arrangements to implement such policy including in the area of avoidance of double taxation.

The President and Prime Minister announce that their two governments will negotiate an agreement on cooperation in the field of nuclear energy, technology and the supply of fuel from the United States under agreed safeguards. This agreement will in particular take account of the intention of the Government of Israel to purchase power-reactors from the United States. These will secure additional and alternative sources of electricity for the rapidly developing Israel economy. As an immediate step, Israel and the United States will in the current month reach provisional agreement on the further sale of nuclear fuel to Israel.

Prime Minister Rabin particularly expressed the view that the supply of oil and other essential raw materials to Israel must be assured on a continuous basis. President Nixon proposed that United States and Israeli representatives meet soon in order to devise ways of meeting this problem.

The President and the Prime Minister stressed as an important mutual aim the further encouragement of the fruitful links already existing between the two countries in the scientific and technical field, including space research. Special emphasis will be put on exchanges of scientists and the sponsorship of joint projects. With this end in view they will explore means to widen the scope and substance of existing agreements and activities including those pertaining to the Bi-National Science Foundation.

In the area of water desalination the two countries will expand their joint projects.

The President and the Prime Minister agreed to develop further the cultural ties between the two countries through exchange of scholars, students, artists, exhibitions, mutual visits and musical and other cultural events. In the near future, Israel will send to the United States an archeological exhibition depicting the Land of the Bible. The Israel Philharmonic Orchestra will visit the United States on the occasion of the American bicentennial celebrations.

The President and the Prime Minister noted with gratification the large number of tourists from their respective countries visiting both the United States and Israel and affirmed that they would continue their efforts to foster this movement. To this end, the two governments will resume negotiations on an agreement granting landing rights to the Israel national carrier in additional major cities in the continental United States.

The President and the Prime Minister discussed the plight of Jewish minorities in various countries in the spirit of the Universal Declaration of Human Rights.[22] The Prime Minister thanked the President for his efforts in support of the right of free emigration for all peoples without harassment, including members of Jewish minorities. The President affirmed that the United States would continue to give active support to these principles in all feasible ways.

The President was particularly pleased at the opportunity to meet with former Prime Minister Golda Meir, whose courage, statesmanship, patience and wisdom he greatly admires. The President expressed his satisfaction at the constructive cooperation between Israel and the United States under Prime Minister Meir's leadership which had led to the conclusion of the agreements between Egypt and Israel and between Israel and Syria respectively on the disengagement of their military forces.

In departing, President and Mrs. Nixon expressed their deep appreciation of the warm reception accorded to them in Israel and their admiration for the achievements of the Israeli people. They were deeply impressed by the manner in which the overwhelming problems of integrating many hundreds of thousands of immigrants of many various backgrounds and cultures were being successfully overcome. Convinced of the determination of this

[22]*Documents, 1948*: 430-35.

valiant people to live in peace, the President gave them renewed assurance of the support of the people of the United States.

The Prime Minister and the President agreed that the cordiality of Israel's reception of the President reflected the long friendship between Israel and the United States and pledged their continued energies to nurture and strengthen that friendship. To this end, the President invited Prime Minister Rabin to pay an early visit to Washington.[23]

[Jordan, the final Middle Eastern country on the presidential itinerary, was another long-time recipient of American economic and military aid. The assurance of continued U.S. support, with special reference to the maintenance of Jordanian military strength, was the central theme of Mr. Nixon's talks with King Hussein in Amman, the Jordanian capital, on June 17-18. More lightly touched upon in the joint statement at the conclusion of the visit was the delicate question of steps toward peace with Israel, an issue severely complicated not merely by the conflicting territorial claims of the two governments but also by the rival pretensions of the Palestine Liberation Organization (PLO) as a spokesman for the Palestinian people in Jordan and elsewhere.]

(19) Joint Statement released at Amman by President Nixon and King Hussein of the Hashemite Kingdom of Jordan at the conclusion of the President's visit, June 18, 1974.[24]

On the invitation of His Majesty King Hussein, President Richard Nixon paid the first visit of a President of the United States of America to the Hashemite Kingdom of Jordan on June 17 and 18, 1974.

During this visit President Nixon and His Majesty King Hussein discussed the full range of common interests which have long bound Jordan and the United States in continued close friendship and cooperation.

The United States reaffirmed its continued active support for the strength and progress of Jordan. The President explained to His Majesty in detail the proposal he has submitted to the Congress of the United States for a substantial increase in American military and economic assistance for Jordan in the coming 12 months.[25] The

[23]Prime Minister Rabin made an official visit to Washington on Sept. 10-13; cf. *Presidential Documents*, 10: 1130-31 and 1145-5, or *Bulletin*, 71: 468-71.

[24]Text from *Presidential Documents*, 10: 646-7.

[25]In his message of Apr. 24 on the foreign assistance program for fiscal year 1975, the President recommended that Jordan be allotted $100 million in military assistance grants, $77.5 million in security supporting assistance, and $30 million in military credit sales; cf. *Presidential Documents*, 10: 434.

President expressed his gratification over the efforts which Jordan is making under its development plan to expand the Jordanian economy, to give significant new impetus to the development of Jordan's mineral and other resources; and production, and to raise the standard of living for all its people.

The President expressed admiration for His Majesty's wise leadership and stated his view that effective and steady development would make a substantial contribution to peace and stability in the Middle East. The President promised a special effort by the United States Government to provide support in a variety of ways for Jordan's development efforts and in this regard welcomed the recent visit to Washington of His Royal Highness Crown Prince Hassan.

His Majesty emphasized the importance of maintaining Jordan's military strength if economic progress and development are to be assured.

His Majesty expressed the view that resources invested in maintaining the security and stability of the Kingdom are related to its economic growth, for without order and peace it is unrealistic to expect to marshal the energies and investment needed for economic progress. The President agreed with His Majesty and promised, in cooperation with the Congress, to play a strong role in maintaining Jordan's military strength.

His Majesty and the President agreed that they will continue to give U.S.-Jordanian relations their personal attention. In this context, it was agreed that a joint Jordanian-U.S. Commission will be established at a high level to oversee and review on a regular basis the various areas of cooperation between Jordan and the United States in the fields of economic development, trade and investment, military assistance and supply, and scientific, social and cultural affairs.[26]

His Majesty and the President have long agreed on the importance of moving toward peace in the Middle East. The President discussed the steps which have been taken in this regard since His Majesty's visit to Washington in March of this year.[27] His Majesty expressed Jordan's support for the very significant diplomatic efforts which the United States has made to help bring peace to the Middle East. His Majesty and the President discussed the strategy of future efforts to achieve peace and the President promised the active support of the United States for agreement between Jordan and Israel on concrete steps toward the just and durable peace call-

[26]The first meetings of the Joint Commission were held in Washington on Aug. 5-8 and 16-17; cf. *Presidential Documents*, 10: 1044-5 or *Bulletin*, 71: 362.
[27]King Hussein paid an unofficial visit to President Nixon on Mar. 12; cf. *Presidential Documents*, 10: 328.

ed for in United Nations Security Council Resolution 338 of October 22, 1973. The President has invited His Majesty to pay a visit to Washington at an early date. The purpose of the visit will be to hold further talks on the strategy of future efforts to achieve peace in accord with the objectives of United Nations Security Council Resolution 338. Further discussions of the details of the establishment of the joint commission will also be held. His Majesty has accepted the invitation and the date of the visit will be announced shortly.[28]

The President expressed his gratitude and that of Mrs. Nixon for the warm hospitality extended by His Majesty, by Her Majesty Queen Alia and by the Jordanian people.

[Returning to the United States by way of the Azores, President Nixon took time for a brief meeting with Portugal's newly inducted President, General Antônio de Spínola, that focused on "the importance that the United States attaches to Portugal's contribution to NATO and to Western security."[29] The position of the Western alliance, and its relationship with the Soviet Union, would be matters of continuing concern in the coming days as Mr. Nixon prepared for new encounters with the leaders of the Western nations in Brussels and with those of the Soviet Union in Moscow.]

---

[28]The visit took place Aug. 15-18; cf. *Presidential Documents*, 10: 1039-40 and 1044-5, or *Bulletin*, 71: 360-62.

[29]*Presidential Documents*, 10: 648; on Portuguese relations cf. Chapter 14 at note 9.

13. PLANS FOR INTERNATIONAL MONETARY REFORM

(June 12-13, 1974)

[Immersed in all the complications of Watergate politics and peripatetic diplomacy, President Nixon was in no position to give detailed attention to the vicissitudes of the international monetary system. Even at a much earlier period of the Watergate story, the President is known to have remarked to his then Chief of Staff, H.R. Haldeman, that the reported floating of the British pound on June 23, 1972 was "too complicated for me to get into"—and that, in his own words, "I don't give a (expletive deleted) about the lira."[1] And yet, as the President himself had pointed out on countless occasions of a more serious character, the struggle for a prosperous world economy and a stable, smoothly functioning monetary system was no less important in its own way than was the struggle for international peace. The crisis in international economic relationships that had developed since the latter part of 1973 had obviously weighed heavily upon the minds of others in the President's official family, however much the President himself may have been absorbed by the struggle for individual survival.

William E. Simon, as the President's most recent appointee to the exacting post of Secretary of the Treasury, was destined to be the key American participant in a series of meetings of financial authorities that took place in Washington during the second week of June, and would go far toward shaping the future evolution of the international monetary system as it continued its adjustment to the novel conditions wrought by the petroleum price breakthrough, the continuing worldwide inflation, and the deepening of global recessionary tendencies. The central responsibility for the planning of this adjustment had remained thus far with the International Monetary Fund's "Committee of Twenty," which, as noted

---

[1]White House transcript, as printed in *New York Times,* Aug. 6, 1974.

earlier, had met at Rome in January and at that time had recommended the adoption of a revised, "evolutionary" approach to monetary reform as well as a strict avoidance of harmful, unilateral trade and monetary measures.[2] Deputies of the Committee of Twenty, chaired by C. Jeremy Morse of the United Kingdom, had since continued their efforts, and had completed by early May a revised "Outline of Reform" that was to be considered by the full committee when it met again in Washington in June.

This sixth and final meeting of the Committee of Twenty, which took place on June 12-13 while President Nixon was in Egypt, was preceded by sessions of two other interested bodies: the Intergovernmental Group of Twenty-four, a leading proponent of developing country interests, and the so-called Group of Ten, which served as an informal caucus of the principal industrial countries. The most significant decisions of the week, however, were those that were taken or motivated by the Committee of Twenty itself and were set forth in the communiqué released at the conclusion of its meeting.]

(20) Committee of the Board of Governors of the International Monetary Fund on Reform of the International Monetary System and Related Issues (Committee of Twenty): Communiqué of the sixth and final meeting, held in Washington June 12-13, 1974.[3]

1. The Committee of the Board of Governors of the International Monetary Fund on Reform of the International Monetary System and Related Issues (the Committee of 20) held its sixth and final meeting in Washington on June 12-13, 1974, under the chairmanship of Mr. Ali Wardhana, Minister of Finance of Indonesia. Mr. H. Johannes Witteveen, Managing Director of the Fund, took part in the meeting which was also attended by Mr. Gamani Corea, Secretary-General of the United Nations Committee on Trade and Development, Mr. Frederic Boyer de la Giroday, Director of Monetary Affairs of the European Economic Community, Mr. René Larre, General Manager of the Bank for International Settlements, Mr. Emile van Lennep, Secretary-General of the Organization for Economic Cooperation and Development, Mr. Olivier Long, Director-General of the General Agreement on Tariffs and Trade (GATT), and Sir Denis Rickett, Vice-President

[2]Cf. Chapter 10 at note 1.
[3]IMF Press Release 74/32, June 13; text from *IMF Survey,* 3:178.

of the International Bank for Reconstruction and Development.

2. The Committee concluded its work on international monetary reform; agreed on a program of immediate action; and reviewed the major problems arising from the current international monetary situation.

3. The program of immediate action is as follows:

(a) Establishment of an Interim Committee of the Board of Governors of the Fund with an advisory role, pending establishment by an amendment of the Articles of Agreement of a Council with such decision-making powers as are conferred on it.

(b) Strengthening of Fund procedures for close international consultation and surveillance of the adjustment process.

(c) Establishment of guidelines for the management of floating exchange rates.

(d) Establishment of a facility in the Fund to assist members in meeting the initial impact of the increase in oil import costs.

(e) Provision for countries to pledge themselves on a voluntary basis not to introduce or intensify trade or other current account measures for balance of payments purposes without a finding by the Fund that there is balance of payments justification for such measures.

(f) Improvement of procedures in the Fund for management of global liquidity.

(g) Further international study in the Fund of arrangements for gold in the light of the agreed objectives of reform.

(h) Adoption for an interim period of a method of valuation of the SDR based on a basket of currencies and of an initial interest rate on the SDR of 5 per cent.

(i) Early formulation and adoption of an extended Fund facility under which developing countries would receive longer-term balance of payments finance.

(j) Reconsideration by the Interim Committee, simultaneously with the preparation by the Executive Board of draft amendments of the Articles of Agreement, of the possibility and modalities of establishing a link between development assistance and SDR allocation.

(k) Establishment of a joint ministerial Committee of the Fund and World Bank to carry forward the study of the broad question of the transfer of real resources to developing countries and to recommend measures.

(l) Preparation by the Executive Board of draft amendments of the Articles of Agreement for further examination by the Interim Committee and for possible recommendation at an appropriate time to the Board of Governors.

These measures are described in more detail in the statement attached to this communiqué.[4]

4. Members of the Committee expressed their serious concern at the acceleration of inflation in many countries. They agreed on the urgent need for stronger action to combat inflation, so as to avoid the grave social, economic and financial problems that would otherwise arise. They recognized that, while international monetary arrangements can help to contain this problem, the main responsibility for avoiding inflation rests with national governments. They affirmed their determination to adopt appropriate fiscal, monetary, and other policies to this end. In the discussion Members of the Committee urged that the multilateral trade negotiations in the framework of GATT[5] should continue to be regarded as a matter of priority.

5. The Committee noted that, as a result of inflation, the energy situation, and other unsettled conditions, many countries are experiencing large current account deficits that need to be financed. The Committee recognized that sustained cooperation would be needed to ensure appropriate financing without endangering the smooth functioning of private financial markets and to avert the danger of adjustment action that merely shifts the problem to other countries. Particular attention was drawn to the pressing difficulties of the most severely affected developing countries. Members of the Committee therefore strongly emphasized their request to all countries with available resources and to development finance institutions to make every effort to increase the flow of financial assistance on concessionary terms to these countries.

6. In concluding its work on international monetary reform, the Committee agreed to transmit a final Report on its work, together with an Outline of Reform,[6] to the Board of Governors.

[The Committee of Twenty was not itself empowered to implement the "program of immediate action" set forth in paragraph 3 of its communiqué. Though some of its recommendations could be put into effect by the IMF's twenty-member Board of Executive Directors, others would have to await the decision of the Board of Governors at its annual meeting later in the year; while any revisions of the IMF's basic Articles of Agreement,[7] which dated from

---

[4]"Detailed Statement of Immediate Steps to Assist the Functioning of the International Monetary System," in *IMF Survey,* 3: 179-80.

[5]Cf. Chapter 10 at note 2.

[6]The text of the "Outline of Reform" is printed, with ten accompanying annexes, in *IMF Survey,* 3: 193-208. The main features of the reform, set forth in the introductory portion of the outline, are virtually identical to those included in the preliminary ouline of Sept. 1973 and printed in *AFR, 1973:* 395 n. 15.

[7]Articles of Agreement of the International Monetary Fund, opened for signature at Washington and entered into force Dec. 27, 1945 (TIAS 1501).

the Bretton Woods Conference of 1944, would necessarily take even more time. Even if the drafting of such a revision could be completed by February 1975, as the Committee of Twenty professed to hope, the subsequent process of approval and ratification by IMF member governments might possibly take years to complete.

Among such steps as could be taken immediately, four were announced by the IMF Executive Directors on the very day the Committee of Twenty completed its work:

1. A recommendation to the Board of Governors that called for the establishment of a twenty-member "Interim Committee of the Board of Governors on the International Monetary System," which would take the place of the Committee of Twenty and serve until a permanent and representative Council of Governors with decision-making powers could be established through an amendment of the Articles of Agreement.[8]

2. Adoption of a new method of valuing the IMF Special Drawing Right (SDR) on the basis of a "basket" of sixteen major world currencies, the U.S. dollar being assigned a weight of 33 percent and a daily rate for the SDR being calculated in terms of each of the sixteen currencies.[9] (The initial value of the SDR in terms of U.S. dollars when the system went into effect on July 1 was $1.20635; by the end of the year it had climbed to $1.22435.)

3. A recommendation to IMF member countries that they help maintain stability and order in exchange matters by adhering to the standards set forth in a special memorandum on "Guidelines for the Management of Floating Rates."[10]

4. Announcement of a decision to establish the proposed IMF "oil facility" to provide resources to member countries that needed help in meeting the balance-of-payments impact of increases in the costs of petroleum and petroleum products. Resources equivalent to about SDR 3 billion ($3.6 billion), it was announced, had already been offered—at 7 percent interest—by various IMF members, including Abu Dhabi, Canada, Iran, Kuwait, Libya, Oman, Saudi Arabia, and Venezuela.[11] (Completion of borrowing arrangements covering the period up to December 31, 1975 was announced August 22, 1974, and the first transactions under the new oil facility actually took place early the following month.)

---

[8]IMF Press Release 74/28, June 13, in *IMF Survey,* 3: 179.
[9]IMF Press Release 74/29, June 13, in same: 177 and 185.
[10]IMF Press Release 74/30, June 13, in same: 181-3.
[11]IMF Press Release 74/31, June 13, in same: 177 and 185-6.

A further recommendation of the Committee of Twenty, the establishment of an "extended Fund facility" under which developing country members could obtain longer-term balance-of-payments financing for periods up to three years, was put into effect in September.[12]

It should be repeated that all of these were provisional measures, aimed at ensuring a degree of order in the operation of the monetary system pending the expected amendment of the IMF Articles of Agreement. Though draft amendments to the Articles were already under consideration by the Executive Directors, the next formal moves in this complicated process would have to await the annual meeting of the Boards of Governors of the Bank and Fund in early autumn.[13]]

---

[12]IMF Press Release 74/43, Sept. 15, in same: 289 and 302.
[13]Cf. Chapter 22.

14. NATO'S TWENTY-FIFTH ANNIVERSARY

(Ottawa and Brussels, June 18-26, 1974)

[The situation of the Western alliance, in its internal aspect as well as its relationship to potential adversaries, had retained a prominent position in American policy calculations throughout this period when Washington was striving to adjust its thoughts and actions to the emerging challenges of the mid-1970s. The Soviet Union, whose actions of the later 1940s had brought about the conclusion of the alliance on April 4, 1949, still seemed to most responsible Americans to challenge the kind of international order to which the United States had remained broadly committed throughout its 198-year history. In equal measure, the fourteen European and North American nations associated with the United States as parties to the North Atlantic Treaty could still be viewed as an essential element of equilibrium not only in the Atlantic area but in the world at large.

Considerable changes had occurred within the Atlantic family since Dr. Kissinger, in his "Year of Europe" speech of April 23, 1973,[1] had urged the Western nations to draw up a "new Atlantic charter" to be adopted as one of the highlights of a projected European trip by President Nixon toward the end of that year. As noted earlier, Dr. Kissinger's original concept, which had particularly stressed the need for cooperation in political and economic as well as defense matters, had met with insuperable opposition on the part of France and other European Community members. But though the original timetable had long since been scrapped, there had remained a hope that agreement might eventually be reached on a pair of common declarations that might be promulgated at a heads of government meeting around the time of NATO's 25th anniversary in April 1974. One such declaration, dealing with security matters, would naturally emanate from NATO itself; the other, on

[1] AFR, 1973: 181-9.

political and economic questions, would have to be negotiated between the United States and the European Community countries.[2]

But even this watered-down plan had in the end turned out to be impracticable, and President Nixon had once again been forced to postpone his hoped-for ceremonial visit to Europe. ". . . The progress in developing declarations on the security front has gone forward on schedule," the President told a Chicago audience on March 15. "However, I regret to report . . . that on the economic and political front the progress has not gone forward, and we face the situation that, therefore, if the heads of government were to meet at this time, for example in the month of April, we would simply be papering over difficulties and not resolving them. . . . And until the Europeans are willing to sit down and cooperate on the economic and political front as well as on the security front, no meeting of heads of government should be scheduled."[3]

Though President Nixon's complaints did not elicit any unequivocal display of European willingness to cooperate on American terms, the subsequent changes of government in France and Germany undoubtedly made it easier for the United States to accept the fact that of the two proposed declarations, only the NATO one was likely to be completed in an acceptable form. Since President Nixon would in any case be traveling to the Soviet Union in June for a meeting with General Secretary Brezhnev and his colleagues, it was eventually decided that the NATO declaration, cast in the form of a 25th anniversary statement, should be reviewed by the North Atlantic Council at its regular ministerial meeting—to be held this year in Ottawa—and endorsed thereafter by the allied heads of government at a special meeting to be convened at NATO Headquarters in Brussels.

No less problematical than the relationships that obtained among the Western governments at this period was the inherently ambiguous situation that still prevailed between the Atlantic alliance and the Soviet-dominated Warsaw Pact, two rival entities upon whose interaction hinged the military fate of Europe and, in all probability, the world. Within the past year, important initiatives looking toward a further relaxation of tension in Europe had been set on foot with the commencement, after many years of preparation, of both the 35-nation Conference on Security and Cooperation in Europe (CSCE) and the 19-nation Conference on Mutual Reduction of Forces and Armaments and Associated Measures in Central Europe (MBFR). As would be noted by the NATO ministers at Ottawa, however, neither of these conferences had yet

[2]*AFR, 1973:* 352-4 and 367-9.
[3]Chicago question-and-answer session, Mar. 15, in *Presidential Documents,* 10: 327 (for further quotation see Chapter 10 at note 6).

got past the fundamental East-West differences on objectives and procedures that had been evident even before they first met.

The European Security Conference, after a ceremonial opening in Helsinki in the summer of 1973,[4] had duly entered upon its second or "working" stage at Geneva and begun detailed discussion of its assigned subject matter, divided for convenience into four "baskets" concerned respectively with (1) security in Europe; (2) cooperation in economics, science and technology, and the environment; (3) cooperation in humanitarian and other fields; and (4) "follow-up" measures. Western delegations to the conference seemed generally resigned to accepting the Soviet demand for formal recognition of the existing territorial frontiers in Europe. But any hope of actually winding up the conference by the summer of 1974, as had been persistently advocated by the Communist states, appeared to be ruled out by those same countries' resistance to Western proposals for broadened informational and cultural exchanges under the so-called "third basket."

The separate East-West talks on mutual force reduction, initiated at Vienna in October 1973,[5] had encountered disagreements that could prove even more intractable. The participating Western governments, whose overall aim was defined in terms of the achievement of "a more stable military balance at lower levels of forces in Central Europe while maintaining undiminished security for all parties," had proposed that their Communist opponents' advantage in manpower and equipment—currently reckoned at 150,000 men and about 10,000 tanks—should be gradually eliminated by working toward a common ceiling for ground force manpower and, in the first phase, reducing both U.S. and Soviet ground forces as well as diminishing the existing disparity in tank strength. The Eastern side, however, had appeared determined to maintain its numerical advantage and had instead proposed a three-stage plan involving the reduction of *all* forces—ground, air, and nuclear—on both sides by equal numbers or percentages.[6] The prospects of transcending this impasse did not seem greatly improved by the offer of the Warsaw Pact nations—renewed at a meeting of the Political Consultative Committee in Warsaw on April 17-18— to disband the Warsaw Pact organization simultaneously with a disbandment of NATO.[7]

What gave their attitude its slightly ominous aspect were the numerous indications that the U.S.S.R. and its allies, far from be-

[4]For background see *AFR, 1973:* 285-8 and 291-8.
[5]Background in same: 285-7, 552-3 and 557-63.
[6]News conference statement by Ambassador Bryan E. Quarles van Ufford of the Netherlands, Apr. 10, in *NATO Letter,* June 1974: 29-32.
[7]*Documents on Disarmament, 1974*: 89.

ing content with their existing military preponderance, were currently engaged in increasing it still further and in enhancing their military readiness both in Europe and in adjacent areas. A sober appraisal of this trend was offered by NATO's Defense Planning Committee at a ministerial session held in Brussels on June 14, immediately before the Ottawa meeting of the North Atlantic Council:

5. Ministers noted with concern the current programmes for the expansion and modernization of Warsaw Pact forces in all fields; these provide the Soviet Union and her Allies with a military power far in excess of that required for self-defence. In particular they drew attention to the expanding capabilities of the Soviet navy which is increasingly being used in support of Soviet world-wide political and strategic objectives. They pointed out that such actions are difficult to reconcile with declared objectives of détente and disarmament and agreed that until assured détente is achieved through equitable and lasting agreements, it will be necessary to make continuing improvements in NATO forces to ensure a stable balance of military power as a necessary premise for achieving a genuine and lasting détente.[8]

Another recent development that would be much on the minds of the NATO Council representatives in Ottawa was the political metamorphosis then taking place in Portugal, where the old-style "corporative" regime of Prime Minister Marcelo Caetano had been overthrown on April 25 by a military junta, led by General Antônio de Spínola, that was pledged to restore political freedom and reach a peaceful settlement of the colonial wars that had been in progress in Portugal's African territories for most of the past dozen years. Inaugurated as President on May 15, General Spínola had enlisted the aid of a coalition cabinet that included such prominent opponents of the former regime as the Socialist Mário Soares and the Communist Alvaro Cunhal. Thus it happened that Senhor Soares, as Minister of Foreign Affairs, was meeting with Secretary Kissinger and the other NATO Foreign Ministers in Ottawa at the very time that President Spínola was talking with President Nixon during the latter's stop in the Azores on his way home from the Middle East.[9]
As was customary, the views expressed by allied representatives at the North Atlantic Council meeting were summarized in a formal communiqué, accompanied in this instance by the final text of the long-pending Declaration on Atlantic Relations.]

[8]NATO Letter, Aug. 1974: 31-2.
[9]Cf. Chapter 12 at note 29.

*(21) Ministerial Session of the North Atlantic Council, Ottawa,
June 18-19, 1974.*

*(a) Communiqué issued at the conclusion of the meeting,
June 19, 1974.*[10]

The North Atlantic Council met in ministerial session in Ottawa
on 18th and 19th June, 1974.

In this, the 25th anniversary year of the Alliance, ministers
declared their countries' continuing dedication to the aims and
ideals of the North Atlantic Treaty.[11] Ministers emphasized the
desirability of developing and deepening the application of the
principles of democracy, respect for human rights, justice and
social progress. Today in Ottawa ministers adopted and published
a Declaration on Atlantic Relations.[12] This important declaration
reaffirms the commitment of all the members to the Alliance and
sets its future course in light of the new perspectives and challenges
of a rapidly changing world.

The Minister of Foreign Affairs of Portugal gave a report on
developments in his country since the change of regime and on the
efforts of his government to promote peace in Africa. Ministers
welcomed the evolution towards the establishment of democratic
and representative government in Portugal.

Ministers reviewed the state of East-West relations. They reaffirmed the determination of their governments patiently to pursue
policies aimed at reducing tensions and promoting greater
understanding and cooperation, not only between states but also
between people. But they recalled that real and lasting improvement in East-West relations calls for a constructive approach by all
concerned. At the same time, in the face of growing Soviet and
Warsaw Pact military power and the risk of renewed tensions the
Allies must, through the Atlantic Alliance, maintain their resolve
and capacity to defend themselves.

Ministers took note of recent developments in relations between
the Federal Republic of Germany and the German Democratic
Republic, including the exchange of permanent representations between the two states in Germany. They expressed the hope that
relations between these states will be further improved for the
benefit of the German people.

As regards Berlin, ministers discussed the further experience
gained in the application of the Quadripartite Agreement of 3rd

---

[10]Department of State Press Release 257, June 20: text from *Bulletin,* 71: 41-2.
[11]Signed at Washington Apr. 4, 1949 and entered into force Aug. 24, 1949 (TIAS
1964); text in *Documents, 1949*: 612-15.
[12]Document 21b.

September, 1971.[13] In doing so, they stressed the essential importance of the provisions of this agreement which stipulate that traffic between the western sectors of Berlin and the Federal Republic of Germany will be unimpeded. Ministers reaffirmed their conviction that progress towards detente in Europe is inseparably linked with the strict observance and full application of the Berlin Agreement.

Ministers reviewed developments in the Conference on Security and Cooperation in Europe. They reaffirmed the importance they attach to increasing security and confidence, to developing further cooperation between the participating states in all spheres and to lowering barriers between people. They noted that in the second stage of the Conference, which should make a thorough examination of all aspects of the Conference agenda, the work has advanced unevenly. Some progress has been made on certain issues, but much work remains to be done, as for example on such key questions as the improvement of human contacts and the freer flow of information, as well as confidence building measures and essential aspects of the principles guiding relations between states. Ministers expressed their governments' determination to pursue the negotiations patiently and constructively in a continuing search for balanced and substantial results acceptable to all participating states. They considered that, to bring the second stage to its conclusion, these results need to be achieved in the various fields of the program of work established by the Foreign Ministers at the first stage of the Conference in Helsinki.

Ministers reviewed developments in the Middle East since their last meeting. They welcomed the recent progress achieved, in particular the disengagement of Syrian and Israeli forces. They affirmed the support of their governments for the relevant resolutions of the United Nations Security Council and for all endeavors directed towards a just and lasting settlement bringing peace to the area; they also welcomed the contributions made by allied governments to UN peace-keeping activities. Ministers took note of the report by the Council in Permanent Session on the situation in the Mediterranean prepared on their instructions. They invited the Council in Permanent Session to continue to keep the situation under review and to report further.

Ministers representing countries which participate in NATO's integrated defense program[14] reviewed the conduct of the negotiations on Mutual and Balanced Force Reductions. These ministers continue to believe that mutual and balanced force reductions achieved through allied solidarity would contribute to the lessening

[13]Excerpt in *AFR, 1971*: 166-9.
[14]In principle, all allied countries except France.

of tensions in Europe and to a more stable peace. They expressed satisfaction at the results so far reached in the continuing consultations in the Council in Permanent Session on questions of objectives and policy. They instructed the Council to continue this work. These ministers noted that the current round of negotiations is proceeding in a businesslike way. They expressed their determination to persist in their efforts to bring the negotiations to a satisfactory conclusion. They recalled that the general objective of the negotiations is to contribute to a more stable relationship at a lower level of forces with the security of all parties undiminished. This objective should be achieved by establishing approximate parity between the two sides in the form of a common ceiling for overall ground force manpower on each side in the area of reductions, taking into account combat capability. These ministers reiterated that a first phase agreement providing for the reduction of United States and Soviet ground forces would be an important initial step forward towards that objective.

In reaffirming their conviction that reductions of allied forces in Europe should take place only within the context of an East-West agreement, these ministers referred to the statements contained in paragraph 4 of the Communique of the Defense Planning Committee in Ministerial Session issued on 14th June, 1974.[15]

Ministers expressed appreciation for continuing consultations on developments with respect to the SALT negotiations. They noted with satisfaction the efforts undertaken by the United States towards limitations of strategic arms and expressed the hope that these efforts would lead to satisfactory results.

The next Ministerial Session of the North Atlantic Council will be held in Brussels in December 1974.[16]

---

[15]The passage in question reads:
"4. Ministers took note of the continuing United States-Soviet talks on the limitation of strategic armaments. They discussed the security aspects of the Conference on Security and Co-operation in Europe. Ministers also reviewed the status of MBFR negotiations now taking place in Vienna. On this last subject they reiterated the importance they attach to the principle of undiminished securtiy for all parties and they confirmed that the fundamental objectives of a more stable military and security situation at lower levels of forces can best be achieved by establishing in the area of reductions approximate parity between the two sides in the form of a common ceiling for overall ground forces. They thus reaffirmed their support for the agreed Alliance approach and noted with satisfaction that Allied representatives are engaged in the talks in a spirit of unity and cohesion. Individually and collectively Ministers reaffirmed the importance they continue to attach to the principle that NATO forces should not be reduced except in the context of an agreement with the East." *NATO Letter,* Aug. 1974: 31.
[16]See Chapter 34, Document 74.

(b) Declaration on Atlantic Relations, adopted by the Council on June 19, 1974.[17]

1. The members of the North Atlantic Alliance declare that the Treaty signed 25 years ago[18] to protect their freedom and independence has confirmed their common destiny. Under the shield of the Treaty, the Allies have maintained their security, permitting them to preserve the values which are the heritage of their civilization and enabling Western Europe to rebuild from its ruins and lay the foundations of its unity.

2. The members of the Alliance reaffirm their conviction that the North Atlantic Treaty provides the indispensable basis for their security, thus making possible the pursuit of detente. They welcome the progress that has been achieved on the road towards detente and harmony among nations, and the fact that a conference of 35 countries of Europe and North America is now seeking to lay down guidelines designed to increase security and cooperation in Europe. They believe that until circumstances permit the introduction of general, complete and controlled disarmament, which alone could provide genuine security for all, the ties uniting them must be maintained. The allies share a common desire to reduce the burden of arms expenditure on their peoples. But states that wish to preserve peace have never achieved this aim by neglecting their own security.

3. The members of the Alliance reaffirm that their common defense is one and indivisible. An attack on one or more of them in the area of application of the Treaty shall be considered an attack against them all. The common aim is to prevent any attempt by a foreign power to threaten the independence or integrity of a member of the Alliance. Such an attempt would not only put in jeopardy the security of all members of the Alliance but also threaten the foundations of world peace.

4. At the same time they realize that the circumstances affecting their common defense have profoundly changed in the last ten years: the strategic relationship between the United States and the Soviet Union has reached a point of near equilibrium. Consequently, although all the countries of the Alliance remain vulnerable to attack, the nature of the danger to which they are exposed has changed. The Alliance's problems in the defense of Europe have thus assumed a different and more distinct character.

5. However, the essential elements in the situation which gave rise to the Treaty have not changed. While the commitment of all

---

[17]Department of State Press Release 258, June 20; text from *Bulletin,* 71: 42-4.
[18]Cf. note 11 above.

the Allies to the common defense reduces the risk of external aggression, the contribution to the security of the entire Alliance provided by the nuclear forces of the United States based in the United States as well as in Europe and by the presence of North American forces in Europe remains indispensable.

6. Nevertheless, the Alliance must pay careful attention to the dangers to which it is exposed in the European region, and must adopt all measures necessary to avert them. The European members who provide three-quarters of the conventional strength of the Alliance in Europe, and two of whom possess nuclear forces capable of playing a deterrent role of their own contributing to the overall strengthening of the deterrence of the Alliance, undertake to make the necessary contribution to maintain the common defense at a level capable of deterring and if necessary repelling all actions directed against the independence and territorial integrity of the members of the Alliance.

7. The United States, for its part, reaffirms its determination not to accept any situation which would expose its Allies to external political or military pressure likely to deprive them of their freedom, and states its resolve, together with its Allies, to maintain forces in Europe at the level required to sustain the credibility of the strategy of deterrence and to maintain the capacity to defend the North Atlantic area should deterrence fail.

8. In this connection the member states of the Alliance affirm that as the ultimate purpose of any defense policy is to deny to a potential adversary the objectives he seeks to attain through an armed conflict, all necessary forces would be used for this purpose. Therefore, while reaffirming that a major aim of their policies is to seek agreements that will reduce the risk of war, they also state that such agreements will not limit their freedom to use all forces at their disposal for the common defense in case of attack. Indeed, they are convinced that their determination to do so continues to be the best assurance that war in all its forms will be prevented.

9. All members of the Alliance agree that the continued presence of Canadian and substantial US forces in Europe plays an irreplaceable role in the defense of North America as well as of Europe. Similarly the substantial forces of the European Allies serve to defend Europe and North America as well. It is also recognized that the further progress towards unity, which the member states of the European Community are determined to make, should in due course have a beneficial effect on the contribution to the common defense of the Alliance of those of them who belong to it. Moreover, the contributions made by members of the Alliance to the preservation of international security and world peace are recognized to be of great importance.

10. The members of the Alliance consider that the will to com-

bine their efforts to ensure their common defense obliges them to maintain and improve the efficiency of their forces and that each should undertake, according to the role that it has assumed in the structure of the Alliance, its proper share of the burden of maintaining the security of all. Conversely, they take the view that in the course of current or future negotiations nothing must be accepted which could diminish this security.

11. The Allies are convinced that the fulfilment of their common aims requires the maintenance of close consultation, cooperation and mutual trust, thus fostering the conditions necessary for defense and favorable for detente, which are complementary. In the spirit of the friendship, equality and solidarity which characterize their relationships, they are firmly resolved to keep each other fully informed and to strengthen the practice of frank and timely consultations by all means which may be appropriate on matters relating to their common interests as members of the Alliance, bearing in mind that these interests can be affected by events in other areas of the world. They wish also to ensure that their essential security relationship is supported by harmonious political and economic relations. In particular they will work to remove sources of conflict between their economic policies and to encourage economic cooperation with one another.

12. They recall that they have proclaimed their dedication to the principles of democracy, respect for human rights, justice and social progress, which are the fruits of their shared spiritual heritage and they declare their intention to develop and deepen the application of these principles in their countries. Since these principles, by their very nature, forbid any recourse to methods incompatible with the promotion of world peace, they reaffirm that the efforts which they make to preserve their independence, to maintain their security and to improve the living standards of their peoples exclude all forms of aggression against anyone, are not directed against any other country, and are designed to bring about the general improvement of international relations. In Europe, their objective continues to be the pursuit of understanding and cooperation with every European country. In the world at large, each Allied country recognizes the duty to help the developing countries. It is in the interest of all that every country benefit from technical and economic progress in an open and equitable world system.

13. They recognize that the cohesion of the Alliance has found expression not only in cooperation among their governments, but also in the free exchange of views among the elected representatives of the peoples of the Alliance. Accordingly, they declare their support for the strengthening of links among Parliamentarians.

14. The members of the Alliance rededicate themselves to the aims and ideals of the North Atlantic Treaty during this year of the twenty-fifth anniversary of its signature. The member nations look to the future, confident that the vitality and creativity of their peoples are commensurate with the challenges which confront them. They declare their conviction that the North Atlantic Alliance continues to serve as an essential element in the lasting structure of peace they are determined to build.

["So far as the United States is concerned," Secretary Kissinger told an Ottawa news conference shortly after the NATO meeting,[19] "we look at this declaration as an expression by the free countries of the Atlantic area that they will gear their policies to the new realities—that they recognize their destiny as common in the next quarter of a century, as it has been in the last quarter of a century." Reminded that his original conception had called for a common expression that would involve not only the NATO powers but also the European Community states and even Japan, Dr. Kissinger stated: "We believe that this document takes care of the necessities in the Atlantic area, though we are prepared to have further discussions with the Nine when they feel ready to do so."[20] "With respect to Japan," he added, "the need to give Japan a sense of belonging to a structure larger than itself continues to be and will remain to be a concern of America's policy."[21]

Revealing incidentally that the United States was also contemplating a declaration of principles with Franco Spain,[22] the Secretary of State went on to elucidate the objectives that President Nixon would be pursuing on his forthcoming visit to NATO Headquarters in Brussels. "The principal purpose of the summit meeting

[19]*Bulletin*, 71:37-41.

[20]No common declaration with the Nine was worked out, the Foreign Ministers of the Community countries having limited themselves, at a meeting in Bonn on June 10, to the adoption of a flexible and pragmatic procedure for future consultations with the United States. (*Keesing's:* 26799-800.)

[21]A bilateral statement of principles was included in the communiqué issued by President Ford and Prime Minister Tanaka on the former's visit to Tokyo on Nov. 20; see Chapter 30, Document 65.

[22]Initiated and carried through entirely outside the NATO framework, the U.S.-Spanish Declaration of Principles was initialed July 9 and signed July 19 by President Nixon at San Clemente and Prince Juan Carlos, Spain's interim Chief of State during the illness of General Franco, in Madrid. Its text (*Bulletin,* 71: 231) particularly stressed the Spanish contribution to Western defense and the determination of the two countries to consolidate still further the bilateral defense collaboration they had initiated as far back as 1953.

to be held next week in Brussels," he explained, "is to give the President an opportunity to discuss personally with his colleagues at the heads-of-government level in NATO our plans for the [U.S.-Soviet] summit and our long-term expectations for Western policy. The President has not had an opportunity to have such a meeting in many years, and it seems to us a logical followup of this declaration [on Atlantic Relations] that he have an opportunity to exchange views with his colleagues before going to Moscow.

"Secondly," Dr. Kissinger added, "the purpose of the meeting—of this visit to Brussels—is to have a formal signing of this document [the Declaration on Atlantic Relations] which will give an adequate solemnity to its importance."

The ceremonial aspect in fact seemed uppermost throughout the presidential party's brief stay in Brussels. Beginning on the evening of June 25 with an airport welcome by Belgium's King Baudouin I and NATO Secretary-General Joseph M.A.H. Luns, it officially concluded—except for private conferences with allied leaders—with the next day's luncheon at the Royal Palace for the participants in the NATO summit. Among the leading statesmen of the alliance, none failed to attend except France's President Giscard d'Estaing and Canada's Prime Minister Pierre Elliott Trudeau. France was represented by its head of government, Premier Jacques Chirac; Canada, by Paul Martin, Government Leader in the Senate.[23] No detailed record of the June 26 meeting at NATO Headquarters was made public, but a summary of President Nixon's remarks was made available in Brussels by Press Secretary Ronald L. Ziegler.]

(22) Heads-of-Government Meeting of the North Atlantic Council, Brussels, June 26, 1974: Summary of the remarks of President Nixon as made public by Ronald L. Ziegler, Press Secretary to the President.[24]

The President was pleased and impressed this morning with the discussions of the North Atlantic Council. All of the delegates in various ways spoke of the vitality of the Alliance, of the continued need of a strong common defense while we pursue better East-West relations.

[23]For full documentation see *Presidential Documents*, 10: 728-35, or (more fully) *Bulletin*, 71: 166-73 and 196-205.
[24]Text from *Presidential Documents*, 10: 730-32.

President Nixon found the general harmony of views expressed in the NATO Council this morning most gratifying. He welcomed the support around the table to full and frank consultation on all issues in which the interest of the allies are involved.

President Nixon also noted with interest, as did others who attended the meeting this morning, the remarks of Chancellor [Helmut] Schmidt regarding the importance of economic problems that the NATO countries are facing. The President, incidentally, also referred to this matter, which I will get into in a moment, in his own remarks.

President Nixon appreciated the positive comments around the table as each representative spoke concerning the role that he had played and that Secretary Kissinger played in the Middle East negotiations and also the expressions of confidence and support for our policies in East-West issues on the eve of the Moscow summit.

The President began his remarks following Secretary Luns' opening comments at about 10 minutes after 10. He spoke for about 25 minutes. We will not provide a text of the President's remarks because this was, of course, a consulting session and a private session, but I will provide to you at this time the general framework of what the President said to the NATO Council and generally the President's views regarding the Declaration[25] that was signed today.

In President Nixon's remarks to the Council, the President, of course, welcomed the signing of the Declaration in this 25th anniversary year of the Alliance, stating to the Council that it lays the groundwork for another quarter century of Atlantic cooperation, solidarity, and security. And the President pointed out that the Declaration forms the foundation for even a brighter future.

The President pointed out that the Declaration signifies that as NATO enters its second quarter century, the Alliance stands stronger and more united than ever before.

In his opening remarks to the Council, the President made the point, which has been made before, that the world we face in 1974 is, of course, very different from the world of 1949. At that time, the President said, peace was in serious jeopardy and the sovereignty of many of the nations of Europe was in jeopardy. The prime need, the President went on to say, was for unity in the common defense so that a period of rebuilding could go forward.

Today, he said that the very success of NATO over the last 25 years provides the security for the pursuit of national, regional, and global interest, but there is no less a need for security and no less a need for unity in pursuing our common objectives.

[25]Document 21b.

Indeed, the President pointed out, it is more important than ever to keep before us the recognition of our common objectives, referring to the Alliance, as to reconcile our interests as individual nations with our interests as allies.

Again, referring to the document signed today, the President pointed out that it demonstrates recognition by all members that if we are to successfully pursue our individual national interests, again referring to the Alliance, then we must do so in essential harmony and, above all, remain united in the common defense of every member of the Alliance.

The President also discussed the significance of the Declaration signed today in the context both of his forthcoming visit to the Soviet Union and his recent visit to the Middle East.

The President, again referring to the Declaration, noted that the Declaration reaffirms the foremost purpose of the Alliance, that of assuring the common defense. He emphasized the importance of each Alliance member devoting the efforts and resources necessary to maintain NATO forces at the proper strength.

He said that for the United States part, that he would again, and did, renew our pledge that the United States will maintain and improve our forces in Europe if there is a similar effort by our allies, and the United States will not reduce forces unless there is a reciprocal action by the other side.

The President pointed out that reductions in conventional forces in Europe can have repercussions far out of proportion to the number of men involved and the amount of money saved. They can set into motion, the President said, a chain of reductions whose consequences could be tragic and went on to make the point that the price of peace is continued strength.

He said that defense and détente are essential to each other and that only by strengthening détente can we eventually reduce the defense burden our people must now support, of course addressing the NATO Conference and referring to the nations involved.

Beyond that, he said the United States is encouraged by the direction and pace of recent efforts, as reflected in the Declaration, to give fresh impetus to NATO's partnership.

In particular, he cited the recognition given to the importance of meaningful consultations to the work of the Alliance, and he indicated the United States' full preparedness to consult on matters of Alliance interest.

He pointed out and reiterated the position that Secretary Kissinger stated in Ottawa[26] and again recently in his press conference, that consultation should not be viewed as a legally binding obligation.

[26]Cf. Ottawa news conference, June 19, in *Bulletin,* 71: 38-40.

That is not the purpose of the Declaration; rather, it is to symbolize a spirit of cooperation within the Alliance which the United States hopes will grow into a recognition that no member of the Alliance should consider taking any actions or action affecting the Alliance without seeking the support and understanding of its members.

He went on to point out—and I am not directly quoting the President but paraphrasing—that while it is true that the legal obligations of the Alliance are confined geographically, events that occur outside the formal area of obligations can affect us all.

This is a point that Secretary Kissinger, as you recall, made in Ottawa, and the United States recognizes this reality and affirms today our determination to consult fully on all matters which affect the interest of the allies.

I call your attention again to Secretary Kissinger's comments and also the pool report last night where reference was made to this point.

The President also said—and this is recognized in the Declaration of our common defense and political association—that these elements of the common defense and political association must be sustained by cooperative and constructive economic relations.

He said that the United States will approach economic issues in a spirit of friendship and in the conviction that the common goal is to benefit all peoples and those of the world at large, including the less developed countries.

A few more concluding comments: The President in his remarks emphasized the importance of the Alliance to the efforts being made toward greater international peace and stability and in this context he cited the importance of the new Declaration to the current efforts being made to ease East-West tensions and to improve relations with the Soviet Union.

Western cohesion, the President said, provides the basis on which the policy of détente can be conducted in the common interest. He noted, for example, the opportunities to bring the arms race under control and to build a network of East-West cooperative agreements contributing to mutual restraint and expanded contacts between peoples and said that the meeting today of the NATO Council provides significant evidence of Western solidarity and forms a vital backdrop for the upcoming summit in Moscow.

In discussing the upcoming Moscow summit,[27] the President made reference, of course, to the extensive briefing that Secretary of State Kissinger provided to the Foreign Ministers in Ottawa and spoke in general and long-range terms about the summit. Addressing the summit specifically, the President told the Council that he

27Cf. Chapter 15.

felt there were three aspects to the Moscow summit. He said that we will exchange views on, of course, the major international issues, and that we will have an extensive review of the entire state of our bilateral relations. He said that he expects that a number of agreements will be signed in various cooperative areas and that there was difficult negotiating ahead in relation to arms control, but that he hoped there would be progress also in that area.

He discussed each of these categories, of course, in more detail than I am providing.

In reference to détente and what détente means to the Alliance and what détente means to the United States, he said that it gives us a chance to try to bring the nuclear arms race under control before it can get out of hand.

Secondly, he said it creates an environment in which problems ranging from energy to peace can be addressed outside the context of bipolar confrontation, and third, it builds up a network of East-West trade and cooperative agreements that should reenforce mutual restraint and may gradually ameliorate conditions in the East.

In discussing also the upcoming Soviet talks, the President assured the NATO Council that the United States would continue to consult fully and again made reference to the fact that Secretary Kissinger will return to Brussels on July 4 to consult with our allies.[28]

In discussing the Conference on Security and Cooperation in Europe and the mutual balanced force reduction and all other issues in which the interests of our allies are engaged, such as strategic arms limitation talks, he said that American positions will continue to be developed in full consultation and in concert with our allies. He made a point of emphasizing that we will never sacrifice the interest of our allies to achieve agreements.

He talked then, in concluding his remarks, about the Middle East and the recent Middle East trip. He pointed out that the recent crisis there and the first tentative steps toward its resolution have provided the clearest possible demonstration that all of us have a stake in maintaining peace outside our own boundaries, of course, referring to the countries present in the NATO Council.

He said that because of its unique position—referring to the United States—and the desires of the parties in the area, the United States must continue to play a central role and will continue to play a central role in the process of seeking realistic diplomatic alternatives to war.

He went on to say that at the same time there is no American intention of attempting to exclude anyone from the area, that we, the

[28]Cf. Brussels news conference, July 4, in *Bulletin,* 71: 225-7.

United States, recognize that our European allies have vital interests there and will wish to play substantial roles of their own, and we hope that our activities in the area, he said, can be coordinated so that we can work together for peace and economic progress.

Then, finally, in summing up, the President feels that this morning's session of the North Atlantic Council provided the President with the occasion to express the very great satisfaction of the United States with the new Declaration on Atlantic Relations which underlines the continuing strength, spirit, and unity of purpose of NATO at a time when the nations of the Alliance are facing major challenges and opportunities.

15. RETURN TO THE U.S.S.R.

(June 27-July 3, 1974)

[The principal objectives of the "Journey for Peace" on which the President was now embarked had been authoritatively listed in the informal talk that preceded his departure from Andrews Air Force Base on June 25:[1]

". . . The purpose of this summit meeting, as was the purpose of the other two—the first in Moscow 2 years ago,[2] and in Washington and in other parts of the United States last year[3]—is threefold:

—first, we expect to strengthen the bilateral relations between the two strongest nations in the world;
—second, we hope to develop areas of cooperation to displace confrontation in other critical areas of the world that might be those places where conflict could develop between the two great powers; and
—third, we hope to make more progress on a goal that we began to achieve and move forward toward in 1972, of limiting both the burden and also the threat of nuclear arms over our two nations and over the world generally."

Like all great goals, the President warned, the objectives he enumerated would be "very difficult to achieve." Their mere recital, in fact, appeared to suggest that there had been some lessening of expectations as compared with the exhilarating days of 1972 and 1973. On Mr. Nixon's previous visit to the U.S.S.R., in 1972, the two governments had not only reached detailed agreements for cooperation in a series of peaceful endeavors, but had concluded

[1]*Presidential Documents,* 10: 727.
[2]*AFR, 1972*: 61-78.
[3]Same, *1973:* 251-83.

two landmark accords growing out of the bilateral Strategic Arms Limitation Talks (SALT) and designed to apply the brakes to what had threatened to become a mutually annihilative strategic arms race. By the Treaty on the Limitation of Anti-Ballistic Missile Systems,[4] both powers had agreed to forgo a competition in the deployment of launcher sites for anti-ballistic missiles (ABMs) and to limit themselves to not more than two sites apiece. By the Interim Agreement on Certain Measures with Respect to the Limitation of Strategic Offensive Arms,[5] they had further undertaken to "freeze" their respective offensive missile armories (with certain specified exceptions) for a five-year period.

This "Interim Agreement" had been explicitly intended to serve as a stopgap that would limit the growth of the two powers' strategic offensive weapons systems while they continued the search for "more complete measures"—in other words, a permanent agreement—limiting strategic offensive arms. But by June of 1973, when General Secretary Brezhnev paid his return visit to the United States, it had already been evident that the road to a permanent agreement would be long and difficult; and the two leaders had to content themselves with a statement of "Basic Principles of Negotiations" in which they affirmed their objective of signing such an agreement in 1974.[6] By the spring of that year, furthermore, the prospects of arriving at a comprehensive, permanent agreement by the time of President Nixon's projected Soviet visit in June had begun to appear more than doubtful. Returning late in March from an exploratory trip to Moscow, in the course of which he had unsuccessfully sought to promote a "conceptual breakthrough" that might clear the way to a comprehensive agreement, Secretary Kissinger had intimated that the new summit meeting was unlikely to produce a full SALT agreement, even though it might well result in what he termed "a substantial agreement of a more limited sphere."[7]

Both technical and political factors had made their contribution to what was beginning to look to some observers like a slowing down of the entire détente process. New technological developments—particularly the advent of the multiple independently targetable reentry vehicle (MIRV) that was now or would soon be entering the armories of both powers—had im-

---

[4]Signed in Moscow May 26, 1972 and entered into force Oct. 3, 1972 (TIAS 7503; 23 UST 3435); text in *AFR, 1972*: 90-95.

[5]Signed in Moscow May 26, 1972 and entered into force Oct. 3, 1972 (TIAS 7504; 23 UST 3462); text in *AFR, 1972*: 97-101.

[6]Signed and entered into force June 21, 1973 (TIAS 7653; 24 UST 1472); text in *AFR, 1973*: 262-3.

[7]News conferences, Mar. 21 and Apr. 12, in *Bulletin,* 70: 353-4 and 457-8.

mensely complicated the task of controlling an arms race which, as Secretary Kissinger was fond of pointing out, must be addressed henceforth in its "qualitative" as well as its "quantitative" aspects. On neither the Soviet nor the American side, moreover, did there seem to be much disposition to delay the introduction of new weapon systems until a SALT agreement was in place. On the contrary, Defense Secretary James R. Schlesinger and other U.S. authorities at the Pentagon and on Capitol Hill were calling alarmed attention to Moscow's apparent determination to "exploit the asymmetries" of the 1972 agreement, and were vigorously advocating a corresponding enhancement of the U.S. strategic posture.[8] Arguments for and against a defense speed-up had been further complicated by an outbreak of controversy about the precise terms of the 1972 agreement and the possibility—repeatedly and vigorously denied by the Secretary of State—of "secret deals" that might have enabled the U.S.S.R. to exceed its nominal limits.[9]

Other aspects of the U.S.-Soviet relationship had been affected by the developments of recent months, particularly since the Yom Kippur War of October 1973. Observing the gradual deterioration of President Nixon's personal position, the Kremlin could hardly have avoided wondering about the policies of any successor. The Soviet leaders were not, presumably, unaware of the fact that their government was being excluded from all but the most nominal participation in current peacemaking efforts in the Middle East. Least of all, moreover, could they conceal their disappointment and irritation over the delayed fulfillment of the glowing economic promises exchanged at the time of President Nixon's earlier visit in 1972.

Central to the whole complex of U.S.-Soviet economic agreements concluded in that year had been the understanding that the American administration would recommend, and Congress would approve, the extension of nondiscriminatory (most-favored-nation) tariff treatment to Soviet products entering the United States; and, in addition, that normal trade credit for the financing of such Soviet exports would be extended through the Export-Import Bank. But Congress, despite repeated prodding by the Nixon administration, had shown itself decidedly unwilling to implement these undertakings at a time when the Soviet Government was attracting worldwide attention by its policy of actively discouraging emigration by its Jewish citizens, particularly to Israel. This issue had already delayed enactment of the basic trade legislation put

[8]Cf. extract from *Annual Report of the Department of Defense, FY 1975* (Mar. 4, 1974), in *Documents on Disarmament, 1974:* 8-54. For further discussion cf. Chapter 31 at notes 6-12.

[9]Cf. *AFR, 1972:* 97.

forward by President Nixon in April 1973 as an essential element in the program for multilateral trade reform under the GATT. As passed by the House of Representatives in December 1973, the proposed Trade Reform Act had specifically barred the extension of nondiscriminatory tariff treatment, or of U.S. Government credits or guarantees, to the U.S.S.R. or any other Communist country that restricted freedom of emigration.[10]

Persistence in this stand, Secretary Kissinger warned once again in testifying before the Senate Finance Committee on March 7, 1974, would not only be counterproductive from the standpoint of liberalizing Soviet emigration policy but would also call in question the U.S. interest in moving toward an improved relationship in other areas. The emigration situation, according to the Secretary of State, had recently shown at least a moderate improvement, with 33,500 Jews arriving in Israel during 1973 out of a total exceeding 81,000 in the 1969-73 period. "The issue," Dr. Kissinger emphasized, "is not whether we condone what the U.S.S.R. does internally; it is whether and to what extent we can risk other objectives—and especially the building of a structure for peace—for these domestic changes. I believe that we cannot and that to do so would obscure, and in the long run defeat, what must remain our overriding objective: the prevention of nuclear war."[11]

Although this key question remained unresolved at the time of the presidential visit, Mr. Nixon's exchanges with the Soviet leaders were marked by at least a superficial cordiality and, despite the hitch in regard to a SALT agreement, produced a number of secondary accords on arms control and other matters. In accordance with past precedent, the highlights of the presidential stay were listed in a final communiqué that was ceremoniously signed as the visit neared its end on July 3.]

(23) Survey of the Visit: Joint communiqué signed at a ceremony in St. Vladimir Hall of the Grand Kremlin Palace, Moscow, July 3, 1974.[12]

In accordance with the agreement to hold regular US-Soviet meetings at the highest level and at the invitation, extended during

---

[10]For background see *AFR, 1972:* 115-16 and 119-30; same, *1973:* 92-3, 421-3, and 617.
[11]*Bulletin,* 70: 323-5.
[12]Text from *Presidential Documents,* 10: 753-63. For additional documentation see same: 735-71, or (more fully), *Bulletin,* 71: 175-223. Narrative highlights will be found in Woodward and Bernstein, *The Final Days:* 222-8.

the visit of General Secretary of the Central Committee of the Communist Party of the Soviet Union L. I. Brezhnev to the USA in June 1973,[13] the President of the United States of America and Mrs. Richard Nixon paid an official visit to the Soviet Union from June 27 to July 3, 1974.

During his stay President Nixon visited, in addition to Moscow, Minsk and the Southern Coast of the Crimea.

The President of the United States and the Soviet leaders held a thorough and useful exchange of views on major aspects of relations between the USA and the USSR and on the present international situation.

On the Soviet side the talks were conducted by L. I. Brezhnev, General Secretary of the Central Committee of the Communist Party of the Soviet Union [CPSU]; N. V. Podgorny, Chairman of the Presidium of the USSR Supreme Soviet; A. N. Kosygin, Chairman of the USSR Council of Ministers; and A. A. Gromyko, Minister of Foreign Affairs of the USSR.

Accompanying the President of the USA and participating in the talks was Dr. Henry A. Kissinger, US Secretary of State and Assistant to the President for National Security Affairs.

Also taking part in the talks were:

On the American Side: Walter J. Stoessel, Jr., American Ambassador to the USSR; General Alexander M. Haig, Jr., Assistant to the President; Mr. Ronald L. Ziegler, Assistant to the President and Press Secretary; Major General Brent Scowcroft, Deputy Assistant to the President for National Security Affairs; Mr. Helmut Sonnenfeldt, Counselor of the Department of State; and Mr. Arthur A. Hartman, Assistant Secretary of State for European Affairs.

On the Soviet Side: A. F. Dobrynin, Soviet Ambassador to the USA; A. M. Aleksandrov, Assistant to the General Secretary of the Central Committee, CPSU; L. M. Zamyatin, Director General of TASS [Telegraphic Agency of the Soviet Union]; and G. M. Korniyenko, Member of the Collegium of the Ministry of Foreign Affairs of the USSR.

The talks were held in a most businesslike and constructive atmosphere and were marked by a mutual desire of both Sides to continue to strengthen understanding, confidence and peaceful cooperation between them and to contribute to the strengthening of international security and world peace.

I. PROGRESS IN IMPROVING US-SOVIET RELATIONS

Having considered in detail the development of relations between

[13]*AFR, 1973:* 283.

the USA and the USSR since the US-Soviet summit meeting in May 1972, both Sides noted with satisfaction that through their vigorous joint efforts they have brought about over this short period a fundamental turn toward peaceful relations and broad, mutually beneficial cooperation in the interests of the peoples of both countries and of all mankind.

They emphasized the special importance for the favorable development of relations between the USA and the USSR of meetings of their leaders at the highest level, which are becoming established practice. These meetings provide opportunities for effective and responsible discussion, for the solution of fundamental and important bilateral questions, and for mutual contributions to the settlement of international problems affecting the interests of both countries.

Both Sides welcome the establishment of official contacts between the Congress of the US and the Supreme Soviet of the USSR.[14] They will encourage a further development of such contacts, believing that they can play an important role.

Both Sides confirmed their mutual determination to continue actively to reshape US-Soviet relations on the basis of peaceful coexistence and equal security, in strict conformity with the spirit and the letter of the agreements achieved between the two countries and their obligations under those agreements. In this connection they noted once again the fundamental importance of the joint documents adopted as a result of the summit meetings in 1972 and 1973, especially of the Basic Principles of Relations Between the USA and the USSR,[15] the Agreement on the Prevention of Nuclear War,[16] the Treaty on the Limitation of Anti-Ballistic Missile Systems, and the Interim Agreement on Certain Measures with Respect to the Limitation of Strategic Offensive Arms.[17]

Both Sides are deeply convinced of the imperative necessity of making the process of improving US-Soviet relations irreversible. They believe that, as a result of their efforts, a real possibility has been created to achieve this goal. This will open new vistas for broad mutually beneficial cooperation, and for strengthening friendship between the American and Soviet peoples, and will thus contribute to the solution of many urgent problems facing the world.

Guided by these worthy goals, both Sides decided to continue

[14]A delegation of the Supreme Soviet led by Poliburo member Boris N. Ponomarev visited the U.S. Congress in May 1974 to inaugurate relations between the two legislative bodies.

[15]*AFR, 1972*: 75-8.

[16]Signed at Washington and entered into force June 22, 1973 (TIAS 7654; 24 UST 1479): text in *AFR, 1973:* 266-9.

steadfastly to apply their joint efforts—in cooperation with other countries concerned, as appropriate—first of all in such important fields as:

—removing the danger of war, including particularly war involving nuclear and other mass-destruction weapons;

—limiting and eventually ending the arms race especially in strategic weapons, having in mind as the ultimate objective the achievement of general and complete disarmament under appropriate international control;

—contributing to the elimination of sources of international tension and military conflict;

—strengthening and extending the process of relaxation of tensions throughout the world;

—developing broad, mutually beneficial cooperation in commercial and economic, scientific-technical and cultural fields on the basis of the principles of sovereignty, equality and noninterference in internal affairs with a view to promoting increased understanding and confidence between the peoples of both countries.

Accordingly, in the course of this summit meeting both Sides considered it possible to take new constructive steps which, they believe, will not only advance further the development of US-Soviet relations but will also make a substantial contribution to strengthening world peace and expanding international cooperation.

II. FURTHER LIMITATION OF STRATEGIC ARMS AND OTHER DISARMAMENT ISSUES

Both sides again carefully analyzed the entire range of their mutual relations connected with the prevention of nuclear war and limitation of strategic armaments. They arrived at the common view that the fundamental agreements concluded between them in this sphere continue to be effective instruments of the general improvement of US-Soviet relations and the international situation as a whole. The USA and the USSR will continue strictly to fulfill the obligations undertaken in those agreements.

In the course of the talks, the two Sides had a thorough review of all aspects of the problem of limitation of strategic arms. They concluded that the Interim Agreement on offensive strategic weapons should be followed by a new agreement between the Soviet Union and the United States on the limitation of strategic arms. They agreed that such an agreement should cover the period until 1985 and deal with both quantitative and qualitative limitations. They agreed that such an agreement should be completed at the earliest possible date, before the expiration of the Interim Agreement.

They hold the common view that such a new agreement would serve not only the interests of the Soviet Union and the United States but also those of a further relaxation of international tensions and of world peace.

Their delegations will reconvene in Geneva in the immediate future on the basis of instructions growing out of the summit.

Taking into consideration the interrelationship between the development of offensive and defensive types of strategic arms and noting the successful implementation of the Treaty on the Limitation of Anti-Ballistic Missile Systems concluded between them in May 1972, both Sides considered it desirable to adopt additional limitations on the deployment of such systems. To that end they concluded a Protocol[18] providing for the limitation of each Side to a single deployment area for ABM systems instead of two such areas as permitted to each Side by the Treaty.

At the same time, two protocols were signed entitled "Procedures Governing Replacement, Dismantling or Destruction and Notification Thereof, for Strategic Offensive Arms" and "Procedures Governing Replacement, Dismantling or Destruction, and Notification Thereof for ABM Systems and their Components." These protocols[19] were worked out by the Standing Consultative Commission which was established to promote the objectives and implementation of the provisions of the Treaty and the Interim Agreement signed on May 26, 1972.

The two Sides emphasized the serious importance which the US and USSR also attach to the realization of other possible measures—both on a bilateral and on a multilateral basis—in the field of arms limitation and disarmament.

Having noted the historic significance of the Treaty Banning Nuclear Weapon Tests in the Atmosphere, in Outer Space and Under Water, concluded in Moscow in 1963,[20] to which the United States and the Soviet Union are parties, both Sides expressed themselves in favor of making the cessation of nuclear weapon tests comprehensive. Desiring to contribute to the achievement of this goal the USA and the USSR concluded, as an important step in this direction, the Treaty on the Limitation of Underground Nuclear Weapon Tests[21] providing for the complete cessation, starting from

[18]Document 24.
[19]Cf. below at note 45.
[20]Done at Moscow Aug. 5, 1963 and entered into force Oct. 10, 1963 (TIAS 5433; 14 UST 1313): text in *Documents, 1963*: 130-32.
[21]Docement 25.

March 31, 1976, of the tests of such weapons above an appropriate yield threshold, and for confining other underground tests to a minimum.

The Parties emphasized the fundamental importance of the Treaty on the Non-Proliferation of Nuclear Weapons.[22] Having reaffirmed their mutual intention to observe the obligations assumed by them under that Treaty, including Article VI thereof, they expressed themselves in favor of increasing its effectiveness.

A joint statement was also signed[23] in which the US and USSR advocate the most effective measures possible to overcome the dangers of the use of environmental modification techniques for military purposes.

Both Sides reaffirmed their interest in an effective international agreement which would exclude from the arsenals of states such dangerous instruments of mass destruction as chemical weapons. Desiring to contribute to early progress in this direction, the USA and the USSR agreed to consider a joint initiative in the Conference of the Committee on Disarmament with respect to the conclusion, as a first step, of an international Convention dealing with the most dangerous, lethal means of chemical warfare.[24]

Both Sides are convinced that the new important steps which they have taken and intend to take in the field of arms limitation as well as further efforts toward disarmament will facilitate the relaxation of international tensions and constitute a tangible contribution to the fulfillment of the historic task of excluding war from the life of human society and thereby of ensuring world peace. The US and the USSR reaffirmed that a world disarmament conference at an appropriate time can play a positive role in this process.

III. PROGRESS IN THE SETTLEMENT OF INTERNATIONAL PROBLEMS

In the course of the meeting detailed discussions were held on major international problems.

Both Sides expressed satisfaction that relaxation of tensions, consolidation of peace, and development of mutually beneficial cooperation are becoming increasingly distinct characteristics of the development of the international situation. They proceed from the assumption that progress in improving the international situation does not occur spontaneously but requires active and pur-

[22]Done at Washington, London, and Moscow July 1, 1968 and entered into force Mar. 5, 1970 (TIAS 6839; 21 UST 483); text in *Documents, 1968-69*: 62-8. Article VI pledges further disarmament negotiations.
[23]Document 26.
[24]Cf. Chapter 33 at notes 11-12.

poseful efforts to overcome obstacles and resolve difficulties that remain from the past.

The paramount objectives of all states and peoples should be to ensure, individually and collectively, lasting security in all parts of the world, the early and complete removal of existing international conflicts and sources of tension and the prevention of new ones from arising.

The United States and the Soviet Union are in favor of the broad and fruitful economic cooperation among all states, large and small, on the basis of full equality and mutual benefit.

The United States and the Soviet Union reaffirm their determination to contribute separately and jointly to the achievement of all these tasks.

Europe

Having discussed the development of the situation in Europe since the last American-Soviet summit meeting, both Sides noted with profound satisfaction the further appreciable advances toward establishing dependable relations of peace, good neighborliness and cooperation on the European continent.

Both Sides welcome the major contribution which the Conference on Security and Cooperation in Europe is making to this beneficial process. They consider that substantial progress has already been achieved at the Conference on many significant questions. They believe that this progress indicates that the present stage of the Conference will produce agreed documents of great international significance expressing the determination of the participating states to build their mutual relations on a solid jointly elaborated basis. The US and USSR will make every effort, in cooperation with the other participants, to find solutions acceptable to all for the remaining problems.

Both Sides expressed their conviction that successful completion of the Conference on Security and Cooperation in Europe would be an outstanding event in the interests of establishing a lasting peace. Proceeding from this assumption the USA and the USSR expressed themselves in favor of the final stage of the Conference taking place at an early date. Both Sides also proceed from the assumption that the results of the negotiations will permit the Conference to be concluded at the highest level, which would correspond to the historic significance of the Conference for the future of Europe and lend greater authority to the importance of the Conference's decisions.

Both Sides reaffirmed the lasting significance for a favorable development of the situation in Europe of the treaties and agreements concluded in recent years between European states with different social systems.

They expressed satisfaction with the admission to the United Nations of the Federal Republic of Germany and the German Democratic Republic.

Both Sides also stressed that the Quadripartite Agreement of September 3, 1971,[25] must continue to play a key role in ensuring stability and detente in Europe. The US and USSR consider that the strict and consistent implementation of this Agreement by all parties concerned is an essential condition for the maintenance and strengthening of mutual confidence and stability in the center of Europe.

The USA and the USSR believe that, in order to strengthen stability and security in Europe, the relaxation of political tension on this continent should be accompanied by measures to reduce military tensions.

They therefore attach importance to the current negotiations on the mutual reduction of forces and armaments and associated measures in Central Europe, in which they are participating. The two Sides expressed the hope that these negotiations will result in concrete decisions ensuring the undiminished security of any of the parties and preventing unilateral military advantage.

Middle East

Both Sides believe that the removal of the danger of war and tension in the Middle East is a task of paramount importance and urgency, and therefore, the only alternative is the achievement, on the basis of UN Security Council Resolution 338,[26] of a just and lasting peace settlement in which should be taken into account the legitimate interests of all peoples in the Middle East, including the Palestinian people, and the right to existence of all states in the area.

As Co-Chairmen of the Geneva Peace Conference on the Middle East, the USA and the USSR consider it important that the Conference resume its work as soon as possible, with the question of other participants from the Middle East area to be discussed at the Conference. Both Sides see the main purpose of the Geneva Peace Conference, the achievement of which they will promote in every way, as the establishment of just and stable peace in the Middle East.

They agreed that the USA and the USSR will continue to remain

---

[25] *AFR, 1971:* 166-70.
[26] Same, *1973:* 459.

in close touch with a view to coordinating the efforts of both countries toward a peaceful settlement in the Middle East.

Indochina

Both Sides noted certain further improvements in the situation in Indochina. In the course of the exchange of views on the situation in Vietnam both Sides emphasized that peace and stability in the region can be preserved and strengthened only on the basis of strict observance by all parties concerned of the provisions of the Paris Agreement of January 27, 1973, and the Act of the International Conference on Vietnam of March 2, 1973.[27]

As regards Laos, they noted progress in the normalization of the situation as a result of the formation there of coalition governmental bodies. Both Sides also pronounced themselves in favor of strict fulfillment of the pertinent agreements.

Both Sides also stressed the need for an early and just settlement of the problem of Cambodia based on respect for the sovereign rights of the Cambodian people to a free and independent development without any outside interference.

Strengthening the Role of the United Nations

The United States of America and the Soviet Union attach great importance to the United Nations as an instrument for maintaining peace and security and the expansion of international cooperation. They reiterate their intention to continue their efforts toward increasing the effectiveness of the United Nations in every possible way, including in regard to peacekeeping, on the basis of strict observance of the United Nations Charter.

IV. COMMERCIAL AND ECONOMIC RELATIONS

In the course of the meeting great attention was devoted to a review of the status of and prospects for relations between the USA and the USSR in the commercial and economic field.

Both Sides reaffirmed that they regard the broadening and deepening of mutually advantageous ties in this field on the basis of equality and nondiscrimination as an important part of the foundation on which the entire structure of US-Soviet relations is built. An increase in the scale of commercial and economic ties correspond-

[27]Same: 39-52 and 58-63.

ing to the potentials of both countries will cement this foundation and benefit the American and Soviet peoples.

The two Sides noted with satisfaction that since the previous summit meeting US-Soviet commercial and economic relations have on the whole shown an upward trend. This was expressed, in particular, in a substantial growth of the exchange of goods between the two countries which approximated $1.5 billion in 1973. It was noted that prospects were favorable for surpassing the goal announced in the joint US-USSR communique of June 24, 1973, of achieving a total bilateral trade turnover of $2-3 billion during the three-year period 1973-1975.[28] The Joint US—USSR Commercial Commission continues to provide an effective mechanism to promote the broad-scale growth of economic relations.

The two Sides noted certain progress in the development of long-term cooperation between American firms and Soviet organizations in carrying out large-scale projects including those on a compensation basis. They are convinced that such cooperation is an important element in the development of commercial and economic ties between the two countries. The two Sides agreed to encourage the conclusion and implementation of appropriate agreements between American and Soviet organizations and firms. Taking into account the progress made in a number of specific projects, such as those concerning truck manufacture, the trade center, and chemical fertilizers, the Sides noted the possibility of concluding appropriate contracts in other areas of mutual interest, such as pulp and paper, timber, ferrous and non-ferrous metallurgy, natural gas, the engineering industry, and the extraction and processing of high energy-consuming minerals.

Both sides noted further development of productive contacts and ties between business circles of the two countries in which a positive role was played by the decisions taken during the previous summit meeting on the opening of a United States commercial office in Moscow as well as the establishment of a U.S.-Soviet Commercial and Economic Council. They expressed their desire to continue to bring about favorable conditions for the successful development of commercial and economic relations between the USA and the USSR.

Both Sides confirmed their interest in bringing into force at the earliest possible time the US-Soviet trade agreement of October 1972.[29]

Desirous of promoting the further expansion of economic relations between the two countries, the two Sides signed a Long-Term Agreement to Facilitate Economic, Industrial and Technical

[28]Same: 279.
[29]Cf. same, *1972:* 119-27.

Cooperation between the USA and the USSR.[30] They believe that a consistent implementation of the cooperation embodied in the Agreement over the ten-year period will be an important factor in strengthening bilateral relations in general and will benefit the peoples of both countries.

Having reviewed the progress in carrying out the Agreement Regarding Certain Maritime Matters concluded in October 1972 for a period of three years,[31] and based on the experience accumulated thus far, the two Sides expressed themselves in favor of concluding before its expiration a new agreement in this field. Negotiations concerning such an agreement will commence this year.

V. PROGRESS IN OTHER FIELDS OF BILATERAL RELATIONS

Having reviewed the progress in the implementation of the cooperative agreements concluded in 1972-1973, both Sides noted the useful work done by joint American-Soviet committees and working groups established under those agreements in developing regular contacts and cooperation between scientific and technical organizations, scientists, specialists and cultural personnel of both countries.

The two Sides note with satisfaction that joint efforts by the USA and USSR in such fields of cooperation as medical science and public health, protection and improvement of man's environment, science and technology, exploration of outer space and the world ocean, peaceful uses of atomic energy, agriculture and transportation create conditions for an accelerated solution of some urgent and complicated problems facing mankind.

Such cooperation makes a substantial contribution to the development of the structure of American-Soviet relations, giving it a more concrete positive content.

Both Sides will strive to broaden and deepen their cooperation in science and technology as well as cultural exchanges on the basis of agreements concluded between them.

On the basis of positive experience accumulated in their scientific and technological cooperation and guided by the desire to ensure further progress in this important sphere of their mutual relations, the two Sides decided to extend such cooperation to the following new areas.

---

[30]Signed and entered into force June 29, 1974 (TIAS 7910; 25 UST 1782); text in *Presidential Documents*, 10: 741-2 and *Bulletin*, 71:219.
[31]Cf. *AFR, 1972:* 119.

Energy

Taking into consideration the growing energy needs of industry, transportation and other branches of the economies of both countries and the consequent need to intensify scientific and technical cooperation in the development of optimal methods of utilizing traditional and new sources of energy, and to improve the understanding of the energy programs and problems of both countries, the two Sides concluded an agreement on cooperation in the field of energy.[32] Responsibility for the implementation of the Agreement is entrusted to a US-USSR Joint Committee on Cooperation in Energy, which will be established for that purpose.

Housing and Other Construction

The two Sides signed an agreement on cooperation in the field of housing and other construction.[33] The aim of this Agreement is to promote the solution by joint effort of problems related to modern techniques of housing and other construction along such lines as the improvement of the reliability and quality of buildings and building materials, the planning and construction of new towns, construction in seismic areas and areas of extreme climatic conditions. For the implementation of this Agreement there will be established a Joint US-USSR Committee on Cooperation in Housing and Other Construction which will determine specific working programs.

For the purpose of enhancing the safety of their peoples living in earthquake-prone areas, the two Sides agreed to undertake on a priority basis a joint research project to increase the safety of buildings and other structures in these areas and, in particular, to study the behavior of prefabricated residential structures during earthquakes.

Artificial Heart Research

In the course of the implementation of joint programs in the field of medical science and public health, scientists and specialists of both countries concluded that there is a need to concentrate their efforts on the solution of one of the most important and humane problems of modern medical science, development of an artificial heart. In view of the great theoretical and technical complexity of the work involved, the two Sides concluded a special agreement on

[32]Signed and entered into force June 28, 1974 (TIAS 7899; 25 UST 1604); text in *Presidential Documents*, 10: 737-9 and *Bulletin*, 71: 219-21.
[33]Signed and entered into force June 28, 1974 (TIAS 7898; 25 UST 1592); text in *Presidential Documents*, 10: 739-40 and *Bulletin*, 71: 221-2.

the subject.[34] The US-USSR Joint Committee for Health Cooperation will assume responsibility for this project.

Cooperation in Space

The two Sides expressed their satisfaction with the successful preparations for the first joint manned flight of the American and Soviet spacecraft, Apollo and Soyuz, which is scheduled for 1975 and envisages their docking and mutual visits of the astronauts in each other's spacecraft. In accordance with existing agreements fruitful cooperation is being carried out in a number of other fields related to the exploration of outer space.

Attaching great importance to further American-Soviet cooperation in the exploration and use of outer space for peaceful purposes, including the development of safety systems for manned flights in space, and considering the desirability of consolidating experience in this field, the two Sides agreed to continue to explore possibilities for further joint space projects following the US-USSR space flight now scheduled for July 1975.

Transport of the Future

Aware of the importance of developing advanced modes of transportation, both Sides agreed that high-speed ground systems of the future, including a magnetically levitated train, which can provide economical, efficient, and reliable forms of transporation, would be a desirable and innovative area for joint activity. A working group to develop a joint research cooperation program in this area under the 1973 Agreement on Cooperation in the Field of Transportation[35] will be established at the Fall meeting of the Joint US-USSR Transportation Committee.

Environmental Protection

Desiring to expand cooperation in the field of environmental protection, which is being successfully carried out under the US-USSR Agreement signed on May 23, 1972,[36] and to contribute to the implementation of the "Man and the Biosphere" international program conducted on the initiative of the United Nations Educational, Scientific and Cultural Organization (UNESCO), both Sides agreed to designate in the territories of their respective countries

[34]Signed and entered into force June 28, 1974 (TIAS 7867: 25 UST 1331); text in *Presidential Documents*, 10: 740-41 and *Bulletin*, 71: 222-3.
[35]Cf. *AFR, 1973*: 282.
[36]Cf. same, *1972*: 71.

certain natural areas as biosphere reserves for protecting valuable plant and animal genetic strains and ecosystems, and for conducting scientific research needed for more effective actions concerned with global environmental protection. Appropriate work for the implementation of this undertaking will be conducted in conformity with the goals of the UNESCO program and under the auspices of the previously established US-USSR Joint Committee on Cooperation in the Field of Environmental Protection.

Cultural Exchanges

The two Parties, aware of the importance of cultural exchanges as a means of promoting mutual understanding, express satisfaction with the agreement between the Metropolitan Museum of Art of New York City and the Ministry of Culture of the USSR leading to a major exchange of works of art. Such an exchange would be in accordance with the General Agreement on Contacts, Exchanges and Cooperation signed July [June] 19, 1973,[37] under which the parties agreed to render assistance for the exchange of exhibitions between the museums of the two countries.

Establishment of New Consulates

Taking into consideration the intensive development of ties between the US and the USSR and the importance of further expanding consular relations on the basis of the US-USSR Consular Convention,[38] and desiring to promote trade, tourism and cooperation between them in various areas, both Sides agreed to open additional Consulates General in two or three cities of each country.

As a first step they agreed in principle to the simultaneous establishment of a United States Consulate General in Kiev and a USSR Consulate General in New York. Negotiations for implementation of this agreement will take place at an early date.

Both Sides highly appreciate the frank and constructive atmosphere and fruitful results of the talks held between them in the course of the present meeting. They are convinced that the results represent a new and important milestone along the road of improving relations between the USA and the USSR to the benefit of the peoples of both countries, and a significant contribution to their efforts aimed at strengthening world peace and security.

[37]Same, *1973*: 283.
[38]Signed at Moscow June 1, 1964 and entered into force July 13, 1968 (TIAS 6503; 19 UST 5018); text in *Documents, 1964*: 125-38.

Having again noted in this connection the exceptional importance and great practical usefulness of US-Soviet summit meetings, both Sides reaffirmed their agreement to hold such meetings regularly and when considered necessary for the discussion and solution of urgent questions. Both Sides also expressed their readiness to continue their active and close contacts and consultations.

The President extended an invitation to General Secretary of the Central Committee of the CPSU, L. I. Brezhnev, to pay an official visit to the United States in 1975. This invitation was accepted with pleasure.[39]

RICHARD NIXON
    President of the United States of America

L. I. BREZHNEV
    General Secretary of the Central Committee CPSU

[In spite of obvious limitations, the most notable achievements listed in the summit communiqué were those concerning strategic arms limitation and the control of nuclear weapons. Admittedly the agreements reached were less impressive than those of 1972. Particularly on the key question of a follow-on agreement on the limitation of strategic offensive arms, the conferees could do little beyond reaffirming their mutual view that such an agreement should be concluded as soon as possible and, in any event, before the expiration of the Interim Agreement in 1977. (Expanding slightly on this theme, they also stated that the new agreement should cover the period until 1985 and should, as was obvious, deal with qualitative as well as quantitative limitations.)

A more concrete, if still limited, achievement was the signature by Messrs. Nixon and Brezhnev of the new Protocol to the 1972 Treaty on the Limitation of Anti-Ballistic Missile Systems. Under that treaty, as already mentioned, each of the two parties had been limited to a maximum of two ABM sites, one of which was to be centered on its national capital and the other on a single ICBM launcher site—in the case of the United States, the ICBM launcher site at Grand Forks, North Dakota.[40] As a practical matter, however, the United States had never been greatly interested in developing a large-scale ABM defense, provided the Russians refrained from doing so. Although construction of the Grand Forks ABM site was now moving toward completion, construction of the Washington site had not even begun. Under the following protocol, sign-

---

[39]Brezhnev did not visit the United States in 1975, but met with President Ford in Vladivostok on Nov. 23-24, 1974; cf. Chapter 31.
[40]*AFR, 1972*: 91-2.

ed on the final day of the President's Moscow visit, it was agreed that the United States would continue for the time being to limit itself to the one site at Grand Forks, and that the U.S.S.R. would similarly limit itself to a single site based on Moscow.]

(24) Limitation of Anti-Ballistic Missile (ABM) Systems: Protocol to the United States-Soviet Treaty on the Limitation of Anti-Ballistic Missile Systems, signed in Moscow July 3, 1974 and entered into force May 24, 1976.[41]

PROTOCOL
TO THE TREATY BETWEEN THE UNITED STATES OF AMERICA AND
THE UNION OF SOVIET SOCIALIST REPUBLICS
ON THE LIMITATION OF ANTI-BALLISTIC MISSILE SYSTEMS

The United States of America and the Union of Soviet Socialist Republics, hereinafter referred to as the Parties,

Proceeding from the Basic Principles of Relations between the United States of America and the Union of Soviet Socialist Republics signed on May 29, 1972,[42]

Desiring to further the objectives of the Treaty between the United States of America and the Union of Soviet Socialist Republics on the Limitation of Anti-Ballistic Missile Systems signed on May 26, 1972,[43] hereinafter referred to as the Treaty,

Reaffirming their conviction that the adoption of further measures for the limitation of strategic arms would contribute to strengthening international peace and security,

Proceeding from the premise that further limitation of anti-ballistic missile systems will create more favorable conditions for the completion of work on a permanent agreement on more complete measures for the limitation of strategic offensive arms,

Have agreed as follows:

Article I

1. Each Party shall be limited at any one time to a single area out of the two provided in Article III of the Treaty for deployment of anti-ballistic missile (ABM) systems or their components and accordingly shall not exercise its right to deploy an ABM system or its components in the second of the two ABM system deployment areas permitted by Article III of the Treaty, except as an exchange

---

[41]Text from TIAS 8276: 3-6. For further comment cf. Document 27 at note 58.
[42]*AFR, 1972*: 75-8.
[43]Same as note 4.

of one permitted area for the other in accordance with Article II of this Protocol.

2. Accordingly, except as permitted by Article II of this Protocol: the United States of America shall not deploy an ABM system or its components in the area centered on its capital, as permitted by Article III (a) of the Treaty, and the Soviet Union shall not deploy an ABM system or its components in the deployment area of intercontinental ballistic missile (ICBM) silo launchers as permitted by Article III (b) of the Treaty.

Article II

1. Each Party shall have the right to dismantle or destroy its ABM system and the components thereof in the area where they are presently deployed and to deploy an ABM system or its components in the alternative area permitted by Article III of the Treaty, provided that prior to initiation of construction, notification is given in accord with the procedure agreed to in the Standing Consultative Commission during the year beginning October 3, 1977 and ending October 2, 1978, or during any year which commences at five year intervals thereafter, those being the years for periodic review of the Treaty, as provided in Article XIV of the Treaty. This right may be exercised only once.

2. Accordingly, in the event of such notice, the United States would have the right to dismantle or destroy the ABM system and its components in the deployment area of ICBM silo launchers and to deploy an ABM system or its components in an area centered on its capital, as permitted by Article III (a) of the Treaty, and the Soviet Union would have the right to dismantle or destroy the ABM system and its components in the area centered on its capital and to deploy an ABM system or its components in an area containing ICBM silo launchers, as permitted by Article III (b) of the Treaty.

3. Dismantling or destruction and deployment of ABM systems or their components and the notification thereof shall be carried out in accordance with Article VIII of the ABM Treaty and procedures agreed to in the Standing Consultative Commission.

Article III

The rights and obligations established by the Treaty remain in force and shall be complied with by the Parties except to the extent modified by this Protocol. In particular, the deployment of an ABM system or its components within the area selected shall remain limited by the levels and other requirements established by the Treaty.

Article IV

This Protocol shall be subject to ratification in accordance with the constitutional procedures of each Party. It shall enter into force on the day of the exchange of instruments of ratification and shall thereafter be considered an integral part of the Treaty.[44]

DONE at Moscow on July 3, 1974, in duplicate, in the English and Russian languages, both texts being equally authentic.

FOR THE UNITED STATES OF AMERICA:	FOR THE UNION OF SOVIET SOCIALIST REPUBLICS:
(*Signed*): Richard Nixon	(*Signed*): L. Brezhnev
President of the United States of America	General Secretary of the Central Committee of the CPSU

[Completing the work of the summit in the field of strategic arms limitation, Secretary Kissinger and Foreign Minister Gromyko signed two protocols that had been worked out in the U.S.-Soviet Standing Consultative Commission set up under the 1972 ABM Treaty and Interim Agreement. One of the two, entitled "Procedures Governing Replacement, Dismantling or Destruction and Notification Thereof, for Strategic Offensive Arms," dealt with the dismantling or destruction of older, land-based ICBM launchers and older submarine ballistic missile launchers that were being replaced, under the terms of the Interim Agreement, by launchers for modern ballistic missiles on nuclear-powered submarines. The second protocol, entitled "Procedures Governing Replacement, Dismantling or Destruction and Notification Thereof for ABM Systems and their Components," set forth guidelines and procedures for dismantling or destroying ABM launchers in excess of treaty limits. The texts of these agreements, which contained specific information bearing on weapon characteristics, were not made public but were later submitted to the appropriate committees of the U.S. Congress.[45]

Of comparable importance to the ABM Protocol was the so-called Threshold Test Ban (TTB) Treaty that was likewise signed by Messrs. Nixon and Brezhnev on July 3, 1974. As a further step in the process of limiting nuclear weapon testing, begun with the 1963 Treaty on the Prohibition of Nuclear Weapon Tests in the Atmosphere, in Outer Space, and Under Water,[46] the new treaty would go at least part way toward satisfying the widespread de-

[44] Instruments of ratification were exchanged and the protocol entered into force May 24, 1976.
[45] Cf. Document 23 at note 19, and Document 27 at note 61.
[46] Same as note 20.

mand for a complete ban on nuclear weapon testing in all environments. Specifically, its terms bound each of the two parties to refrain, as from March 31, 1976, from carrying out any underground nuclear weapon test with a yield exceeding the rather substantial figure of 150 kilotons, equivalent to 150,000 tons of TNT.

Not even this liberal restraint would be effective, however, until such time as the two parties could negotiate a companion treaty fixing comparable limits for peaceful nuclear explosions (PNE). This necessity reflected the fact that, in the words of the U.S. Arms Control and Disarmament Agency (ACDA), "there is no essential distinction between the technology of a nuclear explosive device that could be used as a weapon and a nuclear explosive device used for a peaceful purpose." Negotiation of a PNE treaty was in fact commenced in October 1974 but was not completed until the spring of 1976, and it was only then that President Ford submitted the two treaties to the Senate with a request for its advice and consent to ratification.[47]]

(25) *The Threshold Test Ban (TTB): Treaty Between the United States of America and the Union of Soviet Socialist Republics on the Limitation of Underground Nuclear Weapons Tests, with Protocol, signed in Moscow July 3, 1974.*[48]

(*Not in force as of the close of 1976*)

TREATY BETWEEN THE UNITED STATES OF AMERICA
AND THE UNION OF SOVIET SOCIALIST REPUBLICS
ON THE LIMITATION OF UNDERGROUND NUCLEAR WEAPONS TESTS

The United States of America and the Union of Soviet Socialist Republics, hereinafter referred to as the Parties,

Declaring their intention to achieve at the earliest possible date the cessation of the nuclear arms race and to take effective measures toward reductions in strategic arms, nuclear disarmament, and general and complete disarmament under strict and effective international control,

---

[47]U.S. Arms Control and Disarmament Agency, *Treaties on the Limitation of Underground Nuclear Weapon Tests and on Underground Nuclear Explosions for Peaceful Purposes* (ACDA Publication 87; Washington: ACDA, May 1976): 1-3. The text of the Treaty on Underground Nuclear Explosions for Peaceful Purposes and its accompanying protocol, signed in Washington and Moscow May 28, 1976, appears in same: 5-14, and in *Bulletin,* 74: 802-12 (1976). Cf. also note 52 below.

[48]Text from *Presidential Documents,* 10: 751-2; for further comment see Document 27 at note 59.

Recalling the determination expressed by the Parties to the 1963 Treaty Banning Nuclear Weapon Tests in the Atmosphere, in Outer Space and Under Water[49] in its Preamble to seek to achieve the discontinuance of all test explosions of nuclear weapons for all time, and to continue negotiations to this end,

Nothing that the adoption of measures for the further limitation of underground nuclear weapon tests would contribute to the achievement of these objectives and would meet the interests of strengthening peace and the further relaxation of international tension,

Reaffirming their adherence to the objectives and principles of the Treaty Banning Nuclear Weapon Tests in the Atmosphere, in Outer Space and Under Water and of the Treaty on the Non- Proliferation of Nuclear Weapons,[50]

Have agreed as follows:

Article I

1. Each Party undertakes to prohibit, to prevent, and not to carry out any underground nuclear weapon test having a yield exceeding 150 kilotons at any place under its jurisdiction or control, beginning March 31, 1976.

2. Each Party shall limit the number of its underground nuclear weapon tests to a minimum.

3. The Parties shall continue their negotiations with a view toward achieving a solution to the problem of the cessation of all underground nuclear weapon tests.

Article II

1. For the purpose of providing assurance of compliance with the provisions of this Treaty, each Party shall use national technical means of verification at its disposal in a manner consistent with the generally recognized principles of international law.

2. Each Party undertakes not to interfere with the national technical means of verification of the other Party operating in accordance with paragraph 1 of this Article.

3. To promote the objectives and implementation of the provisions of this Treaty the Parties shall, as necessary, consult with each other, make inquiries and furnish information in response to such inquiries.

---

[49]Same as note 20.
[50]Same as note 22.

Article III

The provisions of this Treaty do not extend to underground nuclear explosions carried out by the Parties for peaceful purposes. Underground nuclear explosions for peaceful purposes shall be governed by an agreement which is to be negotiated and concluded by the Parties at the earliest possible time.[51]

Article IV

This Treaty shall be subject to ratification in accordance with the constitutional procedures of each Party. This Treaty shall enter into force on the day of the exchange of instruments of ratification.[52]

Article V

1. This Treaty shall remain in force for a period of five years. Unless replaced earlier by an agreement in implementation of the objectives specified in paragraph 3 of Article I of this Treaty, it shall be extended for successive five-year periods unless either Party notifies the other of its termination no later than six months prior to the expiration of the Treaty. Before the expiration of this period the Parties may, as necessary, hold consultations to consider the situation relevant to the substance of this Treaty and to introduce possible amendments to the text of the Treaty.

2. Each Party shall, in exercising its national sovereignty, have the right to withdraw from this Treaty if it decides that extraordinary events related to the subject matter of this Treaty have jeopardized its supreme interests. It shall give notice of its decision to the other Party six months prior to withdrawal from this Treaty. Such notice shall include a statement of the extraordinary events the notifying Party regards as having jeopardized its supreme interests.

3. This Treaty shall be registered pursuant to Article 102 of the Charter of the United Nations.

DONE at Moscow on July 3, 1974, in duplicate, in the English and Russian languages, both texts being equally authentic.

---

[51]See above at note 47.

[52]Following the signature of the PNE Treaty on May 28, 1976, the TTB Treaty and Protocol were submitted to the U.S. Senate on July 29, 1976 (Ex. N, 94th Cong., 2d sess.) and to the Supreme Soviet of the U.S.S.R. on August 10, 1976. Ratification was still pending as of the close of 1976.

FOR THE UNITED STATES OF AMERICA:
RICHARD NIXON
The President of the United States of America
FOR THE UNION OF SOVIET SOCIALIST REPUBLICS:
L. I. BREZHNEV
General Secretary of the Central Committee of the CPSU

PROTOCOL TO THE TREATY BETWEEN THE UNITED STATES
OF AMERICA
AND THE UNION OF SOVIET SOCIALIST REPUBLICS
ON THE LIMITATION OF UNDERGROUND NUCLEAR WEAPON TESTS

The United States of America and the Union of Soviet Socialist Republics, hereinafter referred to as the Parties,
Having agreed to limit underground nuclear weapon tests,
Have agreed as follows:

1. For the Purpose of ensuring verification of compliance with the obligations of the Parties under the Treaty by national technical means, the Parties shall on the basis of reciprocity, exchange the following data:

a. The geographic coordinates of the boundaries of each test site and of the boundaries of the geophysically distinct testing areas therein.
b. Information on the geology of the testing areas of the sites (the rock characteristics of geological formations and the basic physical properties of the rock, i.e., density, seismic velocity, water saturation, porosity and depth of water table).
c. The geographic coordinates of underground nuclear weapon tests, after they have been conducted.
d. Yield, date, time, depth and coordinates for two nuclear weapons tests for calibration purposes from each geophysically distinct testing area where underground nuclear weapon tests have been and are to be conducted. In this connection the yield of such explosions for calibration purposes should be as near as possible to the limit defined in Article I of the Treaty and not less than one-tenth of that limit. In the case of testing areas where data are not available on two tests for calibration purposes, the data pertaining to one such test shall be exchanged, if available, and the data pertaining to the second test shall be exchanged as soon as possible after a second test having a yield in the above-mentioned range. The provisions of this Protocol shall not require the Parties to conduct tests solely for calibration purposes.

2. The Parties agree that the exchange of data pursuant to subparagraphs a, b, and d of paragraph 1 shall be carried out simultaneously with the exchange of instruments of ratification of the Treaty, as provided in Article IV of the Treaty, having in mind that the Parties shall, on the basis of reciprocity, afford each other the opportunity to familiarize themselves with these data before the exchange of instruments of ratification.

3. Should a Party specify a new test site or testing area after the entry into force of the Treaty, the data called for by subparagraphs a and b of paragraph 1 shall be transmitted to the other Party in advance of use of that site or area. The data called for by subparagraph d of paragraph 1 shall also be transmitted in advance of use of that site or area if they are available; if they are not available, they shall be transmitted as soon as possible after they have been obtained by the transmitting Party.

4. The Parties agree that the test sites of each Party shall be located at places under its jurisdiction or control and that all nuclear weapon tests shall be conducted solely within the testing areas specified in accordance with paragraph 1.

5. For the purposes of the Treaty, all underground nuclear explosions at the specified test sites shall be considered nuclear weapon tests and shall be subject to all the provisions of the Treaty relating to nuclear weapon tests. The provisions of Article III of the Treaty apply to all underground nuclear explosions conducted outside of the specified test sites, and only to such explosions.

This Protocol shall be considered an integral part of the Treaty.

DONE at Moscow on July 3, 1974.

FOR THE UNITED STATES OF AMERICA:

RICHARD NIXON
   The President of the United States of America

FOR THE UNION OF SOVIET SOCIALIST REPUBLICS:

L. I. BREZHNEV
   General Secretary of the Central Committee of the CPSU

[A third, comparatively novel facet of current arms control efforts had to do with the potential dangers of environmental warfare, or the attempt to influence or modify the environment for military purposes. The desirability of joint steps aimed at preventing such abuse was recognized in the third of the major agreements signed by President Nixon and General Secretary Brezhnev on July 3, 1974.[53]]

---

[53]For further developments see Chapter 33 at note 9.

(26) Dangers of Environmental Warfare: Joint Statement Concerning Future Discussions on the Dangers of Environmental Warfare, signed in Moscow July 3, 1974.[54]

The United States of America and the Union of Soviet Socialist Republics:

Desiring to limit the potential danger to mankind from possible new means of warfare;

Taking into consideration that scientific and technical advances in environmental fields, including climate modification, may open possibilities for using environmental modification techniques for military purposes;

Recognizing that such use could have widespread, long-lasting, and severe effects harmful to human welfare;

Recognizing also that proper utilization of scientific and technical advances could improve the inter-relationship of man and nature;

1. Advocate the most effective measures possible to overcome the dangers of the use of environmental modification techniques for military purposes.

2. Have decided to hold a meeting of United States and Soviet representatives this year for the purpose of exploring this problem.[55]

3. Have decided to discuss also what steps might be taken to bring about the measures referred to in paragraph 1.

Moscow, July 3, 1974

FOR THE UNITED STATES OF AMERICA:

RICHARD NIXON

The President of the United States of America

FOR THE UNION OF SOVIET SOCIALIST REPUBLICS:

L. I. BREZHNEV

General Secretary of the Central Committee of the CPSU

[Some insight into the background and significance of these agreements, and of other business transacted at the summit, was offered by Secretary Kissinger at a news conference held in Moscow's Intourist Hotel shortly before the signing ceremonies on July 3.]

[54]Text from *Presidential Documents,* 10: 753; for further comment cf. Document 27 at note 60.

[55]Bilateral meetings on this isssue were held in Moscow Nov. 1-5, 1974, in Washington Feb. 24-Mar. 5, 1975, and in Geneva June 16-20, 1975 (*Bulletin,* 73: 417n.).

(27) Analysis of the Agreements Reached: News conference statement by Secretary of State Kissinger, Moscow, July 3, 1974. [56]

I thought I would give you a brief summary of the summit as we see it, and I think the best way to start is to look at it in terms of the press conference in which I tried to explain the purposes of the meeting. [57]

I pointed out that there are three fundamental purposes in these summit meetings. One, for the leaders of the Soviet Union and the United States to exchange ideas and to check assessments about international affairs in general. The necessity for this arises because as the two nations capable of destroying humanity, they have a special obligation to prevent conflicts caused by inadvertence, by miscalculation, by misassessment of each other's motives, examples of which history is replete.

The second is to see whether they can, by meeting the needs of their peoples and of mankind, construct a network of positive relationships that will provide an incentive for moderation and for a beneficial and humane conduct of foreign policy.

The second large objective is to prevent the nuclear arms race and the arms race in general from dominating international affairs, and I want to stress again that this objective is no mean goal and one that will occupy American administrations in the absence of comprehensive agreements for as far into the future as we can see.

It is not only the complexity of the weapons and their destructiveness, it is also the justifications that will have to be used in each country to sustain large armament programs that will, over a period of time, present a major obstacle to the humane or even safe conduct of foreign policy.

And the third general goal is to identify those areas of common interests, either produced by the nonmilitary aspects of technology or by others or by the nature of modern life in which the Soviet Union and the United States can cooperate and thereby create a perspective on world affairs that recognizes the interdependence of events and the fact that isolation and confrontation are, over a period of time, inimical to progress and inconsistent with human aspirations.

Now, in terms of these three objectives, a great deal of time was spent by the two leaders in reviewing the international situation, and I will get into details when I go through the various documents.

There were the most extensive discussions at that level of the

[56] Text from *Presidential Documents,* 10: 763-6.
[57] News conference, June 24, in *Bulletin,* 71: 133-45.

arms race that have ever taken place and with a frankness that would have been considered inconceivable 2 years ago, indeed with an amount of detail that would have been considered violating intelligence codes in previous periods.

So, on the issue of SALT, for example, on which I will have more to say in a few minutes, the words of the communique, that far-reaching and deep conversations took place, are of very profound significance, and in the next phase of the discussions, difficulties cannot be caused by misapprehensions about each other's general intentions and general perceptions of the nature of the strategic environment.

And thirdly, there were a series of agreements, about most of which you have already been briefed, in the field of cooperative relationships.

Now, let me speak for myself about the two areas of arms control and the general review of the international situation.

With respect to arms control, let me cover first the agreements that have been made and then let me talk about the strategic arms limitations talks.

With respect to the agreements that have been made, there are three. The agreement that neither side will build the second ABM site, the agreement on the limited threshold test ban, and thirdly, the agreement to begin negotiations on environmental warfare.

With respect to the first agreement in which both sides forgo the second ABM site,[58] you remember that the permanent agreement on defensive weapons, signed in Moscow in 1972, permitted each of the two countries to maintain two ABM sites, one to defend its capital, the second to defend an ICBM field, provided that field was no closer than 1,300 kilometers to the capital.

The United States at that time opted for a defense of an ICBM field. The Soviet Union opted for a defense of its capital. There were provisions of the number of interceptors and radars that could be maintained at each site, but there is no point in going through these.

The United States and the Soviet Union have now decided to forgo that second ABM site and to maintain only the one ABM site that each currently has which is Moscow for the Soviet Union and an ICBM field for the United States. However, because it was thought desirable to keep some flexibility with respect to which area could be defended, each side is permitted at one time during the course of the agreement and once in a 5-year period, to alter its original decision.

In other words, if the United States should decide that it would prefer to defend Washington rather than the ICBM site, we have the option once in a 5-year period to move from the ICBM site to

[58]Document 24.

Washington and equally the Soviet Union has the option of moving once in that 5-year period from Moscow to an ICBM site.

That option, having once been exercised, cannot be exercised the second time. In other words, countries cannot shuttle their ABM sites back and forth between the capital and an ICBM field. Each side, in short, has the option once to reverse its original decision and it may do so once in any 5-year period when the treaty comes up for automatic review.

The significance of this agreement is that it reenforces the original decision implicit in 1972, in fact, explicit in 1972, that neither side would maintain ABM defenses. It makes it even more difficult, if not impossible, to break out of the agreement rapidly, and, in turn, the decision to forgo ABM defenses has profound strategic consequences which are sometimes lost sight of.

You must remember that the original impetus for the multiple warheads derived from the desire or the necessity to overcome ABM defenses and to make sure that the required number of missiles would get through.

In the absence of ABM defenses, the extraordinary number of foreseeable multiple warheads will create a situation in which such terms as superiority should not be lightly thrown around because they may be devoid of any operational meaning.

The notion of nuclear sufficiency of what is necessary under conditions of no ABM defenses requires careful correlation with the number of available warheads. For present purposes, I want to say that any idea that any country can easily achieve strategic superiority is almost devoid, under these conditions, of any operational significance and can only have a numerical significance.

The ABM agreement reenforces the element of strategic stability that was inherent in the original ABM agreement made in 1972. The second agreement on the threshold test ban[59] prohibits underground nuclear explosions above 150 kilotons and will therefore have the tendency to concentrate that competition in the ranges of the lower yield weapons. The date for its going into effect has been put into the future because a number of additional agreements remain to be worked out.

There remains to have an agreement on the peaceful uses of nuclear explosions in which adequate assurance will be given that they will not be used to circumvent the intention of the agreement, and there is an agreement in principle that the inspection of peaceful nuclear explosion, among other things, will involve prior notification, precise definition of the time and place, and the presence of observers which is a major step forward in our discussions.

The second subject that will require further discussion is the ex-

---

59Document 25.

change of geological information which is needed for the adequate verification of this threshold test ban.

The third area in which an agreement was reached was to begin discussions on the dangers of environmental warfare from the point of view of overcoming these dangers.[60] This is a form of warfare that is in its infancy, the nature of which is not properly understood and which obviously, by definition, can have profound consequences for the future of mankind.

The United States and the Soviet Union, in the near future, will open discussions on this problem of environmental warfare.

In addition to these three agreements, two protocols will be signed on the Standing Consultative Commission,[61] and we will certainly make diplomatic history because it will be the first time that secret agreements are publicly signed. The agreements are being kept secret at the request of the Soviet Union because they involve dismantling procedures for replacement missiles under the interim agreement and the ABM agreement. However, they will be submitted to the appropriate Congressional committees upon our return to the United States.

Let me say a word about the Standing Consultative Commission. The Standing Consultative Commission was created in the 1972 agreement in order to implement the provisions for replacement or destruction of weapons under the two agreements on defensive and offensive weapons.[62]

There is a protocol for defensive weapons, because the United States will have to dismantle some deployments that have taken place at a site which under the agreement we can no longer maintain and the Soviet Union will have to dismantle 15 ABM launchers and associated radars on their test ranges.

Secondly, there is a protocol for offensive weapons which discusses dismantling and replacement procedure under the provisions of the interim agreement where all land-based missiles can be traded in for modern sea-based missiles and where older submarine-launched nuclear missiles can be traded in for newer submarine-launched sea-based missiles.

These are the two protocols that have been the subject of illuminating exchange that took place just before I left the United States.

It must be understood that it was the assignment from the beginning of the Standing Consultative Commission to work out precise provisions for replacement and dismantling, that for that purpose

[60]Document 26.
[61]Cf. above at notes 19 and 45.
[62]Cf. AFR, 1972: 94 and 109-12.

they had to go into greater technical detail than was the case in the agreement, and that two protocols will be signed, one to implement the defensive provisions, the other to implement the offensive provisions.

They break no new ground, they change no provisions. If I may say so, they close no loopholes, they deal only with the technical implementation of agreements previously reached. They will be submitted to Congressional committees. They are not policy documents. They are technical documents, in implementation of the 1972 agreement, and they are being signed now as a result of work extending over a period of 18 months because it is only now that the replacement provisions are becoming effective due to the fact that the missiles, the ICBM's, did not have to be dismantled until the submarines containing the 741st missile on the Soviet side underwent sea trial.[63]

Now these are the agreements that have been reached.

Now let me say a word about strategic arms limitation talks. As I pointed out prior to our coming here, the Administration considers the problem of strategic arms limitation one of the central issues of our time. It is one of the central issues because if it runs unchecked the number of warheads will reach proportions astronomical compared to the time when Armageddon seemed near, when there were something less than 1,000 warheads on both sides.

It is important because a perception may grow that these warheads will provide a capability which will not be sustained by any systematic analysis, but because in any event they bring about a gap between the perceived first and second strike capabilities which in itself will fuel a constantly accelerating arms race.

Now the problem we face in these discussions is that under the interim agreement the Soviet Union possesses more missiles, though if you add together the total number of launchers, that is to say, strategic bombers, there is no significant gap, and after all, it was not the Soviet Union that made us build bombers, that was our own decision, and therefore, an attempt has been made to establish a correlation between the number of MIRV missiles and the number of launchers in which perhaps to some extent the larger numbers of missiles on one side can be offset by a larger number of MIRV's on the other.

The difficulty with this approach has been the limited time frame within which it was attempted to be implemented so that during the

---

[63]Under the 1972 Interim Agreement, the U.S.S.R. was permitted to add to its existing total of 740 SLBMs (up to a maximum of 950) on condition of retiring equal numbers of older ICBM launchers or of ballistic missile launchers on older submarines (AFR, 1972: 96-7).

maximum deployment period it would not be clear whether any of these limitations would not simply be to provide a base for a breakout when the agreement lapsed.

Therefore, the two leaders have decided that the principal focus of the discussions would not be on a brief extension of the interim agreement tied to an equally brief MIRV agreement, but to see whether the three factors, time, quantity of launchers, and quantity of warheads cannot be related in a more constructive and stabilizing fashion over a longer period of time, that is to say, by 1985.

And in the context, some of the difficulty of relating the various asymmetries in number can be taken care of and a stability can be perhaps achieved in deployment rates that would remove, to a considerable extent, the insecurities inherent in an unchecked arms race.

As the communique says, the two sides will reconvene their delegations in Geneva on the basis of this approach and on the basis of instructions growing out of the summit meeting.

With respect to the review of the international situation implicit in the communique, I think I will confine myself to a few observations and primarily answer your questions.

The basic purpose of this review was, as I have pointed out, to attempt to avoid miscalculation and where possible, bring about cooperative action.

In Europe, the principal focus were two subjects: the European Security Conference and the mutual balanced force reductions.

With respect to the European Security Conference, the United States repeated its position, which is that we are prepared to have that security conference end at the summit level if the results of the conference warrant it, and that we would believe that such a conference, with adequate results, could make a contribution to European security.

That phrase has been used by Western statesmen now for 2 years, and it will not in itself advance matters until we can define for ourselves what results we constitute justifying a summit conference. We have put that question to our European allies at Ottawa, discussions of it have begun in Brussels, and we hope to be able to have at least a Western answer to this in the relatively near future.

[At this point, the Secretary read the Middle East section of the communiqué, Document 23.]

Finally, the communique lists the area of bilateral relations that have already been covered in previous briefings on which separate agreements were signed. In addition to the ones that have been signed, there will be additional cooperation in space and technology of high-speed transportation and in the area of environmental protection where both sides will create biosphere areas, that is, areas which are kept free of the encroachment of modern technology to use for purposes of comparison with areas in which major environmental problems are posed.

Now, these are the main outlines of the conference and of the agreements that have been signed. They should be seen in the context of what is now and what will remain for the decades ahead, the problem of preserving the peace, namely, that the United States and the Soviet Union make every honorable effort to avoid the catastrophe of war, and every endeavor to improve the lot of humanity, and that for this purpose the regular meeting of their leaders—which the communique points out can be supplemented for special occasions between the yearly intervals that have been set—performs an essential role.

[President Nixon's own views concerning his recent travels were set forth in his reply to the welcoming address of Vice-President Gerald R. Ford as the presidential party arrived at Loring Air Force Base, Maine (minus Secretary Kissinger, who had embarked on a further tour of Western European capitals) on the evening of July 3.]

(28) *Report to the Nation: Remarks by Vice-President Gerald R. Ford and President Nixon, Loring Air Force Base, Maine, July 3, 1974.* [64]

THE VICE PRESIDENT. *Mr. President, Mrs. Nixon:*

It is a very high honor and a very great privilege for me to welcome you home again and to say what better way could the American people celebrate our 198th Fourth of July than with the assurance that you bring our world a little safer and a little saner tonight than it was when you left.

You know, Mr. President, that it was my life-long goal to be Speaker of the House of Representatives until you upset it last October.[65] The great State of Maine has given us two very distinguished Republican Speakers during the 19th century, and I would like to recall something Speaker Tom Reed said almost prophetically

---

[64]*Presidential Documents,* 10: 766-71.
[65]The then Representative Ford had been designated to succeed Vice-President Spiro T. Agnew following the latter's resignation on Oct. 10, 1974.

here in 1885, and I quote, "The reason why the race of man moves so slowly," Speaker Reed said, "is because it must move all together."

From your first mission to Moscow, Mr. President, in the days that you had the job that I now have,[66] you have seen the global dimension of peace and pursued it with patience, preparation, and performance.

As our President, you have not only demonstrated the truth of Speaker Reed's observation but you have permitted us to see much of mankind moving slowly, but perceptibly, all together in the direction of peace.

Your strategy for peace, Mr. President, has been bold but never rash, courageous but never foolhardy, tough but never rude, gentle but never soft. One by one, from China through Southeast Asia, through the Middle East, through the Soviet Union, through the NATO Alliance, you have emplaced the building blocks of a solid foundation for a better understanding of international relations than we have had in our lifetime and perhaps in the history of our country.

Permit me to say, Mr. President, and say particularly to Mrs. Nixon, who has been your faithful partner throughout literally millions and millions of miles of air travel, and sometimes on her own, that she has charmed and captivated both the officials and the citizens of every country she has visited and surely is entitled to be saluted in her own right again as First Lady of the World.

Mr. President, I wished you Godspeed last week and urged all of our countrymen to pray for you, for your safety and success on this historic mission. My prayers, and those of our fellow countrymen, have been answered many-fold. I cannot escape the conclusion that the Biblical injunction, "Blessed are the peacemakers," has again been confirmed.

Ladies and gentlemen, the President of the United States.

THE PRESIDENT. Mr. Vice President, I want to express appreciation not only on my own behalf but also on Mrs. Nixon's behalf for your very gracious and generous words.

Governor [Kenneth M.] Curtis and Mrs. Curtis and to all of our friends here in Maine, I want to thank you for giving us such a splendid welcome as we return.

[66]Cf. *Documents, 1959:* 177-93.

I know that as I see cars parked what a real effort it is to come out to an air base. It took a lot of time, and we appreciate that effort, and we thank you very much.

To each and every one of you, and to perhaps millions who are listening on television and radio, I can assure you of one thing, and that is, it is always good to come home to America. That is particularly so when one comes home from a journey that has advanced the cause of peace in the world.

We left Moscow earlier today, and as we did there were hundreds of United States and Soviet flags flying side by side, and I thought of the fact that tomorrow millions of Americans will be flying the flag from their homes on the Fourth of July. And you will be flying those flags proudly because of what it means in your own lives and in our lives and also because of what our flag means in the world. We can be very proud of the American flag all over the world today.

I thought also of how much more that flag means to the world because of the role the United States has been playing in building a structure of peace from which all nations can benefit, a role which was symbolized so dramatically by those flags flying side by side in the Soviet Union.

Our generation, which has known so much war and destruction—four wars in this century—now has an opportunity to build for the next generation a structure of peace in which we hope war will have no part whatever.

This is the great task before us, and this is the greatest task in which any people could be summoned. In the past month, Mrs. Nixon and I have traveled over 25,000 miles visiting nine countries in Western Europe and the Middle East, as well as, of course, the Soviet Union. The visit to each of these areas had a separate purpose but in a larger sense all of these visits were directed toward the same purpose, and they are all interacted and interconnected.

Among the nations of the Middle East, among those of the Western Alliance, and between the United States and the Soviet Union, new patterns are emerging, patterns that hold out to the world the brightest hopes in a generation for a just and lasting peace that all of us can enjoy.

In the Middle East a generation of bitter hostility, punctuated by four wars, is now giving way to a new spirit in which both sides are searching earnestly for the keys to a peaceful resolution of their differences.

In the Western Alliance, 25 years after NATO was founded,

there has been given a new birth, a new life to that organization as embodied in the Declaration on Atlantic Relations[67] that we signed 7 days ago in Brussels at the NATO heads-of-government meeting[68] before going on to Moscow. In the series of United States-Soviet summits that we began in 1972, we have been charting a new relationship between the world's two most powerful nations, a new relationship which is designed to insure that these two nations will work together in peace rather than to confront each other in an atmosphere of distrust and tension, which could lead, if it were not corrected, to war.

At this year's summit, we advanced further the relationship that we began two years ago in Moscow and that we continued at last year's summit in the United States. In the communique we issued earlier today in Moscow,[69] both sides committed themselves to this goal, the imperative necessity of making the process of improving United States-Soviet relations irreversible.

This sums up what the whole broad pattern of our expanding range of agreements is designed to achieve, to make the improvement not just a one-day headline, not just a one-day sensation, but a continuing, irreversible process that will build its own momentum and will develop into a permanent peace.

At this year's meeting, we reached a number of important agreements both in the field of arms limitation and also in the field of peaceful cooperation. In the field of arms limitation, three of the agreements we reached are of special note. One of those involves the exceedingly difficult question of offensive strategic nuclear arms, and this base, as we know, is involved in that particular kind of operation.

Two years ago we signed an interim agreement on offensive strategic weapons covering the 5-year period until 1977. This year we decided that this interim agreement should be followed by a new agreement to cover the period until 1985. We agreed that this should deal with both quantitative and qualitative aspects of strategic nuclear weapons, that it should be concluded well above and well before, I should say, the expiration of the present agreement.

We also agreed that the extensive work we have already done toward hammering out such a long-range agreement should go for-

[67]Document 21b.
[68]Cf. Document 22.
[69]Document 23.

ward at Geneva in the immediate future on the basis of instructions growing out of our talks at the highest level during the past week.

Now, the two sides have not yet reached a final accord on the terms of an agreement. This is a difficult and a very complex subject, but we did bring such an accord significantly closer, and we committed both sides firmly to the resolution of our remaining differences.

The second important arms control agreement that we reached deals with the anti-ballistic missile systems.[70] You will recall that 2 years ago we agreed that each country should be limited to two ABM sites. The agreement we signed earlier today in Moscow strengthens and extends the scope of that earlier measure by restricting each country to one ABM site.

And then the third arms limitation agreement deals with underground testing of nuclear weapons.[71] It extends significantly the earlier steps toward limiting tests that began with the 1963 test-ban treaty. That original treaty barred the signatories from conducting tests in the atmosphere, in outer space, and underwater. Today, we concluded a new treaty that for the first time will also cover tests underground. It will bar both the Soviet Union and the United States, after March 31, 1976, from conducting any underground test of weapons above a certain explosive power, and it will also require both countries to keep tests of weapons below that power to the very minimum number.

This is not only another major step toward bringing the arms race under control, it is also a significant additional step toward reducing the number of nuclear and thermonuclear explosions in the world.

Now, arms limitations, of course, are enormously and crucially important, but the work of these summit meetings is much broader, just as the nature of the new United States-Soviet relationship is much broader. This year, the important new agreements we reached in the area of peaceful progress included new programs for cooperation between our two countries in energy, in housing, in health, and also an agreement on long-term economic cooperation designed to facilitate increasing mutually beneficial trade between our two countries.[72]

The significance of these agreements goes beyond the advances

---

[70]Document 24.
[71]Document 25.
[72]Cf. Document 23 at notes 28-38.

each will bring to its particular field, just as the significance of our summit meetings goes beyond the individual agreements themselves. With this growing network of agreements, we are creating new habits of cooperation and new patterns of consultation, and we are also giving the people of the Soviet Union, as well as our own people in the United States, not just a negative but a positive stake in peace.

We are creating a stable new base on which to build peace, not just through the fear of war but through sharing the benefits of peace, of working together for a better life for the people of both of our countries.

The United States-Soviet agreements at the summit contribute importantly to the structure of peace we are trying to build between our two countries and in the world. The continued strength of the Western Alliance is also an essential and major element of that structure and, so too, is the development of a new pattern of relationships and a new attitude toward peace in areas of tension such as the Middle East.

The fact that the NATO meeting in Brussels came midway between the trip to the Middle East and the one to the Soviet Union is symbolic of the central role that the Western Alliance must play in building the new structure of peace.

It is clearly understood by the leaders of the Soviet Union that in forging the new relationship between the United States and the Soviet Union, we will not proceed at the expense of traditional allies. On the contrary, the continued strength of the Western Alliance is essential to the success and to the process in which we are engaged of maintaining and developing the new relationship to the Soviet Union.

The development of that new relationship provides an opportunity to deepen the unity of the Western Alliance. We must not neglect our alliances, and we must not assume that our new relationship with the Soviet Union allows us to neglect our own military strength. It is because we are strong that such a relationship that we are now developing is possible.

In his first annual message to the Congress, George Washington said, "To be prepared for war is one of the most effective means of preserving peace." That statement is true today as it was then, and that is why all of you who are serving in our Armed Forces today are actually serving in the peace forces for America and the world. We thank you for your service.

We are prepared, we in the United States, to reduce our military strength but only through a process in which that reduction is mutual and one that does not diminish the security of the United States of America. It is to that end that we have been working.

Twenty-five years ago when the NATO Treaty was signed, it was called "an act of faith in the destiny of Western Civilization." That description was prophetic as well as accurate, and now, 25 years later, we might well say the new structure of peace we are building in the world is an act of faith in the destiny of mankind. Like anything built to be permanent, that structure must be built step by careful step. It must be built solidly. It must be such a structure that those who use it will preserve it because they treasure it, because it responds to their needs, and because it reflects their hopes.

Two years ago in my report to the Congress on returning from the first of the United States-Soviet summits, I expressed the hope that historians of some future age will write of the year 1972, not that this was the year America went up to the summit and then down to the depths of the valley again, but that this was the year when America helped to lead the world up out of the lowlands of war and on to the high plateau of lasting peace.[73]

And now, 2 years, two summits later, the realization of that hope has been brought closer. The process of peace is going steadily forward. It is strengthened by the new and expanding patterns of cooperation between the United States and the Soviet Union. It is reinforced by the new vitality of our Western Alliance and bringing such encouraging results as the new turn toward peace in the Middle East.

In all of our travels, to which the Vice President has referred, one message has come through more clearly than any other. We have seen millions and millions of people over these past few weeks, and, from their faces as well as the words of those we have seen and the thousands we have met in every part of the world, this is the message, and that is, that the desire to end war, to build peace is one that knows no national boundaries and that unites people everywhere.

Something else also comes through very loud and very clear: The people of the nations that we visited—and we saw them, as I have indicated, not only by the thousands but by the millions—want to be friends of the American people and we reciprocate. We want to be their friends, too.

In the early years of our Nation's history, after America had won its independence, Thomas Jefferson said: We act not just for ourselves alone but for the whole human race.

[73]*AFR, 1972:* 86.

As we prepare tomorrow to celebrate the anniversary of that independence, the 198th anniversary, we as Americans can be proud that we have been true to Jefferson's vision and that, as a result of America's initiative, that universal goal of peace is now closer, closer not only for ourselves but for all mankind.

Thank you very much and good evening.

16. CYPRUS CRISIS, PHASE I

(July 15-August 1, 1974)

[The most serious international conflict of 1974 began within a fortnight of President Nixon's "Journey for Peace" and less than a month before his final departure from office. In contrast to the Mideast crisis of 1973, the conflict over Cyprus that broke out in the early hours of Monday, July 15, did not involve a direct threat of confrontation between the Soviet Union and the United States. Other interests, possibly not less weighty, were nevertheless at stake in this triangular quarrel among the governments of Cyprus, Greece, and Turkey. Among them were not only the strength and solidarity of the Atlantic alliance, so recently acclaimed at Ottawa and Brussels, but the politico-strategic situation of the entire Eastern Mediterranean, in which the U.S.S.R. as well as the Western governments had become an active element in recent years. While much of the immediate responsibility for "crisis management" could in this instance be left to Foreign Secretary Callaghan and the British Foreign Office, the United States was intimately involved not only through its close relationships with Greece and Turkey but also by reason of its interest in the stability of the entire region.

What first precipitated the latest in the lengthy series of international crises over Cyprus was a frontal attack upon the delicately balanced arrangements that had made possible the emergence, and the survival since 1960, of an independent Cypriot Republic that was dominated by members of the local ethnic Greek community but afforded at least nominal guarantees for the rights of the ethnic Turkish minority, comprising some 18 percent of the island's population of around 650,000. The visible symbol of the 1960 arrangements was Archbishop Makarios III, who, as leader of the Greek Cypriot community and President of the Republic, commanded the loyalty of most Greek Cypriots but was detested not only by Turkish Cypriots but also by those Greek Cypriot elements, mainly of right-wing nationalist outlook, who rejected the whole idea of Cypriot independence and sought instead to promote political union (*enosis*) of Cyprus with Greece. Greece and Turkey, hereditary foes as well as fellow members of NATO, had repeatedly come close to war over Cyprus in the past and, as mentioned earlier, were currently at odds with one another over Aegean offshore oil exploration rights and other matters as well. The United Kingdom was directly involved as Cyprus' former ruler and a guarantor of the 1960 independence arrangements, under which Britain retained certain "sovereign base areas" and continued to garrison troops on the island. In addition, a U.N. Peacekeeping force, currently consisting of some 2,341 men from eight countries, had operated since 1964 as a buffer between the hostile Greek and Turkish Cypriot communities.

This already precarious situation had become virtually unmanageable when the military junta that had ruled Greece since 1967 was replaced late in 1973 by a new group of military leaders that was dominated from behind the scenes by the head of the military police, Brigadier General Dimitrios Ioannides. With a singular disregard for international obligations, this group was soon providing open moral and material support to those right-wing Greek Cypriot elements that were engaged in fighting the elected regime of President Makarios. His patience exhausted by the recurrent intrigues and plots against his government and his own person, Makarios on July 2, 1974, took the extraordinary step of addressing an open letter to the Greek President, General Phaedon Gizikis, in which he demanded the withdrawal of the 650 Greek officers who controlled the Cypriot National Guard in conformity with the 1960 arrangements but, as the Cypriot leader bitterly pointed out, had converted what was supposed to be an internal security force into what amounted to a machine directed against his government.[1]

The response of Makarios' enemies was the mounting of still another attempted coup, this one initiated by the Cypriot National Guard on the morning of July 15 and crowned with what at first appeared to be complete success. President Makarios, marked for assassination and initially presumed dead (though actually unscathed, and soon afterward evacuated from Cyprus with British assistance), was promptly replaced as head of the Cypriot Government by Nikos Georgiades Sampson, a former terrorist and right-wing newspaper publisher.

---

[1] Text in *Keesing's:* 26661-2. For background see especially Stern, "Bitter Lessons," especially pp. 34-56; also the report of the Select Committee on Intelligence of the U.S. House of Representatives, 94th Cong., excerpted in *Village Voice* (New York), Feb. 16, 1976: 80-81.

This patently illegal action, which had been openly supported by the military regime in Greece, was widely denounced in Europe and elsewhere. Considerable criticism was also directed against the U.S. Government and particularly its intelligence agencies, which were widely believed—though without convincing proof—to have at least tacitly acquiesced in the attempt to get rid of Makarios. The prevalent impression of U.S. complicity was heightened by the seeming equanimity of the American Government in face of so open a challenge to international law and order. No explicit condemnation of the coup or of the insurgent regime in Nicosia was heard in official Washington, which took the position that the change of government in Cyprus was virtually an "accomplished fact" and that the prime U.S. objective must be merely to "prevent further exacerbation of the situation" by "urging restraint on all concerned."[2]

A similar emphasis marked Ambassador Scali's initial comment to the U.N. Security Council, which convened on Tuesday, July 16, on the initiative of Secretary-General Waldheim.]

(29) Discussion in the United Nations Security Council, July 16-19, 1974.

(a) Statement by Ambassador Scali to the Security Council, July 16, 1974.[3]

The United States strongly deplores the violence which has upset the delicate balance on the island of Cyprus. Unhappily, such violence and bloodshed have all too often influenced the fate of this Republic.

We have listened with keen attention to the report of the Secretary General on recent developments there. I am sure that all of us share a common sense of relief that Archbishop Makarios is alive and free. Unfortunately, there is much more we still do not know about the emerging situation on Cyprus, and it is difficult at this moment to see clearly whether and how the Council can make a positive contribution.

We continue to support the independence and territorial integrity of Cyprus and its existing constitutional arrangements. We urge all other states to support a similar policy. We wish to urge in particular that all interested parties exercise the utmost restraint and

---

[2]*New York Times,* July 16, 1974.
[3]USUN Press Release 88, July 16; text from *Bulletin,* 71: 262.

statesmanship and avoid actions which might further worsen the situation.

[The most immediate danger in this situation lay in the possibility that Turkey—which, with Greece and Britain, was a guarantor of the 1960 settlement—would feel constrained to intervene militarily in Cyprus in an attempt to protect its own rights, and those of the Turkish Cypriots, against the Greek Cypriot extremists who now appeared to be in power. As in the earlier Cyprus crises of 1964 and 1967, any such move by Turkey could very easily provoke a countermove by Greece that would result in open warfare between these two NATO allies. In an attempt to forestall such dangers, Under Secretary of State Joseph J. Sisco was dispatched to the area by Secretary Kissinger, breaking his journey in London to join in the urgent consultations already initiated by the British and Turkish governments. The importance of giving free play to these diplomatic efforts was emphasized by Ambassador Scali when the Security Council met again on Friday, July 19, to listen to statements by the rescued President Makarios and others. In view of the intensive consultations already taking place in London and in the area, the U.S. Representative urged, the Security Council should refrain from "overhasty actions" that might compromise the "efforts and processes" going forward elsewhere.]

(b) Statement by Ambassador Scali to the Security Council, July 19, 1974.[4]

We are gathered at a moment when peace is clearly threatened in the eastern Mediterranean. As responsible members of the Security Council I believe that we all have an obligation to ask ourselves what is the most useful contribution we can make to avoid conflict and to stabilize peace.

We have listened with great attentiveness to the words of Archbishop Makarios. We join in the sense of relief that all of us feel that he is able to be with us today and to express his views so eloquently.

My government looks forward to welcoming President Makarios in Washington to discuss with him what additional steps can be taken to resolve this crisis and to help end the suffering and the agony of the Cypriot people.

Let there be no misunderstanding about the attitude of the U.S.

[4]USUN Press Release 91, July 19; text from *Bulletin,* 71: 262-3.

Government in this situation. As I stated in the Council on Tuesday, the U.S. Government continues to support the independence, the sovereignty, and the territorial integrity of Cyprus and the existing constitutional arrangements.

Further, I would like to emphasize a fundamental point. The United States does not consider *enosis*, or union between Greece and Cyprus, as an acceptable solution of the Cyprus problem. The United States continues to believe in the future of a free and independent Cyprus as a sovereign nation capable of making its own decisions in full equality with the rest of the independent countries of the world.

We do not consider military intervention by any party for any reason to be justified in the present situation. In our view, Mr. President,[5] the first and very important step is that all interested parties continue to exercise the utmost restraint and good judgment to prevent this crisis from taking further unfortunate turns. In particular, the U.S. Government is firmly opposed to any attempt to bring about a military solution to the present problem. Such attempts would severely, perhaps irretrievably, set back the negotiating process, which alone can bring about the peaceful and constitutional solution which we all desire.

Therefore we most earnestly appeal to all governments concerned to resist the temptation to settle this issue by force. We ask them instead to pursue the much harder but wiser course of negotiation.

Having said this, however, I am sure that all of us around this table will recognize that there are many critical uncertainties in the present situation. We are gratified to note that the fighting on the island apparently has ceased. Yet the threat of military action in this area remains a grim prospect.

I note with considerable interest that the Representative of the Soviet Union [Vasily Safronchuk] is impressed by the fact that American citizens have sent messages to his Embassy expressing their view on this crisis. I am not surprised that he is impressed; American citizens have the right to communicate with anyone, regardless of the point of view they wish to express.

We are all aware of the special treaty provisions which govern the relationships of the governments concerned in Cyprus and the historically unique constitutional arrangements which were established to provide an acceptable basis of association between the Greek and Turkish communities.

Given the forcible overthrow of the existing government, it is quite understandable that strong emotions are widely felt about how to resolve the problem. It is also quite natural that many

[5]Jovier Perez de Cuellar of Peru, President of the Security Council for July.

members feel compelled to pronounce themselves quickly on some of the very complicated issues involved.

At the same time, the Security Council does have very definite responsibilities which we must always keep clearly in mind. Our obligation is first and foremost to contribute to a peaceful resolution of disputes. Thus in considering what action we should take, we should ask ourselves precisely what it is that we are trying to achieve. What we clearly should not be seeking are pronouncements which serve only propaganda purposes or are without practical effect or which because of their nature would serve to inflame an already aggravated situation.

For example, one suggestion proposed in informal consultations is to have the Council demand that Greece remove its officers in the Cypriot National Guard. At this point I merely suggest that if such a proposal is pursued, members of the Council should carefully weigh the implications. Would it perhaps lead to an even more unstable situation? What would be the prospects of compliance with such an appeal? I raise these questions without foreshadowing or prejudicing my government's ultimate position on this matter.

And lest there be any misunderstanding about the general attitude of the United States, my government has always opposed intervention in the internal affairs of one country by another, and to the extent that this may be the case in Cyprus, I repeat we deplore it. We believe that this Council is unanimous in its view that the Cyprus crisis demands a peaceful and constitutional solution. But what we need to search for, of course, before we can pronounce wisely, is the best way to achieve this result.

In our view, it can only be accomplished through discussions among the parties who are themselves directly involved. These discussions are already underway. Intensive consultations have been taking place in London between the British and Turkish Governments and a representative of my own government. Other consultations are taking place urgently in the area.

Under these circumstances, the United States considers it to be a serious error to rush to judgment on an issue of this gravity. We have an obligation to peace, to statesmanship, to allow enough time for a peaceful resolution of this crisis, no matter how difficult or insurmountable the deadlock may seem.

My government has had some experience in bridging differences which have defied solution in this part of the world. Let us not at this stage permit overhasty actions in another crisis in this important region [to] complicate and delay efforts and processes outside this chamber. Together, we can achieve what neither can achieve alone. Let us give peace a chance.

[Negotiations among the guarantor powers failed, however, to

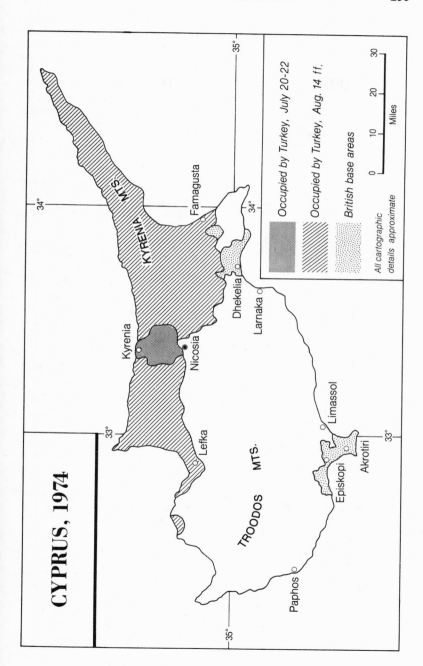

CYPRUS, 1974

Occupied by Turkey, July 20-22

Occupied by Turkey, Aug. 14 ff.

British base areas

All cartographic
details approximate

Miles
0   10   20   30

Famagusta

Dhekelia

Larnaka

Kyrenia

Nicosia

Limassol

KYRENIA MTS.

Lefka

Akrotiri

Episkopi

TROODOS MTS.

Paphos

avert a widening of the conflict, and Turkish military forces did intervene in Cyprus by sea and air in the early hours of Saturday, July 20. While Turkish troops and tanks poured ashore near the northern port of Kyrenia, waves of Turkish paratroops secured strategic points along the Kyrenia-Nicosia highway and seized the Turkish quarter of the capital. In two days' fighting with units of the Cypriot National Guard and Greek Cypriot irregulars, over 30,000 Turkish troops were landed in what had obviously been a well-planned operation aimed, at the very least, at creating a "position of strength" for any future discussion involving Turkish and Turkish Cypriot interests.

The United States, like other governments, voiced lively disapproval of these Turkish moves. At the same time, it must be noted that the American Government both then and later was widely thought to have been less shocked than it should have been by Turkey's resort to military force in the midst of an ongoing effort to resolve the situation by diplomatic means. At first condemned for overleniency with respect to the Greek-inspired coup against Makarios, the United States from this time on was to be even more sharply criticized for alleged overindulgence toward the military intervention carried out by its Turkish ally.

These trends, however, had not yet crystallized fully when the Security Council reassembled in the course of July 20 to consider the state of affairs created by Turkey's military moves. The Council's initial response to the new situation, worked out in prolonged off-the-record consultation, was the adoption of a rather ambiguously worded resolution that called for a cease-fire, a withdrawal of unauthorized military forces, and prompt negotiations among the guarantor powers.]

(30) *Reaction to the Turkish Invasion: Meeting of the Security Council, July 20, 1974.*

(a) *Call for a cease-fire: Security Council Resolution 353 (1974), July 20, 1974.*[6]

The Security Council,

Having considered the report of the Secretary-General, at its 1779th meeting [July 16], about the recent developments in Cyprus,

Having heard the statement of the President of Republic of

---

[6]Text from Security Council, *Official Records: 29th Year, Resolutions and Decisions 1974:* 7; adopted unanimously.

Cyprus and the statements of the representatives of Cyprus, Turkey, Greece and other Member States,

Having considered at its present meeting further developments in the island,

Deeply deploring the outbreak of violence and the continuing bloodshed,

Gravely concerned about the situation which has led to a serious threat to international peace and security, and which has created a most explosive situation in the whole Eastern Mediterranean area,

Equally concerned about the necessity to restore the constitutional structure of the Republic of Cyprus, established and guaranteed by international agreements,

Recalling its resolution 186 (1964) of 4 March 1964[7] and its subsequent resolutions on this matter,

Conscious of its primary responsibility for the maintenance of international peace and security in accordance with Article 24 of the Charter of the United Nations,

1. *Calls upon* all States to respect the sovereignty, independence and territorial integrity of Cyprus;

2. *Calls upon* all parties to the present fighting as a first step to cease all firing and requests all States to exercise the utmost restraint and to refrain from any action which might further aggravate the situation;

3. *Demands* an immediate end to foreign military intervention in the Republic of Cyprus that is in contravention of the provisions of paragraph 1 above;

4. *Requests* the withdrawal without delay from the Republic of Cyprus of foreign military personnel present otherwise than under the authority of international agreements, including those whose withdrawal was requested by the President of the Republic of Cyprus, Archbishop Makarios, in his letter of 2 July 1974;[8]

5. *Calls upon* Greece, Turkey and the United Kingdom of Great Britain and Northern Ireland to enter into negotiations without delay for the restoration of peace in the area and constitutional government in Cyprus and to keep the Secretary-General informed;

6. *Calls upon* all parties to co-operate fully with the United Nations Peace-keeping Force in Cyprus to enable it to carry out its mandate;

7. *Decides* to keep the situation under constant review and asks the Secretary-General to report as appropriate with a view to

---

[7]Establishing the U.N. Force in Cyprus (UNFICYP); text in *Documents, 1964:* 103-5.

[8]Cf. above at note 1.

adopting further measures in order to ensure that peaceful conditions are restored as soon as possible.

[American views on the situation were expounded by Ambassador Scali following adoption of the foregoing resolution.]

(b) Comment on the cease-fire resolution: Statement by Ambassador Scali to the Security Council, July 20, 1974.[9]

We convene here today in the wake of open military action in the eastern Mediterranean. To our deep regret, Turkish troops have landed on Cyprus. This Council, all too familiar with the antagonisms which have shaped Greek-Turkish relations on Cyprus, needs no reminder of what the Turkish landing forebodes for the stability of the island and what a serious threat is posed for peace in the area. Regrettably the process of diplomacy was not given a chance to run its course. The people of Cyprus are the tragic losers, once more overtaken by events sadly beyond their capability to control. Indeed, Mr. President, we are all losers as international peace hangs most precariously and dramatically in the balance.

My government deplores the pressures and interventions which contributed to the Turkish action on Cyprus and for which Greece must bear a heavy share of the responsibility. However, this invasion in no way serves the hopes for peace of the Turkish community on Cyprus or, indeed, the cause of peace in the world. Neither can we be convinced that foreign military intervention in Cyprus, from whatever quarter and by whatever means, has at any time been justifiable.

We oppose any intervention in the internal affairs of a member state of these United Nations.

My government has worked untiringly these past days in an attempt to forestall the escalation toward intervention in the eastern Mediterranean. Tragically, with the Turkish intervention last night, another step has been taken toward exactly that which we have attempted to forestall.

Turkey is and will remain an ally of the United States; Greece is and will remain an ally of the United States.

It is in the interest of the people of Greece and the people of Turkey to insure that Greece remains the ally of Turkey. As friends for a generation, both peoples have made giant strides; as enemies, they stand to lose all.

It is in the interest of the people of Cyprus as well as those of Greece and Turkey and all members of this Council that Cyprus not become a Mediterranean battleground.

The United States will continue to work with its friends toward this goal. We urge the Governments of Greece and Turkey to display to the members of this Council the maximum spirit of restraint and compromise in the interest of peace.

We believe that with good will, common sense, and extraordinary statesmanship by all concerned, it is still not too late to avert major tragedy.

We appreciate that all members of the Security Council have joined in calling for an immediate cease-fire. We owe the embattled people of Cyprus no less.

All the members of this Council have wisely joined with us in a request to the Governments of Greece and Turkey to accept immediately the United Kingdom proposal for negotiations among the guarantor powers. We believe that at this time the Security Council can make no greater contribution to the cause of peace and constitutional government in Cyprus.

[The failure of the Turkish invasion to precipitate actual full-scale war with Greece could be attributed in part to the latter's lack of military preparedness and in part to the precarious situation within the Greek military junta, where the "strong man" position of General Ioannides had been disastrously impaired in consequence of the failure of his intrigues against Makarios and the resultant Turkish military moves. Although Ioannides was by this time agitating for all-out military action against Turkey, his demands were now beginning to meet decisive if somewhat belated resistance from the responsible heads of the Greek military services.[10] Rumors of an impending coup against the junta were, in fact, already beginning to circulate as Secretary Kissinger met with the press on Monday morning, July 22, to confirm reports that a cease-fire in Cyprus had been agreed upon the evening before and was due to go into effect that day.]

(31) Plans for a Cease-fire: News conference remarks by Secretary Kissinger, July 22, 1974.[11]

(Excerpts)

Secretary Kissinger: I thought I would review for you the events of the last 36 hours to tell you where we are and what is likely to

---

[10]Stern, "Bitter Lessions": 66-7.
[11]Department of State Press Release 309, July 22; text from *Bulletin,* 71: 257-61.

happen now and take a few questions confined to the Cyprus situation, Greece, and Turkey on a somewhat informal basis.

On Saturday [July 20] in San Clemente I gave a review of the diplomacy of last week;[12] so let me pick it up from Saturday. After the Turkish landing, our efforts were:

—First, to prevent a Greek-Turkish war from erupting;
—Secondly, to keep open the possibility of a settlement of the Cyprus issues along constitutional lines; and
—Thirdly, to prevent a further internationalization of the conflict.

Obviously, the prime necessity for this was to bring about a cease-fire. We operated with great intensity, both in Ankara and Athens.

Joe Sisco was in Athens when the invasion occurred. And when the Turkish landings in Cyprus occurred he spent Saturday morning in Athens and then went back to Ankara. He received a Turkish agreement in principle to a cease-fire, which he then took back to Athens—at which point all the parties discovered that it was easy to telephone Washington, and we were in very intensive contact with [Turkish] Prime Minister [Bülent] Ecevit, the Greek Prime Minister, Foreign Minister Callaghan, the French Foreign Minister, and toward the end the German Foreign Minister.

Our effort throughout was that this was an issue affecting NATO, affecting Western Europe, in which we should work in the closest cooperation with our allies and particularly with Great Britain, which had a relationship as one of the guarantors of the Zurich agreement.[13] Throughout the period, as I pointed out Saturday, there has been a complete unanimity as to objective and very substantial agreement between the United Kingdom and the United States in every facet of the diplomatic process and a complete coordination of our efforts.

There has also been a very close cooperation with the French Foreign Minister in his capacity of President of the Communities' Council of Ministers. And it was in this manner that we proceeded.

Now, I won't go through all the complications of the negotiations during the day, which were pursued on two tracks. The United States concentrated on getting the cease-fire; the United

[12]The Secretary of State held a news briefing for attribution, but not for direct quotation, at San Clemente on Saturday, July 20; cf. David Binder in *New York Times,* July 21, 1974.
[13]Cf. U.K. declaration, Feb. 17, 1959, in *Documents, 1959:* 390-92. The Zürich agreement of Feb. 11, 1959 (same, pp. 381-90) set forth the basic arrangements under which Cyprus became independent on Aug. 16, 1960.

Kingdom concentrated on getting the negotiating process started after the cease-fire. The attempt has been made to get a cease-fire established and then have the United Kingdom invite Greece and Turkey to a meeting.

The difficulties during the day arose because, as always in these cease-fire negotiations, there were infinite technical disputes—for example, at one point the Turks thought that a Greek fleet was approaching Cyprus and were reluctant to make a cease-fire while the Greek fleet was approaching Cyprus; the Greeks denied that there was a Greek fleet. To do all of this on transatlantic telephone had many complexities. There was, in fact, some dispute on whether it might be a Turkish fleet.

I won't pursue the complexity of military operations in a confused situation. All I want to say is that this has delayed matters somewhat.

Then in the afternoon, the Turkish Prime Minister called over here with a proposal that he would accept a cease-fire in principle provided the Greeks would send a representative to any place in Europe and then at that place they would negotiate the modalities of the cease-fire, after which the cease-fire would go into effect.

Each one of these phone calls—and a complex series of phone calls—then, involved Sisco in Athens. And it was apparent that we weren't going to get anywhere on this basis, because the Greeks, predictably, rejected this.

And so about 6 o'clock yesterday afternoon we thought it might be time to come up with an American proposal; and therefore we proposed to the Turkish Prime Minister that—after consultation with Foreign Minister Callaghan and the French Foreign Minister, we proposed to the Turkish Foreign Minister that a cease-fire go into effect.

We gave the time at 1400 today Greenwich mean time and that this should be followed almost immediately by negotiations between Greece and Turkey under United Kingdom auspices. This was supported by the United Kingdom and by France; and France, in turn, was backed by the Nine.

Turkey accepted this around 9 o'clock last night—or 8 o'clock last night—and then we had to get Greek acceptance.

Having obtained Greek acceptance, the problem was to find a means between two parties that have no great confidence in each other to achieve a simultaneous announcement so that each party would have enough confidence that an announcement would, in fact, be made.

And this led to the solution that we would make the announcement here and, after that, each party would confirm our announcement.

But these are the mechanics of how the cease-fire was achieved.

The problem now is, "Where do we go from here?" Our expectation is that within the next few days, hopefully by Wednesday [July 24], probably the Foreign Ministers of Greece and Turkey will meet under British auspices in Geneva and these talks can settle the constitutional arrangements of Cyprus and all other issues that stem from recent events. And we believe, therefore, that a rather complicated crisis which had dangers of internationalization has been overcome.

We have been in touch with the Soviet Union throughout, and we believe that there will be no complications from that side. And these exchanges have been constructive.

So we hope that during the course of the week we can move the situation toward a solution that will be acceptable. There have been reports, with which you're familiar, that there may be a coup in Greece at this moment. But we have very sketchy reports, and we can't form any clear judgment as to the complexion of the forces that will take over the government. And I'm not confirming that either officially. We've had no official word; we have had the fragmentary reports that you always get at the beginning of a crisis.

So this is where we are. I'll be glad to answer a few questions.

Q. Mr. Secretary, did you threaten to cut off military aid to both Greece and Turkey in order to get them to accept the cease-fire?

Secretary Kissinger: I made clear on Saturday in San Clemente that no war would be fought between NATO allies with an open American supply line. So this put a limit to the escalation that could be conducted.

As to the other steps that were taken, there were no specific threats made. It was very clear that we would consider a continuation of a military confrontation between NATO allies as a very grave matter.

* * *

Q. Mr. Kissinger, there was a report of a joint British-U.S. note to the Greek and Turkish Governments calling for a cease-fire, a toughly worded note.

Secretary Kissinger: The exact sequence is that I first made the proposal on the telephone to Prime Minister Ecevit around 6 o'clock U.S. time last night. And it was the first time that the United States made a concrete proposal in which it said something other than we propose a cease-fire—we said we propose a cease-fire at this hour to be implemented in this manner.

This was followed up by a Presidential letter to the Presidents of Greece and Turkey, and this in turn was backed by a British note and a Common Market note.

I believe that several of these notes arrived after the parties had already accepted the cease-fire. But given the staggered timing for first an American announcement and then a confirmation of this announcement by Greece and Turkey, we permitted these notes that did express the urgency everyone felt to be delivered by all the parties—by all our friends and ourselves—so that the parties knew that this was a matter that was not taken lightly in the United States and in Europe and that there was total unanimity of view between Europe and the United States on this issue.

Q. Mr. Secretary, your expectations that the Geneva talks may in fact take place with only a 24-hour slippage would seem to indicate that whatever may or may not be happening in Greece did not take you by complete surprise.

Secretary Kissinger: If I answer this question, I get into major difficulties, because if I say it took us by complete surprise, you will say "intelligence failure." And if I say it didn't take us by complete surprise, you will say other things. [Laughter.]

May I make one general point. I have read many learned articles during the week of why we were taken by surprise by the coup in Cyprus, and I simply would like to point out to you ladies and gentlemen that obviously the man most concerned in Cyprus—namely, Archbishop Makarios—also was taken by surprise, so that the information was not exactly lying on the street.

Late in the day yesterday it became apparent in Athens that there was a certain restiveness, so that in this sense, we were aware of the fact that the events of the last week were not considered unanimously in Athens as a complete success. And this gave a particular urgency to the need to bring about a cease-fire during the night and it was one of the reasons why we took a rather active and even more active role toward the end of the day. So we had some general information.

Marilyn [Marilyn Berger, Washington Post]. I'll take two more questions.

Q. Mr. Secretary, before the Turkish invasion, did the United States warn the Turkish Government that it would lose aid if it moved, military aid?

Secretary Kissinger: No, but we made very clear that we were very strongly opposed to military action.

Q. Mr. Secretary, what are we doing about the 3,000 Americans on the island? Are they going to be taken out?

Secretary Kissinger: The Americans are being evacuated. I think—

Q. By U.S. forces?

Secretary Kissinger: By American helicopters. We have offered the British that we would be willing to send in a marine company to the British base if that would help them, if their facilities were overloaded. I don't believe they have accepted it yet, and it may not be necessary, but American helicopters will take them off the British base, and then there is an enclave near Kyrenia about which we have now begun negotiations for their removal.

I might also say that we have been asked by the Soviet Government to help them in the evacuation of some of their 150 civilians in Nicosia. A Soviet ship is going into the port—I never can remember the name—in the south of Cyprus, and we are cooperating with the Soviet Union to bring this about.

* * *

[From London, Secretary Kissinger's account was confirmed by Foreign Secretary Callaghan, who informed the House of Commons on July 22 that in accepting a cease-fire to be effective that day, Greece and Turkey had also agreed to a tripartite Foreign Ministers' meeting such as had been foreseen in the Security Council resolution of July 20 (Document 30a). Noting that he personally would preside at these talks, which were to take place in Geneva, Mr. Callaghan expressed the hope that they could begin on Tuesday, July 23, or at latest by Wednesday, July 24.

But neither the military situation in Cyprus nor the political situation in Greece had yet been clarified sufficiently for this program to be carried out on schedule. Although the cease-fire in Cyprus was supposed to go into effect on Monday at 4:00 P.M. local time (1400 GMT), Secretary-General Waldheim told the Security Council later that day that fighting was still going on, that the Turkish air force had made a second attack on Nicosia airport at 5:15 P.M., and that combat was reported from other sectors as well. The urgency of stopping hostilities was again stressed by Ambassador W. Tapley Bennett, Jr., the Deputy U.S. Representative, at a Council meeting that was marked by growing recriminations, including mutual charges of atrocities on the part of the belligerents.]

(32) *Urgency of Observing the Cease-fire: Statement by Ambassador W. Tapley Bennett, Jr., United States Deputy Representative, to the Security Council, July 22, 1974.*[14]

It is indeed high time that the cease-fire take effect. My government, as is well known, has taken a very active part in trying to supplement the work of this Council and to arrange a cease-fire, with very active diplomacy in the capitals concerned.

All parties in the fighting, certainly the two governments away from Cyprus, have publicly accepted the cease-fire. Now, the firing did not immediately cease at 10 o'clock. I believe that is fairly usual in such circumstances. There are many technical complications. But I would call on the parties to give their best efforts, and I would call on the population of Cyprus similarly. To the best of our most recent information, the two armed forces involved, Greece and Turkey, have begun to observe the cease-fire. There is still communal fighting going on. That may be the most difficult to stop. But I would hope that we can, before this day is over, have a genuine cease-fire.

Let the killing cease! It seems to me that is our priority and primary purpose and objective at this time. And then let us go forward with the negotiations, as our British colleague [Ivor Richard] has described them, negotiations which hold such tremendous importance for the future, if we are going to have some resolution of this age-old problem and allow the decent people of Cyprus, whatever their historical or ethnic origin, to have a life of their own and to live in peace in their own way.

The Secretary General has described to us the extreme tests which are being imposed on UNFICYP [United Nations Peace-keeping Force in Cyprus]. My government has always supported UNFICYP. It continues to do so, and if more men are needed there, as circumstances would seem to dictate, then we would support what the Secretary General has outlined as the means of supplementing the present force.

And so, Mr. President, despite the tragedy through which we have been living—the people of Cyprus living it most intensely of all—this past week, I would agree with our British colleague that this is a time for looking forward. Let us bind up the wounds of war. Let us try to look at this in an objective way to give to each side of this communal situation its own right to exist. We can look forward to an independent and single Cyprus. Let us go forward toward a better fate for Cyprus.

---

[14]USUN Press Release 94, July 22; text from *Bulletin*, 71: 265.

[But violations of the cease-fire were still being reported when the Security Council convened again on Tuesday, July 23, to adopt a more urgent cease-fire demand and listen to further statements by Ambassador Bennett and others.]

(33) Further Discussion in the Security Council, July 23, 1974.

(a) Demand for compliance with the cease-fire: Security Council Resolution 354 (1974), July 23, 1974.[15]

The Security Council,
Reaffirming the provisions of its resolution 353 (1974) of 20 July 1974,[16]
Demands that all parties to the present fighting comply immediately with the provisions of paragraph 2 of Security Council resolution 353 (1974) calling for an immediate cessation of all firing in the area and requesting all States to exercise the utmost restraint and to refrain from any action which might further aggravate the situation.

(b) Comment on the second cease-fire resolution: Statement by Ambassador Bennett to the Security Council, July 23, 1974.[17]

I think that little needs to be said here. The facts as we know them and as we have just heard them from the Secretary General speak for themselves, and they are somber enough for all of us. The cease-fire in Cyprus agreed to yesterday by all the parties is not being observed. The guns are still firing; the innocent are still dying.

The resolution which this Council has just adopted, as the resolution we adopted on the 20th, was unanimously adopted. The new resolution is short and to the point. In this resolution we demand that the parties, all the parties, comply immediately with the cease-fire provisions of Resolution 353 and cease the hostilities in Cyprus, hostilities which have brought suffering and death to countless innocent people and which so clearly threaten international peace and security.

The United States has joined in supporting the resolution adopted by this Council because of our determination that the cease-fire ordered by the Council on July 20 should be made fully effective at

---

[15]Text from Security Council, *Official Records: 29th Year, Resolutions and Decisions 1974:* 7; adopted unanimously.
[16]Document 30a.
[17]USUN Press Release 95, July 23; text from *Bulletin,* 71: 265-6.

the earliest possible moment. My government believes that the governments and peoples of Cyprus, Greece, and Turkey, as well as all the rest of us, want an end to the fighting and that they want it now.

Nothing is more difficult, Mr. President, nothing requires greater political leadership and courage, than to stop hostilities once they have started. I call on the parties to exercise that leadership and that courage now. I call on the parties to stop the bloodletting and turn to the negotiating table. The cease-fire has to be the first step toward peace. It must be the basis for other efforts toward conciliation and for other developments which can lead on to a brighter future for the people of Cyprus.

[Though nothing could erase the damage and human suffering that had already occurred in Cyprus, hopes for a peaceful outcome in the near future were now buoyed by governmental changes in two of the three contending nations. In Cyprus, the bankrupt Nikos Sampson regime resigned on July 23 in favor of an administration led by the moderate Glafkos Clerides, presiding officer of the House of Representatives and previously Greek Cypriot delegate in intercommunal talks with Turkish Cypriot community leaders. In Greece, meanwhile, the military junta had reached the end of the road and, faced with the proofs of its own impotence, had determined to return power to the civilian politicians from whom authority had been wrested in 1967. Constantine Caramanlis, Greece's elder statesman and one of the architects of the 1960 Cyprus settlement, was summoned from exile in Paris and arrived on July 24 to try to rebuild a democratic government on the ruins of seven years' military rule. Thus it fell to George Mavros, leader of Greece's Center Union party and newly designated Deputy Prime Minister and Minister of Foreign Affairs, to represent Greece at the tripartite talks with British and Turkish representatives that finally got under way in Geneva on Thursday, July 25.

Nominally aimed at "the restoration of peace in the area and constitutional government in Cyprus," the Geneva talks were handicapped from the beginning by conflicting Greek and Turkish views not only on the immediate situation but on the long-term future of Cyprus. To Greece's insistence on immediate withdrawal of the Turkish invasion force, Turkish Prime Minister Bülent Eçevit in Ankara (and Foreign Minister Turan Günes in Geneva) replied in effect that the troops must remain on hand until the Cyprus question was resolved in a manner satisfactory to Turkey and the Turkish Cypriots.[18] By the time the talks recessed on July 30, the three Foreign Ministers had agreed only on certain pre-

[18]*Keesing's:* 26709.

liminary measures to stabilize the military situation pending a second round of talks, dealing with constitutional and other matters, that was scheduled to begin on August 8.]

(34) **Tripartite Agreement in Geneva: Declaration and statement by the Foreign Ministers of Greece, Turkey, and the United Kingdom, Geneva, July 30, 1974.** [19]

DECLARATION BY THE FOREIGN MINISTERS
OF GREECE, TURKEY AND THE UNITED
KINGDOM OF GREAT BRITAIN AND
NORTHERN IRELAND

1. The Foreign Ministers of Greece, Turkey and the United Kingdom of Great Britain and Northern Ireland held discussions in Geneva from 25 to 30 July 1974. They recognized the importance of setting in train, as a matter of urgency, measures to adjust and to regularize within a reasonable period of time the situation in the Republic of Cyprus on a lasting basis, having regard to the international agreements signed at Nicosia on 16 August 1960 and to resolution 353 (1974) of the Security Council.[20] They were, however, agreed on the need to decide first on certain immediate measures.

2. The three Foreign Ministers declared that in order to stabilize the situation, the areas in the Republic of Cyprus controlled by opposing armed forces on 30 July 1974 at 2200 hours (Geneva time) should not be extended; they called on all forces, including irregular forces, to desist from all offensive or hostile activities.

3. The three Foreign Ministers also concluded that the following measures should be put into immediate effect:

(a) A security zone of size to be determined by representatives of Greece, Turkey and the United Kingdom in consultation with the United Nations Peace-keeping Force in Cyprus (UNFICYP) should be established at the limit of the areas occupied by the Turkish armed forces at the time specified in paragraph 2 above. This zone should be entered by no forces other than those of UNFICYP, which should supervise the prohibition of entry. Pending the determination of the size and character of the security zone, the existing area between the two

---

[19]Text from U.N. document S/11398, July 30, in Security Council, *Official Records: 29th Year, Supplement for July, Aug., Sept. 1974*: 74.
[20]Document 30a.

forces should be entered by no forces.

(b)   All the Turkish enclaves occupied by Greek or Greek-Cypriot forces should be immediately evacuated. These enclaves will continue to be protected by UNFICYP and to have their previous security arrangements. Other Turkish enclaves outside the area controlled by the Turkish armed forces shall continue to be protected by an UNFICYP security zone and may, as before, maintain their own police and security forces.

(c)   In mixed villages the functions of security and police will be carried out by UNFICYP.

(d)   Military personnel and civilians detained as a result of the recent hostilities shall be either exchanged or released under the supervision of the International Committee of the Red Cross within the shortest time possible.

4.   The three Foreign Ministers, reaffirming that resolution 353 (1974) of the Security Council should be implemented in the shortest possible time, agreed that, within the framework of a just and lasting solution acceptable to all the parties concerned and as peace, security and mutual confidence are established in the island, measures should be elaborated which will lead to the timely and phased reduction of the number of armed forces and the amounts of armaments, munitions and other war material in the Republic of Cyprus.

5.   Deeply conscious of their responsibilities as regards the maintenance of the independence, territorial integrity and security of the Republic of Cyprus, the three Foreign Ministers agreed that negotiations, as provided for in resolution 353 (1974) of the Security Council, should be carried on with the least possible delay to secure the restoration of peace in the area and the re-establishment of constitutional government in Cyprus. To this end they agreed that further talks should begin on 8 August 1974 at Geneva. They also agreed that representative of the Greek Cypriot and Turkish Cypriot communities should, at an early stage, be invited to participate in the talks relating to the constitution. Among the constitutional questions to be discussed should be that of an immediate return to constitutional legitimacy, the Vice-President assuming the functions provided for under the 1960 Constitution.[21] The Ministers noted the existence in practice in the Republic of Cyprus

[21]The 1960 constitution provided for a mixed administration under a Greek Cypriot President and a Turkish Cypriot Vice-President; but Vice-President Fazil Küçük, the leader of the Turkish Cypriot community, had ceased to exercise his functions on the cessation of Turkish Cypriot participation in the national government in Jan. 1964. Rauf Denktash, Turkish Cypriot representative in the intercommunal talks, had nominally succeeded to the vice-presidency early in 1973.

of two autonomous administrations, that of the Greek Cypriot community and that of the Turkish Cypriot community. Without any prejudice to the conclusions to be drawn from this situation, the Ministers agreed to consider the problems raised by their existence at their next meeting.

6. The three Foreign Ministers agreed to convey the contents of this Declaration to the Secretary-General of the United Nations and to invite him to take appropriate action in the light of it. They also expressed their conviction of the necessity that the fullest co-operation should be extended by all concerned in the Republic of Cyprus in carrying out its terms.

STATEMENT BY THE FOREIGN MINISTERS OF
GREECE, TURKEY AND THE UNITED
KINGDOM OF GREAT BRITAIN AND
NORTHERN IRELAND

The Foreign Ministers of Greece, Turkey and the United Kingdom of Great Britain and Northern Ireland made it clear that the adherence of their Governments to the Declaration of today's date in no way prejudiced their respective views on the interpretation or application of the 1960 Treaty of Guarantee or their rights and obligations under that Treaty.

Done in duplicate at Geneva the 30th day of July, 1974, in the English and French languages, both texts being equally authoritative.

(*Signed*) George MAVROS
Minister of Foreign Affairs of Greece

(Signed) Turan GÜNEŞ
Minister of Foreign Affairs of Turkey

(*Signed*) James CALLAGHAN
*Secretary of State for Foreign
and Commonwealth Affairs of the
United Kingdom of Great Britain
and Northern Ireland*

[A key feature of the July 30 agreement was a further enlargement of the responsibilities of the U.N. Peace-keeping Force (UN-FICYP), already stretched to the limit as a result of the recent fighting. Proposals for a further expansion of UNFICYP were thus the principal subject of discussion at two further meetings of the Security Council on July 31 and August 1.]

(35) New Tasks for the United Nations: Discussion in the Security Council, July 31-August 1, 1974.

(a) Statement by Secretary-General Kurt Waldheim to the Security Council, July 31, 1974.[22]

As members of the Council are aware, at 5 p.m. New York time on July 30, that is, yesterday, I received a communication from Mr. Callaghan, the Secretary of State for Foreign and Commonwealth Affairs of the United Kingdom, on behalf of the three Foreign Ministers who had been negotiating in Geneva, communicating to me the text of the declaration and statement which have been agreed to by the Foreign Ministers of Greece, Turkey, and the United Kingdom. The texts of the declaration and statement[23] have been circulated as an official document (S/11398). I am sure the members of the Council will wish to give their urgent consideration to that document. I hope that the agreement reached in Geneva on the cease-fire will be a first step to the full implementation of Security Council Resolution 353 (1974).[24]

Members of the Council will note that the declaration envisages certain tasks for UNFICYP. In particular, the declaration calls for action in consultation with UNFICYP to determine the size and character of the security zone, which will be entered by no forces other than those of UNFICYP. Other important functions are also foreseen for UNFICYP.

I wish to inform the Council that I have requested my Special Representative and the Force Commander of UNFICYP[25] to give me a preliminary assessment of the practical implications of the declaration as far as UNFICYP is concerned. I shall report to the Council on the practical consequences involved.

The total strength of UNFICYP as of July 31 is 3,484 men. That total comprises 3,332 military personnel and 152 civilian police. By August 7 the total strength of UNFICYP will, it is estimated, be 4,238 men. When all the reinforcements currently pledged have arrived—by about August 12—the total strength of UNFICYP will be approximately 4,443.

I take this opportunity to draw the attention of members of the Council to the question of the nature of UNFICYP's continued presence in the Turkish area of control, which I mentioned to the

---

[22]Text from *Bulletin,* 71: 331.
[23]Document 34.
[24]Document 30a.
[25]Respectively Luis Weckmann Muñoz (Mexico) and Maj. Gen. Prem Chand (India).

Council on July 29 and which needs clarification. As you know, UNFICYP has been playing, and should continue to play, a most useful humanitarian role in all parts of the island of Cyprus in assisting the civilian population—Turkish and Greek Cypriots alike—who have been afflicted by the recent hostilities. This matter is now under discussion by UNFICYP with the Turkish Military Command in Cyprus. I am confident that these discussions will enable UNFICYP to continue to perform its role in all parts of the island with the full agreement of all the parties concerned.

I think that is as much as I should say at this stage. I am sure that the members of the Council are fully aware of the complexity of the situation. I do not have to say that I and my colleagues in the Secretariat, both here and in Cyprus, are prepared fully to cooperate with the parties in order to restore peaceful conditions in the island, so that negotiations can continue and Security Council Resolution 353 (1974) can be fully implemented.

[A draft resolution requesting the Secretary-General to "take appropriate action" to carry out the Geneva provisions was promptly placed before the Council and was endorsed by Ambassador Bennett, among others, in a highly positive appraisal of the tripartite agreement.]

(b) Statement by Ambassador Bennett to the Security Council, July 31, 1974.[26]

The United States is deeply gratified by the agreement reached in Geneva among the Foreign Ministers of Greece, Turkey, and the United Kingdom.[27] In that connection, Mr. President, I should like to read a statement issued yesterday by the White House in Washington:

The United States welcomes the announcement in Geneva of the agreement reached by the Foreign Ministers of the United Kingdom, Greece, and Turkey. We consider this an important step toward the restoration of peace and stability in Cyprus.

We commend the intensive and patient efforts of the three governments concerned which brought about this achievement. In particular, we wish to pay tribute to the skill and persistence of Mr. Callaghan, the Minister of State of Great Britain, who, as leader of the conference, deserves great credit for its success, and to the Foreign Ministers of Greece and Turkey.

[26]Text from Bulletin, 71: 329-30.
[27]Document 34.

We believe this agreement justifies the wisdom of this Council in adopting Resolution 353[28] and thereafter in supporting the intensive efforts at Geneva to negotiate the serious issues involved in this Cyprus crisis.

I want to reiterate the view of my government that we consider this agreement an important step toward the restoration of peace and stability in Cyprus.

We particularly welcome the recognition by the three Foreign Ministers of the "importance of setting in train, as a matter of urgency, measures to adjust and regularize within a reasonable period of time the situation in the Republic of Cyprus on a lasting basis," having regard to the international agreements of 1960 and Resolution 353 of the Security Council. My government wants to see strict maintenance of the cease-fire in the area and the prompt implementation of other portions of the agreement signed in Geneva. My government very much hopes that this agreement foreshadows a quick return to more normal conditions in Cyprus, conditions which will bring to all the people of Cyprus a return to constitutional government and a new measure of political stability and general well-being.

We note that the United Nations Peace-keeping Force in Cyprus is asked to undertake certain responsibilities under the terms of the agreement of July 30. UNFICYP has been on duty now for more than 10 years. And we may recall that Security Council Resolution 186 of March 4, 1964,[29] recommended in paragraph 5 "that the function of the Force should be, in the interest of preserving international peace and security, to use its best efforts to prevent a recurrence of fighting and, as necessary, to contribute to the maintenance and restoration of law and order and a return to normal conditions." We consequently believe it appropriate to urge the Secretary General to take immediately any necessary steps to this end. Consistent with this view, my delegation supports the resolution before the Council requesting the Secretary General to take appropriate action, and we urge its approval without delay.

Mr. President, an important first step has been taken toward the normalization of conditions in Cyprus, and it points the way toward the full implementation of Security Council Resolution 353 of July 20. We believe it is now the obligation of this Council to maintain and encourage the momentum toward peace which has now been generated. We strongly urge members of this Council to support the efforts of the parties and to place no doctrinal or procedural barriers in their way. Our individual and collective support for this Geneva agreement and its continuing implementation will

[28]Document 30a.
[29]Cf. note 7.

be our most important contribution to the maintenance of international peace and security in the area.

[Despite its approval by a majority of the Security Council, adoption of the pending resolution was blocked by a procedural objection on the part of Soviet Representative Yakov A. Malik, who employed the U.S.S.R.'s 109th veto to prevent approval after the Council had declined to heed his complaint that time had not been allowed to obtain instructions from Moscow. Next day, however, a virtually identical resolution was adopted by a vote of 12 to 0, with the U.S.S.R. and Byelorussia abstaining and China, which invariably took a dim view of U.N. peacekeeping ventures, not participating.]

(c) Instructions to the Secretary-General: Security Council Resolution 355 (1974), August 1, 1974.[30]

The Security Council,

Recalling its resolutions 186 (1964) of 4 March 1964,[31] 353 (1974) of 20 July and 354 (1974) of 23 July 1974,[32]

Noting that all States have declared their respect for the sovereignty, independence and territorial integrity of Cyprus,

Taking note of the Secretary-General's statement made at the 1788th meeting of the Security Council,[33]

Requests the Secretary-General to take appropriate action in the light of his statement and to present a full report to the Council, taking into account that the cease-fire will be the first step in the full implementation of Security Council resolution 353 (1974).

[A statement by Ambassador Scali expressed American satisfaction at what appeared—deceptively, as matters turned out—to mark the close of one of the more tumultuous episodes in recent international affairs.]

(d) Statement of Ambassador Scali to the Security Council, August 1, 1974.[34]

[30]Text from Security Council, *Official Records: 29th Year, Resolutions and Decisions 1974:* 8.

[31]Cf. note 7.

[32]Documents 30a and 33a.

[33]Document 35 a.

[34]Text from *Bulletin,* 71: 330. For further developments see Chapter 18.

Mr. President:[35] I salute you as you return refreshed and relaxed from the Soviet Union in time to assume the Presidency of the Security Council. I express the hope that with your broad experience we can all join together in this month to help promote the peace. I wish to pay particular tribute to the skill and the wisdom with which Ambassador Perez de Cuellar[36] has guided our deliberations in this past rather difficult month. This Council has seen many distinguished Presidents, but I am sure that the performance and the gentle wisdom of the Ambassador of Peru will rank among the very highest.

I am glad that we have done today what we should have done yesterday.

As Ambassador Bennett told this Council last night,[37] the U.S. delegation believes it entirely appropriate to urge the Secretary General to take immediately any steps necessary to fulfill the recommendation in paragraph 5 of Security Council Resolution 186 of March 4, 1964. It reads as follows: "that the function of the Force should be, in the interest of preserving international peace and security, to use its best efforts to prevent a recurrence of fighting and, as necessary, to contribute to the maintenance and restoration of law and order and a return to normal conditions."

Mr. President, in voting the two previous resolutions which this Council has considered in the past few days, some important first steps already have been taken to normalize conditions on Cyprus. In approving today's resolution, we can speed up the full implementation of Security Council Resolution 353 of July 20.[38] The Council has now acted to maintain and to encourage the momentum toward peace which has been generated. We are confident that all parties involved in the complex Cyprus situation will do their utmost to keep the peace, to maintain the cease-fire without which prospects for negotiation toward a just and durable settlement would remain dim.

As we have done throughout these debates, we urge all members of this Council to support the efforts of the parties and to place no barriers of doctrine or procedure in their way. Our individual and collective support for the resolutions of the Security Council and the Geneva declaration[39]—a roadmap for peace—will be a most important contribution to the maintenance of international peace and security in the area.

[35]Yakov A. Malik of the U.S.S.R., President of the Security Council for Aug. 1974.
[36]Cf. note 5.
[37]Document 35b.
[38]Document 30a.
[39]Document 34.

Mr. President, like the majority of the Council, my delegation was disappointed and concerned when it proved impossible yesterday to take prompt action of the kind needed to help make the cease-fire effective and thus to enhance the propects for peace. We are concerned that delay offered opportunity for further violence. Today we have acted, and I believe we can congratulate ourselves that the Security Council has again acted as it should in a moment of crisis.

17. A CHANGE OF PRESIDENTS

(August 9, 1974)

[Phase I of the Cyprus crisis turned out to be the last among the international dramas of the Nixon administration. By the time Phase II commenced with the breakdown of the Geneva talks and the opening of a second Turkish offensive extending throughout northern Cyprus, Mr. Nixon was back in San Clemente as a private citizen and President Ford was fingering the levers of office under the guidance of Secretary Kissinger and other members of the former Nixon cabinet.

Two separate events, both occuring in Washington on Wednesday, July 24, initiated the final debacle of a presidency that had already been largely discredited through piecemeal revelation of its various improprieties. The Judiciary Committee of the House of Representatives began on that day its televised debates on the question of a presidential impeachment; and the Supreme Court unanimously affirmed Judge Sirica's earlier ruling that the White House must comply with Special Prosecutor Jaworski's demand for the tapes of 64 specified presidential conversations.

For most of the 21 Democrats and 17 Republicans who made up the House Judiciary Committee, the case for impeachment of the President was already so clear as to require no further tape-recorded evidence. Proceeding with the preparation of its recommendations to the House of Representatives, the committee approved on Saturday, July 27, by 27 votes to 11, a first, detailed article of impeachment in which Mr. Nixon was accused of having "prevented, obstructed, and impeded the administration of justice" in the Watergate cover-up. On Monday, July 29, the committee voted 28 to 10 to recommend a second article of impeachment, detailing numerous abuses of presidential authority in regard to the Internal Revenue Service, the Federal Bureau of Investigation, the Central Intelligence Agency, and other Federal agencies. A third article, citing the President's defiance of four committee subpoenas, was voted by 21 to 17 on Tuesday, July 30, while two further articles, dealing with the secret bombing of Cambodia and with financial and tax irregularities, were rejected on that day, by votes of 12 in favor and 26 opposed. Debate on the committee's charges in the House of Representatives was expected to begin not later than Monday, August 19, by which time it could be assumed that any new information contained in the 64 subpoenaed conversations would also be available to supplement the committee's findings.

That the subpoenaed tapes in fact contained still further, highly damaging information—information that directly belied the President's public statements over many months—was made known on Monday, August 5, when Mr. Nixon personally released the transcripts of three conversations he had held with H. R. Haldeman on June 23, 1972, six days after the Watergate break-in. Portions of these tapes, the President now acknowledged,[1] were "at variance with certain of my previous statements"—notably, with a formal written statement of May 22, 1973,[2] in which he had asserted that the FBI investigation of the Watergate break-in had been restricted only to the extent thought necessary to avoid exposing certain operations of the CIA or the White House "investigations unit," better known as the "Plumbers." In reality, Mr. Nixon now conceded, it was clearly evident from the June 23 tapes "that at the time I gave these instructions I also discussed the political aspects of the situation, and . . . was aware of the advantages this course of action would have with respect to limiting possible exposure of involvement by persons connected with the re-election committee." Still "firmly convinced that the record, in its entirety, does not justify the extreme step of impeachment and removal of a President," Mr. Nixon nevertheless admitted "that a House vote of impeachment is, as a practical matter, virtually a foregone conclusion, and that the issue will therefore go to trial in the Senate."[3]

Not yet brought home to the President, apparently, was the virtual certainty of his conviction in the latter body by more than the constitutionally necessary two-thirds of the Senators present. At a meeting with Republican congressional leaders on Wednesday afternoon, August 7, he was finally made to realize that not more than twelve to fifteen Senators could be counted upon to stand in his defense. Bereft in this way of practically his last hope of political survival, Mr. Nixon went to the Oval Office on Thursday evening, August 8, to announce to a waiting world that rather than

[1] *Presidential Documents,* 10: 1008-9.
[2] *Presidential Documents,* 9: 693-8 (1973); cf. *AFR, 1973:* 196-7.
[3] *Presidential Documents,* 10: 1008-9.

subject the country to a prolonged impeachment battle, he had determined to become the first American President to resign his office before the expiration of his constitutional term. His speech is here reprinted in its entirety because, like so many of Mr. Nixon's major pronouncements, it emphasizes the international aspects of a presidency whose successive moves had invariably been laden with international significance.]

(36) *President Nixon's Resignation Speech: Radio-television address from the Oval Office at the White House, August 8, 1974.*[4]

Good evening.

This is the 37th time I have spoken to you from this office, where so many decisions have been made that shaped the history of this Nation. Each time I have done so to discuss with you some matter that I believe affected the national interest.

In all the decisions I have made in my public life, I have always tried to do what was best for the Nation. Throughout the long and difficult period of Watergate, I have felt it was my duty to persevere, to make every possible effort to complete the term of office to which you elected me.

In the past few days, however, it has become evident to me that I no longer have a strong enough political base in the Congress to justify continuing that effort. As long as there was such a base, I felt strongly that it was necessary to see the constitutional process through to its conclusion, that to do otherwise would be unfaithful to the spirit of that deliberately difficult process and a dangerously destabilizing precedent for the future.

But with the disappearance of that base, I now believe that the constitutional purpose has been served, and there is no longer a need for the process to be prolonged.

I would have preferred to carry through to the finish whatever the personal agony it would have involved, and my family unanimously urged me to do so. But the interest of the Nation must always come before any personal considerations.

From the discussions I have had with Congressional and other leaders, I have concluded that because of the Watergate matter I might not have the support of the Congress that I would consider necessary to back the very difficult decisions and carry out the duties of this office in the way the interests of the Nation would require.

[4]Text from *Presidential Documents,* 10: 1014-17.

I have never been a quitter. To leave office before my term is completed is abhorrent to every instinct in my body. But as President, I must put the interest of America first. America needs a full-time President and a full-time Congress, particularly at this time with problems we face at home and abroad.

To continue to fight through the months ahead for my personal vindication would almost totally absorb the time and attention of both the President and the Congress in a period when our entire focus should be on the great issues of peace abroad and prosperity without inflation at home.

Therefore, I shall resign the Presidency effective at noon tomorrow. Vice President Ford will be sworn in as President at that hour in this office.[5]

As I recall the high hopes for America with which we began this second term,[6] I feel a great sadness that I will not be here in this office working on your behalf to achieve those hopes in the next 2½ years. But in turning over direction of the Government to Vice President Ford, I know, as I told the Nation when I nominated him for that office 10 months ago, that the leadership of America will be in good hands.

In passing this office to the Vice President, I also do so with the profound sense of the weight of responsibility that will fall on his shoulders tomorrow and, therefore, of the understanding, the patience, the cooperation he will need from all Americans.

As he assumes that responsibility, he will deserve the help and the support of all of us. As we look to the future, the first essential is to begin healing the wounds of this Nation, to put the bitterness and divisions of the recent past behind us, and to rediscover those shared ideals that lie at the heart of our strength and unity as a great and as a free people.

By taking this action, I hope that I will have hastened the start of that process of healing which is so desperately needed in America.

I regret deeply any injuries that may have been done in the course of the events that led to this decision. I would say only that if some of my judgments were wrong, and some were wrong, they were made in what I believed at the time to be the best interest of the Nation.

To those who have stood with me during these past difficult months, to my family, my friends, to many others who joined in supporting my cause because they believed it was right, I will be eternally grateful for your support.

And to those who have not felt able to give me your support, let

[5]President Ford took the oath of office in the East Room of the White House.
[6]Cf. *AFR, 1973:* 8-12.

me say I leave with no bitterness toward those who have opposed me, because all of us, in the final analysis, have been concerned with the good of the country, however our judgments might differ.

So, let us all now join together in affirming that common commitment and in helping our new President succeed for the benefit of all Americans.

I shall leave this office with regret at not completing my term, but with gratitude for the privilege of serving as your President for the past 5½ years. These years have been a momentous time in the history of our Nation and the World. They have been a time of achievement in which we can all be proud, achievements that represent the shared efforts of the Administration, the Congress and the people.

But the challenges ahead are equally great, and they, too, will require the support and the efforts of the Congress and the people working in cooperation with the new Administration.

We have ended America's longest war, but in the work of securing a lasting peace in the world, the goals ahead are even more far-reaching and more difficult. We must complete a structure of peace so that it will be said of this generation, our generation of Americans, by the people of all nations, not only that we ended one war but that we prevented future wars.

We have unlocked the doors that for a quarter of a century stood between the United States and the People's Republic of China.

We must now ensure that the one quarter of the world's people who live in the People's Republic of China will be and remain not our enemies but our friends.

In the Middle East, 100 million people in the Arab countries, many of whom have considered us their enemy for nearly 20 years, now look on us as their friends. We must continue to build on that friendship so that peace can settle at last over the Middle East and so that the cradle of civilization will not become its grave.

Together with the Soviet Union we have made the crucial breakthroughs that have begun the process of limiting nuclear arms. But we must set as our goal not just limiting but reducing and finally destroying these terrible weapons so that they cannot destroy civilization and so that the threat of nuclear war will no longer hang over the world and the people.

We have opened the new relation with the Soviet Union. We must continue to develop and expand that new relationship so that the two strongest nations of the world will live together in cooperation rather than confrontation.

Around the world, in Asia, in Africa, in Latin America, in the Middle East, there are millions of people who live in terrible poverty, even starvation. We must keep as our goal turning away from production for war and expanding production for peace so that people everywhere on this earth can at last look forward in their children's time, if not in our own time, to having the necessities for a decent life.

Here in America, we are fortunate that most of our people have not only the blessings of liberty but also the means to live full and good and, by the world's standards, even abundant lives. We must press on, however, toward a goal of not only more and better jobs but of full opportunity for every American and of what we are striving so hard right now to achieve, prosperity without inflation.

For more than a quarter of a century in public life I have shared in the turbulent history of this era. I have fought for what I believed in. I have tried to the best of my ability to discharge those duties and meet those responsibilities that were entrusted to me.

Sometimes I have succeeded and sometimes I have failed, but always I have taken heart from what Theodore Roosevelt once said about the man in the arena, "whose face is marred by dust and sweat and blood, who strives valiantly, who errs and comes short again and again because there is not effort without error and shortcoming, but who does actually strive to do the deed, who knows the great enthusiasms, the great devotions, who spends himself in a worthy cause, who at the best knows in the end the triumphs of high achievements and who at the worst, if he fails, at least fails while daring greatly."

I pledge to you tonight that as long as I have a breath of life in my body, I shall continue in that spirit. I shall continue to work for the great causes to which I have been dedicated throughout my years as a Congressman, a Senator, a Vice President, and President, the cause of peace not just for America but among all nations, prosperity, justice, and opportunity for all of our people.

There is one cause above all to which I have been devoted and to which I shall always be devoted for as long as I live.

When I first took the oath of office as President 5½ years ago, I made this sacred commitment, to "consecrate my office, my energies, and all the wisdom I can summon to the cause of peace among nations."[7]

I have done my very best in all the days since to be true to that pledge. As a result of these efforts, I am confident that the world is a safer place today, not only for the people of America but for the people of all nations, and that all of our children have a better chance than before of living in peace rather than dying in war.

This, more than anything, is what I hoped to achieve when I sought the Presidency. This, more than anything, is what I hope will be my legacy to you, to our country, as I leave the Presidency.

---

[7] *Documents, 1968-69*: 42.

To have served in this office is to have felt a very personal sense of kinship with each and every American. In leaving it, I do so with this prayer: May God's grace be with you in all the days ahead.

[Mr. Nixon's formal resignation of the presidency, communicated in a one-sentence letter to the Secretary of State, became effective at noon on August 9 as Gerald R. Ford took the oath of office as the nation's 38th President. Mr. Ford's remarks, though eloquent in their appeal for national reconciliation, included only the briefest reference to foreign affairs:

To the peoples and governments of all friendly nations, and I hope that could encompass the whole world, I pledge an uninterrupted and sincere search for peace. America will remain strong and united, but its strength will remain dedicated to the safety and sanity of the entire family of man, as well as to our own precious freedom.[8]

Reassuring to many in the United States and abroad was the knowledge that the new President had requested Dr. Kissinger to remain as head of the nation's foreign affairs establishment, a mark of continuity that was understood to have been specially recommended by the departing President Nixon.

A slightly fuller account of the new President's views on foreign and defense policy was included in the address he delivered before a joint session of the Congress the following Monday evening (August 12),[9] in the course of which he urged prompt action on the pending trade reform bill and other items of current legislation.]

(37) President Ford's Intentions: Address delivered before a Joint Session of the Congress, August 12, 1974.[10]

(Excerpt)

*   *   *

The economy of our country is critically dependent on how we interact with the economies of other countries. It is little comfort that our inflation is only a part of a worldwide problem or that American families need less of their paychecks for groceries than most of our foreign friends.

[8]*Presidential Documents,* 10: 1024.
[9]Same: 1029-35.
[10]Text from same: 1032-4.

As one of the building blocks of peace, we have taken the lead in working toward a more open and a more equitable world economic system. A new round of international trade negotiations started last September among 105 nations in Tokyo. The others are waiting for the United States Congress to grant the necessary authority to the executive branch to proceed.[11]

With modifications, the trade reform bill passed by the House last year would do a good job.[12] I understand good progress has been made in the Senate Committee on Finance. But I am optimistic, as always, that the Senate will pass an acceptable bill quickly as a key part of our joint prosperity campaign.

I am determined to expedite other international economic plans. We will be working together with other nations to find better ways to prevent shortages of food and fuel. We must not let last winter's energy crisis happen again. I will push Project Independence[13] for our own good and the good of others. In that, too, I will need your help.

Successful foreign policy is an extension of the hopes of the whole American people for a world of peace and orderly reform and orderly freedom. So, I would say a few words to our distinguished guests from the governments of other nations where, as at home, it is my determination to deal openly with allies and adversaries.

Over the past 5½ years in Congress and as Vice President, I have fully supported the outstanding foreign policy of President Nixon. This policy I intend to continue.

Throughout my public service, starting with wartime naval duty under the command of President Franklin D. Roosevelt, I have upheld all our Presidents when they spoke for my country to the world. I believe the Constitution commands this. I know that in this crucial area of international policy I can count on your firm support.

Now, let there be no doubt or any misunderstanding anywhere, and I emphasize anywhere: There are no opportunities to exploit, should anyone so desire. There will be no change of course, no relaxation of vigilance, no abandonment of the helm of our Ship of State as the watch changes.

We stand by our commitments and we will live up to our responsibilities in our formal alliances, in our friendships, and in our improving relations with potential adversaries.

On this, Americans are united and strong. Under my term of

---

[11]Cf. Chapter 10 at note 2.
[12]Cf. Chapter 15 at notes 10-11.
[13]Cf. Chapter 3 at note 1.

leadership, I hope we will become more united. I am certain America will remain strong.

A strong defense is the surest way to peace. Strength makes détente attainable. Weakness invites war as my generation—my generation—knows from four very bitter experiences.

Just as America's will for peace is second to none, so will America's strength be second to none.

We cannot rely on the forbearance of others to protect this Nation. The power and diversity of the Armed Forces, active guard, and reserve, the resolve of our fellow citizens, the flexibility in our command to navigate international waters that remain troubled are all essential to our security.

I shall continue to insist on civilian control of our superb military establishment. The Constitution plainly requires the President to be Commander in Chief, and I will be.

Our job will not be easy. In promising continuity, I cannot promise simplicity. The problems and challenges of the world remain complex and difficult. But we have set out on a path of reason, of fairness, and we will continue on it.

As guideposts on that path, I offer the following:

—To our allies of a generation in the Atlantic community and Japan, I pledge continuity in the loyal collaboration on our many mutual endeavors.

—To our friends and allies in this hemisphere, I pledge continuity in the deepening dialog to define renewed relationships of equality and justice.

—To our allies and friends in Asia, I pledge a continuity in our support for their security, independence, and economic development. In Indochina, we are determined to see the observance of the Paris agreement on Vietnam and the cease-fire and negotiated settlement in Laos. We hope to see an early compromise settlement in Cambodia.

—To the Soviet Union, I pledge continuity in our commitment to the course of the past 3 years. To our two peoples, and to all mankind, we owe a continued effort to live and, where possible, to work together in peace; for in a thermonuclear age there can be no alternative to a positive and peaceful relationship between our nations.

—To the People's Republic of China, whose legendary hospitality I enjoyed,[14] I pledge continuity in our commitment to the principles of the Shanghai communique.[15] The new relationship built

[14]Cf. *AFR, 1972*: 320 n. 38.
[15]Same: 307-11.

on those principles has demonstrated that it serves serious and objective mutual interests and has become an enduring feature of the world scene.

—To the nations in the Middle East, I pledge continuity in our vigorous efforts to advance the progress which has brought hopes of peace to that region after 25 years as a hotbed of war. We shall carry out our promise to promote continuing negotiations among all parties for a complete, just, and lasting settlement.

—To all nations, I pledge continuity in seeking a common global goal: a stable international structure of trade and finance which reflects the interdependence of all peoples.

—To the entire international community—to the United Nations, to the world's nonaligned nations, and to all others—I pledge continuity in our dedication to the humane goals which throughout our history have been so much of America's contribution to mankind.

So long as the peoples of the world have confidence in our purposes and faith in our word, the age-old vision of peace on earth will grow brighter.

I pledge myself unreservedly to that goal. I say to you in words that cannot be improved upon: Let us never negotiate out of fear, but let us never fear to negotiate.[16]

* * *

[In an address to the Veterans of Foreign Wars convention in Chicago on August 19,[17] President Ford reiterated his commitment to a strong national defense and also made known his intention to review the status of an estimated 50,000 young Americans convicted, charged or under investigation, or still sought in connection with "offenses loosely described as desertion and draft-dodging." It fell to Secretary Kissinger, in an August 20 address before the American Legion in Miami, to provide a more detailed, authoritative statement emphasizing the continuity of America's aims and attitudes vis-à-vis the outside world.]

(38) *"America's Strength and America's Purposes": Address by Secretary of State Kissinger before the American Legion National Convention, Miami, August 20, 1974.*[18]

---

[16]*Documents, 1961*: 14.
[17]*Presidential Documents,* 10: 1045-9.
[18]Department of State Press Release 335; title and text from *Bulletin,* 71: 373-8.

I bring you the greetings of President Ford, who has asked that I tell you that he looks forward to being with you at your national convention next year.[19]

I am proud to accept the honor you do me this evening. The basic objective of this organization, the maintenance of our national security, has been the central concern of my life for over two decades as a teacher and writer as well as a public servant. Your unswerving dedication to that goal for half a century, through good times and bad, reflects not only the striving of a single organization but also the purposes of an entire nation.

The greatness of a nation is measured not only by its courage in an hour of crisis but by its response to a prolonged ordeal. After a decade of national tragedy and travail, America and the American people have now emerged strong and united.

For two decades after the Second World War we believed that we could do everything; more recently some spoke of overinvolvement and began to believe that we could do nothing. But as we approach our 200th anniversary our faith in ourselves has returned. We are the better for our experience. By learning our limits, we have learned our possibilities as well. We have rejected the extremes of world policeman and isolation which have too long dominated our debate. This has enabled us to move toward the definition of a foreign policy that the American people can support and sustain over the decades to come.

Our constancy is the hope of the world. As President Ford stated in his first address to the Congress last week:[20]

So long as the peoples of the world have confidence in our purposes and faith in our word, the age-old vision of peace on earth will grow brighter.

Each age has striven for peace; yet wars inevitably came either by decision or miscalculation. No generation in this century has avoided it. This age must be different. For the first time in history, man has the capacity quite literally to destroy mankind. In our era, miscalculation could end life itself.

No group of men understands better the meaning of peace than those who have experienced personally the agonies of war.

The greatest of America's military leaders have always been in the forefront of those who have sought to turn man's eternal

---

[19]President Ford addressed the Legion's 57th National Convention in Minneapolis on Aug. 19, 1975; cf. *Presidential Documents,* 11: 869-74 (1975).
[20]Document 36.

history of conflict into a new international order of justice and cooperation and peace.

Thus George Marshall's contribution to mankind after the Second World War may have surpassed even his historic contribution during the war. He helped forge the national conviction that America's security is inseparable from the world's security and that the great issues of national defense transcend party and partisan purpose. This tradition has served us well through five administrations.

Dwight Eisenhower added another dimension. He called attention to the necessity of a strong standing defense. In his words "the weak have no assurance of peace. They can only accept the future without influence upon it." But he also understood that in the nuclear age strength cannot be an end in itself. He proclaimed what no President since has ever forgotten: "There is no longer any alternative to peace."

So our search for peace begins with America's strength. For other nations to have confidence in our purposes and faith in our word, America must remain a military power second to none. As I can attest from experience, in time of crisis and at the conference table, America's military might is the foundation of our diplomatic strength. We have made progress toward peace in recent years because we have been flexible, but also because we have been resolute. Let us never forget that conciliation is a virtue only in those who are thought to have a choice.

—A strong defense is the essential deterrent to aggression. By demonstrating that there is no alternative to negotiation, it is the precondition of our policy of relaxing tensions with our adversaries.

—A strong defense is the cement of our alliances, reinforcing our partners' will to join in the common defense. It is the basis of mutual confidence and thus of our cooperation across the whole spectrum of our common interests.

Since the Second World War, each administration regardless of party has supported the maintenance of our military strength. And on every major question of national defense for the past quarter century Congress has supported the President. This is a proud record which we must and will sustain.

But we are living in an age when the issues of defense are of unprecedented complexity. In the nuclear age we must:

—Allocate resources between strategic and tactical forces.

—Relate military strength to foreign policy goals.

—Maintain our security while ending and ultimately reversing the arms race.

In an era of rough strategic balance, the threat to launch an all-out nuclear war grows less and less credible; hence it is less and less likely to deter the full range of potential conflicts. Military challenges at the conventional level may become more difficult to prevent. Thus the political and military importance of tactical forces grows correspondingly.

Our conventional forces must therefore be strong. They keep the nuclear threshold high by helping to contain, discourage, or altogether prevent hostilities. They are the essential tool of our diplomacy in times of crisis. In no recent crisis did we come close to using our strategic forces, but on many occasions our tactical forces were alerted or deployed to deter aggressive actions or to defend the interests of America and its allies. About one-third of our conventional forces are deployed abroad. They are there to serve these purposes. They are not overseas as a favor to foreigners; they are abroad as part of our defense.

American forces in Europe are a vivid illustration of these principles. Reducing our forces there unilaterally would risk serious military and political instability in the center of Europe, enhance Soviet political influence by default, and, ironically, make reliance on nuclear weapons more necessary. It would undercut promising negotiations for the mutual reduction of forces. The defense of Western Europe remains—as it has been throughout the postwar period—the cornerstone of our own security.

Just as we must assure a balance of conventional forces, so we must also assure a nuclear balance. We are determined never to fall behind in nuclear arms. We will never accept the strategic preponderance of another power. We will maintain our strategic weapons program at whatever level is required to achieve this end.

The definition of adequacy or sufficiency or equivalence is not simple, however. Throughout history the essential task of national security was to accumulate military power. It would have seemed inconceivable even a generation ago that such power, once gained, could not be translated directly into foreign policy advantage.

Today we, as well as the Soviet Union, must start from the premise that in the nuclear era an increase in certain categories of military power does not necessarily represent an increase of usable political strength. When two nations are already capable of destroying each other, an upper limit exists beyond which additional weapons lose their political significance. The overwhelming destructiveness of nuclear weapons makes it difficult to relate their use to specific political objectives and may indeed generate new political problems.

A continual expansion of strategic forces by both sides will not result in greater security. It will only lead to new balances at higher levels of complexity and risk and at exorbitant cost. It will generate an atmosphere of hostility and suspicion that makes political conflict more likely and that will over time thwart aspirations for a more tranquil and secure world.

This is why President Ford, an ardent advocate of national defense, as one of his first acts as President has invited the Soviet leaders to join with us in an intensified effort to negotiate an effective and equitable limitation of strategic arms.

We will be guided by two basic principles:

—First, until further arms limits are negotiated we will maintain American strategic strength, whatever the cost. Our power will not falter through lack of resolve or sacrifice.

—Second, we will pursue the Strategic Arms Limitation Talks with an energy and conviction equal to the challenge before us. We are determined to become the masters of our own technology, not its slave.

The President has asked me to emphasize that in his view the choice is clear. We will maintain the nuclear balance by unilateral actions if we must and by negotiations if at all possible. I can assure you that these negotiations will not fail for lack of good will and readiness to explore new solutions on our part.

Winston Churchill once said to the American people:

The destiny of mankind is not decided by material computation. When great causes are on the move . . . we learn that something is going on in space and time, and beyond space and time, which, whether we like it or not, spells duty.

America now has an opportunity—and hence a duty—which comes rarely to a nation: to help shape a new peaceful international order. This challenge exists for us as a people, not as partisans of any cause. This is why this effort—even in periods of great domestic strain—has had bipartisan support. The leaders of both parties in Congress deserve the nation's gratitude for having insulated our foreign and security policies from our recent domestic travails.

President Nixon's legacy to President Ford is a world safer than the one he found. President Ford has dedicated himself to leaving to his successor a world at peace and living with a consciousness of peace.

Many of the conflicts that have haunted the past three decades have been overcome. We have muted the constant crises over Berlin; for the first time it is possible to conceive of a lasting settlement in the Middle East; our combat involvement in the Viet-Nam war has been ended honorably and the level of fighting reduced. The United States and the Soviet Union, after decades of profound suspicion, have perceived a common interest in avoiding nuclear holocaust and in establishing a broad web of constructive relationships. And two decades of estrangement between the United States and the People's Republic of China have given way to constructive dialogue and productive exchanges.

But if this world is better than our fears, it is still far short of our hopes. We have eased many crises; we have not yet eliminated their roots. Our achievements, solid as they are, have not yet resolved the dangers and divisions of the postwar era. We have begun but not completed the journey from confrontation to cooperation, from coexistence to community. We are determined to complete that journey.

In pursuing our course we shall encounter many obstacles. There will be turmoil in many parts of the world, such as the current situation in Cyprus. Our attitude will be that we cannot be the world's policeman but that we will always use our influence for peace and conciliation. We will not yield to pressure groups but we will always listen to reason. We will act in foreign policy as trustee of the future, conscious that we will be judged on how well we built an enduring peace and not how often we bowed to the emotional demands of the moment.

America is still the hope of the world, not only because of our physical resources and military might but because of the creativity of our people, the vitality of our institutions, and the ideals of our nation.

At a time when some in this country doubted our ability to cope with the challenges of our future, most of the world perceived that America was emerging stronger than at any period in the past decade. Our alliances are strong. A nation once preoccupied with Viet-Nam is now addressing its broader purposes. A nation once isolated from one major Communist power and in a posture of confrontation with the other has opened a constructive dialogue with both. And a nation facing the crises of a world grown economically interdependent has, unsatisfactory as it is, one of the lowest rates of inflation in the world and is less dependent on foreign sources of energy than any other industrialized nation.

Thus we have a firm base on which to build.

—We must insure that the heart of American foreign policy, our alliances with the Atlantic community and Japan, can meet the challenges of the next generation. America's principal alliances have overcome a period of strain brought about by the inevitable adjustment to new conditions. We now have an opportunity for a new period of creativity in joint efforts to deal with the problems and opportunities of an increasingly interdependent world. Maintaining the vitality of our alliances and giving even greater impetus to their joint efforts will be one of the principal goals of President Ford's foreign policy.

—We must insure that a history in which brief moments of improved Soviet-American relations gave way to prolonged periods of confrontation is replaced by an irreversible commitment to the maintenance of peace. We will spare no effort to reconcile the reality of competition with the imperative of cooperation. In the nuclear era there is no rational alternative.

—We must sustain the process of growing understanding and respect which we have launched with the People's Republic of China. Deep differences in ideology and policy remain. But we believe the new relationship serves fundamental national purposes of both countries; it can be strengthened with dedication and care, and it will endure.

—We must create in the Middle East a lasting peace, not just another cease-fire. My trips throughout that tragically torn area have convinced me of one essential fact above all others: The peoples of the Middle East, be they Arab or Jew, have had enough of bloodshed; they cry out for peace. And peace can be theirs if they and we have the will and patience to achieve it. For the Arabs, there can be no peace without a recovery of territory and the redress of grievances of a displaced people. For Israel, peace requires both security and recognition by its neighbors of its legitimacy as a nation. Our Arab and Israeli friends have, with our help over the past six months, taken the first difficult steps down the road toward fulfillment of these aspirations. We have a long distance yet to travel, but with patience and hard work we will complete the journey. The people of the Middle East deserve it; the peace of the world demands it.

—We must work with our friends in Africa and the nonaligned world in support of their national independence, economic growth, and social progress.

—We must build in the Western Hemisphere a new relationship of equality and partnership. We shall be guided by the conviction that a shared history creates an opportunity and common aspirations provide the basis for fresh approaches. The relationship between industrialized and developing nations cannot be solved creatively anywhere if not in this hemisphere.

—We must strengthen the ability of the peoples of Indochina to determine their own destiny. After the Second World War we spent hundreds of billions to help former ally and enemy alike to recover from the devastation of six years of war. After the Korean war we spent billions to assist in the rebuilding of South Korea. Yet today, after a decade of war and the loss of 50,000 American lives, some hesitate to give South Viet-Nam—for whom the war has not yet ended—the help it so desperately needs to maintain itself as an independent nation. It would be tragic; it would break faith with all those Americans who have fought and died there if we now fail to make the relatively modest effort that the administration has proposed to the Congress to enable South Viet-Nam to survive.

There is an item of unfinished business in Indochina that I know is of special concern to this audience: the accounting for our men who are missing in action, including the dead whose bodies were never recovered. I have met periodically with the families of our missing men continually over the past five years; I know how difficult it is for them to live without knowing the fate of their loved ones. More than 18 months have passed since the signing of the Paris agreement, which specified that there should be cooperation on this humanitarian problem.[21] Surely there should be no political or military advantage in a proper accounting for the missing and the return of the remains of the dead. Our efforts will continue until we have obtained the fullest possible accounting as required by solemn agreements.

Peace, however, is something more than the absence of armed conflict. It is something deeper than the establishment of stability. To enlist the support of humanity it must reflect man's eternal hopes for a humane and prosperous world.

The excitement of creation, of crossing new frontiers, has characterized every major period of American history. Now we face an unprecedented new challenge.

The products of man's technical genius—weapons of incalculable power, a global economic system, a technology that consumes finite resources at an ever-expanding rate—have compressed this planet and multiplied our mutual dependence. In an age of instantaneous communication the quest for justice and dignity has become universal. The national interest can no longer be pursued in isolation from the global interest, as the problems of energy, food, and inflation have recently made clear.

Man has made his world interdependent. Now the challenge is to make it whole.

An enlightened national self-interest requires major American initiatives for an open and cooperative world. Without global solutions our own economy will stagnate. Without an American contribution there can be no global solution. Industrially, we are the most advanced nation in the world. We are still a pioneering nation, on the frontiers of the most important revolutions of the last third of the 20th century in technology, communications, agriculture, and health.

[21]*AFR, 1973:* 42.

With your support and the support of the American people we will contribute to:

—Cooperative efforts to insure an expanding supply of energy and other essential materials at an equitable price.

—Overcoming rampant global inflation by cooperating in building a trade, monetary, and investment system that stimulates global economic growth.

—Fashioning a long-term policy for dealing with chronic global food shortages and striking a balance between food production and population growth.

—Helping the third of mankind threatened with starvation and permanent underdevelopment create a better future.

We in the United States cannot alone assure that the overriding need of cooperation will overcome the historic selfishness of the nation-state. But it is equally clear that mankind cannot fulfill its needs without the faith, the dynamism, and the creativity of our country.

We have a long tradition in this country of arming with great haste when war comes upon us and disarming with even greater haste when the war is over. We have tended to view our relations with nations in terms of absolutes—friend or foe, ally or adversary, unlimited war or permanent peace. We have acted in cycles of overcommitment and withdrawal, enthusiasm and cynicism

This we can no longer afford. We must commit ourselves for the long haul. The search for peace is not a part-time job.

We must learn to deal with nuance, to strive for what is good while never forgetting what is best. Fate has offered us an unprecedented opportunity for creativity in the search for peace.

Let us not rest on the achievements of recent years, but let us summon new hope and new faith in ourselves to go beyond.

If we are true to ourselves, America can be both strong and purposeful, principled and realistic, equally devoted to deterring war and to achieving man's greatest hopes. Over three decades ago President Roosevelt said of his generation that it had a rendezvous with destiny. Let it be said of our generation that it had—and met—a rendezvous with peace.

[While Secretary Kissinger was preparing to address the American Legion in Miami, President Ford in Washington had been making known his choice of Nelson A. Rockefeller, former Governor of New York and a representative of the Republican Party's internationalist wing, to fill the vacant post of Vice-President. In a more sensational move, apparently inspired by a combination of humanitarian feeling and desire to close the Watergate chapter, President Ford on September 8 took action to accord the ailing Richard M. Nixon a "full, free, and absolute pardon" for all offenses against the United States that he had or might have committed or taken part in during his term of office.

Two further actions by the new President require mention in any account of the presidential transition. In a follow-up to his August 19 speech to the Veterans of Foreign Wars, Mr. Ford on September 16 announced an elaborate but, from the first, exceedingly controversial program for the return of Vietnam era draft evaders and military deserters.[22] Its principal features were, for those not yet convicted or punished, the performance of 24 months' alternate service; for those already convicted by a civilian or military court, a review of their cases by a Presidential Clemency Board that would be chaired by former Republican Senator Charles E. Goodell of New York.

Also on September 16, the President announced the appointment of General Alexander M. Haig, Jr., to succeed General Andrew J. Goodpaster as Supreme Allied Commander, Europe and Commander of U.S. Forces in Europe. General Haig, who had served successively as Deputy Assistant to the President for National Security Affairs, Vice-Chief of Staff of the Army, and successor to H. R. Haldeman as Chief of Staff to the President, had been intimately involved in the history of the past few years and would take to Brussels an unrivaled knowledge of political and security issues as seen from a White House vantage point. His nearest equivalent in the Ford administration would be Ambassador Donald H. Rumsfeld, another former Nixon aide who had been serving as U.S. Representative on the North Atlantic Council and was now being brought back to Washington as Assistant to the President with special responsibility for coordinating White House operations.]

18. CYPRUS CRISIS, PHASE II

(August 8-30, 1974)

[After closing out the Nixon administration with a final, furious paroxysm, the parties to the Cyprus conflict inaugurated President Ford's regime with an even more dismaying exhibition of national and ethnic violence. The tentative agreements announced at Geneva by the British, Greek, and Turkish Foreign Ministers on July 30[1] had soon proved insufficient to contain the disruptive elements in the situation. Within little more than a fortnight, the Turkish forces in Cyprus, which had been built up to an estimated strength of some 40,000, were once again upon the offensive and would not rest until the whole northern third of the island had been subjected to Turkish military control.

Like every earlier attempt to solve the problem, the tripartite diplomatic talks that formally resumed in Geneva on August 8—the day of President Nixon's resignation announcement—soon foundered on the irreconcilably opposed demands of the Greek and Turkish Cypriot communities, whose leaders, Acting President Clerides for the Greek and Vice-President Denktash for the Turkish Cypriots, had been invited to join the talks as they turned to the matter of the country's constitutional future. A Turkish Cypriot demand for the formation of a binational state, with an autonomous Turkish area in the north that would encompass 34 percent of the entire Cypriot land area, was promptly rejected by the Greek Cypriot spokesman; while a "compromise" plan put forward by Turkish Foreign Minister Güneş, in which the Turkish Cypriots would still get 34 percent of the territory but would be concentrated in a number of autonomous enclaves, was flatly rejected when its author refused to permit a 36-hour adjournment to enable the Greek and Greek Cypriot representatives to consult their

[1]Chapter 16, Document 34.

governments. The Turkish representative's "unreasonable" and "entirely arbitrary" stand, as Foreign Secretary Callaghan was to call it, occasioned the break up of the Geneva talks at 2:15 A.M. on Wednesday, August 14.

Within two hours of the Geneva debacle, the Turkish military forces in Cyprus were opening a new offensive whose aim, according to Prime Minister Eçevit, was nothing less than to gain control of an area large enough to ensure an unmolested future for the Turkish Cypriot population. While Turkish tanks and infantry, preceded by air and artillery bombardments, thrust east and west from their Kyrenia bridgehead, the Security Council hastily assembled in New York for a pre-dawn meeting at which it unanimously adopted a British-sponsored resolution reaffirming the earlier demand for a cease-fire and a resumption of negotiations.]

(39) Renewal of the Turkish Offensive: Meeting of the Security Council, August 14, 1974.

(a) Renewed demand for a cease-fire: Security Council Resolution 357 (1974), August 14, 1974.[2]

The Security Council,

Recalling its resolutions 353 (1974) of 20 July, 354 (1974) of 23 July, and 355 (1974) of 1 August 1974,[3]

Deeply deploring the resumption of fighting in Cyprus, contrary to the provisions of its resolution 353 (1974),

1. *Reaffirms* its resolution 353 (1974) in all its provisions and calls upon the parties concerned to implement those provisions without delay;

2. *Demands* that all parties to the present fighting cease all firing and military action forthwith;

3. *Calls* for the resumption of negotiations without delay for the restoration of peace in the area and constitutional government in Cyprus, in accordance with resolution 353 (1974);

4. *Decides* to remain seized of the situation and on instant call to meet as necessary to consider what more effective measures may be required if the cease-fire is not respected.

[Following the adoption of this resolution, Ambassador Scali

---

[2]Text from Security Council, *Official Records: 29th Year, Resolutions and Decisions 1974*: 8.
[3]Respectively Documents 30a, 33a, and 35c.

joined with other delegates in expressing his government's indignation at the Turkish action, as well as its conviction that the United Nations must maintain its authority and persevere in its efforts to promote a peaceful and workable settlement.]

(b) Statement by Ambassador Scali to the Council, August 14, 1974.[4]

My delegation deeply regrets that almost a month after the approval of Security Council Resolution 353, we have found it necessary to meet once again in this hall to consider new steps to end violence on the island of Cyprus. We regret this all the more because this return of violence was so unnecessary. Promising negotiations had been going forward in Geneva pursuant to Resolution 353 and in keeping with the Charter of the United Nations and treaties of guarantee establishing the state of Cyprus. But, unhappily, in the absence of a conciliatory spirit at the conference table, these negotiations have been interrupted and the guns of war are speaking again.

The United States, Mr. President,[5] is convinced that only through such negotiations can a settlement emerge which will restore constitutional government to Cyprus and peace and stability in the eastern Mediterranean. As this Council is aware, the United States has lent its total support to this process. My government did this because of its close relations with its allies Greece and Turkey, because of its commitment to the independence and territorial integrity of Cyprus, because of its concern for the welfare of the Cypriot people of both communities, and also, but not least, because of its overriding concern for peace in the area.

We have given our full support to the valiant and tireless efforts of the United Kingdom, a guarantor power under the London-Zurich agreement, to bring about a measure of common understanding at Geneva which would point the way toward a new constitutional arrangement in Cyprus which takes into account the new realities. In this role we have been in constant touch with all of the parties to do whatever we could to encourage the negotiating process.

The United States has taken heart from the restoration of constitutional government in Greece so ably led by Prime Minister Karamanlis. The Greek Government has pursued with diligence the search for arrangements to restore constitutional government in

---

Cyprus. As a guarantor power, Greece has legitimate interests which must be fully recognized.

We also pay tribute to the people of Cyprus of both communities, who have endured many hardships in the past month. The Acting President of Cyprus, Mr. Clerides, and the Turkish Vice President, Mr. Denktash, have both made major contributions in this complicated process of negotiation.

Turkey also has legitimate interests which must be fully recognized. My government made clear yesterday in a public statement its view that the position of the Turkish community on Cyprus requires considerable improvement and protection as well as a greater degree of autonomy.[6]

My government, Mr. President, considers that it is the duty of this Council to do everything in keeping with Resolution 353 to aid in bringing the parties back to the negotiating table. It is only at that table that a consensus can emerge leading to a settlement which will be satisfactory to all the parties and which will bring peace and stability once again to this area.

The duty of this Council tonight is simply this: We must call for an immediate end to the fighting, and we must call for the earliest resumption of negotiations. My government pledges that it will continue its own efforts toward the end that the voice of reason will again be heard and the voice of the cannons once more stilled.

[Ambassador Scali's implicit criticism of the Turkish action was made explicit by the Department of State, which issued a formal statement declaring the resort to military action "unjustified" and stating that "We deplore the Turkish resort to force."[7] Once again, however, insistent questions were raised about the sincerity of the American Government and its Secretary of State. As in the Indo-Pakistan war of 1971,[8] there seemed to be a widespread impression that the United States, in spite of its professions of impartiality,

---

[6]In a news briefing on Aug. 13, Robert Anderson, Special Assistant to the Secretary of State for Press Relations, said:

"The U.S. position is as follows:

"We recognize the position of the Turkish community of Cyprus requires considerable improvement and protection. We have supported a greater degree of autonomy for them.

"The parties are negotiating on one or more Turkish autonomous areas. The avenues of diplomacy have not been exhausted. And therefore the United States would consider a resort to military action unjustified.

"We have made this clear to all parties." *(Bulletin,* 71: 367n.)

[7]*New York Times,* Aug. 15, 1974.

[8]Cf. *AFR, 1971:* 225.

was actually "tilting" in the direction of one of the two opposing governments—in this case, that it was favoring Turkey because it rated that country's contribution to Western security as more important than its adherence to accepted standards of international behavior.

The new Greek Government, which appeared particularly prone to such suspicions, was already showing lively dissatisfaction not only with the United States but with the entire Atlantic alliance. Within hours of the new Turkish attack, Athens had announced its determination to withdraw its armed forces from NATO and to limit its alliance membership thenceforward to the "political aspects." So far as going to war with Turkey was concerned, however, the Greek authorities felt driven to a negative conclusion. As Turkish forces continued their advance in open defiance of the Security Council resolutions, Prime Minister Caramanlis broke the painful news that Greece was simply not in a position to offer military resistance, in part because of the distances involved and in part because mismanagement by the previous Greek regime had made it impossible to intervene in Cyprus without imperiling the defense of Greece itself.

But if even Greece, the patron and protector of the Greek Cypriots, was unable to move, no other outside power seemed likely to do so. As the Turkish offensive continued for a second day, the Security Council in New York could do little beyond reaffirming past admonitions. In this spirit, two further resolutions were adopted at the meeting of Thursday, August 15: a unanimous demand for observance of the cease-fire, and a demand for cooperation with the U.N. Peace-keeping Force.]

(40) Continuation of the Turkish Offensive: Meeting of the Security Council, August 15, 1974.

(a) Insisting on the implementation of previous resolutions: Security Council Resolution 358 (1974), August 15, 1974.[9]

The Security Council,

Deeply concerned about the continuation of violence and bloodshed in Cyprus,

Deeply deploring the non-compliance with its resolution 357 (1974) of 14 August 1974,[10]

---

[9]Text from Security Council, *Official Records: 29th Year, Resolutions and Decisions 1974*: 8.

[10]Document 39a.

1. *Recalls* its resolutions 353 (1974) of 20 July, 354 (1974) of 23 July, 355 (1974) of 1 August 1974[11] and 357 (1974);

2. *Insists* on the full implementation of the above resolutions by all parties and on the immediate and strict observance of the cease-fire.

(b) Demanding respect for UNFICYP: Security Council Resolution 359 (1974), August 15, 1974.[12]

The Security Council,

Noting with concern from the Secretary-General's report on developments in Cyprus, in particular documents S/11353/Add.24 and 25,[13] that casualties are increasing among the personnel of the United Nations Peace-keeping Force in Cyprus as a direct result of the military action which is still continuing in Cyprus,

Recalling that the United Nations Force was stationed in Cyprus with the full consent of the Governments of Cyprus, Turkey and Greece,

Bearing in mind that the Secretary-General was requested by the Security Council in resolution 355 (1974) of 1 August 1974[14] to take appropriate action in the light of his statement made at the 1788th meeting of the Council in which he dealt with the role, functions and strength of the Force and related issues arising out of the most recent political developments in respect of Cyprus,

1. *Deeply deplores* the fact that members of the United Nations Peace-keeping Force in Cyprus have been killed and wounded;

2. *Demands* that all parties concerned fully respect the international status of the United Nations Force and refrain from any action which might endanger the lives and safety of its members;

3. *Urges* the parties concerned to demonstrate in a firm, clear and unequivocal manner their willingness to fulfil the commitments they have entered into in this regard;

4. *Demands further* that all parties co-operate with the United Nations Force in carrying out its tasks, including humanitarian functions, in all areas of Cyprus and in regard to all sections of the population of Cyprus;

[11]Respectively Documents 30a, 33a, and 35c.
[12]Text from Security Council, *Official Records: 29th Year, Resolutions and Decisions 1974:* 8-9. Sponsored by Australia, Austria, Cameroon, France, and Peru, the resolution was adopted by a vote of 14-0-0 with China not participating.
[13]Security Council, *Official Records: 29th Year, Supplement for July, Aug. and Sept. 1974:* 45-7.
[14]Document 35c.

5. *Emphasizes* the fundamental principle that the status and safety of the members of the United Nations Peace-keeping Force in Cyprus, and for that matter of any United Nations peace-keeping force, must be respected by the parties under all circumstances.

(c) Statement by Ambassador Scali to the Council, August 15, 1974.[15]

It is with a sense of deep appreciation to those who seek to keep the peace on behalf of the United Nations that we have voted for this resolution [359] tonight, which was sponsored by five member countries. It is also with a sense of grief, however, because of the tragic news that three Austrian members of UNFICYP have been killed while carrying out their duties on Cyprus. Our government extends its profound condolences to the Austrian Government and to the families of these brave men who have sacrificed their lives for the peace which is the goal of us all.

We further note with a feeling of deepest sorrow that an additional number of UNFICYP troops have been wounded in the fighting, 27 by the latest count of the Secretariat. These men are international heroes. They deserve not only our gratitude but our support so that their task can be facilitated, not hampered, as they carry out their tasks far from home, like other United Nations peacekeepers in the Middle East and in other areas. We, the representatives of our governments, who sit here in the safety of this chamber, must remember them because, regardless of nationality, they are our sons. We must make sure that they and their successors patrolling distant battlefields have the capacity and the mandate to carry out their dangerous assignments without requiring of them that they give up their lives.

[By August 16, the third day of their offensive, Turkish forces had virtually completed their occupation of the northern third of the island, comprising all of the territory north of the so-called "Attila Line" between Lefka in the west and Famagusta in the east. Asserting that the foundation had thus been laid for a federal Cypriot state with autonomous Turkish and Greek administrations, Prime Minister Eçevit now at length announced that a cease-fire would be effective at 7:00 P.M. local time that evening, Friday, August 16. The Security Council, angered by the disregard of its previous resolutions and dismayed by the growing devastation and human suffering reported from Cyprus, recorded its views in a

French-sponsored resolution that was adopted by a vote of 11 to 0, with 3 abstentions (the U.S.S.R., Byelorussia, and Iraq) and with China not participating.]

(41) Renewal of the Cease-fire: Meeting of the Security Council, August 16, 1974.

(a) Urging resumption of negotiations: Security Council Resolution 360 (1974), August 16, 1974.[16]

The Security Council,

Recalling its resolutions 353(1974) of 20 July, 354 (1974) of 23 July, 355 (1974) of 1 August,[17] 357 (1974) of 14 August and 358 (1974) of 15 August 1974,[18]

Noting that all States have declared their respect for the sovereignty, independence and territorial integrity of the Republic of Cyprus,

Gravely concerned at the deterioration of the situation in Cyprus, resulting from the further military operations, which constituted a most serious threat to peace and security in the Eastern Mediterranean area,

1. *Records its formal disapproval* of the unilateral military actions undertaken against the Republic of Cyprus;

2. *Urges* the parties to comply with all the provisions of previous resolutions of the Security Council, including those concerning the withdrawal without delay from the Republic of Cyprus of foreign military personnel present otherwise than under the authority of international agreements;

3. *Urges* the parties to resume without delay, in an atmosphere of constructive co-operation, the negotiations called for in resolution 353 (1974) whose outcome should not be impeded or prejudged by the acquisition of advantages resulting from military operations;

4. *Requests* the Secretary-General to report to the Council, as necessary, with a view to the possible adoption of further measures designed to promote the restoration of peaceful conditions;

5. *Decides* to remain seized of the question permanently and to meet at any time to consider measures which may be required in the light of the developing situation.

---

[16]Text from Security Council, *Official Records: 29th Year, Resolutions and Decisions 1974*: 9.
[17]Respectively Documents 30a, 33a, and 35c.
[18]Respectively Documents 39a and 40a.

[Ambassador Scali, in a statement in explanation of vote, particularly stressed the hope that the tripartite negotiations in Geneva would now be promptly resumed.]

(b) Statement by Ambassador Scali to the Council, August 16, 1974.[19]

We can all take satisfaction from the Secretary General's report that at long last the guns are stilled on Cyprus. The cease-fire seems finally to be in effect. Regrettably, the U.N. peace forces, UNFICYP, have suffered further casualties. We extend our deepest sympathy to the Danish Government and to the bereaved families of these soldiers of peace who have given their lives selflessly in the service of others.[20]

Mr. President, with the cease-fire now taking hold, we must also turn our attention to forging the peace, to establishing conditions under which the good people of Cyprus may live undisturbed and walk in paths of their own choosing.

My delegation hopes that, on reflection, all parties to the Cyprus dispute will decide it is in their own national interests to move on to Geneva without delay to resume the peace negotiations suspended earlier this week.

The success of these talks, under the chairmanship of the distinguished British Foreign Secretary, involves the peace of the eastern Mediterranean. The world is watching. The participants have an obligation to mankind to enter into negotiations in a spirit of conciliation and fairminded compromise to reach an understanding which will renew and indeed reinforce the historic friendship of the peoples of the area.

[But neither the Greek nor the Cypriot Government was keen to resume negotiations at a time when Turkish military forces maintained their manifestly illegal occupation of a large part of the Cypriot national territory, and when upward of one-third of the Cypriot population had become refugees. Little attempt was made in Athens or Nicosia to hide the prevalent dissatisfaction with the United States for having permitted such a state of affairs to develop—the assumption being, obviously, that Washington could have prevented it had it cared to do so. A tragic consequence of this

[19]USUN Press Release 108, Aug. 16; text from *Bulletin,* 71: 367-8.
[20]Secretary-General Waldheim had reported that a vehicle with five Danish UNFICYP soldiers had run into a minefield in which two were killed and three wounded, two of them seriously.

feeling was the fatal shooting of the new U.S. Ambassador to Cyprus, Rodger P. Davies, in the course of an anti-American demonstration in front of the U.S. Embassy in Nicosia on Monday, August 19. This and other aspects of the situation were discussed by Secretary Kissinger at a Washington news conference that same day.]

(42) Recapitulation of United States Policy: News conference statement by Secretary of State Kissinger, August 19, 1974.[21]

(Excerpts)

Secretary Kissinger: I would like to begin with a few observations about the tragic death of Ambassador Davies.

Ambassador Davies has been a close associate for all the years that I have been in Washington. He worked closely with me on Middle East problems when he was Deputy Assistant Secretary. His performance after he was appointed Ambassador in Cyprus has been outstanding. I think I can do no better than to read to you two cables which I sent to him, one on July 22, the other on August 10.

On July 22 I sent him the following cable:

I would like to express my thanks for your performance and that of your staff during the last week. I relied heavily on your good judgment and on the excellent reporting from Nicosia. The steadiness and courage displayed by you and your staff under dangerous conditions were examplary. The Embassy's overall performance deserves the highest commendation. Please convey my congratulations and profound thanks to all members of your staff. Hopefully, and in great measure due to your efforts, the situation will calm in Cyprus.

Then on August 10 I sent him another cable:

Art Hartman [Arthur A. Hartman, Assistant Secretary for European Affairs] has just reported to me in some detail on the magnificent performance of all of you under the most dangerous and trying circumstances. Your courage under fire, your accurate, perceptive and calm reporting, and your continued efforts to further our policy and protect American citizens with a reduced and overworked staff are a credit to you and are in the finest tradition of the Service.

[21]Department of State Press Release 331, Aug. 19; text from *Bulletin,* 71: 353-6.

My associates will tell you that the highest praise they usually get from me is the absence of criticism. And I want to call your attention to these two cables which express the extraordinary performance of Ambassador Davies. Those of us who have known him will miss him for his outstanding human qualities.

The Foreign Service, which is often criticized, has produced no better representative. And his work is in the best traditions of a Service to which dedication and the performance of a national duty are the principal objectives.

I have sent the following message to Ambassador Davies' children:

You both have my deepest sympathy in this tragic time. While there is little that anyone can say at a moment such as this to lessen the sorrow, I want you to know that we share your deep sense of loss. Your father was loved, respected and admired by all of his colleagues in the Foreign Service and the State Department. You should be very proud of him; we are. Mrs. Kissinger and I stand ready to do anything we can to help in the difficult months ahead.

You know that the White House has already announced that the President has ordered that a plane be sent for the children. I have asked our Deputy Under Secretary of State, [L. Dean] Brown, whose distinguished service includes service as Ambassador in Jordan in very difficult circumstances, to go out with this plane, to represent the United States in Cyprus until we can appoint an Ambassador and get him in place. The designation of an officer of the distinction of Ambassador Brown leaves no doubt of the importance we attach to a speedy and peaceful resolution of the Cyprus issue.

This morning also, President Clerides called me to express his personal sorrow at the loss of Ambassador Davies, whom he described as a close personal and very trusted friend. I assured President Clerides that the United States fully understood the lack of responsibility of the Cyprus Government for this tragic event. I assured him that the United States would continue a major effort to bring about peace, and he urged us to make such an effort. I emphasized to him, however, that these efforts would not be helped by anti-American demonstrations that were unjustified by the record and that could only create conditions to hamper these efforts.

I also have had an opportunity this morning to speak with President Ford about the situation in the eastern Mediterranean. We were in close touch by telephone yesterday, and we have met personally several times in the preceding days. President Ford has asked me to make the following statement on behalf of the United States:

First, the United States shall insist on the strict maintenance of the cease-fire on Cyprus.

Second, the imperative and urgent need is to begin negotiations.

Third, we will continue to support efforts to bring the parties to the negotiating table.

Fourth, the United States will play any role requested by the parties. We are also prepared to support the able efforts of the British Foreign Secretary, Callaghan, in this regard.

Fifth, in these negotiations, we believe it will be necessary for Turkey, as the stronger power on the ground, to display flexibility and a concern for Greek sensitivities, both in terms of territory and the size of military forces on the island. I have made this point directly this morning to the Prime Minister of Turkey. I have been assured that the Turkish Government considers the demarcation line negotiable and that it will carry out the provisions of the Geneva agreement calling for phased reductions of troops on Cyprus.

Sixth, the United States greatly values the traditional friendship of Greece. It has the highest regard for Prime Minister Karamanlis and wishes every success to his democratic government. We will use our influence in any negotiation to take into full account Greek honor and national dignity. At the same time, we assume that all of our allies, including Greece, join in collective defense in their own interests. We are willing to strengthen these common alliance ties and to help the Greek Government in any way possible. We will not be pressured by threat of withdrawal from the alliance, or anti-American demonstrations, which in any event are totally unjustified by our record.

I repeat that this statement has been gone over by President Ford.

*   *   *

Q. Will you take questions?

Secretary Kissinger: Reluctantly.

Q. Last week, one of your associates described as plain "baloney" suggestions that the United States has tilted toward

Turkey. Do you share in that view? And can you tell us specifically the consideration that was given to cutting off arms to Turkey and why arms were not cut off during the building crisis?

Secretary Kissinger: With the speaker sitting here and looking balefully at me, my options, as they say, are severely limited—I completely support the statement of Mr. McCloskey.[22]

The situation on Cyprus tilted toward Turkey not as a result of American policy but as a result of the actions of the previous Greek Government which destroyed the balance of forces as it had existed on the island.

The United States did not threaten the cutoff of military aid to Turkey, for these reasons: First, it was considered that such an action would be ineffective and would not prevent the threatening eventuality; secondly, as was pointed out in this statement, we are giving economic and military aid as a reflection of our common interest in the defense of the eastern Mediterranean. Once such a decision is taken, it will have the most drastic consequences and not just over a period of time covering a few days but over an extended period of time.

For all these reasons, it was judged that the United States would be both ineffective and counterproductive to threaten the cutoff of aid.

Short of this, however, we made the most repeated and urgent representations to Turkey in order to prevent the military action that happened. We have criticized the action, and we believe also that the inflexibility of all of the parties in Geneva contributed to it.

* * *

Q. Mr. Secretary, there has been widespread criticism around the world from diplomats, as well as from public demonstrators, that the United States used "quiet diplomacy" which was so quiet during the past four weeks that it was ineffective. Can you address yourself to whether the United States at an earlier point might have done what it has done today, if it had issued a firm, specific statement?

Also, you have been burned in effigy on Lafayette Square, I believe for the first time.

Secretary Kissinger: Well, I am honored—is it really only the first time? [Laughter.]

Q. In Lafayette Square, I believe.

[22]Ambassador at Large Robert J. McCloskey.

Secretary Kissinger: I hope you all realize that half of the demonstrators were State Department employees. [Laughter.]

Let us understand the context within which the negotiations have taken place.

Until early August, until in fact August 8, it was the general judgment of all those dealing with the negotiations, including specifically that of the United Kingdom, that the conference in Geneva would lead to a settlement and that in fact it would, after an initial phase which would be conducted by Foreign Ministers, break up into working groups that would settle the issue.

Under those circumstances, it would have been highly inappropriate for the United States to make a public statement of the solution that it advocated.

After it became apparent that the negotiations in Geneva were heading for a stalemate, the United States, first, responded to every request by the principal mediator, the British Foreign Secretary, for specific assistance and specific proposals. In addition, the United States made many demarches to Turkey to prevent the threatened military action.

And it [the United States] would have preferred if, perhaps, some more flexibility could have been shown by all of the parties in Geneva.

Our judgment was that a public statement would freeze the positions and that it would not achieve the objective of thwarting a military attack.

After the event, it is never possible to prove whether some other course might not have been successful. Our judgment was that under the circumstances quiet diplomacy would lead to these results. But there is a limit to what diplomacy can achieve. It cannot substitute for an existing relationship of forces.

We understand the frustrations of the Greek community. We understand also the frustrations and disappointments of the Greek Government—but it is important to remember that the original dislocations were not of our own making and that the United States, while it will try to be helpful, cannot solve all problems around the world.

With respect to the demonstrations, it is worth while to remember that a few years ago the demonstrations were complaining about excessive American involvement. Now the complaint seems to be the opposite.

Q. Mr. Secretary, has the perception of the United States as "tilting toward Turkey," regardless of whether it's correct or incorrect, in any way hampered your efforts to serve as an effective mediator between the two sides?

Secretary Kissinger: I think that it is understandable that Greek emotions run very deep at this moment.

I believe that upon calmer reflection the responsible Greek leaders will recognize that the United States has shown deep sympathy for the Greek Government, that we welcome the present democratic government in Greece, and that within the limits of what was possible we have attempted to play a constructive role.

I think the Greek Government will also realize that the U.S. roles can be very important in bringing about a result consistent with the dignity and honor of all of the parties—and we hope it will realize that anti-American demonstrations and anti-American gestures do not contribute to our effectiveness.

* * *

[Secretary Kissinger's observations did not entirely dispel the view that the United States had been and was being unduly lenient to Turkey, particularly in light of that country's use of U.S.- supplied military equipment in ways that seemed to contravene bilateral agreements as well as the provisions of the foreign assistance legislation. Nor did there seem to be any early prospect of reconvening the Geneva talks, although Secretary-General Waldheim succeeded late in August in persuading Glafkos Clerides and Rauf Denktash, leaders respectively of the Greek and Turkish Cypriot communities, to initiate bilateral talks on prisoners of war and other humanitarian problems.

The most serious of these humanitarian concerns, the plight of the estimated 225,600 persons displaced by the recent fighting, was meanwhile being handled on behalf of the U.N. Secretary-General by Prince Sadruddin Aga Khan, the U.N. High Commissioner for Refugees and Coordinator of U.N. Humanitarian Assistance in Cyprus. The importance of doing what was possible to alleviate human suffering on the island was the focus of still another Security Council resolution that was unanimously adopted on August 30.]

(43) Political and Humanitarian Problems: Meeting of the Security Council, August 30, 1974.

(a) Humanitarian assistance to the people of Cyprus: Security Council Resolution 361 (1974), August 30, 1974.[23]

---

[23]Text from Security Council, *Official Records: 29th Year, Resolutions and Decisions 1974*: 9.

The Security Council,

Conscious of its special responsibilities under the United Nations Charter,

Recalling its resolutions 186 (1964) of 4 March 1964,[24] 353 (1974) of 20 July, 354 (1974) of 23 July, 355 (1974) of 1 August,[25] 357 (1974) of 14 August, 358 (1974) and 359 (1974) of 15 August and 360 (1974) of 16 August 1974,[26]

Noting that a large number of people in Cyprus have been displaced, and are in dire need of humanitarian assistance,

Mindful of the fact that it is one of the foremost purposes of the United Nations to lend humanitarian assistance in situations such as the one currently prevailing in Cyprus,

Noting also that the United Nations High Commissioner for Refugees has already been appointed Co-ordinator for United Nations Humanitarian Assistance for Cyprus, with the task of co-ordinating relief assistance to be provided by United Nations programmes and agencies and from other sources,

Having considered the report of the Secretary-General contained in document S/11473,[27]

1. *Expresses its appreciation* to the Secretary-General for the part he has played in bringing about talks between the leaders of the two communities in Cyprus;

2. *Warmly welcomes* this development and calls upon those concerned in the talks to pursue them actively with the help of the Secretary-General and in the interests of the Cypriot people as a whole;

3. *Calls upon* all parties to do everything in their power to alleviate human suffering, to ensure the respect of fundamental human rights for every person and to refrain from all action likely to aggravate the situation;

4. *Expresses its grave concern* at the plight of the refugees and other persons displaced as a result of the situation in Cyprus and urges the parties concerned, in conjunction with the Secretary-General, to search for peaceful solutions to the problems of refugees and take appropriate measures to provide for their relief and welfare and to permit persons who wish to do so to return to their homes in safety;

5. *Requests* the Secretary-General to submit at the earliest possible opportunity a full report on the situation of the refugees and

[24] *Documents, 1964:* 103-5.
[25] Respectively Documents 30a, 33a, and 35c.
[26] Respectively Documents 39a, 40a, 40b, and 41a.
[27] Security Council, *Official Records: 29th Year, Supplement for July, Aug. and Sept. 1974:* 125-6.

other persons referred to in paragraph 4 above and decides to keep that situation under constant review;

6. *Further requests* the Secretary-General to continue to provide emergency United Nations humanitarian assistance to all parts of the population of the island in need of such assistance;

7. *Calls upon* all parties, as a demonstration of good faith, to take, both individually and in co-operation with each other, all steps which may promote comprehensive and successful negotiations;

8. *Reiterates* its call to all parties to co-operate fully with the United Nations Peace-keeping Force in Cyprus in carrying out its tasks;

9. *Expresses the conviction* that the speedy implementation of the provisions of the present resolution will assist the achievement of a satisfactory settlement in Cyprus.

[In his statement in explanation of his vote, Ambassador Scali offered some sarcastic comments on the attitude of the Soviet Government, which had persisted in its traditional tactic of attributing the Cyprus problem to sinister machinations by the NATO powers. In a statement made public August 22, the U.S.S.R. had urged the submission of the problem to an international conference, to be convened within the U.N. framework and with the participation of all Security Council members together with Cyprus, Greece, and Turkey. (The proposal was accepted in principle by the Greek and Cypriot governments, but was unacceptable to Turkey.)]

(b) *Statement by Ambassador Scali to the Council, August 30, 1974.*[28]

First I would like to express to the Secretary General the thanks of my delegation and my government for his recent visits to Cyprus, Greece, and Turkey to discuss the situation on that island. In particular, we commend him for his statesmanlike role in bringing about a meeting on humanitarian questions in which Acting President Clerides, Vice President Denktash, and the High Commissioner for Refugees have participated. The value of such talks between the leaders of the Greek Cypriot and Turkish Cypriot communities cannot be overemphasized.

For the sake of all of the people of Cyprus, we urge the international community to make every effort to help create a negotiating climate which can produce constructive solutions, particularly of humanitarian questions.

Mr. President, we have heard at length today from one delegate of a special formula for peace which his government is going to sell. To persuade others to accept it, we have heard some fairy tales from another era—the bold charges of mysterious machinations by unidentified members of NATO. Mr. President, these stories might amuse or titillate the readers of summertime fiction on the beaches of the Crimea, but such fairy tales will not help us solve the real problems of Cyprus. I think in this regard that we can all agree that an absolute prerequisite for solving the critical humanitarian problems on Cyprus is strict compliance with the cease-fire as called for in previous Security Council resolutions.

The United States shares the concern of the Secretary General and the parties for the plight of the refugees from both communities who have been made homeless. We commend the International Committee of the Red Cross and the U.N. High Commissioner for Refugees, as well as other humanitarian organizations, for their outstanding efforts to give emergency assistance particularly to those whose lives have been dislocated. We urge all of the parties concerned to adhere scrupulously to international agreements concerning the human rights of civilians during times of conflict.

Upon the recommendation of the late American Ambassador to Cyprus, Rodger Davies, the United States has responded to appeals from the International Committee of the Red Cross for emergency humanitarian assistance. We have donated $3.1 million as of now. This sum includes a cash contribution of $725,000 plus airlifts of relief supplies, and emergency equipment such as tents, blankets, and other provisions. The United States stands ready to provide additional assistance based on recommendations from the International Red Cross and the U.N. High Commissioner for Refugees. It is our view that such assistance goes to the heart of the issues before the Council today. We therefore appeal to the international community to join with us in responding to this humanitarian effort.

The United Nations Peace-keeping Force in Cyprus (UNFICYP) has performed courageously in assisting the parties and international relief agencies in carrying out their crucial humanitarian responsibilities. The United States underscores its support for Security Council Resolution 359,[29] which demands that all parties cooperate with UNFICYP in carrying out all of its tasks, "including humanitarian functions, in all areas of Cyprus and in regard to all sections of the population."

[29]Document 40b.

The effort to render assistance to the people of Cyprus is a necessary emergency measure. However, the imperative and urgent need is to resume negotiations. A negotiated settlement of the Cyprus dispute offers the best hope for all of the people on the island to live in peace and security.

The U.S. delegation supports the resolution before this Council and commends the spirit of compromise with which various points of view converged to produce it. Perhaps each delegation—and I would not exclude my own—would have preferred some variations in the text. Nonetheless, in our view, passage of this resolution can make positive contributions to easing the plight of refugees and should pave the way for further efforts to get broader negotiations under way again.

In closing, Mr. President, may I say a simple but no less heartfelt "thank you" to those who have spoken words of condolence on the memory of Ambassador Rodger Davies.[30]

---

[30]For further developments cf. Chapter 24 at notes 14-16.

19. CONFERENCE ON THE LAW OF THE SEA: SECOND SESSION

(Caracas, June 20-August 29, 1974)

[Amid the recurring shocks of confrontation and conflict, the international community had not entirely overlooked the existence of other issues, less dramatic but possibly even more momentous, that already were affecting the life of the planet and would certainly present new threats to civilized existence unless addressed with wisdom and promptitude. One such issue had been exhaustively examined at the United Nations Conference on the Human Environment, held in Stockholm in 1972.[1] Another—or, rather, a whole group of interconnected issues—formed the subject matter of the Third United Nations Conference on the Law of the Sea, which had opened in New York in December 1973 and was scheduled to continue with a second session in Caracas, Venezuela, in the summer of 1974.[2] Also in 1974, a majority of the world's nations planned to be represented at a United Nations World Population Conference in Bucharest, and a World Food Conference in Rome.[3] Noting that the General Assembly itself had just completed a special session on the burning issue of raw materials and development,[4] Secretary-General Waldheim could justifiably claim that the United Nations was currently being given both the opportunity and responsibility to create a new global strategy based on all of the elements essential for the survival of mankind.[5]

Active preparation for the Third United Nations Conference on the Law of the Sea went all the way back to 1970, when the General

---

[1]Cf. *AFR, 1972*: 467-77.
[2]Same, *1973*: 581-2 and 598-601.
[3]Cf. below, Chapters 20 and 27.
[4]Cf. Chapter 7.
[5]*Un Monthly Chronicle,* July 1974: 32.

Assembly, aware that two earlier Law of the Sea conferences in 1958 and 1960 had left unsolved a number of critical issues that by now were in urgent need of resolution, had decided to convene in 1973 a third such conference to deal with a complicated agenda encompassing, in the formal language of the Assembly's resolution, "the establishment of an equitable international régime—including an international machinery—for the area and the resources of the sea-bed and the ocean floor and the subsoil thereof beyond the limits of national jurisdiction, a precise definition of the area, and a broad range of related issues including those concerning the régimes of the high seas, the continental shelf, the territorial sea (including the question of its breadth and the question of international straits) and contiguous zone, fishing and conservation of the living resources of the high seas (including the question of the preferential rights of coastal States), the preservation of the marine environment (including, *inter alia*, the prevention of pollution) and scientific research."[6]

At a more recent session in the fall of 1973, the General Assembly had further decided that the mandate of the forthcoming conference should be "to adopt a convention dealing with all matters relating to the law of the sea"; that its first session, which would deal exclusively with organizational matters, should be convened in New York on December 3-14, 1973, while the second session, dealing with the substantive work of the conference, should be convened at Caracas for a ten-week period extending from June 20 to August 29, 1974; and that any subsequent session or sessions that might prove necessary should be convened not later than 1975.[7]

It was this second, substantive session of the conference, attended by representatives of over 140 nations and presided over by H.S. Amerasinghe of Sri Lanka, that was called to order in Caracas on June 20, 1974. Although the achievements of the next ten weeks fell short of implementing the General Assembly's mandate to complete a law of the sea convention, it was agreed by most of the participants that the conference made visible progress in that direction. Preliminary texts of more than 250 draft articles or provisions—many of them, it is true, in competing, alternative versions—were produced by the three committees set up to deal with the conference's major subjects: (1) the international regime and machinery for the seabed beyond the jurisdiction of individual states; (2) general aspects of the law of the sea, from the territorial sea and the proposed economic zone to the rights of landlocked

⁶Resolution 2750 C (XXV), Dec. 17, 1970.
⁷Resolution 3067 (XXVIII), Nov. 16, 1973, in *AFR, 1973*: 598-601. For further background cf. *AFR, 1971*:533-6 and 543-8; same, *1972*: 477-85; same, *1973*: 581-2.

countries and the special problems of archipelagoes; and (3) preservation of the marine environment and scientific research.

Though none of the more controversial issues before the conference was finally resolved at Caracas, there was at least an approach to consensus on the long-vexed question of the breadth of the territorial sea and the adjacent waters in which many states claimed exclusive jurisdiction. After years of bitter feuding, most countries at length seemed ready to settle for a twelve-mile territorial sea plus a 200-mile economic zone, although the United States—historically identified with a three-mile territorial sea—gave notice that its assent would be conditioned on an assurance of unimpeded transit of international straits. Much further from agreement, it appeared, were the principles that should govern the exploitation of the mineral wealth of the seabed. Here there was a definite clash of opinions between the developing countries, which saw in the resources of the seabed an important source of future economic benefits, and the more advanced industrial countries which alone possessed the capital and technological resources required for their exploitation.

In the hope that these and other outstanding issues could be resolved in the course of one more period of negotiations, it was agreed at Caracas that a further session of up to eight weeks' duration should be convened in Geneva on March 17, 1975, and that the conference should then return to Caracas for signature of the final documents. Most delegates were undoubtedly aware that the search for multilateral agreements was increasingly taking the form of a race against time as pressures mounted, in the United States and elsewhere, for unilateral action to protect those interests that had failed thus far to find acceptable protection on an international level. American companies were already gearing up for deep-sea mining ventures, with or without international sanction, and American fishing interests were already pressing Congress to proclaim a 200-mile exclusive fishing zone such as had long been claimed by various South American countries.

An early appraisal of the Caracas session was given the Senate Foreign Relations Committee on September 5, 1974, by Ambassador John R. Stevenson, the President's Special Representative for the Law of the Sea Conference and chief of the U.S. delegation.]

(44) Report on the Caracas Session: Statement of Ambassador John R. Stevenson, Special Representative of the President and Chairman of the United States Delegation, before the Senate Committee on Foreign Relations, September 5, 1974.[8]

---

[8]Text and subtitles from *Bulletin,* 71: 389-95.

I welcome this opportunity to appear before the Senate Foreign Relations Committee to report on the progress made at the first substantive session of the Third U.N. Conference on the Law of the Sea, held in Caracas, Venezuela, from June 20 to August 29, 1974. Before proceeding with this report, I would like to say how much we appreciated the attendance at the conference of three members of this committee, Senators Clifford Case, Edmund Muskie, and Claiborne Pell, as well as members of their and the committee's staffs. We are deeply grateful for their willingness to attend the conference and for the advice and assistance that they and other members of the committee have given to our efforts to achieve an agreed constitution and supporting legal regime for two-thirds of this planet. It has been and will remain a fundamental part of our policy to work closely with the Congress and this committee to achieve a law of the sea treaty that fully protects the basic interests of the United States.

Accomplishments of Caracas Session

I want to emphasize at the outset that, while the results of the Caracas session were not all we hoped for, the session was not a failure.

A most significant result was the apparent agreement of most nations represented there that the interests of all will be best served by an acceptable and timely treaty.

To that end, the conference has scheduled not only the next session in the spring in Geneva but a return to Caracas for the signing of this agreement in the expectation that this will take place in accordance with the U.N. timetable. That timetable provides for conclusion of the treaty in 1975.

Further evidence of this desire to achieve promptly a widely acceptable treaty was reflected in the adoption by consensus of the rules of procedure early in the session. These rules make several changes in normal procedures that are designed to promote widespread agreement.

The tone of the general debate and the informal meetings was moderate and serious and reflected wide agreement on the broad outlines of a comprehensive general agreement.

Finally, I am sure the members of the Senate who were with us will agree that the delegates from all regions worked hard. Three or four simultaneous meetings were common, and there were some night sessions. The number of papers worked on was enormous, but this time the object—largely achieved—was organizing and reducing the alternatives, not proliferating them.

Other accomplishments of the session were considerable. Among the most important are the following:

a. The vast array of critical law of the sea issues and proposals within the mandate of Committee II—including, among others, the territorial sea, economic zone, straits, fisheries, and the continental margin—was organized by the committee into a comprehensive set of working papers containing precise treaty texts reflecting main trends on each precise issue. All states can now focus on each issue, and the alternative solutions, with relative ease.

A similar development occurred with respect to marine scientific research in Committee III. Committee I, dealing with the novel subject of a legal regime for exploiting the deep seabed, had previously agreed to alternative treaty texts in the preparatory committee and further refined these texts at the Caracas session.

b. The transition from a preparatory committee of about 90 to a conference of almost 150, including many newly independent states, was achieved without major new stumbling blocks and with a minimum of delay.

c. The inclusion in the treaty of a 12-mile territorial sea and a 200-mile economic zone was all but formally agreed, subject of course to acceptable resolution of other issues, including unimpeded transit of straits. Accordingly, expanded coastal state jurisdiction over living and nonliving resources appears assured as part of the comprehensive treaty.

d. With respect to the deep seabeds, the first steps have been taken into real negotiation of the basic questions of the system of exploitation and the conditions of exploitation.

e. Traditional regional and political alignments of states are being replaced by informal groups whose membership is based on similarities of interest on a particular issue. This has greatly facilitated clarification of issues and is necessary for finding effective accommodations.

f. The number and tempo of private meetings has increased considerably and moved beyond formal positions. This is essential to a successful negotiation. Of course, by their very nature, the results of such meetings cannot be discussed publicly.

With few exceptions, the conference papers now make it clear what the structure and general content of the treaty will be. The alternatives to choose from and the blanks to be filled in, and even the relative importance attached to different issues, are well known.

Accommodation on Critical Issues Required

What was missing in Caracas was sufficient political will to make hard negotiating choices. A principal reason for this was the conviction that this would not be the last session. The absence prior to the completion of this session of organized alternate treaty texts on many issues also inhibited such decisionmaking.

The next step is for governments to make the political decisions necessary to resolve a small number of critical issues. In short, we must now move from the technical drafting and preliminary exploratory exchanges of views at this just-completed session, which has laid bare both the outlines of agreement and the details of disagreement, to the highest political levels, involving heads of states themselves, to make accommodation on these critical issues possible.

The fundamental problem is that most states believe the major decisions must be put together in a single package. Every state has different priorities, and agreement on one issue is frequently conditioned on agreement on another. Thus it might have been possible—and might have been helpful to the executive branch in its efforts here today—to adopt a general declaration of principles in Caracas endorsing, among other things, a 12-mile territorial sea and a 200-mile economic zone.

Our delegation opposed such an idea because it would have diverted us from negotiating the key details of an economic zone that can spell the difference between true agreement and the mere appearance of agreement and because our willingness to support such concepts is also conditioned on satisfactory resolution of other issues, including unimpeded passage of straits. In choosing to concentrate on precise texts and alternatives, our delegation believed we were in fact best promoting widespread agreement on schedule. However, we recognized that the absence of tangible symbols of agreement would place us in a politically difficult situation between sessions.

In his closing statement before the Caracas session, the President of the conference, recognizing the problem, stated, "we should restrain ourselves in the face of the temptation to take unilateral action," and then urged states to prepare to reach agreement "without delay" since governments cannot be expected to exercise "infinite patience."

We regret that for a variety of reasons the conference was unable to capitalize upon the initial prevailing good will to produce a final treaty at the Caracas session. Nevertheless the political parameters of an overall agreement were made much clearer at Caracas, and we are at the stage where differences in approaches are embodied in specific treaty articles expressed as alternative formulations on almost all the major issues.

Rights and Duties in the Economic Zone

On July 11 at a plenary session, we noted there was a growing consensus on the limits of national jurisdiction, which we expressed in the following terms:

A maximum outer limit of 12 miles for the territorial sea and of 200 miles for the economic zone . . . conditional on a satisfactory overall treaty package and, more specifically, on provisions for unimpeded transit of international straits and a balance between coastal state rights and duties within the economic zone.[9]

To promote negotiations on the essential balance of coastal state rights and duties the United States submitted draft articles proposing the establishment of a 200-mile economic zone in the treaty. The U.S. draft articles consist of three sections: the economic zone, fishing, and the continental shelf.[10]

The economic zone section provides for a 200-mile outer limit with coastal state sovereign and exclusive rights over resources, exclusive rights over drilling and economic installations, and other rights and duties regarding scientific research and pollution to be specified. There would be coastal state environmental duties with respect to installations and seabed activities. All states would enjoy freedom of navigation and other rights recognized by international law within the economic zone.

The fishing section gives the coastal state exclusive rights for the purpose of regulating fishing in the 200-mile economic zone subject to a duty to conserve, and to insure full utilization of, fishery stocks taking into account environmental and economic factors.

In substance, there is no significant difference between the objectives of S. 1988[11] and the U.S. proposal at the conference. Fishing for anadromous species such as salmon beyond the 12-mile territorial sea would be prohibited except as authorized by the host state. Highly migratory species such as tuna would be regulated by the coastal state in the zone and by the flag state outside the zone, in both cases in accordance with regulations established by ap-

[9]*Bulletin,* 71: 233; full text of statement in same: 232-6.
[10]Texts in *Digest of United States Practice in International Law, 1974*: 295-300 and 306-10.
[11]The proposed Emergency Marine Fisheries Act of 1974, extending U.S. fishery jurisdiction from 12 to 200 miles on an interim basis in order to protect the domestic fishing industry. Approved by a 68-27 vote of the Senate on Dec. 11, 1974, the measure did not come before the House during the 1973-74 congressional session.

propriate international or regional organizations. Membership in the organization would be mandatory, and the coastal state would receive reasonable fees for the highly migratory fish caught in its zone by foreign vessels. The international organization, in establishing equitable allocation regulations, would be obligated to insure full utilization of the resource and to take into account the special interests of the coastal states within whose economic zones highly migratory fish are caught.

The continental shelf section provides for coastal state sovereign rights over exploration and exploitation of continental shelf resources. The continental shelf is defined as extending to the limit of the economic zone or beyond to a precisely defined outer limit of the continental margin.

The coastal state would have a duty to respect the integrity of foreign investment on the shelf and to make payments from mineral resource exploitation for international community purposes, particularly for the economic benefit of developing countries. In our plenary statement we suggested that these payments should be at a modest and uniform rate. The revenue-sharing area would begin seaward of 12 miles or 200 meters' water depth, whichever is further seaward.

The draft articles on the economic zone place the United States in the mainstream of the predominant trends in the conference, and we were pleased with the favorable reaction to our proposal.

We were disappointed, however, at the support, particularly among a number of African countries, for an economic zone in which there would be plenary coastal state jurisdiction not only over resources but over scientific research and vessel-source pollution as well and in all of these areas there would be no international standards except provisions for freedom of navigation and overflight and the right to lay submarine cables and pipelines. Many of the same countries are saying that if a pattern of unilateral action by individual countries emerges before a treaty is agreed they would go further and opt for a full 200-mile territorial sea.

We believe that specifying the rights and duties of both coastal states and other states in the economic zone is the approach best designed to avoid the sterile debate over abstract concepts.

At the final meeting of the Second Committee on August 28, the chairman, Ambassador Andres Aguilar of Venezuela, made a constructive and challenging statement summing up its work. On its own initiative, the committee decided to have the statement circulated as an official committee document. This occurred after initial opposition by the 200-mile territorial sea supporters, which was withdrawn in the face of other delegations' willingness to proceed to a vote if necessary. Because of its great importance and the universal respect and admiration earned by Chairman Aguilar for his strong and effective leadership, I would like to quote briefly from that statement:

No decision on substantive issues has been taken at this session, nor has a single article of the future convention been adopted, but the states represented here know perfectly well which are at this time the positions that enjoy support and which are the ones that have not managed to make any headway.

The paper that sums up the main trends does not pronounce on the degree of support which each of them has enlisted at the preparatory meetings and the conference itself, but it is now easy for anyone who has followed our work closely to discern the outline of the future convention.

So far each state has put forward in general terms the positions which would ideally satisfy its own range of interests in the seas and oceans. Once these positions are established, we have before us the opportunity of negotiation based on an objective and realistic evaluation of the relative strength of the different opinions.

It is not my intention in this statement to present a complete picture of the situation as I see it personally, but I can offer some general evaluations and comments.

The idea of a territorial sea of 12 miles and an exclusive economic zone beyond the territorial sea up to a total maximum distance of 200 miles is, at least at this time, the keystone of the compromise solution favored by the majority of the states participating in the conference, as is apparent from the general debate in the plenary meetings and the discussions held in our committee.

Acceptance of this idea is, of course, dependent on the satisfactory solution of other issues, especially the issue of passage through straits used for international navigation, the outermost limit of the continental shelf and the actual retention of this concept, and, last but not least, the aspirations of the landlocked countries and of other countries which, for one reason or another, consider themselves geographically disadvantaged.

There are, in addition, other problems to be studied and solved in connection with this idea; for example, those relating to archipelagoes and the regime of islands in general.

It is also necessary to go further into the matter of the nature and characteristics of the concept of the exclusive economic zone, a subject on which important differences of opinion still persist.

On all these subjects substantial progress has been made which lays the foundations for negotiation during the intersessional period and at the next session of the conference.

Deep Seabed Resources

Mr. Chairman,[12] perhaps the most marked differences between the position of the United States and that of a majority of other states at the conference emerged in the First Committee, which deals principally with the mining of manganese nodules in the deep seabed for the production of nickel, copper, cobalt, and perhaps certain other metals. The basic differences relate to who will exploit the deep seabed resources and how this exploitation will take place.

The United States took the position that access to the resources should be guaranteed on a nondiscriminatory basis under reasonable conditions that provide the security of expectations needed to attract the investment for development of the resources. This would generate international revenues to be used for international community purposes, particularly for developing countries. A number of developing countries have supported a concept under which the international seabed authority would itself undertake exploration and exploitation and which, under the new formula introduced by the developing countries at Caracas, would in addition have discretion to contract with states and private companies to operate under its direct and effective control and under basic conditions of exploitation set forth in the convention itself.

During the last few weeks of the conference real negotiations began on the basic conditions for exploitation when the First Committee agreed to establish a small informal negotiating group. This group will resume its work at the next session of the conference, and we hope that negotiations in this context and during the intersessional period will lead to a narrowing of differences and a realistic approach that will promote access by industrialized consumer countries and the development of the mineral resources of the deep seabeds.

The differences between what we call regulation and what others call control may be narrowed if we can agree on the conditions of exploitation, including measures to insure that exploitation on a nondiscriminatory basis will take place, and if agreement can be reached on protecting relevant interests in the decisionmaking process.

Marine Environment and Scientific Research

In the Third Committee of the conference, there were mixed

---

[12]Senator J. William Fulbright (Democrat of Arkansas).

results on formulating treaty texts for protection of the marine environment and oceanographic scientific research.

We were pleased that texts concerning the preservation of the marine environment were prepared on several points, including basic obligations, particular obligations, global and regional cooperation, and technical assistance. But basic political issues remain to be resolved on the jurisdiction of port and coastal states with respect to vessel-source pollution and on whether there will be different obligations for states depending upon their stage of economic development—the so-called double standard.

We believe that the Caracas session broadened the basis of understanding of the complex problems involved in drafting new legal obligations to protect the marine environment, and there were indications that all states were analyzing their environmental policies in detail.

On the scientific research issue, the various proposals were reduced to four principal alternatives regarding scientific research within the areas of national jurisdiction. Some states advocated a regime requiring coastal state consent for all research. Others supported a modified consent regime. The United States supported a regime which places obligations on the state conducting the research to notify the coastal state, provide for its participation, and insure sharing of the data and assistance in interpreting such data. Other states proposed complete freedom of scientific research.

We were encouraged by the fact that for the first time states appeared to be moving toward serious negotiations on this subject, including serious consideration of our proposal.

Provisions for Settlement of Disputes

Mr. Chairman, we know there will be disputes with respect to the interpretation and application of the provisions of the treaty. The willingness of the United States and many others to agree to a particular balance of the rights and duties of states and the international authority is predicated upon reasonable confidence that the balance will be fairly maintained. Accordingly, the establishment of an impartial system of peaceful and compulsory third-party dispute settlement is critical.

We were encouraged to find at the Caracas session that there were states from all regional groups that support the need for comprehensive dispute-settlement provisions. At the end of the session, the United States cosponsored, with eight other states from different regions, a working paper containing alternative texts of draft treaty articles. This document was prepared, and is in general supported, by a broader informal group chaired by the Representatives of Australia and El Salvador, for which Professor Louis Sohn of the Harvard Law School served as rapporteur. We hope this document will facilitate the drafting of treaty articles on this important element of the convention.

With your permission, Mr. Chairman, I will submit for the record a copy of the report transmitted by the delegation to the Secretary of State on August 30 and copies of all draft articles sponsored or cosponsored by the United States. The consolidated treaty texts in Committee II and other documents will be transmitted to the committee as soon as we receive them from the U.N. Secretariat.

Mr. Chairman, it is my firm conviction that a comprehensive treaty is obtainable by the end of 1975 as contemplated in last year's U.N. General Assembly resolution. To do so, however, governments must begin serious negotiation the first day at Geneva; and to prepare for that, they must during the intersessional period appraise the alternatives, meet informally to explore possible accommodations that go beyond stated positions, and supply their delegates with instructions that permit a successful negotiation.

A multilateral convention of unparalleled complexity affecting some of our nation's most vital economic and strategic interests is within our reach. We cannot and will not sign just any treaty, but in my judgment we would be terribly remiss in our responsibilities to the United States and to the international community as a whole if we were now to overlook broader and longer range perspectives.

In the year ahead we intend to work diligently and carefully for a convention that will protect our interests in the broadest sense of that term. In this endeavor, Mr. Chairman, we trust that we shall have the guidance and support of the Congress and of your committee.

Through our mutual cooperative efforts I am certain that we can take the necessary steps and develop constructive initiatives so that all will agree that the United States has done all it could to foster a successful outcome of the Third U.N. Conference on the Law of the Sea on schedule in 1975.

[Like innumerable other forecasts of the 1970s, the windup of the Law of the Sea Conference failed to occur in 1975 or even in 1976, when two further sessions in New York found the conferees still short of agreement on fundamental issues. In the meantime, the United States took independent action in one important area of conference responsibility as Congress enacted and President Ford signed the Fishery Conservation and Management Act of 1976,[13] extending U.S. fishery jurisdiction on a unilateral basis to a distance of 200 miles from the American coast with effect from March 1, 1977.]

[13]Public Law 94-265, Apr. 13, 1976.

20. THE UNITED NATIONS WORLD POPULATION CONFERENCE

(Bucharest, August 19-30, 1974)

[Ideological considerations, which had thus far exerted only a muted influence in the deliberations on the Law of the Sea, emerged in full crescendo at the United Nations World Population Conference that took place in Bucharest, Romania, on August 19-30. Few among the 136 governments that sent delegates to this first government-level conference on global population problems would have challenged President Ford's assertion, in a message of greeting, that "The rapid growth of the human race presents one of the greatest challenges to man's ingenuity that we have ever encountered."[1] A world population that was currently increasing by 2 percent a year would necessarily double every 35 years as long as the rate of increase was maintained; and the resultant economic and social dislocations would be accentuated many times over in consequence of the fact that the highest growth rates tended to occur in the countries that were poorest, least developed, and least able to support even their existing populations. But even though these basic facts were generally recognized, there still remained wide areas of disagreement concerning their significance and, above all, concerning the methods that might properly be employed in trying to avert potentially harmful consequences.

The nature of these differences had become increasingly well defined in the course of discussions relating to the population problem that had been going forward in the United Nations throughout the past two decades—particularly since 1970, when the Economic

Bulletin, 71: 431.

328 AMERICAN FOREIGN RELATIONS 1974

and Social Council (ECOSOC) had recommended that the year 1974 be designated as World Population Year and that there be convened during that year a U.N.-sponsored World Population Conference to consider "basic demographic problems, their relationship with economic and social development, and population policies and action programmes needed to promote human welfare and development."[2] For most of the more developed countries, the key to limiting runaway population increase lay in a wider, more consistent use of so-called family planning techniques. But though this approach had made a certain amount of headway in some of the developing countries, it continued to encounter strong resistance from several directions. Opposed by the Vatican on theological grounds, it was also opposed for ideological reasons by some of the Communist governments and, in addition, was frequently denounced by those of the third world governments that tended to see in such suggestions an intrusion on their sovereignty. The only real solution, such governments maintained, was more rapid economic development. More rapid development, they said, would automatically bring with it a decline in birth rates such as had already occurred in the developed countries.

The discussions at Bucharest, which were organized by Antonio Carillo-Flores of Mexico in his capacity as Secretary-General of the Conference, had as their point of departure a so-called "Draft World Population Plan of Action," a lengthy analysis and programmatic statement drawn up by the U.N. Secretariat under Mr. Waldheim's direction.[3] While it obviously sought to do justice to all of the contending points of view, this document particularly stressed the thought that family planning information and assistance should be made available by 1980, or at latest by 1985, in those countries where it was not already provided.

Such a recommendation, which could hardly fail to provoke a lively debate at Bucharest, was assured the support of the American delegation, which was headed by Caspar W. Weinberger, the Secretary of Health, Education, and Welfare, and also included Russell W. Peterson, the Chairman of the Council on Environmental Quality, and Christian A. Herter, Jr., the Special Assistant to the Secretary of State for Environmental Affairs. Outlining the thinking of the U.S. delegation in his opening statement, Secretary Weinberger not only expressed approval of the Secretariat plan but offered the bold suggestion that countries represented at the conference seek to attain "a replacement level of fertility"—i.e., an average of two children per family—by the year 2000.]

[2]ECOSOC Resolution 1484 (XVIII), Apr. 3, 1970.
[3]U.N. document E/CONF.60/7.

(45)   The United Nations World Population Conference, Bucharest, August 19-30, 1974: Statements by Caspar W. Weinberger, Secretary of Health, Education, and Welfare and Head of the United States Delegation.

(a) Statement to the Conference, August 20, 1974.[4]

I welcome this opportunity to thank Secretary General Waldheim for his stimulating address and the guidance he has given us. I should also like to declare to this distinguished body the admiration I have already expressed to our dedicated and indefatigable Conference Secretary General, Don Antonio Carillo-Flores, for the thorough and valuable preparations he and his able colleagues have made for this largest of all U.N. conferences. Mr. President,[5] we are grateful to your government and its many able officials who have provided the magnificent arrangements here and deeply appreciate the warm traditional hospitality of the Romanian people.

The Charter of the United Nations announces our determination to provide social progress and better standards of life in larger freedom. For some time now, the nations represented here have been engaged in a common endeavor to improve the quality of life of our peoples and of mankind generally.

Many nations have made plans for themselves individually and collectively in the strategies for the U.N. Development Decade and Second Development Decade.[6] Together we have passed resolutions and declarations in support of human rights, social development, improvement in the status of women, aid from science and technology, protection of the environment. There has been a special U.N. General Assembly on the use of resources. Preparations are being made for a conference to assure food supply.[7]

Taken together, these actions cover essentially all aspects of the supply side of the population and development equation.

This great conference brings governments from all over the world for the first time to address the demand side of that equation: people. It is a momentous occasion to deal with a subject that is at the same time the most personal and the most public.

I should like to report to you first on the population situation in the United States. Our long-term downward trend of fertility, inter-

[4]Text and subtitles from *Bulletin,* 71: 429-33. For other statements by members of the U.S. delegation see same: 433-9.

[5]George Macovescu, Minister of Foreign Affairs of Romania, was elected by acclamation as President of the Conference.

[6]General Assembly Resolutions 1710 (XVI), Dec. 19, 1961 (*Documents, 1961*: 535-8), and 2626 (XXV), Oct. 24, 1970 (excerpts in same, *1970*: 324-31).

[7]Cf. respectively Chapters 7 and 27.

rupted by the post-World War II baby boom, has resumed. Laws that existed in some of our states against sale or use of contraceptives have been declared invalid by many of our courts. A Commission on Population Growth and the American Future,[8] authorized by the Congress and appointed by the President, has produced a landmark study. The Congress has enacted and the executive branch is administering a family planning services program. Organized family planning programs now reach over 3 million women who otherwise would not have access to them. Some form of government-subsidized family planning service is now available in 85 percent of the counties in the United States, and efforts are being made to reach into the others. A national Center for Population Research supports a large biomedical and social service program of research in human fertility and its control. The U.S. Agency for International Development also sponsors general research programs.

Our government-supported programs insist that the voluntary choice of each individual participant must be fully safeguarded. We believe this choice is strengthened by information and by a full range of fertility controls. We are concerned about growing numbers, but we are equally concerned to help parents avoid the conception of an unwanted child—which I call a population crisis all its own.

Although the United States does not have a written population policy as such, the attitudes of the American people and the programs I have mentioned are as effective as a mere statement of policy. They have contributed to the drop in the U.S. birth rate in 1973 to 15 per 1,000 and even less for the first five months of this year. Fertility has been below the level of replacement for 2½ years. It seems likely, though by no means certain, that the country will report a stable population not long after the year 2000.

Elsewhere in the world, while developing countries have achieved commendable success in their strenuous efforts to increase the supply of goods and services for their peoples, their very success in reducing early mortality and extending life has, ironically, generated the very rapid population growth that in many nations absorbs a half, two-thirds, sometimes all of their increased economic growth.

This rapid population growth makes development more difficult in many countries. Immediate consumption diverts resources from social and economic improvement. Importation of food depletes limited foreign exchange. The number of children for whom basic education cannot be provided continues to increase. Chronic and growing underemployment and unemployment are becoming more tragic for individuals and more serious for nations.

[8]Chaired by John D. Rockefeller, 3rd; cf. *Presidential Documents,* 8: 823 (1972).

These are of course the major reasons that within the last decade 30 nations with 75 percent of the peoples of the developing world have undertaken programs to slow their population growth. Fifteen other developing nations have begun to provide family planning as a health service.

We agree with those nations that have decided the process of modernization itself requires that birth rates be reduced just as death rates have been and are being reduced. We agree with them further that as rapid population growth is slowed, national income per person will increase.

We also see population programs not as a substitute for development, but as a proper and integral part of development—whatever style it may follow. Whatever action nations take on population matters, it will be essential to move even more rapidly with programs of development to care for the growing numbers that will be inevitable.

Food and Natural Resource Requirements

The sudden, enormous requirements of many nations in 1972 for imported food have alarmed the world. The most urgent needs were met; but world food reserves are the lowest in decades, and prices of basic foods have risen sharply. All U.S. farmland formerly held out of production has been returned to production. There is little margin of safety anywhere. Part of this increased demand is due to the growing affluence of many countries, but part is due to population increase.

The annual increase of some 80 million people, nearly all in countries which already must import part of their food supply, plus slight improvements in diets for some, will increase world food requirements about 2½ percent per year on the average. But within many developing countries the annual increase in demand may be closer to 4 percent. The U.N. Second Development Decade of the seventies calls for a 4 percent annual increase in agricultural production. Unfortunately, in the first three years of the Decade the increase has only averaged 1 percent.

Agricultural specialists tell us that if all goes well with weather, soil, water, fuel, fertilizer, and if incentives are provided to the farmers, the world can produce the food requirements for the U.N. medium projection for the populations of 1985 and 2000.

Unfortunately, even if it works, much of this food will not be where the people are. The countries with the greatest needs simply will not be able to produce food to meet their needs. In many of them, most of the good land with adequate water is already in use. Fuel and fertilizer are scarce, expensive, and usually require foreign exchange. In some large regions, population growth weakens an already fragile environment in ways that threaten longer term food production. Thus, overgrazing, deforestation, land exhaustion, soil erosion, and water pollution of many kinds increase in areas that can least afford any of these problems. In addition, the impact of natural or other disaster[s] is greater because more people are trying to exist under marginal and quite vulnerable conditions.

Most developing countries will be dependent on continually increasing imports. If their populations grow as projected, their import requirements for basic cereals alone will rise from the 24 million tons in 1970 to some 95-112 million tons in 2000. The costs of these import requirements would rise from about $2.5 billion in 1970 to $15-$18 billion (in 1974 prices) in 2000.

We will be moving toward the debacle described by Dr. Norman Borlaug, Nobel Peace Prize laureate, who has solemnly warned:

By the green revolution we have only delayed the world food crisis for another 30 years. If the world population continues to increase at the same rate we will destroy the species.

We all know that many predictions do not come true, but surely there is cause not only for grave concern but—even more important—for specific action in family planning and increasing the world's food supply.

We are all aware of the growing demands made on the world's natural resources, especially by the industrialized countries. In the United States 87 percent of the natural resources we use come from within the country, and a considerable part of these as well as imported resources are sent to other countries as finished products. Population growth, increasing affluence, and expanding industrialization in all countries are increasing these demands for resources.

Many human activities in both the industrialized countries and the less developed countries harm the natural environment. Most of the nations here have agreed in the Action Plan for the Human Environment adopted at the U.N. World Conference on the Environment in 1972[9] to take measures to minimize these adverse effects. In the United States we are taking specific actions to make more efficient use of resources, reduce waste, reuse products, recycle materials, curb pollution, repair damage already done to the environment, and to plan developments so as to minimize adverse impacts on the world ecosystem. We will continue to strengthen these actions.

Individual and National Welfare

There is a temptation to think of the effects of too rapid population growth in national or world terms. But the actual suffering is

[9]Cf. *AFR, 1972*: 468.

in the individual family—mothers worn by too frequent childbearing, infants affected by malnutrition, children deprived of an education, young adults jobless and frustrated. These are great personal tragedies that affect millions.

The draft World Population Plan of Action quite rightly gives first attention to goals to reduce infant mortality, extend expectations of life, and erase the difference in expectation of life between more developed and less developed regions of the world. We strongly support these goals.

The draft plan of action also asserts the basic human right, recognized by repeated U.N. resolutions, of couples to determine freely and responsibly the number and spacing of their children and to have information, education, and means to do so. The plan urges each country to assure that such information, education, and means of family planning are made available to all its people by the end of this Second Development Decade or at the latest by 1985. This recommendation is the foundation of the plan. We support it, emphasizing the urgency of providing these services by the end of the Second Development Decade as called for by Economic and Social Council (ECOSOC) Resolution 1672 (LII), June 2, 1972, and the Declaration on Population and Development of the Second Asian Population Conference.[10] We think it is important also that couples, in having children, recognize their responsibility to consider the welfare of the children and of their community.

We are glad to find in the plan of action recognition that nations, in addition to providing family planning services, should give attention in their development programs to aspects of development that are desirable in themselves and may also motivate couples toward smaller families: reduction of infant and child mortality; basic education, equally for women; improved status of women, including wider opportunities for employment; promotion of social justice; improvement of life in rural areas; provision for old-age security; education of the rising generation of children as to the desirability of small families; establishment of an appropriate lower limit for age of marriage.

We are all aware of the repeated, almost constant argument as to the relative merits of family planning services and of economic and social development for reducing fertility. Our own conclusion is that both are important. We think the draft plan of action presents both in a sensible balance.

Couples have both rights and responsibilities of parenthood. We believe, similarly, nations in exercising their sovereign right to determine their own population policies have a responsibility toward their neighbors and the world.

[10]Adopted at Tokyo Nov. 13, 1972; text in *Bulletin,* 68: 19-20 (1973).

Reaching Population Goals

We commend the Secretary Genral and all who have been involved in the drafting of the World Population Plan of Action. We support it fully but believe it can and should be strengthened in a few important respects.

My delegation will suggest in the Working Group on the World Population Plan of Action national goals together with a world goal of replacement level of fertility by the year 2000.

We believe the plan should be the commencement of a serious effort by both developed and developing countries to consider the various means of arriving at chosen goals. The choice may make the difference between a decent life or early death for hundreds of millions of the next generation and even greater numbers in the following generation.

For example, according to the U.N. medium projection, the world's population will reach about 6.4 billion by 2000 and over 11 billion by 2050. If, however, delegates agree at this conference and are able to persuade their countries to endeavor to attain the practicable goal of a replacement level of fertility—an average of two children per family—by 2000, the world's population in that year will be approximately 5.9 billion. Countries with high fertility will still double or treble their populations, but the world total in 2050 will be about 8.2 billion rather than in excess of 11 billion. The difference is, of course, a half billion people in the year 2000 and over 3 billion in 2050. The quality of life our children enjoy or suffer in 2000, and our grandchildren in 2050, will be deeply affected by the course we take at this conference and later in our countries.

With this lower population size by 2000, food import requirements of the less developed countries would be reduced by 100 million tons of cereals, thereby making self-sufficiency in food a real possibility. They will be able to divert enormous funds from food imports to development needs.

As a contribution toward these goals, the United States offers four undertakings:

—First, we will carry out the provision of the World Population Plan of Action to the best of our ability. Especially we will continue our effort to assure the availability of family planning services to all our people.

—Second, we will undertake a collaborative effort with other interested donor countries and U.N. agencies—especially the World Health Organization (WHO), the U.N. Fund for Population Activities (UNFPA), the International Bank for Reconstruction and Development (IBRD), and the U.N. Children's Fund (UNICEF)—to assist poorer countries to develop low-cost basic preventive and curative health services, including maternal and child health and family planning services, reaching out into remote rural areas. We have already begun to use our communications satellites for medical consultation and diagnosis. If desired, we could extend these new techniques to family planning organizations and administration.

—Third, we will join with other interested countries in a further collaborative effort of national research in human reproduction and fertility control covering biomedical and socioeconomic factors.

—Fourth, my government will be glad to join other countries in order to seek increased funds for assistance to bilateral and multilateral health and population programs in developing countries that desire our help and our voluntary contributions to the U.N. Fund for Population Activities. If other donor countries—especially the newly wealthy countries—indicate an interest in providing a steady increase in such funds over the next 10 years, my delegation will bring that message home from this conference, and given some evidence of world interest, it is quite possible our Congress will respond favorably.

Mr. President, I believe we all realize the awesome responsibility that falls on us who represent our governments here. We have a unique opportunity to offer guidance by which nations can set their own course toward a brighter future for their peoples. With the cooperative spirit I feel here, we can achieve a success for this conference that will benefit generations to come.

[It may be doubted whether the U.S. delegation had seriously expected the conference to endorse the goal of a "replacement level of fertility" by the end of the century. As the Action Plan emerged from the process of amendment by the conference,[11] it lacked not only this feature but even the suggested interim deadline of 1980 or 1985 for the general availability of family planning services. It did, however, invite those countries that thought their birth rates too high to consider setting quantitative goals and implementing policies with a view to their achievement by 1985. Even this formulation was unacceptable to the delegation of the Holy See, which formally recorded its dissent. Other delegations also expressed a variety of reservations concerning the final version of the Action Plan, but did not oppose its adoption by a consensus procedure. In

---

[11]*Report of the United Nations World Population Conference, 1974* (U.N. document E/CONF.60/19; U.N. sales no. E.75.XIII.3): 3-26; also in *Bulletin,* 71: 440-53. For a detailed analysis see same: 649-54.

supplemental resolutions reflecting a broad range of ideological influences, the conference called among other things for a more equitable distribution of world resources, equality of the sexes, support for a proposed Charter of Economic Rights and Duties of States, participation in the forthcoming World Food Conference, independence for Portuguese territories, and the elimination of *apartheid* in Southern Africa.[12]

In a concluding statement to the press, Secretary Weinberger ignored these ancillary issues and concentrated on an evaluation of the revised Action Plan.]

(b) Statement to the press, August 30, 1974.[13]

At the end of this World Population Conference, it is apparent that it has achieved a great success in carrying out the purposes for which it was established by the resolution of the Economic and Social Council four years ago. The fact that a Population Conference of 135 nations has been held at all has been a great accomplishment. It has been a real educational process for all those who have attended.

It has successfully adopted a meaningful World Population Plan of Action. After two weeks, including a long weekend of intensive effort, a consensus was reached on a plan which is a landmark advance in international understanding and agreement on population matters. The plan itself says:

(It) must be considered as an important component of the system of international strategies and as an instrument of the international community for the promotion of economic development, quality of life, human rights and fundamental freedom.

Although, understandably, much attention has been given to the controversial paragraphs in the plan, the totality of the plan is most important. For example, the sections on collection and analysis of information, on research, on training and education and the spreading of knowledge have received little attention outside of the working group itself, but they are fundamental to any plan for guidance to nations in the preparation of their own population programs.

Polemics and ideological statements in the first few days of the conference almost obscured the substance of the plan of action. The content of some of these statements were included in the plan; they added little of value but did not impair the substance.

[12]Report of the Conference, as cited, pp. 27-49.
[13]U.S. Embassy Press Release, Bucharest, Aug. 30; text from *Bulletin,* 71: 439-40.

The plan has not been injured and in a number of ways has been improved by the two weeks of consideration.

    a. It confirms the basic human right of couples and individuals to decide freely and responsibly the number and spacing of their children and to have the information, education, and means to do so.

    b. It calls on nations to assure the provision of such information and means to their peoples.

    c. The plan recognizes for the first time that the responsibility of couples and individuals in the exercise of this right takes into account the needs of their living and future children and their responsibility to the community.

    d. It recognizes, at the national level, the sovereign right of each nation to formulate and implement population policies and also recognizes that in exercising their sovereign rights nations should take into account international cooperation in order to improve the quality of life of the peoples of the world.

The plan also recognizes that population goals and policies are recognized to be integral parts of social, economic, and cultural development with the principal aim to improve levels of living and the quality of life of the people.

There has been introduced into the plan, with the leadership of the U.S. delegation and others, a strong recognition of the right of women to complete integration in the development process, particularly by means of an equal participation in educational, social, economic, cultural, and political life. An entire new section in the recommendations has also been added concerning strengthening the status of women as essential in its own right and conducive to lower fertility.

The document also recommends priority in economic development programs to those sectors which, while valuable in their own right, will also be particularly conducive to moderating fertility. As noted earlier, the plan calls upon nations to assure the provision of means to assist responsible parenthood, but it omits the reference in the draft to achievement of this objective by 1980 or 1985. A new paragraph (37), however, invites countries which consider their birth rates detrimental to their national purposes to consider quantitative goals and implementing policies that may lead to the attainment of such goals by 1985. It recognizes of course that nothing in this invitation should interfere with the sovereignty of any government to adopt or not to adopt such quantitative goals. The inclusion of 1985 as a specific date was hotly debated in the working group but was sustained by a vote.

A strong statement concerning the relation of population matters to resources and environment has also been added.

The close relationship between population and food was recognized, and all governments were urged to participate actively in the World Food Conference in November in Rome.

The adoption of the plan of action by consensus should not be considered a victory or a defeat for any country or group of countries. We think it is a real triumph for the process of international negotiations under U.N. auspices and that it can lead to a better future for all peoples and all countries.

21. OPENING THE 29TH GENERAL ASSEMBLY

(New York, September 17-23, 1974)

[The differences and shared preoccupations of the world community of the 1970s habitually achieved their most authoritative expression at the regular annual sessions of the U.N. General Assembly, which had served since 1946 both as "town meeting of the world" and as sounding board for the views of virtually every kind of government. These annual convocations had not, in recent years, been specially happy occasions for the American Government, whose own opinions had been increasingly overborne by a coalition of Communist and third world nations to which even some close allies of the United States had occasionally attached themselves. In 1971, the United States had sustained a special humiliation in the defeat of its proposal to admit the People's Republic of China to U.N. representation while preserving a seat for the Republic of China on Taiwan.[1] In 1972, the American delegation had been unable to gain the Assembly's backing for its proposals aimed at curbing certain forms of international terrorism.[2] In 1973, the United States had incurred the direct censure of the Assembly for its breach of the mandatory economic sanctions imposed by the Security Council against the breakaway British colony of Southern Rhodesia.[3] Yet in spite of these and other discomfitures, American authorities had continued to maintain that participation in the General Assembly and most other U.N. bodies brought advantages to the United States that decisively outweighed the drawbacks.

[1]Cf. *AFR, 1971*: 500-515.
[2]Cf. same, *1972*: 490-515.
[3]Cf. same, *1973*: 579-80 and 583-6.

The 29th Regular Session of the General Assembly, which opened at U.N. Headquarters in New York on September 17, 1974, was destined to produce the usual crop of frictions, which this year would center primarily around the membership status of the Republic of South Africa, the claims of the Palestine Liberation Organization, and the content of the proposed Charter of Economic Rights and Duties of States.[4] These difficulties, however, were still not clearly foreseeable as delegates gathered in the Assembly chamber for opening-day ceremonies that included the election of Algeria's Foreign Minister, Abdelaziz Bouteflika, as President of the 29th Session, followed by the admission of Bangladesh, Grenada, and Guinea-Bissau (formerly Portuguese Guinea) as the organization's 136th, 137th, and 138th members.

Delegates to the Assembly's previous Regular Session, in 1973, had experienced the novelty of listening to the first significant statement of American foreign policy to be delivered by Dr. Kissinger in his then newly assumed role as Secretary of State.[5] The 29th Session was witness to an even more illustrious American debut as President Ford himself, still less than six weeks in office, approached the Assembly's rostrum to deliver an address of welcome that seemed to aim at reducing the complexities of world affairs to a few timely truths.]

(46) Address of Welcome to the Assembly by President Ford, September 18, 1974.[6]

Mr. President, Mr. Secretary General, your Excellencies:

In 1946, President Harry Truman welcomed representatives of 55 nations to the first General Assembly of the United Nations.[7] Since then, every American President has had the great honor of addressing this Assembly.

Today, with pleasure and humility, I take my turn in welcoming you, the distinguished representatives of 138 nations.

When I took office, I told the American people that my remarks would be "just a little straight talk among friends."[8] Straight talk is what I propose here today in the first of my addresses to the representatives of the world.

Next week, Secretary of State Henry Kissinger will present in

[4]Cf. Chapters 25, 26, and 32.
[5]*AFR, 1973*: 359-66.
[6]Text from *Presidential Documents,* 10: 1165-9.
[7]*Documents, 1945-46*: 40-44.
[8]*Presidential Documents,* 10: 1023.

specifics the overall principles which I will outline in my remarks today.[9] It should be emphatically understood that the Secretary of State has my full support and the unquestioned backing of the American people.

As a party leader in the Congress of the United States, as Vice President, and now as President of the United States of America, I have had the closest working relationship with Secretary of State Kissinger. I have supported and will continue to endorse his many efforts as Secretary of State and in our National Security Council system to build a world of peace.

Since the United Nations was founded, the world has experienced conflicts and threats to peace, but we have avoided the greatest danger—another world war. Today, we have the opportunity to make the remainder of this century an era of peace and cooperation and economic well-being.

The harsh hostilities which once held great powers in their rigid grasp have now begun to moderate. Many of the crises which dominated past General Assemblies are fortunately behind us. And technological progress holds out the hope that one day all men can achieve a decent life.

Nations too often have had no choice but to be either hammer or anvil, to strike or to be struck. Now we have a new opportunity—to forge, in concert with others, a framework of international cooperation. That is the course the United States has chosen for itself.

On behalf of the American people, I renew these basic pledges to you today.

—We are committed to a pursuit of a more peaceful, stable, and cooperative world. While we are determined never to be bested in a test of strength, we will devote our strength to what is best. And in the nuclear era, there is no rational alternative to accords of mutual restraint between the United States and the Soviet Union, two nations which have the power to destroy mankind.

—We will bolster our partnerships with traditional friends in Europe, Asia, and Latin America to meet new challenges in a rapidly changing world. The maintenance of such relationships underpins rather than undercuts the search for peace.

—We will seek out, we will expand our relations with old adversaries. For example, our new rapport with the People's Republic of China best serves the purposes of each nation and the interests of the entire world.

[9]Document 47.

—We will strive to heal old wounds, reopened in recent conflicts in Cyprus, the Middle East, and in Indochina. Peace cannot be imposed from without, but we will do whatever is within our capacity to help achieve it.

—We rededicate ourselves to the search for justice, equality, and freedom. Recent developments in Africa signal the welcome end of colonialism.[10] Behavior appropriate to an era of dependence must give way to the new responsibilities of an era of interdependence.

No single nation, no single group of nations, no single organization can meet all of the challenges before the community of nations. We must act in concert. Progress toward a better world must come through cooperative efforts across the whole range of bilateral and multilateral relations.

America's revolutionary birth and centuries of experience in adjusting democratic government to changing conditions have made Americans practical as well as idealistic. As idealists, we are proud of our role in the founding of the United Nations and in supporting its many accomplishments. As practical people, we are sometimes impatient at what we see as shortcomings.

In my 25 years as a Member of the Congress of the United States, I learned two basic practical lessons:

First, men of differing political persuasions can find common ground for cooperation. We need not agree on all issues in order to agree on most. Differences of principle, of purpose, of perspective will not disappear. But neither will our mutual problems disappear unless we are determined to find mutually helpful solutions.

Second, a majority must take into account the proper interest of a minority if the decisions of the majority are to be accepted. We who believe in and live by majority rule must always be alert to the danger of the "tyranny of the majority." Majority rule thrives on the habits of accommodation, moderation, and consideration of the interests of others.

A very stark reality has tempered America's actions for decades and must now temper the actions of all nations. Prevention of full-scale warfare in the nuclear age has become everybody's responsibility. Today's regional conflict must not become tomorrow's world disaster. We must assure by every means at our disposal that local crises are quickly contained and resolved.

[10]Cf. Chapter 25, introductory paragraphs.

The challenge before the United States [Nations] is very clear. This organization can place the weight of the world community on the side of world peace. And this organization can provide impartial forces to maintain the peace.

And at this point I wish to pay tribute on behalf of the American people to the 37 members of the United Nations peacekeeping forces who have given their lives in the Middle East and in Cyprus in the past 10 months, and I convey our deepest sympathies to their loved ones.

Let the quality of our response measure up to the magnitude of the challenge that we face. I pledge to you that America will continue to be constructive, innovative, and responsive to the work of this great body.

The nations in this hall are united by a deep concern for peace. We are united as well by our desire to ensure a better life for all people.

Today, the economy of the world is under unprecedented stress. We need new approaches to international cooperation to respond effectively to the problems that we face. Developing and developed countries, market and nonmarket countries—we are all a part of one interdependent economic system.

The food and oil crises demonstrate the extent of our interdependence. Many developing nations need the food surplus of a few developed nations. And many industrialized nations need the oil production of a few developing nations.

Energy is required to produce food and food to produce energy—and both to provide a decent life for everyone. The problems of food and energy can be resolved on the basis of cooperation, or can, I should say, [be] made unmanageable on the basis of confrontation. Runaway inflation, propelled by food and oil price increases, is an early warning signal to all of us.

Let us not delude ourselves. Failure to cooperate on oil and food and inflation could spell disaster for every nation represented in this room. The United Nations must not and need not allow this to occur. A global strategy for food and energy is urgently required.

The United States believes four principles should guide a global approach:

First, all nations must substantially increase production. Just to maintain the present standards of living the world must almost double its output of food and energy to match the expected increase in the world's population by the end of this century. To meet aspirations for a better life, production will have to expand at a significantly faster rate than population growth.

Second, all nations must seek to achieve a level of prices which not only provides an incentive to producers but which consumers can afford. It should now be clear that the developed nations are not the only countries which demand and receive [*sic*] an adequate return for their goods. But it should also be clear that by confronting consumers with production restrictions, artificial pricing, and the prospect of ultimate bankruptcy, producers will eventually become the victims of their own actions.

Third, all nations must avoid the abuse of man's fundamental needs for the sake of narrow national or bloc advantage. The attempt by any nation to use one commodity for political purposes will inevitably tempt other countries to use their commodities for their own purposes.

Fourth, the nations of the world must assure that the poorest among us are not overwhelmed by rising prices of the imports necessary for their survival. The traditional aid donors and the increasingly wealthy oil producers must join in this effort.

The United States recognizes the special responsibility we bear as the world's largest producer of food. That is why Secretary of State Kissinger proposed from this very podium last year a world food conference to define a global food policy.[11] And that is one reason why we have removed domestic restrictions on food productions in the United States.

It has not been our policy to use food as a political weapon, despite the oil embargo and recent oil prices and production decisions.

It would be tempting for the United States—beset by inflation and soaring energy prices—to turn a deaf ear to external appeals for food assistance, or to respond with internal appeals for export controls. But however difficult our own economic situation, we recognize that the plight of others is worse.

Americans have always responded to human emergencies in the past, and we respond again here today. In response to Secretary General Waldheim's appeal and to help meet the long-term challenge in food, I reiterate: To help developing nations realize their aspirations to grow more of their own food, the United States will substantially increase its assistance to agricultural production programs in other countries.

Next, to ensure that the survival of millions of our fellow men does not depend upon the vagaries of weather, the United States is prepared to join in a worldwide effort to negotiate, establish, and maintain an international system of food reserves. This system will

[11]*AFR, 1973*: 365.

work best if each nation is made responsible for managing the reserves that it will have available.

Finally, to make certain that the more immediate needs for food are met this year, the United States will not only maintain the amount it spends for food shipments to nations in need but it will increase this amount this year.

Thus, the United States is striving to help define and help contribute to a cooperative global policy to meet man's immediate and long-term need for food. We will set forth our comprehensive proposals at the World Food Conference in November.[12]

Now is the time for oil producers to define their conception of a global policy on energy to meet the growing need and to do this without imposing unacceptable burdens on the international monetary and trade system.

A world of economic confrontation cannot be a world of political cooperation. If we fail to satisfy man's fundamental needs for energy and food, we face a threat not just to our aspirations for a better life for all our peoples but to our hopes for a more stable and a more peaceful world. By working together to overcome our common problems, mankind can turn from fear towards hope.

From the time of the founding of the United Nations, America volunteered to help nations in need, frequently as the main benefactor. We were able to do it. We were glad to do it. But as new economic forces alter and reshape today's complex world, no nation can be expected to feed all the world's hungry peoples.

Fortunately, however, many nations are increasingly able to help. And I call on them to join with us as truly united nations in the struggle to produce, to provide more food at lower prices for the hungry and, in general, a better life for the needy of this world.

America will continue to do more than its share. But there are realistic limits to our capacities. There is no limit, however, to our determination to act in concert with other nations to fulfill the vision of the United Nations Charter, to save succeeding generations from the scourge of war, and to promote social progress and better standards, better standards of life in a larger freedom.

Thank you very, very much.

[The emphasis on food and energy problems in President Ford's remarks was maintained by Secretary Kissinger in his address to the Assembly the following week. As the principal U.S. contribution to the annual "general debate," the Kissinger speech touched also on some of the leading political issues of the period, including the

---

[12]Cf. Chapter 27.

danger of nuclear proliferation, on which India's recent nuclear test had focused anxious attention.]

(47) "An Age of Interdependence—Common Disaster or Community": Address to the Assembly by Secretary of State Kissinger, September 23, 1974.[13]

Last year, in my first address as Secretary of State, I spoke to this Assembly about American purposes.[14] I said that the United States seeks a comprehensive, institutionalized peace, not an armistice. I asked other nations to join us in moving the world from détente to cooperation, from coexistence to community.

In the year that has passed, some progress has been made in dealing with particular crises. But many fundamental issues persist, and new issues threaten the very structure of world stability.

Our deepest problem—going far beyond the items on our agenda—is whether our vision can keep pace with our challenges. Will history recall the 20th century as a time of mounting global conflict or as the beginning of a global conception? Will our age of interdependence spur joint progress or common disaster?

The answer is not yet clear. New realities have not yet overcome old patterns of thought and action. Traditional concepts—of national sovereignty, social struggle, and the relation between the old and the new nations—too often guide our course. And so we have managed but not advanced; we have endured but not prospered; and we have continued the luxury of political contention.

This condition has been dramatized in the brief period since last fall's regular session. War has ravaged the Middle East and Cyprus. The technology of nuclear explosives has resumed its dangerous spread. Inflation and the threat of global decline hang over the economies of rich and poor alike.

We cannot permit this trend to continue. Conflict between nations once devastated continents; the struggle between blocs may destroy humanity. Ideologies and doctrines drawn from the last century do not even address, let alone solve, the unprecedented problems of today. As a result, events challenge habits; a gulf grows between rhetoric and reality.

The world has dealt with local conflicts as if they were perpetually manageable. We have permitted too many of the underlying causes to fester unattended until the parties believed that their only

[13]News release, Office of Media Services, Department of State; titles and text from *Bulletin*, 71: 498-504.
[14]*AFR, 1973*: 359-66.

recourse was war. And because each crisis ultimately has been contained we have remained complacent. But tolerance of local conflict tempts world holocaust. We have no guarantee that some local crisis—perhaps the next—will not explode beyond control.

The world has dealt with nuclear weapons as if restraint were automatic. Their very awesomeness has chained these weapons for almost three decades; their sophistication and expense have helped to keep constant for a decade the number of states who possess them. Now, as was quite foreseeable, political inhibitions are in danger of crumbling. Nuclear catastrophe looms more plausible— whether through design or miscalculation; accident, theft, or blackmail.

The world has dealt with the economy as if its constant advance were inexorable. While postwar growth has been uneven and some parts of the world have lagged, our attention was focused on how to increase participation in a general advance. We continue to deal with economic issues on a national, regional, or bloc basis at the precise moment that our interdependence is multiplying. Strains on the fabric and institutions of the world economy threaten to engulf us all in a general depression.

The delicate structure of international cooperation so laboriously constructed over the last quarter century can hardly survive—and certainly cannot be strengthened—if it is continually subjected to the shocks of political conflict, war, and economic crisis.

The time has come, then, for the nations assembled here to act together on the recognition that continued reliance on old slogans and traditional rivalries will lead us toward:

—A world ever more torn between rich and poor, East and West, producer and consumer.

—A world where local crises threaten global confrontation and where the spreading atom threatens global peril.

—A world of rising costs and dwindling supplies, of growing populations and declining production.

There is another course. Last week before this Assembly, President Ford dedicated our country to a cooperative, open approach to build a more secure and more prosperous world.[15] The United States will assume the obligations that our values and strength impose upon us.

But the building of a cooperative world is beyond the grasp of any one nation. An interdependent world requires not merely the resources but the vision and creativity of us all. Nations cannot simultaneously confront and cooperate with one another.

[15]Document 46.

We must recognize that the common interest is the only valid test of the national interest. It is in the common interest, and thus in the interest of each nation:

—That local conflicts be resolved short of force and their root causes removed by political means.

—That the spread of nuclear technology be achieved without the spread of nuclear weapons.

—That growing economic interdependence lift all nations and not drag them down together.

We will not solve these problems, during this session, or any one session, of the General Assembly.

But we must at least begin to remedy problems, not just manage them; to shape events, rather than endure them; to confront our challenges instead of one another.

The Political Dimension

The urgent political responsibility of our era is to resolve conflicts without war. History is replete with examples of the tragedy that sweeps nations when ancient enmities and the inertia of habit freeze the scope for decision. Equally, history is marked by brief moments when an old order is giving way to a pattern new and unforeseen; these are times of potential disorder and danger but also of opportunity for fresh creation. We face such a moment today. Together let us face its realities:

—First, a certain momentum toward peace has been created— in East-West relations and in certain regional conflicts. It must be maintained. But we are only at the beginning of the process. If we do not continue to advance, we will slip back.

—Second, progress in negotiation of difficult issues comes only through patience, perseverance, and recognition of the tolerable limits of the other side. Peace is a process, not a condition. It can only be reached in steps.

—Third, failure to recognize and grasp the attainable will prevent the achievement of the ideal. Attempts to resolve all issues at one time are a certain prescription for stagnation. Progress toward peace can be thwarted by asking too much as surely as by asking too little.

—Fourth, the world community can help resolve chronic conflicts, but exaggerated expectations will prevent essential accommodation among the parties. This Assembly can help or hinder the negotiating process. It can seek a scapegoat or a solution. It can offer the parties an excuse to escape reality or sturdy support in search of a compromise. It can decide on propaganda or contribute to realistic approaches that are responsive to man's yearning for peace.

The Middle East starkly demonstrates these considerations. In the past year we have witnessed both the fourth Arab-Israeli war in a generation and the hopeful beginnings of a political process toward a lasting and just peace.

We have achieved the respite of a cease-fire and of two disengagement agreements,[16] but the shadow of war remains. The legacy of hatred and suffering, the sense of irreconcilability, have begun to yield—however haltingly—to the process of negotiation. But we still have a long road ahead.

One side seeks the recovery of territory and justice for a displaced people. The other side seeks security and recognition by its neighbors of its legitimacy as a nation. In the end, the common goal of peace surely is broad enough to embrace all these aspirations.

Let us be realistic about what must be done. The art of negotiation is to set goals that can be achieved at a given time and to reach them with determination. Each step forward modifies old perceptions and brings about a new situation that improves the chances of a comprehensive settlement.

Because these principles were followed in the Middle East, agreements have been reached in the past year which many thought impossible. They were achieved, above all, because of the wisdom of the leaders of the Middle East who decided that there had been enough stalemate and war, that more might be gained by testing each other in negotiation than by testing each other on the battlefield.

The members of this body, both collectively and individually, have a solemn responsibility to encourage and support the parties in the Middle East on their present course. We have as well an obligation to give our support to the U.N. peacekeeping forces in the Middle East and elsewhere. The United States applauds their indispensable role, as well as the outstanding contribution of Secretary General Waldheim in the cause of peace.

During the past year my country has made a major effort to promote peace in the Middle East. President Ford has asked me to reaffirm today that we are determined to press forward with these efforts. We will work closely with the parties, and we will cooperate with all interested countries within the framework of the Geneva Conference.

[16]Chapters 1 and 11.

The tormented island of Cyprus is another area where peace requires a spirit of compromise, accommodation, and justice. The United States is convinced that the sovereignty, political independence, and territorial integrity of Cyprus must be maintained. It will be up to the parties to decide on the form of government they believe best suited to the particular conditions of Cyprus. They must reach accommodation on the areas to be administered by the Greek and Turkish Cypriot communities as well as on the conditions under which refugees can return to their homes and reside in safety. Finally, no lasting peace is possible unless provisions are agreed upon which will lead to the timely and phased reduction of armed forces and armaments and other war materiel.

The United States is prepared to play an even more active role than in the past in helping the parties find a solution to the centuries-old problem of Cyprus. We will do all we can, but it is those most directly concerned whose effort is most crucial. Third parties should not be asked to produce miraculous outcomes not anchored in reality. Third parties *can* encourage those directly involved to perceive their broader interests; they can assist in the search for elements of agreement by interpreting each side's views and motives to the other. But no mediator can succeed unless the parties genuinely want mediation and are ready to make the difficult decisions needed for a settlement.

The United States is already making a major contribution to help relieve the human suffering of the people of Cyprus. We urge the international community to continue and, if possible, to increase its own humanitarian relief effort.

The United States notes with particular satisfaction the continuing process of change in Africa. We welcome the positive demonstration of cooperation between the old rulers and the new free. The United States shares and pledges its support for the aspirations of all Africans to participate in the fruits of freedom and human dignity.

The Nuclear Dimension

The second new dimension on our agenda concerns the problem of nuclear proliferation.

The world has grown so accustomed to the existence of nuclear weapons that it assumes they will never be used. But today, technology is rapidly expanding the number of nuclear weapons in the hands of major powers and threatens to put nuclear-explosive technology at the disposal of an increasing number of other countries.

In a world where many nations possess nuclear weapons, dangers would be vastly compounded. It would be infinitely more difficult, if not impossible, to maintain stability among a large number of nuclear powers. Local wars would take on a new dimension. Nuclear weapons would be introduced into regions where political conflict remains intense and the parties consider their vital interests overwhelmingly involved. There would, as well, be a vastly heightened risk of direct involvement of the major nuclear powers.

This problem does not concern one country, one region, or one bloc alone. No nation can be indifferent to the spread of nuclear technology; every nation's security is directly affected.

The challenge before the world is to realize the peaceful benefits of nuclear technology without contributing to the growth of nuclear weapons or to the number of states possessing them.

As a major nuclear power, the United States recognizes its special responsibility. We realize that we cannot expect others to show restraint if we do not ourselves practice restraint. Together with the Soviet Union we are seeking to negotiate new quantitative and qualitative limitations on strategic arms. Last week our delegations reconvened in Geneva, and we intend to pursue these negotiations with the seriousness of purpose they deserve. The United States has no higher priority than controlling and reducing the levels of nuclear arms.

Beyond the relations of the nuclear powers to each other lies the need to curb the spread of nuclear explosives. We must take into account that plutonium is an essential ingredient of nuclear explosives and that in the immediate future the amount of plutonium generated by peaceful nuclear reactors will be multiplied many times. Heretofore the United States and a number of other countries have widely supplied nuclear fuels and other nuclear materials in order to promote the use of nuclear energy for peaceful purposes. This policy cannot continue if it leads to the proliferation of nuclear explosives. Sales of these materials can no longer be treated by anyone as a purely commercial competitive enterprise.

The world community therefore must work urgently toward a system of effective international safeguards against the diversion of plutonium or its byproducts. The United States is prepared to join with others in a comprehensive effort.

Let us together agree on the practical steps which must be taken to assure the benefits of nuclear energy free of its terrors:

—The United States will shortly offer specific proposals to strengthen safeguards to the other principal supplier countries.

—We shall intensify our efforts to gain the broadest possible acceptance of International Atomic Energy Agency (IAEA) safeguards, to establish practical controls on the transfer of nuclear materials, and to insure the effectiveness of these procedures.

—The United States will urge the IAEA to draft an international convention for enhancing physical security against theft or diversion of nuclear material. Such a convention should set forth specific standards and techniques for protecting materials while in use, storage, and transfer.

—The Treaty on the Non-Proliferation of Nuclear Weapons, which this assembly has endorsed,[17] warrants continuing support. The treaty contains not only a broad commitment to limit the spread of nuclear explosives but specific obligations to accept and implement IAEA safeguards and to control the transfer of nuclear materials.

Mr. President, whatever advantages seem to accrue from the acquisition of nuclear-explosive technology will prove to be ephemeral. When Pandora's box has been opened, no country will be the beneficiary and all mankind will have lost. This is not inevitable. If we act decisively now, we can still control the future.

The Economic Dimension

Lord Keynes wrote:

The power to become habituated to his surroundings is a marked characteristic of mankind. Very few of us realize with conviction the intensely unusual, unstable, complicated, unreliable, temporary nature of the economic organization . . . .

The economic history of the postwar period has been one of sustained growth, for developing as well as developed nations. The universal expectation of our peoples, the foundation of our political institutions, and the assumption underlying the evolving structure of peace are all based on the belief that this growth will continue.

But will it? The increasingly open and cooperative global economic system that we have come to take for granted is now under unprecedented attack. The world is poised on the brink of a return to the unrestrained economic nationalism which accompanied the collapse of economic order in the thirties. And should that occur, all would suffer—poor as well as rich, producer as well as consumer.

So let us no longer fear to confront in public the facts which have come to dominate our private discussions and concerns.

The early warning signs of a major economic crisis are evident.

[17]Resolution 2373 (XXII), June 12, 1968, in *Documents, 1968-69*: 54-5. For the non-proliferation treaty see note 22 to Chapter 15.

Rates of inflation unprecedented in the past quarter century are sweeping developing and developed nations alike. The world's financial institutions are staggering under the most massive and rapid movements of reserves in history. And profound questions have arisen about meeting man's most fundamental needs for energy and food.

While the present situation threatens every individual and nation, it is the poor who suffer the most. While the wealthier adjust their living standards, the poor see the hopes of a lifetime collapse around them. While others tighten their belts, the poor starve. While others can hope for a better future, the poor see only despair ahead.

It can be in the interest of no country or group of countries to base policies on a test of strength; for a policy of confrontation would end in disaster for all. Meeting man's basic needs for energy and food and assuring economic growth while mastering inflation require international cooperation to an unprecedented degree.

Let us apply these principles first to the energy situation:

—Oil producers seek a better life for their peoples and a just return for their diminishing resources.

—The developing nations less well-endowed by nature face the disintegration of the results of decades of striving for development as the result of a price policy over which they have no control.

—The developed nations find the industrial civilization built over centuries in jeopardy.

Both producers and consumers have legitimate claims. The problem is to reconcile them for the common good.

The United States is working closely with several oil producers to help diversify their economies. We have established commissions to facilitate the transfer of technology and to assist with industrialization. We are prepared to accept substantial investments in the United States, and we welcome a greater role for the oil producers in the management of international economic institutions.

The investment of surplus oil revenues presents a great challenge. The countries which most need these revenues are generally the least likely to receive them. The world's financial institutions have coped thus far, but ways must be found to assure assistance for those countries most in need of it. And the full brunt of the surplus revenues is yet to come.

Despite our best efforts to meet the oil producers' legitimate needs and to channel their resources into constructive uses, the world cannot sustain even the present level of prices, much less continuing increases. The prices of other commodities will inevitably rise in a never-ending inflationary spiral. Nobody will benefit. The oil producers will be forced to spend more for their own imports. Many nations will not be able to withstand the pace, and the poorer could be overwhelmed. The complex, fragile structure of global economic cooperation required to sustain national economic growth stands in danger of being shattered.

The United States will work with other consuming nations on means of conservation and on ways to cushion the impact of massive investments from abroad. The preliminary agreement on a program of solidarity and cooperation signed a few days ago in Brussels by the major consumer countries[18] is an encouraging first step.

But the long-range solution requires a new understanding between consumers and producers. Unlike food prices, the high cost of oil is not the result of economic factors—of an actual shortage of capacity or of the free play of supply and demand. Rather it is caused by deliberate decisions to restrict production and maintain an artificial price level. We recognize that the producers should have a fair share; the fact remains that the present price level even threatens the economic well-being of producers. Ultimately they depend upon the vitality of the world economy for the security of their markets and their investments. And it cannot be in the interest of any nation to magnify the despair of the least developed, who are uniquely vulnerable to exorbitant prices and who have no recourse but to pay.

What has gone up by political decision can be reduced by political decision.

Last week President Ford called upon the oil producers to join with consumers in defining a strategy which will meet the world's long-term need for both energy and food at reasonable prices. He set forth the principles which should guide such a policy. And he announced to this Assembly America's determination to meet our responsibilities to help alleviate another grim reality: world hunger.

At a time of universal concern for justice and in an age of advanced technology, it is intolerable that millions are starving and hundreds of millions remain undernourished.

The magnitude of the long-term problem is clear. At present rates of population growth, world food production must double by the end of this century to maintain even the present inadequate dietary level. And an adequate diet for all would require that we triple world production. If we are true to our principles, we have an

[18]Cf. Chapter 29 at note 15.

obligation to strive for an adequate supply of food to every man, woman, and child in the world. This is a technical possibility, a political necessity, and a moral imperative.

The United States is prepared to join with all nations at the World Food Conference in Rome[19] to launch the truly massive effort which is required. We will present a number of specific proposals:

—To help developing nations. They have the lowest yields and the largest amounts of unused land and water; their potential in food production must be made to match their growing need.

—To increase substantially global fertilizer production. We must end once and for all the world's chronic fertilizer shortage.

—To expand international, regional, and national research programs. Scientific and technical resources must be mobilized now to meet the demands of the year 2000 and beyond.

—To rebuild the world's food reserves. Our capacity for dealing with famine must be freed from the vagaries of weather.

—To provide a substantial level of concessionary food aid. The United States will in the coming year increase the value of our own food aid shipments to countries in need. We make this commitment, despite great pressures on our economy and at a time when we are seeking to cut our own government budget, because we realize the dimensions of the tragedy with which we are faced. All of us here have a common obligation to prevent the poorest nations from being overwhelmed and enable them to build the social, economic, and political base for self-sufficiency.

The hopes of every nation for a life of peace and plenty rest on an effective international resolution of the crises of inflation, fuel, and food. We must act now, and we must act together.

The Human Dimension

Mr. President, let us never forget that all of our political endeavors are ultimately judged by one standard—to translate our actions into human concerns.

The United States will never be satisfied with a world where man's fears overshadow his hopes. We support the U.N.'s efforts in the fields of international law and human rights. We approve of the activities of the United Nations in social, economic, and

[19]Cf. Chapter 27.
[20]Cf. respectively Chapters 20, 27, and 19.

humanitarian realms around the world. The United States considers the U.N. World Population Conference last month, the World Food Conference a month from now, and the continuing Law of the Sea Conference[20] of fundamental importance to our common future.

In coming months the United States will make specific proposals for the United Nations to initiate a major international effort to prohibit torture; a concerted campaign to control the disease which afflicts and debilitates over 200 million people in 70 countries, schistosomiasis; and a substantial strengthening of the world's capacity to deal with natural disaster, especially the improvement of the U.N. Disaster Relief Organization.

Mr. President, we have long lived in a world where the consequences of our failures were manageable—a world where local conflicts were contained, nuclear weapons threatened primarily those nations which possessed them, and the cycle of economic growth and decline seemed principally a national concern.

But this is no longer the case. It is no longer possible to imagine that conflicts, weapons, and recession will not spread.

We must now decide. The problems we face will be with us the greater part of the century. But will they be with us as challenges to be overcome or as adversaries that have vanquished us?

It is easy to agree to yet another set of principles or to actions *other* nations should take. But the needs of the poor will not be met by slogans; the needs of an expanding global economy will not be met by new restrictions; the search for peace cannot be conducted on the basis of confrontation. So each nation must ask what it can do, what contribution it is finally prepared to make to the common good.

Mr. President, beyond peace, beyond prosperity, lie man's deepest aspirations for a life of dignity and justice. And beyond our pride, beyond our concern for the national purpose we are called upon to serve, there must be a concern for the betterment of the human condition. While we cannot, in the brief span allowed to each of us, undo the accumulated problems of centuries, we dare not do less than try. So let us now get on with our tasks.

Let us act in the spirit of Thucydides that "the bravest are surely those who have the clearest vision of what is before them, glory and danger alike, and yet notwithstanding go out to meet it."

[The somber if resolute tone of Secretary Kissinger's address was not uncharacteristic of the mood of thoughtful people during this final third of 1974. It was a period when, as noted earlier, the serious implications of recent events were beginning to be more

[20] Cf. respectively Chapters 20, 27, and 19.

widely understood, signs of a world recession were becoming daily more evident, and the long-term threats to economic and political order were being viewed in an unusually pessimistic light. In appealing to the Assembly to display a sense of realism commensurate with its wide-ranging responsibilities, the Secretary of State undoubtedly had in mind a number of issues on which American and majority views would come into conflict as the session advanced, and which will be examined in future chapters.]

22. MEETING OF THE BANK AND FUND

(Washington, September 30-October 4, 1974)

[Almost as prestigious as the U.N. Assembly—and even more authoritative in their own field—were the annual meetings of the Boards of Governors of the International Bank for Reconstruction and Development (IBRD) and the International Monetary Fund (IMF), the two institutions conceived at Bretton Woods in 1944 and still regarded, at least in the non-Communist nations, as twin pillars of the international economic system. The 29th annual meeting of the two organizations, occurring at a time of acknowledged crisis in both economic development and monetary affairs, would obviously represent a milestone of more than ordinary importance, the more so because it would be up to the Board of Governors of the 126-member International Monetary Fund to take a position on the far-reaching proposals advanced in June by the "Committee of Twenty" on Reform of the International Monetary System and Related Issues.[1]

That group, it will be recalled, had concluded its labors with the publication of a "program of immediate action" that included, among other things, (1) the establishment of an "oil facility" to help IMF members meet the initial impact of increased oil prices, and of an "extended facility" to provide developing country members with longer-term balance-of-payments financing; (2) the adoption of a new method of valuation of the IMF special drawing right (SDR); (3) the establishment of a 20-member Interim Committee of the IMF Board of Governors to serve in an advisory role pending a projected amendment of the IMF Articles of Agreement; and (4) the establishment of a joint ministerial committee of the IMF and the World Bank "to carry forward the study of the broad question of the transfer of real resources to developing countries and to recommend measures." Steps (1) and (2) had meanwhile

[1]Cf. Chapter 13.

358

been put into effect by the IMF Executive Directors; steps (3) and (4) awaited action by the Board of Governors at the autumn meeting. In what could be read as an important gesture of support, the Ministers and Central Bank Governors of the "Group of Ten" agreed at a private meeting in Washington on September 29 to renew for a five-year period, beginning October 24, 1975, the so-called "General Arrangements to Borrow," which reinforced the lending capacity of the IMF by providing an assurance of substantial supplementary resources should they be needed.[2]

For many of the worried participants in the Boards of Governors meeting, the long-term issues of institutional reform had increasingly been overshadowed by the more immediate, double-barreled menace of rampant worldwide inflation and global recessionary dangers. "We in America view these problems very soberly and without any rose-tinted glasses," President Ford assured the delegates in his traditional address of welcome.[3] "But we believe at the same time the spirit of international cooperation which brought about the Bretton Woods Agreement a generation ago can resolve the problems today effectively and constructively."

Secretary of the Treasury Simon, in his formal presentation of American views next day, adopted a somber tone that would be echoed by many a speaker from both industrial and developed countries. In his appraisal of the global economic scene, the new Treasury head also gave evidence of a characteristic determination to accord the highest priority to anti-inflationary measures, even where some postponement of other objectives might be required.]

(48) *Meeting of Boards of Governors of the International Monetary Fund (IMF) and the International Bank for Reconstruction and Development (IBRD): Statement by Secretary of the Treasury William E. Simon, United States Governor of the Fund and Bank, October 1, 1974.*[4]

Our recent annual meetings have reflected encouraging changes in the international economic scene. Three years ago our attention was focused on the new economic policy introduced by the United States to eliminate a longstanding imbalance in the world economy. Two years ago we launched a major reform of the international trade and payments system. Last year we developed the broad outlines of monetary reform.[5]

---

[2]Communiqué, Sept. 29, in *IMF Survey*, 3: 334.

[3]*Presidential Documents*, 10: 1211-12.

[4]Department of the Treasury Press Release, Oct. 1; text and subtitles from *Bulletin*, 71: 575-80.

[5]Cf. *AFR, 1971*: 591-604; same, *1972*: 528-42; same, *1973*: 381-3 and 394-406.

This year circumstances are different. We face a world economic situation that is the most difficult since the years immediately after World War II.

Our predecessors in those early postwar years responded well to the great challenges of that period. I am confident we can also respond appropriately to the challenges of our day. But first we must identify the issues correctly.

Let me declare myself now on three of these key issues:

—First, I *do not* believe the world is in imminent danger of a drift into cumulative recession, though we must be alert and ready to act quickly should the situation change unexpectedly. I *do* believe the world must concentrate its attention and its efforts on the devastating inflation that confronts us.

—Second, I *do not* believe the international financial market is about to collapse. I *do* believe that situations can arise in which individual countries may face serious problems in borrowing to cover oil and other needs. For that reason we must all stand prepared to take cooperative action should the need arise.

—Third, I firmly believe that undue restrictions on the production of raw materials and commodities in order to bring about temporary increases in their prices threaten the prosperity of all nations and call into question our ability to maintain and strengthen an equitable and effective world trading order.

With respect to the first of these issues, it is clear that most countries are no longer dealing with the familiar trade-off of the past—balancing a little more or less inflation against [a] little more or less growth and employment. We are confronted with the threat of inflationary forces so strong and so persistent that they could jeopardize not only the prosperity but even the stability of our societies. A protracted continuation of inflation at present rates would place destructive strains on the framework of our present institutions—financial, social, and political.

Our current inflation developed from a combination of factors. In addition to pressures emanating from cartel pricing practices in oil, we have suffered from misfortune including bad weather affecting crops around the world; bad timing in the cyclical convergence of a worldwide boom; and bad policies reflected in years of excessive government spending and monetary expansion. As financial officials, we cannot be held responsible for the weather, but we must accept responsibility for government policies, and we must recommend policies that take fully into account the circumstances of the world in which we find ourselves.

In today's circumstances in most countries there is, in my view, no alternative to policies of balanced fiscal and monetary restraint.

We must steer a course of firm, patient, persistent restraint of both public and private demand, and we must maintain this course for an extended period of time, until inflation rates decrease. We must restore the confidence of our citizens in our economic future and our ability to maintain strong and stable currencies.

Some are concerned that a determined international attack on inflation by fiscal and monetary restraint might push the world into a deep recession, even depression. I recognize this concern, but I do not believe we should let it distort our judgment.

Of course we must watch for evidence of excessive slack. The day is long past when the fight against inflation can be waged in any country by tolerating recession. We must remain vigilant to the danger of cumulative recession. But if there is some risk in moving too slowly to relax restraints, there is also a risk—and I believe a much greater risk—in moving too rapidly toward expansive policies. If we fail to persevere in our anti-inflation policies now, with the result that inflation becomes more severe, then in time countermeasures will be required that would be so drastic as to risk sharp downturns and disruptions in economic activity.

There is a tendency to lay much of the blame on the international transmission of inflation. Certainly with present high levels of world trade and investment, developments in any economy, be they adverse or favorable, are quickly carried to other economies. But that does not absolve any nation from responsibility to adapt its financial policies so as to limit inflation and to shield its people from the ultimate damage which inflation inflicts on employment, productivity, and social justice in our societies.

Financial Mechanisms To Recycle Oil Funds

In addition to inflation, public concern has centered on methods of recycling oil funds and on whether we need new institutions to manage those flows.

So far, our existing complex of financial mechanisms, private and intergovernmental, has proved adequate to the task of recycling the large volumes of oil monies already moving in the system. Initially, the private financial markets played the major role, adapting in imaginative and constructive ways. More recently, government-to-government channels have increasingly been opened, and they will play a more important role as time goes by. New financing organizations have also been established by OPEC countries [Organization of Petroleum Exporting Countries]. Our international institutions, and specifically the IMF and World Bank, have redirected their efforts to provide additional ways of shifting funds from lenders to borrowers. The IMF responded rapidly in setting up its special oil facility.

In our experience over the period since the sharp increase in oil prices, three points stand out:

—First, the amount of new investments abroad being accumulated by the oil-exporting countries is very large; we estimate approximately $30 billion thus far in 1974.

—Second, the net capital flow into the United States from all foreign sources, as measured by the U.S. current account deficit, has been small, about $2 billion so far this year. During the same period our oil import bill has been about $12 billion larger than it was in the comparable period last year.

—Third, markets in the United States are channeling very large sums of money from foreign lenders to foreign borrowers. Our banks have increased their loans to foreigners by approximately $15 billion since the beginning of the year, while incurring liabilities to foreigners of a slightly larger amount. This is one kind of effective recycling. And while some have expressed concern that excessive oil funds would seek to flow to the United States and would require special recycling efforts to move them out, the picture thus far has been quite different.

No one can predict for sure what inflows of funds to the United States will be in the future. But it is our firm intention to maintain open capital markets, and foreign borrowers will have free access to any funds which come here. The U.S. Government offers no special subsidies or inducements to attract capital here; neither do we place obstacles to outflows.

Nonetheless some have expressed concern that the banking structure may not be able to cope with strains from the large financial flows expected in the period ahead. A major factor in these doubts has been the highly publicized difficulties of a small number of European banks and one American bank, which have raised fears of widespread financial collapse.

The difficulties of these banks developed in an atmosphere of worldwide inflation and of rapid increases in interest rates. In these circumstances, and in these relatively few instances, serious management defects emerged. These difficulties were in no way the result of irresponsible or disruptive investment shifts by oil- exporting countries. Nor were they the result of any failure in recycling or of any general financial crisis in any country.

The lesson to be learned is this: In a time of rapid change in interest rates and in the amounts and directions of money flows, financial institutions must monitor their practices carefully. Regulatory and supervisory authorities, too, must be particularly vigilant. We must watch carefully to guard against mismanagement and speculative excesses, for example, in the forward exchange markets. And we must make certain that procedures for assuring the liquidity of our financial systems are maintained in good working order. Central banks have taken major steps to assure this result.

Although existing financial arrangements have responded reasonably well to the strains of the present situation—and we believe they will continue to do so—we recognize that this situation could change. We should remain alert to the potential need for new departures. We do not believe in an attitude of laissez-faire, come what may. If there is a clear need for additional international lending mechanisms, the United States will support their establishment.

We believe that various alternatives for providing such supplementary mechanisms should be given careful study. Whatever decision is made will have profound consequences for the future course of the world economy. We must carefully assess what our options are and carefully consider the full consequences of alternative courses of action. The range of possible future problems is a wide one, and many problems can be envisaged that will never come to pass. What is urgently needed now is careful preparation and probing analysis.

We must recognize that no recycling mechanism will insure that every country can borrow unlimited amounts. Of course, countries continue to have the responsibility to follow monetary, fiscal, and other policies such that their requirements for foreign borrowing are limited.

But we know that facilities for loans on commercial or near-commercial terms are not likely to be sufficient for some developing countries whose economic situation requires that they continue to find funds on concessional terms. Traditional donors have continued to make their contributions of such funds, and oil-exporting countries have made some commitments to provide such assistance. Although the remaining financing problem for these countries is small in comparison with many other international flows, it is of immense importance for those countries affected. The new Development Committee which we are now establishing must give priority attention to the problems confronting these most seriously affected developing countries.

Trade in Primary Products

For the past two years, world trade in primary commodities has been subject to abnormal uncertainties and strains. Poor crops, unusually high industrial demand for raw materials, transport problems, and limited new investment in extractive industries have all contributed to tremendous changes in commodity prices. Unfortunately, new forms of trade restraint have also begun to appear.

In the past, efforts to build a world trading system were concentrated in opening national markets to imports. Clearly we need now also to address the other side of the equation, that of supply. The oil embargo, and the sudden and sharp increase in the price of oil, with their disruptive effects throughout the world economy, have of course brought these problems to the forefront of our attention.

The world faces a critical decision on access to many primary products. In the United States we have sought in those areas where we are exporters to show the way by maximum efforts to increase production. Market forces today result in the export of many items, from wheat to coal, which some believe we should keep at home. But we believe an open market in commodities will provide the best route to the investment and increased production needed by all nations.

We believe that cooperative, market-oriented solutions to materials problems will be most equitable and beneficial to all nations. We intend to work for such cooperative solutions.

Prospects for the Future

In the face of our current difficulties—inflation, recycling, commodity problems—I remain firmly confident that with commitment, cooperation, and coordination, reasonable price stability and financial stability can be restored.

The experience of the past year has demonstrated that although our economies have been disturbed by serious troubles, the international trade and payments system has stood the test.

Flexible exchange rates during this period have served us well. Despite enormous overall uncertainties and sudden change in the prospects for particular economies, exchange markets have escaped crises that beset them in past years. The exchange rate structure has no longer been an easy mark for the speculator, and governments have not been limited to the dismal choice of either financing speculative flows or trying to hold them down by controls.

Another encouraging fact is that the framework of international cooperation has remained strong. Faced with the prospect of severe balance of payments deterioration, deficit countries have, on the whole, avoided shortsighted efforts to strengthen their current account positions by introducing restrictions and curtailing trade.

In the longer run, we look forward to reinforcing this framework of cooperation through a broad-gauged multilateral negotiation to strengthen the international trading system. In the Tokyo round,[6] we hope to reach widespread agreement both on trade liberalization

---

[6]Cf. Chapter 10 at note 2.

measures—helping all countries to use resources more efficiently through greater opportunities for exchange of goods and services—and on trade management measures—helping to solidify practices and procedures to deal with serious trade problems in a spirit of equity and joint endeavor. It is gratifying that more and more governments have recognized the opportunities and the necessity for successful, creative negotiations on trade.

We in the U.S. Government recognize our own responsibility to move these negotiations along. Early last year we proposed to our Congress the Trade Reform Act[7] to permit full U.S. participation in the trade negotiations. It is clear that in the intervening months the need for such negotiations has become all the more urgent. We have threrefore been working closely with the Congress on this crucial legislation, and we shall continue to work to insure its enactment before the end of this year.[8]

In the whole field of international economic relations, I believe we are beginning to achieve a common understanding of the nature of the problems we face. There is greater public recognition that there lies ahead a long, hard worldwide struggle to bring inflation under control. Inflation is an international problem in our interdependent world, but the cure begins with the policies of national governments.

Success will require on the part of governments uncommon determination and persistence. There is today increasing awareness that unreasonable short-term exploitation of a strong bargaining position to raise prices and costs, whether domestically or internationally, inevitably intensifies our problems.

Finally, I am encouraged that our several years of intensive work to agree on improvements in the international monetary system have now begun to bear fruit. The discussions of the Committee of Twenty led to agreement on many important changes, some of which are to be introduced in an evolutionary manner and others of which we are beginning to implement at this meeting.

For the immediate future, the IMF's new Interim Committee will bring to the Fund structure a needed involvement of world financial leaders on a regular basis, providing for them an important new forum for consideration of the financing of massive oil bills and the better coordination of national policies. The Interim Committee shculd also increasingly exercise surveillance over nations' policies affecting international payments, thereby gaining the experience from which additional agreed guidelines for responsible behavior may be derived.

Moreover, discussions in the Interim Committee can speed the consideration of needed amendments to the Fund's Articles of Agreement. These amendments, stemming from the work of the Committee of Twenty, will help to modernize the IMF and better equip it to deal with today's problems. For example, the articles should be amended so as to remove inhibitions on IMF sales of gold in the private markets, so that the Fund, like other official financial institutions, can mobilize its resources when they are needed. In order to facilitate future quota increases, the package of amendments should also include a provision to modify the present requirement that 25 percent of a quota subscription be in gold. Such an amendment will be a prerequisite for the quota increase now under consideration. And the amendment will be necessary in any event for us to achieve the objectives shared by all the participants in the Committee of Twenty of removing gold from a central role in the system and of assuring that the SDR becomes the basis of valuation for all obligations to and from the IMF.

Preparation of an amendment to embody the results of the current quinquennial review of quotas offers us still another opportunity to reassess the Fund's role in helping to meet the payments problems of member nations in light of today's needs and under present conditions of relative flexibility in exchange rates.

The trade pledge agreed by the Committee of Twenty[9] provides an additional framework for cooperative action in today's troubled economic environment. It will mitigate the potential danger in the present situation of self-defeating competitive trade actions and bilateralism. The United States has notified its adherence to the pledge, and I urge other nations to join promptly in subscribing.

The new Development Committee, still another outgrowth of the work of the Committee of Twenty, will give us an independent forum that will improve our ability to examine comprehensively the broad spectrum of development issues. We look forward to positive results from this new committee's critical work on the problems of the countries most seriously affected by the increase in commodity prices and on ways to insure that the private capital markets make a maximum contribution to development.

The World Bank and Its Affiliates

International cooperation for development is also being strengthened in other ways, notably through the replenishment of IDA [International Development Association]. A U.S. contribution of $1.5 billion to the fourth IDA replenishment has been authorized by Congress, and we are working with our congressional leaders to

⁹Cf. Chapter 10 at note 1.

find a way to complete our ratification at the earliest possible date. [10] A significant new group of countries has become financially able to join those extending development assistance on a major scale. We would welcome an increase in their World Bank capital accompanied by a commensurate participation in IDA.

The United States is proud of its role in the development of the World Bank over the past quarter century. We are confident that the Bank will respond to the challenges of the future as it has so successfully responded in the past.

One of these challenges is to concentrate the Bank's resources to accelerate growth in those developing countries with the greatest need.

A second challenge is to continue the Bank's annual transfer of a portion of its income to IDA. The recent increase in interest rates charged by the Bank is not sufficient to enable the Bank to continue transfers to IDA in needed amounts. We urge that the Bank's Board promptly find a way to increase significantly the average return from new lending.

A third challenge is that the Bank find ways to strengthen its commitment to the principle that project financing makes sense only in a setting of appropriate national economic policies, of effective mobilization and use of domestic resources, and of effective utilization of the private capital and the modern technology that is available internationally on a commercial basis.

I should mention also that we are concerned about the Bank's capital position. We should encourage the Bank to seek ways to assist in the mobilization of funds by techniques which do not require the backing of the Bank's callable capital.

Within the Bank Group, we are accustomed to thinking mainly of the IFC [International Finance Corporation] in considering private capital financing. While now small, the IFC is, in my view, a key element in the total equation and should be even more important in the future. But the Bank itself needs to renew its own commitment to stimulation of the private sectors of developing countries.

Finally, let me emphasize that the capable and dedicated leadership and staff of the World Bank have the full confidence and support of the United States as they face the difficult challenges of the current situation.

Ladies and gentlemen, the most prosperous period in the history of mankind was made possible by an international framework which was a response to the vivid memories of the period of a beggar-thy-neighbor world. Faced with staggering problems, the

[10]Cf. Chapter 24 at note 8.

founders of Bretton Woods were inspired to seek cooperative solutions in the framework of a liberal international economic order. Out of that experience evolved an awareness that our economic and political destinies are inextricably linked.

Today, in the face of another set of problems, we must again shape policies which reflect the great stake each nation has in the growth and prosperity of others. Because I believe that interdependence is a reality—one that all must sooner or later come to recognize—I remain confident that we will work out our problems in a cooperative manner.

The course which the United States will follow is clear. Domestically, we will manage our economy firmly and responsibly, resigning ourselves neither to the inequities of continued inflation nor to the wastefulness of recession. We will strengthen our productive base; we will develop our own energy resources; we will expand our agricultural output. We will give the American people grounds for confidence in their future.

Internationally, let there be no doubt as to our course. We will work with those who would work with us. We make no pretense that we can, or should, try to solve these problems alone, but neither will we abdicate our responsibility to contribute to their solution. Together, we can solve our problems. Let me reaffirm our desire and total commitment to work with all nations to coordinate our policies to assure the lasting prosperity of all our peoples.

[The formal decisions of the IMF Board of Governors were set forth in a "Composite Resolution"[11] in which were announced, among other things, (1) the dissolution of the Committee of Twenty and the establishment of the new Interim Committee of the Board of Governors on the International Monetary System; (2) the establishment of a second group, the Joint Ministerial Committee of the Board of Governors of the Bank and the Fund on the Transfer of Real Resources to Developing Countries; and (3) the endorsement of various recommendations respecting the conduct to be observed by IMF members pending revision of the IMF Articles of Agreement. Expressing the hope that draft amendments to the Articles of Agreement would be presented by the IMF Executive Directors as early as February 1975, the Board of Governors also asked the Executive Directors to complete as soon as possible their review of the quotas subscribed to the IMF by its member states.

Once again, however, the timetable laid down by high authority was to prove overoptimistic. The proposed "Second Amendment to the Articles of Agreement'' was actually not ready for submission to the Board of Governors until April 2, 1976, and its acceptance by the IMF member governments would still be pending at the end of that year. Likewise still awaiting implementation at the end of 1976 was a proposed 32.5 percent increase in members' quotas, which was expected to take effect once the amendment had been ratified and entered into force. [12]]

"IMF Survey, 5: 97-9 and 113-16 (1976).

23. MEETING OF THE SEATO COUNCIL

(New York, October 3, 1974)

[Still another recurring item on the international calendar was the annual meeting of the SEATO Council, that monument to the regional security concepts that had guided American foreign policy in the 1950s. Originally set up by the Western "Big Three" (the United States, Britain, and France) in concert with Australia, New Zealand, and the three Asian states of Pakistan, the Philippines, and Thailand, the South-East Asia Treaty Organization—to give it its full name—had experienced a number of vicissitudes over the twenty-year period that had seen the rise and fall of the American involvement in Vietnam, the advent of the Gaullist Fifth Republic in France, the promulgation of the Nixon Doctrine, and the U.S. opening to China. France, for all practical purposes, had ceased to be a SEATO member during the 1960s, while Pakistan had formally withdrawn in consequence of the loss of its eastern province (now the People's Republic of Bangladesh) in 1971.

To many observers, the SEATO organization itself had appeared in recent years to be increasingly devoid of any valid reason for existence. In a far-reaching reorientation that followed the advent to power of new governments in Australia and New Zealand at the end of 1972, the SEATO Council had decided at its eighteenth meeting, held in New York on September 28, 1973, that it was indeed time to soft-pedal the military aspect of the alliance and to devote increased attention to internal stability and development in its two "regional" members, the Philippines and Thailand.[1] This trend had subsequently been accentuated by the overthrow of Thailand's military government within a few days of the New York meeting.

Despite the far-reaching changes that had been and were still occurring in Southeast Asia, however, the United States had remained a steadfast believer in the regional security arrangements established in this part of the world, including SEATO. The State Department's reasoning was vigorously expounded by Robert S. Ingersoll, a former Ambassador to Japan who had recently become Assistant Secretary of State for East Asian and Pacific Affairs, in an appearance before the Senate Foreign Relations Committee on March 6, 1974. "Our view," Mr. Ingersoll emphasized, "is that the [Manila] pact[2] and SEATO have not outlived their usefulness in the present era of transition. We believe that in a period that has seen the withdrawal of half a million U.S. troops from the Asian mainland and a significant reduction in the U.S. military presence elsewhere in East Asia, it would create doubt and uncertainty were the United States to urge the dismantling of the Manila Pact and SEATO at this time. . . . The pact has a residual role to play in preserving equilibrium as Southeast Asia moves to a still- undetermined future by restraining U.S.S.R.-P.R.C. [People's Republic of China] rivalry in the area and providing international support for Thailand. The Thais continue to attach importance to the organization and its headquarters in Bangkok. The annual price for maintaining the organization remains small."[3]

An impartial observer of developments in the SEATO area would have had to admit that there was still much room for improvement in regard to stability and development in the two "regional" member countries, even though the political trends they exhibited at the moment appeared to point in opposite directions. Thailand, still readjusting after its latest period of military rule, was experiencing obvious difficulty in trying to elaborate a democratic constitution; while the Philippines, whose people still seemed far from reconciled to the dictatorial rule imposed by President Ferdinand E. Marcos in 1972, was tormented in addition by persistent civil strife between Muslim and Christian elements in Mindanao and the Sulu Archipelago. Even in Australia, an already confused political situation was further complicated during 1974 by a constitutional conflict between the Whitlam administration and the opposition-controlled Senate, which occasioned a new election on May 18 in which Labor managed to cling to power but failed to improve its precarious parliamentary position. In New Zealand, Prime Minister Kirk died of a heart attack on August 31 and was succeeded by former Finance Minister Wallace (Bill) Rowling, who was little known abroad, as Prime Minister and Minister of Foreign Affairs.

Such was the background of the nineteenth meeting of the SEATO Council, held in New York on October 3 with Mr. Inger-

---

[2]Southeast Asia Collective Defense Treaty, signed at Manila Sept. 8, 1954 and entered into force Feb. 19, 1955 (TIAS 3170; 6 UST 81); text in *Documents, 1954*: 319-23.
[3]*Bulletin*, 70: 346-8. (A further statement appears in same: 470-74.)

soll (who had meanwhile succeeded Kenneth Rush as Deputy Secretary of State) heading the U.S. delegation. Absent, as in 1973, was the lengthy political communiqué that had traditionally marked this annual event. To judge from the press statement issued by Secretary-General Sunthorn Hongladarom of Thailand, the participating delegates would seem to have confined themselves for the most part to expressing satisfaction with the way the organization had been refocused since their meeting the year before. Few of them perhaps foresaw that within another twelve months, following the definitive Communist takeover of South Vietnam and Cambodia, they would be deciding that the SEATO organization itself (as distinct from the underlying collective defense treaty) should be "phased out" in response to "changing circumstances."[4]]

(49) The South-East Asia Treaty Organization (SEATO): Press statement issued at the conclusion of the Nineteenth Annual Meeting of the SEATO Council, New York, October 3, 1974.[5]

The Council of the South-East Asia Treaty Organization (SEATO), comprised of ministerial representatives from Australia, New Zealand, the Philippines, Thailand, the United Kingdom, and the United States, held its nineteenth annual meeting in New York on 3 October.

The Secretary-General announced that the Council held an informal and wide-ranging exchange of views on the situation in Southeast Asia and agreed to continue to uphold the objectives of the Manila Pact and its basic purpose of strengthening the fabric of peace in the region.

The Council affirmed that the recently reorganized structure and programmes of SEATO accorded with the goal of the treaty that member nations co-operate in promising economic progress, social well-being and peace in the treaty area, and were consonant with the currently prevailing conditions in Southeast Asia.

Satisfaction was expressed by the Council with the Secretary-General's reorganization of the staff at SEATO Headquarters in Bangkok in accordance with the directives of the Eighteenth Council Meeting held last year.[6] It agreed that the integration of the civilian and military staffs of the organization, which came into effect on 1 February 1974, facilitated SEATO's current emphasis upon supporting the internal security and development pro-

[4]Press statement, New York, Sept. 24, 1975, in Bulletin, 73: 575 (1975).
[5]Text from Bulletin, 71: 616.
[6]AFR, 1973: 376-7.

grammes of the two regional members, the Philippines and Thailand.

The Council also noted that SEATO assistance to projects in the social and economic fields had been increased, with greater emphasis upon the rural economic development and rural education sectors. Member countries will continue multilateral or bilateral social and economic aid to the regional members under SEATO auspices.

24. CONGRESS, TURKEY, AND DÉTENTE (I)

(October 1-27, 1974)

[The conduct of American foreign relations can be described in terms of a tripartite pattern in which two separate branches of the American Government—the executive and the legislative—are locked in a continuing struggle to control the nation's dealings with the outside world. Seen from a different angle, the diplomatic resources of the executive branch are permanently committed to a two-front relationship in which the search for agreement with foreign governments is matched by an unending quest for agreement with those possessed of the decisive authority on Capitol Hill. The influence of Congress on the design and execution of American foreign policy, though sharply reduced in the years of World War II and its aftermath, had reemerged dramatically in the course of the Vietnam struggle, attaining an historic peak in 1973 with the enactment of legislation that not only terminated American combat activity in Indochina but sharply limited the President's authority to order the armed forces into other combat situations.[1]

Flushed by the success of these essays in limiting the nation's international role, the Democratic-controlled 93rd Congress had begun its second session in January 1974 amid indications that it would not feel inhibited in cutting back or even repudiating other overseas programs with which it disagreed. A startling index to the congressional mood was the action of the House of Representatives on January 23 in rejecting, by a surprise vote of 248 to 155, legislation authorizing the appropriation of $1.5 billion as the U.S. share in the Fourth Replenishment of the resources of the International Development Association (IDA), plans for which had been agreed at the international level in 1973.[2]

---

[1] *AFR, 1973*: 335-47 and 481-94.
[2] For background cf. *AFR, 1973*: 497 and 510-14, and see below at note 8.

Though reversed later in the session, this action was widely viewed at the time as a rejection of the whole philosophy of economic development of which the United States had been a leading supporter for nearly three decades. The sense of a growing isolationist trend in Congress was reinforced a few days later, on February 5 and 6, when a minority of Senate opponents succeeded in blocking two attempts to force a vote on ratification of the 1948 Convention on the Prevention and Punishment of the Crime of Genocide.

Despite its overwhelming preoccupation with Watergate and impeachment matters, Congress did enact a number of legislative measures with foreign policy implications during the closing months of the Nixon era. Especially noteworthy from the point of view of future foreign policy operations was the Congressional Budget and Impoundment Control Act of 1974,[3] which provided among other things for (1) the setting by Congress of overall appropriation targets for each fiscal year, and (2) the commencement of the 1977 and later fiscal years on October 1 instead of the traditional July 1. Under this arrangement, the fiscal year 1976 would terminate as usual on June 30, 1976, after which a three-month "transition quarter" would precede the opening of the new fiscal year 1977, which would begin October 1, 1976 and terminate September 30, 1977.

Among other pieces of legislation enacted in time for President Nixon's signature, the Antihijacking Act of 1974[4] sought to implement the provisions of the Hague Antihijacking Convention of 1970[5] by establishing severe penalties for hijacking offenses and authorizing the suspension of civil air traffic between the United States and any nation that failed to cooperate in antihijacking efforts. In working over the military procurement legislation for fiscal year 1975, Congress reduced the administration's overall funding estimate of $23.1 billion to $22.2 billion; slashed military assistance for South Vietnam from $1.6 billion to $1.0 billion; reduced funds for weapons research, development, and procurement on such projects as the Airborne Warning and Control System (AWACS), the B-1 bomber, and an improved submarine-launched ballistic missile (SLBM) system; and slightly lowered the year-end authorized military personnel strength to 2,149,000.[6] A criticism of

---

[3]Public Law 93-344, July 12, 1974.
[4]Public Law 93-366, Aug. 5, 1974.
[5]Convention for the Suppression of Unlawful Seizure of Aircraft, done at The Hague Dec. 16, 1970 and entered into force Oct. 14, 1971 (TIAS 7192; 22 UST 1641); text in *Documents, 1970*: 350-55.
[6]Department of Defense Appropriation Authorization Act, 1975, Public Law 93-365, Aug. 5, 1974.

some features of this legislation was one of Mr. Nixon's last statements as President.[7]

Another important enactment, signed by President Ford a few days after taking office, reversed the January action of the House of Representatives by authorizing the $1.5 billion requested for the International Development Association and also—somewhat incongruously—permitting U.S. citizens to buy and sell gold after December 31, 1974.[8] But though it authorized the full appropriation for IDA in four annual installments of $375 million each, this measure did not actually provide any funds, and almost another two years were to elapse before the first appropriations were made available in support of the U.S. commitment. In the meantime, Congress also approved late in 1974 a plan for increased U.S. participation in the Asian Development Bank, including a $50 million contribution (in addition to $100 million previously authorized) to that institution's Special Funds for concessional lending to less wealthy countries.[9]

By October, a further series of bills was emerging from Congress and arriving on the desk of President Ford. The Department of Defense Appropriation Act, 1975, signed by the new President on October 8,[10] trimmed total obligational authority for the ongoing fiscal year from the Pentagon's amended estimate of $87.1 billion to $82.6 billion; although no major weapon system was eliminated or sharply reduced, military aid for South Vietnam was trimmed again, this time to $700 million. By the Energy Reorganization Act of 1974, signed October 11,[11] Congress abolished the old Atomic Energy Commission (AEC) and set up two new agencies, the Energy Research and Development Administration (ERDA) and the Nuclear Regulatory Commission (NRC). In passing the State Department/USIA [U.S. Information Agency] Authorization Act, Fiscal Year 1975, signed October 26,[12] Congress urged a "phased reduction" of economic as well as military assistance to South Vietnam; in addition, it repealed the long-forgotten Formosa Resolution of 1955, which had authorized the use of U.S. armed forces to protect Formosa (Taiwan) and the Pescadores Islands off the China coast.[13]

None of this legislation impinged upon what had emerged as the two most controversial foreign policy issues of the year and, as

[7]Signature statement, Aug. 5, in *Presidential Documents,* 10: 1007.
[8]Public Law 93-373, Aug. 14, 1974.
[9]Public Law 93-537, Dec. 22, 1974.
[10]Public Law 93-437, Oct. 8, 1974.
[11]Public Law 93-438, Oct. 11, 1974.
[12]Public Law 93-475, Oct. 26, 1974.
[13]Public Law 84-4, Jan. 29, 1955; text in *Documents, 1955*: 298-9.

such, were to provoke the first important collisions between the new Republican President and the opposition-controlled Congress. One of these issues was the familiar matter of most-favored-nation commercial treatment for the U.S.S.R., as affected by the latter's policy regarding Jewish emigration. A second major problem had arisen more recently with the Turkish invasion of Cyprus and the determination of some members of Congress, particularly younger members and those with Greek backgrounds, to exert pressure for a removal of the Turkish forces and a return to peaceful conditions in the island. Proponents of this effort seemed, by and large, to share the view that recent U.S. policy in this area had been doubly at fault, first in maintaining excessively warm relations with the Greek military junta and then in failing to oppose and condemn the Turkish Government's resort to force.

The method chosen by congressional critics of the Greek-Turkish policy consisted mainly in the attachment of amendments to the pending foreign aid legislation that would have the effect of suspending U.S. military aid to Turkey so long as Ankara persisted in its current line of policy. Since the most recent long-term foreign aid appropriation had expired on June 30, the program was currently being carried on under the authority of successive continuing resolutions until work on the aid appropriation for the new fiscal year could be completed. But the attempt to make an exception of the Turkish military aid program encountered an unexpectedly vigorous opponent in the person of President Ford. On two successive occasions in mid-October, the new chief executive went so far as to veto the resolutions passed by Congress because of "harmful" and "reckless" amendments which, he claimed, would deprive the United States of its negotiating leverage, "imperil our relationships with our Turkish ally and weaken us in the crucial Eastern Mediterranean," "directly" jeopardize the NATO alliance—and, at the same time, afford no help to Greece or to "the Greek Cypriot people who have suffered so tragically over the past several months."[14]

Attempts to override these presidential vetoes having failed in the House—the first by 16 votes, the second by 2 votes—Congress proceeded on October 17 to enact a third continuing resolution (House Joint Resolution 1167) which, though it again decreed a cutoff of military aid to Turkey, empowered the President to suspend its application until December 10 if Turkey meanwhile observed the cease-fire and refrained from increasing its forces in Cyprus or transferring U.S.-supplied arms to the island.[15] "With serious

---

[14]Messages to the House, Oct. 14 and 17, in *Presidential Documents,* 10: 1282-3 and 1316-17 (also in *Bulletin,* 71: 656-8).
[15]Sec. 6, Public Law 93-448, Oct. 17, 1974; text in *Bulletin,* 71: 658n.

reservations" over this persistence in a course he still considered "ill advised and dangerous," President Ford signed this resolution on October 18. " . . . This bill," he complained, "can only hinder progress toward a settlement of the Cyprus dispute. . . . Whatever we can still do to assist in resolving the Cyprus dispute will be done. But if we fail despite our best efforts, those in the Congress who overrode the congressional leadership must bear the full responsibility for that failure."[16]

Still larger matters had meanwhile come into focus with an approach to executive-legislative agreement on the terms of the pending Trade Reform Act, the basic measure required to authorize U.S. participation in the ongoing multilateral trade negotiations as well as the implementation of the U.S.-Soviet economic bargains negotiated in 1972. As already pointed out,[17] a version of this key enactment had passed the House of Representatives late in 1973, and the only serious obstacle to passage by the Senate was the prevalent disapproval of the Soviet Union's policy of restricting the emigration of Soviet Jews to Israel. In an attempt to bring about the lifting of such restrictions, the House of Representatives had included as Section 402 of the Trade Reform Act the so-called Jackson-Vanik amendment, named for Democratic Senator Henry M. Jackson of Washington and Democratic Representative Charles A. Vanik of Ohio, which undertook to bar the extension of most-favored-nation tariff treatment or U.S. Government credits to any Communist country that restricted freedom of emigration.

Foreseeing that the U.S.S.R. would react unfavorably to any attempt at outside interference with its emigration policies, Secretary Kissinger had repeatedly advised the Congress to discontinue its efforts and leave such matters to the administration's "quiet diplomacy." Since early 1974, moreover, he had been actively engaged in trying to eliminate, or at least reduce, the gap in viewpoints between the Soviet Government and its congressional critics. His efforts were not made easier by the indications that the U.S.S.R. was curbing its would-be Jewish emigrants with even greater rigor than the year before: according to one later tabulation, total Jewish emigration from the Soviet Union decreased from about 35,000 in 1973 to 20,000 in 1974, while emigration to Israel decreased from 30,604 to 16,849 in the same years. Despite these discouraging portents, however, Secretary Kissinger's efforts appeared by mid-October of 1974 to be on the point of bearing good fruit. Some of the details were later disclosed by Dr. Kissinger himself in an appearance before the Senate Finance Committee.]

---

[16]Signature statement, Oct. 18, in *Presidential Documents,* 10: 1320-21 and *Bulletin,* 71: 658-9. For further developments see Chapter 35 at notes 21-25.
[17]Cf. Chapter 15 at notes 10-11.

(50) *Negotiations on Soviet Emigration Policy: Statement by Secretary of State Kissinger before the Senate Committee on Finance, December 3, 1974.* [18]

(Excerpt)

* * *

As you are well aware, the administration since the beginning of detente had been making quiet representations on the issue of emigration. We were never indifferent to, nor did we condone, restrictions placed on emigration. We understood the concerns of those private American groups that expressed their views on this troubling subject. We believed, based on repeated Soviet statements and experience, that making this issue a subject of state-to-state relations might have an adverse effect on emigration from the U.S.S.R. as well as jeopardize the basic relationship which had made the steadily rising emigration possible in the first place. We were convinced that our most effective means for exerting beneficial influence was by working for a broad improvement in relations and dealing with emigration by informal means.

It is difficult, of course, to know the precise causes for changes in emigration rates. We know that during the period of improving relations and quiet representations, it rose from 400 in 1968 to about 33,500 in 1973. We believe that increase as well as recent favorable actions on longstanding hardship cases was due at least in part to what we had done privately and unobtrusively. We are also convinced that these methods led to the suspension of the emigration tax in 1973. We can only speculate whether the decline by about 40 percent in 1974 was the result of decisions of potential applicants or whether it was also affected by the administration's inability to live up to the terms of the trade agreement we had negotiated with the Soviet Union in 1972.

Nevertheless, we were aware that substantial opinion in the Congress favored a different approach. We recognized that if our government was to be equipped with the necessary means for conducting an effective foreign policy it would be necessary to deal with the emigration issue in the trade bill. As I stated in my previous testimony before this committee,[19] we regard mutually beneficial economic contact with the U.S.S.R. as an important element in our overall effort to develop incentives for responsible and restrained international conduct.

[18]Department of State Press Release 516; text from *Bulletin,* 71: 936-8. The opening and concluding portions of the statement appear in Chapter 35 as Document 76.
[19]Statement of Mar. 7, in *Bulletin,* 70: 321-5 (cf. Chapter 15 at note 11).

I therefore remained in close contact with leaders of the Congress in an effort to find a means of reconciling the different points of view. I remember that I was urged to do so by several members of this committee when I testified before you on March 7 of this year. Shortly afterwards, I began meeting regularly with Senators Jackson, Ribicoff, and Javits[20] to see whether a compromise was possible on the basis of assurances that did not reflect formal governmental commitments but nevertheless met widespread humanitarian concerns.

We had, as you know, been told repeatedly that the Soviet Union considered the issue of emigration a matter of its own domestic legislation and practices not subject to international negotiation. With this as a background, I must state flatly that if I were to assert here that a formal agreement on emigration from the U.S.S.R. exists between our governments, that statement would immediately be repudiated by the Soviet Government.

In early April [1974], the three Senators agreed to an approach in which I would attempt to obtain clarifications of Soviet domestic practices from Soviet leaders. These explanations could then be transmitted to them in the form of a letter behind which our government would stand.

My point of departure was statements by General Secretary Brezhnev during his visit to the United States in 1973 to both our executive and Members of Congress to the effect that Soviet domestic law and practice placed no obstacles in the way of emigration. In conversations with Foreign Minister Gromyko in Geneva in April, in Cyprus in May, and in Moscow in July, we sought to clarify Soviet emigration practices and Soviet intentions with respect to them. It was in these discussions that information was obtained which subsequently formed the basis of the correspondence with Senator Jackson,[21] with which you are familiar.

In particular, we were assured that Soviet law and practice placed no unreasonable impediments in the way of persons wishing to apply for emigration; that all who wished to emigrate would be permitted to do so except for those holding security clearances; that there would be no harassment or punishment of those who applied for emigration; that there would be no discriminatory criteria applied to applicants for emigration; and that the so-called emigration tax, which was suspended in 1973, would remain suspended.

It was consistently made clear to us that Soviet explanations applied to the definition of criteria and did not represent a commitment as to numbers. If any number was used in regard to Soviet

[20]Henry M. Jackson (Democrat, Washington), Abraham Ribicoff (Democrat, Connecticut), and Jacob K. Javits (Republican, New York).
[21]Document 51.

emigration this would be wholly our responsibility; that is, the Soviet Government could not be held accountable for or bound by any such figure. This point has been consistently made clear to Members of Congress with whom we have dealt.

Finally, the discussions with Soviet leaders indicated that we would have an opportunity to raise informally with Soviet authorities any indication we might have that emigration was in fact being interfered with or that applicants for emigration were being subjected to harassment or punitive action.

The points I have just cited have always been the basis for my contacts with Senators Jackson, Javits, and Ribicoff. I may add that these points have been reiterated to us by Soviet leaders on several occasions, including in President Ford's initial contacts with Soviet representatives and most recently at Vladivostok.[22]

All these clarifications were conveyed to the three Senators and eventually led to the drafting of the exchange of correspondence published by Senator Jackson on October 18. The process took much time, however, because of the administration's concern that there be no misleading inference—specifically that there be no claim to commitments either in form or substance which in fact had not been made.

Within a week of being sworn in, President Ford took a direct and personal interest in settling the issues yet outstanding. He met or had direct contact with the three Senators (as well as with you, Mr. Chairman)[23] on several occasions. He discussed the subject with leading Soviet officials. These contacts and conversations eventually resulted in the drafting of two letters, one from me to Senator Jackson and one from the Senator to me. The first of these letters[24] contains the sum total of the assurances which the administration felt in a position to make on the basis of discussions with Soviet representatives. The second letter[25] contained certain interpretations and elaborations by Senator Jackson which were never stated to us by Soviet officials. They will, however, as my letter to Senator Jackson indicated, be among the considerations which the President will apply in judging Soviet performance when he makes his determination on whether to continue the measures provided for in the trade bill; i.e., extension of governmental credit facilities and of most-favored-nation (MFN) treatment. We recognize of course that these same points may be applied by the Congress in reaching its own decisions under the procedures to be provided in the trade bill.

[22]Cf. Chapter 31.
[23]Senator Russell B. Long (Democrat, Louisiana).
[24]Document 51a.
[25]Document 51b.

* * *

[As Dr. Kissinger stated, the result of his endeavors was embodied in an exchange of letters with Senator Jackson, dated October 18 and made public by the Senator on that day.]

(51)   American Expectations Regarding Soviet Emigration Policy: Exchange of letters between Secretary of State Kissinger and Senator Henry M. Jackson, October 18, 1974.[26]

(a)   Secretary Kissinger to Senator Jackson.

OCTOBER 18, 1974

DEAR SENATOR JACKSON: I am writing to you, as the sponsor of the Jackson Amendment, in regard to the Trade Bill (H.R. 10710) which is currently before the Senate and in whose early passage the administration is deeply interested. As you know, Title IV of that bill, as it emerged from the House,[27] is not acceptable to the administration. At the same time, the administration respects the objectives with regard to emigration from the U.S.S.R. that are sought by means of the stipulations in Title IV, even if it cannot accept the means employed. It respects in particular your own leadership in this field.

To advance the purposes we share both with regard to passage of the trade bill and to emigration from the U.S.S.R., and on the basis of discussions that have been conducted with Soviet representatives, I should like on behalf of the administration to inform you that we have been assured that the following criteria and practices will henceforth govern emigration from the U.S.S.R.

First, punitive actions against individuals seeking to emigrate from the U.S.S.R. would be violations of Soviet laws and regulations and will therefore not be permitted by the government of the U.S.S.R. In particular, this applies to various kinds of intimidation or reprisal, such as, for example, the firing of a person from his job, his demotion to tasks beneath his professional qualifications, and his subjection to public or other kinds of recrimination.

Second, no unreasonable or unlawful impediments will be placed

[26]Text from U.S. Senate, 93rd Cong., 2nd sess., Committee on Finance, *Trade Reform Act of 1974: Report* . . . together with additional views on H.R. 10710 (S. Rept. 93-1298; Washington: GPO, 1974): 203-6.
[27]"Trade Relations with Countries Not Enjoying Nondiscriminatory Treatment." For text see U.S. Senate, 93rd Cong., 2nd sess., Committee on Finance, *Emigration Amendment to the Trade Reform Act of 1974: Hearing,* Dec. 3, 1974 (Washington: GPO, 1974): 14-33.

in the way of persons desiring to make application for emigration, such as interference with travel or communications necessary to complete an application, the withholding of necessary documentation and other obstacles including kinds frequently employed in the past.

Third, applications for emigration will be processed in order of receipt, including those previously filed, and on a non-discriminatory basis as regards the place of residence, race, religion, national origin and professional status of the applicant. Concerning professional status, we are informed that there are limitations on emigration under Soviet law in the case of individuals holding certain security clearances, but that such individuals who desire to emigrate will be informed of the date on which they may expect to become eligible for emigration.

Fourth, hardship cases will be processed sympathetically and expeditiously; persons imprisoned who, prior to imprisonment, expressed an interest in emigrating, will be given prompt consideration for emigration upon their release; and sympathetic consideration may be given to the early release of such persons.

Fifth, the collection of the so-called emigration tax on emigrants which was suspended last year will remain suspended.

Sixth, with respect to all the foregoing points, we will be in a position to bring to the attention of the Soviet leadership indications that we may have that these criteria and practices are not being applied. Our representations, which would include but not necessarily be limited to the precise matters enumerated in the foregoing points, will receive sympathetic consideration and response.

Finally, it will be our assumption that with the application of the criteria, practices, and procedures set forth in this letter, the rate of emigration from the U.S.S.R. would begin to rise promptly from the 1973 level and would continue to rise to correspond to the number of applicants.

I understand that you and your associates have, in addition, certain understandings incorporated in a letter dated today[28] respecting the foregoing criteria and practices which will henceforth govern emigration from the U.S.S.R. which you wish the President to accept as appropriate guidelines to determine whether the purposes sought through Title IV of the trade bill and further specified in our exchange of correspondence in regard to the emigration practices of non-market economy countries are being fulfilled. You have submitted this letter to me and I wish to advise you on behalf of the President that the understandings in your letter will be

[28]Document 51b.

among the considerations to be applied by the President in exercising the authority provided for in Sec. 402[29] of Title IV of the trade bill.

I believe that the contents of this letter represent a good basis, consistent with our shared purposes, for proceeding with an acceptable formulation of Title IV of the trade bill, including procedures for periodic review, so that normal trading relations may go forward for the mutual benefit of the U.S. and the U.S.S.R.

Best regards,

HENRY A. KISSINGER

(b) Senator Jackson to Secretary Kissinger.

OCTOBER 18, 1974

DEAR MR. SECRETARY: Thank you for your letter of Oct. 18[30] which I have now had an opportunity to review. Subject to the further understandings and interpretations outlined in this letter, I agree that we have achieved a suitable basis upon which to modify Title IV by incorporating within it a provision that would enable the President to waive subsections designated (a) and (b) in Sec. 402 of Title IV as passed by the House[31] in circumstances that would substantially promote the objectives of Title IV.

It is our understanding that the punitive actions, intimidation or reprisals that will not be permitted by the government of the U.S.S.R. include the use of punitive conscription against persons seeking to emigrate, or members of their families; and the bringing of criminal actions against persons in circumstances that suggest a relationship between their desire to emigrate and the criminal prosecution against them.

Second, we understand that among the unreasonable impediments that will no longer be placed in the way of persons seeking to emigrate is the requirement that adult applicants receive the permission of their parents or other relatives.

Third, we understand that the special regulations to be applied to persons who have had access to genuinely sensitive classified in-

---

[29]Statutory language authorizing the President to waive the restrictions in Title IV of the Trade Bill under certain conditions will be added as a new (and as yet undesignated) subsection. [Footnote in original.]

[30]Document 51a.

[31]Subsection (a) barred nondiscriminatory treatment or credits to Communist countries restricting freedom of emigration; subsection (b) required the President to report semiannually on the emigration policies of those countries to which such treatment or credits were extended.

formation will not constitute an unreasonable impediment to emigration. In this connection we would expect such persons to become eligible for emigration within three years of the date on which they last were exposed to sensitive and classified information.

Fourth, we understand that the actual number of emigrants would rise promptly from the 1973 level and would continue to rise to correspond to the number of applicants, and may therefore exceed 60,000 per annum. We would consider a benchmark—a minimum standard of initial compliance—to be the issuance of visas at the rate of 60,000 per annum; and we understand that the President proposes to use the same benchmark as the minimum standard of initial compliance. Until such time as the actual number of emigrants corresponds to the number of applicants the benchmark figure will not include categories of persons whose emigration has been the subject of discussion between Soviet officials and other European governments.

In agreeing to provide discretionary authority to waive the provisions of subsections designated (a) and (b) in Sec. 402 of Title IV as passed by the House, we share your anticipation of good faith in the implementation of the assurances contained in your letter of Oct. 18 and the understandings conveyed by this letter. In particular, with respect to paragraphs three and four of your letter we wish it to be understood that the enumeration of types of punitive action and unreasonable impediments is not and cannot be considered comprehensive or complete, and that nothing in this exchange of correspondence shall be construed as permitting types of punitive action or unreasonable impediments not enumerated therein.

Finally, in order adequately to verify compliance with the standard set forth in these letters, we understand that communication by telephone, telegraph and post will be permitted.

Sincerely yours,

HENRY M. JACKSON

[The Soviet Government was obviously not committed in any legal sense by the terms of this correspondence between Americans. Brezhnev, in fact, had seemed to repudiate them in advance in warning Secretary of the Treasury Simon a few days earlier against the imposition of "utterly irrelevant and unacceptable conditions" on trade. Nevertheless, it was the view of Senator Jackson and his associates that the concessions obtained by Dr. Kissinger eliminated the last serious obstacle to passage of the Trade Reform Act. Plans were accordingly made to submit a floor amendment permitting a waiver of the requirements of Section 402 for specified periods, assuming that the conditions specified in the letters were in fact met.[32]

What the world did not realize until much later, however, was the fact that Moscow formally advised the United States of its rejection of these conditions almost as soon as they had been made public. Visiting the Soviet capital late in October for a general review of U.S.-Soviet relations following the change in the leadership of the American Government, Secretary Kissinger was handed a communication from Foreign Minister Gromyko that took sharp exception to the Kissinger-Jackson exchange and specifically disclaimed any obligation to permit an increase in the emigration level.]

(52) Rejection of the Kissinger-Jackson Correspondence: Letter from Soviet Foreign Minister Andrei A. Gromyko to Secretary of State Kissinger, presented in Moscow October 26 and published by the Soviet Government December 18, 1974.[33]

I believe it to be necessary to draw your attention to the question of the publication in the United States of materials of which you are aware and which touch on the departure from the Soviet Union of a certain category of Soviet citizens.

I must say straightforwardly that the above-mentioned materials, including the correspondence between you and Senator Jackson,[34] create a distorted picture of our position and also of what we told the American side with regard to this matter.

When clarifying the actual state of affairs in response to your request, we emphasised that the question as such was entirely within the internal competence of our state. We gave a warning at the time that in this matter we had acted and would continue to act strictly in conformity with our present legislation on this subject.

However, silence is now being preserved precisely about this. At the same time, attempts are being made to ascribe to the elucidations that were furnished by us the character of assurances of some kind and almost commitments on our part regarding the procedure for the departure of Soviet citizens from the USSR, and certain figures are even being cited with regard to the supposed number of such citizens, and there is talk about an anticipated increase in that number as compared with previous years.

We resolutely reject such an interpretation. What we said—and

[32]For further developments see Chapter 35 at notes 2-20.
[33]Text from *Soviet News*, 1974: 486.
[34]Document 51.

you, Mr. Secretary of State, are well aware of this—concerned solely and exclusively the real situation regarding this particular question. And when we did mention figures—in order to inform you of the real situation—the point was quite the contrary, namely, concerning the present tendency towards a decrease in the number of persons wishing to leave the USSR and seek permanent residence in other countries.

We believe it to be important that in this whole matter having regard to its importance in principle, no ambiguities should remain as regards the position of the Soviet Union.

[In other respects, Dr. Kissinger's conversations in Moscow would seem to have passed off in the "businesslike and constructive spirit" referred to in the official communiqué. Their most sensational result was the announcement that President Ford and General Secretary Brezhnev intended to hold a face-to-face meeting in Vladivostok at the end of November.]

(53) Review of United States-Soviet Relations: Joint communiqué issued at the conclusion of Secretary Kissinger's visit to Moscow, October 27, 1974.[35]

As previously agreed, Henry A. Kissinger, Secretary of State of the United States of America and Assistant to the President for National Security Affairs, visited Moscow from October 23 to October 27.

He had discussions with Leonid I. Brezhnev, General Secretary of the Central Committee of the Communist Party of the Soviet Union, and Andrei A. Gromyko, Member of the Politburo of the Central Committee of the Communist Party of the Soviet Union, Minister of Foreign Affairs of the USSR.

Taking part in the discussions on the Soviet side were:

The Ambassador of the USSR in the United States, A.F. Dobrynin
Assistant to the General Secretary of the Central Committee of the Communist Party of the Soviet Union, A.M. Alexandrov
Member of the Collegium of the Ministry of Foreign Affairs of the USSR, G.M. Korniyenko.

On the American side:

The Ambassador of the United States to the USSR, Walter J. Stoessel, Jr.

[35]Department of State Press Release 442; text from *Bulletin,* 71: 703-4.

Officials of the Department of State: Helmut Sonnenfeldt, Arthur A. Hartman, Alfred A. Atherton, William G. Hyland, Winston Lord; and Jan M. Lodal and A. Denis Clift of the staff of the National Security Council.

In the course of the discussions, a thorough exchange of views took place on a wide range of issues concerning American-Soviet relations and on a number of current international problems. The two sides noted with satisfaction that the relations between the USA and the USSR continue to improve steadily, in accordance with the course previously established.

In this connection they again emphasized the fundamental importance of the decisions taken as a result of the U.S.-Soviet summit meetings, and expressed their mutual determination to continue to make energetic efforts to ensure uninterrupted progress in U.S.-Soviet relations.

Particular attention was given to the problem of the further limitation of strategic arms. In their consideration of this problem the two sides were guided by the fundamental understanding with regard to developing a new long-term agreement which is to follow the Interim Agreement of May 26, 1972. Useful exchanges took place on the details involved in such an agreement. Discussions on these matters will continue.

The two sides noted that as a whole ties in various spheres between the USA and the USSR have been developing successfully. They agreed that full implementation of the agreements already concluded will open favorable prospects for further expansion of mutually beneficial cooperation between the two countries.

The two sides continue to be concerned over the situation in the Middle East. They reaffirmed their determination to make efforts to find solutions to the key questions of a just and lasting settlement in the area. The two sides agreed that the early reconvening of the Geneva Conference should play a useful role in finding such a settlement.

Noting the progress achieved by the Conference on Security and Cooperation in Europe, the two sides will continue to work actively for its successful conclusion at an early date. They also believe that it is possible to achieve progress at the talks on mutual reduction of armed forces and armaments in Central Europe.

The exchange of views was marked by a businesslike and constructive spirit. Both sides consider it highly useful. In this connection they reaffirmed the positive value of the established practice of regular consultations between the two countries. Both sides emphasized the special importance of summit meetings for a constructive development of relations between the USA and the USSR. As has been announced, Gerald R. Ford, President of the United States, and L.I. Brezhnev, General Secretary of the Central Committee of the CPSU, will hold a working meeting in the vicinity of Vladivostok at the end of November 1974.[36]

[36]Cf. Chapter 31.

25. AFRICA AT THE UNITED NATIONS

(New York, September-December 1974)

[Revolution came to Africa in 1974, as unmistakably as it had come to America in 1776 and to Russia in 1917. The political changes that now began to gain momentum on the African continent were of a different order from the more or less voluntary decolonization processes that had resulted, over the past fifteen or twenty years, in the advent to national independence of most of the former British, French, and Belgian possessions in Africa. Radically as they had transformed the political map, those processes had failed to disrupt in any significant degree the pattern of white European dominance that still persisted in the southern third of the continent, where white minorities continued to hold sway in South Africa, Namibia (South West Africa), and Southern Rhodesia, and where Portugal still devoted its efforts to preserving a centuries-old hegemony in Mozambique and Angola as well as the more northerly territory of Portuguese Guinea (Guinea-Bissau).

By 1974, however, established patterns were beginning to crumble even where they had hitherto proved most resistant to change. A portent of things to come might be seen in the ancient empire of Ethiopia, where a military mutiny in February initiated a train of events that rapidly exposed the weakness and decrepitude of Africa's one traditional monarchy. The assumption of supreme power by Major General Aman Andom in July was followed in September by the deposition of the Emperor Haile Selassie in favor of his son, Crown Prince Asfa Wossen, and in November by the execution of General Andom and much of the country's former leadership in a new overturn that precipitated Brigadier General Teferi Benti into the presidency of the ruling Provisional Military Council. Among the side effects of this upheaval was a sense of increased instability throughout the so-called "Horn of Africa," where the U.S.S.R. and other Communist countries had already attracted notice by their assiduous cultivation of the Somali Government headed by President Muhammad Siad Barre.

More drastic repercussions followed the April 25 coup in Portugal and the advent to temporary supreme power of General Spínola, already known as a vigorous critic of Portugal's colonial wars in Africa. The right to self-determination and independence of the inhabitants of Portugal's overseas territories promptly took rank as one of the fundamental elements in the policy of the short-lived Spínola government, which formally recognized the independence of Guinea-Bissau on September 10 and shortly afterward installed in Mozambique a nationalist-dominated transitional government of distinctly leftist complexion to prepare that territory for independence in July 1975. Later in the year, after the leadership of the Portuguese revolution had passed from the conservative hands of General Spínola into those of the leftist Brigadier General Vasco dos Santos Gonçalves (who became Prime Minister in July and continued in that capacity under the middle-of-the-road presidency of General Francisco da Costa Gomes), it was announced that São Tomé and Principe would also become independent in 1975. A similar arrangement for Angola appeared to have been delayed only by lack of agreement among the three rival liberation movements that were contending for the mastery of that large and potentially wealthy territory.

The impending liquidation of Portugal's African empire gave natural satisfaction to the anticolonial elements that had for years been raising their voices in the United Nations in the interests of speeding just such a result. But while the change of policy in Lisbon served to defuse what had been one of the more contentious items on the U.N. agenda, it also heightened the already vociferous demand for parallel changes in other Southern African areas. Militarily, white-ruled Namibia and Rhodesia seemed likely to find themselves in a most uncomfortable position as the adjacent Portuguese territories, which thus far had helped to shield them from serious encroachment, came under the control of hostile nationalist elements. Politically, the anticolonial governments already gave evidence of their determination to exert all possible pressure upon the white regimes—not only in those two territories but also in South Africa itself, which now stood out more conspicuously than ever as the patron and ultimate defense of white majority rule throughout the area.

Partly because of tactical considerations, it was the government of the Republic of South Africa itself that bore the brunt of the anticolonial assault in the United Nations in 1974—an assault that admittedly sought to bring about the outright expulsion of South

Africa from the world organization or, failing that, to reduce its participation as nearly as possible to the vanishing point. Because the United States considered this effort to be ill-judged and indefensible from both a legal and a practical point of view, the U.S. delegation in New York was destined once again to find itself cast in an opposition role that could only widen the rift already dividing it from the majority of U.N. members.

A preliminary skirmish early in the General Assembly's regular session hinged upon the familiar question of the credentials of the South African delegation. Though regularly challenged at each new session by spokesmen for the anticolonial nations, the rights of the delegation accredited by the Pretoria government had thus far been as regularly upheld on the authority of the Assembly's elected President. This year, however, the Assembly's nine-member Credentials Committee was no longer willing to confine itself, as in the past, to verifying the authenticity of the South African credentials in conformity with the Assembly's rules of procedure. Over the dissenting votes of the United States and others, the committee instead decided on September 27 to make a recommendation that the Assembly *decline to accept* the South African credentials, on the ground that the South African delegation—and the government that had appointed it—were representative of only a small fraction of the South African population.

Again opposed by the United States on the floor of the General Assembly, this proposal was nevertheless accepted by that body on September 30 by a vote of 98 to 23, with 14 abstentions.[1] Immediately thereafter, the Assembly proceeded to adopt a second and even more far-reaching resolution, sponsored by 52 states, which called on the Security Council to review the whole relationship between the United Nations and South Africa in light of the latter's "constant violation" of the principles of the Charter and the Universal Declaration of Human Rights. This second resolution, reproduced as Document 54a below, was adopted by a vote of 125 to 1, with South Africa voting "No" and with 9 states abstaining—among them France, the United Kingdom, and the United States.]

(54) *Review of South Africa's Position in the United Nations: Action by the General Assembly, September 30, 1974.*

(a) *Relationship between the United Nations and South Africa: General Assembly Resolution 3207 (XXIX), September 30, 1974.*[2]

'Resolution 3206 (XXIX), Sept. 30, 1974.
[2]Text from General Assembly, *Official Records: 29th Year, Supplement No. 31* (A/9631): 2.

The General Assembly,

Recalling its resolutions 2636 A (XXV) of 13 November 1970, 2862 (XXVI) of 20 December 1971 and 2948 (XXVII) of 8 December 1972 and its decision of 5 October 1973, by which it decided to reject the credentials of South Africa,[3]

Recalling that South Africa did not heed any of the aforementioned decisions and has continued to practise its policy of *apartheid* and racial discrimination against the majority of the population in South Africa,

Reaffirming, once again, that the policy of *apartheid* and racial discrimination of the Government of South Africa is a flagrant violation of the principles of the Charter of the United Nations and the Universal Declaration of Human Rights,[4]

Noting the persistent refusal of South Africa to abandon its policy of *apartheid* and racial discrimination in compliance with relevant resolutions and decisions of the General Assembly,

Calls upon the Security Council to review the relationship between the United Nations and South Africa in the light of the constant violation by South Africa of the principles of the Charter and the Universal Declaration of Human Rights.

[The difference in the positions adopted by the United States on these two resolutions—opposition on the credentials, abstention on referral to the Security Council—was explained in a brief statement by Ambassador Scali.]

(b) Position of the United States: Statement to the Assembly by Ambassador Scali, September 30, 1974.[5]

My delegation finds the policy of apartheid an illegal and obnoxious violation of fundamental human rights. It is as contrary to that for which my government stands as it is to that for which the United Nations stands.

We understand why many seek this opportunity to assert their moral outrage at this heinous policy. We for our part, however, do not believe the question of credentials was an appropriate one for this purpose. The purpose of evaluating the authenticity of the

---

[3]During the period 1970-73, the Assembly had annually rejected the credentials of the South African delegation by amending the report of the Credentials Committee; but the Assembly's President had then ruled in each instance that while the vote amounted to a severe condemnation and warning, the South African delgation could nevertheless continue to participate.

[4]General Assembly Resolution 217 A (III), Dec. 10, 1948, in *Documents, 1948*: 430-35.

[5]USUN Press Release 121, Sept. 30; text from *Bulletin,* 71: 594.

credentials submitted to the Secretary General is clearly to insure that the individuals representing states in this body have been authorized to do so by the government of the country they are here to represent.

The policies of those governments are not a legitimate consideration in this context. There are other times and other contexts in which they may be. But what is unquestionably true is that here they are not. No one can reasonably argue with the facts that South Africa is a member of the United Nations, that the government which has sent representatives to this Assembly is indeed the government in power in that country, that an appropriate official of that country signed the necessary credential documents, and that they were submitted in a proper, timely way.

Since we do not regard this as the appropriate item for expressing the Assembly's views on the policy of apartheid or the representative nature of the Government of South Africa or other members who do not elect governments by universal, free elections, our vote against this report does not diminish our opposition to these unfortunate practices.

My delegation abstained on the resolution sending this matter to the Security Council.[6] The preambular paragraphs contained statements of undeniable and tragic accuracy. As I said, the policy of apartheid we believe is illegal, immoral, and fundamentally repugnant. It is the obligation of the United Nations to be concerned and to seek to take steps to eliminate such outrages.

We are not convinced, however, that the Security Council is the appropriate forum for discussing such issues. For this reason we did not believe it appropriate to cast a positive vote. Since others wished to discuss this question in the Security Council—and we favor wherever legally possible the right of all members to state their views in the forum of their choice—we did not believe it appropriate for us to cast a negative vote. Since we were neither in a position to vote in favor nor of a mind to oppose, we have abstained.

Of course our abstention is without prejudice to the position my government will take in the Security Council when this matter is discussed there.

[The Security Council's consideration of the relationship between the United Nations and South Africa, initiated in response to the foregoing request, occupied that body at no fewer than eleven meetings during the second half of October, eliciting statements by

36 guest delegations as well as spokesmen for five African liberation movements. A majority of the speakers insisted that South
Africa did in fact merit outright expulsion from the United Nations
under Article 6 of the Charter, which reads: "A Member of the
United Nations which has persistently violated the principles contained in the present Charter may be expelled from the organization
by the General Assembly upon the recommendation of the Security
Council."

In his response to these charges, South African Ambassador
Roelof F. Botha did not deny that discriminatory practices existed
in his country; but he did insist that progress was occurring both
there and in Namibia, and that such changes should be encouraged
"by communication, by discussion and understanding, not by
threats and a course of confrontation."[7]

Such reasoning failed, however, to deter the representatives of
Kenya, Mauritania, and Cameroon, later joined by Iraq, from introducing a resolution[8] recommending South Africa's immediate expulsion in compliance with Article 6. U.N. historians were
quick to note that this was the first explicit call for the expulsion of
a member state in all the 29-year experience of the United Nations.
The views of the United States on this proposal were outlined
by Ambassador Scali as the time for voting approached on
October 30.]

(55) Proposed Expulsion of South Africa from the United Nations: Action in the Security Council, October 30, 1974.

(a) Views of the United States: Statement to the Council by Ambassador Scali, October 30, 1974.[9]

Over the past two weeks, distinguished members of our organization and individual petitioners to this Council have expressed their
opposition to the South African Government's practice of apartheid. In virtually all cases, their arguments were predicated on the
abhorrence of the unequal treatment of peoples within a society
and a minority rule which discriminates against the majority on the
basis of color.

Let there be no doubt or confusion, despite the efforts of some,
about the attitude of the U.S. Government concerning apartheid.

---

[7]Summary in *UN Monthly Chronicle,* Nov. 1974: 19-23.
[8]Document 55b.
[9]USUN Press Release 154, Oct. 30; text from *Bulletin,* 71: 775-7.

In simplest terms, Mr. President,[10] the Government of the United States opposes it categorically and absolutely. It is evil. It is ugly. The United States shares the indignation of those who during this debate have decried South Africa's persistence in holding on to the iniquitous and callous policy of apartheid. The system of legislated racial discrimination and associated repressive legislation that prevails in South Africa is an indefensible affront to the spirit and principles of the charter and to human dignity around the world. It denies what the U.N. Charter proclaims—the dignity and worth of every person and the equal rights of all men and women. It is a matter of profound concern to the United States that the South African Government has ignored calls in the Security Council and in the General Assembly to put an end to its inhumane, outmoded, and shortsighted policies.

Despite all warnings and admonitions, the South African Government continues to practice apartheid. It continues to uproot non-whites and consign them to often-barren "homelands" in order to preserve the supremacy of the fifth of the population who are white. It maintains draconian restrictions on the movement of non-whites. It persists in providing to non-whites inferior education, keeping them in a disadvantageous position. Segregation and inequality in all areas of life are pervasive. Non-whites are not represented in the government that dominates and intrudes into almost every aspect of their lives.

South Africa's denial of basic human rights is compounded in Namibia by its illegal occupation of that territory. The United States finds it reprehensible that South Africa has failed to honor its obligations under international law to withdraw from Namibia in accordance with General Assembly and Security Council resolutions and the 1971 opinion of the International Court of Justice.[11]

South Africa's continuing illegal occupation of Namibia is made all the more outrageous by the manner in which it administers the territory. The repression of peaceful political activity, the flogging of dissidents by the South African administration's surrogates, and the division of the territory into so-called homelands are indefensible and inconsistent with the responsibilities South Africa had assumed as administrator of a mandated territory.

But, Mr. President, I am obliged to point out that even in this grievous case, the United States continues strongly to adhere to the view that resorts to force and other forms of violence are not acceptable means to induce change. This is our view with regard to other serious problems throughout the world, and it is our view

[10]Michel Njine (Cameroon).
[11]*AFR, 1971*: 403-5.

with respect to South Africa. Armed confrontation is no substitute for communication.

The description of South Africa's transgressions I have just presented is not new. Observers have agreed about the essential facts of apartheid for many years.

Some of the words I have just used are borrowed. Members of the Council may be familiar with the statement made in the Special Political Committee of the General Assembly on October 17 on the issue of apartheid by my distinguished co-delegate Mr. Joseph Segel.[12] This is a personal statement, as well as an official one, delivered from the heart by a man now serving as a public member—I repeat, a public member—of the U.S. delegation. It is also a statement to which I subscribe, to which the U.S. Government subscribes.

We are heartened indeed by some encouraging words in this chamber voiced by the Permanent Representative of South Africa. On October 24, he himself implied that South Africa is responding not in a vacuum but in reaction to world events, not the least of which has been the condemnation of South Africa's apartheid, Namibian, and Rhodesian policies within this international organization. I have noted with special interest that a distinguished African leader, whose bitter experiences in the past make him an impressive witness today, has also found hopeful aspects in the new South African voices.

We believe that a just solution of South Africa's racial dilemma indeed lies within South Africa itself. Taking practical steps toward improving the condition of non-whites and seeking change through communication seem to us more likely to have impact than some other measures suggested.

American firms in South Africa, for example, have had notable success in improving the pay and working conditions of their non-white workers. They do this as a matter of enlightened policy—with the support of the U.S. Government. The United States believes that through its current cultural exchange program prominent South Africans of all races have gained a new, more accurate perspective of their country's problems and a determination to seek a solution to them.

At the same time, the United States continues to bar the sale of military equipment to South Africa. In this regard, I would like to state flatly that the United States has not collaborated with South Africa on military or naval matters for over a decade and has no intention of beginning such cooperation in the future.

The situation in southern Africa is significantly different now

[12]*Bulletin*, 71: 672-3.

from that of six months ago. South Africa has no alternative but to reassess its position in light of recent events. The United States urges that in doing so, the South African Government look at the realities of the future.

We call on South Africa to make good the assurances it gave Secretary General Waldheim in April last year[13] to allow the people of Namibia to determine the future of the territory by exercising their right of self-determination, and to withdraw from Namibia. We urge that South Africa simultaneously begin to bring an end to its apartheid policies and to establish the basis for a just society and government where all are equal. We believe that after a quarter of a century of warnings it is time for the South African Government to adopt the measures which will lead to a society of equal opportunity, equal rewards, and equal justice for all. We call on South Africa to fulfill its obligations under article 25 of the charter[14] and to comply with Security Council resolutions on Southern Rhodesia.

Mr. President, some speakers have argued that the best way to bring the Government of South Africa to accomplish these objectives—to bring the South African Government to heel—is for this Council to recommend to the General Assembly that South Africa be expelled from membership in the United Nations organization.

My government believes that this kind of all-or-nothing approach would be a major strategic mistake, especially at a time when we have been hearing what may be new voices of conciliation out of South Africa. These new voices should be tested. We must not be discouraged, as we may have been last December when we instructed the Secretary General to abandon his contacts with the South Africans on Namibia.[15]

Mr. President, many of our colleagues during the past weeks have cited time and time again the poetic reference to "winds of change." With the fresh winds of change blowing from an enlightened Portuguese policy toward Angola and Mozambique, effecting important and progressive changes in southern Africa, the United States believes that it is incumbent upon this organization not to deflect those very winds as they rush toward South Africa. By doing so, we confess that this organization is powerless to influence change there. My government does not accept the view that the United Nations is powerless; rather, we strongly believe that it is through both increased bilateral contacts and the strong will of a

[13]Cf. *AFR, 1973*: 152.

[14]Article 25 of the U.N. Charter reads: "The Members of the United Nations agree to accept and carry out the decisions of the Security Council in accordance with the present Charter."

[15]Security Council Resolution 342 (1973), Dec. 11, 1973; cf. *AFR, 1973*: 581.

determined United Nations that peaceful change will occur in South Africa.

Mr. President, the United Nations was not founded to be simply a league of the just. Rather, in our view, it is a unique international forum for the exchanging of ideas, where those practicing obnoxious doctrines and policies may be made to feel the full weight of world opinion. There is therefore a clear, positive, and indispensable role for the United Nations in bringing change to South Africa.

My delegation believes that South Africa should continue to be exposed, over and over again, to the blunt expressions of the abhorrence of mankind for apartheid. South Africans could hear of this abhorrence only from afar were we to cast them from our ranks, beyond the range of our voices.

Our analysis is that expulsion would say to the most hardened racist elements in South Africa that their indifference to our words and resolutions had been justified. We think it would say to the South Africans that we have not heard, or do not wish to encourage, the new voices—the voices that augur hope of change.

We believe that the United Nations must continue its pressure upon South Africa, moving step by step until right has triumphed. It is self-defeating to fire a single last dramatic salvo with only silence to follow. History holds no example of a pariah state that reformed itself in exile. The pariah is by definition an outlaw, free of restraint. There is no record of good citizenship in the land of Nod, east of Eden, where Cain, the first pariah, was banished.

My delegation has another grave concern about the wisdom of expelling South Africa. Even if this would help thwart the ugly crime of apartheid, expulsion would set a shattering precedent which could gravely damage the U.N. structure. It would bring into question one cf the most fundamental concepts on which our charter is based—the concept of a forum in which ideas and ideals are voiced and revoiced along with conflicting views until elements of injustice and oppression are forced to give way to reason.

This, in sum, is the appeal of my delegation. Let us continue to hold the evils of apartheid under the light of world opinion until all our fellow human beings have seen it for what it is. Let us continue to press South Africa in this U.N. forum and others to move rapidly toward an era of equality and justice.

[Many of Ambassador Scali's arguments were echoed later in the debate by Ambassadors Louis de Guiringaud of France and Ivor Richard of the United Kingdom. When the draft resolution recommending South Africa's expulsion (Document 55b) was put to a vote later on October 30, ten of the Council's fifteen members voted for adoption, but all three Western powers voted against it, thus casting what was in effect the first triple veto in Security Council history. The complete vote was 10 in favor with 3 opposed (France, United Kingdom, and United States) and 2 abstentions (Austria and Costa Rica).]

(b) Draft Resolution Vetoed by France, the United Kingdom, and the United States, October 30, 1974.[16]

Iraq, Kenya, Mauritania and United Republic of Cameroon: draft resolution

[Original: English]
[24 October 1974]

The Security Council,

Having considered General Assembly resolution 3207 (XXIX) of 30 September 1974,[17] in which the Assembly called upon the Security Council "to review the relationship between the United Nations and South Africa in the light of the constant violation by South Africa of the principles of the Charter and the Universal Declaration of Human Rights",

Having heard the statements of the persons invited to address the Council on this issue,[18]

Taking note of the report of the Special Committee on Apartheid entitled "Violations of the Charter of the United Nations and resolutions of the General Assembly and the Security Council by the South African régime" [S/11537],

Mindful of the provisions of the Charter concerning the rights and obligations of Member States, particularly those of Articles 1, 2, 6, 55 and 56,

Recalling its resolutions 134 (1960), 181 (1963), 182 (1963), 190 (1964), 282 (1970),[19] and 311 (1972), on the question of the policies of apartheid of the Government of the Republic of South Africa,

---

[16]U.N. document S/11543, Oct. 24; text from Security Council, Official Records: 29th Year, Supplement for Oct., Nov. and Dec. 1974: 34-5.
[17]Document 54a.
[18]In addition to 36 U.N. member countries invited to participate in the debate without the right to vote, invitations to address the Council in conformity with its provisional rules of procedure were extended to representatives of the Pan Africanist Congress of Azania (South Africa), African National Congress, Zimbabwe African National Union, Zimbabwe African People's Union, and South West Africa People's Organization.
[19]Documents, 1960: 350-51; same, 1963: 355-9; same, 1964: 370-72; same, 1970: 251-3.

Reaffirming that the policies of *apartheid* are contrary to the principles and purposes of the Charter and inconsistent with the provisions of the Universal Declaration of Human Rights, as well as with South Africa's obligations under the Charter,

Recalling that the General Assembly and the Security Council have more than once condemned the South African Government for its persistent refusal to abandon its policies of *apartheid* and to abide by its obligations under the Charter, as called for by the Council and the Assembly,

Noting with concern South Africa's refusal to withdraw its police and military forces, as well as its civilian personnel, from the Mandated Territory of Namibia and to co-operate with the United Nations in enabling the people of Namibia as a whole to attain self-determination and independence,

Noting further that, in violation of the pertinent resolutions of the Security Council, particularly resolution 253 (1968) of 29 May 1968, South Africa has not only given support to the illegal régime in Southern Rhodesia, but has also sent into that Territory military and police personnel for the purpose of strengthening that régime in its attempt to impede the exercise by the people of the Territory of their inalienable rights,

Considering that effective measures should be taken to resolve the present situation arising out of the policies of *apartheid* of the Government of South Africa,

Recommends to the General Assembly the immediate expulsion of South Africa from the United Nations, in compliance with Article 6 of the Charter.

[Speaking after the vote as the representative of his country, the President of the Security Council, Ambassador Michel Njine of Cameroon, declared that the defeat of the expulsion resolution had clarified the position of South Africa in the sense that it now continued as a U.N. member only thanks to the veto power. The outcome of the debate, so the Cameroon representative declared, was not only a moral victory for the foes of apartheid but the prelude to a continuing fight and a great source of comfort to the suffering people of "Azania," the African nationalist name for South Africa.[20]

The foes of South African participation did not in fact abandon their efforts at this point, but mounted still another attack in the General Assembly when that body came to consider the implications of the Security Council vote. Although South Africa had not actually been taking part in the work of the Assembly since the Sep-

---

[20]*UN Monthly Chronicle*, Nov. 1974: 40.

tember 30 vote on the credentials question, it was hoped that its exclusion might now be formally pinned down by means of a ruling from the Assembly's President, Foreign Minister Abdelaziz Bouteflika of Algeria. Ambassador Scali, speaking in opposition to this trend at a plenary session of the Assembly on November 12, again insisted on the United States' abhorrence of South African racial policies, but contended nevertheless that the legal position with regard to South African participation remained unchanged by recent developments.]

(56) Suspension of South Africa from Participation in the Work of the 29th Assembly Session: Action in the General Assembly, November 12, 1974.

    (a) Statement by Ambassador Scali to the Assembly, November 12, 1974.[21]

My delegation cannot accept the argument that the vote in the Security Council on the South African issue last October 30 in any way changes the clear wording of articles 5 and 6 of the charter.[22] Nor, in our view, does it in any way permit this or any other Assembly to deprive a member of the rights and privileges of membership.

I am deeply concerned with the criticism of my delegation's vote in the Security Council on the South African matter. I categorically reject any implication that our vote was anti-African, anti-United Nations, or was motivated by any support whatsoever for apartheid.

As I had hoped was clear from the many times my delegation has expressed this view, the U.S. Government thoroughly opposes the policy of apartheid. We support the self-determination as soon as possible of Namibia. We call on South Africa to fulfill its obligations under article 25 of the charter[23] and to comply with Security Council resolutions on Southern Rhodesia.

---

[21]USUN Press Release 166, November 12; text from *Bulletin,* 71: 811-12.

[22]Article 5 of the U.N. Charter reads: "A Member of the United Nations against which preventive or enforcement action has been taken by the Security Council may be suspended from the exercise of the rights and privileges of membership by the General Assembly upon the recommendation of the Security Council. The exercise of these rights and privileges may be restored by the Security Council." Article 6 of the Charter is quoted in the text preceding Document 55a.

[23]Cf. note 14.

Has it been forgotten that the United States imposed its own arms embargo on South Africa before the United Nations did?

Our vote in the Security Council, Mr. President, reflected our strong belief that the continued presence in the United Nations of South Africa would best allow members to continue pressure for necessary reforms in that nation as well as changes in Namibia and Rhodesia.

As I said in my explanation of vote before the Security Council last October 30,[24] Mr. President:

[Quoted here are the concluding portions of Document 54a, from "My delegation believes" to "damage the U.N. structure."]

Mr. President, my delegation further believes that the expulsion of South Africa would reverse the evolution of the United Nations toward ever wider membership.

These were our reasons and our only reasons. We hold them no less deeply than those who hold a different view. We respect that different view, and we expect no less in return. We also expect that the clear words of the charter will be honored. This Assembly may be master of its procedures, but not of our charter, which remains the paramount document governing our existence as an organization based on law.

[But Foreign Minister Bouteflika seemed unimpressed by this reasoning. Asked by the Tanzanian representative for his guidance on the point at issue, the Algerian statesman delivered himself of a ruling that was generally interpreted as banning further South African participation in the work of the 29th Session. "On the basis of the consistency with which the General Assembly has regularly refused to accept the credentials of the delegation of South Africa," Mr. Bouteflika stated, "one may legitimately infer that the General Assembly would in the same way reject the credentials of any other delegation authorized by the Government of the Republic of South Africa to represent it, which is tantamount to saying in explicit terms that the General Assembly refuses to allow the delegation of South Africa to participate in its work."[25]]

Ambassador Scali was quick to challenge the Bouteflika ruling, contending that it was incompatible with the relevant provisions of the Charter as interpreted in connection with an earlier discussion of the issue in 1970.]

[24]Document 55a.
[25]*U.S. Participation, 1974*: 117.

(b) Challenge to the ruling of the Assembly's President: Second statement by Ambassador Scali to the Assembly, November 12, 1974.[26]

Mr. President: My delegation regrets that we have no choice but to challenge your ruling. We did not come to this decision lightly, and we do so only because of the overriding importance of the issue, the fundamental rights of a member state under the Charter of the United Nations.

There is also an obvious conflict, Mr. President, between your ruling and the legal opinion given to this Assembly on November 11, 1970, at the 25th session.[27] Further, there is a conflict between your ruling and the practice that the General Assembly has consistently followed in the four years since then, at the 25th, the 26th, the 27th, and the 28th sessions and at the 6th special session held in spring this year. In addition, as we all know, during this 29th session, South Africa was allowed to vote without objection after the Assembly's decision on its credentials was made.

The legal opinion given at the 25th session remains as valid today, in our view, as it was then. It affirms that under the charter the Assembly may not deprive a member of any of the rights of membership. The Assembly may be master of its rules of procedure, but no majority, no matter how large, can ignore or change the clear provisions of the charter in this way.

We consider it to be a violation of the rules of procedure and of articles 5 and 6 of the charter for the Assembly to attempt to deny a member state of the United Nations its right to participate in the Assembly, through this type of unprecedented action. Article 5 of the charter expressly lays down rules by which a member may be suspended. Article 6 of the charter specifically provides the process by which a member may be expelled. The Assembly is not empowered to deprive a member of the rights and privileges of membership other than in accordance with articles 5, 6, and 19 of the charter. In our view, none of these circumstances applies in this case.

At the 25th session of this Assembly, the then Legal Counsel of the United Nations ruled:

Article 5 of the Charter lays down the following requirements for the suspension of a Member State from the rights and privileges of membership:

[26]USUN Press Release 167, November 12; text from *Bulletin,* 71: 812-13.
[27]The relevant portion of this opinion, submitted by the U.N. Legal Counsel, Constantin A. Stavropoulos, at the request of the then President of the Assembly (Edvard Hambro of Norway), is quoted in the body of the document.

(a) Preventive or enforcement action has to be taken by the Security Council against the Member State concerned;

(b) The Security Council has to recommend to the General Assembly that the Member State concerned be suspended from the exercise of the rights and privileges of membership;

(c) The General Assembly has to act affirmatively on the foregoing recommendation by a two-thirds vote, in accordance with Article 18, paragraph 2, of the Charter, which lists "the suspension of the rights and privileges of membership" as an "important question".

The participation in meetings of the General Assembly is quite clearly one of the important rights and privileges of membership. Suspension of this right through the rejection of credentials would not satisfy the foregoing requirements and would therefore be contrary to the Charter.

It is our view that nothing has transpired in the General Assembly or the Security Council to affect the validity of that ruling. Since the Security Council remains seized of the range of South African questions, there is all the more reason why the Assembly cannot properly seek to take action to deprive South Africa of its rights of membership. The effect of the resolution of September 30, 1974, on credentials[28] has the same effect as resolutions of previous years.

Mr. President, your action is taken in the context of the Assembly's action on the credentials item. The policy of a government is not a legitimate consideration in this context. Those policies may rightly be examined at other times and in other contexts but not here. In the present case no one can reasonably argue with the technical propriety of the credentials of the South African delegation. South Africa is not the only member state whose government is not chosen by free elections where all adults are entitled to vote.

In our view, we must not seek to change the membership regulations to convert this into an organization of like-minded governments. Were we to apply that criterion, we should cease to be a universal institution and would become very different indeed.

Those facts and a respect for the charter have led past Presidents of the General Assembly to rule that decisions involving the nonacceptance or rejection of South African credentials constitute an expression of international outrage at the heinous policy of apartheid. But each of those Presidents has also ruled that such decisions do not serve to deprive South Africa of its fundamental rights of membership—rights which include the right to take its seat

---

[28]Cf. note 1.

in the General Assembly, to speak, to raise questions and make proposals, and to vote.

Mr. President, we consider that your ruling fails to take into account that law of the charter, the existing legal opinion, and the consistent series of applicable precedents. For those reasons and pursuant to rule 71 [of the Assembly's rules of procedure], we must respectfully challenge your ruling. We request that, in accordance with rule 71, you put this challenge immediately to a vote. I request that a recorded vote be taken.

[In accordance with Ambassador Scali's request, the issue was then put to a vote of the entire Assembly, which upheld its President's ruling by a majority of 91 to 22 with 19 abstentions. With the Communist and most third world countries voting "Yes," the allies and close associates of the United States were divided between the "No" and "Abstain" columns. Even Portugal, once the most steadfast opponent of anti-South African moves in the United Nations, abstained in this instance. Israel, whose own position of semi-ostracism within the world organization was coming to resemble that of South Africa in some respects, was among those voting "No."

Though subsequent Assembly actions on the substantive problems of Southern Africa provoked no further major clashes involving the United States, there were repeated reminders of the gulf now separating the latter from the Communist and third world majority. Out of five Assembly resolutions relating to South Africa's apartheid policies, for instance, the United States supported one, abstained on two, and voted against two, one of which urged a mandatory arms embargo against South Africa while the other called for that country's isolation from various kinds of international contact.[29] The U.S. delegation also abstained on the Assembly's principal resolution regarding Namibia, in part because of what it considered a somewhat arbitrary designation of the South West African People's Organization (SWAPO) as the "authentic representative of the Namibian people."[30] The United States did, however, join on December 17 in the unanimous adoption by the Security Council of a resolution renewing the demand for South African withdrawal from Namibia and setting a further meeting on or before May 30, 1975, to review South African compliance.[31]

As on earlier occasions in the 1970s, the United States itself incurred the Assembly's censure as the result of its persistence, in line

---

[29]For details see U.S. Participation, 1974: 42-6.
[30]Resolution 3295 (XXIX), Dec. 13, 1974, adopted by a vote of 112-0-15 (U.S.).
[31]Resolution 366 (1974), Dec. 17, 1974.

with the so-called Byrd amendment of 1971, in importing limited amounts of chrome ore and other strategic materials from Rhodesia in violation of the mandatory economic sanctions imposed by the Security Council. Although a bill to repeal the Byrd amendment had passed the Senate late in 1973, a parallel effort in the House in 1974 proved unsuccessful in spite of the announced support of President Ford. Approved by the relevant House committees and twice scheduled for a floor vote, the bill was withdrawn shortly before it was due to come up for final consideration in December. The General Assembly, meanwhile, in a resolution adopted on December 13 by a vote of 112 to 0 with 18 abstentions, again condemned "the continued importation of chrome and nickel from Southern Rhodesia (Zimbabwe) into the United States of America" and called upon the latter "to repeal speedily any legislation permitting such importation."[32] Abstaining rather than voting against this resolution, the U.S. delegation nevertheless registered an objection to the singling out of the United States for condemnation while sanctions violations by other countries were largely ignored.]

[32]Resolution 3298 (XXIX), Dec. 13. For background cf. *AFR, 1971*: 412-29; same, *1972*: 394-405; same, *1973*: 579-80.

26. THE U.N. VIEWS THE MIDEAST CONFLICT

(New York, October-November 1974)

[The General Assembly's repeated rejection of U.S. views on Africa had its counterpart in an even more decisive repudiation of some of the central features of U.S. policy regarding the Arab-Israeli conflict. Thanks largely to U.S. peacemaking efforts since the 1973 war, the world was spared the horrors of another full-scale military encounter between Israelis and Arabs in 1974. But despite the disengagement arrangements in effect on both the Egyptian and the Syrian fronts, tension in the area had failed to abate as recurrent incidents in northern Israel and southern Lebanon, in the occupied West Bank territories, and on the international airways continued to remind the world how fragile was the existing armistice structure. Possibly even more significant was the increasingly conspicuous isolation of Israel—and, to a considerable degree, the United States—as international favor increasingly forsook the 26-year-old Jewish state and the world began to accept its most intransigent foe, the quasi-governmental Palestine Liberation Organization (PLO), as the legitimate representative of the Palestine Arab people who had, unquestionably, become the principal losers by Israel's emergence.

The tendency to identify Israel and the United States as parts of a political and military continuum was only partially justified by the facts. Washington, in reality, continued to differ sharply with the Israelis concerning the territorial and other features of an eventual peace settlement. For many weeks it had been causing great discomfort in Israeli quarters by its pressure to begin a disengagement process on the Jordanian front, notwithstanding the reluctance of many Israelis to relinquish territory in that historic region. At the same time, however, the United States had also thought it proper to meet at least a substantial part of Israel's requests for modern arms, all the more so when Syria and (to a lesser degree) Egypt were benefiting from still another Soviet arms build-up in the wake of the 1973 war. Important assurances bearing on future arms supplies were undoubtedly conveyed to Prime Minister Yitzhak Rabin when he met with President Ford and other American representatives in Washington just prior to the opening of the new General Assembly session.

By early October, Secretary Kissinger was preparing to undertake another of his frequent Middle Eastern tours with a view to exploring current peace prospects and, if possible, encouraging such countries as Saudi Arabia to begin thinking in terms of a reduction of petroleum prices.[1] By the time the Secretary of State returned to Washington on October 15, the General Assembly was already launched upon a course of action which, within a few weeks' time, would reduce Israel's political standing to its nadir while elevating the Palestine Liberation Organization to a position scarcely distinguishable from that of a U.N. member state. Following an initial break with precedent in deciding to include in its agenda an item dealing specifically with the "Question of Palestine," the Assembly on October 14 embarked upon the even more portentous step of inviting the PLO, as "the representative of the Palestinian people," to participate in its deliberations on the Palestine issue. A resolution to that effect, introduced with the sponsorship of 72 nations, was adopted by the substantial vote of 105 to 4, with only Bolivia, the Dominican Republic, Israel, and the United States recorded in opposition while 20 countries abstained.]

(57) Status of the Palestine Liberation Organization (PLO): Action by the General Assembly, October 14, 1974.

(a) Invitation to the Palestine Liberation Organization: General Assembly Resolution 3210 (XXIX), October 14, 1974.[2]

The General Assembly,

Considering that the Palestinian people is the principal party to the question of Palestine,

Invites the Palestine Liberation Organization, the representative of the Palestinian people, to participate in the deliberations of the General Assembly on the question of Palestine in plenary meetings.

[The opposition of the United Sates to this procedure was explained by Ambassador Scali in a brief statement after the vote.]

---

[1]Secretary Kissinger visited Egypt, Syria, Jordan, Israel, Saudi Arabia, Algeria, and Morocco on Oct. 9-15; cf. *Bulletin,* 71: 607-16.

[2]Text from General Assembly, *Official Records:Supplement No. 31* (A/9631): 3.

(b) The Position of the United States: Statement by Ambassador Scali to the Assembly, October 14, 1974.[3]

It should be clear from many statements by my government over the past months and years that our vote today in no way reflects a lack of understanding or sympathy for the very real concerns and yearning for justice of the Palestinian people. Rather, it reflects our consistent conviction that the justice they seek will come only as part of a peace that is just for all the parties. This just peace must be negotiated with utmost care and must lead to an overall settlement of the Arab-Israeli conflict, at the heart of which we all recognize lies the Palestinian problem.

Our vote also reflects a deep concern that the resolution before us could be interpreted by some as prejudging that negotiating process and make a durable settlement more difficult to achieve. In that sense, the resolution could have the ultimate effect of working against the interests of a Palestinian settlement.

The world knows how tirelessly we have sought to move the Middle East from the scourge of war to the path of peace. For us to have voted other than we did would be inconsistent with and harmful to our efforts to help promote a just and lasting peace that takes into account the legitimate needs of all the states and peoples in the Middle East.

I should also like to express my government's profound concern over the resolution's departure from the longstanding precedent that only representatives of governments should be allowed to participate in plenary deliberations. Have we created a dangerous precedent which may return to haunt this organization—perhaps cripple its effectiveness?

Mr. President, I want to make clear that the only basis for a just negotiated settlement is and must remain Security Council Resolutions 242 and 338.[4] The resolution passed today cannot alter the basis, and our efforts will go forward in that established and widely accepted framework.

[The commencement of actual debate on the Palestine question was delayed until mid-November, in part because the Arab heads of state had still to clarify their views on some of the pertinent issues at a summit meeting scheduled to take place in Rabat, Morocco, in the last week of October. In the meantime, the Security Council was called upon to renew the expiring mandate of the

---

[3]USUN Press Release 135, Oct. 14; text from *Bulletin*, 71: 622-3.
[4]Security Council Resolution 242 (1967), Nov. 22, 1967, in *Documents, 1967*: 169-70; Security Council Resolution 338 (1973), Oct. 22, 1973, in *AFR, 1973*: 459.

U.N. Emergency Force (UNEF) in the Sinai Peninsula, originally set up in October 1973 and since renewed for a six-month period ending October 24.[5] Assured of the indispensable support of Egypt and Israel, the Council on October 23 adopted a resolution extending the mandate of the force for a further six months, until April 24, 1975. As with earlier resolutions on UNEF, the vote was 13 to 0, with China and Iraq not participating.]

(58) *Continuation of the United Nations Emergency Force (UNEF): Action by the Security Council, October 23, 1974.*

(a) *Extension of UNEF's mandate: Security Council Resolution 362 (1974), October 23, 1974.[6]*

The Security Council,

Recalling its resolutions 338 (1973) of 22 October, 340 (1973) of 25 October, 341 (1973) of 27 October 1973[7] and 346 (1974) of 8 April 1974,

Having examined the report of the Secretary-General on the activities of the United Nations Emergency Force (S/11536),

Noting the opinion of the Secretary-General that "although quiet now prevails in the Egypt-Israel sector, the over-all situation in the Middle East will remain fundamentally unstable as long as the underlying problems are unresolved",

Noting also from the report of the Secretary-General that in the present circumstances the operation of the United Nations Emergency Force is still required,

1. *Decides* that the mandate of the United Nations Emergency Force should be extended for an additional period of six months, that is, until 24 April 1975, in order to assist in further efforts for the establishment of a just and lasting peace in the Middle East;

2. *Commends* the United Nations Emergency Force and those Governments supplying contingents to it for their contribution towards the achievement of a just and lasting peace in the Middle East;

3. *Expresses its confidence* that the Force will be maintained with maximum efficiency and economy;

4. *Reaffirms* that the United Nations Emergency Force must be

[5]Security Council Resolution 341 (1973), Oct. 27, 1973, in *AFR, 1973*: 475-6; Security Council Resolution 346 (1974), Apr. 8, 1974.
[6]Text from Security Council, *Official Records: 29th Year, Resolutions and Decisions*: 5.
[7]*AFR, 1973*: 459, 469-70, and 475-6.

able to function as an integral and efficient military unit in the whole Egypt-Israel sector of operations without differentiation regarding the United Nations status of the various contingents, as stated in paragraph 26 of the report of the Secretary-General (S/11536) and requests the Secretary-General to continue his efforts to that end.

[Ambassador Scali was among the delegates who emphasized, in statements following the vote on this resolution, that UNEF should not be regarded as a substitute for peace but rather as a means of providing time for necessary negotiations.]

(b) Views of the United States: Statement by Ambassador Scali to the Council, October 23, 1974.[8]

Mr. President:[9] It is with great pleasure that I congratulate you for the good will and the patience and the leadership that you have demonstrated in leading us to this happy result—13 affirmative votes and no dissenting voices in approving this important resolution. At a time when there were dissenting and differing views, you have successfully led us to a consensus I think of which we can all be proud.

One year ago, renewed war broke out between Israel and her Arab neighbors, endangering the peace and the security of the entire area. Today, a year later, the Security Council has made a second important contribution to preserving the present ceasefire and disengagement and, hopefully, to moving us closer to a lasting peace. By extending the mandate of the U.N. Emergency Force (UNEF) for another six months, we seek to allow the necessary time and opportunity for negotiations, which are indispensable.

This U.N. peace force has already made a historic impact for good in this highly strategic part of the world. It has a record of which we can all be proud. Despite some problems, UNEF has not only separated the combatants but has helped create the climate of peace that is essential to successful negotiations.

With this renewed mandate and our vote of confidence, we are confident these soldiers for peace will overcome any difficulties as successfully as they solved the inevitable problems that occurred in the first 12 months of the existence of the Force. No force of this kind can expect perfect conditions for its task. The important point is that it has been an effective force for good, and we are confident that it can continue its effective role.

[8]USUN Press Release 147, Oct. 23; text from *Bulletin,* 71: 674-6.
[9]Michel Njine (Cameroon).

Last year's tragic conflict brought about a realization by the parties that the only realistic means of settling disputes is by a process of step-by-step negotiations based on Security Council Resolutions 242 and 338.[10] For the first time in 26 years, this approach has produced concrete progress toward such a settlement. Significant steps have been taken, particularly in the Egyptian-Israeli and the Israeli-Syrian disengagement agreements.

The United States has been privileged to participate actively in the negotiating process. Our government is convinced, and the successes of the past year have strengthened our conviction, that the only way to break through existing stalemates and move concretely toward peace is through a progressive series of agreements. Each step helps to change attitudes and create new situations in which further steps toward an equitable and permanent settlement can be agreed upon. The United States pledges to continue strenuous efforts to achieve this goal.

We thus note with approval that the Secretary General in his report, document S/11536, states that he considers the continued operation of UNEF essential not only for the maintenance of the present quiet but also to assist, if required, in further efforts for the establishment of peace in the Middle East as called for by the Security Council.

I am grateful for the opportunity to commend the UNEF for its outstanding work in maintaining the peace and preserving the climate in which the negotiating process can go forward. It is difficult to exaggerate the constructive role played by the soldiers for peace in these important first steps.

Therefore, I am pleased to extend my government's highest appreciation to the Secretary General and his headquarters staff and to the Commander in Chief of UNEF[11] for their faithful and dedicated performance. I also wish to commend the civilian staff, the UNTSO [U.N. Truce Supervision Organization] observers, and most of all, the UNEF troops, who daily risk their lives far from their homes and families in the tasks of peace.

Our deepest sympathy is extended to the Governments of Canada, Peru, Finland, Panama, Indonesia, and Austria for the tragic loss of lives of members of their contingents who in the past few months have given their lives in the service of peace. We ask the delegations of these countries to convey our condolences to the bereaved families of these brave men. May their sacrifice inspire our efforts to achieve a permanent settlement.

[10]Cf. note 4.
[11]Lieutenant General Ensio Siilasvuo (Finland).

We also wish to commend the troop-contributing countries[12] for their commitment to international peace and security, for the beliefs which have motivated them to contribute troops for this peacekeeping operation.

The operation of UNEF has demonstrated effectively that the willingness of U.N. members to assume collective responsibility for international peacekeeping is important. All of us have agreed that it is vitally important that UNEF should operate with a maximum possible efficiency and at the lowest cost to U.N. members, all of whom share the financial burdens of peacekeeping.

We also are aware that the Secretary General, the troop contributors, all U.N. members, the Security Council, and the General Assembly are vitally interested in the effective and efficient operation of this Force. Efficient operation, in my government's view, must be coupled with maximum attention to economy. Indeed, the most efficient force is usually the leanest. My government strongly urges the Secretary General to continue his policy of keeping UNEF costs as low as possible consistent with efficient operation and fair compensation to troop-contributing governments. My delegation will be working to achieve these ends in the responsible organ of the General Assembly, the Fifth Committee.

Mr. President, the United States has voted in favor of the resolution just adopted[13] which extends UNEF's mandate for another six months in the belief that further progress toward a Middle East settlement can be made during this period. We know that peacekeeping operations in the Middle East are essential to maintaining stability during the negotiations among the parties. But we also firmly believe that peacekeeping must not become a substitute for a just and permanent settlement.

[Contrasting with the conciliatory temper of the Security Council's proceedings was the stormy atmosphere engendered by the meeting of Arab heads of state that took place in Rabat on October 26-29. The main result of this meeting was a further heightening of the tension that already surrounded the question of Palestinian national rights, both in the Israeli-occupied territories of the West Bank and the Gaza Strip and also—at least by implication—in the national territory that Israel had held since 1948-49. Not content with affirming "the right of the Palestinian people to return to its

---

[12]As of Oct. 12, UNEF had a strength of 4,491 made up of contingents from Austria, Canada, Finland, Ghana, Indonesia, Panama, Poland, Senegal, Sweden, and Ireland. (The bulk of the Irish contingent had, however, been repatriated in May 1974.)

[13]Document 58a.

homeland and to define its self-determination," the Rabat conference went on to underwrite the claims of the PLO by asserting
that the Palestinians had the "right . . . to establish an independent national authority under the leadership of the Palestine
Liberation Organization as the sole legitimate representative of the
Palestinian people in all liberated Palestinian territory."[14]

In thus endorsing what would seemingly amount to the establishment of a Palestinian state under the rule of the PLO, the Rabat
meeting launched a formidable challenge not only to the future of
Israel but also to that of Jordan, the state that had long claimed the
sovereignty of the West Bank territories and the allegiance of their
people. A long-time foe of the PLO and its leader, Yasir Arafat,
the outmaneuvered King Hussein nevertheless lost little time in
signifying his acquiescence in the Rabat decisions. Israeli Prime
Minister Rabin, on the other hand, was vehement in rejecting any
negotiation with "terrorist organizations whose avowed policy is to
strive for Israel's destruction and whose method is terrorist
violence."[15] Yet if they were to maintain this stand, the Israelis
would have to breast a tide that was setting more and more strongly
against them. Even President Ford expressed the view, in a news
conference on October 29, that "there must be movement toward
settlement of the problems between Israel and Egypt on the one
hand, between Israel and Jordan *or the PLO* on the other, and the
problems between Israel and Syria in the other category."[16]

The strength of the sentiment that had been building up in favor
of the PLO, to the detriment of both Israel and the United States as
its principal foreign sponsor, was fully evidenced in the course of
the General Assembly debate that began on November 13. Setting
the tone of the proceedings was the ceremonial welcome accorded
Mr. Arafat, the Chairman of the PLO Executive Committee, on
the responsibility of Assembly President Bouteflika. The statement
of the PLO leader was later described in the following terms by an
official U.S. Government publication:

> The debate on Palestine began November 13 with the highly
> publicized appearance of Yasir Arafat, head of the PLO. He
> gave a long and impassioned speech detailing his view of the
> world struggle against imperialism and colonialism and the in-
> justices perpetrated on the Palestinians. He called for the cre-
> ation of a secular, democratic state in Palestine where Moslem,
> Jew, and Christian could live together in equality. He ended his

[14]*Keesing's*: 26813.
[15]Same: 26814.
[16]*Presidential Documents,* 10:1379 (emphasis supplied).

speech by saying that he stood before the world with an olive branch in one hand and a gun in the other, and he asked that the olive branch not be allowed to drop from his hand.[17]

Representatives of 82 U.N. member states took part in the ensuing debate, which continued through November 21 and coincided with a sharp though temporary threat of renewed hostilities between Israel and Syria. Although both of those countries made known their desire to be heard on each day of debate, Assembly President Bouteflika, in still another action sharply questioned by the United States, proposed on November 14 that each participating country be limited to a single intervention. Upheld by a vote of 75 to 23 with 18 abstentions, this action reduced the number of speeches but did not limit the right of reply enjoyed by every delegation under the Assembly's rules of procedure.

Speaking for the United States on the final day of debate, Ambassador Scali stressed the fundamental importance of the negotiating processes already under way and the dangers of any action—such as the questioning of Israel's right to exist—that might make negotiation more difficult.]

(59) The Question of Palestine: Action in the General Assembly, November 21-22, 1974.

(a) Views of the United States: Statement by Ambassador Scali to the Assembly, November 21, 1974.[18]

The question of Palestine, as the speakers who have preceded me have amply demonstrated, has commanded more attention from the United Nations than almost any other single issue. The United Nations has not resolved the basic conflict in the Middle East, but it has limited the terrible consequences of this dispute. As we once again confront this issue, it is fitting that we remind ourselves of the long and honorable history of the U.N.'s efforts to maintain the peace. We also should pay tribute to those who serve in the U.N. peace forces in the area and to those who provide humanitarian assistance to the victims of war.

We must not forget the thousands of human beings who have suffered and who continue to suffer from this conflict.

Those who seek a genuine resolution of the Middle East problem must keep ever in mind the continuing plight of people who have

[17]*U.S. Participation, 1974*: 14-15.
[18]USUN Press Release 176, Nov. 21; text from *Bulletin,* 71: 857-9.

left their homes because of this conflict and have been unable to return. Continuing efforts by the international community to alleviate the hardships of these people are essential, but these efforts alone are not a solution.

Only a just and lasting solution of the Arab-Israeli dispute can halt the killing, stop the suffering, and heal the wounds. The goal of this organization must be to seek ways to promote movement to that end while avoiding any measure which might make such movement more difficult.

Last year's outbreak of war in the Middle East demonstrated for the fourth time in a quarter century that military force cannot resolve the issues which divide Arab and Israeli. It must be clear by now that more violence cannot bring peace. It will only intensify hatreds, complicate differences, and add to the sum of human misery.

The sole alternative to the sterile pursuit of change through violence is negotiation. This path is less dramatic, but in the end it is far more likely to produce acceptable change. The great achievement of the past year has been that the parties to the conflict have at last accepted this alternative and that they have for the first time begun to make it work. A landmark in this effort, and in Arab-Israeli relations, is set forth in Security Council Resolution 338,[19] in which the Security Council for the first time called for immediate negotiations "between the parties concerned under appropriate auspices aimed at establishing a just and durable peace."

The acceptance by the parties of the negotiating process set in motion by Resolution 338 has led to the convening of the Geneva Peace Conference and to the subsequent, successful efforts to negotiate separate disengagement agreements between the forces of Egypt and Israel, and Syria and Israel.[20] In each of these disengagement agreements the parties reaffirmed their acceptance of the principle of a step-by-step negotiated settlement. They did so by agreeing to include the following statement as the final paragraph of each accord:

This agreement is not regarded . . . as a final peace agreement. It constitutes a first step toward a final, just and durable peace according to the provisions of Security Council Resolution 338 and within the framework of the Geneva Conference.

The consequences of a possible breakdown in this negotiating process cannot be overemphasized. War has ravaged the Middle

[19]Cf. note 4.
[20]Chapters 1 and 11.

East four times in 26 years because people did not believe that constructive dialogue between the parties was possible. A fifth war would threaten the security of every country and produce no permanent gains for any.

The primary objective of the U.S. Government therefore has been to maintain the momentum of the negotiating process. Secretary Kissinger recently returned from a visit to the Middle East[21] where he explored with every leader he consulted in the area the vital question of how to continue building on the progress already achieved. The answer to this paramount question still hangs in the balance.

If the negotiating process is to continue, each party must remain committed to negotiating. Each must be prepared to accept a negotiated peace with the others, and each must be prepared to see decisions on how to proceed evolve through understandings among the parties. This is how the Geneva Peace Conference was convened, under the cochairmanship of the Soviet Union and the United States. This is why, when the parties agreed to attend that conference, they also agreed that the role of other participants would be discussed at the conference.[22]

The foundation of such steps toward peace is the acceptance by all parties of the principles of Resolution 338—to engage in the give-and-take of negotiation with the objective of achieving a permanent peace settlement among them on a basis that all parties can accept. If any of the parties rejects this governing principle or questions the right to exist of any of the parties to the negotiation, our best hopes for negotiation and for peace are lost. Certainly it must be understood by all that Israel has a right to exist as a sovereign, independent state within secure and recognized boundaries.

In the course of this debate there have been speakers who have sought to equate terror with revolution, who profess to see no difference between the slaughter of innocents and a struggle for national liberation. There are those who wish to compare the American Revolution and the many other wars of liberation of the past 200 years with indiscriminate terrorism.

If there were instances during the American Revolution where innocent people suffered, there was no instance where the revolutionary leadership boasted of or condoned such crimes. There were no victims, on either side, of a deliberate policy of terror. Those

[21]Secretary Kissinger again visited Egypt, Saudi Arabia, Jordan, Syria, Israel, and Tunisia on Nov. 5-9; see *Bulletin,* 71: 757-64.
[22]Cf. *AFR, 1973*: 603-6.

who molded our nation and fought for our freedom never succumbed to the easy excuse that the end justifies the means.

We hope that all member nations will reaffirm their support for a negotiated settlement in the Middle East and their support for Security Council Resolutions 242 and 338. We know that these resolutions are the basis on which progress so far has been possible. We believe they remain the best hope for continued progress. To seek to alter them not only risks dangerous delay but could destroy prospects for peace in the foreseeable future.

Certainly we can all accept the fact that negotiations can take place only when the parties are willing to negotiate. My government is convinced—and the successes of the past year strengthen our conviction—that the only way to keep the parties committed to negotiations is to move forward through a series of agreements, each substantial enough to represent significant progress, yet each limited enough for governments and peoples to assimilate and accept. Each of these steps helps attitudes to evolve, creates new confidence, and establishes new situations in which still further steps can be taken. With this approach, the parties have, over the past year, succeeded in taking the first substantial steps in decades toward reconciling their differences.

It is my government's firm conviction that the way to move toward a situation more responsive to Palestinian interests is not through new resolutions or dramatic parliamentary maneuvers, but by weaving the Palestinian interests into the give-and-take of the negotiating process. Through this evolutionary process, Palestinian interests can be better reflected in the new situations which are created.

The U.S. Government thus believes that the most important contribution this Assembly can now make toward resolving the issue before us is to help establish an international climate in which the parties will be encouraged to maintain the momentum toward peace. We are equally convinced that the legitimate interests of the Palestinian people can be promoted in this negotiating process and that these negotiations will lead to a just and lasting peace for all peoples in the Middle East.

[No trace of the cautious deliberation recommended by Ambassador Scali could be discerned in the two draft resolutions that had meanwhile been in preparation by advocates of a strong pro-Palestinian stand. The first, a 47-power statement on the "Question of Palestine," included a vigorous affirmation of the rights of the "Palestinian people," while pointedly omitting any reference to the State of Israel. Belatedly circulated only hours before a vote was scheduled, this resolution was adopted by a vote of 89 in favor and 8 opposed (including Israel and the United States), with 37 nations (including most of the United States' allies) abstaining.]

(b) Question of Palestine: General Assembly Resolution 3236 (XXIX), November 22, 1974.[23]

The General Assembly,

Having considered the question of Palestine,

Having heard the statement of the Palestine Liberation Organization, the representative of the Palestinian people,[24]

Having also heard other statements made during the debate,

Deeply concerned that no just solution to the problem of Palestine has yet been achieved and recognizing that the problem of Palestine continues to endanger international peace and security,

Recognizing that the Palestinian people is entitled to self-determination in accordance with the Charter of the United Nations,

Expressing its grave concern that the Palestinian people has been prevented from enjoying its inalienable rights, in particular its right to self-determination,

Guided by the purposes and principles of the Charter,

Recalling its relevant resolutions which affirm the right of the Palestinian people to self-determination,

1. *Reaffirms* the inalienable rights of the Palestinian people in Palestine, including:

(a)   The right to self-determination without external interference;

(b)   The right to national independence and sovereignty;

2. *Reaffirms also* the inalienable right of the Palestinians to return to their homes and property from which they have been displaced and uprooted, and calls for their return;

3. *Emphasizes* that full respect for and the realization of these inalienable rights of the Palestinian people are indispensable for the solution of the question of Palestine;

4. *Recognizes* that the Palestinian people is a principal party in the establishment of a just and lasting peace in the Middle East;

5. *Further recognizes* the right of the Palestinian people to regain its rights by all means in accordance with the purposes and principles of the Charter of the United Nations;

6. *Appeals* to all States and international organizations to ex-

---

[23]Text from General Assembly, *Official Records: 29th Year, Supplement No. 31* (A/9631): 4.

[24]Cf. above at note 17.

tend their support to the Palestinian people in its struggle to restore its rights, in accordance with the Charter;

7. *Requests* the Secretary-General to establish contacts with the Palestine Liberation Organization on all matters concerning the question of Palestine;

8. *Requests* the Secretary-General to report to the General Assembly at its thirtieth session on the implementation of the present resolution;

9. *Decides* to include the item entitled "Question of Palestine" in the provisional agenda of its thirtieth session.

[The second resolution on the Palestine question, a 36-power draft on "Observer Status for the Palestine Liberation Organization," invited the PLO to participate henceforth as an observer in the sessions and work not only of the General Assembly itself but of all international conferences convened under its auspices—a privilege hitherto granted only to states or associations of states. This resolution, which also recommended PLO observer status in international conferences convened by other U.N. organs, was adopted by a vote of 95 in favor to 17 against (including Israel, the United States, and several NATO countries), with 19 abstentions.]

(c) Observer Status for the Palestine Liberation Organization: General Assembly Resolution 3237 (XXIX), November 22, 1974.[25]

The General Assembly,

Having considered the question of Palestine,

Taking into consideration the universality of the United Nations prescribed in the Charter,

Recalling its resolution 3102 (XXVIII) of 12 December 1973,[26]

Taking into account Economic and Social Council resolutions 1835 (LVI) of 14 May 1974 and 1840 (LVI) of 15 May 1974,[27]

Noting that the Diplomatic Conference on the Reaffirmation and Development of International Humanitarian Law Applicable

---

[25]Text from General Assembly, *Official Records: 29th Year, Supplement No. 31* (A/9631): 4.

[26]Urging that "the national liberation movements recognized by the various regional intergovernmental organizations concerned" be invited to participate as observers in the Diplomatic Conference on the Reaffirmation and Development of International Humanitarian Law Applicable in Armed Conflicts, the first session of which was to be held in Geneva Feb. 20-Mar. 29, 1974.

[27]Inviting national liberation movements recognized by the Organization of African Unity (OAU) and the League of Arab States to participate in the world conferences on food and population.

in Armed Conflicts, the World Population Conference and the World Food Conference have in effect invited the Palestine Liberation Organization to participate in their respective deliberations,

Noting also that the Third United Nations Conference on the Law of the Sea has invited the Palestine Liberation Organization to participate in its deliberations as an observer,

1. *Invites* the Palestine Liberation Organization to participate in the sessions and the work of the General Assembly in the capacity of observer;

2. *Invites* the Palestine Liberation Organization to participate in the sessions and the work of all international conferences convened under the auspices of the General Assembly in the capacity of observer;

3. *Considers* that the Palestine Liberation Organization is entitled to participate as an observer in the sessions and the work of all international conferences convened under the auspices of other organs of the United Nations;

4. *Requests* the Secretary-General to take the necessary steps for the implementation of the present resolution.

[The United States did not take part in the series of "explanations of vote" that followed these actions. While Israel's delegate spoke of "days of degradation and disgrace, of surrender and humiliation for the international community," a PLO spokesman retorted that reconciliation with "Zionist terrorism and usurpation was out of the question" and that Israel offered the Palestinians only "death and destruction, with the assistance and encouragement of the United States."[28]

The tendency to link the United States and Israel in a mutual bond of "guilt by association" was also evident at the biennial General Conference of the U.N. Educational, Scientific and Cultural Organization (UNESCO), which had been taking place in Paris while the General Assembly was meeting in New York. In addition to approving a two-year budget of $170 million and electing Amadou Mahtar M'Bow of Senegal to succeed René Maheu of France as UNESCO Director-General, UNESCO's 18th Conference took a number of anti-Israeli actions despite warnings from U.S. Permanent Representative William B. Jones that the organization was overstepping its mandate and jeopardizing its own future. On November 20, the conference decreed a suspension of UNESCO assistance to Israel, pending a discontinuance of certain archeological activities carried on by the latter that were allegedly altering historic features of Jerusalem and damaging some of its

[28]*UN Monthly Chronicle*, Dec. 1974: 41 and 44.

monuments. Next day, the conference also rejected Israel's request for assignment to UNESCO's European regional group, one of five such groups set up in 1964 to stimulate regional program activities. These actions, which were vigorously condemned in Europe as well as the United States, were to result among other things in a cutoff of U.S. financial support of UNESCO under an amendment to the pending Foreign Assistance Act.[29]

In the General Assembly, meanwhile, the United States had taken a rather selective position on a group of resolutions relating to alleged Israeli practices affecting the human rights of the population of occupied territories. A special committee of the General Assembly, set up in 1968 to investigate such practices but never admitted either to Israel or to the occupied lands, had nevertheless submitted a mass of information purporting to show Israel to be in violation of the relevant Geneva convention and, among other things, to have deliberately destroyed the Syrian city of El Quneitra before withdrawing its forces under the recent disengagement agreement. Three resolutions admonishing Israel on the basis of this unverified information had already been approved by the Assembly's Special Political Committee, and were adopted by the Assembly on November 29. For technical reasons explained at the time, the United States opposed one resolution, supported a second, and abstained on the third.[30]

In this explosive and recriminatory atmosphere, it was a relief to know that at least the military disengagement agreements on the Egyptian and Syrian fronts held firm and that Syria, as well as Egypt, was willing to accept a six-month extension of the U.N. force that had been interposed between its forces and those of Israel. All of the governments concerned were anxious to reach a settlement through negotiations, Secretary-General Waldheim assured the Security Council on his return from a brief visit to Syria, Israel, and Egypt. Though peacekeeping operations were not an end in themselves, he added, they did help create conditions needed for progress toward a political settlement. Assured that both Syria and Israel were favorable to the extension, the Security Council on November 29 adopted the appropriate resolution by the customary vote of 13 to 0, with China and Iraq not participating.]

(60) Continuation of the United Nations Disengagement Observer Force (UNDOF): Action by the Security Council, November 29, 1974.

---

[29]Cf. Chapter 35 at note 26.
[30]*U.S. Participation, 1974*: 23-6.

(a) Renewal of UNDOF's mandate: Security Council Resolution 363 (1974), November 29, 1974.[31]

The Security Council,

Having considered the report of the Secretary-General on the United Nations Disengagement Observer Force (S/11563),

Having noted the efforts made to establish a durable and just peace in the Middle East area and the developments in the situation in the area,

Expressing concern over the prevailing state of tension in the area,

Reaffirming that the two agreements on disengagement of forces are only a step towards the implementation of Security Council resolution 338 (1973) of 22 October 1973,[32]

Decides:

(a)   To call upon the parties concerned to implement immediately Security Council resolution 338 (1973);

(b)   To renew the mandate of the United Nations Disengagement Observer Force for another period of six months;

(c)   That the Secretary-General will submit at the end of this period a report on the developments in the situation and the measures taken to implement resolution 338 (1973).

[In a brief statement following the vote on this resolution, Ambassador Scali stressed the interest of the United States in ensuring that the time thus gained was utilized to promote a lasting settlement.]

(b) Views of the United States: Statement by Ambassador Scali to the Council, November 29, 1974.[33]

Since there are no additional members who wish to speak, I should like to express the views of the United States on the subject before us.

---

[31]Text from Security Council, *Official Records: 29th Year, Resolutions and Decisions*: 5.

[32]*AFR, 1973*: 459-60.

[33]USUN Press Release 181, Nov. 29; text from *Bulletin*, 71: 940-41. Ambassador Scali was President of the Security Council for Nov. 1974, but spoke as representative of the U.S.

The establishment of UNDOF six months ago,[34] like that of UNEF before it,[35] marked a major step forward on the path to a lasting Middle East peace. That this road was long and difficult, that it would try men's patience and test their good will, no one doubted then or doubts now. Nevertheless what this Council did in establishing the two Middle East peacekeeping forces was no small thing. The U.N. peacekeeping provides a deterrent to renewed war after four tragic devastating conflicts. It offers time for passions to cool and for prudence and reason to prevail. In short, it offers to those who would grasp it an opportunity to move ahead toward peace.

By extending UNDOF's mandate today, the Security Council has demonstrated anew its awareness of the critical role this Force plays in helping to preserve the disengagement between Syrian and Israeli forces. My government at this time wishes to pledge anew that we will continue the search for a just and enduring peace through negotiations under Security Council Resolutions 242 and 338.

My government warmly welcomes the Council's action today in extending the mandate of UNDOF. The resolution we have adopted[36] with no dissenting votes assures the continuing operation of UNDOF for another six months under the same mandate in accordance with the recommendation which the Secretary General has made in his lucid and comprehensive report of November 27.[37]

I have spoken already of the patience and good will that are so indispensable to peace in the Middle East. These qualities were sorely needed in the recent negotiations leading to agreement on the extension of UNDOF. My government is pleased to have been of assistance in this effort. May I take this opportunity, on behalf of my government, to pay a sincere tribute to the Governments of Syria and Israel for their determination to overcome all obstacles in the cause of peace and justice for their peoples.

I take special pleasure in extending my government's deep appreciation to the Secretary General for his continuing efforts and to his Headquarters staff. Their dedicated, tireless efforts have kept UNDOF operating efficiently. Our congratulations go also to the interim Force commander,[38] to the officers and men of UNDOF,

---

[34]Chapter 11, Document 14b.

[35]*AFR, 1973*: 475-6.

[36]Document 60a.

[37]U.N. document S/11563, Nov. 27, in Security Council, *Official Records: 29th Year, Supplement for Oct., Nov. and Dec. 1974*: 43-7.

[38]Brigadier General Gonzalo Briceño Zevallos (Peru). As of Nov. 26, UNDOF's total strength of 1,224 included contingents from Austria, Canada, Peru, and Poland.

and to the UNTSO [United Nations Truce Supervision Organization] Military Observers assigned to UNDOF for the exemplary manner in which they have performed their duties. I have spoken on a number of occasions of our admiration for these men and of our appreciation for the hardships and sacrifice which they must endure. Some of these soldiers have given their lives so that other men, women, and children in the Middle East might live. We mourn in particular at this time the brave men who have died on the UNDOF front, and we ask the delegations of Canada and Austria to convey our sincere condolences to their bereaved families.

The Secretary General in his report and many members of this Council in their statements have emphasized the importance of moving toward settlement of the underlying problems of the Middle East conflict. My government shares this sense of urgency. In the months ahead we shall be bending every effort to advance step by step along the road that leads to a just and lasting peace in the Middle East.

27. THE WORLD FOOD CONFERENCE

(Rome, November 5-16, 1974)

[Not to be overlooked among the diplomatic commitments of this crowded year was the World Food Conference which Secretary Kissinger had proposed to the U.N. General Assembly on September 24, 1973,[1] and which duly took place in Rome, the headquarters city of the Food and Agriculture Organization of the United Nations (FAO), on November 5-16, 1974. Food was one of those basic subjects that none of the world's governments could safely ignore, and the attendance of representatives from 133 states, together with numerous international organizations, national liberation movements, and nongovernmental bodies, bore witness to a general recognition that the problems involved in trying to feed a rapidly expanding global population could not possibly be longer postponed.

Dramatically brought to public notice by the poor harvests of 1972 and the subsequent disclosure of famine conditions in Sahelian Africa, Bangladesh, and elsewhere, the vulnerability of the world food supply situation continued to preoccupy responsible authorities during the preparations for the Rome conference, which were superintended by a team appointed by Secretary-General Waldheim and headed by Sayed Ahmed Marei of Egypt as conference Secretary-General. United States participation, which involved a multitude of agencies concerned with food, development, and trade matters, was coordinated by Ambassador Edwin M. Martin, while Secretary of Agriculture Earl L. Butz headed a U.S. delegation that included strong congressional as well as executive representation.

Secretary of State Kissinger, as the first prominent international figure to have espoused the conference idea, delivered an opening day address that combined an analysis of the world food problem

AFR, 1973: 365; for further background see same: 497-8 and 514-20.

with a listing of the numerous areas the United States considered ripe for international action.]

(61) The Global Food Problem: Address to the World Food Conference by Secretary of State Kissinger, November 5, 1974. [2]

We meet to address man's most fundamental need. The threat of famine, the fact of hunger, have haunted men and nations throughout history. Our presence here is recognition that this eternal problem has now taken on unprecedented scale and urgency and that it can only be dealt with by concerted worldwide action.

Our challenge goes far deeper than one area of human endeavor or one international conference. We are faced not just with the problem of food but with the accelerating momentum of our interdependence. The world is midway between the end of the Second World War and the beginning of the 21st century. We are stranded between old conceptions of political conduct and a wholly new environment, between the inadequacy of the nation-state and the emerging imperative of global community.

In the past 30 years the world came to assume that a stable economic system and spreading prosperity would continue indefinitely. New nations launched themselves confidently on the path of economic and social development; technical innovation and industrial expansion promised steady improvement in the standard of living of all nations; surpluses of fuel, food, and raw materials were considered a burden rather than a blessing. While poverty and misery still afflicted many parts of the globe, over the long run there was universal hope; the period was fairly characterized as a "revolution of rising expectations."

That time has ended. Now there are fundamental questions about our capacity to meet even our most basic needs. In 1972, partly due to bad weather around the globe, world grain production declined for the first time in two decades. We were made ominously conscious of the thin edge between hope and hunger, and of the world's dependence on the surplus production of a few nations. In 1973, first a political embargo and then abruptly raised prices for oil curbed production in the world's factories and farms and sharply accelerated a global inflation that was already at the margin of governments' ability to control. In 1974, the international monetary and trading system continues under mounting stress, not yet

[2]Department of State Press Release 477, Nov. 5; text and subtitles from *Bulletin*, 71: 821-9.

able to absorb the accumulated weight of repeated shocks, its institutions still struggling to respond. The same interdependence that brought common advance now threatens us with common decline.

We must act now and we must act together to regain control over our shared destiny. Catastrophe when it cannot be foreseen can be blamed on a failure of vision or on forces beyond our control. But the current trend is obvious, and the remedy is within our power. If we do not act boldly, disaster will result from a failure of will; normal culpability will be inherent in our foreknowledge.

The political challenge is straightforward: Will the nations of the world cooperate to confront a crisis which is both self-evident and global in nature? Or will each nation or region or bloc see its special advantage as a weapon instead of as a contribution? Will we pool our strengths and progress together or test our strengths and sink together?

President Ford has instructed me to declare on behalf of the United States: We regard our good fortune and strength in the field of food as a global trust. We recognize the responsibilities we bear by virtue of our extraordinary productivity, our advanced technology, and our tradition of assistance. That is why we proposed this conference. That is why a Secretary of State is giving this address. The United States will make a major effort to match its capacity to the magnitude of the challenge. We are convinced that the collective response will have an important influence on the nature of the world that our children inherit.

As we move toward the next century the nations assembled here must begin to fashion a global conception. For we are irreversibly linked to each other—by interdependent economies and human aspirations, by instant communications and nuclear peril. The contemporary agenda of energy, food, and inflation exceeds the capacity of any single government, or even of a few governments together, to resolve.

All nations—East and West, North and South—are linked to a single economic system. Preoccupation with narrow advantage is foredoomed. It is bound to lead to sterile confrontations, undermining the international cooperation upon which achievement of national objectives depends. The poorest and weakest nations will suffer most. Discontent and instabilities will be magnified in all countries. New dangers will be posed to recent progress in reducing international tensions.

But this need not be our future. There is great opportunity as well as grave danger in the present crisis. Recognition of our condition can disenthrall us from outdated conceptions, from institutional inertia, from sterile rivalries. If we comprehend our reality and act upon it, we can usher in a period of unprecedented advance with consequences far transcending the issues before this conference. We will have built an international system worthy of the capacities and aspirations of mankind.

The Food Challenge

We must begin here with the challenge of food. No social system, ideology, or principle of justice can tolerate a world in which the spiritual and physical potential of hundreds of millions is stunted from elemental hunger or inadequate nutrition. National pride or regional suspicions lose any moral and practical justification if they prevent us from overcoming this scourge.

A generation ago many farmers were self-sufficient; today fuel, fertilizer, capital, and technology are essential for their economic survival. A generation ago many nations were self-sufficient; today a few food exporters provide the margin between life and death for many millions.

Thus food has become a central element of the international economy. A world of energy shortages, rampant inflation, and a weakening trade and monetary system will be a world of food shortages as well. And food shortages in turn sabotage growth and accelerate inflation.

The food problem has two levels—first, coping with food emergencies, and second, assuring long-term supplies and an adequate standard of nutrition for our growing populations.

During the 1950's and 1960's, global food production grew with great consistency. Per capita output expanded even in the food-deficit nations; the world's total output increased by more than half. But at the precise moment when growing populations and rising expectations made a continuation of this trend essential, a dramatic change occurred: during the past three years, world cereal production has fallen; reserves have dropped to the point where significant crop failure can spell a major disaster.

The longer term picture is, if anything, starker still. Even today hundreds of millions of people do not eat enough for decent and productive lives. Since increases in production are not evenly distributed, the absolute numbers of malnourished people are, in fact, probably greater today than ever before except in times of famine. In many parts of the world 30 to 50 percent of the children die before the age of five, millions of them from malnutrition. Many survive only with permanent damage to their intellectual and physical capacities.

World population is projected to double by the end of the century. It is clear that we must meet the food need that this entails. But it is equally clear that population cannot continue indefinitely to double every generation. At some point we will inevitably exceed the earth's capacity to sustain human life.

The near- as well as the long-term challenges of food have three components:

—There is the problem of production. In the face of population trends, maintaining even current inadequate levels of nutrition and food security will require that we produce twice as much food by the end of this century. Adequate nutrition would require 150 percent more food, or a total annual output of 3 billion tons of grain.

—There is the problem of distribution. Secretary General Marei estimates that at the present rate of growth of 2½ percent a year the gap between what the developing countries produce themselves and what they need will rise from 25 million to 85 million tons a year by 1985. For the foreseeable future, food will have to be transferred on a substantial scale from where it is in surplus to where it is in shortage.

—There is the problem of reserves. Protection against the vagaries of weather and disaster urgently requires a food reserve. Our estimate is that as much as 60 million tons over current carryover levels may be required.

In short, we are convinced that the world faces a challenge new in its severity, its pervasiveness, and its global dimension. Our minimum objective of the next quarter century must be to more than double world food production and to improve its quality. To meet this objective the United States proposes to this conference a comprehensive program of urgent cooperative worldwide action on five fronts:

—Increasing the production of food exporters.
—Accelerating the production in developing countries.
—Improving means of food distribution and financing.
—Enhancing food quality.
—Insuring security against food emergencies.

Let me deal with each of these in turn.

Increased Production by Food Exporters

A handful of countries, through good fortune and technology, can produce more than they need and thus are able to export. Reliance on this production is certain to grow through the next decade and perhaps beyond. Unless we are to doom the world to chronic famine, the major exporting nations must rapidly expand their potential and seek to insure the dependable long-term growth of their supplies.

They must begin by adjusting their agricultural policies to a new economic reality. For years these policies were based on the premise that production to full capacity created undesirable surpluses and depressed markets, depriving farmers of incentives to invest and produce. It is now abundantly clear that this is not the problem we face; there is no surplus so long as there is an unmet need. In that sense, no real surplus has ever existed. The problem has always been a collective failure to transfer apparent surpluses to areas of shortage. In current and foreseeable conditions this can surely be accomplished without dampening incentives for production in either area.

The United States has taken sweeping steps to expand its output to the maximum. It already has 167 million acres under grain production alone, an increase of 23 million acres from two years ago. In an address to the Congress last month, President Ford asked for a greater effort still; he called upon every American farmer to produce to full capacity. He directed the elimination of all restrictive practices which raise food prices; he assured farmers that he will use present authority and seek additional authority to allocate the fuel and fertilizer they require; and he urged the removal of remaining acreage limitations.[3]

These efforts should be matched by all exporting countries.

Maximum production will require a substantial increase in investment. The best land, the most accessible water, and the most obvious improvements are already in use. Last year the United States raised its investment in agriculture by $2.5 billion. The U.S. Government is launching a systematic survey of additional investment requirements and of ways to insure that they are met.

A comparable effort by other nations is essential.

The United States believes that cooperative action among exporting countries is required to stimulate rational planning and the necessary increases in output. We are prepared to join with other major exporters in a common commitment to raise production, to make the necessary investment, and to begin rebuilding reserves for food security. Immediately following the conclusion of this conference, the United States proposes to convene a group of major exporters—an Export Planning Group—to shape a concrete and coordinated program to achieve these goals.

[3]Address on the economy before a Joint Session of the Congress, Oct. 8; referenced passage in *Presidential Documents*, 10: 1240.

Production in Developing Countries

The food-exporting nations alone will simply not be able to meet the world's basic needs. Ironically but fortunately, it is the nations with the most rapidly growing food deficits which also possess the greatest capacity for increased production. They have the largest amounts of unused land and water. While they now have 35 percent more land in grain production than the developed nations, they produce 20 percent less on this land. In short, the largest growth in world food production can and must take place in the chronic deficit countries.

Yet the gap between supply and demand in these countries is growing, not narrowing. At the current growth rate, the grain supply deficit is estimated to more than triple and reach some 85 million tons by 1985. To cut this gap in half would require accelerating their growth rate from the historically high average of 2½ percent per annum to 3½ percent—an increase in the rate of growth of 40 percent.

Two key areas need major emphasis to achieve even this minimum goal: new research and new investment.

International and national research programs must be concentrated on the special needs of the chronic food-deficit nations, and they must be intensified. New technologies must be developed to increase yields and reduce costs, making use of the special features of their labor-intensive, capital-short economies.

On the international plane, we must strengthen and expand the research network linking the less developed countries with research institutions in the industrialized countries and with the existing eight international agricultural research centers. We propose that resources for these centers be more than doubled by 1980. For its part, the United States will in the same period triple its own contribution for the international centers, for agricultural research efforts in the less developed countries, and for research by American universities on the agricultural problems of developing nations. The existing Consultative Group on International Agricultural Research can play an important coordinating role in this effort.

The United States is gratified by the progress of two initiatives which we proposed at the sixth special session of the U.N. General Assembly last April:[4] the International Fertilizer Development Center and the study on the impact of climate change on food supply. The fertilizer center opened its doors last month in the United States with funds provided by Canada and the United States; we invite wider participation and pledge its resources to the needs of the developing nations. And the important study on climate and food

[4]Chapter 7, Document 8a.

supply has been taken on by the U.N. World Meteorological Organization (WMO).

National as well as international research efforts must be brought to bear. The United States offers to share with developing nations the results of its advanced research. We already have underway a considerable range of promising projects: to increase the protein content of common cereals; to fortify staple foods with inexpensive nutrients; to improve plant fixation of atmospheric nitrogen to reduce the need for costly fertilizers; to develop new low-cost, small-scale tools and machines for the world's millions of small farmers.

We also plan a number of new projects. Next year our space, agriculture, and weather agencies will test advanced satellite techniques for surveying and forecasting important food crops. We will begin in North America and then broaden the project to other parts of the world. To supplement the WMO study on climate, we have begun our own analysis of the relationship between climatic patterns and crop yields over a statistically significant period. This is a promising and potentially vital contribution to rational planning of global production.

The United States will also make available the results of these projects for other nations.

Finally, President Ford is requesting the National Academy of Sciences, in cooperation with the Department of Agriculture and other governmental agencies, to design a far-reaching food and nutrition research program to mobilize America's talent. It is the President's aim to dedicate America's resources and America's scientific talent to finding new solutions, commensurate both with the magnitude of the human need and the wealth of our scientific capacities.

While we can hope for technological breakthroughs, we cannot count on them. There is no substitute for additional investment in chronic food-deficit countries. New irrigation systems, storage and distribution systems, production facilities for fertilizer, pesticide, and seed, and agricultural credit institutions are all urgently needed. Much of this can be stimulated and financed locally. But substantial outside resources will be needed for some time to come.

The United States believes that investment should be concentrated in strategic areas, applying existing, and in some cases very simple, technologies to critical variables in the process of food production. Among these are fertilizer, better storage facilities, and pesticides.

Modern fertilizer is probably the most critical single input for increasing crop yields; it is also the most dependent on new investment. In our view, fertilizer production is an ideal area for collaboration between wealthier and poorer nations, especially combining the technology of the developed countries, the capital and raw materials of the oil producers, and the growing needs of the least developed countries. Existing production capacity is inadequate worldwide; new fertilizer industries should be created, especially in the developing countries, to meet local and regional needs for the long term. This could be done most efficiently on the basis of regional cooperation.

The United States will strongly support such regional efforts. In our investment and assistance programs we will give priority to the building of fertilizer industries and will share our advanced technology.

Another major priority must be to reduce losses from inadequate storage, transport, and pest control. Tragically, as much as 15 percent of a country's food production is often lost after harvesting because of pests that attack grains in substandard storage facilities. Better methods of safe storage must be taught and spread as widely as possible. Existing pesticides must be made more generally available. Many of these techniques are simple and inexpensive; investment in these areas could have a rapid and substantial impact on the world's food supply.

To plan a coherent investment strategy, the United States proposes the immediate formation of a Coordinating Group for Food Production and Investment. We recommend that the World Bank join with the Food and Agriculture Organization and the U.N. Development Program to convene such a group this year. It should bring together representatives from both traditional donors and new financial powers, from multilateral agencies, and from developing countries, with the following mandate:

—To encourage bilateral and international assistance programs to provide the required external resources.
—To help governments stimulate greater internal resources for agriculture.
—To promote the most effective uses of new investment by the chronic deficit countries.

The United States has long been a major contributor to agricultural development. We intend to expand this contribution. We have reordered our development assistance priorities to place the central emphasis on food and nutrition programs. We have requested an increase of almost $350 million for them in our current budget. This new emphasis will continue for as long as the need exists.

For all these international measures to be effective, governments must reexamine their overall agricultural policies and practices.

Outside countries can assist with technology and the transfer of resources; the setting of priorities properly remains the province of national authorities. In far too many countries, farmers have no incentive to make the investment required for increased production because prices are set at unremunerative levels, because credit is unavailable, or because transportation and distribution facilities are inadequate. Just as the exporting countries must adjust their own policies to new realities, so must developing countries give a higher priority for food production in their development budgets and in their tax, credit, and investment policies.

Improving Food Distribution and Financing

While we must urgently produce more food, the problem of its distribution will remain crucial. Even with maximum foreseeable agricultural growth in the developing countries, their food import requirement is likely to amount to some 40 million tons a year in the mid-1980's, or nearly twice the current level.

How is the cost of these imports to be met?

The earnings of the developing countries themselves of course remain the principal source. The industrialized nations can make a significant contribution simply by improving access to their markets. With the imminent passage of the trade bill,[5] the United States reaffirms its commitment to institute a system of generalized tariff preferences for the developing nations and to pay special attention to their needs in the coming multilateral trade negotiations.

Nevertheless an expanded flow of food aid will clearly be necessary. During this fiscal year the United States will increase its food aid contribution, despite the adverse weather conditions which have affected our crops. The American people have a deep and enduring commitment to help feed the starving and the hungry. We will do everything humanly possible to assure that our future contribution will be responsive to the growing needs.

The responsibility for financing food imports cannot, however, rest with the food exporters alone. Over the next few years in particular, the financing needs of the food-deficit developing countries will simply be too large for either their own limited resources or the traditional food aid donors.

The oil exporters have a special responsibility in this regard. Many of them have income far in excess of that needed to balance their international payments or to finance their economic development. The continuing massive transfer of wealth and the resulting impetus to worldwide inflation have shattered the ability of the

[5]Cf. Chapter 35 at note 19.

developing countries to purchase food, fertilizer, and other goods. And the economic crisis has severely reduced the imports of the industrialized countries from the developing nations.

The United States recommends that the traditional donors and the new financial powers participating in the Coordinating Group for Food Production and Investment make a major effort to provide the food and funds required. They could form a subcommittee on food financing which, as a first task, would negotiate a minimum global quantity of food for whose transfer to food-deficit developing countries over the next three years they are prepared to find the necessary finances.

I have outlined various measures to expand production, to improve the earning capacity of developing countries, to generate new sources of external assistance. But it is not clear that even these measures will be sufficient to meet the longer term challenge, particularly if our current estimates of the gap by 1985 and beyond prove to be too conservative.

Therefore ways must be found to move more of the surplus oil revenue into long-term lending or grants to the poorer countries. The United States proposes that the Development Committee created at the recent session of the Governors of the World Bank and International Monetary Fund[6] be charged with the urgent study of whether existing sources of financing are sufficient to meet the expected import requirements of developing countries. If these sources are not sufficient, new means must be found to supplement them. This must become one of the priority objectives of the countries and institutions that have the major influence in the international monetary system.

Enhancing Food Quality

Supplies alone do not guarantee man's nutritional requirements. Even in developed countries with ample supplies, serious health problems are caused by the wrong kinds and amounts of food. In developing countries, the problem is magnified. Not only inadequate distribution but also the rising cost of food dooms the poorest and most vulnerable groups—children and mothers—to inferior quality as well as insufficient quantity of food. Even with massive gains in food production, the world could still be haunted by the specter of inadequate nutrition.

First, we must understand the problem better. We know a good deal about the state of global production. But our knowledge of the state of global nutrition is abysmal. Therefore the United States proposes that a global nutrition surveillance system be established

---

[6]Cf. Chapter 22 at note 11.

by the World Health Organization (WHO), the Food and Agriculture Organization (FAO), and the United Nations Children's Fund (UNICEF). Particular attention should be devoted to the special needs of mothers and young children and to responding quickly to local emergencies affecting these particularly vulnerable groups. Nutrition surveying is a field with which the United States has considerable experience; we are ready to share our knowledge and techniques.

Second, we need new methods for combating malnutrition. The United States invites the WHO, FAO, and UNICEF to arrange for an internationally coordinated program in applied nutritional research. Such a program should set priorities, identify the best centers for research, and generate the necessary funding. The United States is willing to contribute $5 million to initiate such a program.

Third, we need to act on problems which are already clear. The United States proposes an immediate campaign against two of the most prevalent and blighting effects of malnutrition: vitamin A blindness and iron-deficiency anemia. The former is responsible for well over half of the millions of cases of blindness in less developed countries; the current food shortages will predictably increase this number. Iron-deficiency anemia is responsible for low productivity in many parts of the world. Just as the world has come close to eradicating smallpox, yellow fever, and polio, it can conquer these diseases. There are available new and relatively inexpensive techniques which could have a substantial impact. The United States is ready to cooperate with developing countries and international donors to carry out the necessary programs. We are prepared to contribute $10 million to an international effort.

Finally, we need to reflect our concern for food quality in existing programs. This conference should devote special attention to food aid programs explicitly designed to fight malnutrition among the most vulnerable groups. The United States will increase funding for such programs by at least $50 million this year.

Insuring Against Food Emergencies

The events of the past few years have brought home the grave vulnerability of mankind to food emergencies caused by crop failures, floods, wars, and other disasters. The world has come to depend on a few exporting countries, and particularly the United States, to maintain the necessary reserves. But reserves no longer exist, despite the fact that the United States has removed virtually all of its restrictions on production and our farmers have made an all-out effort to maximize output. A worldwide reserve of as much as 60 million tons of food above present carryover levels may be needed to assure adequate food security.

It is neither prudent nor practical for one or even a few countries to be the world's sole holder of reserves. Nations with a history of radical fluctuations in import requirements have an obligation, both to their own people and to the world community, to participate in a system which shares that responsibility more widely. And exporting countries can no longer afford to be caught by surprise. They must have advance information to plan production and exports.

We commend FAO Director General [Addeke H.] Boerma for his initiative in the area of reserves. The United States shares his view that a cooperative multilateral system is essential for greater equity and efficiency. We therefore propose that this conference organize a Reserves Coordinating Group to negotiate a detailed agreement on an international system of nationally held grain reserves at the earliest possible time. It should include all the major exporters as well as those whose import needs are likely to be greatest. This group's work should be carried out in close cooperation with other international efforts to improve the world trading system.

An international reserve system should include the following elements:

—Exchange of information on levels of reserve and working stocks, on crop prospects, and on intentions regarding imports or exports.

—Agreement on the size of global reserves required to protect against famine and price fluctuations.

—Sharing of the responsibility for holding reserves.

—Guidelines on the management of national reserves, defining the conditions for adding to reserves, and for releasing from them.

—Preference for cooperating countries in the distribution of reserves.

—Procedures for adjustment of targets and settlement of disputes and measures for dealing with noncompliance.

The Promise of Our Era

The challenge before this conference is to translate needs into programs and programs into results. We have no time to lose.

I have set forth a five-point platform for joint action:

—To concert the efforts of the major surplus countries to help meet the global demand.

—To expand the capacity of chronic food-deficit developing nations for growth and greater self-sufficiency.

—To transfer resources and food to meet the gaps which remain.

—To improve the quality of food to insure adequate nutrition.

—To safeguard men and nations from sudden emergencies and the vagaries of weather.

I have outlined the contribution that the United States is prepared to make in national or multilateral programs to achieve each of these goals. And I have proposed three new international groups to strengthen national efforts, coordinate them, and give them global focus:

—The Exporters Planning Group.

—The Food Production and Investment Coordinating Group.

—The Reserves Coordinating Group.

A number of suggestions have been made for a central body to fuse our efforts and provide leadership. The United States is open-minded about such an institution. We strongly believe, however, that whatever the mechanisms, a unified, concerted, and comprehensive approach is an absolute requirement. The American delegation, headed by our distinguished Secretary of Agriculture, Earl Butz, is prepared to begin urgent discussions to implement our proposals. We welcome the suggestions of other nations gathered. here. We will work hard, and we will work cooperatively.

Nothing more overwhelms the human spirit, or mocks our values and our dreams, than the desperate struggle for sustenance. No tragedy is more wounding than the look of despair in the eyes of a starving child.

Once famine was considered part of the normal cycle of man's existence, a local or at worst a national tragedy. Now our consciousness is global. Our achievements, our expectations, and our moral convictions have made this issue into a universal political concern.

The profound promise of our era is that for the first time we may have the technical capacity to free mankind from the scourge of hunger. Therefore, today we must proclaim a bold objective—that within a decade no child will go to bed hungry, that no family will fear for its next day's bread, and that no human being's future and capacities will be stunted by malnutrition.

Our responsibility is clear. Let the nations gathered here resolve to confront the challenge, not each other. Let us agree that the scale and severity of the task require a collaborative effort unprecedented in history. And let us make global cooperation in food a model for our response to other challenges of an interdependent world: energy, inflation, population, protection of the environment.

William Faulkner expressed the confidence that "man will not merely endure: he will prevail." We live today in a world so complex that even only to endure, man must prevail. Global community is no longer a sentimental ideal, but a practical necessity. National purposes, international realities, and human needs all summon man to a new test of his capacity and his morality.

We cannot turn back or turn away.

"Human reason," Thomas Mann wrote, "needs only to will more strongly than fate and it *is* fate."

[Language from Dr. Kissinger's address was subsequently incorporated into Resolution I of the Rome conference, in which was set forth the resolve "that all Governments . . . should accept the goal that within a decade no child will go to bed hungry, that no family will fear for its next day's bread, and that no human being's future and capacities will be stunted by malnutrition."[7] The conference's other statements, comprising a "Universal Declaration on the Eradication of Hunger and Malnutrition" and 21 further resolutions—all adopted without vote—on specific aspects of the world food problem, could be regarded as an elaboration of this fundamental theme as well as a reflection of the fact that the elimination of hunger, unlike the limitation of births, had no declared opponents.

Although the comparatively generous tone of Secretary Kissinger's presentation helped spare the United States some part of the unpopularity it was currently experiencing in other U.N. forums, the conference at Rome was not without echoes of the prevailing ideological and policy clash between developed and developing nations. Even within the U.S. delegation, there were obvious differences of opinion between Secretary Butz, who held to a noticeably cautious position on the matter of food reserves and emergency food aid,[8] and the more openhanded approach favored by such congressional observers as Senator Hubert H. Humphrey and Senator George McGovern, a former Food for Peace Administrator. Conference Secretary-General Marei, in his concluding

---

[7]*Bulletin*, 71: 832. Texts of this and all other conference statements will be found in *Report of the World Food Conference, Rome, 5-16 November 1974* (U.N. document E/CONF.65/20; U.N. sales no. 75.II.A.3): 1-19.

[8]Cf. Butz statement, Nov. 6, in *Bulletin*, 71: 829-31.

remarks, expressed particular disappointment that no specific aid had been offered to countries already suffering from famine; while FAO Director-General Boerma, in describing the results of the conference as "extremely promising" for the long term, observed that there remained "a very grave problem affecting the food supply of millions of people over the next few months."[9]

Included among the conference's specific recommendations, as later summarized in condensed form in the official monthly of the United Nations, were "an international fund for agricultural development to channel investments towards the improvement of agriculture in the developing world with contributions on a voluntary basis from traditional assistance-granting nations and those developing countries with ample means; an international undertaking on world food security based on a co-ordinated system of nationally-held cereal reserves, supported by a world-wide food information and food shortage detection service; and a commitment to provide, on a three-year forward plan basis, commodities and financing for food aid to a minimum level of 10 million tons of cereal each year plus other food commodities."[10]

On the institutional side, the major recommendation of the conference was the creation of a World Food Council, to be established at ministerial level, to review and coordinate all food policy matters in the areas of food production, nutrition, security, trade, food aid, and other related matters. (In its follow-up resolution endorsing the results of the Rome conference, the General Assembly on December 17 took action to establish the World Food Council with a membership of 36, and called for an early meeting to work out details of the proposed International Fund for Agricultural Development.[11]) All in all, Secretary-General Marei observed in his concluding remarks, he was convinced that "the Conference would be an important milestone in man's perennial fight against hunger, and he only hoped the system whose foundations it had laid would secure the world against a recurrence of the kind of crises that had occurred in the last two decades."[12]]

[9]*Keesing's*: 26834.
[10]*UN Monthly Chronicle*, Dec. 1974: 59.
[11]Resolution 3348 (XXIX), Dec. 17, adopted without vote.
[12]*Report of the World Food Conference*: 64.

28. AMERICAN DIALOGUE, PART III

(Quito, November 8-12, 1974)

[Within the life of the larger global community, the nations of the Americas continued to cultivate the narrower yet still substantial interests that found expression through the institutions of the inter-American system. The new American dialogue, proposed by Secretary Kissinger in October 1973 and initiated at Tlatelolco in February 1974, had remained a matter of particularly lively interest throughout the following months.[1] A full-dress resumption of this inter-American discussion had been scheduled to take place at a Foreign Ministers' meeting to be held in Buenos Aires in 1975; and some of the Latin American governments had suggested that the Buenos Aires session might prove especially rewarding if the roster of participating countries could be widened in such a way that the Cuban regime of Fidel Castro could take part alongside the countries that had brought about that nation's present ostracism within the inter-American system.

The legal position of the Cuban Government in relation to the other members of the OAS was governed primarily by two resolutions that had been adopted at two separate meetings of American Foreign Ministers in the early 1960s. The first of these resolutions, adopted at the Eighth Meeting of Consultation on January 31, 1962, had declared "the present government of Cuba" excluded from participation in the inter-American system by reason of its ideological and military ties with the "Sino-Soviet bloc."[2] The other, adopted July 26, 1964 as Resolution I of the Ninth Meeting

---

[1] Cf. Chapters 4 and 8.
[2] *Documents, 1962*: 344-6.

443

of Consultation, had ordered the discontinuance of diplomatic and consular relations, trade, and maritime transportation between the other American states and Cuba in view of the latter's responsibility for acts of "intervention and aggression" against Venezuela that conflicted with the principles and aims of the inter-American system.[3] Though Premier Castro still showed nothing but contempt for the inter-American organization that had thus blackballed his government, the severity of the Cuban threat to the peace and order of the hemisphere appeared to have diminished of late years, and the justification for continuing the diplomatic and economic boycott declared in 1964 had been increasingly questioned by various Latin American and Caribbean governments. By the early 1970s, several of the latter had begun to disregard the OAS prohibitions even without their formal revocation.

By the time of the Atlanta meeting of the OAS General Assembly in the spring of 1974, the United States itself would seem to have concluded that notwithstanding its own continued detestation of the Castro regime, any further insistence on the latter's isolation within the hemisphere would be impractical as well as inconsistent with the spirit of the new dialogue. It therefore offered no opposition to moves by other American governments that were actively interested in bringing about a change. An initiative by the Presidents of Colombia and Venezuela at the end of July was accordingly followed in September by a unanimous decision on the part of the OAS Permanent Council to convoke still another Meeting of Consultation of American Foreign Ministers, this one to be held in Quito, Ecuador, in the second week of November in order to decide whether the change in circumstances over the past decade justified the annulment of the Cuba sanctions.[4]

The business of this Fifteenth Meeting of Consultation, which convened in Quito on November 8 and would continue to November 12, consisted essentially in the consideration of a single resolution that had previously been drafted in OAS circles in Washington and was jointly submitted by the delegations of Colombia, Costa Rica, and Venezuela. Assuming it was adopted by the necessary two-thirds majority, it would simply "discontinue the application" of the sanctions resolution and reaffirm the historic inter-American principle of nonintervention.]

[3]Same, *1964*: 294-5.
[4]OAS Council Resolution CP/RES. 117 (133/74), Sept. 20, in *Fifteenth Meeting of Consultation of Ministers of Foreign Affairs . . . Final Act* (OAS document OEA/Ser.C/11.15): 1-2.

(62) Fifteenth Meeting of Consultation of Ministers of Foreign Affairs of the American States, Quito, November 8-12, 1974.

(a) Proposal to discontinue sanctions against Cuba: Draft resolution submitted by the delegations of Colombia, Costa Rica, and Venezuela.[5]

DRAFT RESOLUTION SUBMITTED BY THE DELEGATIONS
OF COLOMBIA, COSTA RICA AND VENEZUELA

WHEREAS:

The Permanent Council of the Organization of American States, by resolution CP/RES. 117 (133/74) of September 20, 1974,[6] which was approved unanimously, convoked this Meeting so that the Organ of Consultation of the Inter-American Treaty of Reciprocal Assistance, in strict observance of the principle of nonintervention by one state in the affairs of other states, and bearing in mind the change in the circumstances that existed when the measures against the Government of Cuba were adopted, might decide whether there is justification for discontinuing the application of Resolution I of the Ninth Meeting of Consultation of Ministers of Foreign Affairs,[7] held in Washington, D.C., in 1964; and

The Ministers of Foreign Affairs and the Special Delegates have stated the positions of their respective governments with regard to the subject matter of the resolution convoking the meeting,

THE FIFTEENTH MEETING OF CONSULTATION OF MINISTERS
OF FOREIGN AFFAIRS, SERVING AS ORGAN OF CONSULTATION IN
APPLICATION OF THE INTER-AMERICAN TREATY
OF RECIPROCAL ASSISTANCE,[8]

RESOLVES:

1. To discontinue the application of Resolution I of the Ninth Meeting of Consultation of Ministers of Foreign Affairs, held in Washington, D.C., in 1974 [1964].

[5]OAS document OEA/Ser.F/11.15, Document 19/74 corr. 1, Nov. 10; text from *Fifteenth Meeting of Consultation*, cited: 27.
[6]Cf. note 4.
[7]Cf. above at note 3.
[8]Cf. Chapter 4 at note 1.

2. To request the governments of the American states faithfully to observe the principle of nonintervention and to abstain from any act inconsistent therewith.

3. To transmit the text of the present resolution to the Security Council of the United Nations.

[Proponents of this resolution had some reason to believe that of the 21 OAS members entitled to vote on the matter, a two-thirds majority would indeed consider that the time was ripe for lifting OAS sanctions against Cuba and leaving it to the individual American states to determine the nature of their relations with that country. Although the sanctions program still counted some supporters among conservative and military-dominated governments in South and Central America, theirs had clearly become a minority position. Among the prominent advocates of a revocation of sanctions was the Peronist government of Argentina, which had remained in the pro-Cuban column even after the recent death of President Perón and the accession to office of his widow, Isabel.

A reasonably sympathetic attitude toward the new initiative was also expected of the United States, which had recently reorganized the conduct of its Latin American relations through the installation of William D. Rogers, a former administrator of the Alliance for Progress, as Assistant Secretary of State for Inter-American Affairs and of William S. Mailliard, a former member of the House of Representatives, as Ambassador to the OAS. President Ford himself had intimated, shortly after assuming office, that the United States expected to "act in accord" with the other OAS members on the Cuban issue—although he had also stated at a later meeting with Mexican President Echeverría that the United States had detected no change in Premier Castro's attitude and consequently did not expect to change its own attitude either.[9]

Secretary Kissinger was involved in another of his visits to the Middle East at the time of the Quito conference,[10] and it therefore fell to Deputy Secretary Ingersoll to head the U.S. delegation with the support of Assistant Secretary Rogers and Ambassador Mailliard. Judging by the post-conference explanations offered by the two latter officials,[11] the most genuinely novel element in the U.S. approach was a determination to refrain from "arm-twisting" and pressure and, in effect, permit the Latin American governments to resolve the issue in accordance with their own best judgment. This

[9]News conferences, Aug. 28 and Oct. 21, in *Presidential Documents*, 10: 1073 and 1343.
[10]Cf. note 21 to Chapter 26.
[11]Rogers-Mailliard news conference, Quito, Aug. 12, in *Bulletin*, 72: 9-18.

hands-off attitude would stand in dramatic contrast to some of the recent manifestations of U.S. policy toward Latin America—one of which, the allocation of millions of dollars in clandestine support of parties and media opposed to the late President Allende, was even then being aired in the world press following the disclosure of secret testimony given before a committee of the House of Representatives.[12] Such revelations, though lacking any direct bearing on the business of the Quito meeting, could hardly fail to suggest the reflection that not all of the conspiracies against elected governments in the Americas had originated in Havana.

From the statements of Messrs. Rogers and Mailliard, it would appear that the U.S. delegation had decided in advance that it would abstain on the pending resolution, perhaps assuming that it would in any case fall short of the necessary two-thirds majority. There had, however, been no advance announcement of the U.S. position, since even an announcement of abstention, according to Assistant Secretary Rogers, "would have been inconsistent with the neutrality of a non-arm-twisting policy."[13] This act of self- abnegation did not exempt the United States from angry accusations of Machiavellian duplicity when it was found that the advocates of the resolution in fact had failed to muster the 14 votes required for a two-thirds majority. Of the 21 delegations that participated in the voting on November 12, only 12 were recorded in support of the resolution, while 3 were opposed and 6 (including the United States) abstained.[14]

"An absurd procedure . . . contrary to the democratic spirit," the twelve supporters of the resolution protested. This flaunting of the majority's will, they asserted, would further undermine the authority of the inter-American system and encourage additional states to renew relations with Cuba in defiance of OAS sanctions.[15] In more temperate language, Deputy Secretary Ingersoll set forth the official view of the U.S. delegation.]

(b) Position of the United States: Statement to the meeting by Deputy Secretary of State Ingersoll, Chairman of the U.S. delegation, November 12, 1974.[16]

[12]Seymour M. Hersh in *New York Times*, Sept. 8, 1974; further references in *AFR, 1973*: 409-10.
[13]*Bulletin*, 72:11.
[14]The complete vote was as follow:
    In favor: Argentina, Colombia, Costa Rica, Dominican Republic, Ecuador, El Salvador, Honduras, Mexico, Panama, Peru, Trinidad and Tobago, Venezuela.
    Opposed: Chile, Paraguay, Uruguay.
    Abstaining: Bolivia, Brazil, Guatemala, Haiti, Nicaragua, U.S.
[15]*Fifteenth Meeting of Consultation*, cited: 12.
[16]Text from *Bulletin*, 72: 8-9.

Mr. Chairman,[17] distinguished Foreign Ministers and Special Delegates: We have remained silent prior to the vote because we wished to avoid even the appearance of influencing by our remarks or by our actions the outcome of this Meeting of Consultation. Now I think a word of explanation of our vote is in order.

As most of you are aware, the United States was initially opposed to a review of Resolution I at this time. We were persuaded by other nations that the issue should be discussed. We voted for the convocation of this meeting.[18] And we have carefully attended these sessions and considered the statements of each of the members.

The resolution convoking this meeting received unanimous approval in the Permanent Council of the OAS. It placed before us the important question of sanctions against Cuba. Ten years have passed since Resolution I was enacted by the Ninth Meeting of Consultation of the Ministers of Foreign Affairs. It is natural that we should review that decision.

We recognize that a majority now exists for lifting sanctions. On the other hand, we also recall that the measures contained in Resolution I were adopted in 1964 by an overwhelming majority of the OAS member states. Some states here today were, with good reason, among the most persuasive advocates of sanctions. For some of us, evidence of Cuban hostility is fresh in our minds. Though 10 years have passed, the states of the Americas have still received no clear satisfaction that Cuba has abandoned the export of revolution.

We have also taken into account another consideration. It is of the essence of the new dialogue not merely that we consider the major issues confronting this hemisphere, but that we do so in the spirit President [Guillermo] Rodriguez Lara of our host country, Ecuador, so well laid before us Friday [November 8], when he said that a fundamental part of our responsibility was to:

. . . openly and freely express the position of our countries. —While at the same time seeing that the possible differences of opinion that may arise in no way affect the Inter-American solidarity that we seek to strengthen.

We have considered all these factors in coming to our decision to abstain. But our abstention should not be taken as a sign of anything other than the fact that the United States has voted in accordance with its own perception of this question at this time. We respect the views of the majority who have voted for this resolu-

[17]Antonio José Lucio Paredes, Minister of Foreign Affairs of Ecuador.
[18]Cf. above at note 4.

tion. We have not voted "no," and we have not worked against the resolution. We also respect the views of those who entertain such serious reservations with respect to Cuba and who therefore have felt it necessary to vote against.

If this Meeting of Consultation has not produced a conclusive result, it has at least aired in a constructive way the fact that there is no easy solution to the problem of a country which deals with some on the basis of hostility and with others on the basis of a more normal relationship.

I should add that the United States looks forward to the day when the Cuban issue is no longer a divisive issue for us. Cuba has absorbed far too much of our attention in recent years. We need to turn our energies to the more important questions. We must not let a failure of agreement on the Cuban issue at this time obscure our common interest in working together toward mutually beneficial relationships on the major issues of this decade.

Finally, I would like to express my appreciation to the Government of Ecuador, to President Rodriguez Lara, and to Foreign Minister Lucio-Paredes, for acting as hosts of this important inter-American meeting. We are fortunate to have such an able and experienced chairman in Foreign Minister Lucio-Paredes. We are grateful for your excellent preparations and hospitality. Your high sense of responsibility toward the inter-American system should be an example to us all.

[The advocates of the defeated resolution were right when they predicted an intensified movement by Latin American governments toward normalization of their relations with Cuba. In addition to the seven OAS members that currently had diplomatic relations with the Havana regime (Argentina, Barbados, Jamaica, Mexico, Panama, Peru, and Trinidad and Tobago, together with Guyana, an OAS observer country), four more (Colombia, Ecuador, Honduras, and Venezuela) indicated that they would move to open relations shortly. Not many months were to pass before the American Foreign Ministers, holding still another Meeting of Consultation (the sixteenth) at San José, Costa Rica, on July 29, 1975, would formally decide—this time with the support of the United States—that the states parties to the Rio Treaty were "free to normalize or conduct in accordance with the national policy and interests of each their relations with the Republic of Cuba at the level and in the form that each State deems advisable."[19]

There was another sense in which the Quito meeting, to quote the disappointed delegations once again, marked "the end of a stage in

[19]*Sixteenth Meeting of Consultation of Ministers of Foreign Affairs . . . Final Act* (OAS document OEA/Ser.C/11.16): 4.

inter-American relations, a historical event that has taken place here in Quito.''[20] Evident from this time on was a growing tendency on the part of Latin American governments to organize themselves and pursue their objectives independently of both the United States and the OAS. Already being actively promoted by Presidents Echeverría of Mexico and Carlos Andrés Pérez of Venezuela, this idea was to lead in less than a year to the signature in Panama, on October 18, 1975, of a treaty establishing a 23-nation Latin American Economic System (SELA) whose most distinctive feature was the absence of the United States. This project, however, was not to take form before the United States had aroused additional resentment in Latin America by reason of the insistence of Congress on excluding Ecuador and Venezuela, as members of the Organization of Petroleum Exporting Countries (OPEC), from certain benefits that were to be accorded most developing countries under the Trade Act belatedly enacted at the end of 1974.[21]

---

[20]*Fifteenth Meeting of Consultation*, cited: 13.
[21]Cf. Chapter 35 at note 19.

29. SHAPING AN ENERGY POLICY

(Chicago and Paris, November 14-18, 1974)

[In the midst of their preoccupation with more dramatic issues, the global energy crisis had remained a source of constant worry both to the United States and to an overwhelming majority of the world's nations at every stage of development. It was true that the critical petroleum shortages of the winter of 1973-74 had long since been overcome, and that production by the summer of 1974 was again outstripping demand on a worldwide basis. But the new price structure imposed by the petroleum exporting countries in late 1973 was also beginning to be felt in an increasingly painful manner as an inflation-ridden world slid deeper into the global recession of the mid-decade. Although the darkening prospects of the world economy might reasonably have been thought to justify a reduction in the posted price of $11.651 per barrel (for Saudi Arabian light crude) that had taken effect at the beginning of 1974, the OPEC members took no such action at a September meeting at which, in fact, they decided to add a further 3.5 percent to their oil revenues through an increase in royalty and tax payments. While Saudi Arabia was understood to have favored a modest price reduction, Iran, on the other hand, was described as having urged that prices be set still higher.

The potentially devastating impact of these increases on all classes of oil importing countries had, of course, been widely recognized, and plans for drastic remedial action had proliferated at both national and international levels. President Nixon's "Project Independence," originally aimed at assuring energy self-sufficiency by 1980,[1] had by now been more or less superseded by a modified program, set forth by President Ford in an October 8 address to Congress, which featured among other things a reduction

AFR, 1973: 520-28.

of a million barrels in the nation's daily petroleum imports—from 7 to 6 million barrels—by the end of 1975.[2]

At the international level, meanwhile, the twelve-nation Energy Coordinating Group set up in February at the Washington Energy Conference[3] had been developing plans for long-term cooperation in various phases of energy policy through the machinery of a new International Energy Agency (IEA) that was to be set up within the framework of the Organization for Economic Cooperation and Development (OECD). Measures for coping with the flood of "petrodollars" that were now flowing to the oil producing countries and, from there, sloshing back into the developed world were being discussed in various forums, among them a two-day meeting of the Foreign and Finance Ministers of the "Big Five"—Britain, France, West Germany, Japan, and the United States—that took place in Washington on September 28-29 just before the annual meetings of the International Bank and Fund.

The nine-nation European Community, most of whose members (except France) were participating in the Coordinating Group under OECD, was also engaged in drawing up its own long-term energy policy, one that generally paralleled American thinking in its emphasis on the need for conservation, for development of energy sources other than oil, and for assistance to countries experiencing balance-of-payments difficulties as a result of increased import costs. A further element in the European approach, one that had originated at least as far back as the Mideast war of October 1973, was a deliberate attempt to cultivate the good will of the Arab nations—including, of course, the oil exporting countries—through regular consultations looking toward long-term economic, technical, and cultural cooperation.

Although both Europeans and Americans were evidently pursuing similar aims, their differences of approach continued to throw off overtones suggestive of the "confrontation-negotiation" antithesis so frequently emphasized by former President Nixon. Though strenuously disclaiming any thought of "confrontation" with the oil producing countries, the United States was obviously giving top priority to the organization of a solid front of consumer countries that would be endowed with sufficient bargaining power to hold its own in future price negotiations and even, perhaps, to secure a reduction in the current inflated price of oil. Unofficially, there was persistent talk in American quarters about the possibility of "breaking up the oil cartel" by refusing to bow to its demands and giving free play to its inherently divisive tendencies.

[2]*Presidential Documents*, 10: 1240-41, 1246.
[3]Cf. Chapter 3.

President Giscard d'Estaing, perhaps the leading exponent of the opposite tendency, actually made use of such words as "domination" and "confrontation" at his October 24 press conference, contrasting such an approach with what he described as France's preference for solutions based on "concertation" and "negotiation." France, Giscard emphasized, did not intend to take part in a bloc of rich consuming nations, perceived by the producing countries as an instrument of "confrontation" rather than "concertation." Insisting that there could be no solution without dialogue, President Giscard proposed a different approach: the convening in 1975 of a conference of ten or twelve countries, based on equal representation of exporting, industrialized, and developing nations, to examine both the problems of petroleum pricing and the required adjustments of the world economy as a whole.

This French proposal initiated a process that would ultimately lead to the convening of the 27-member "North-South conference" or Conference on International Economic Cooperation (CIEC), which held its inaugural session in Paris on December 16-19, 1975. At the time it was made, however, M. Giscard d'Estaing's proposal impressed American authorities as decidedly premature—the more so at a time when the proposed organization of industrialized petroleum-consuming countries was just about to come to birth. Secretary Kissinger's reaction to the French proposal found a place in the comprehensive account of steps to meet the energy challenge that he delivered at a Board of Trustees banquet at the University of Chicago on November 14.]

(63) "The Energy Crisis—Strategy for Cooperative Action": Address by Secretary of State Kissinger before a University of Chicago Board of Trustees banquet, Chicago, November 14, 1974.[4]

A generation ago the Western world faced a historic crisis—the breakdown of international order in the wake of world war. Threatened by economic chaos and political upheaval, the nations of the West built a system of security relations and cooperative institutions that have nourished our safety, our prosperity, and our freedom ever since. A moment of grave crisis was transformed into an act of lasting creativity.

We face another such moment today. The stakes are as high as they were 25 years ago. The challenge to our courage, our vision, and our will is as profound. And our opportunity is as great.

[4]Department of State Press Release 500; text and titles from *Bulletin*, 71: 749-56.

What will be our response?

I speak, of course, of the energy crisis. Tonight I want to discuss how the administration views this problem, what we have been doing about it, and where we must now go. I will stress two themes that this government has emphasized for a year and a half:

—First, the problem is grave but it is soluble.

—Second, international collaboration, particularly among the industrial nations of North America, Western Europe, and Japan, is an inescapable necessity.

The economic facts are stark. By 1973, worldwide industrial expansion was outstripping energy supply; the threat of shortages was already real. Then, without warning, we were faced first with a political embargo, followed quickly by massive increases in the price of oil. In the course of a single year the price of the world's most strategic commodity was raised 400 percent. The impact has been drastic and global:

—The industrial nations now face a collective payments deficit of $40 billion, the largest in history and beyond the experience or capacity of our financial institutions. We suffer simultaneously a slowdown of production and speedup of an inflation that was already straining the ability of governments to control.

—The nations of the developing world face a collective yearly deficit of $20 billion, over half of which is due to increases in oil prices. The rise in energy costs in fact roughly equals the total flow of external aid. In other words, the new oil bill threatens hopes for progress and advancement and renders problematical the ability to finance even basic human needs such as food.

—The oil producers now enjoy a surplus of $60 billion, far beyond their payments or development needs and manifestly more than they can invest. Enormous unabsorbed surplus revenues now jeopardize the very functioning of the international monetary system.

Yet this is only the first year of inflated oil prices. The full brunt of the petrodollar flood is yet to come. If current economic trends continue, we face further and mounting worldwide shortages, unemployment, poverty, and hunger. No nation, East or West, North or South, consumer or producer, will be spared the consequences.

An economic crisis of such magnitude would inevitably produce dangerous political consequences. Mounting inflation and recession—brought on by remote decisions over which consumers have no influence—will fuel the frustration of all whose hopes for economic progress are suddenly and cruelly rebuffed. This is fertile ground for social conflict and political turmoil. Moderate governments and moderate solutions will be under severe attack. Democratic societies could become vulnerable to extremist pressures from right or left to a degree not experienced since the twenties and thirties. The great achievements of this generation in preserving our institutions and constructing an international order will be imperiled.

The destinies of consumers and producers are joined in the same global economic system, on which the progress of both depends. If either attempts to wield economic power aggressively, both run grave risks. Political cooperation, the prerequisite of a thriving international economy, is shattered. New tensions will engulf the world just when the antagonisms of two decades of the cold war have begun to diminish.

The potentially most serious international consequences could occur in relations between North America, Europe, and Japan. If the energy crisis is permitted to continue unchecked, some countries will be tempted to secure unilateral benefit through separate arrangements with producers at the expense of the collaboration that offers the only hope for survival over the long term. Such unilateral arrangements are guaranteed to enshrine inflated prices, dilute the bargaining power of the consumers, and perpetuate the economic burden for all. The political consequences of disarray would be pervasive. Traditional patterns of policy may be abandoned because of dependence on a strategic commodity. Even the hopeful process of easing tensions with our adversaries could suffer, because it has always presupposed the political unity of the Atlantic nations and Japan.

The Need for Consumer Cooperation

This need not be our fate. On the contrary, the energy crisis should summon once again the cooperative effort which sustained the policies of North America, Western Europe, and Japan for a quarter century. The Atlantic nations and Japan have the ability, if we have the will, not only to master the energy crisis but to shape from it a new era of creativity and common progress.

In fact we have no other alternative. The energy crisis is not a problem of transitional adjustment. Our financial institutions and mechanisms of cooperation were never designed to handle so abrupt and artificially sustained a price rise of so essential a commodity with such massive economic and political ramifications. We face a long-term drain which challenges us to common action or dooms us to perpetual crisis.

The problem will not go away by permitting inflation to proceed to redress the balance between oil producers and producers of other goods. Inflation is the most grotesque kind of adjustment, in which all other elements in the domestic structure are upset in an attempt to balance one—the oil bill. In any event, the producers could and would respond by raising prices, thereby accelerating all the political and social dangers I have described.

Nor can consumers finance their oil bill by going into debt to the producers without making their domestic structure hostage to the decisions of others. Already, producers have the power to cause major financial upheavals simply by shifting investment funds from one country to another or even from one institution to another. The political implications are ominous and unpredictable. Those who wield financial power would sooner or later seek to dictate the political terms of the new relationships.

Finally, price reductions will not be brought about by consumer-producer dialogue alone. The price of oil will come down only when objective conditions for a reduction are created, and not before. Today the producers are able to manipulate prices at will and with apparent impunity. They are not persuaded by our protestations of damage to our societies and economies, because we have taken scant action to defend them ourselves. They are not moved by our alarms about the health of the Western world, which never included and sometimes exploited them. And even if the producers learn eventually that their long-term interest requires a cooperative adjustment of the price structure, it would be foolhardy to count on it or passively wait for it.

We agree that a consumer-producer dialogue is essential. But it must be accompanied by the elaboration of greater consumer solidarity. The heart of our approach must be collaboration among the consuming nations. No one else will do the job for us.

Blueprint for Consumer Cooperation

Consumer cooperation has been the central element of U.S. policy for the past year and a half.

In April 1973 the United States warned that energy was becoming a problem of unprecedented proportions and that collaboration among the nations of the West and Japan was essential.[5] In December of the same year, we proposed a program of collective action.[6] This led to the Washington Energy Conference in February 1974,[7] at which the major consumers established new machinery for consultation with a mandate to create, as soon as possible, institutions for the pooling of effort, risk, and technology.

[5]Nixon message, Apr. 18, 1973, in *Presidential Documents*, 9: 389-406 (1973).
[6]Kissinger address, Dec. 12, 1973, in *AFR, 1973*: 573-4.
[7]Chapter 3.

In April 1974 and then again this fall before the U.N. General Assembly,[8] President Ford and I reiterated the American philosophy that global cooperation offered the only long-term solution and that our efforts with fellow consumers were designed to pave the way for constructive dialogue with the producers. In September 1974 we convened a meeting of the Foreign and Finance Ministers of the United Kingdom, Japan, the Federal Republic of Germany, France, and the United States to consider further measures of consumer cooperation. And last month President Ford announced a long-term national policy of conservation and development[9] to reinforce our international efforts to meet the energy challenge.

In our view, a concerted consumer strategy has two basic elements:

—First, we must create the objective conditions necessary to bring about lower oil prices. Since the industrialized nations are the principal consumers, their actions can have a decisive impact. Determined national action, reinforced by collective efforts, can transform the market by reducing our consumption of oil and accelerating development of new sources of energy. Over time this will create a powerful pressure on prices.

—Second, in the interim we must protect the vitality of our economies. Effective action on conservation will require months; development of alternative sources will take years. In the meantime, we will face two great dangers. One is the threat of a new embargo. The other is that our financial system may be unable to manage chronic deficits and to recycle the huge flows of oil dollars that producers will invest each year in our economies. A financial collapse—or the threat of it—somewhere in the system could result in restrictive monetary, fiscal, and trade measures and a downward spiral of income and jobs.

The consumers have taken two major steps to safeguard themselves against these dangers by collaborative action.

One of the results of the Washington Energy Conference was a new permanent institution for consumer energy cooperation—the International Energy Agency (IEA). This agency will oversee a comprehensive common effort—in conservation, cooperative research and development, broad new action in nuclear enrichment, investment in new energy supplies, and the elaboration of consumer positions for the consumer-producer dialogue.

Equally significant is the unprecedented agreement to share oil supplies among principal consumers in the event of another crisis.

[8]Chapter 7, Document 8a, and Chapter 21, Documents 46 and 47.
[9]Cf. above at note 2.

The International Energy Program that grew out of the Washington Energy Conference and that we shall formally adopt next week[10] is a historic step toward consumer solidarity. It provides a detailed blueprint for common action should either a general or selective embargo occur. It is a defensive arrangement, not a challenge to producers. But producing countries must know that it expresses the determination of the consumers to shape their own future and not to remain vulnerable to outside pressures.

The International Energy Agency and the International Energy Program are the first fruits of our efforts. But they are only foundations. We must now bring our blueprint to life.

To carry through the overall design, the consuming countries must act in five interrelated areas:

—First, we must accelerate our national programs of energy conservation, and we must coordinate them to insure their effectiveness.

—Second, we must press on with the development of new supplies of oil and alternative sources of energy.

—Third, we must strengthen economic security—to protect against oil emergencies and to safeguard the international financial system.

—Fourth, we must assist the poor nations whose hopes and efforts for progress have been cruelly blunted by the oil price rises of the past year.

—Fifth, on the basis of consumer solidarity we should enter a dialogue with the producers to establish a fair and durable long-term relationship.

Let me deal with each of these points in turn.

Coordination of Conservation Programs

Conservation and the development of new sources of energy are basic to the solution. The industrialized countries as a whole now import nearly two-thirds of their oil and over one-third of their total energy. Over the next decade, we must conserve enough oil and develop sufficient alternative supplies to reduce these imports to no more than one-fifth of the total energy consumption. This requires that the industrialized countries manage the growth of their economies without increasing the volume of their oil imports.

The effect of this reduced dependence will be crucial. If it succeeds, the demand of the industrialized countries for imported oil will remain static while new sources of energy will become available

[10]Cf. below at note 15.

both inside and outside of OPEC. OPEC may attempt to offset efforts to strengthen conservation and develop alternative sources by deeper and deeper cuts in production, reducing the income of producers who seek greater revenues for their development. The majority of producers will then see their interest in expanding supply and seeking a new equilibrium between supply and demand at a fair price.

Limiting oil imports into industrial countries to a roughly constant figure is an extremely demanding goal requiring discipline for conservation and investment for the development of new energy sources. The United States, which now imports a third of its oil and a sixth of its total energy, will have to become largely self-sufficient. Specifically, we shall set as a target that we reduce our imports over the next decade from 7 million barrels a day to no more than 1 million barrels, or less than 2 percent of our total energy consumption.

Conservation is of course the most immediate road to relief. President Ford has stated that the United States will reduce oil imports by 1 million barrels per day by the end of 1975—a 15 percent reduction.

But one country's reduction in consumption can be negated if other major consumers do not follow suit. Fortunately, other nations have begun conservation programs of their own. What is needed now is to relate these programs to common goals and an overall design. Therefore, the United States proposes an international agreement to set consumption goals. The United States is prepared to join an international conservation agreement that would lead to systematic and long-term savings on an equitable basis.

As part of such a program, we propose that by the end of 1975 the industrialized countries reduce their consumption of oil by 3 million barrels a day over what it would be otherwise—a reduction of approximately 10 percent of the total imports of the group. This reduction can be carried out without prejudice to economic growth and jobs by cutting back on wasteful and inefficient uses of energy both in personal consumption and in industry. The United States is prepared to assume a fair share of the total reduction.

The principal consumer nations should meet each year to determine appropriate annual targets.

Development of Alternative Energy Sources

Conservation measures will be effective to the extent that they are part of a dynamic program for the development of alternative energy sources. All countries must make a major shift toward nuclear power, coal, gas, and other sources. If we are to assure substantial amounts of new energy in the 1980's, we must start now. If the industrialized nations take the steps which are within their power, they will be able to transform energy shortages into energy surpluses by the 1980's.

Project Independence is the American contribution to this effort. It represents the investment of hundreds of billions of dollars, public and private—dwarfing our moon-landing program and the Manhattan Project, two previous examples of American technology mobilized for a great goal. Project Independence demonstrates that the United States will never permit itself to be held hostage to a strategic commodity.

Project Independence will be complemented by an active policy of supporting cooperative projects with other consumers. The International Energy Agency to be established next week is well designed to launch and coordinate such programs. Plans are already drawn up for joint projects in coal technology and solar energy. The United States is prepared to expand these collective activities substantially to include such fields as uranium enrichment.

The area of controlled thermonuclear fusion is particularly promising for joint ventures, for it would make available abundant energy from virtually inexhaustible resources. The United States is prepared to join with other IEA members in a broad program of joint planning, exchange of scientific personnel, shared use of national facilities, and the development of joint facilities to accelerate the advent of fusion power.

Finally, we shall recommend to the IEA that it create a common fund to finance or guarantee investment in promising energy projects in participating countries and in those ready to cooperate with the IEA on a long-term basis.

Financial Solidarity

The most serious immediate problem facing the consuming countries is the economic and financial strain resulting from high oil prices. Producer revenues will inevitably be reinvested in the industrialized world; there is no other outlet. But they will not necessarily flow back to the countries whose balance of payments problems are most acute. Thus many countries will remain unable to finance their deficits and all will be vulnerable to massive sudden withdrawals.

The industrialized nations, acting together, can correct this imbalance and reduce their vulnerability. Just as producers are free to choose where they place their funds, so the consumers must be free to redistribute these funds to meet their own needs and those of the developing countries.

Private financial institutions are already deeply involved in this process. To buttress their efforts, central banks are assuring that necessary support is available to the private institutions, particularly since so much of the oil money has been invested in relatively short-term obligations. Private institutions should not bear all the risks indefinitely, however. We cannot afford to test the limits of their capacity.

Therefore the governments of Western Europe, North America, and Japan should move now to put in place a system of mutual support that will augment and buttress private channels whenever necessary. The United States proposes that a common loan and guarantee facility be created to provide for redistributing up to $25 billion in 1975, and as much again the next year if necessary.

The facility will not be a new aid institution to be funded by additional taxes. It will be a mechanism for recycling, at commercial interest rates, funds flowing back to the industrial world from the oil producers. Support from the facility would not be automatic, but contingent on full resort to private financing and on reasonable self-help measures. No country should expect financial assistance that is not moving effectively to lessen its dependence on imported oil.

Such a facility will help assure the stability of the entire financial system and the credit-worthiness of participating governments; in the long run it would reduce the need for official financing. If implemented rapidly it would:

—Protect financial institutions from the excessive risks posed by an enormous volume of funds beyond their control or capacity;
—Insure that no nation is forced to pursue disruptive and restrictive policies for lack of adequate financing;
—Assure that no consuming country will be compelled to accept financing on intolerable political or economic terms; and
—Enable each participating country to demonstrate to people that efforts and sacrifices are being shared equitably—that the national survival is buttressed by consumer solidarity.

We have already begun discussion of this proposal; it was a principal focus of the meeting of the Foreign and Finance Ministers of the Federal Republic of Germany, the United States, Japan, the United Kingdom, and France in September in Washington.

Easing the Plight of Developing Countries

The strategy I have outlined here is also essential to ease the serious plight of many developing countries. All consuming nations are in need of relief from excessive oil prices, but the developing world cannot wait for the process to unfold. For them, the oil crisis has already produced an emergency. The oil bill has wiped out the external assistance of the poorer developing countries, halted agricultural and industrial development, and inflated the prices for their most fundamental needs, including food. Unlike the industrial nations, developing countries do not have many options of self-help; their margin for reducing energy consumption is limited; they have little capacity to develop alternative sources.

For both moral and practical reasons, we cannot permit hopes for development to die or cut ourselves off from the political and economic needs of so great a part of mankind. At the very least, the industrial nations must maintain the present level of their aid to the developing world and take special account of its needs in the multilateral trade negotiations.

We must also look for ways to help in the critical area of food. At the World Food Conference, I outlined a strategy for meeting the food and agricultural needs of the least developed countries.[11] The United States is uniquely equipped to make a contribution in this field and will make a contribution worthy of its special strength.

A major responsibility must rest with those oil producers whose actions aggravated the problems of the developing countries and who, because of their new-found wealth, now have greatly increased resources for assistance.

But even after all presently available resources have been drawn upon, an unfinanced payments deficit of between $1 and $2 billion will remain for the 25 or 30 countries most seriously affected by high oil prices. It could grow in 1976.

We need new international mechanisms to meet this deficit. One possibility would be to supplement regular International Monetary Fund facilities by the creation of a separate trust fund managed by the IMF to lend at interest rates recipient countries could afford. Funds would be provided by national contributions from interested countries, including especially oil producers. The IMF itself could contribute the profits from IMF gold sales undertaken for this purpose. We urge the Interim Committee of the IMF and the joint IMF-IBRD Development Committee[12] to examine this proposal on an urgent basis.

Constructive Dialogue With Producers

When the consumers have taken some collective steps toward a durable solution—that is, measures to further conservation and the

[11]Chapter 27, Document 61.
[12]Cf. Chapter 22 at note 11.

development of new supplies—and for our interim protection through emergency planning and financial solidarity, the conditions for a constructive dialogue with producers will have been created.

We do not see consumer cooperation as antagonistic to consumer-producer cooperation. Rather we view it as a necessary prerequisite to a constructive dialogue, as do many of the producers themselves, who have urged the consumers to curb inflation, conserve energy, and preserve international financial stability.

A dialogue that is not carefully prepared will compound the problems which it is supposed to solve. Until the consumers develop a coherent approach to their own problems, discussions with the producers will only repeat in a multilateral forum the many bilateral exchanges which are already taking place. When consumer solidarity has been developed and there are realistic prospects for significant progress, the United States is prepared to participate in a consumer-producer meeting.

The main subject of such a dialogue must inevitably be price. Clearly the stability of the system on which the economic health of even the producers depends requires a price reduction. But an equitable solution must also take account of the producers' need for long-term income security and economic growth. This we are prepared to discuss sympathetically.

In the meantime the producers must recognize that further increases in the prices while this dialogue is being prepared and when the system has not even absorbed the previous price rises would be disruptive and dangerous.

On this basis—consumer solidarity in conservation, the development of alternative supplies, and financial security; producer policies of restraint and responsibility; and a mutual recognition of interdependence and a long-term common interest—there can be justifiable hope that a consumer-producer dialogue will bring an end to the crisis that has shaken the world to its economic foundations.

The Next Step

It is now a year and a month since the oil crisis began. We have made a good beginning, but the major test is still ahead.

The United States in the immediate future intends to make further proposals to implement the program I have outlined.

Next week, we will propose to the new International Energy Agency a specific program for cooperative action in conservation, the development of new supplies, nuclear enrichment, and the preparation of consumer positions for the eventual consumer-producer dialogue.

Simultaneously, Secretary [of the Treasury] Simon will spell out our ideas for financial solidarity in detail,[13] and our representative at the Group of Ten will present them to his colleagues.

We will, as well, ask the Chairman of the Interim Committee of the IMF as well as the new joint IMF-IBRD Development Committee to consider an urgent program for concessional assistance to the poorest countries.

Yesterday, Secretary [of the Interior Rogers C. B.] Morton announced an accelerated program for domestic oil exploration and exploitation.

President Ford will submit a detailed and comprehensive energy program to the new Congress.[14]

Let there be no doubt, the energy problem is soluble. It will overwhelm us only if we retreat from its reality. But there can be no solution without the collective efforts of the nations of North America, Western Europe, and Japan—the very nations whose cooperation over the course of more than two decades has brought prosperity and peace to the postwar world. Nor, in the last analysis, can there be a solution without a dialogue with the producers carried on in a spirit of reconciliation and compromise.

A great responsibility rests upon America, for without our dedication and leadership no progress is possible. This nation for many years has carried the major responsibility for maintaining the peace, feeding the hungry, sustaining international economic growth, and inspiring those who would be free. We did not seek this heavy burden, and we have often been tempted to put it down. But we have never done so, and we cannot afford to do so now—or the generations that follow us will pay the price for our self-indulgence.

For more than a decade America has been torn by war, social and generational turbulence, and constitutional crisis. Yet the most striking lesson from these events is our fundamental stability and strength. During our upheavals, we still managed to ease tensions around the globe. Our people and our institutions have come through our domestic travails with an extraordinary resiliency. And now, once again, our leadership in technology, agriculture, industry, and communications has become vital to the world's recovery.

Woodrow Wilson once remarked that "wrapped up with the liberty of the world is the continuous perfection of that liberty by

---

[13]Address before the 61st National Foreign Trade Convention, New York, Nov. 18, in *Bulletin*, 71: 794-802.
[14]Message on the State of the Union, Jan. 15, 1975, in *Presidential Documents*, 11: 48-51 (1975).

the concerted powers of all civilized people." That, in the last analysis, is what the energy crisis is all about. For it is our liberty that in the end is at stake and it is only through the concerted action of the industrial democracies that it will be maintained. The dangers that Woodrow Wilson and his generation faced were, by today's standards, relatively simple and straightforward. The dangers we face now are more subtle and more profound. The context in which we act is more complex than even the period following the Second World War. Then we drew inspiration from stewardship; now we must find it in partnership. Then we and our allies were brought together by an external threat, now we must find it in our devotion to the political and economic institutions of free peoples working together for a common goal. Our challenge is to maintain the cooperative spirit among like-minded nations that has served us so well for a generation and to prove, as Woodrow Wilson said in another time and place, that "The highest and best form of efficiency is the spontaneous cooperation of a free people."

[A number of the proposals embodied in Secretary Kissinger's comprehensive statement would obviously call for prolonged and intricate negotiations; and at least one of them, the $25 billion "safety net" to reinforce the position of the industrialized countries, was destined ultimately to fall by the wayside. Negotiations relating to the proposed International Energy Program and International Energy Agency, in contrast, had already been completed, and nothing now remained but to bring the pertinent agreement into effect. The establishment of the new IEA within the framework of the Organization for Economic Cooperation and Development was accordingly sanctioned by the OECD Council (with Finland, France, and Greece abstaining) on November 15, and the "Agreement on an International Energy Program" was signed in Paris three days later, November 18, on behalf of 16 of the 24 OECD member countries,[15] France and Norway being the most conspicuous holdouts. Signing for the United States was Thomas O. Enders, Assistant Secretary of State for Economic and Business Affairs, who had headed the U.S. delegation at the decisive negotiating sessions of the Energy Coordinating Group. At a meeting immediately following the signature ceremony, the Governing Board of the new IAE elected Viscount Etienne Davignon of Belgium as its Chairman and appointed Ulf Lantzke of West Germany as the agency's Executive Director.]

---

[15]The signatory states are listed in the preamble to the agreement (Document 64).

(64) Agreement on an International Energy Program, done at Paris and entered into force provisionally November 18, 1974; entered into force definitively January 19, 1976.[16]

(Excerpts)

AGREEMENT
ON AN
INTERNATIONAL ENERGY PROGRAM

THE GOVERNMENTS OF THE REPUBLIC OF AUSTRIA, THE KINGDOM OF BELGIUM, CANADA, THE KINGDOM OF DENMARK, THE FEDERAL REPUBLIC OF GERMANY, IRELAND, THE ITALIAN REPUBLIC, JAPAN, THE GRAND DUCHY OF LUXEMBOURG, THE KINGDOM OF THE NETHERLANDS, SPAIN, THE KINGDOM OF SWEDEN, THE SWISS CONFEDERATION, THE REPUBLIC OF TURKEY, THE UNITED KINGDOM OF GREAT BRITAIN AND NORTHERN IRELAND, AND THE UNITED STATES OF AMERICA,

DESIRING to promote secure oil supplies on reasonable and equitable terms,

DETERMINED to take common effective measures to meet oil supply emergencies by developing an emergency self-sufficiency in oil supplies, restraining demand and allocating available oil among their countries on an equitable basis,

DESIRING to promote co-operative relations with oil producing countries and with other oil consuming countries, including those of the developing world, through a purposeful dialogue, as well as through other forms of co-operation, to further the opportunities for a better understanding between consumer and producer countries,

MINDFUL of the interests of other oil consuming countries, including those of the developing world,

DESIRING to play a more active role in relation to the oil industry by establishing a comprehensive international information system and a permanent framework for consultation with oil companies,

DETERMINED to reduce their dependence on imported oil by undertaking long term co-operative efforts on conservation of energy, on accelerated development of alternative sources of energy, on

---

[16]TIAS 8278.

research and development in the energy field and on uranium enrichment,

CONVINCED that these objectives can only be reached through continued co-operative efforts within effective organs,

EXPRESSING the intention that such organs be created within the framework of the Organisation for Economic Co-operation and Development,

RECOGNISING that other Member countries of the Organisation for Economic Co-operation and Development may desire to join in their efforts,

CONSIDERING the special responsibility of governments for energy supply,

CONCLUDE that it is necessary to establish an International Energy Program to be implemented through an International Energy Agency, and to that end,

HAVE AGREED as follows:

Article 1

1. The Participating Countries shall implement the International Energy Program as provided for in this Agreement through the International Energy Agency, described in Chapter IX, hereinafter referred to as the "Agency".

2. The term "Participating Countries" means States to which this Agreement applies provisionally and States for which the Agreement has entered into and remains in force.

3. The term "group" means the Participating Countries as a group.

Chapter I

EMERGENCY SELF-SUFFICIENCY

Article 2

1. The Participating Countries shall establish a common emergency self-sufficiency in oil supplies. To this end, each Participating Country shall maintain emergency reserves sufficient to sustain consumption for at least 60 days with no net oil imports. Both consumption and net oil imports shall be reckoned at the average daily level of the preceding calendar year.

2. The Governing Board shall, acting by special majority, not later than 1st July, 1975, decide the date from which the emergency reserve commitment of each Participating Country shall, for the purpose of calculating its supply right referred to in Article 7, be deemed to be raised to a level of 90 days. Each Participating Country shall increase its actual level of emergency reserves to 90 days and shall endeavour to do so by the date so decided.

3. The term "emergency reserve commitment" means the emergency reserves equivalent to 60 days of net oil imports as set out in paragraph 1 and, from the date to be decided according to paragraph 2, to 90 days of net oil imports as set out in paragraph 2.

Article 3

1. The emergency reserve commitment set out in Article 2 may be satisfied by:
 — oil stocks,
 — fuel switching capacity,
 — stand-by oil production,
in accordance with the provisions of the Annex which forms an integral part of this Agreement.[17]

2. The Governing Board shall, acting by majority, not later than 1st July, 1975, decide the extent to which the emergency reserve commitment may be satisfied by the elements mentioned in paragraph 1.

Article 4

1. The Standing Group on Emergency Questions shall, on a continuing basis, review the effectiveness of the measures taken by each Participating Country to meet its emergency reserve commitment.

2. The Standing Group on Emergency Questions shall report to the Management Committee, which shall make proposals, as appropriate, to the Governing Board. The Governing Board may, acting by majority, adopt recommendations to Participating Countries.

Chapter II

DEMAND RESTRAINT

Article 5

1. Each participating Country shall at all times have ready a pro-

---

[17]The Annex, not reprinted here, sets forth technical criteria relating to the definition and measurement of emergency reserves.

gram of contingent oil demand restraint measures enabling it to reduce its rate of final consumption in accordance with Chapter IV.

2. The Standing Group on Emergency Questions shall, on a continuing basis, review and assess:

— each Participating Country's program of demand restraint measures,

—the effectiveness of measures actually taken by each Participating Country.

3. The Standing Group on Emergency Questions shall report to the Management Committee, which shall make proposals, as appropriate, to the Governing Board. The Governing Board may, acting by majority, adopt recommendations to Participating Countries.

Chapter III

ALLOCATION

Article 6

1. Each Participating Country shall take the necessary measures in order that allocation of oil will be carried out pursuant to this Chapter and Chapter IV.

2. The Standing Group on Emergency Questions shall, on a continuing basis, review and assess:

— each Participating Country's measures in order that allocation of oil will be carried out pursuant to this Chapter and Chapter IV,

— the effectiveness of measures actually taken by each Participating Country.

3. The Standing Group on Emergency Questions shall report to the Management Committee, which shall make proposals, as appropriate, to the Governing Board. The Governing Board may, acting by majority, adopt recommendations to Participating Countries.

4. The Governing Board shall, acting by majority, decide promptly on the practical procedures for the allocation of oil and on the procedures and modalities for the participation of oil companies therein within the framework of this Agreement.

Article 7

1. When allocation of oil is carried out pursuant to Article 13, 14, or 15, each Participating Country shall have a supply right equal to

its permissible consumption less its emergency reserve drawdown obligation.

2. A Participating Country whose supply right exceeds the sum of its normal domestic production and actual net imports available during an emergency shall have an allocation right which entitles it to additional net imports equal to that excess.

3. A Participating Country in which the sum of normal domestic production and actual net imports available during an emergency exceeds its supply right shall have an allocation obligation which requires it to supply, directly or indirectly, the quantity of oil equal to that excess to other Participating Countries. This would not preclude any Participating Country from maintaining exports of oil to non-participating countries.

4. The term "permissible consumption" means the average daily rate of final consumption allowed when emergency demand restraint at the applicable level has been activated; possible further voluntary demand restraint by any Participating Country shall not affect its allocation right or obligation.

5. The term "emergency reserve drawdown obligation" means the emergency reserve commitment of any Participating Country divided by the total emergency reserve commitment of the group and multiplied by the group supply shortfall.

6. The term "group supply shortfall" means the shortfall for the group as measured by the aggregate permissible consumption for the group minus the daily rate of oil supplies available to the group during an emergency.

7. The term "oil supplies available to the group" means

— all crude oil available to the group,

— all petroleum products imported from outside the group, and

— all finished products and refinery feedstocks which are produced in association with natural gas and crude oil and are available to the group.

8. The term "final consumption" means total domestic consumption of all finished petroleum products.

Article 8

1. When allocation of oil to a Participating Country is carried out pursuant to Article 17, that Participating Country shall

— sustain from its final consumption the reduction in its oil supplies up to a level equal to 7 per cent of its final consumption during the base period,

— have an allocation right equal to the reduction in its oil supplies which results in a reduction of its final consumption over and above that level.

2. The obligation to allocate this amount of oil is shared among the other Participating Countries on the basis of their final consumption during the base period.

3. The Participating Countries may meet their allocation obligations by any measures of their own choosing, including demand restraint measures or use of emergency reserves.

Article 9

1. For purposes of satisfying allocation rights and allocation obligations, the following elements will be included:

— all crude oil,
— all petroleum products,
— all refinery feedstocks, and
— all finished products produced in association with natural gas and crude oil.

2. To calculate a Participating Country's allocation right, petroleum products normally imported by that Participating Country, whether from other Participating Countries or from non-participating countries, shall be expressed in crude oil equivalents and treated as though they were imports of crude oil to that Participating Country.

3. Insofar as possible, normal channels of supply will be maintained as well as the normal supply proportions between crude oil and products and among different categories of crude oil and products.

4. When allocation takes place, an objective of the Program shall be that available crude oil and products shall, insofar as possible, be shared within the refining and distributing industries as well as between refining and distributing companies in accordance with historical supply patterns.

Article 10

1. The objectives of the Program shall include ensuring fair treatment for all Participating Countries and basing the price for allocated oil on the price conditions prevailing for comparable commercial transactions.

2. Questions relating to the price of oil allocated during an emergency shall be examined by the Standing Group on Emergency Questions.

Article 11

1. It is not an objective of the Program to seek to increase, in an emergency, the share of world oil supply that the group had under normal market conditions. Historical oil trade patterns should be preserved as far as is reasonable, and due account should be taken of the position of individual non-participating countries.

2. In order to maintain the principles set out in paragraph 1, the Management Committee shall make proposals, as appropriate, to the Governing Board, which, acting by majority, shall decide on such proposals.

Chapter IV

ACTIVATION

ACTIVATION

Article 12

Whenever the group as a whole or any Participating Country sustains or can reasonably be expected to sustain a reduction in its oil supplies, the emergency measures, which are the mandatory demand restraint referred to in Chapter II and the allocation of available oil referred to in Chapter III, shall be activated in accordance with this Chapter.

Article 13

Whenever the group sustains or can reasonably be expected to sustain a reduction in the daily rate of its oil supplies at least equal to 7 per cent of the average daily rate of its final consumption during the base period, each Participating Country shall implement demand restraint measures sufficient to reduce its final consumption by an amount equal to 7 per cent of its final consumption during the base period, and allocation of available oil among the Participating Countries shall take place in accordance with Articles 7, 9, 10 and 11.

Article 14

Whenever the group sustains or can reasonably be expected to sustain a reduction in the daily rate of its oil supplies at least equal to 12 per cent of the average daily rate of its final consumption during the base period, each Participating Country shall implement demand restraint measures sufficient to reduce its final consumption by an amount equal to 10 per cent of its final consumption during the base period, and allocation of available oil among the Participating Countries shall take place in accordance with Articles 7, 9, 10 and 11.

Article 15

When cumulative daily emergency reserve drawdown obligations as defined in Article 7 have reached 50 per cent of emergency reserve commitments and a decision has been taken in accordance with Article 20, each Participating Country shall take the measures so decided, and allocation of available oil among the Participating Countries shall take place in accordance with Articles 7, 9, 10 and 11.

Article 16

When demand restraint is activated in accordance with this Chapter, a Participating Country may substitute for demand restraint measures use of emergency reserves held in excess of its emergency reserve commitment as provided in the Program.

Article 17

1. Whenever any Participating Country sustains or can reasonably be expected to sustain a reduction in the daily rate of its oil supplies which results in a reduction of the daily rate of its final consumption by an amount exceeding 7 per cent of the average daily rate of its final consumption during the base period, allocation of available oil to that Participating Country shall take place in accordance with Articles 8 to 11.

2. Allocation of available oil shall also take place when the conditions in paragraph 1 are fulfilled in a major region of a Participating Country whose oil market is incompletely integrated. In this case, the allocation obligation of other Participating Countries shall be reduced by the theoretical allocation obligation of any other major region or regions of the Participating Country concerned.

Article 18

1. The term "base period" means the most recent four quarters with a delay of one quarter necessary to collect information. While emergency measures are applied with regard to the group or to a Participating Country, the base period shall remain fixed.

2. The Standing Group on Emergency Questions shall examine the base period set out in paragraph 1, taking into account in particular such factors as growth, seasonal variations in consumption and cyclical changes and shall, not later than 1st April, 1975, report to the Management Committee. The Management Committee shall make proposals, as appropriate, to the Governing Board, which, acting by majority, shall decide on these proposals not later than 1st July, 1975.

Article 19

1. The Secretariat shall make a finding when a reduction of oil supplies as mentioned in Article 13, 14 or 17 has occurred or can reasonably be expected to occur, and shall establish the amount of the reduction or expected reduction for each Participating Country and for the group. The Secretariat shall keep the Management Committee informed of its deliberations, and shall immediately report its finding to the members of the Committee and inform the Participating Countries thereof. The report shall include information on the nature of the reduction.

2. Within 48 hours of the Secretariat's reporting a finding, the Committee shall meet to review the accuracy of the data compiled and the information provided. The Committee shall report to the Governing Board within a further 48 hours. The report shall set out the views expressed by the members of the Committee, including any views regarding the handling of the emergency.

3. Within 48 hours of receiving the Management Committee's report, the Governing Board shall meet to review the finding of the Secretariat in the light of that report. The activation of emergency measures shall be considered confirmed and Participating Countries shall implement such measures within 15 days of such confirmation unless the Governing Board, acting by special majority, decides within a further 48 hours not to activate the emergency measures, to activate them only in part or to fix another time limit for their implementation.

4. If, according to the finding of the Secretariat, the conditions of more than one of the Articles 14, 13 and 17 are fulfilled, any decision not to activate emergency measures shall be taken separately

for each Article and in the above order. If the conditions in Article 17 are fulfilled with regard to more than one Participating Country any decision not to activate allocation shall be taken separately with respect to each Country.

5. Decisions pursuant to paragraphs 3 and 4 may at any time be reversed by the Governing Board, acting by majority.

6. In making its finding under this Article, the Secretariat shall consult with oil companies to obtain their views regarding the situation and the appropriateness of the measures to be taken.

7. An international advisory board from the oil industry shall be convened, not later than the activation of emergency measures, to assist the Agency in ensuring the effective operation of such measures.

Article 20

1. The Secretariat shall make a finding when cumulative daily emergency reserve drawdown obligations have reached or can reasonably be expected to reach 50 per cent of emergency reserve commitments. The Secretariat shall immediately report its finding to the members of the Management Committee and inform the Participating Countries thereof. The report shall include information on the oil situation.

2. Within 72 hours of the Secretariat's reporting such a finding, the Management Committee shall meet to review the data compiled and the information provided. On the basis of available information the Committee shall report to the Governing Board within a further 48 hours proposing measures required for meeting the necessities of the situation, including the increase in the level of mandatory demand restraint that may be necessary. The report shall set out the views expressed by the members of the Committee.

3. The Governing Board shall meet within 48 hours of receiving the Committee's report and proposal. The Governing Board shall review the finding of the Secretariat and the report of the Management Committee and shall within a further 48 hours, acting by special majority, decide on the measures required for meeting the necessities of the situation, including the increase in the level of mandatory demand restraint that may be necessary.

Article 21

1. Any Participating Country may request the Secretariat to make a finding under Article 19 or 20.

2. If, within 72 hours of such request, the Secretariat does not make such a finding, the Participating Country may request the Management Committee to meet and consider the situation in accordance with the provisions of this Agreement.

3. The Management Committee shall meet within 48 hours of such request in order to consider the situation. It shall, at the request of any Participating Country, report to the Governing Board within a further 48 hours. The report shall set out the views expressed by the members of the Committee and by the Secretariat, including any views regarding the handling of the situation.

4. The Governing Board shall meet within 48 hours of receiving the Management Committee's report. If it finds, acting by majority, that the conditions set out in Article 13, 14, 15 or 17 are fulfilled, emergency measures shall be activated accordingly.

Article 22

The Governing Board may at any time decide by unanimity to activate any appropriate emergency measures not provided for in this Agreement, if the situation so requires.

DEACTIVATION

Article 23

1. The Secretariat shall make a finding when a reduction of supplies as mentioned in Article 13, 14 or 17 has decreased or can reasonably be expected to decrease below the level referred to in the relevant Article. The Secretariat shall keep the Management Committee informed of its deliberations and shall immediately report its finding to the members of the Committee and inform the Participating Countries thereof.

2. Within 72 hours of the Secretariat's reporting a finding, the Management Committee shall meet to review the data compiled and the information provided. It shall report to the Governing Board within a further 48 hours. The report shall set out the views expressed by the members of the Committee, including any views regarding the handling of the emergency.

3. Within 48 hours of receiving the Committee's report, the Governing Board shall meet to review the finding of the Secretariat in the light of the report from the Management Committee. The deactivation of emergency measures or the applicable reduction of the demand restraint level shall be considered confirmed unless the

Governing Board, acting by special majority, decides within a further 48 hours to maintain the emergency measures or to deactivate them only in part.

4. In making its finding under this Article, the Secretariat shall consult with the international advisory board, mentioned in Article 19, paragraph 7, to obtain its views regarding the situation and the appropriateness of the measures to be taken.

5. Any Participating Country may request the Secretariat to make a finding under this Article.

Article 24

When emergency measures are in force, and the Secretariat has not made a finding under Article 23, the Governing Board, acting by special majority, may at any time decide to deactivate the measures either wholly or in part.

Chapter V

INFORMATION SYSTEM ON THE INTERNATIONAL OIL MARKET

Article 25

1. The Participating Countries shall establish an Information System consisting of two sections:

- a General Section on the situation in the international oil market and activities of all companies,
- a Special Section designed to ensure the efficient operation of the measures described in Chapters I to IV.

2. The System shall be operated on a permanent basis, both under normal conditions and during emergencies, and in a manner which ensures the confidentiality of the information made available.

3. The Secretariat shall be responsible for the operation of the Information System and shall make the information compiled available to the Participating Countries.

* * *

Chapter VI

FRAMEWORK FOR CONSULTATION WITH OIL COMPANIES

Article 37

1. The Participating Countries shall establish within the Agency a permanent framework for consultation within which one or more Participating Countries may, in an appropriate manner, consult with and request information from individual oil companies on all important aspects of the oil industry, and within which the Participating Countries may share among themselves on a co-operative basis the results of such consultations.

2. The framework for consultation shall be established under the auspices of the Standing Group on the Oil Market.

3. Within 60 days of the first day of the provisional application of this Agreement, and as appropriate thereafter, the Standing Group on the Oil Market, after consultation with oil companies, shall submit a report to the Management Committee on the procedures for such consultations. The Management Committee shall review the report and make proposals to the Governing Board, which, within 30 days of the submission of the report to the Management Committee, and acting by majority, shall decide on such procedures.

* * *

Chapter VII

LONG TERM CO-OPERATION ON ENERGY

Article 41

1. The Participating Countries are determined to reduce over the longer term their dependence on imported oil for meeting their total energy requirements.

2. To this end, the Participating Countries will undertake national programs and promote the adoption of co-operative programs, including, as appropriate, the sharing of means and efforts, while concerting national policies, in the areas set out in Article 42.

Article 42

1. The Standing Group on Long Term Co-operation shall examine and report to the Management Committee on co-operative action. The following areas shall in particular be considered:

*(a)*Conservation of energy, including co-operative programs on
—exchange of national experiences and information on energy conservation;
—ways and means for reducing the growth of energy consumption through conservation.

*(b)*Development of alternative sources of energy such as domestic oil, coal, natural gas, nuclear energy and hydroelectric power, including co-operative programs on
—exchange of information on such matters as resources, supply and demand, price and taxation;
—ways and means for reducing the growth of consumption of imported oil through the development of alternative sources of energy;
—concrete projects, including jointly financed projects;
—criteria, quality objectives and standards for environmental protection.

*(c)*Energy research and development, including as a matter of priority co-operative programs on
—coal technology;
—solar energy;
—radioactive waste management;
—controlled thermonuclear fusion;
—production of hydrogen from water;
—nuclear safety;
—waste heat utilisation;
—conservation of energy;
—municipal and industrial waste utilisation for energy conservation;
—overall energy system analysis and general studies.

*(d)*Uranium enrichment, including co-operative programs
—to monitor developments in natural and enriched uranium supply;
—to facilitate development of natural uranium resources and enrichment services;
—to encourage such consultations as may be required to deal with international issues that may arise in relation to the expansion of enriched uranium supply;
—to arrange for the requisite collection, analysis and dissemination of data related to the planning of enrichment services.

2. In examining the areas of co-operative action, the Standing Group shall take due account of ongoing activities elsewhere.

3. Programs developed under paragraph 1 may be jointly financed. Such joint financing may take place in accordance with Article 64, paragraph 2.

Article 43

1. The Management Committee shall review the reports of the Standing Group and make appropriate proposals to the Governing Board, which shall decide on these proposals not later than 1st July, 1975.

2. The Governing Board shall take into account possibilities for co-operation within a broader framework.

Chapter VIII

RELATIONS WITH PRODUCER COUNTRIES AND WITH OTHER CONSUMER COUNTRIES

Article 44

The Participating Countries will endeavour to promote co-operative relations with oil producing countries and with other oil consuming countries, including developing countries. They will keep under review developments in the energy field with a view to identifying opportunities for and promoting a purposeful dialogue, as well as other forms of co-operation, with producer countries and with other consumer countries.

Article 45

To achieve the objectives set out in Article 44, the Participating Countries will give full consideration to the needs and interests of other oil consuming countries, particularly those of the developing countries.

Article 46

The Participating Countries will, in the context of the Program, exchange views on their relations with oil producing countries. To this end, the Participating Countries should inform each other of co-operative action on their part with producer countries which is relevant to the objectives of the Program.

Article 47

The Participating Countries will, in the context of the Program

— seek, in the light of their continuous review of developments in the international energy situation and its effect on the world economy, opportunities and means of encouraging stable international trade in oil and of promoting secure oil supplies on reasonable and equitable terms for each Participating Country;

— consider, in the light of work going on in other international organisations, other possible fields of co-operation including the prospects for co-operation in accelerated industrialisation and socio-economic development in the principal producing areas and the implications of this for international trade and investment;

— keep under review the prospects for co-operation with oil producing countries on energy questions of mutual interest, such as conservation of energy, the development of alternative sources, and research and development.

Article 48

1. The Standing Group on Relations with Producer and other Consumer Countries will examine and report to the Management Committee on the matters described in this Chapter.

2. The Management Committee may make proposals on appropriate co-operative action regarding these matters to the Governing Board, which shall decide on such proposals.

Chapter IX

INSTITUTIONAL AND GENERAL PROVISIONS

Article 49

1. The Agency shall have the following organs:
—a Governing Board

—a Management Committee
—Standing Groups on
—Emergency Questions
—The Oil Market
—Long Term Co-operation
—Relations with Producer and Other Consumer Countries.

2. The Governing Board or the Management Committee may, acting by majority, establish any other organ necessary for the implementation of the Program.

3. The Agency shall have a Secretariat to assist the organs mentioned in paragraphs 1 and 2.

GOVERNING BOARD

Article 50

1. The Governing Board shall be composed of one or more ministers or their delegates from each Participating Country.

2. The Governing Board, acting by majority, shall adopt its own rules of procedure. Unless otherwise decided in the rules of procedure, these rules shall also apply to the Management Committee and the Standing Groups.

3. The Governing Board, acting by majority, shall elect its Chairman and Vice-Chairmen.

Article 51

1. The Governing Board shall adopt decisions and make recommendations which are necessary for the proper functioning of the Program.

2. The Governing Board shall review periodically and take appropriate action concerning developments in the international energy situation, including problems relating to the oil supplies of any Participating Country or Countries, and the economic and monetary implications of these developments. In its activities concerning the economic and monetary implications of developments in the international energy situation, the Governing Board shall take into account the competence and activities of international institutions responsible for overall economic and monetary questions.

3. The Governing Board, acting by majority, may delegate any of its functions to any other organ of the Agency.

Article 52

1. Subject to Article 61, paragraph 2, and Article 65, decisions adopted pursuant to this Agreement by the Governing Board or by any other organ by delegation from the Board shall be binding on the Participating Countries.

2. Recommendations shall not be binding.

MANAGEMENT COMMITTEE

Article 53

1. The Management Committee shall be composed of one or more senior representatives of the Government of each Participating Country.

2. The Management Committee shall carry out the functions assigned to it in this Agreement and any other function delegated to it by the Governing Board.

3. The Management Committee may examine and make proposals to the Governing Board, as appropriate, on any matter within the scope of this Agreement.

4. The Management Committee shall be convened upon the request of any Participating Country.

5. The Management Committee, acting by majority, shall elect its Chairman and Vice-Chairmen.

*   *   *

SECRETARIAT

Article 59

1. The Secretariat shall be composed of an Executive Director and such staff as is necessary.

2. The Executive Director shall be appointed by the Governing Board.

3. In the performance of their duties under this Agreement the Executive Director and the staff shall be responsible to and report to the organs of the Agency.

4. The Governing Board, acting by majority, shall take all decisions necessary for the establishment and the functioning of the Secretariat.

Article 60

The Secretariat shall carry out the functions assigned to it in this Agreement and any other function assigned to it by the Governing Board.

VOTING

Article 61

1. The Governing Board shall adopt decisions and recommendations for which no express voting provision is made in this Agreement, as follows:
   (a) by majority:
     —decisions on the management of the Program, including decisions applying provisions of this Agreement which already impose specific obligations on Participating Countries
     —decisions on procedural questions
     —recommendations
   (b) by unanimity:
     —all other decisions, including in particular decisions which impose on Participating Countries new obligations not already specified in this Agreement.

2. Decisions mentioned in paragraph 1 (b) may provide:
   (a) that they shall not be binding on one or more Participating Countries;
   (b) that they shall be binding only under certain conditions.

Article 62

1. Unanimity shall require all of the votes of the Participating Countries present and voting. Countries abstaining shall be considered as not voting.

2. When majority or special majority is required, the Participating Countries shall have the following voting weights:

	General voting weights	Oil consumption voting weights	Combined voting weights
Austria	3	1	4
Belgium	3	2	5
Canada	3	5	8
Denmark	3	1	4
Germany	3	8	11
Ireland	3	0	3
Italy	3	6	9
Japan	3	15	18
Luxembourg	3	0	3
The Netherlands	3	2	5
Spain	3	2	5
Sweden	3	2	5
Switzerland	3	1	4
Turkey	3	1	4
United Kingdom	3	6	9
United States	3	48	51
Totals	48	100	148

3. Majority shall require 60 per cent of the total combined voting weights and 50 per cent of the general voting weights cast.

4. Special majority shall require:

(a) 60 per cent of the total combined voting weights and 36 general voting weights for:

—the decision under Article 2, paragraph 2, relating to the increase in the emergency reserve commitment;

—decisions under Article 19, paragraph 3, not to activate the emergency measures referred to in Articles 13 and 14;

—decisions under Article 20, paragraph 3, on the measures required for meeting the necessities of the situation;

—decisions under Article 23, paragraph 3, to maintain the emergency measures referred to in Articles 13 and 14;

—decisions under Article 24 to deactivate the emergency measures referred to in Articles 13 and 14.

(b) 42 general voting weights for:

—decisions under Article 19, paragraph 3, not to activate the emergency measures referred to in Article 17;

—decisions under Article 23, paragraph 3, to maintain the emergency measures referred to in Article 17;

—decisions under Article 24 to deactivate the emergency measures referred to in Article 17.

5. The Governing Board, acting by unanimity, shall decide on the necessary increase, decrease, and redistribution of the voting weights referred to in paragraph 2, as well as on amendment of the voting requirements set out in paragraphs 3 and 4 in the event that

—a Country accedes to this Agreement in accordance with Article 71, or

—a Country withdraws from this Agreement in accordance with Article 68, paragraph 2, or Article 69, paragraph 2.

6. The Governing Board shall review annually the number and distribution of voting weights specified in paragraph 2, and, on the basis of such review, acting by unanimity, shall decide whether such voting weights should be increased or decreased, or redistributed, or both, because a change in any Participating Country's share in total oil consumption has occurred or for any other reason.

7. Any change in paragraph 2, 3 or 4 shall be based on the concepts underlying those paragraphs and paragraph 6.

RELATIONS WITH OTHER ENTITIES

Article 63

In order to achieve the objectives of the Program, the Agency may establish appropriate relations with non-participating countries, international organisations, whether governmental or nongovernmental, other entities and individuals.

FINANCIAL ARRANGEMENTS

Article 64

1. The expenses of the Secretariat and all other common expenses shall be shared among all Participating Countries according to a scale of contributions elaborated according to the principles and rules set out in the Annex to the "OECD Resolution of the Council on Determination of the Scale of Contributions by Member Countries to the Budget of the Organisation" of 10th December, 1963. After the first year of application of this Agreement, the Governing

Board shall review this scale of contributions and, acting by unanimity, shall decide upon any appropriate changes in accordance with Article 73.

2. Special expenses incurred in connection with special activities carried out pursuant to Article 65 shall be shared by the Participating Countries taking part in such special activities in such proportions as shall be determined by unanimous agreement between them.

3. The Executive Director shall, in accordance with the financial regulations adopted by the Governing Board and not later than 1st October of each year, submit to the Governing Board a draft budget including personnel requirements. The Governing Board, acting by majority, shall adopt the budget.

4. The Governing Board, acting by majority, shall take all other necessary decisions regarding the financial administration of the Agency.

5. The financial year shall begin on 1st January and end on 31st December of each year. At the end of each financial year, revenues and expenditures shall be submitted to audit.

SPECIAL ACTIVITIES

Article 65

1. Any two or more Participating Countries may decide to carry out within the scope of this Agreement special activities, other than activities which are required to be carried out by all Participating Countries under Chapters I to V. Participating Countries which do not wish to take part in such special activities shall abstain from taking part in such decisions and shall not be bound by them. Participating Countries carrying out such activities shall keep the Governing Board informed thereof.

2. For the implementation of such special activities, the Participating Countries concerned may agree upon voting procedures other than those provided for in Articles 61 and 62.

IMPLEMENTATION OF THE AGREEMENT

Article 66

Each Participating Country shall take the necessary measures, including any necessary legislative measures, to implement this Agreement and decisions taken by the Governing Board.

Chapter X

FINAL PROVISIONS

Article 67

1. Each Signatory State shall, not later than 1st May, 1975, notify the Government of the Kingdom of Belgium that, having complied with its constitutional procedures, it consents to be bound by this Agreement.

2. On the tenth day following the day on which at least six States holding at least 60 per cent of the combined voting weights mentioned in Article 62 have deposited a notification of consent to be bound or an instrument of accession, this Agreement shall enter into force for such States.[18]

3. For each Signatory State which deposits its notification thereafter, this Agreement shall enter into force on the tenth day following the day of deposit.

4. The Governing Board, acting by majority, may upon request from any Signatory State decide to extend, with respect to that State, the time limit for notification beyond 1st May, 1975.

Article 68

1. Notwithstanding the provisions of Article 67, this Agreement shall be applied provisionally by all Signatory States, to the extent possible not inconsistent with their legislation, as from 18th November, 1974 following the first meeting of the Governing Board.

2. Provisional application of the Agreement shall continue until:

— the Agreement enters into force for the State concerned in accordance with Article 67, or
— 60 days after the Government of the Kingdom of Belgium receives notification that the State concerned will not consent to be bound by the Agreement, or
— the time limit for notification of consent by the State concerned referred to in Article 67 expires.

---

[18]Following deposit of the U.S. notification on Jan. 9, 1976, the agreement entered into force definitively Jan. 19, 1976.

Article 69

1. This Agreement shall remain in force for a period of ten years from the date of its entry into force and shall continue in force thereafter unless and until the Governing Board, acting by majority, decides on its termination.

2. Any Participating Country may terminate the application of this Agreement for its part upon twelve months' written notice to the Government of the Kingdom of Belgium to that effect, given not less than three years after the first day of the provisional application of this Agreement.

Article 70

1. Any State may, at the time of signature, notification of consent to be bound in accordance with Article 67, accession or at any later date, declare by notification addressed to the Government of the Kingdom of Belgium that this Agreement shall apply to all or any of the territories for whose international relations it is responsible, or to any territories within its frontiers for whose oil supplies it is legally responsible.

2. Any declaration made pursuant to paragraph 1 may, in respect of any territory mentioned in such declaration, be withdrawn in accordance with the provisions of Article 69, paragraph 2.

Article 71

1. This Agreement shall be open for accession by any Member of the Organisation for Economic Co-operation and Development which is able and willing to meet the requirements of the Program. The Governing Board, acting by majority, shall decide on any request for accession.[19]

2. This Agreement shall enter into force for any State whose request for accession has been granted on the tenth day following the deposit of its instrument of accession with the Government of the Kingdom of Belgium, or on the date of entry into force of the Agreement pursuant to Article 67, paragraph 2, whichever is the later.

3. Until 1st May, 1975, accession may take place on a provisional basis under the conditions set out in Article 68.

[19]New Zealand acceded to the agreement effective Mar. 21, 1975, and Norway was admitted to participation as an associate member.

Article 72

1. This Agreement shall be open for accession by the European Communities.

2. This Agreement shall not in any way impede the further implementation of the treaties establishing the European Communities.

Article 73

This Agreement may at any time be amended by the Governing Board, acting by unanimity. Such amendment shall come into force in a manner determined by the Governing Board, acting by unanimity and making provision for Participating Countries to comply with their respective constitutional procedures.

Article 74

This Agreement shall be subject to a general review after 1st May, 1980.

Article 75

The Government of the Kingdom of Belgium shall notify all Participating Countries of the deposit of each notification of consent to be bound in accordance with Article 67, and of each instrument of accession, of the entry into force of this Agreement or any amendment thereto, of any denunciation thereof, and of any other declaration or notification received.

Article 76

The original of this Agreement, of which the English, French and German texts are equally authentic, shall be deposited with the Government of the Kingdom of Belgium, and a certified copy thereof shall be furnished to each other Participating Country by the Government of the Kingdom of Belgium.

IN WITNESS WHEREOF the undersigned, being duly authorized thereto by their respective Governments, have signed this Agreement.

DONE at Paris, this eighteenth day of November, Nineteen Hundred and Seventy Four.

30. A VISIT TO EAST ASIA

(November 18-29, 1974)

[Nineteen seventy-four was an extraordinary year for presidential travels and summit diplomacy. President Nixon, before his resignation, had been twice to Western Europe, once to the Middle East and the Azores, and once to the Soviet Union. President Ford, in addition to numerous meetings with foreign leaders in Washington, had gone to the Mexican border to meet with President Echeverría and now, in mid-November, was about to embark upon a week-long visit to the Far East in the course of which he would hold talks with the leaders of two allied countries, Japan and the Republic of Korea, as well as the ranking political authority in the Soviet Union. The presidential calendar for December would include an important meeting with President Giscard d'Estaing in Martinique and talks in Washington with Canadian Prime Minister Trudeau and Chancellor Schmidt.[1]

The journey to Alaska and across the Pacific occurred at a moment when events in Washington and elsewhere had accentuated the need to reassure allied governments about the steadfastness of American purposes. As Watergate and President Nixon faded into history, uncertainties about the trend of U.S. foreign policy had persisted and even increased in view of the comparative inexperience of the new President, the constantly deepening economic crisis, and the heavy losses sustained by Republican candidates in the November 5 congressional elections. Japan and Korea, too, had been experiencing internal convulsions and currently found themselves in a condition where any display of American solidarity—or its absence—might have important repercussions in their domestic as well as foreign affairs.

The trip to Japan, originally planned by President Nixon though

[1]Cf. Chapter 34.

491

ultimately undertaken by his successor, occurred midway in the political decline and fall of Prime Minister Kakuei Tanaka, the self-made politician who had thrust his way to leadership of Japan's ruling Liberal Democratic Party in 1972, achieved at least a temporary stabilization of relations with mainland China, but more recently had lost political momentum and, by the fall of 1974, was already being charged with large-scale financial improprieties and corrupt political practices. A cabinet reorganization carried out in Tokyo just a week before President Ford's arrival had failed to temper the anti-Tanaka fervor of such rival Liberal Democratic leaders as Takeo Fukuda and Takeo Miki, the latter of whom was to succeed Tanaka as party President and Prime Minister not many days after Mr. Ford's departure.

This presidential visit also marked the final stage of the long and tortuous processes initiated by Dr. Kissinger's "Year of Europe" address of April 23, 1973, in which he had urged agreement on a written statement of the principles underlying the U.S.-European-Japanese association.[2] The quest for a universally acceptable formula having ultimately proved fruitless, the United States had been forced to settle, on the European side, for the NATO "Declaration on Atlantic Relations"[3] and, on the Japanese side, for a vaguely worded declaration setting forth principles ostensibly held in common by the United States and its Pacific associate. An enumeration of "the . . . common purposes underlying future relations between the United States and Japan" thus made up the bulk of the joint communiqué that was issued on behalf of President Ford and Prime Minister Tanaka as they concluded their formal discussions on November 20.]

(65) Presidential Visit to Japan, November 18-22, 1974: Joint communiqué issued by President Ford and Prime Minister Kakuei Tanaka, Tokyo, November 20, 1974.[4]

I

President Ford of the United States of America paid an official visit to Japan between November 18 and 22 at the invitation of the Government of Japan. President Ford met Their Majesties the Emperor and Empress of Japan at the Imperial Palace on November 19.

---

[2]*AFR, 1973*: 181-9.
[3]Chapter 14, Document 21b.
[4]Text from *Presidential Documents*, 10: 1481-3. Activities during the remainder of the President's visit to Japan are listed in same: 1508.

II

In discussions held on November 19 and 20, President Ford and Prime Minister Tanaka agreed on the following common purposes underlying future relations between the United States and Japan.

1. The United States and Japan, Pacific nations sharing many political and economic interests, have developed a close and mutually beneficial relationship based on the principle of equality. Their friendship and cooperation are founded upon a common determination to maintain political systems respecting individual freedom and fundamental human rights as well as market economies which enhance the scope for creativity and the prospect of assuring the well-being of their peoples.

2. Dedicated to the maintenance of peace and the evolution of a stable international order reflecting the high purposes and principles of the Charter of the United Nations, the United States and Japan will continue to encourage the development of conditions in the Asia-Pacific area which will facilitate peaceful settlement of outstanding issues by the parties most concerned, reduce international tensions, promote the sustained and orderly growth of developing countries, and encourage constructive relationships among countries in the area. Each country will contribute to this task in the light of its own responsibilities and capabilities. Both countries recognize that cooperative relations between the United States and Japan under the Treaty of Mutual Cooperation and Security[5] constitute an important and durable element in the evolution of the international situation in Asia and will continue to plan [*sic*: play?] an effective and meaningful role in promoting peace and stability in that area.

3. The United States and Japan recognize the need for dedicated efforts by all countries to pursue additional arms limitation and arms reduction measures, in particular controls over nuclear armaments, and to prevent the further spread of nuclear weapons or other explosive devices while facilitating the expanded use of nuclear energy for peaceful purposes. Both countries underline the high responsibility of all nuclear-weapon states in such efforts, and note the importance of protecting non-nuclear-weapon states against nuclear threats.

4. The United States and Japan recognize the remarkable range of their interdependence and the need for coordinated responses to new problems confronting the international community. They will intensify efforts to promote close cooperation among industrialized

[5]Signed at Washington Jan. 19, 1960 and entered into force June 23, 1960 (TIAS 4509; 11 UST 1632); text and related documents in *Documents, 1960*: 425-31.

democracies while striving steadily to encourage a further relaxation of tensions in the world through dialogue and exchanges with countries of different social systems.

5. In view of the growing interdependence of all countries and present global economic difficulties, it is becoming increasingly important to strengthen international economic cooperation. The United States and Japan recognize the necessity of the constructive use of their human and material resources to bring about solutions to major economic problems. The establishment of an open and harmonious world economic system is indispensable for international peace and prosperity and a primary goal of both nations. The United States and Japan will, to this end, continue to promote close economic and trade relations between the two countries and participate constructively in international efforts to ensure a continuing expansion of world trade through negotiations to reduce tariff and other trade distortions and to create a stable and balanced international monetary order. Both countries will remain committed to their international pledges to avoid actions which adversely affect the economies of other nations.

6. The United States and Japan recognize the need for a more efficient and rational utilization and distribution of world resources. Realizing the importance of stable supplies of energy at reasonable prices they will seek, in a manner suitable to their economies, to expand and diversify energy supplies, develop new energy sources, and conserve on the use of scarce fuels. They both attach great importance to enhancing cooperation among consuming countries and they intend, in concert with other nations, to pursue harmonious relations with producing nations. Both countries agree that further international cooperative efforts are necessary to forestall an economic and financial crisis and to lead to a new era of creativity and common progress. Recognizing the urgency of the world food problem and the need for an international framework to ensure stable food supplies, the United States and Japan will participate constructively in multilateral efforts to seek ways to strengthen assistance to developing countries in the field of agriculture, to improve the supply situation of agricultural products, and to assure an adequate level of food reserves. They recognize the need for cooperation among food producers and consumers to deal with shortage situations.

7. For the well-being of the peoples of the world, a steady improvement in the technological and economic capabilities of developing countries must be a matter of common concern to all nations. In recognition of the importance of assisting developing countries, particularly those without significant natural resources, the United States and Japan will, individually and with the par-

ticipation and support of other traditional aid-donors and those newly able to assist, maintain and expand programs of cooperation through assistance and trade as those nations seek to achieve sound and orderly growth.

8. The United States and Japan face many new challenges common to mankind as they endeavor to preserve the natural environment and to open new areas for exploration such as space and the oceans. In broad cooperation with other countries, they will promote research and facilitate the exchange of information in such fields as science, technology and environmental protection, in an effort to meet the needs of modern society, improve the quality of life and attain more balanced economic growth.

9. The United States and Japan recognize that their durable friendship has been based upon the continued development of mutual understanding and enhanced communication between their peoples, at many levels and in many aspects of their lives. They will seek therefore to expand further cultural and educational interchange which fosters and serves to increase such understanding.

10. In the spirit of friendship and mutual trust, the United States and Japan are determined to keep each other fully informed and to strengthen the practice of frank and timely consultations on potential bilateral issues and pressing global problems of common concern.

11. Friendly and cooperative relations between the United States and Japan have grown and deepened over the years in many diverse fields of human endeavor. Both countries reaffirm that, in their totality, these varied relationships constitute major foundation stones on which the two countries base their respective foreign policies and form an indispensable element supporting stable international political and economic relations.

III

This first visit to Japan by an incumbent President of the United States of America will add a new page to the history of amity between the two countries.

[Not mentioned in the official communiqué was the acceptance by Emperor Hirohito and Empress Nagako of a renewed invitation to undertake a state visit to the United States, a commitment ultimately carried out on September 30-October 13, 1975. Some of the other questions touched on by the President and Prime Minister were mentioned to the press by Secretary Kissinger, who stressed cooperation in energy and food matters but failed to illuminate significantly a controversy that had recently broken out with regard to the alleged presence of nuclear weapons on U.S. naval vessels using Japanese ports. This matter, the Secretary indicated, would be handled within the framework of the Mutual Security Treaty and with what he described as the usual American understanding of Japanese sensitivities.[6]

A presidential visit to the Republic of Korea in 1974 was bound to assume a rather more controversial character than the visit to America's major Far Eastern ally. Never especially sympathetic to democratic ways, the South Korean Government of President Park Chung Hee had lately incurred increasing criticism both at home and abroad by reason of the political trials, curtailments of civil liberties, and other authoritarian practices allegedly made necessary by the threat from Communist North Korea. Symptomatic in some ways of the unease that currently prevailed in South Korea had been the fatal shooting of President Park's wife on August 15 in an unsuccessful attempt to assassinate the President by a Korean resident of Japan. While South Korean liberals demanded repeal of the authoritarian constitution imposed in 1972, increasing doubts were being expressed within the United States about the justification for maintaining nearly 40,000 American troops in South Korea and shoring up its authoritarian government with substantial annual increments of U.S. military aid. A presidential visit at such a time, it had been suggested, might seem to place a stamp of American approval on the Park regime's internal practices.

The other side of the question was briefly expounded by Secretary Kissinger at a news conference in Tokyo. South Korea, he pointed out, was after all an accredited ally of the United States, one whose security was important both to the United States and to Japan as well. It "would have created all the wrong impressions," in Dr. Kissinger's opinion, "for the President to be in Japan and not pay the visit over such a short distance to Korea." Asked whether President Ford was "going to express any degree of dissatisfaction with the degree of political oppression in South Korea," the Secretary of State replied: "We have stated the importance that we attach to the security of South Korea. We have also, I believe, made clear our general view with respect to the form of domestic conduct we prefer, but I do not want to predict now what the President will discuss in his private talks with President Park. We are not," he added, "going to South Korea in order to discuss—much less to announce—any reduction of forces."[7]

Anything that President Ford may actually have said on this delicate issue was carefully excluded from the official communiqué

[6] *Bulletin*, 71: 883-6.
[7] *Bulletin*, 71: 892.

released at the conclusion of his Korean visit, during which he found time for a meeting with American forces and was able to assure President Park that the United States had no plan to reduce their current level. Observing the lack of recent progress in the three-year-old "dialogue" between North and South Korea, the two leaders also reviewed the status of the annual debate on the Korean problem in the U.N. General Assembly, where a group of Communist and "third world" countries was as usual calling for the withdrawal of American forces from Korea, whereas the United States and other friends of the Seoul government continued to urge dialogue and eventual peaceful reunification. The major emphasis of the Ford-Park discussions, however, was clearly directed to the continued underwriting by the United States of South Korea's military position, in part by American troop deployments and in part, it was understood, by further support (subject to congressional concurrence) of Seoul's $400-500 million military modernization program.[8]]

(66) *Visit to the Republic of Korea, November 22-23, 1974: Joint communiqué of President Ford and President Park Chung Hee, Seoul, November 22, 1974.*[9]

At the invitation of President Park Chung Hee of the Republic of Korea, President Gerald R. Ford of the United States of America visited the Republic of Korea on November 22 and 23, 1974, to exchange views on the current international situation and to discuss matters of mutual interest and concern to the two nations.

During the visit the two Presidents held discussions on two occasions. Present at these meetings were Prime Minister Kim Chong Pil, Secretary of State Henry Kissinger, Foreign Minister Kim Dong Jo, Presidential Secretary General Kim Chung Yum, Ambassador Richard L. Sneider, Ambassador Hahm Pyong Choon and other high officials of both Governments. President Ford also visited American forces stationed in the Republic of Korea.

President Ford laid a wreath at the Memorial of the Unknown Soldiers. He also visited the grave of Madame Park Chung Hee and expressed his deepest personal condolences to President Park on her tragic and untimely death.

The two Presidents reaffirmed the strong bonds of friendship and cooperation between their two countries. They agreed to continue the close cooperation and regular consultation on security matters and other subjects of mutual interest which have characterized the relationship between the Republic of Korea and the United States.

The two Presidents took note of significant political and economic changes in the situation in Asia in recent years. They recognized that the allied countries in the area are growing stronger and more prosperous and are making increasing contributions to their security as well as to that of the region. President Ford explained that the United States, as a Pacific power, is vitally interested in Asia and the Pacific and will continue its best effort to ensure the peace and security of the region. President Park expressed his understanding and full support for United States policies directed toward these ends.

President Park described the efforts being made by the Republic of Korea to maintain a dialogue with North Korea, designed to reduce tensions and establish peace on the Korean Peninsula, and to lead eventually to the peaceful unification of Korea. President Park affirmed the intention of the Republic of Korea to continue to pursue the dialogue despite the failure of the North Korean authorities to respond with sincerity thus far. President Ford gave assurance that the United States will continue to support these efforts by the Republic of Korea and expressed the hope that the constructive initiatives by the Republic of Korea would meet with positive responses by all concerned.

The two Presidents discussed the current United Nations General Assembly consideration of the Korean question. They agreed on the importance of favorable General Assembly action on the Draft Resolution introduced by the United States and other member countries.[10] Both expressed the hope that the General Assembly would base its consideration of the Korean question on a recognition of the importance of the security arrangements which have preserved peace on the Korean Peninsula for more than two decades.

President Park explained in detail the situation on the Korean Peninsula, and described the threat to peace and stability of hostile acts by North Korea, exemplified most recently by the construction of an underground tunnel inside the southern sector of the Demilitarized Zone.

The two Presidents agreed that the Republic of Korea forces and American forces stationed in Korea must maintain a high degree of strength and readiness in order to deter aggression. President Ford reaffirmed the determination of the United States to render prompt and effective assistance to repel armed attack against the Republic of Korea in accordance with the Mutual Defense Treaty of 1954

---

[10]Cf. Chapter 32 at note 7.

between the Republic of Korea and the United States.[11] In this connection, President Ford assured President Park that the United States has no plan to reduce the present level of United States forces in Korea.

The two Presidents discussed the progress of the Modernization Program for the Republic of Korea armed forces and agreed that implementation of the program is of major importance to the security of the Republic of Korea and peace on the Korean Peninsula. President Ford took note of the increasing share of the defense burden which the Republic of Korea is able and willing to assume and affirmed the readiness of the United States to continue to render appropriate support to the further development of defense industries in the Republic of Korea.

President Ford expressed his admiration for the rapid and sustained economic progress of the Republic of Korea, accomplished in the face of various obstacles, including the lack of sufficient indigenous natural resources and continuing tensions in the area. President Park noted with appreciation the United States contribution to Korea's development in the economic, scientific and technological fields.

The two Presidents examined the impact of recent international economic developments. They agreed that the two countries should continue to foster close economic cooperation for their mutual benefit, and that they should guide their economic policies toward each other in the spirit of closer interdependence among all nations. They shared the view that coordination of their policies on new problems confronting the international community is necessary. Both Presidents expressed mutual satisfaction over the continuing growth of substantial bilateral economic relations which have been beneficial to both countries. They agreed that continued private foreign investment in Korea by the United States and other foreign countries is desirable. It was agreed that international efforts should focus on the reduction of trade distortions, establishment of a framework for ensuring stable food supplies, and realization of stable supplies of energy at reasonable prices.

President Park expressed his high expectations and respect for the efforts being made by President Ford to establish world peace and to restore world economic order.

On behalf of the members of his Party and the American people, President Ford extended his deepest thanks to President Park and all the people of the Republic of Korea for the warmth of their reception and the many courtesies extended to him during the visit.

President Ford cordially invited President Park to visit the Unit-

---

[11]Signed at Washington Oct. 1, 1953 and entered into force Nov. 17, 1954 (TIAS 3097; 5 UST 2368); text in *Documents, 1953*: 312-13.

ed States of America and President Park accepted the invitation with pleasure. The two Presidents agreed that the visit would take place at a time of mutual convenience.

[From Seoul, the presidential party flew on to Vladivostok for the meeting with General Secretary Brezhnev, which will be described in the next chapter. President Ford, his mission completed, returned on November 24 to Andrews Air Force Base outside Washington, where he assured a welcoming crowd that he had "traveled some 17,000 miles for the purpose of peace and not a single step toward war."[12] Secretary Kissinger, meanwhile, returned to Tokyo and thence went on to Peking for a round of meetings with leaders of the People's Republic of China on November 25-29.

The object of this "regular annual visit" to the People's Republic—where George Bush now served as head of the U.S. Liaison Office—was defined by Dr. Kissinger as an exchange of views and a periodic review of the international situation with particular reference to Chinese-American relations.[13] While disclaiming any need for "specific reassurance" of the Peking leadership, the Secretary of State endeavored none the less to share with Prime Minister Chou En-lai, Vice-Premier Teng Hsiao-ping, and Foreign Minister Chiao Kuan-hua his own certitude "that the process of improving relations between the People's Republic and the United States is a fixed principle of American foreign policy." "It was no accident," he said on one occasion during his stay in Peking, "that the new American President saw your ambassador the first afternoon he was in office, within a few hours of having taken his oath of office, and that he reaffirmed on that occasion that we would continue to pursue the principles of the Shanghai communique and that we would continue to follow the goal of normalization of relations with the People's Republic of China."[14] The unchanged commitment of both sides to the principles of the Shanghai communiqué was reaffirmed again in a brief joint statement as the Kissinger visit concluded on November 29. President Ford himself, the two governments also announced, would be visiting the People's Republic in 1975.[15]]

[12]*Presidential Documents*, 10: 1498.
[13]*Bulletin*, 71: 905.
[14]Same, 906-7. For the Shanghai communiqué see *AFR, 1972*: 307-11.
[15]*Bulletin*, 71: 907. President Ford visited the People's Republic of China on Dec. 1-5, 1975; cf. *Presidential Documents*, 11: 1339-46 (1975).

31. REUNION IN VLADIVOSTOK

(November 23-24, 1974)

[If it was important to assure the Japanese and Chinese governments of the continuity of U.S. foreign policy, a parallel assurance to the leaders of the Soviet Union might well have been considered even more essential. The policy of détente in which the two governments had invested so heavily could flourish only in so far as it was identified not with the fortunes of individual political leaders but with the permanent interests of the two nations and of international peace. In recent months, the rhythm of détente had slowed perceptibly in consequence of the uncertainties attendant on the change of Presidents as well as the congressional furor over Soviet emigration policy and most-favored-nation commercial treatment. Reinvigoration of the détente process was thus a prime objective of the meeting between President Ford and General Secretary Brezhnev that took place in the area of Vladivostok, the capital of the Soviet Far East, on November 23-24 at the conclusion of the President's Far Eastern tour.

Although the Vladivostok meeting is remembered primarily as the occasion when the two governments announced their agreement on a formula for the limitation of strategic offensive arms, the range of their joint concern was more broadly reflected in the official communiqué that was signed by the two leaders on Sunday, November 24, in the conference hall of Vladivostok's Okeanskiy Sanitarium.]

(67) The Vladivostok Meeting: Joint communiqué of President Ford and Leonid I. Brezhnev, General Secretary of the Central Committee of the Communist Party of the Soviet Union, Vladivostok, November 24, 1974.[1]

In accordance with the previously announced agreement, a working meeting between the President of the United States of America Gerald R. Ford and the General Secretary of the Central Committee of the Communist Party of the Soviet Union L. I. Brezhnev took place in the area of Vladivostok on November 23 and 24, 1974. Taking part in the talks were the Secretary of State of the United States of America and Assistant to the President for National Security Affairs, Henry A. Kissinger and Member of the Politburo of the Central Committee of the CPSU, Minister of Foreign Affairs of the USSR, A. A. Gromyko.

They discussed a broad range of questions dealing with American-Soviet relations and the current international situation.

Also taking part in the talks were:

On the American side Walter J. Stoessel, Jr., Ambassador of the USA to the USSR; Helmut Sonnenfeldt, Counselor of the Department of State; Arthur A. Hartman, Assistant Secretary of State for. European Affairs; Lieutenant General Brent Scowcroft, Deputy Assistant to the President for National Security Affairs; and William Hyland, official of the Department of State.

On the Soviet side A. F. Dobrynin, Ambassador of the USSR to the USA; A. M. Aleksandrov, Assistant to the General Secretary of the Central Committee of the CPSU; and G. M. Korniyenko, Member of the Collegium of the Ministry of Foreign Affairs of the USSR.

I

The United States of America and the Soviet Union reaffirmed their determination to develop further their relations in the direction defined by the fundamental joint decisions and basic treaties and agreements concluded between the two States in recent years.

They are convinced that the course of American-Soviet relations, directed towards strengthening world peace, deepening the relaxation of international tensions and expanding mutually beneficial cooperation of states with different social systems meets the vital interests of the peoples of both States and other peoples.

Both Sides consider that based on the agreements reached between them important results have been achieved in fundamentally reshaping American-Soviet relations on the basis of peaceful coexistence and equal security. These results are a solid foundation for progress in reshaping Soviet-American relations.

Accordingly, they intend to continue, without a loss in momentum, to expand the scale and intensity of their cooperative efforts in all spheres as set forth in the agreements they have signed so that the process of improving relations between the US and the USSR will continue without interruption and will become irreversible.

Mutual determination was expressed to carry out strictly and fully the mutual obligations undertaken by the US and the USSR in accordance with the treaties and agreements concluded between them.

II

Special consideration was given in the course of the talks to a pivotal aspect of Soviet-American relations: measures to eliminate the threat of war and to halt the arms race.

Both sides reaffirm that the Agreements reached between the US and the USSR on the prevention of nuclear war and the limitation of strategic arms are a good beginning in the process of creating guarantees against the outbreak of nuclear conflict and war in general. They expressed their deep belief in the necessity of promoting this process and expressed their hope that other states would contribute to it as well. For their part the US and the USSR will continue to exert vigorous efforts to achieve this historic task.

A joint statement on the question of limiting strategic offensive arms is being released separately.[2]

Both sides stressed once again the importance and necessity of a serious effort aimed at preventing the dangers connected with the spread of nuclear weapons in the world. In this connection they stressed the importance of increasing the effectiveness of the Treaty on the Non-Proliferation of Nuclear Weapons.[3]

It was noted that, in accordance with previous agreements, initial contacts were established between representatives of the US and of the USSR on questions related to underground nuclear explosions for peaceful purposes, to measures to overcome the dangers of the use of environmental modification techniques for military purposes, as well as measures dealing with the most dangerous lethal means of chemical warfare. It was agreed to continue an active search for mutually acceptable solutions of these questions.[4]

III

In the course of the meeting an exchange of views was held on a number of international issues: special attention was given to negotiations already in progress in which the two Sides are participants and which are designed to remove existing sources of tension and to

[2]Document 68.
[3]Cf. note 22 to Chapter 15.
[4]Cf. Chapter 33 at notes 6-12.

bring about the strengthening of international security and world peace.

Having reviewed the situation at the Conference on Security and Cooperation in Europe, both Sides concluded that there is a possibility for its early successful conclusion. They proceed from the assumption that the results achieved in the course of the Conference will permit its conclusion at the highest level and thus be commensurate with its importance in ensuring the peaceful future of Europe.

The USA and the USSR also attach high importance to the negotiations on mutual reduction of forces and armaments and associated measures in Central Europe. They agree to contribute actively to the search for mutually acceptable solutions on the basis of [the] principle of undiminished security for any of the parties and the prevention of unilateral military advantages.

Having discussed the situation existing in the Eastern Mediterranean, both Sides state their firm support for the independence, sovereignty and territorial integrity of Cyprus and will make every effort in this direction. They consider that a just settlement of the Cyprus question must be based on the strict implementation of the resolutions adopted by the Security Council and the General Assembly of the United Nations regarding Cyprus.

In the course of the exchange of views on the Middle East both Sides expressed their concern with regard to the dangerous situation in that region. They reaffirmed their intention to make every effort to promote a solution of the key issues of a just and lasting peace in that area on the basis of the United Nations resolution 338,[5] taking into account the legitimate interests of all the peoples of the area, including the Palestinian people, and respect for the right to independent existence of all states in the area.

The Sides believe that the Geneva Conference should play an important part in the establishment of a just and lasting peace in the Middle East, and should resume its work as soon as possible.

IV

The state of relations was reviewed in the field of commercial, economic, scientific and technical ties between the USA and the USSR. Both Sides confirmed the great importance which further progress in these fields would have for Soviet-American relations, and expressed their firm intention to continue the broadening and deepening of mutually advantageous cooperation.

The two Sides emphasized the special importance accorded by

[5]*AFR, 1973*: 459.

them to the development on a long term basis of commercial and economic cooperation, including mutually beneficial large-scale projects. They believe that such commercial and economic cooperation will serve the cause of increasing the stability of Soviet-American relations.

Both Sides noted with satisfaction the progress in the implementation of agreements and in the development of ties and cooperation between the US and the USSR in the fields of science, technology and culture. They are convinced that the continued expansion of such cooperation will benefit the peoples of both countries and will be an important contribution to the solution of worldwide scientific and technical problems.

The talks were held in an atmosphere of frankness and mutual understanding, reflecting the constructive desire of both Sides to strengthen and develop further the peaceful cooperative relationship between the USA and the USSR, and to ensure progress in the solution of outstanding international problems in the interests of preserving and strengthening peace.

The results of the talks provided a convincing demonstration of the practical value of Soviet-American summit meetings and their exceptional importance in the shaping of a new relationship between the United States of America and the Soviet Union.

President Ford reaffirmed the invitation to L. I. Brezhnev to pay an official visit to the United States in 1975. The exact date of the visit will be agreed upon later.

FOR THE UNITED STATES OF AMERICA
GERALD R. FORD
President of the United States of America

FOR THE UNION OF SOVIET SOCIALIST REPUBLICS
L. I. BREZHNEV
General Secretary of the Central Committee of the CPSU

November 24, 1974

[Despite this optimistic forecast, General Secretary Brezhnev was destined not to visit the United States in 1975, a year when his contacts with President Ford would be limited to brief and superficial meetings during the concluding phase of the European Security Conference in Helsinki. The failure to carry out the plan announced at Vladivostok would be due primarily to unforeseen difficulties in implementing the preliminary accord on strategic arms limitation that loomed as the principal accomplishment of the Vladivostok sessions.

It will be recalled that the Interim Agreement on the Limitation of Strategic Offensive Arms,[6] concluded during President Nixon's earlier visit to Moscow on May 26, 1972, had undertaken to "freeze" the long-range missile forces of the two powers for a period of up to five years at the levels operational or under construction as of the date of signature. During the lifetime of this agreement, expiring at latest on October 3, 1977, the United States would for practical purposes be limited to its existing inventory of 1,054 intercontinental ballistic missile (ICBM) launchers together with 656 submarine-launched ballistic missile (SLBM) launchers, making 1,710 launchers in all. The Soviet Union, on its side, would be permitted a higher total of 2,358 launchers, consisting—subject to certain permitted substitutions—of 1,618 ICBM launchers and 740 SLBM launchers.

Although the Interim Agreement thus allowed the U.S.S.R. substantially more missile launchers than were permitted the United States, this disparity was largely offset by two related considerations that tended to favor the American side. First, the United States retained a substantial advantage over the U.S.S.R. in terms of long-range bombers, which were not covered by the agreement; as of 1974, in fact, the American long-range bomber force amounted to some 496 aircraft to the U.S.S.R.'s 140. Second, the United States had been well ahead of the Soviet Union in commencing the equipment of its long-range missiles with multiple warheads or "multiple independently targetable reentry vehicles" (MIRVs). In consequence of its early start, the United States by 1974 possessed as many as 5,700 operational warheads (as distinguished from missiles) to the U.S.S.R.'s 2,250. The Soviet Union, on the other hand, retained a pronounced lead not only in the number of missiles but in their "throw-weight" or carrying capacity, in which it held an advantage of three to one or more, thanks mainly to its 300 large SS-9 missiles.[7]

In concluding the Interim Agreement in 1972, the American and Soviet governments had also undertaken to conduct "active follow-on negotiations" looking toward an agreement on more complete measures limiting strategic offensive arms. Such an agreement, they had said, should be concluded as soon as possible, presumably well before the expiration of the Interim Agreement in 1977. In the

[6]*AFR, 1972:* 95-7; cf. also note 63 to Chapter 15 above.
[7]Walter Slocombe, *Controlling Strategic Nuclear Weapons* (Foreign Policy Association *Headline Series,* No. 226, June 1975): 19-21.

meantime, however, the two powers had also remained free to press forward with the development of larger and more sophisticated weapons such as might prove useful whether or not a follow-on agreement was achieved. Examples of such new weapon systems were the United States' Minuteman III missile, Trident submarine, and B-1 bomber and the Soviets' SS-18 missile, a successor to the SS-9 which was credited by Secretary of Defense James R. Schlesinger with "a very respectable hard target killing capability" that "could pose a serious threat to our ICBM's in their silos."[8]

In entering upon the follow-on strategic arms talks (SALT II), it had been a fundamental objective of the United States to do away with the disparities that characterized the Interim Agreement and to insist upon what it called "an essential equivalency in strategic forces." Congress, in approving the Interim Agreement, had clearly intended as much when it called upon the President "to seek a future treaty that, inter alia, would not limit the United States to levels of intercontinental strategic forces inferior to the limits provided for the Soviet Union."[9] "There is mutual agreement," President Nixon had written in 1973, "that permanent limitations must meet the basic security interests of both sides equitably if they are to endure in an era of great technological change and in a fluid international environment. There obviously can be no agreement that creates or preserves strategic advantages. But each side perceives the strategic balance differently and therefore holds differing concepts of an equitable framework for a permanent agreement."[10]

It was basically because of these differing perceptions that the SALT II negotiations had progressed more slowly than had been hoped, thus preventing Messrs. Nixon and Brezhnev from signing any follow-on agreement at their meetings in 1973 or 1974. In the former year, as previously noted, they had been compelled to settle for an agreement on "Basic Principles of Negotiations" for a future accord;[11] in the latter, for a mere announcement that the new agreement, when made, should extend to 1985.[12] Thus it was with some surprise that the world now read the announcement from Vladivostok that President Ford and General Secretary Brezhnev had actually agreed upon the outlines of a new accord that could be completed in 1975 and enter into force on the expiration of the Interim Agreement in October 1977.]

---

[8]Same: 19.
[9]Public Law 92-448, Sept. 30, 1972, in *AFR, 1972*: 107.
[10]*Nixon Report, 1973*: 202.
[11]*AFR, 1973*: 262-3.
[12]Chapter 15, Document 23.

(68) Limitation of Strategic Offensive Arms: Joint United States-Soviet statement released in Vladivostok November 24, 1974.[13]

During their working meeting in the area of Vladivostok on November 23-24, the President of the USA Gerald R. Ford and General Secretary of the Central Committee of the CPSU L. I. Brezhnev discussed in detail the question of further limitations of strategic offensive arms.

They reaffirmed the great significance that both the United States and the USSR attach to the limitation of strategic offensive arms. They are convinced that a long-term agreement on this question would be a significant contribution to improving relations between the US and the USSR, to reducing the danger of war and to enhancing world peace. Having noted the value of previous agreements on this question, including the Interim Agreement of May 26, 1972, they reaffirm the intention to conclude a new agreement on the limitation of strategic offensive arms, to last through 1985.

As a result of the exchange of views on the substance of such a new agreement the President of the United States of America and the General Secretary of the Central Committee of the CPSU concluded that favorable prospects exist for completing the work on this agreement in 1975.

Agreement was reached that further negotiations will be based on the following provisions.

1. The new agreement will incorporate the relevant provisions of the Interim Agreement of May 26, 1972, which will remain in force until October 1977.

2. The new agreement will cover the period from October 1977 through December 31, 1985.

3. Based on the principle of equality and equal security, the new agreement will include the following limitations:

a. Both sides will be entitled to have a certain agreed aggregate number of strategic delivery vehicles;

b. Both sides will be entitled to have a certain agreed aggregate number of ICBMs and SLBMs equipped with multiple independently targetable warheads (MIRVs).

4. The new agreement will include a provision for further negotiations beginning no later than 1980-1981 on the question

---

[13]Text from *Presidential Documents*, 10: 1489.

of further limitations and possible reductions of strategic arms in the period after 1985.

5. Negotiations between the delegations of the U.S. and USSR to work out the new agreement incorporating the foregoing points will resume in Geneva in January 1975.

November 24, 1974

[The text of the announcement released at Vladivostok was replete with obvious lacunae and ambiguities. Even the basic fact that the two powers were to be permitted equal numbers of strategic delivery vehicles and MIRVed vehicles was not clearly evident from the text, although it was noted by Secretary Kissinger at a news conference following the release (Document 69a). The actual number of missiles and/or bombers to be permitted each side—2,400 strategic delivery vehicles, of which 1,320 could be MIRVed—was kept secret until it was disclosed by President Ford at his news conference on December 2 (Document 69b). Still another possible misapprehension was later corrected in an unpublished U.S.-Soviet aide-memoire which noted that there was no bar to negotiations or reductions of strategic arms even before 1985.[14]]

(69) Interpretation of the Agreement on Limiting Strategic Offensive Arms.

(a) News conference statement by Secretary of State Kissinger, Vladivostok, November 24, 1976.[15]

(Excerpt)

SECRETARY KISSINGER. If you are all through with reading the joint statement,[16] let me deal with that. There is also a communique[17] which we will distribute and if it should not be finished by the time when I get through with the joint statement, I will talk from it.

The joint statement, in our judgment, marks the breakthrough

---

[14]Kissinger interview, Dec. 18, in *Bulletin*, 72: 58. The aide-memoire was initialed by Secretary Kissinger and Soviet Ambassador A. F. Dobrynin in Washington on Dec. 10 (*New York Times*, Dec. 11, 1974).

[15]Text from *Presidential Documents*, 10: 1489-91. (For full text see same: 1489-94 or *Bulletin*, 71: 898-905.)

[16]Document 68.

[17]Document 67.

with the SALT negotiations that we have sought to achieve in recent years and produces a very strong possibility of agreement, to be signed in 1975.

Perhaps the best way to talk about it would be to go back to the history of the negotiations, starting with the summit in July [18] and the conclusion of the discussions since then, in relation to some specific issues before us.

In all of the discussions on SALT, there is the problem of aggregate numbers, and then there is the problem of the numbers of weapons with certain special characteristics such as MIRV's, and, finally, there is the problem of duration of the agreement.

In July, we were talking about an extension of the interim agreement for a period of 2 to 3 years, and we attempted to compensate for the inequality of numbers in the interim agreement by negotiating a differential in our favor of missiles with multiple warheads.

This negotiation was making some progress, but it was very difficult to establish a relationship between aggregate numbers. It would be an advantage on aggregate numbers on one side and an advantage in multiple warheads on the other, all the more so as we were talking about a time period between 1974 and at the end of 1979 during which various new programs of both sides were going into production at the precise moment that the agreement would have lapsed. That is to say, the United States was developing the Trident and the B-1, both of which will be deployed in the period after 1979, and the Soviet MIRV development would really not reach its full evolution until the period 1978 to 1979.

In other words, while we were negotiating the 5-year agreement we became extremely conscious of the fact that it would lapse at the moment that both sides would have the greatest concern about the weapons programs of the other. And this was the origin of the 10-year proposal and the negotiation for a 10-year agreement that emerged out of the July summit.

No preparatory work of any significance could be undertaken in July on the summit, so that when President Ford came into office, the preparations for a 10-year agreement started practically from scratch.

Now, in a period of 10 years, the problem of numbers has a different significance than in the shorter period because over that period of time, one would have to account, really, for two deployments of a cycle that is usually a 5-year effort. And also, inequalities that might be bearable for either side in a 5-year period would become much more difficult if they were trying over a 10-year period.

[18]Chapter 15.

Finally, since we considered that any agreement that we signed with respect to numbers should be the prelude to further negotiations about reduction, it was very important the debates for reduction for both sides represent some equivalence that permitted a reasonable calculation.

I won't repeat on this occasion all the internal deliberations through which we went, the various options that were considered. There were five in number, but various combinations of quantitative and qualitative restraints seem possible for the United States.

Finally, prior to my visit to the Soviet Union in October, President Ford decided on a proposal which did not reflect any of the options precisely, but represented an amalgamation of several of the approaches. This we submitted to the Soviet leaders about a week before my visit to the Soviet Union in October, and it led to a Soviet counterproposal which was in the general framework of our proposal, and which I have indicated to you marked a substantial step forward on the road to an agreement.

It was discussed in great detail on the occasion of my visit in October.[19] The Soviet counterproposal was studied by the President and his advisers, and it caused us to submit another refinement or an answer to the Soviet counterproposal about a week before we came here. And then, most of the discussions last night, all of the discussions last night, and 2½ hours this morning, were devoted to the issue of SALT.

President Ford and the General Secretary, in the course of these discussions, agreed that a number of the issues that had been standing in the way of progress should be resolved and that guidelines should be issued to the negotiators in Geneva, who we expect to reconvene in early January.

They agreed that obviously, as the joint statement says, the new agreement will cover a period of 10 years, that for the first 2 years of that period, the provisions of the interim agreement will remain in force, as was foreseen in the interim agreement; that after the lapse of the interim agreement, both sides could have equal numbers of strategic vehicles. And President Ford and Secretary General Brezhnev agreed substantially on the definition of strategic delivery vehicles.

During the 10-year period of this agreement, they would also have equal numbers of weapons with multiple, independent reentry vehicles, and that number is substantially less than the total number of strategic vehicles.

There is no compensation for forward-based systems and no other compensations. In other words, we are talking about equal

[19]Cf. Chapter 24, Document 53.

numbers on both sides for both MIRV's and for strategic delivery vehicles and these numbers have been agreed to and will be discussed with Congressional leaders after the President returns.

The negotiations will have to go into the details of verifications of what restraints will be necessary, how one can define and verify missiles which are independently targeted. But we believe that with good will on both sides, it should be possible to conclude a 10-year agreement by the time that the General Secretary visits the United States at the summit, and, at any rate, we will make a major effort in that direction.

As I said, the negotiations could be difficult and will have many technical complexities, but we believe that the target is achievable. If it is achieved, it will mean that a cap has been put on the arms race for a period of 10 years, that this cap is substantially below the capabilities of either side, that the element of insecurity inherent in an arms race in which both sides are attempting to anticipate not only the actual programs but the capabilities of the other side will be substantially reduced with levels achieved over a 10-year period by agreement.

The negotiations for reductions can take place in a better atmosphere, and, therefore, we hope that we will be able to look back to this occasion here as the period or as the turning point that led to putting a cap on the arms race and was the first step to a reduction of arms.

Now, I will be glad to take your questions.

* * *

(b) News conference statement by President Ford, Washington, December 2, 1974.[20]

(Excerpt)

THE PRESIDENT. Good evening.

Perhaps I can anticipate some of your questions by summarizing my recent visits to Japan, the Republic of Korea, and the Soviet Union.

In Japan, we succeeded in establishing a new era of relations between our two countries. We demonstrated our continuing commitment to the independence and to the security of South Korea.

At Vladivostok we put a firm ceiling on the strategic arms race, which heretofore has eluded us since the nuclear age began. I

[20]Text from *Presidential Documents*, 10: 1514. (For full text see same: 1514-19; relevant portions appear also in *Bulletin*, 71: 861-6.)

believe this is something for which future generations will thank us.

Finally, Secretary Kissinger's mission maintained the momentum in China with the People's Republic of China.

My meetings at Vladivostok with General Secretary Brezhnev were a valuable opportunity to review Soviet-American relations and chart their future course. Although this was our original purpose, Secretary Brezhnev and I found it possible to go beyond this get-acquainted stage.

Building on the achievements of the past 3 years, we agreed that the prospects were favorable for more substantial and, may I say, very intensive negotiations on the primary issue of a limitation of strategic arms. In the end, we agreed on the general framework for a new agreement that will last through 1985.

We agreed it is realistic to aim at completing this agreement next year. This is possible because we made major breakthroughs on two critical issues:

Number one, we agreed to put a ceiling of 2,400 each on the total number of intercontinental ballistic missiles, submarine-launched missiles, and heavy bombers.

Two, we agreed to limit the number of missiles that can be armed with multiple warheads—MIRV's. Of each side's total of 2,400, 1,320 can be so armed.

These ceilings are well below the force levels which would otherwise have been expected over the next 10 years and very substantially below the forces which would result from an all-out arms race over that same period.

What we have done is to set firm and equal limits on the strategic forces of each side, thus preventing an arms race with all its terror, instability, war-breeding tension, and economic waste.

We have, in addition, created the solid basis from which future arms reductions can be made and, hopefully, will be negotiated.

It will take more detailed negotiations to convert this agreed framework into a comprehensive accord. But we have made a long step toward peace on a basis of equality, the only basis on which an agreement was possible.

Beyond this, our improved relations with the other nations of Asia developed on this journey will continue to serve the interests of the United States and the cause of peace for months to come. Economy, energy, security, and trade relations were discussed, which will be of mutual benefit to us all.

I would like to repeat publicly my thanks and gratitude for the hospitality extended to me by all of my hosts and, through me, to the American people.

*   *   *

[Secretary Kissinger, at his own news conference on December 7, took the opportunity to respond to some of the early criticisms of the Vladivostok agreement.]

(c) News conference statement by Secretary of State Kissinger, Washington, December 7, 1974.[21]

(Excerpt)

* * *

Q. Mr. Secretary, I wonder if you would care to use this, what I assume is a first public opportunity to answer the critics of the Vladivostok agreement. I had in mind especially two points. One, the argument that the number you agreed upon in Vladivostok is too high and really wouldn't stop the nuclear arms race. And, second, that the throw-weight issue, which a senior official called a phony issue, wouldn't be phony, would be more serious, if the Soviets started MIRV'ing their large missiles.

The Vladivostok Strategic Arms Agreement

Secretary Kissinger: Let me make a few comments about the Vladivostok agreement.

Throughout the SALT Two negotiations, our negotiators strove for the following objectives:

—One, to achieve a ceiling on the number of total delivery vehicles.

—Second, to achieve a ceiling on the number of MIRV'ed delivery vehicles.

—Third, to have these ceilings equal.

—Fourth, not to count forward-based systems.

—Fifth, not to count the British and French nuclear forces.

—Sixth, not to give compensation to any other geographic factors.

—And then we thought [sought] other technical objectives, such as the freedom to mix, which means that each side should be free to compose its strategic forces substantially according to its best judgment.

All of these objectives were achieved in the SALT Two negotiations.

[21]Department of State Press Release 518, Dec. 7; text from *Bulletin*, 71: 909-11. (For full text see same: 909-19.)

Now, with respect to the total numbers. The significance of the numbers is that for the first time in the nuclear age, a ceiling has been put on the strategic forces of both sides. For the first time in the nuclear age, for a 10-year period the arms race will not be driven by the fear of what the other side might be able to do but only by the agreed ceilings that have been established.

This can be justly described as a major breakthrough, and its significance becomes all the more clear if one compares the numbers not with some hypothetical model that one might have in mind but with what would have happened in the absence of this agreement.

In order to reach these numbers, the Soviet Union will have slightly to reduce its strategic forces, by some 5 percent, I would guess. If this agreement had not been reached, all our intelligence estimates agreed that both with respect to MIRV's and with respect to total numbers of forces that the Soviet Union would build would be considerably larger than those foreseen in the agreement, giving us the problem of whether we were to match these forces or whether we would permit a growing numerical gap against us to arise. So it is not a fair comparison to compare these figures with some abstract model but only with, one, the reality of existing strategic forces, and, second, what would, according to the best judgment of our intelligence community, have happened in the absence of such an agreement.

With respect to the argument that at this level a substantial capacity for overkill exists, this would be true at almost any foreseeable level, or at any level that has been publicly suggested by any of the protagonists in this debate. This is a problem that is inherent in the nature of nuclear weapons and in the size of existing nuclear stockpiles.

So, I repeat, the significance of this agreement is that for a 10-year period it means that the arms race will not be driven by the fear of each side of the building capabilities of the other side.

Now the argument that it does not stop the qualitative arms race. It is of course extremely difficult to stop qualitative changes in the best of circumstances, because it is very difficult to control what one is not able to describe, which is inherent in the nature of technological change.

However, it reduces substantially the incentive of an unlimited qualitative arms race. The nightmare in qualitative changes has always been the linkage of qualitative change with quantity. And it is the combination of technological improvement with increases in numbers that has produced the various models for strategic superiority that people were concerned about.

It is extremely difficult to conceive how, under the provisions of this agreement, foreseeable technological changes, if either side acts with a moderate—with even a modicum of circumspection—can produce strategic superiority.

And this gets to the throw-weight point and to the adjective "phony" as applied to the throw-weight point. It is rather difficult to be drawn into a debate about an adjective taken out of context from a deep-background discussion. But let me sum up my views with respect to throw weight.

Throw weight is, of course, one measure of strategic power. Throw weight is significant when it is converted into numbers of warheads and if these warheads are of sufficient accuracy to threaten a definable part of the opposing side's target system. It therefore is a function both of the power of the weapons and of the vulnerability of the targets. If one side acquires additional throw weight, the other side has the choice either of increasing its throw weight or reducing the vulnerability of the targets. For example, putting larger throw-weight missiles into our holes does not reduce the vulnerability of our silos. It increases the vulnerability of Soviet silos.

The major target system that is threatened by increases of throw weights are land-based silos. Over a period of 10 years, these are likely to become vulnerable on both sides, regardless of the throw weight that either side has, simply by improvement in accuracy and improvements in yield.

Under the agreement, the United States has the ability to increase its throw weight substantially if it is judged in our interests to do so. Even though there is a limitation on building new silos, our existing silos can accommodate missiles of a throw weight many times larger than the one we now have. And if we increased them by the permitted 15 percent, we can increase the throw weight even more. So there is no effective limit on the increase in our throw weight if we decide to match the Soviet throw weight.

We must remember, moreover, that the decision to accept the differential in throw weight was made six years ago, or 10 years ago, as a unilateral decision by the United States and has nothing to do with this agreement.

But the major point I want to make is this: We have the possibility of increasing our throw weight. We have also the possibility of increasing the invulnerability of our forces by reducing reliance on land-based silos and increasing the number of our submarine-based missiles.

We will not match throw weight simply for the abstract purpose of being equal in every category. We will take whatever measures are necessary to assure the invulnerability of our forces and to maintain strategic equivalence. If we should determine that we need to increase our throw weight, we will do so, and there is nothing in this agreement to constrain us from doing so. And therefore from this point of view, the throw-weight argument is an unreal issue.

* * *

[Scarcely noticed in the early discussions of the Vladivostok accord was the one issue which, more than any other, was to frustrate the hope of reaching a definitive agreement in 1975. This was the problem of defining the "strategic delivery vehicles" to be counted under each side's 2,400 ceiling, particularly as it related to such intermediate-class weapons as the Soviets' "Backfire" bomber and the U.S. cruise missile. Attempts by each power to exclude its own weapons from the 2,400 limitation while including those of its adversary were to occupy the SALT negotiators throughout the following year and even beyond, resulting not only in a deferral of Brezhnev's projected visit to the United States but, eventually, in a further slackening in the pace of détente as American attention turned increasingly toward the presidential election of November 1976.]

32. THE GENERAL ASSEMBLY REVISITED

(New York, December 6-12, 1974)

[While U.S. leaders concentrated their attention on the major powers of Europe and Asia, American relations with the numerous "third world" countries at the United Nations had continued to deteriorate. The opposition, not to say contempt, for American views displayed by this group at the 29th General Assembly—most frequently with the enthusiastic encouragement of the Communist members—was if anything even more marked than in 1971, when the Republic of China on Taiwan had been peremptorily ousted from its seat in the United Nations in order to make room for the mainland China regime. Events surrounding the appearance of Yasir Arafat in the Assembly on November 13,[1] for example, had touched American nerves as sensitive as any affected by the China question.

In riding roughshod over American sensibilities, the General Assembly came close to sacrificing public recognition of its more positive achievements—among them, such considerable accomplishments as the completion of a convention on the registration of objects launched into outer space;[2] the formulation, after many years of effort, of an agreed definition of the term "aggression";[3] and the adoption, with no opposing votes, of a resolution calling for specific measures to curb the use of torture and other cruel, inhuman, degrading treatment or punishment.[4] In the international political field, the United States and other like-minded governments scored a victory of some importance in blocking for the sec-

---

[1]Cf. Chapter 26 at note 17.

[2]Commended by General Assembly Resolution 3235 (XXIX) of Nov. 12, 1974, the convention was opened for signature at U.N. Headquarters in New York on Jan. 14, 1975 and entered into force with the deposit of the U.S. instrument of ratification on Sept. 15, 1976.

[3]Annexed to Resolution 3314 (XXIX) of Dec. 14, 1974.

[4]Resolution 3218 (XXIX), Nov. 6, 1974, adopted by a vote of 125 (U.S.)-0-1 (Zaïre).

ond successive year a move to oust the representatives of the Khmer Republic (Cambodia) and substitute those of the exiled government of former Chief of State Prince Norodom Sihanouk.[5] In addition, the United States and other friends of the Republic of Korea eventually succeeded in their efforts to sidetrack a 40-nation move to demand withdrawal of the American forces stationed in that country with the sanction of the United Nations.[6]

But these hard-won successes in no way lessened the feeling of American authorities that the Assembly, by and large, was daily growing more unmanageable, more doctrinaire, and more in need of cautionary advice. An admonitory statement of the sort that was felt in Washington to have become essential was at length delivered by Ambassador Scali on December 6 as the U.S. contribution to a debate on ''strengthening the role of the United Nations''—a recurrent topic that traditionally provided the opportunity for general reflections on the U.N. role and performance.]

(70) Voting Trends in the General Assembly: Statement by Ambassador Scali in Plenary Session, December 6, 1974.[7]

Last year the U.S. delegation sought to call attention to a trend which we believed threatened the U.N.'s potential as an instrument for international cooperation. We were deeply concerned then over the growing tendency of this organization to adopt one-sided, unrealistic resolutions that cannot be implemented.

Today, more than a year later, my delegation feels that we must return to this subject because this trend has not only continued but accelerated. Added to this, there is now a new threat—an arbitrary disregard of U.N. rules, even of its charter. What my delegation spoke of 12 months ago as a potential threat to this organization, unhappily, has become today a clear and present danger.

The U.S. Government has already made clear from this rostrum its concern over a number of Assembly decisions taken during the sixth special session last spring and during the current session.[8] These decisions have dealt with some of the most important, the most controversial, and the most vexing issues of our day: the

[5]Action on this matter was postponed to 1975 by Resolution 3238 (XXIX) of Nov. 29, 1974, adopted by a vote of 56 (U.S.)-54-24.

[6]A substitute Resolution 3333 (XXIX) of Dec. 17, 1974, adopted by a vote of 61 (U.S.)-43-31, voiced a renewed appeal for North-South dialogue leading to peaceful reunification of Korea.

[7]USUN Press Release 191, Dec. 6; text from *Bulletin*, 72: 114-18.

[8]For the Sixth Special Session see Chapter 7; for earlier developments at the 29th Regular Session, Chapters 20, 25, and 26.

global economic crisis, the turmoil in the Middle East, and the injustice in southern Africa. I will not today discuss again our main concerns with each of these decisions. Rather, I wish to take this opportunity to discuss the more general question of how self-centered actions endanger the future of this organization.

The United Nations, and this Assembly in particular, can walk one of two paths. The Assembly can seek to represent the views of the numerical majority of the day, or it can try to act as a spokesman of a more general global opinion. To do the first is easy. To do the second is infinitely more difficult. But, if we look ahead, it is infinitely more useful.

There is certainly nothing wrong with like-minded groups of nations giving voice to the views they hold in common. However, organizations other than the United Nations exist for that purpose. Thus, there are organizations of African states, of Asian states, of Arab states, of European states, and of American states. There are groups of industrialized nations, of developing nations, of Western and Eastern nations, and of nonaligned nations. Each of these organizations exists to promote the views of its membership.

The United Nations, however, exists not to serve one or more of these special-interest groups while remaining insensitive to the others. The challenge of the United Nations is to meld and reflect the views of all of them. The only victories with meaning are those which are victories for us all.

The General Assembly fulfills its true function when it reconciles opposing views and seeks to bridge the differences among its member states. The most meaningful test of whether the Assembly has succeeded in this task is not whether a majority can be mobilized behind any single draft resolution, but whether those states whose cooperation is vital to implement a decision will support it in fact. A better world can only be constructed on negotiation and compromise, not on confrontation, which inevitably sows the seeds of new conflicts. In the words of our charter, the United Nations is "to be a center for harmonizing the actions of nations in the attainment of these common ends."

No observer should be misled by the coincidental similarities between the General Assembly and a legislature. A legislature passes laws. The General Assembly passes resolutions, which are in most cases advisory in nature. These resolutions are sometimes adopted by Assembly majorities which represent only a small fraction of the people of the world, its wealth, or its territory. Sometimes they brutally disregard the sensitivity of the minority.

Because the General Assembly is an advisory body on matters of world policy, the pursuit of mathematical majorities can be a particularly sterile form of international activity. Sovereign nations, and the other international organs which the Assembly advises through its resolutions, sometimes accept and sometimes reject that advice. Often they do not ask how many nations voted for a resolution, but who those nations were, what they represented, and what they advocated.

Members of the United Nations are endowed with sovereign equality; that is, they are equally entitled to their independence, to their rights under the charter. They are not equal in size, in population, or in wealth. They have different capabilities and therefore different responsibilities, as the charter makes clear.

Similarly, because the majority can directly affect only the internal administration of this organization, it is the United Nations itself which suffers most when a majority, in pursuit of an objective it believes overriding, forgets that responsibility must bear a reasonable relationship to capability and to authority.

Each time this Assembly adopts a resolution which it knows will not be implemented, it damages the credibility of the United Nations. Each time that this Assembly makes a decision which a significant minority of members regards as unfair or one-sided, it further erodes vital support for the United Nations among that minority. But the minority which is so offended may in fact be a practical majority in terms of its capacity to support this organization and implement its decisions.

Unenforceable, one-sided resolutions destroy the authority of the United Nations. Far more serious, however, they encourage disrespect for the charter and for the traditions of our organization.

No organization can function without an agreed-upon framework of rules and regulations. The framework for this organization was built in the light of painful lessons learned from the disastrous failure of its predecessor, the League of Nations. Thus, the U.N. Charter was designed to insure that the important decisions of this organization reflected real power relationships and that decisions, once adoped, could be enforced.

One of the principal aims of the United Nations, expressed in the preamble of its charter, is "to practice tolerance and live together in peace with one another as good neighbors." The promise the American people and the peoples of the other founding nations made to each other—not as a matter of law, but as a matter of solemn moral and political obligation—was to live up to the charter and the duly made rules unless or until they were modified in an orderly, constitutional manner.

The function of all parliaments is to provide expression to the majority will. Yet, when the rule of the majority becomes the tyranny of the majority, the minority will cease to respect or obey it, and the parliament will cease to function. Every majority must recognize that its authority does not extend beyond the point where the minority becomes so outraged that it is no longer willing to maintain the covenant which binds them.

My countrymen have made a great investment in this world organization over the years—as host country, as the leading financial contributor, and as a conscientious participant in its debates and negotiations and operational programs. Americans have loyally continued these efforts in a spirit of good faith and tolerance, knowing that there would be words spoken which we did not always like and resolutions adopted which we could not always support.

As the 29th General Assembly draws to a close, however, many Americans are questioning their belief in the United Nations. They are deeply disturbed.

During this 29th General Assembly, resolutions have been passed which uncritically endorse the most far-reaching claims of one side in dangerous international disputes. With this has come a sharply increased tendency in this Assembly to disregard its normal procedures to benefit the side which enjoys the favor of the majority and to silence, and even exclude, the representatives of member states whose policies the majority condemns. In the wake of some of the examples of this Assembly, the General Conference of UNESCO has strayed down the same path,[9] with the predictable consequences of adverse reaction against the United Nations. Innocent bystanders such as UNICEF [United Nations Children's Fund] already have been affected.

We are all aware that true compromise is difficult and time consuming, while bloc voting is fast and easy. But real progress on contentious issues must be earned. Paper triumphs are, in the end, expensive even for the victors. The cost is borne first of all by the United Nations as an institution and, in the end, by all of us. Our achievements cannot be measured in paper.

A strong and vital United Nations is important to every member state; and actions which weaken it weaken us all, particularly the smaller and the developing nations. Their security is particularly dependent on a collective response to aggression. Their prosperity particularly depends on access to an open and expanding international economy. Their ability to project their influence in the world is particularly enhanced by membership in international bodies such as the United Nations.

In calling attention to the dangerous trends, I wish also to call attention to the successes of the United Nations during the past year.

U.N. members overcame many differences at the World Popula-

---

[9]Cf. Chapter 26 at note 29.

tion Conference and the World Food Conference.[10] There was also progress at the Law of the Sea Conference.[11] There was agreement on programs encouraging states to maintain a population which they can feed and feed the population which they maintain. As a result of these U.N. conferences the world community has at last begun to grapple with the two fundamental issues which are central to any meaningful attempt to provide a better life for most of mankind.

In the Middle East a unique combination of multilateral and bilateral diplomacy has succeeded in halting last year's war and in separating the combatants. With good will and cooperation, the Security Council has renewed the mandate for the peace forces,[12] allowing time for a step-by-step negotiating process to bear fruit. My government believes that this negotiating process continues to hold the best hope in more than a quarter of a century for a just and lasting peace in that area.

On Cyprus, the Security Council, the Assembly, and our Secretary General have all contributed to progress toward peace and reconciliation.[13] Much remains to be done, but movement toward peace has been encouraged.

Perhaps the U.N.'s most overlooked success of the past year resulted from the mission of the Secretary General's representative, Mr. Weckmann-Munoz.[14] This effort, which was undertaken at the request of the Security Council, succeeded in mediating a particularly dangerous border dispute between Iran and Iraq. This example of how to prevent a small conflict from blowing up into a much bigger war must rank among the U.N.'s finest, if least heralded, achievements.

Thus, despite the disturbing trend toward the sterile pursuit of empty majorities, recent U.N. achievements demonstrate that this organization can still operate in the real world in the interests of all its members. Unfortunately, failure and controversy are threatening to overshadow the record of successes. Its lapses are long remembered and remain a source of lasting grievance for those who feel wronged.

Before concluding my remarks, I would like to say a few words, not as the U.S. Representative to this organization but as an American who has believed deeply in the United Nations since 1945 when, as a young reporter just returned from the war, I observed the birth of this organization.

[10]Cf. respectively Chapters 20 and 27.
[11]Cf. Chapter 19.
[12]Chapter 26, Documents 58 and 60.
[13]Cf. Chapters 16 and 18.
[14]Cf. Chapter 9 following note 2.

I must tell you that recent decisions of this Assembly and of other U.N. bodies have deeply affected public opinion in my country. The American people are deeply disturbed by decisions to exclude member states and to restrict their participation in discussions of matters of vital concern to them. They are concerned by moves to convert humanitarian and cultural programs into tools of political reprisal. Neither the American public nor the American Congress believes that such actions can be reconciled with the spirit or letter of the U.N. Charter. They do not believe that these decisions are in accord with the purposes for which this organization was founded. They believe the United Nations, in its forums, must show the same understanding, fair play, and responsibility which its resolutions ask of individual members.

My country cannot participate effectively in the United Nations without the support of the American people and of the American Congress. For years they have provided that support generously. But I must tell you honestly that this support is eroding—in our Congress and among our people. Some of the foremost American champions of this organization are deeply distressed at the trend of recent events.

A majority of our Congress and our people are still committed to a strong United Nations. They are still committed to achieving peaceful solutions to the issues which confront this organization— in the Middle East, in South Africa, and elsewhere. They are still committed to building a more just world economic order. But the trends and decisions of the past few months are causing many to reflect and reassess what our role should be.

I have not come to the General Assembly today to suggest that the American people are going to turn away from the United Nations. I believe that World War II taught Americans the tragic cost of standing aside from an organized international effort to bring international law and justice to bear on world problems. But, like every nation, we must from time to time reassess our priorities, review our commitments, and redirect our energies. In the months ahead, I will do all in my power to persuade my countrymen that the United Nations can return to the path the charter has laid out and that it can continue to serve the interests of *all* of its members.

If the United Nations ceases to work for the benefit of all of its members, it will become increasingly irrelevant. It will fade into the shadow world of rhetoric, abandoning its important role in the real world of negotiation and compromise.

We must join to prevent this. The reasons for which this world organization was founded remain as valid and as compelling today as they were in 1945. If anything, there is added reason: the specters of nuclear holocaust, world depression, mass famine, overpopulation, and a permanently ravaged environment.

If we are to succeed, we must now renew our commitment to the central principles of tolerance and harmony upon which the U.N. Charter was built. We must redouble our efforts to use this organization as the world's ultimate instrument for compromise and negotiation. I pledge my nation to these efforts.

[Although Ambassador Scali's remarks elicited some cries of "duplicity, double standards," and "blackmail and intimidation,"[15] the U.S. Representative later expressed appreciation for the serious tone of the discussion initiated by his statement. "I am encouraged," he said, "that the debate has turned into a constructive dialogue with sober reflection. If we can maintain this willingness to listen carefully to one another, we can write a record that peoples everywhere can applaud."[16]

What may, however, have been the most serious clash of the session was still to come as the Assembly moved toward final action on one of the most controversial items on its agenda, the proposed Charter of Economic Rights and Duties of States. A brain child of Mexican President Echeverría that had been zealously embraced by the countries of the so-called "Group of 77," this evangelistically worded document provided an admirable statement of third world views on economic questions but flew in the face of accepted economic doctrine in the industrialized countries. Prolonged discussion in the U.N. Conference on Trade and Development (UNCTAD) and in the Assembly's own Second (Economic and Financial) Committee had quite failed to resolve the deep-rooted differences between the sponsoring governments and the United States and its industrial allies; and a proposal by the Common Market countries to postpone the issue to the Assembly's 1975 session was formally rejected on December 6 by a committee vote of 20 in favor (including the United States) to 81 opposed, with 15 abstentions.

Having thus determined that the matter must be settled without delay, the Second Committee then went on to reject, in seventeen separate votes, a series of proposed amendments cosponsored by the United States and other like-minded countries. That done, the committee next proceeded to adopt, by further separate votes, the very different draft provisions recommended by the Group of 77. Finally, the Charter as a whole was approved by a committee vote of 115 in favor to 6 opposed (including the United States), with 10

[15]*New York Times*, Dec. 12, 1974.
[16]*Bulletin*, 72: 118.

abstentions—a majority sufficient to ensure its later adoption by the full Assembly.[17]

The nature of the U.S. objections to this procedure, and to the provisions of the Charter as approved, was indicated by Senator Charles H. Percy of the U.S. Delegation in a statement following the committee vote.]

(71) Charter of Economic Rights and Duties of States, Adopted by the General Assembly December 12, 1974.

(a) Views of the United States: Statement to the Second (Economic and Financial) Committee of the General Assembly by Senator Charles H. Percy, United States Representative, December 6, 1974.[18]

It is with deep regret that my delegation could not support the proposed Charter of Economic Rights and Duties of States.

When President Echeverría of Mexico initiated the concept of such a charter two years ago,[19] he had what is indeed a worthy vision. The U.S. Government shares the conviction that there is a real need for basic improvements in the international economic system, and we supported in principle the formulation of new guidelines to this end. We welcomed President Echeverría's initiative. Secretary of State Kissinger, in addressing this Assembly last year, confirmed the fact that the United States favored the concept of a charter. He said it would make a significant and historic contribution if it reflected the true aspirations of all nations. He added that, to command general support—and to be implemented—the proposed rights and duties must be defined equitably and take into account the concerns of industrialized as well as of developing countries.[20]

In extensive negotiations in Mexico City, Geneva, and here in New York, the United States worked hard and sincerely with other countries in trying to formulate a charter that would achieve such a balance. We tried to go the extra mile in particular because of our close and friendly relations with Mexico. We are indebted, as I believe is the entire Assembly, to Foreign Minister [Emilio O.]

---

[17]For details see U.S. Participation, 1974: 156-9 and Bulletin, 72: 146-7 (footnotes). "No" votes and abstentions were identical to those on final adoption, as listed below.

[18]USUN Press Release 192, Dec. 6; text from Bulletin, 72: 146-7.

[19]The charter was originally proposed at the Third Ministerial Session of the U.N. Conference on Trade and Development (UNCTAD III), held in Santiago, Chile, on Apr. 13-May 21, 1972.

[20]AFR, 1973: 365.

Rabasa [of Mexico] for his patient and tireless efforts as a negotiator. One must recognize the difficulty of his tasks in seeking to reconcile such fundamentally divergent views as have been apparent in a group of this size and disparity. Despite the chasm which it has thus far proved impossible to bridge, he labored up to the last moment seeking an agreed consensus. Indeed, agreement was reached on many important articles, and our support for those was shown in the vote we have just taken.

On others, however, agreement has not been reached. Our views on these provisions are apparent in the amendments proposed by the United States and certain other countries, but these regrettably have been rejected by the majority here. Many of the unagreed provisions, in the view of my government, are fundamental and are unacceptable in their present form. To cite a few: the treatment of foreign investment in terms which do not fully take into account respect for agreements and international obligations, and the endorsement of concepts of producer cartels and indexation of prices. As a result, Mr. Chairman,[21] we have before us a draft charter which is unbalanced and which fails to achieve the purpose of encouraging harmonious economic relations and needed development. Moreover, the provisions of the charter would discourage rather than encourage the capital flow which is vital for development.

There is much in the charter which the United States supports. The bulk of it is the result of sincere negotiations, as demonstrated by the voting pattern today. It was to demonstrate this fact that the United States asked for an article-by-article vote on the charter.

Mr. Chairman, my government was prepared to continue these negotiations until agreement could be reached, as we much preferred agreement to confrontation. For that reason, we supported the proposed resolution to continue negotiating next year with a view to acting on a generally agreed charter in the Assembly next September.

For all these reasons, Mr. Chairman, my delegation felt compelled to vote against the charter as a whole. We have not closed our minds, however, to the possibility of further reconsideration at some future date should others come to the conclusion that an agreed charter would still be far preferable to one that is meaningless without the agreement of countries whose numbers may be small but whose significance in international economic relations and development can hardly be ignored. We stand ready to resume negotiations on a charter which could command the support of all countries.

[21] Jihad Karam (Iraq).

[No votes were changed as a result of Senator Percy's statement. When the resolution containing the proposed charter was taken up in plenary session on December 12, it was adopted by the overwhelming vote of 120 in favor, to 6 opposed and 10 abstentions. Once again the United States voted "No," as did Belgium, Denmark, the Federal Republic of Germany, Luxembourg, and the United Kingdom. The remaining Common Market countries abstained, as did Austria, Canada, Israel, Japan, Norway, and Spain. Countries voting for adoption of the charter, on the other hand, included six allies of the United States (Australia and New Zealand, Greece and Turkey, Iceland and Portugal) as well as Finland, Sweden, the Communist countries, and the Latin American and Caribbean group.]

(b) **Charter of Economic Rights and Duties of States: General Assembly Resolution 3281 (XXIX), December 12, 1974.**[22]

The General Assembly,

Recalling that the United Nations Conference on Trade and Development, in its resolution 45 (III) of 18 May 1972, stressed the urgency to establish generally accepted norms to govern international economic relations systematically and recognized that it is not feasible to establish a just order and a stable world as long as a charter to protect the rights of all countries, and in particular the developing States, is not formulated,

Recalling further that in the same resolution it was decided to establish a Working Group of governmental representatives to draw up a draft Charter of Economic Rights and Duties of States, which the General Assembly, in its resolution 3037 (XXVII) of 19 December 1972, decided should be composed of forty Member States,

Noting that, in its resolution 3082 (XXVIII) of 6 December 1973, it reaffirmed its conviction of the urgent need to establish or improve norms of universal application for the development of international economic relations on a just and equitable basis and urged the Working Group on the Charter of Economic Rights and Duties of States to complete, as the first step in the codification and development of the matter, the elaboration of a final draft Charter of Economic Rights and Duties of States, to be considered and approved by the General Assembly at its twenty-ninth session,

Bearing in mind the spirit and terms of its resolutions 3201 (S-

[22]Text from General Assembly, *Official Records: 29th Year, Supplement 31* (A/9631): 50-55.

VI)[23] and 3202 (S-VI) of 1 May 1974, containing, respectively, the Declaration and the Programme of Action on the Establishment of a New International Economic Order, which underlined the vital importance of the Charter to be adopted by the General Assembly at its twenty-ninth session and stressed the fact that the Charter shall constitute an effective instrument towards the establishment of a new system of international economic relations based on equity, sovereign equality and interdependence of the interests of developed and developing countries,

Having examined the report of the Working Group on the Charter of Economic Rights and Duties of States on its fourth session,[24] transmitted to the General Assembly by the Trade and Development Board at its fourteenth session,

Expressing its appreciation to the Working Group on the Charter of Economic Rights and Duties of States which, as a result of the task performed in its four sessions held between February 1973 and June 1974, assembled the elements required for the completion and adoption of the Charter of Economic Rights and Duties of States at the twenty-ninth session of the General Assembly, as previously recommended,

Adopts and solemnly proclaims the following Charter:

CHARTER OF ECONOMIC RIGHTS
AND DUTIES OF STATES

PREAMBLE

The General Assembly,

Reaffirming the fundamental purposes of the United Nations, in particular the maintenance of international peace and security, the development of friendly relations among nations and the achievement of international co-operation in solving international problems in the economic and social fields,

Affirming the need for strengthening international co-operation in these fields,

Reaffirming further the need for strengthening international co-operation for development,

Declaring that it is a fundamental purpose of the present Charter to promote the establishment of the new international economic order, based on equity, sovereign equality, interdependence, com-

---

[23]Chapter 7, Document 8b.
[24]U.N. document TD/B/AC.12/4 and Corr.1.

mon interest and co-operation among all States, irrespective of their economic and social systems,

Desirous of contributing to the creation of conditions for:

(a) The attainment of wider prosperity among all countries and of higher standards of living for all peoples,

(b) The promotion by the entire international community of the economic and social progress of all countries, especially developing countries,

(c) The encouragement of co-operation, on the basis of mutual advantage and equitable benefits for all peace-loving States which are willing to carry out the provisions of the present Charter, in the economic, trade, scientific and technical fields, regardless of political, economic or social systems,

(d) The overcoming of main obstacles in the way of the economic development of the developing countries,

(e) The acceleration of the economic growth of developing countries with a view to bridging the economic gap between developing and developed countries,

(f) The protection, preservation and enhancement of the environment,

Mindful of the need to establish and maintain a just and equitable economic and social order through:

(a) The achievement of more rational and equitable international economic relations and the encouragement of structural changes in the world economy,

(b) The creation of conditions which permit the further expansion of trade and intensification of economic co-operation among all nations,

(c) The strengthening of the economic independence of developing countries,

(d) The establishment and promotion of international economic relations, taking into account the agreed differences in development of the developing countries and their specific needs,

Determined to promote collective economic security for development, in particular of the developing countries, with strict respect for the sovereign equality of each State and through the co-operation of the entire international community,

Considering that genuine co-operation among States, based on joint consideration of and concerted action regarding international economic problems, is essential for fulfilling the international community's common desire to achieve a just and rational development of all parts of the world,

Stressing the importance of ensuring appropriate conditions for the conduct of normal economic relations among all States, irrespective of differences in social and economic systems, and for the full respect of the rights of all peoples, as well as strengthening instruments of international economic co-operation as a means for the consolidation of peace for the benefit of all,

Convinced of the need to develop a system of international economic relations on the basis of sovereign equality, mutual and equitable benefit and the close interrelationship of the interests of all States,

Reiterating that the responsibility for the development of every country rests primarily upon itself but that concomitant and effective international co-operation is an essential factor for the full achievement of its own development goals,

Firmly convinced of the urgent need to evolve a substantially improved system of international economic relations,

Solemnly adopts the present Charter of Economic Rights and Duties of States.

CHAPTER I

FUNDAMENTALS OF INTERNATIONAL ECONOMIC RELATIONS

Economic as well as political and other relations among States shall be governed, *inter alia*, by the following principles:

(a) Sovereignty, territorial integrity and political independence of States;

(b) Sovereign equality of all States;

(c) Non-aggression;

(d) Non-intervention;

(e) Mutual and equitable benefit;

(f) Peaceful coexistence;

(g) Equal rights and self-determination of peoples;

(h) Peaceful settlement of disputes;

(i) Remedying of injustices which have been brought about by force and which deprive a nation of the natural means necessary for its normal development;

(j) Fulfilment in good faith of international obligations;

(k) Respect for human rights and fundamental freedoms;

(l) No attempt to seek hegemony and spheres of influence;

(m) Promotion of international social justice;

(n) International co-operation for development;

(o) Free access to and from the sea by land-locked countries within the framework of the above principles.

CHAPTER II

ECONOMIC RIGHTS AND DUTIES OF STATES

Article 1

Every State has the sovereign and inalienable right to choose its economic system as well as its political, social and cultural systems in accordance with the will of its people, without outside interference, coercion or threat in any form whatsoever.

Article 2

1. Every State has and shall freely exercise full permanent sovereignty, including possession, use and disposal, over all its wealth, natural resources and economic activities.
2. Each State has the right:

(a) To regulate and exercise authority over foreign investment within its national jurisdiction in accordance with its laws and regulations and in conformity with its national objectives and priorities. No State shall be compelled to grant preferential treatment to foreign investment;

(b) To regulate and supervise the activities of transnational corporations within its national jurisdiction and take measures to ensure that such activities comply with its laws, rules and regulations and conform with its economic and social policies. Transnational corporations shall not intervene in the internal affairs of a host State. Every State should, with full regard for its sovereign rights, co-operate with other States in the exercise of the right set forth in this subparagraph;

(c) To nationalize, expropriate or transfer ownership of foreign property, in which case appropriate compensation should be paid by the State adopting such measures, taking into account its relevant laws and regulations and all circumstances that the State considers pertinent. In any case where the question of compensation gives rise to a controversy, it shall be settled under the domestic law of the nationalizing State and by its tribunals, unless it is freely and mutually agreed by all States concerned that other peaceful means be sought on the basis of the sovereign equality of States and in accordance with the principle of free choice of means.

Article 3

In the exploitation of natural resources shared by two or more countries, each State must co-operate on the basis of a system of information and prior consultations in order to achieve optimum use of such resources without causing damage to the legitimate interest of others.

Article 4

Every State has the right to engage in international trade and other forms of economic co-operation irrespective of any differences in political, economic and social systems. No State shall be subjected to discrimination of any kind based solely on such differences. In the pursuit of international trade and other forms of economic co-operation, every State is free to choose the forms of organization of its foreign economic relations and to enter into bilateral and multilateral arrangements consistent with its international obligations and with the needs of international economic co-operation.

Article 5

All States have the right to associate in organizations of primary commodity producers in order to develop their national economies, to achieve stable financing for their development and, in pursuance of their aims, to assist in the promotion of sustained growth of the world economy, in particular accelerating the development of developing countries. Correspondingly, all States have the duty to respect that right by refraining from applying economic and political measures that would limit it.

Article 6

It is the duty of States to contribute to the development of international trade of goods, particularly by means of arrangements and by the conclusion of long-term multilateral commodity agreements, where appropriate, and taking into account the interests of producers and consumers. All States share the responsibility to promote the regular flow and access of all commercial goods traded at stable, remunerative and equitable prices, thus contributing to the equitable development of the world economy, taking into account, in particular, the interests of developing countries.

Article 7

Every State has the primary responsibility to promote the

economic, social and cultural development of its people. To this end, each State has the right and the responsibility to choose its means and goals of development, fully to mobilize and use its resources, to implement progressive economic and social reforms and to ensure the full participation of its people in the process and benefits of development. All States have the duty, individually and collectively, to co-operate in eliminating obstacles that hinder such mobilization and use.

Article 8

States should co-operate in facilitating more rational and equitable international economic relations and in encouraging structural changes in the context of a balanced world economy in harmony with the needs and interests of all countries, especially developing countries, and should take appropriate measures to this end.

Article 9

All States have the responsibility to co-operate in the economic, social, cultural, scientific and technological fields for the promotion of economic and social progress throughout the world, especially that of the developing countries.

Article 10

All States are juridically equal and, as equal members of the international community, have the right to participate fully and effectively in the international decision-making process in the solution of world economic, financial and monetary problems, *inter alia*, through the appropriate international organizations, in accordance with their existing and evolving rules, and to share equitably in the benefits resulting therefrom.

Article 11

All States should co-operate to strengthen and continuously improve the efficiency of international organizations in implementing measures to stimulate the general economic progress of all countries, particularly of developing countries, and therefore should co-operate to adapt them, when appropriate, to the changing needs of international economic co-operation.

Article 12

1. States have the right, in agreement with the parties concerned, to participate in subregional, regional and interregional co-operation in the pursuit of their economic and social development. All States engaged in such co-operation have the duty to ensure that the policies of those groupings to which they belong correspond to the provisions of the present Charter and are outward-looking, consistent with their international obligations and with the needs of international economic co-operation, and have full regard for the legitimate interests of third countries, especially developing countries.

2. In the case of groupings to which the States concerned have transferred or may transfer certain competences as regards matters that come within the scope of the present Charter, its provisions shall also apply to those groupings in regard to such matters, consistent with the responsibilities of such States as members of such groupings. Those States shall co-operate in the observance by the groupings of the provisions of this Charter.

Article 13

1. Every State has the right to benefit from the advances and developments in science and technology for the acceleration of its economic and social development.

2. All States should promote international scientific and technological co-operation and the transfer of technology, with proper regard for all legitimate interests including, *inter alia*, the rights and duties of holders, suppliers and recipients of technology. In particular, all States should facilitate the access of developing countries to the achievements of modern science and technology, the transfer of technology and the creation of indigenous technology for the benefit of the developing countries in forms and in accordance with procedures which are suited to their economies and their needs.

3. Accordingly, developed countries should co-operate with the developing countries in the establishment, strengthening and development of their scientific and technological infrastructures and their scientific research and technological activities so as to help to expand and transform the economies of developing countries.

4. All States should co-operate in research with a view to evolving further internationally accepted guidelines or regulations for the transfer of technology, taking fully into account the interests of developing countries.

Article 14

Every State has the duty to co-operate in promoting a steady and increasing expansion and liberalization of world trade and an improvement in the welfare and living standards of all peoples, in particular those of developing countries. Accordingly, all States should co-operate, *inter alia*, towards the progressive dismantling of obstacles to trade and the improvement of the international framework for the conduct of world trade and, to these ends, co-ordinated efforts shall be made to solve in an equitable way the trade problems of all countries, taking into account the specific trade problems of the developing countries. In this connexion, States shall take measures aimed at securing additional benefits for the international trade of developing countries so as to achieve a substantial increase in their foreign exchange earnings, the diversification of their exports, the acceleration of the rate of growth of their trade, taking into account their development needs, an improvement in the possibilities for these countries to participate in the expansion of world trade and a balance more favourable to developing countries in the sharing of the advantages resulting from this expansion, through, in the largest possible measure, a substantial improvement in the conditions of access for the products of interest to the developing countries and, wherever appropriate, measures designed to attain stable, equitable and remunerative prices for primary products.

Article 15

All States have the duty to promote the achievement of general and complete disarmament under effective international control and to utilize the resources released by effective disarmament measures for the economic and social development of countries, allocating a substantial portion of such resources as additional means for the development needs of developing countries.

Article 16

1. It is the right and duty of all States, individually and collectively, to eliminate colonialism, *apartheid*, racial discrimination, neo-colonialism and all forms of foreign aggression, occupation and domination, and the economic and social consequences thereof, as a prerequisite for development. States which practise such coercive policies are economically responsible to the countries, territories and peoples affected for the restitution and full compensation for

the exploitation and depletion of, and damages to, the natural and all other resources of those countries, territories and peoples. It is the duty of all States to extend assistance to them.

2. No State has the right to promote or encourage investments that may constitute an obstacle to the liberation of a territory occupied by force.

Article 17

International co-operation for development is the shared goal and common duty of all States. Every State should co-operate with the efforts of developing countries to accelerate their economic and social development by providing favourable external conditions and by extending active assistance to them, consistent with their development needs and objectives, with strict respect for the sovereign equality of States and free of any conditions derogating from their sovereignty.

Article 18

Developed countries should extend, improve and enlarge the system of generalized non-reciprocal and non-discriminatory tariff preferences to the developing countries consistent with the relevant agreed conclusions and relevant decisions as adopted on this subject, in the framework of the competent international organizations. Developed countries should also give serious consideration to the adoption of other differential measures, in areas where this is feasible and appropriate and in ways which will provide special and more favourable treatment, in order to meet the trade and development needs of the developing countries. In the conduct of international economic relations the developed countries should endeavour to avoid measures having a negative effect on the development of the national economies of the developing countries, as promoted by generalized tariff preferences and other generally agreed differential measures in their favour.

Article 19

With a view to accelerating the economic growth of developing countries and bridging the economic gap between developed and developing countries, developed countries should grant generalized preferential, non-reciprocal and non-discriminatory treatment to developing countries in those fields of international economic co-operation where it may be feasible.

Article 20

Developing countries should, in their efforts to increase their over-all trade, give due attention to the possibility of expanding their trade with socialist countries, by granting to these countries conditions for trade not inferior to those granted normally to the developed market economy countries.

Article 21

Developing countries should endeavour to promote the expansion of their mutual trade and to this end may, in accordance with the existing and evolving provisions and procedures of international agreements where applicable, grant trade preferences to other developing countries without being obliged to extend such preferences to developed countries, provided these arrangements do not constitute an impediment to general trade liberalization and expansion.

Article 22

1. All States should respond to the generally recognized or mutually agreed development needs and objectives of developing countries by promoting increased net flows of real resources to the developing countries from all sources, taking into account any obligations and commitments undertaken by the States concerned, in order to reinforce the efforts of developing countries to accelerate their economic and social development.

2. In this context, consistent with the aims and objectives mentioned above and taking into account any obligations and commitments undertaken in this regard, it should be their endeavour to increase the net amount of financial flows from official sources to developing countries and to improve the terms and conditions thereof.

3. The flow of development assistance resources should include economic and technical assistance.

Article 23

To enhance the effective mobilization of their own resources, the developing countries should strengthen their economic co-operation and expand their mutual trade so as to accelerate their economic and social development. All countries, especially developed countries, individually as well as through the competent international organizations of which they are members, should provide appropriate and effective support and co-operation.

Article 24

All States have the duty to conduct their mutual economic relations in a manner which takes into account the interests of other countries. In particular, all States should avoid prejudicing the interests of developing countries.

Article 25

In furtherance of world economic development, the international community, especially its developed members, shall pay special attention to the particular needs and problems of the least developed among the developing countries, of land-locked developing countries and also island developing countries, with a view to helping them to overcome their particular difficulties and thus contribute to their economic and social development.

Article 26

All States have the duty to coexist in tolerance and live together in peace, irrespective of differences in political, economic, social and cultural systems, and to facilitate trade between States having different economic and social systems. International trade should be conducted without prejudice to generalized non-discriminatory and non-reciprocal preferences in favour of developing countries, on the basis of mutual advantage, equitable benefits and the exchange of most-favoured-nation treatment.

Article 27

1. Every State has the right to enjoy fully the benefits of world invisible trade and to engage in the expansion of such trade.
2. World invisible trade, based on efficiency and mutual and equitable benefit, furthering the expansion of the world economy, is the common goal of all States. The role of developing countries in world invisible trade should be enhanced and strengthened consistent with the above objectives, particular attention being paid to the special needs of developing countries.
3. All States should co-operate with developing countries in their endeavours to increase their capacity to earn foreign exchange from invisible transactions, in accordance with the potential and needs of

each developing country and consistent with the objectives mentioned above.

Article 28

All States have the duty to co-operate in achieving adjustments in the prices of exports of developing countries in relation to prices of their imports so as to promote just and equitable terms of trade for them, in a manner which is remunerative for producers and equitable for producers and consumers.

CHAPTER III

COMMON RESPONSIBILITIES TOWARDS THE INTERNATIONAL COMMUNITY

Article 29

The sea-bed and ocean floor and the subsoil thereof, beyond the limits of national jurisdiction, as well as the resources of the area, are the common heritage of mankind. On the basis of the principles adopted by the General Assembly in resolution 2749 (XXV) of 17 December 1970, all States shall ensure that the exploration of the area and exploitation of its resources are carried out exclusively for peaceful purposes and that the benefits derived therefrom are shared equitably by all States, taking into account the particular interests and needs of developing countries; an international régime applying to the area and its resources and including appropriate international machinery to give effect to its provisions shall be established by an international treaty of a universal character, generally agreed upon.

Article 30

The protection, preservation and enhancement of the environment for the present and future generations is the responsibility of all States. All States shall endeavour to establish their own environmental and developmental policies in conformity with such responsibility. The environmental policies of all States should enhance and not adversely affect the present and future development potential of developing countries. All States have the responsibility to ensure that activities within their jurisdiction or control do not cause damage to the environment of other States or of areas beyond the limits of national jurisdiction. All States should co-operate in evolving international norms and regulations in the field of the environment.

CHAPTER IV

FINAL PROVISIONS

Article 31

All States have the duty to contribute to the balanced expansion of the world economy, taking duly into account the close interrelationship between the well-being of the developed countries and the growth and development of the developing countries, and the fact that the prosperity of the international community as a whole depends upon the prosperity of its constituent parts.

Article 32

No State may use or encourage the use of economic, political or any other type of measures to coerce another State in order to obtain from it the subordination of the exercise of its sovereign rights.

Article 33

1. Nothing in the present Charter shall be construed as impairing or derogating from the provisions of the Charter of the United Nations or actions taken in pursuance thereof.
2. In their interpretation and application, the provisions of the present Charter are interrelated and each provision should be construed in the context of the other provisions.

Article 34

An item on the Charter of Economic Rights and Duties of States shall be included in the agenda of the General Assembly at its thirtieth session, and thereafter on the agenda of every fifth session. In this way a systematic and comprehensive consideration of the implementation of the Charter, covering both progress achieved and any improvements and additions which might become necessary, would be carried out and appropriate measures recommended. Such consideration should take into account the evolution of all the economic, social, legal and other factors related to the principles upon which the present Charter is based and on its purpose.

33. CURBING CHEMICAL AND BIOLOGICAL WARFARE

(December 10-16, 1974)

[Absent from the foregoing survey of the 29th General Assembly is an account of its deliberations in the field of arms control and disarmament, a permanent U.N. concern that gave rise in 1974 to 21 separate resolutions, among which the United States supported or voted in favor of eleven while abstaining on the remainder.[1] But though these actions bore witness to the importance of disarmament in the eyes of the U.N. membership, they represented no more than a minor front in a struggle whose more decisive engagements were taking place elsewhere—primarily in such specialized forums as the bilateral Strategic Arms Limitation Talks (SALT), the Vienna conference on mutual force reduction (MBFR), and the 26-nation, Geneva-based Conference of the Committee on Disarmament (CCD)—whose membership was scheduled to increase to 31 with the addition of the two German states, Iran, Peru, and Zaïre on January 1, 1975.[2]

Four substantive issues attracted special attention during 1974 in the area of multilateral arms control that constituted the special concern of both the CCD and the General Assembly. India's nuclear explosion of May 18 focused renewed and anxious attention on the problems of nuclear proliferation. Despite the inhibitions embodied in the 1968 nuclear nonproliferation treaty, it was realized, numerous countries were now approaching the point where they might be able to acquire nuclear weapons as a by-product of the development of nuclear power. To some observers it seemed that the likelihood of such dangerous developments had been accentuated by President Nixon's promise, in the course of his journey to the Middle East, to furnish nuclear reactors and fuel to Egypt and Israel.[3] Though Secretary Kissinger and other U.S. offi-

[1]Details in *U.S. Participation, 1974*: 55-78.
[2]For a review of the work of the CCD in 1974 see same: 46-55.
[3]Cf. Chapter 12.

cials insisted that the detailed agreements to be negotiated with those two countries would preclude diversion of nuclear material for military purposes,[4] the Secretary of State in his September 23 address to the General Assembly[5] particularly stressed the need to strengthen existing restraints on nuclear proliferation on a world-wide basis. No specific proposals, however, seemed likely to be forthcoming in advance of the conference to review the non-proliferation treaty that was scheduled to take place in May 1975.

The Indian explosion also stimulated renewed discussion of the familiar question of a treaty that would prohibit underground nuclear weapon tests and thus complete the system of prohibitions initiated in 1963 with the treaty banning nuclear weapon tests in the atmosphere, in outer space and under water. The main development in this area during 1974 was the signature by President Nixon and General Secretary Brezhnev of the so-called Threshold Test Ban (TTB) Treaty pledging the two powers not to conduct underground nuclear weapon tests with an explosive yield of more than 150 kilotons.[6] But this bilateral treaty between the two leading nuclear powers—which would not enter into force until a parallel limitation on peaceful underground explosions could be negotiated—would have little if any relevance to the problem presented by countries in the early stages of nuclear technology. As Secretary Kissinger pointed out to a congressional subcommittee, it was "unrealistic to make a distinction at the early stages of nuclear development between peaceful uses and potential military applications because any capacity to produce an explosion has obvious military application, no matter what purpose the country concerned asserts it is attempting to serve."[7]

Another outgrowth of the Moscow summit of 1974 was a heightened awareness of the perils involved in any attempt to modify the natural environment for military purposes, a danger highlighted in a special statement by Messrs. Nixon and Brezhnev.[8] In a bid for early action in this new and unfamiliar field, the Soviet Union later submitted to the General Assembly the text of a fully worked-out draft convention "on the prohibition of action to influence the environment and climate for military and other purposes incompatible with the maintenance of international security, human well-being and health." Although the United States maintained that much additional study was required, the Assembly decided to pass the Soviet draft to the CCD with a request for early

[4]*Bulletin*, 71: 123-4 and 484-6.
[5]Chapter 21, Document 47.
[6]Chapter 15, Document 25.
[7]Quoted in *U.S. Participation, 1974*: 51.
[8]Chapter 15, Document 26.

consideration and action. (Subsequently, in August 1975, the United States and the Soviet Union submitted to the CCD identical drafts of a Convention on the Prohibition of Military or Any Other Hostile Use of Environmental Modification Techniques. The final test of such a convention was approved by the General Assembly on December 10, 1976.)[9]

Significant progress was achieved in 1974 in the longstanding campaign to inhibit any future resort to chemical or bacteriological (biological) warfare. The easier part of this problem had been dealt with through the recent conclusion of a Convention on the Prohibition of the Development, Production and Stockpiling of Bacteriological (Biological) and Toxin Weapons and on Their Destruction,[10] which had been opened for signature in Washington, London, and Moscow on April 10, 1972 and, by December 1974, had been signed by 110 states and ratified by 37. Although the convention was not yet in force and none of the three depositary governments (U.S.S.R., U.K., and U.S.) had deposited its instrument of ratification, the United Kingdom had completed the necessary parliamentary procedures and the U.S.S.R. had also announced its intention to ratify before the end of 1974.

A parallel endeavor, aimed at the prohibition and destruction of chemical weapons, had been fraught with much greater difficulty, primarily because of more complicated verification requirements. In recognition of the likelihood that a comprehensive convention in this area would take some time to complete, Messrs. Nixon and Brezhnev had agreed at their Moscow summit meeting to consider the possibility of adopting a step-by-step approach that could commence with a convention limited to "the most dangerous, lethal means of chemical warfare."[11] No action along these lines, however, was reported during 1974—or, for that matter, until August 1976, when initial consultations on the subject were held in Moscow.[12]

For the American Government, the problems of chemical and bacteriological warfare presented a special dimension as a result of its failure, thus far, to become a party to the so-called Geneva Protocol or "Protocol for the Prohibition of the Use in War of Asphyxiating, Poisonous or other Gases, and of Bacteriological

[9]Text of Soviet draft convention annexed to Resolution 3264 (XXIX), Dec. 9, 1974; U.S. views in *Bulletin*, 72: 77-8. For later developments see same, 73: 419-20 (1975). The final text of the convention was annexed to General Assembly Resolution 31/72 of Dec. 10, 1976, and can be found in *Bulletin*, 76: 27-9 (1977).

[10]TIAS 8062 (26 UST 583); text in *AFR, 1971*: 90-95.

[11]Chapter 15, Document 23.

[12]*Bulletin*, 75: 423 (1976).

Warfare.''[13] Originally concluded at Geneva in 1925 with the aim of prohibiting a resort to either chemical or bacteriological methods of warfare, the protocol had failed to win the endorsement of the U.S. Senate in 1926 but had nevertheless been ratified in course of time by no fewer than 103 other governments, including all major powers except the United States. (Most governments had accepted with reservations stating, in effect, that they would not resort to such methods unless they were first used by other powers against them.)

As part of a general readjustment of U.S. policies in the field of chemical and bacteriological warfare, President Nixon in 1970 had renewed the administration's request for Senate approval of the Geneva Protocol. He had, however, offered no response to a subsequent request from Chairman J.W. Fulbright of the Senate Foreign Relations Committee for a reconsideration of the administration's announced view on certain points of interpretation. Particularly troubling to the committee and its chairman was the administration's contention that, contrary to the prevailing opinion as expressed in various resolutions of the U.N. Assembly, the terms of the Geneva Protocol did *not* prohibit the use in war of "riot-control agents and chemical herbicides" such as the United States had used on a large scale in Vietnam.[14]

Now that the war in Vietnam was over and President Nixon had left the White House, a significant modification of the administration stand was authorized by President Ford and communicated to the Foreign Relations Committee by Fred C. Iklé, the Director of the U.S. Arms Control and Disarmament Agency (ACDA). In outlining the new policy in a statement to the committee on December 10, Dr. Iklé also urged early approval of the Biological Weapons Convention, "so that we will not be the ones who prevent the treaty from coming into force."]

(72) The Geneva Protocol of 1925 and the Biological Weapons Convention of 1972: Statement by Fred C. Iklé, Director of the United States Arms Control and Disarmament Agency (ACDA), before the Senate Committee on Foreign Relations, December 10, 1974. [15]

I appreciate the opportunity to testify this morning on the Geneva Protocol of 1925 and the Biological Weapons Convention

---

[13]Done at Geneva June 17, 1925 and entered into force for the U.S. Apr. 10, 1975 (TIAS 8061; 26 UST 571); partial text in *Documents, 1968-69*: 107n.
[14]*AFR, 1971*: 72-3 and 80-83.
[15]ACDA Press Release 74-10, Dec. 10; text from *Bulletin*, 72: 93-5.

of 1972. Ratification of these two arms control agreements in the field of chemical and biological warfare has the strong support of the President and the executive branch. We welcome the initiative of the committee in holding this hearing, which we hope will lead to prompt ratification of both agreements.

As you know, the Geneva Protocol of 1925 prohibits the use—in effect, the first use—of chemical and biological agents of war. Except for the United States, all militarily important countries are parties to the protocol.

The extensive hearings on the protocol held by this committee in March 1971[16] examined the reasons why U.S. ratification of the protocol has been so long delayed. In the interest of brevity, I shall not go back over this record now, although I would of course be happy to respond to any questions regarding the history of the protocol.

During the 1971 hearings, differing views were expressed on the question of including riot control agents and herbicides within the scope of the protocol. As a result, the committee requested that the executive branch reexamine its interpretation of the protocol's scope.[17]

In response to the committee's request, the executive branch has undertaken a comprehensive review. We have reconsidered our legal interpretation and analyzed possible alternatives for resolving differences of opinion on the scope of the protocol. We have evaluated the military utility of riot control agents and herbicides. And we have of course carefully considered alternative approaches that would accomplish our arms control objectives.

Mr. Chairman,[18] the President considers it important that the United States ratify the Geneva Protocol at the earliest possible date. On the basis of an interagency review he has very recently taken decisions with a view to achieving Senate advice and consent to ratification. The President has authorized me to announce those decisions today.

The President has authorized me to state on his behalf that he is prepared, in reaffirming the current U.S. understanding of the scope of the protocol, to renounce as a matter of national policy:

1. First use of herbicides in war except use, under regulations applicable to their domestic use, for control of vegetation within U.S. bases and installations or around their immediate defensive perimeters.

2. First use of riot control agents in war except in defensive military modes to save lives such as:

[16]Cf. *AFR, 1971*: 74-80.
[17]Same: 80-83.
[18]Senator J. William Fulbright (Democrat of Arkansas).

a. Use of riot control agents in riot control circumstances to include controlling rioting prisoners of war. This exception would permit use of riot control agents in riot situations in areas under direct and distinct U.S. military control.

b. Use of riot control agents in situations where civilian casualties can be reduced or avoided. This use would be restricted to situations in which civilians are used to mask or screen attacks.

c. Use of riot control agents in rescue missions. The use of riot control agents would be permissible in the recovery of remotely isolated personnel such as downed aircrews (and passengers).

d. Use of riot control agents in rear-echelon areas outside the combat zone to protect convoys from civil disturbances, terrorists, and paramilitary organizations.

The President intends to conform U.S. policy to this position, assuming the Senate consents.

Finally, the President, under an earlier directive still in force, must approve in advance any use of riot control agents and chemical herbicides in war.

Mr. Chairman, I believe that you may have several specific questions concerning this policy. I would be happy to respond to such questions at this time before I proceed to the section of my statement dealing with the Biological Weapons Convention.

The second agreement before the committee is the Biological Weapons Convention of 1972. The full title is the Convention on the Prohibition of the Development, Production and Stockpiling of Bacteriological (Biological) and Toxin Weapons and on Their Destruction. As the title suggests, this convention completely prohibits biological and toxin weapons. Since it provides for the elimination of existing weapons, it is a true disarmament measure.

The convention is entirely consistent with U.S. policy concerning biological and toxin weapons, since the U.S. had already unilaterally renounced these weapons before the convention was negotiated.[19] In fact, our entire stockpile of biological and toxin agents and weapons has already been destroyed. Our biological warfare facilities have been converted to peaceful uses.

Since opening the convention for signature in April 1972, 110 nations have become signatories. This includes all members of the Warsaw Pact and all members of NATO except France. In order for this treaty to come into force it must be ratified by the three depositaries—the United States, the United Kingdom, and the U.S.S.R.—and at least 19 other countries. Enough countries have

---

[19]Nixon statement, Nov. 29, 1969, in *Documents, 1968-69*: 106-9; Nixon statement, Feb. 14, 1970, in same, *1970*: 75-6.

now ratified, some 36, so that only ratification by depositaries is still required. The British have completed all the parliamentary procedures for ratification and the Soviet Union has announced that it intends to ratify before the end of 1974. It is particularly important that U.S. ratification be accomplished in the near future so that we will not be the ones who prevent this treaty from coming into force.

There is one aspect of the convention to which I would like to give particular attention: the question of verification. Verification of compliance with this convention in countries with relatively closed societies is difficult, particularly for the prohibition of the development of these weapons.

Nevertheless, in our judgment, it is in the net interest of the United States to enter into this convention, basically for three reasons:

—First, the military utility of these weapons is dubious at best: the effects are unpredictable and potentially uncontrollable, and there exists no military experience concerning them. Hence the prohibitions of this convention do not deny us a militarily viable option, and verifiability is therefore less important.

—Second, biological weapons are particularly repugnant from a moral point of view.

—Third, widespread adherence to the convention can help discourage some misguided competition in biological weapons.

It is to be feared that without such a prohibition, new developments in the biological sciences might give rise to concern because they could be abused for weapons purposes. Such anxieties could foster secretive military competition in a field of science that would otherwise remain open to international cooperation and be used solely for the benefit of mankind.

It is important, however, that the limited verifiability of this convention should not be misconstrued as a precedent for other arms limitation agreements where these special conditions would not obtain.

Mr. Chairman, the administration believes that the Biological Weapons Convention represents a useful arms control measure. We hope the United States will not prevent the treaty from entering into force through its failure to ratify. By failing to ratify, we would deny ourselves the benefit of having other countries legally committed not to produce weapons that we have already given up. And we would deny 109 other countries the benefit of a treaty that they have already signed.

This completes my prepared statement. I would be happy to respond to any further questions on either the Geneva Protocol or the Biological Weapons Convention.

[In light of these clarifications, the Senate Foreign Relations Committee on December 13 signified its approval of both the Geneva Protocol and the Biological Weapons Convention. In recommending ratification of the Geneva Protocol, the committee endorsed a single reservation, originally proposed by former Secretary of State Rogers, whereby the United States reserved the right to make retaliatory use of chemical weapons and agents, though not of biological methods of warfare. The reservation was phrased as follows:

That the said Protocol shall cease to be binding on the Government of the United States with respect to the use in war of asphyxiating, poisonous or other gases, and of all analogous liquids, materials, or devices, in regard to an enemy State if such State or any of its allies fails to respect the prohibitions laid down in the Protocol.[20]

With this reservation, the Protocol was approved by a 90 to 0 vote of the Senate on December 16, was ratified by President Ford on January 22, 1975, and entered into force for the United States with the deposit of its instrument of ratification on April 10, 1975.

The Biological Weapons Convention, likewise recommended by the Foreign Relations Committee and approved by a Senate vote of 90 to 0 on December 16, was also ratified by President Ford on January 22, 1975, and entered into force with the simultaneous deposit of instruments of ratification by the Soviet Union, the United Kingdom, and the United States on March 26, 1975.]

[20]Senate Executive Report 93-35, Dec. 13, in *Documents on Disarmament, 1974*: 833.

34. NEW START FOR THE WEST

(December 4-16, 1974)

[Throughout the year, American foreign policy had been deprived of full effectiveness by a continuance of the transatlantic dissensions that had simmered since the beginning of the decade, had boiled over at the time of the October War and the oil embargo of 1973, and had been only partially allayed by the diplomatic processes that culminated in the signature of the Declaration on Atlantic Relations at Brussels on June 26, 1974.[1] By December, however, the new administrations that had taken office in several of the Western capitals were more firmly seated, and some of the year's more controversial issues, such as those involved in the establishment of a common energy policy, had been at least provisionally settled. The time seemed ripe for a new attempt at alleviating the remaining differences and attempting to meet in common the challenge of the deepening world recession.

As always, the process of mutual accommodation was significantly furthered by personal meetings among senior governmental leaders, some of whom had enjoyed little if any direct acquaintance in the past. Premier Pierre Elliott Trudeau of Canada, who visited Washington at President Ford's invitation on December 4, struck a characteristic if unexpectedly positive note in responding to the President's toast at a White House dinner. ". . . I think we would both agree," the visitor declared, "that our peoples, Canadian and the American peoples, would cease to support us overnight if they thought that we were embarking on courses which were not friendly, which were not based on cooperation and understanding, on the desire to solve any differences that arise in that spirit of friendship rather than the spirit of hostility . . . . We know that in matters of Atlantic security, détente, and disarmament—we know that we can

[1] Cf. Chapter 14.

follow your lead because the principles on which your policies are based are the same as ours.''[2]

A visit to Washington by Chancellor Helmut Schmidt of the Federal Republic of Germany on December 5-6 gave rise to a lengthier, more formal statement that touched on many of the issues of current Western concern.]

(73) Visit of Chancellor Helmut Schmidt of the Federal Republic of Germany, December 5-6, 1974: Joint communiqué issued at the conclusion of the visit, December 6, 1974. [3]

The President of the United States of America Gerald R. Ford and the Chancellor of the Federal Republic of Germany Helmut Schmidt met in Washington on December 5 and 6, 1974. They reaffirmed the relationship of friendship and trust and confidence between the United States and the Federal Republic of Germany, and they held wide-ranging talks embracing international and economic problems, security and defense policy, and current East-West discussions. Secretary of State and Assistant to the President for National Security Affairs Henry A. Kissinger and Foreign Minister Hans Dietrich Genscher participated in the discussions between the President and the Chancellor and held complementary talks. In the economic talks, the President was joined by members of his Economic Policy Board and the Chancellor was accompanied by representatives of labor and business.

The President and the Chancellor reviewed the world economic situation in depth and explored effective solutions for current economic problems. They were agreed that international energy problems, the sharp increases in world prices, the contraction of economic activities, and large-scale payments imbalance constitute a severe threat to political and social stability in many countries. A creative new effort to coordinate economic policies between the United States and the Federal Republic of Germany, together with its partners in the European Community, will be required to master these difficulties.

The United States of America and the Federal Republic of Germany recognize the responsibility which falls to them for ensuring a prosperous international economy and safeguarding world trade. In this context they attach great significance to the upcoming multilateral trade negotiations. They reaffirmed their international pledges to avoid trade and payments restrictions which adversely affect other countries.

[2]*Presidential Documents*, 10: 1534.
[3]Text from *Presidential Documents*, 10: 1541-4.

The President and the Chancellor agreed that in current circumstances they both have a responsibility to manage their domestic economic policies so as simultaneously to strengthen output and employment and to avoid new inflationary impulses. They affirmed that both countries have a need to encourage investment, to combat rising unemployment, and to act to increase confidence in the financial and economic outlook. They recognized that the two countries are at different points in their fight against inflation, and that policies will take that fact into account. They are determined not to permit a serious deterioration in their economies to occur. If necessary, they will step in with adequate measures to prevent it.

The United States and the Federal Republic of Germany agreed that determination and cooperation are also necessary in dealing with energy-related problems. They underlined the importance of the International Energy Agency set up within the framework of the Organization for Economic Cooperation and Development to coordinate the energy policies of the industrialized countries.[4] They attach particular importance to measures to reduce dependence on imported energy through conservation, more economic use of energy, and opening up of alternative sources. They stressed the need for cooperation in the field of research, notably in relation to coal processing and gasification.

Despite cooperative efforts to reduce dependence on energy imports, the President and the Chancellor recognized that in the coming year there will continue to be large scale imbalances in trade among nations and a corresponding necessity for large international flows of funds. They recognized that these flows for the most part have been, and in all probability will continue to be, handled by existing private and official channels. At the same time they agreed on the necessity of close cooperation among the financial authorities to insure the continued safe and orderly functioning of financial institutions in their expanding international roles. They agreed on the importance of the International Monetary Fund and other multilateral financial agencies being in a position in 1975 to provide flexible responsive financial assistance to any member nation facing international payments difficulties arising from the rapidly changing world economic situation. In addition, to insure that industrial countries which follow prudent and cooperative economic and energy policies have access to adequate financial resources in case of need, the President and the Chancellor agreed that early consideration should be given by these nations to the establishment of a supplementary financial safety net in the framework of the OECD.

[4]Cf. Chapter 29.

The President and the Chancellor also stressed their determination to improve cooperation with the oil-producing countries. They expressed the conviction that further economic progress in the world, both in the developing and the developed countries, can only be resolved by means of world-wide cooperation.

The United States and the Federal Republic of Germany recognize the necessity of international cooperation to improve the international food situation. They will undertake prompt discussions on an international system of nationally-held grain reserves, increased global food production and substantial growth in food output in developing countries in order to prevent the recurrence of major food problems in the future. Both recognize the need for cooperation between food producers and consumers to ensure equitable adjustment to shortages and deficits.

The discussions on political questions centered on the North Atlantic Alliance, the evolution of East-West relations, and the situation in the Mediterranean and in the Near East.

The President and the Chancellor reviewed the progress of matters before the Alliance on the eve of the NATO Ministerial meeting to be convened next week in Brussels.[5] They agreed on the continuing importance to the Allies of maintaining their political cohesion and strong defenses as the indispensable prerequisites for continued efforts to advance the process of East-West détente. Against the background of current challenges to their strength and solidarity, they reaffirmed their support for the principles of the Declaration on Atlantic Relations signed by Allied Heads of Government in June 1974.[6]

The President and the Chancellor reiterated their resolve to contribute to the process of détente and the growth of cooperation between East and West. President Ford reviewed the SALT negotiations in the light of his talks with General Secretary Brezhnev in Vladivostok.[7] They noted with satisfaction that it has been agreed to aim for limitations on strategic nuclear weapons on the basis of equality. The Chancellor expressed his appreciation for the progress achieved in Vladivostok which he considered most important for the pursuit of the policy of détente and safeguarding peace. President Ford and Chancellor Schmidt agreed that the understandings of Vladivostok would have a salutary effect on the overall development of East-West relations.

The two delegations also discussed the state of negotiations in Vienna on mutual and balanced force reductions in Central Europe. They confirmed their shared view that the aim of MBFR

[5]Cf. Document 74.
[6]Chapter 14, Document 21b.
[7]Cf. Chapter 31.

should be to arrive at a common ceiling for forces of both alliance systems.

Both sides expressed the hope that the Conference on Security and Cooperation in Europe would soon complete its initial consideration of texts dealing with all items on the agenda. It would then be possible to enter into the final stage of the negotiations. They agreed that certain progress had recently been made in reaching agreement on such areas as family reunification and improved access to printed information. They noted, however, that important texts still remain to be agreed, especially with regard to the Declaration of Principles governing Relations between States.

The President and Secretary of State Kissinger reviewed the United States' efforts to contribute to progress toward the achievement of a just and lasting peace in the Middle East. Both sides emphasized the importance of the disengagement agreements and of further results in the negotiating process.

As to developments in the Eastern Mediterranean, both sides stressed the responsibility of the parties immediately concerned. They stated their readiness to encourage Greece, Turkey, and Cyprus in the search for a mutually acceptable settlement of the dispute on the basis of the independence and territorial integrity of the Republic of Cyprus.

The German side reviewed the state of the relations of the Federal Republic of Germany with the GDR [German Democratic Republic] and of the issue of foreign representation of West Berlin by the Federal Republic of Germany. Both sides were agreed on the importance of maintaining and developing the ties between the Federal Republic of Germany and West Berlin as well as full and complete implementation of all other parts of the Quadripartite Agreement.[8]

The President and the Federal Chancellor reaffirmed the attachment of their Governments and peoples to the high purposes of the United Nations. They reviewed the proceedings of the current General Assembly and expressed their hope that the spirit of cooperation would prevail over divergences and divisions so that the cause of international harmony, cooperation and a sound and enduring peace would be furthered.

The President and the Chancellor agreed to remain in close touch with one another, and to consult on all matters of mutual interest as might be required in the future.

[His Washington visit concluded, Chancellor Schmidt was due in Paris for a summit meeting of European Community leaders on

[8]Cf. *AFR, 1971*: 162-70.

December 9-10. Its main result would be a decision to try to in-
vigorate the process of political consolidation in Europe by scheduling at least three summit meetings a year in the framework of the
Council of the Communities.

Overlapping the Paris summit was a series of important meetings
at NATO Headquarters in Brussels, where the ten-nation "Euro-
group" and the NATO Nuclear Planning Group and Defense Planning Committee were engaged in periodic sessions that would be
followed by the semiannual ministerial meeting of the North Atlantic Council. A highlight of the discussion of defense issues, in
which the United States was represented by Defense Secretary
James R. Schlesinger, was a report on the Warsaw Pact forces that
stressed the continuing build-up of Soviet and allied military
capabilities even while the U.S.S.R. pursued its détente policy on
the political level. Not for the first time, the NATO Defense Ministers felt called upon to express "their deep concern at the scale of
resources which the Soviet Union is continuing to devote to military
purposes, which indicates its determination to seek military superiority over the West, and . . . that these resources already provide
the Soviet Union and its Allies with a military power far in excess of
that required for self-defence."[9]

However ominous the long-range military picture, it still took
second place to economic dangers when Secretary Kissinger and the
other allied Foreign Ministers assembled in Brussels for the 58th
ministerial session of the North Atlantic Council, held on
December 12-13 under a new format that favored sustained and intimate discussion rather than set speeches.[10] The fundamental importance of economic factors at this period of incipient world recession was given special recognition in the communiqué that listed
the main achievements of the session.]

(74) Ministerial Meeting of the North Atlantic Council, Brussels, December 12-13, 1974: Final communiqué.[11]

1. The North Atlantic Council met in Ministerial session in
Brussels on 12th and 13th December, 1974. At the close of the year
which marked the 25th Anniversary of the Alliance, Ministers
noted with satisfaction that member countries remain firmly committed to the Alliance and that this had found solemn expression in
the Ottawa Declaration.[12]

[9]Communiqué, Dec. 11, in *NATO Review*, Jan. 1975: 25.
[10]Same: 3.
[11]Department of State Press Release 532, Dec. 16; text from *Bulletin*, 72: 5-7.
[12]Chapter 14, Document 21b.

2. Ministers reviewed developments in East-West relations. They noted the progress, albeit uneven, towards détente over the past six months. They stated their readiness to continue their efforts to make progress in their negotiations and exchanges with the Soviet Union and Warsaw Pact countries aimed at steady improvement in East-West relations. Noting, however, the increase in the military strength of the Warsaw Pact countries, and bearing in mind that security is the prerequisite for the policy of détente, they expressed their determination to maintain their own defensive military strength.

3. Ministers had a broad discussion on the implications of the current economic situation for the maintenance of Alliance defense and noted the efforts made at both the national and international levels to overcome the difficulties confronting the economies of the allied countries. They reaffirmed their determination to seek appropriate solutions in the spirit of cooperation and mutual confidence which characterizes their relations. Ministers decided to continue to consult on the repercussions of economic developments on areas within the direct sphere of competence of the Alliance.

4. Ministers noted that at the Conference on Security and Cooperation in Europe there had been enough progress to show that substantial results were possible. Nonetheless, important questions remain to be resolved. Ministers expressed the undiminished determination of their Governments to work patiently and constructively towards balanced and substantial results under all the agenda headings of the Conference, so as to bring about a satisfactory conclusion to the Conference as a whole as soon as may be possible.

5. Ministers of the participating countries reviewed the state of the negotiations in Vienna on Mutual and Balanced Force Reductions. These negotiations have as their general objective to contribute to a more stable relationship and to the strengthening of peace and security in Europe, and their success would advance détente. These Ministers were resolved to pursue these negotiations with a view to ensuring undiminished security for all parties, at a lower level of forces in Central Europe. They reaffirmed their commitment to the establishment of approximate parity in the form of an agreed common ceiling for the ground force manpower of NATO and the Warsaw Pact in the area of reductions. They considered that a first phase reduction agreement covering United States and Soviet ground forces would be an important and practical first step in this direction. They noted that the negotiations have, so far, not produced results and expressed the hope that a constructive response to the Allied proposals would soon be forthcoming. They reaffirmed the importance they attach to the princi-

ple to which they adhere in these negotiations that NATO forces should not be reduced except in the context of a Mutual and Balanced Force Reduction Agreement with the East.

6. Ministers heard a report from the United States Secretary of State on the continuing United States efforts towards the further limitation of strategic offensive arms in the light of President Ford's recent talks with Mr. Brezhnev.[13] They noted with satisfaction the significant progress towards limitation of strategic nuclear weapons achieved in Vladivostok. They expressed the hope that this progress will lead to the early conclusion of a satisfactory SALT II Agreement. They also expressed appreciation for continuing consultations within the Alliance with respect to the SALT negotiations.

7. The Ministers reviewed the developments concerning Berlin and Germany which have taken place since their last meeting in June 1974, especially as regards the application of those provisions of the Quadripartite Agreement[14] relating to the Western Sectors of Berlin. They considered, in particular, traffic and ties between the Western Sectors and the Federal Republic of Germany and the representation abroad of the interests of those sectors by the Federal Republic of Germany. They emphasized the importance to the viability and security of the city of all provisions of the Quadripartite Agreement. The Ministers also emphasized that there is an essential connection between détente in Europe and the situation relating to Berlin.

8. Ministers expressed their concern about the situation in the Middle East which could have dangerous consequences for world peace and thus for the security of the members of the Alliance. They reaffirmed the overriding importance they attach to fresh progress towards a just and lasting peace in this area. They likewise welcomed the contributions which Allied Governments continue to make to United Nations peace-keeping activities. Ministers noted the report on the situation in the Mediterranean prepared by the Permanent Council on their instructions. They found the instability in the area disquieting, warranting special vigilance on the part of the Allies. They invited the Permanent Council to continue consultations on this subject and to report further.

9. As regards Greek-Turkish relations, Ministers heard a report by the Secretary General[15] under the terms of his watching brief established by the Ministerial session of May 1964. They expressed the firm hope that relations between these two Allied countries would rapidly return to normal.

[13] Cf. Chapter 31.
[14] Cf. note 8 above.
[15] Joseph M.A.H. Luns (The Netherlands).

10. Ministers noted the progress of the work of the Committee on the Challenges of Modern Society, especially on solar and geothermal energy resources as well as on coastal water pollution, improved sewage disposal, urban transport and health care. Ministers also noted the start of projects on the disposal of hazardous wastes and action to follow up completed CCMS studies on the prevention of ocean oil spills, road safety improvement, cleaner air and purer river water, thus enhancing the quality of life for their citizens.

11. The Ministers directed the Council in permanent session to consider and decide on the date and place of the Spring session of the Ministerial Meeting of the North Atlantic Council.[16]

[A contribution to the slightly easier international atmosphere prevailing during these pre-Christmas weeks was the action of the OPEC ministerial representatives, meeting at the organization's Vienna headquarters on December 12-13, in refraining from a further increase in petroleum prices and freezing the price of oil at current levels for the next nine months in order to give the consuming countries time to adjust their differences and prepare for a "constructive dialogue."[17] Not less contributory to a moderating international climate was the successful meeting of Presidents Ford and Giscard d'Estaing that took place December 14-16 on the French West Indian island of Martinique. Like Presidents Nixon and Pompidou at their meeting in the Azores in 1971,[18] the French and American leaders appeared to experience no great difficulty in compromising on the central issue that had kept their governments at loggerheads for months past—in this case, the issue of when and how to commence a dialogue with the oil exporting countries. Accepting President Giscard's acknowledgment of the need for close cooperation among consuming nations, President Ford agreed in turn that a meeting of consumers and producers should take place at an early date—a decision that paved the way for the "Preparatory Meeting for the International Conference Proposed by the President of France" (Prepcon) that was actually to take place in Paris on April 7-15, 1975. Possibly even more significant than this agreement of detail was the measure of personal rapport established between the leaders of two countries that so often represented opposite extremes in the affairs of the West.]

---

[16]The North Atlantic Council met in Brussels with the participation of heads of state and government on May 29-30, 1975; for the communiqué see *Bulletin*, 72: 889-90.
[17]*Keesing's*: 27350-51 (1975).
[18]Cf. *AFR, 1971*: 181 and 605-7.

*(75) Meeting in Martinique between President Ford and President
Valéry Giscard d'Estaing of the French Republic, December
14-16, 1974: Joint communiqué issued at the conclusion of
the meeting.* [19]

The President of the United States, Gerald R. Ford, and the
President of the French Republic, Valery Giscard d'Estaing, met in
Martinique December 14-16, 1974, to discuss current issues of
mutual concern. They were joined in their discussions by the
Secretary of State and Assistant to the President for National
Security Affairs Henry A. Kissinger and Minister of Foreign Af-
fairs Jean Sauvagnargues, and by Secretary of the Treasury
William Simon and Minister of Finance Jean-Pierre Fourcade. The
Ministers also held complementary side talks.

The meeting took place in an atmosphere of cordiality and mutual confidence. President Ford and President Giscard d'Estaing
welcomed the opportunity to conduct detailed substantive discussions on the whole range of subjects of mutual concern. As traditional friends and allies, the two nations share common values and
goals and the two Presidents expressed their determination to
cooperate on this basis in efforts to solve common problems.

They reviewed the international situation in the economic, financial and monetary fields.

The two Presidents agreed that the Governments of the United
States and of the European Community, in the name of which the
French President spoke on this subject, must adopt consistent
economic policies in order to be effective in avoiding unemployment while fighting inflation. In particular, they agreed on the importance of avoiding measures of a protectionist nature. And they
decided to take the initiative in calling additional intergovernmental meetings should they prove necessary for achievement of
the desired consistency of basic economic policies among industrial
nations.

In the light of the rapid pace of change in international financial
positions in the world today, the Presidents were in full agreement
on the desirability of maintaining the momentum of consideration
of closer financial cooperation both within the International Monetary Fund and through supplementary measures. As one specific
measure to strengthen the existing financial framework, the Presidents agreed that it would be appropriate for any Government
which wished to do so to adopt current market prices as the basis of
valuation for its gold holdings.

The two Presidents considered in depth the energy problem and
its serious and disturbing effects on the world economy. They

[19]Text from *Presidential Documents*, 10: 1571-3.

recognized the importance for the USA, the EEC [European Economic Community] and other industrialized nations of implementing policies for the conservation of energy, the development of existing and alternative sources of energy, and the setting up of new mechanisms of financial solidarity. They stressed the importance of solidarity among oil importing nations on these issues.

The two Presidents also exchanged views on the desirability of a dialogue between consumers and producers and in that connection discussed the proposal of the President of the French Republic of October 24 for a conference of oil exporting and importing countries.[20] They agreed that it would be desirable to convene such a meeting at the earliest possible date. They regard it as important that all parties concerned should be better informed of their respective interests and concerns and that harmonious relations should be established among them in order to promote a healthy development of the world economy.

The two Presidents noted that their views on these matters are complementary and, in this context, they agreed that the following interrelated steps should be taken in sequence:

—They agreed that additional steps should be taken, within the framework of existing institutions and agreements to which they are a party, and in consultation with other interested consumers, to strengthen their cooperation. In particular, such cooperation should include programs of energy conservation, for the development of existing and alternative sources of energy and for financial solidarity.

—Based on substantial progress in the foregoing areas, the two Presidents agreed that it will be desirable to propose holding a preparatory meeting between consumers and producers to develop an agenda and procedures for a consumer/producer conference. The target date for such a preparatory meeting should be March 1975.

—The preparatory discussions will be followed by intensive consultations among consumer countries in order to prepare positions for the conference.

The two Presidents agreed that the actions enumerated above will be carried out in the most expeditious manner possible and in full awareness of the common interest in meeting this critical situation shared by the United States and France and all other countries involved.

President Ford and President Giscard d'Estaing reviewed current developments in East-West relations. They discussed their respec-

[20]Cf. Chapter 29.

tive meetings with General Secretary Brezhnev, and Secretary Kiss-singer reported on his discussions with leaders of the People's Republic of China. They exchanged views on developments in East-West negotiations, including the Conference on Security and Coop-eration in Europe. They expressed their conviction that progress in easing tensions was being made.

The two Presidents exchanged views on the present situation in the Middle East. They agreed on the importance of early progress toward a just and lasting peace in that area.

President Giscard d'Estaing described current efforts by France and other members of the European Community to further the pro-cess of European unity. President Ford reaffirmed the continuing support of the United States for efforts to achieve European unity.

The two Presidents discussed the situation in Indochina.[21] They noted that progress in Laos toward reconciliation and reunification was encouraging.

The two Presidents agreed on the need for all parties to support fully the Paris Peace Agreements on Vietnam.[22] Regarding Cam-bodia, they expressed the hope that the contending parties would enter into negotiations in the near future rather than continuing the military struggle. They expressed the hope that following Laos, Cambodia and Vietnam might also find their political way towards civil peace.

The two Presidents renewed the pledges of both Governments to continue close relations in the field of defense as members of the Atlantic Alliance. They agreed that the cooperation between France and NATO is a significant factor in the security of Europe.

They noted with satisfaction that the positive steps in negotia-tions on SALT taken during the Soviet-American meeting at Vladivostok have reduced the threat of a nuclear arms race. The two Presidents explored how, as exporters of nuclear materials and technology, their two countries could coordinate their efforts to assure improved safeguards of nuclear materials.

The President of France indicated that his Government was pre-pared to reach a financial settlement in connection with the relo-cation of American forces and bases committed to NATO from France to other countries in 1967. The French offer of $100 million in full settlement was formally accepted by President Ford.

The two Presidents concluded that the personal contact and discussion in this meeting had demonstrated accord on many ques-tions and expressed their determination to maintain close contact for the purpose of broad cooperation in areas of common concern to the two countries.

[21]Cf. Chapter 6.
[22]*AFR, 1973*: 39-63 and 239-46.

35. CONGRESS, TURKEY, AND DÉTENTE (II)

(December 3-30, 1974)

[The year-end détente in the relations between the United States and its Atlantic allies found no parallel in the relationship between the American executive and legislative branches. On the contrary, it was during these closing weeks of 1974 that the expiring 93rd Congress directed some of its most devastating blows against the foreign policy arrangements of the Nixon-Ford administration and Secretary Kissinger. The Senate's unanimous approval of the Geneva Protocol and the Bacteriological Warfare Convention, an action made possible in part by President Ford's abandonment of an interpretive position enunciated by President Nixon,[1] involved no relaxation of legislative vigilance. More characteristic of the diverging attitudes of the administration and Congress were their continuing differences on two questions that specially involved the ethical content of American foreign policy: the question of trade relations with the Soviet Union and the question of military assistance to Turkey.

In principle, the conditions under which most-favored-nation commercial treatment might be accorded to the Soviet Union and other Communist countries under the pending Trade Reform Act appeared to have been settled by the so-called "Jackson compromise," the exchange of letters dated October 18 in which Secretary Kissinger and Senator Jackson had set forth their respective anticipations regarding future Jewish emigration from the Soviet Union.[2] Not generally known as yet was the fact that the understandings set forth in this correspondence had not only been denounced in general terms by Brezhnev and other Soviet spokesmen but had been specifically repudiated by Foreign Minister Gromyko in the secret letter handed to Secretary Kissinger during his latest visit to Moscow.[3]

[1]Cf. Chapter 33 at note 14.
[2]Chapter 24, Document 51.
[3]Chapter 24, Document 52.

By December, a showdown on the issue was rapidly approaching. The Senate Finance Committee approved the pending trade bill in late November in a version which—like the version passed by the House of Representatives in December 1973—included the controversial Jackson-Vanik amendment denying nondiscriminatory treatment or government credits to any Communist country that limited freedom of emigration.[4] By prior agreement, however, those Senators who had been particularly involved in the negotiation of the Jackson compromise had promptly introduced an amendment authorizing the President to waive the application of these provisions for a period of eighteen months (provided he could furnish the Congress with suitable assurances regarding the country's emigration practices) and thereafter to recommend further extensions for twelve-month periods.[5]

In the course of its work on the Trade Reform Act, the Senate Finance Committee also modified important features of the administration plan for a system of generalized trade preferences for developing countries, a key element in its strategy for dealing with global development problems. Specifically, the Finance Committee undertook to declare that several different types of countries would not be eligible to benefit from such preferences: Communist countries, countries belonging to OPEC and similar cartel-type arrangements, countries that improperly expropriated U.S.-owned property or failed to cooperate in U.S. anti-drug programs, and countries that gave so-called "reverse preferences" to developed countries.

Secretary Kissinger voiced a word of caution regarding such exclusions when he appeared before the Senate Finance Committee on December 3 for a general review of the trade legislation in advance of its consideration by the full Senate.]

(76) The Pending Trade Reform Bill: Statement by Secretary of State Kissinger before the Senate Committee on Finance, December 3, 1974.[6]

(Excerpts)

Thank you, Mr. Chairman,[7] for this opportunity to appear

---

[4]Senate Report 93-1298, Nov. 26, 1974 (for full reference see note 26 to Chapter 24). The text of the Jackson-Vanik provision appears as sec. 402 (a) and (b) of the Trade Act of 1974 (Public Law 93-618, Jan. 3, 1975).

[5]Amendment No. 2,000, introduced by Senators Jackson, Ribicoff, and Javits; text in *Emigration Amendment to the Trade Reform Act* (cited in note 27 to Chapter 24), pp. 2-13. The text of this amendment as enacted appears as sec. 402 (c) of Public Law 93-618.

[6]Department of State Press Release 516; text and subtitles from *Bulletin*, 71: 935-9. (The omitted portion of the statement appears in Chapter 24 as Document 50.)

[7]Senator Russell B. Long (Democrat, Louisiana).

before your committee and particularly for your patience while scheduling difficulties were being worked out.

Let me first address the question of why the administration places such a high priority on passage of the Trade Reform Act—a priority which has increased since the bill was first introduced. At a time when the economic stability of the world has been severely shaken and difficult times still lie ahead, it is of critical importance to demonstrate that the nations of the world can still resolve critical economic problems and conduct their trading relationships in a spirit of compromise and a recognition of interdependence.

There are many causes of the current worldwide economic crisis. But one of the principal problems is the unwillingness of too many nations to face the facts of interdependence. The application of ever more restrictive trade practices, the insistence on the unfettered exploitation of national advantage, threatens the world with a return to the beggar-thy-neighbor policies of the thirties.

The U.S. Government has repeatedly urged the nations of the world to raise their sights and to avoid ruinous confrontation. In the fields of food and energy we have made far-reaching and detailed proposals to give effect to the principles of interdependence for the common benefit. The trade negotiations which will be made possible by the bill before you are part of this overall design.

The major trading nations stand today uneasily poised between liberalized trade and unilateral restrictive actions leading toward autarky. If they choose the second course, global economic difficulties will be magnified and an international economic crisis will be upon us. This in turn will make all other international problems more difficult to solve. For such a catastrophe to result from our failure to act would be a blow to international stability of potentially historic proportions.

In my testimony before this committee of March 7, 1974,[8] I stated the objectives of the Trade Act to be as follows:

—A mutual reduction of trade barriers among industrialized countries.

—A joint response by industrialized countries to the aspirations of developing countries which require the expansion of exports to sustain their development programs.

—A normalization of trade relations between the United States and the countries of Eastern Europe and the Soviet Union.

—A new start on emerging trade issues that are not covered under the present trade rules and procedures.

—Finally, the preservation and enhancement of a global

multilateral economic relationship and the dampening of tendencies toward discriminatory arrangements among selected groups of countries.

Mr. Chairman, the importance of these objectives has been emphasized by events since. I am confident that current economic problems can be solved. We should bear in mind that the foreign policy implications of the Trade Reform Act are not limited to those provisions on which I wish to direct my main comments—our trade relations with Communist countries and generalized preferences for developing countries. The bill in its entirety is an absolutely essential tool if the United States is to be in a position to manage effectively its overall relations—political and economic— at a time when the world economy is at a critical point.

The Emigration Issue

Mr. Chairman, you have asked me to return to your committee to comment specifically on the emigration issue as it relates to title IV of the trade bill,[9] a problem dealt with in the Jackson-Vanik amendment to title IV.

Let me state at the outset that I deal with this matter with considerable misgiving because what is said on this occasion could, if not handled with utmost care, deal a serious setback both to the cause of freer emigration from the U.S.S.R. and to the more hopeful trend in U.S.-Soviet relations that has been maintained for the last few years and was recently strengthened in the President's meeting with Mr. Brezhnev in Vladivostok.

[Secretary Kissinger's account of the negotiations that preceded his exchange of letters with Senator Jackson appears in Chapter 24 as Document 50.]

With the exchange of correspondence [with Senator Jackson][10] agreed, it became possible to work out a set of procedures—which, I understand, has now been offered as Senate amendment 2000— whereby the President will be authorized to waive the provisions of the original Jackson-Vanik amendment and to proceed with the granting of MFN [most-favored-nation treatment] and Eximbank [Export-Import Bank] facilities for at least an initial period of 18 months. These procedures will also provide for means whereby the initial grants can be continued for additional one-year periods.

---

[9]"Trade Relations with Countries Not Currently Receiving Nondiscriminatory Treatment."
[10]Chapter 24, Document 51.

Thus, Mr. Chairman, I believe a satisfactory compromise was achieved on an unprecedented and extraordinarily sensitive set of issues. I cannot give you any assurance concerning the precise emigration rate that may result, assuming that the trade bill is passed and MFN is extended to the U.S.S.R. As I noted earlier, it is difficult to know fully the causes of past changes in Soviet emigration rates. However, I do believe that we have every right to expect, as my letter to Senator Jackson said, that the emigration rate will correspond to the number of applicants and that there will be no interference with applications. If some of the current estimates about potential applicants are correct, this should lead to an increase in emigration.

I believe it is now essential to let the provisions and understandings of the compromise proceed in practice. I am convinced that additional public commentary, or continued claims that this or that protagonist has won, can only jeopardize the results we all seek. We should not delude ourselves that the commercial measures to be authorized by the trade bill will lead a powerful state like the Soviet Union to be indifferent to constant and demonstrative efforts to picture it as yielding in the face of external pressure; nor can we expect extended debates of domestic Soviet practices by responsible U.S. public figures and officials to remain indefinitely without reaction. We should keep in mind that the ultimate victims of such claims will be those whom all of us are trying to help.

Therefore I respectfully ask that your questions take account of the sensitivity of the issues. There will be ample opportunity to test in practice what has been set down on paper and to debate these matters again when the time for stocktaking foreseen in the legislation comes. With this caveat, I shall of course answer your questions to the best of my ability.

As I indicated to this committee in March, we seek improved relations with the Soviet Union because in the nuclear age we and the Soviets have an overriding obligation to reduce the likelihood of confrontation. We have profound differences with the Soviet Union, and it is these very differences which compel any responsible administration to make a major effort to create a more constructive relationship. In pursuing this policy, we are mindful that the benefits must be mutual and that our national security must be protected. With respect to title IV of the trade reform bill, we believe we are now in a position to meet these vital concerns adequately while at the same time bringing important economic and political benefits to the United States.

Generalized Tariff Preferences

I would be remiss if I did not also take this opportunity to comment briefly on another part of the trade bill which has important foreign policy implications.

You will recall, Mr. Chairman, that I wrote to you in September to express my strong support for title V of the Trade Reform Act[11] because I consider the prompt implementation of a meaningful system of generalized preferences important to U.S. relations with developing countries. I am gratified that this committee has agreed to endorse the concept of generalized tariff preferences. I have, however, serious questions about the decision of your committee to exclude automatically certain categories of developing countries from the benefits of these preferences.

The concerns which these amendments reflect are, I believe, shared by all in both the executive and legislative branches of our government. I am not opposed to having these concerns put on the record.

However, these amendments, as we understand them, would result in the automatic denial of preferences to a number of important developing countries. Such automaticity could work to our disadvantage. For example, would it be in our interest to exclude all members of the Organization of Petroleum Exporting Countries, including those which did not participate in last year's oil embargo?

Moreover, many of the countries affected—including those who can play a role in helping prevent renewed conflict in the Middle East—are just those with which we are now actively engaged in efforts to strengthen our relations and to work out mutually acceptable solutions to difficult economic and political problems.

With respect to the automatic denial of preferences to countries expropriating U.S. property, the Congress recognized last year that inflexible sanctions are not effective in promoting the interests of American citizens or businesses abroad and modified the Hickenlooper amendment to authorize the President to waive its sanctions when required for our national interest.[12] The same authority should be provided in the Trade Act.

This committee has made several changes in title V which we consider to be distinct improvements. At the same time, I believe that title V, as passed by the House, contains ample authority to provide or to deny generalized preferences to any country whenever it is in the overall interest of the United States to do so. I can assure you that the administration will keep Congress fully informed in advance of the basis for any decisions on beneficiary status. I am confident that you and your committee will give serious consideration to the problems I have raised.

The trade bill is one of the most important measures to come

[11] "Generalized System of Preferences."

[12] Sec. 15, Foreign Assistance Act of 1973 (Public Law 93-189, Dec. 17, 1973).

before the Congress in many years. It is essential to our hopes for a more stable, more prosperous world. This Congress in the time remaining to it thus has an opportunity to contribute to the construction of a safer and more peaceful world.

[Though seemingly unconvinced by Secretary Kissinger's representations regarding trade preferences, the Senate did give unanimous endorsement to the Jackson compromise before going on to approve the Trade Act as a whole, in the version recommended by the Finance Committee, by a 77 to 4 vote on December 13. Again, however, this action seemed to underrate the opposition to be expected from the U.S.S.R., the country whose emigration practices it was hoped to liberalize. With final congressional votes expected as soon as a committee of conference had reconciled the differences between the House and Senate bills, the Soviet Union on December 18 reiterated its objections by releasing the text of Gromyko's secret letter together with a new blast from the TASS Agency.]

(77) The Soviet Viewpoint: Statement issued by TASS (Telegraphic Agency of the Soviet Union), December 18, 1974. [13]

As is well known, Bills concerning Soviet-U.S. commercial and economic relations have been under discussion for some time now in United States official circles, including the U.S. Congress. These Bills have now been approved separately by the House of Representatives and the Senate and, after the finalising of the texts in the House-Senate conference committee, they are subject to final endorsement by the two houses.

Under the agreement on principles reached between the USSR and the USA in 1972[14] it was intended that discriminatory restrictions in the sphere of commercial and economic relations, introduced in the United States during the years of the cold war, would be removed.

However, those opposed to normalising Soviet-American trade, and also to improving Soviet-American relations in general, began from the very outset actively to hinder this process, seeking to prevent the development of mutually-beneficial Soviet-U.S. economic relations, including the reciprocal granting of most-favoured-nation treatment in trade and trade crediting, or, to be more precise, the removal of the discriminatory regime applied in the USA with regard to the Soviet Union.

[13]Text from *Soviet News*, 1974: 486. (The letter from Foreign Minister Gromyko appears as Document 52 in Chapter 24.)
[14]*AFR, 1972*: 75-8.

Matters reached a point where the favourable settlement of these questions was made dependent on all kinds of qualifications and demands, which were nothing but gross interference in the Soviet Union's internal affairs.

This is the only way to describe the attempts to include in the Bills provisions concerning, for instance, the departure of Soviet citizens for other countries, concerning economic information of a purely domestic nature being made available to American institutions, etc., and it was certainly only as a result of the loss of a sense of reality that one could conceive of the idea of creating in the United States certain organs to supervise the implementation of those provisions by the Soviet Union.[15]

The adoption by the U.S. Congress of reservations of this kind and of restrictive conditions would be in direct contradiction with the clear-cut commitments undertaken by the two sides under the Soviet-U.S. agreement on trade of 1972,[16] which envisages the unconditional termination of the discriminatory legislation against the Soviet Union.

Tass is authorised to state that any attempts, from whomsoever they may come, to interfere in internal affairs that are entirely the concern of the Soviet state and no one else are flatly rejected as unacceptable in leading circles in the Soviet Union. The same circles believe that the complications artificially created with regard to questions of normalising trade and economic relations between the USSR and the United States are not in keeping with the interests of either side. Mutually-beneficial co-operation and trade are undoubtedly in the interests of both the Soviet and the American peoples.

There is only one basis on which Soviet-American relations in general, and commercial and economic relations in particular, can be built successfully. It is clearly formulated in the appropriate Soviet-American documents, including the above-mentioned agreement. This is complete equality of the two sides and non-interference in one another's internal affairs. It is precisely on this basis, and on this basis alone, that one can work confidently towards the further development of commercial and economic relations between the USSR and the United States, just as in the case of relations between them in general.

As for the Soviet Union, it intends to continue to adhere strictly to this principle.

---

[15]Secs. 410 and 411 of the Trade Act provide respectively for the establishment of an "East-West Trade Statistics Monitoring System" and of an East-West Foreign Trade Board, charged with monitoring East-West trade and ensuring "that such trade will be in the national interest of the United States."

[16]Cf. *AFR, 1972*: 119-25.

[Discounted by many Americans as a typical face-saving exercise, the Soviet statement failed to deter the Congress from final passage of the trade measure, now "in the works" for more than twenty months. As reported from the conference committee on December 19 and passed by both houses on December 20—the final day of the 1974 session—the newly titled "Trade Act of 1974"[17] belatedly provided the bulk of the authority requested in President Nixon's trade message of April 10, 1973—above all, the five-year grant of negotiating authority required for full engagement in the multilateral trade negotiations now going forward under the General Agreement on Tariffs and Trade (GATT).

In its final version, the lengthy section of the Act devoted to "Freedom of Emigration in East-West Trade" (Sec. 402) incorporated both (1) the original Jackson-Vanik amendment on the denial of MFN treatment and credits, and (2) the later Jackson-Ribicoff-Javits amendment authorizing a temporary waiver of these restrictions in line with the Jackson compromise. In addition, a separate section on "Limitation of Credit to Russia" (Sec. 613) imposed a ceiling of $300 million on the amount of trade credits to the U.S.S.R. (except credits from the Commodity Credit Corporation) that could be approved without prior congressional approval. (This provision was also reaffirmed, with other restrictions, in the separate Export-Import Bank Amendments of 1974.)[18]

Also included, in the separate Title V of the Trade Act, were (1) an authorization to the President to extend duty-free preferential treatment to imports from "beneficiary developing countries" over a ten-year period, and (2) a definition of the term "beneficiary developing country" (Sec. 502) which listed at some length the various groups of countries that were considered ineligible for such classification. Particularly noticed was the denial of "beneficiary developing country" status to any country which, to quote the language of the statute, "is a member of the Organization of Petroleum Exporting Countries, or a party to any other arrangement of foreign countries, and such country participates in any action pursuant to such arrangement the effect of which is to withhold supplies of vital commodity resources from international trade or to raise the price of such commodities to an unreasonable level and to cause serious disruption of the world economy." This definition seemed clearly to encompass not only the Arab oil producing states but also the Western Hemisphere countries of Ecuador and Venezuela, which had not participated in the Arab oil embargo but had been parties to the successive price increases imposed by OPEC since 1973.

[17]Public Law 93-618, Jan. 3, 1975.
[18]Public Law 93-646, Jan. 4, 1975.

The misgivings voiced by President Ford in signing this legislation on January 3, 1975,[19] were to be amply justified by events. Just a week later, on January 10, 1975, the Soviet Government would formally advise the United States that it was unable to accept a trading relationship based on legislation incompatible, in its view, with the bilateral trade agreement of 1972 as well as the principle of noninterference in domestic affairs. In giving notice that under such circumstances it would not put the 1972 trade agreement into force,[20] the Soviet Union also doomed the settlement of its longstanding lend-lease obligations to the United States, concluded in 1972 on the assumption that most-favored-nation treatment would not be long delayed. The separate provision of the Trade Act regarding membership in OPEC, meanwhile, occasioned an explosion of anger in Latin America and led, among other things, to a postponement of the Foreign Ministers' meeting that was to have convened at Buenos Aires in March for a continuation of the U.S.-Latin American "dialogue."

The Washington debate on military aid to Turkey, meanwhile, had followed a roughly parallel course in the weeks since Congress had voted in mid-October to cut off military assistance to that country so long as it persevered in its present line of action in regard to Cyprus—but to delay the implementation of the cutoff until December 10 if the President determined that this would further negotiations for a peaceful solution.[21] The current Turkish Government, the product of a series of cabinet crises which had placed the elderly Professor Sadi Irmak in office as head of a caretaker cabinet, was far too weak to deviate from the nationalist line laid down by the previous Eçevit administration. Turkish military forces thus continued their occupation of the northern third of Cyprus, while Ankara reiterated its insistence on the establishment of a federal Cypriot state with guarantees for the security of the Turkish minority. The Greek Government and public, meanwhile, continued to manifest their lively dissatisfaction with the United States as well as Turkey. Even more dissatisfied with the fruits of American policy to date was the legal government of Cyprus, where President Makarios resumed his official functions early in December.

Under these circumstances, the future of American military aid to Turkey was bound to become a point of strenuous contention in Congress, which was now engaged in putting the final touches to the Foreign Assistance Act of 1974, the bill to authorize essential

[19]Text of statement in *Presidential Documents*, 11: 10-11 and *Bulletin*, 72: 137-8.
[20]Kissinger statement, Jan. 14, 1975, in *Bulletin*, 72: 139-40.
[21]Cf. Chapter 24 at note 15.

parts of the global foreign aid program during the ongoing fiscal year 1975.[22] Included in the Senate version of the bill (S. 3394), as passed December 4 by a vote of 46 to 45, was an amendment proposed by Democratic Senator Thomas F. Eagleton of Missouri—but softened at the suggestion of Democratic Senator Hubert H. Humphrey of Minnesota—that reaffirmed the cutoff of aid to Turkey but once again suspended its operation for a further period ending 30 days after the new 94th Congress convened in mid-January.

Although he obviously would have preferred a longer extension, Secretary Kissinger three days later convened a Saturday news conference at which he pleaded for similar action by the House in advance of the impending December 10 deadline.]

(78) Military Aid to Turkey: News conference statement by Secretary of State Kissinger, December 7, 1974.[23]

Secretary Kissinger: First of all, my apologies for having made you come in on Saturday. I had planned to do this on Monday [December 9] but forgot that I have a congressional appearance on Monday afternoon and Foreign Minister [of Israel Yigal] Allon on Monday morning.

I'd like to begin by reading a brief statement on military aid to Turkey, which I am doing on behalf of the President as well as myself.

As you know, Congress in October enacted legislation which will cut off military assistance to Turkey on December 10. As you are also aware, the Senate has now acted to extend the period prior to such a cutoff. It is absolutely essential, and the President and I strongly urge, that the House take similar action immediately.

To begin with, the congressional decision to terminate military assistance to Turkey has not served the purpose it was designed to accomplish. Rather, it undermines the ability of the U.S. Government to assist in bringing about a just settlement of the tragic conflict on Cyprus.

We had made progress with the Turkish Government in the development of steps designed to make possible the initiation of negotiations.

Congressional action in October setting a terminal date for

---

[22]Economic aid for fiscal years 1974 and 1975 had already been authorized by the Foreign Assistance Act of 1973 (Public Law 93-189, Dec. 17, 1973); hence the new act was concerned primarily with military assistance in fiscal 1975.

[23]Department of State Press Release 518, Dec. 7; text from *Bulletin*, 71: 909.

military assistance contributed substantially to the difficulties that have prevented the beginning of negotiations. Unless the Congress acts now to permit the continued flow of military assistance, further efforts by the United States to assist in resolving the crisis will be thwarted and our ability to play a future useful role will be undermined.

The United States has made it clear that it does not approve of actions taken by Turkey on Cyprus. We have equally made clear that Turkey should display flexibility and a concern for the interests of the other parties in that dispute.

The United States will continue to do all it can to assist the parties in arriving at an equitable and enduring resolution of the Cyprus problem. But if we are deprived of diplomatic flexibility, there will be little that we will be able to accomplish.

Even more important, the U.S. military assistance to Turkey is not, and has never been, granted as a favor. It has been the view of the U.S. Government since 1947 that the security of Turkey is vital to the security of the eastern Mediterranean, to NATO Europe, and therefore to the security of the Atlantic community.

These are the reasons, and these alone, that we grant military assistance. They were compelling when we first decided to grant such aid. They are equally compelling today.

In 1947, our commitment to assist Greece and Turkey marked the turning point in the building of a security system which has contributed to Western security. Are we now to establish a new turning point which will mark the end of our commitment to a system which has served the free countries so well?

The security interests of the West may be irreparably damaged unless the Congress takes immediate action to permit military assistance to Turkey to continue.

This statement is made on behalf of the President as well as myself.

[In the background of administration concern was a fear that Turkey, if sufficiently upset by American actions, might retaliate by altering the status of the important U.S. bases and electronic monitoring installations situated on its territory. ". . . Given the foreseeable crises in the eastern Mediterranean," Secretary Kissinger observed at a later point in his December 7 news conference, "it would seem to us axiomatic that one should not drive Turkey out of a defense relationship with the United States [sic] at this particularly crucial period." Asserting that he remained hopeful there would be progress over the next few months in getting negotiations for a Cyprus settlement under way, the Secretary mentioned his intention of talking at some length with the Turkish and Greek Foreign

Ministers during the NATO meeting in Brussels[24]—a discussion which would later result in a resumption of the intercommunal talks between Greek and Turkish Cypriot representatives.

In spite of Dr. Kissinger's admonitions, American military aid to Turkey had to be legally halted at midnight on December 10 in the absence of any new legislation continuing the suspension. It was not until next day, December 11, that the House of Representatives took action in the matter by approving, with 297 votes to 98, an amendment to the foreign aid bill, proposed by Democratic Representative Benjamin S. Rosenthal of New York, that ran directly counter to the Kissinger recommendations by continuing the *cutoff* of military aid—rather than the suspension of the cutoff—through the end of the fiscal year on June 30, 1975. With this and other amendments, the House version of the foreign aid legislation was then adopted by a final vote of 201 to 190.

The danger of a drastic Turkish reaction was nevertheless postponed—though hardly averted—by the subsequent action of the Senate-House committee of conference, which met to reconcile the differences between the two bills and advanced a compromise recommendation that the aid cutoff be once again suspended until February 5, 1975. As recommended by the conference committee on December 17, the relevant Section 22 of the Foreign Assistance Act was phrased as follows:

SUSPENSION OF MILITARY ASSISTANCE TO TURKEY

SEC. 22. Section 620 of the Foreign Assistance Act of 1961 is amended by adding at the end thereof the following new subsection:

"(x) All military assistance, all sales of defense articles and services (whether for cash or by credit, guaranty, or any other means), and all licenses with respect to the transportation of arms, ammunitions, and implements of war (including technical data relating thereto) to the Government of Turkey, shall be suspended on the date of enactment of this subsection unless and until the President determines and certifies to the Congress that the Government of Turkey is in compliance with the Foreign Assistance Act of 1961, the Foreign Military Sales Act, and any agreement entered into under such Acts, and that substantial progress toward agreement has been made regarding military forces in Cyprus: *Provided,* that the President is authorized to suspend the provisions of this section and such Acts if he determines that such suspension will further negotiations for a peaceful solution of the Cyprus conflict. Any such suspension shall be effective only until February 5, 1975, and only if, during that time, Turkey shall observe the ceasefire and shall neither increase its forces on Cyprus nor transfer to Cyprus any United States supplied implements of war.''

A similar provision was included in the joint resolution providing funds to carry on the foreign aid program pending enactment of a new appropriation bill.[25]

Other noteworthy features of the Foreign Assistance Act, as it emerged from the conference committee on December 17, included authorizations of $500 million for food and nutrition assistance; $600 million for military assistance, and $660 million for security supporting assistance, chiefly in the Middle East; and $617 million for postwar reconstruction in Indochina. Aid to the Indochinese countries was, however, sharply curtailed as compared with administration recommendations, while assistance to Chile was limited to $25 million, none of it military; aid to South Korea and to India was also limited; and any further funding for UNESCO was barred until that organization returned to its assigned objectives and took "concrete steps to correct its recent actions of a primarily political character."[26] Indicative of growing disenchantment with the entire structure of security-oriented relationships abroad, Congress urged a reexamination of the whole military assistance program and its reduction and termination "as rapidly as feasible consistent with the security and foreign policy requirements of the United States.''

Approved by the Senate on December 17 and by the House the following day, this final version of the Foreign Assistance Act of 1974[27] was signed by President Ford on December 30 with the following statement:]

(79) The Foreign Assistance Act of 1974: Statement by President Ford, December 30, 1974.[28]

I have signed S. 3394, the Foreign Assistance Act of 1974, with

[25]Section 5, Public Law 93-570, Dec. 31, 1974. The Foreign Assistance and Related Programs Appropriations Act, 1975 was later enacted as Public Law 94-11, Mar. 26, 1975.
[26]Cf. Chapter 26 at note 29.
[27]Public Law 93-559, Dec. 30, 1974.
[28]Text from Presidential Documents, 11: 3-4 (1975). The statement was released at Vail, Colorado.

some reservations, but with appreciation for the spirit of constructive compromise which motivated the Congress.

I sought a bill which would serve the interests of the United States in an increasingly interdependent world in which the strength and vitality of our own policies and society require purposeful and responsible participation in the international community. Foreign assistance is indispensable in exercising the role of leadership in the cooperative and peaceful resolution of conflicts, in pursuing political stability and economic progress, and in expressing the American spirit of helping those less fortunate than we are.

In most respects, the Foreign Assistance Act of 1974 will serve those ends. It includes, however, several restrictions that may pose severe problems to our interests. I must bring them to the attention of the Congress as matters which will be of continuing concern and which may require our joint efforts to remedy if circumstances require.

First, are the numerous and detailed limitations on assistance to Indochina. The economic and military assistance levels for Cambodia,[29] particularly, are clearly inadequate to meet minimum basic needs. Our support is vital to help effect an early end to the fighting and a negotiated settlement. This is also the objective of the United Nations General Assembly which approved a resolution calling for a negotiated settlement.[30] I intend to discuss this critical issue with the Congressional leadership at the earliest possible time.

In South Vietnam, we have consistently sought to assure the right of the Vietnamese people to determine their own futures free from enemy interference. It would be tragic indeed if we endangered, or even lost, the progress we have achieved by failing to provide the relatively modest but crucial aid which is so badly needed there. Our objective is to help South Vietnam to develop a viable, self-sufficient economy and the climate of security which will make that development possible. To this end, the economic aid requested represented the amount needed to support crucial capital development and agricultural productivity efforts. The lower amount finally approved[31] makes less likely the achievement of our objectives and will significantly prolong the period needed for essential development.

I appreciate the spirit of compromise which motivated the Congress to extend to February 5, 1975, the period during which military assistance to Turkey may continue under specified cir-

---

[29]Economic and military assistance to Cambodia was set at $377 million, of which not more than $200 million was to be available for military assistance.
[30]Cf. Chapter 32 at note 5.
[31]Economic assistance to South Vietnam under this act was limited to $449.9 million for relief and rehabilitation.

cumstances. I regret, however, that the restriction was imposed at all. Turkey remains a key element of U.S. security and political interests in the eastern Mediterranean. The threat of cutoff of aid, even if unfulfilled, cannot fail to have a damaging effect on our relations with one of our staunch NATO allies whose geographic position is of great strategic importance. This, in turn, could have a detrimental effect on our efforts to help achieve a negotiated solution of the Cyprus problem.

I regret the action of the Congress in cutting off the modest program of military assistance to Chile. Although I share the concern of the Congress for the protection of human rights and look forward to continuing consultation with the Chilean Government on this matter, I do not regard this measure as an effective means for promoting that interest.

Finally, the Congress has directed that during the current fiscal year no more than 30 percent of concessional food aid should be allocated to countries which are not among those most seriously affected by food shortages—unless the President demonstrates that such food is required solely for humanitarian purposes. I understand and share the spirit of humanitarianism that prompted a statement of Congressional policy on this subject. But that policy could unduly bind the flexibility of the United States in an arbitrary way in meeting the needs of friendly countries and in pursuing our various interests abroad.

As with other differences which the Congress and the executive branch worked out in consideration of this bill, I look forward to working with the 94th Congress in meeting and solving the problems that are still before us. We share the common goal of best serving the interests of the people of the United States. Working together, we shall continue to serve them responsibly.

36. THE MEANING OF IT ALL

(December 18, 1974)

[Each Secretary of State must personally carry an important share of the responsibility for keeping Congress and the public informed about the underlying principles, operations, and aspirations of American foreign policy. To the normal duties of his position were added, in Secretary Kissinger's case, those special responsibilities that flowed from long-established preeminence in the analysis and interpretation of international processes. This merging of the detached philosopher with the practicing statesman imparted a characteristic weight and depth not only to the Secretary's formal speeches but, equally, to his frequent congressional appearances, interviews, and news conferences.

Particularly noteworthy, for its insights into the mind of the Secretary of State as well as its intimations of the movement of world history, had been the two-day interview conducted by James Reston which had been published in the *New York Times* of October 13 and was quoted early in this volume.[1] Similar in format and tone, though pitched at a somewhat lower level of abstraction, was a further series of Kissinger interviews that took place at the end of 1974 and the beginning of 1975—a conversation with members of *Newsweek* on December 18, with representatives of *Business Week* on December 23, and with Bill Moyers of the Public Broadcasting Service on January 15, 1975.[2]

Most vividly remembered among the Secretary's comments at this period was his acknowledgment, in answer to questions raised in the *Business Week* interview,[3] that the United States might in extreme circumstances consider the possibility of using military force to assure the flow of Middle East oil. But such a contingency—to

---

[1]Cf. Introduction at notes 2-3.
[2]Texts in *Bulletin*, 72: 57-63, 97-106, and 165-78.
[3]Published in *Business Week*, Jan. 13, 1975 and released in Department of State Press Release 2, Jan. 2, 1975.

be contemplated only "where there is some actual strangulation of the industrialized world"—was treated by Dr. Kissinger as so remote as to be practically unthinkable. The central interest of these year-end interviews—particularly the *Newsweek* interview—lies rather in their identification of some of the dominant themes in the history of the year just closing as well as the period ahead.]

(80) Thoughts of the Secretary of State: Interview with Dr. Kissinger by representatives of Newsweek, December 18, 1974.[4]

(Excerpts)

Q. Looking back over the conduct of American foreign policy in 1974, what have been your greatest satisfactions and greatest disappointments?

Secretary Kissinger: Strangely enough, the greatest satisfaction was that we managed the Presidential transition without a disaster. This was a rather heartbreaking period. I was extremely worried that while the central authority was in severe jeopardy, the transition might create basic weaknesses in the structure of our foreign policy. I considered our ability to continue an effective foreign policy the most satisfying thing. Of course, individual events were important, too: I got great satisfaction from the Syrian disengagement.

Q. In that transition period, was there a hiatus in which you could not function very well?

Secretary Kissinger: I would say from July to October was a period in which we could not act with decisiveness. Every negotiation was getting more and more difficult because it involved the question of whether we could, in fact, carry out what we were negotiating. Secondly, we were not in a position to press matters that might involve serious domestic disputes. And I think this affected to some extent the summit in Moscow in July. But it affected many other things in more intangible ways.

Q. How do you rank the SALT agreement in Vladivostok in the list of achievements for this past year?

Secretary Kissinger: Very high, and of more permanent signifi-

[4]Department of State Press Release 3, Jan. 2, 1975; text from *Bulletin*, 72: 57-63. The interview, conducted by *Newsweek* Executive Editor Kenneth Auchincloss, Foreign Editor Edward Klein, and diplomatic correspondent Bruce van Voorst, was published in *Newsweek*, Dec. 30, 1974: 29-32.

cance than perhaps anything else that was achieved. The various disengagement agreements in the Middle East were dramatic and important because they reversed a trend toward another outbreak of a war and may have set the stage for making some important progress. But I think in terms of permanent achievements, I would rank the outline for a second SALT agreement at or near the top. And I think it will be so viewed by history.

Q. How do you account for all the criticism of SALT Two?

Secretary Kissinger: I think we have a difficult domestic situation right now. Many people remember, or think they remember, that foreign policy had certain domestic effects in '71 or '72. I don't agree with this. But I think it is in the back of some people's minds.

Secondly, there is a general atmosphere of disillusionment with government.

Thirdly, the liberal intellectual community, which used to lead American foreign policy, was alienated for a variety of reasons from the Johnson administration and then from the Nixon administration, and therefore from this administration as well, at least at first.

Now, what in fact is the significance of this agreement? The nightmare of the nuclear age is the fear of strategic arms based on the expectation of what the other side is doing. One has to get one's priorities right. The first objective must be to get that cycle of self-fulfilling prophecies interrupted. That has now been substantially achieved. Once that is built into the planning of both sides, I think the negotiations on reductions will be easier.

*   *   *

Q. The Soviets have issued a statement that they are not going to make any guarantees about Jewish emigration from the Soviet Union.⁵ Does this statement and its possible impact on the trade bill concern you?

Secretary Kissinger: Yes, it concerns me. Certainly there is no one in Washington who has not heard me warn about this for years. Without saying anything, without making any claims for it, we managed to increase Jewish emigration from 400 a year in 1968 to 35,000 before any of this debate started. We had managed to intercede quietly in behalf of a list of hardship cases, of which more than half were dealt with successfully. We never claimed a success; we never took credit for it. We never said this was a result of détente. We just encouraged it to happen. We have warned con-

⁵Cf. Chapter 35, Document 77.

stantly not to make this an issue of state-to-state relations, because we were afraid it would lead to a formal confrontation and defeat the objective of promoting emigration. Despite our deep misgivings, we acquiesced when statements were made by some which implied that the Soviet Union had yielded to pressure, because we thought it was the result that was important, and we wanted to avoid a domestic debate that might have jeopardized the trade bill.

The issue of Jewish emigration is, above all, a human problem. There is no legal agreement we can make with the Soviet Union that we can enforce. Whether the Soviet Union permits emigration depends on the importance they attach to their relationship with the United States and therefore on the whole context of the East-West relationship.

If we can maintain a Soviet commitment to détente, and if we can make clear that this is related to the emigration question, existing understandings will have a chance. But what we have had is, first, excessive claims. And now the Export-Import Bank bill has been encumbered with amendments that, to all practical purposes, virtually prevent loans of any substantial size to the Soviet Union.[6]

Loans are more important to the Soviet Union than most-favored-nation status, and in this respect the Soviets are worse off now, after three years of détente and even after increased Jewish emigration, than they were to begin with. We cannot simply keep saying that the Soviets must pay something for détente, and then not provide anything from our side to give them an interest in its continuance.

Q. Do you see any signs that détente has led Moscow to play a more positive role in the Mideast?

Secretary Kissinger: The Middle East is a very complicated issue for them and for us. I do not believe evidence supports the proposition that the Soviet Union produced the 1973 war. On the other hand, the Soviet Union has not been prepared to risk its relationship to some of the Arab states for the sake of Middle East tranquillity. What this proves is that détente does not mean that the Soviet Union and we have become collaborators, but that we are partly rivals, partly ideologically incompatible, and partly edging toward cooperation. The Middle East has been an area where cooperation has been far from satisfactory.

Q. Will détente help in the next round in the Mideast?

Secretary Kissinger: Generally, yes, if all parties proceed with circumspection. Some of the participants in the Middle East conflict

---

[6]Cf. Chapter 35 at note 18.

did not want an extremely active Soviet role. This was one inhibiting feature. The second is that a cooperative effort with the Soviet Union depends on the actual positions the Soviet Union takes. If the Soviet Union takes positions which are identical with one of the parties, then we are better off dealing with those parties directly.

Q. What would be the necessary condition before the Palestine Liberation Organization (PLO) and Israel could sit down together and talk?

Secretary Kissinger: It is impossible for the United States to recommend negotiation with the PLO until the PLO accepts the existence of Israel as a legitimate state. As long as the PLO proposals envisage, in one form or another, the destruction of Israel, we don't see much hope for negotiation with the PLO.

Q. Do you share the concern of many people now who feel that both sides are hardening their positions?

Secretary Kissinger: I have been through several Mideast negotiations, and they run a fever cycle. There is a great deal of excessive talk on both sides to prove that they have been tough, unyielding, and didn't make any concessions. We are now in the relatively early phases of these exchanges. I am not pessimistic. On the contrary, I believe another step is quite possible. Obviously, because of the Rabat meeting, and the increasing complexity of the domestic situation of almost all of the participants, negotiations are more difficult now than they were a year ago. The stakes are also higher. But I believe that progress is possible. We have to do it now by somewhat different methods than we did last year. If I compare where we are now with where we were at various stages during the Syrian negotiations, I think it looks far more encouraging than it did then. I am in fact quite hopeful.

Q. Are you going to deemphasize "shuttle diplomacy"?

Secretary Kissinger: There was a time for shuttle diplomacy, and there is a time for quiet diplomacy. I cannot accept the principle that whenever there is something to be settled, the Secretary of State must go to the area and stake his personal prestige on the conduct of the negotiations. I don't think that is a healthy situation. And therefore, while I don't exclude that in a concluding phase, or in a critical phase, I might go to the Middle East for three or four days, I will not do so unless conditions are right and the stakes are important enough.

*   *   *

Q. Some people say that it would be to Israel's advantage to find an excuse to launch a preemptive strike.

Secretary Kissinger: Based on my talks with Israeli leaders, I do not believe that any responsible Israeli leader operates on this assumption. They know that if a war starts it may start events of incalculable consequences.

I think the responsible people in Israel realize that improved American relations with Arab countries are also in the interests of Israel, because they enable us to be a moderating influence. The Israeli leaders with whom I am dealing are genuinely interested in moving toward peace. It is a very complicated problem because their margin of survival is so much narrower than ours that it is hard for Americans to understand some Israeli concerns. But I do not believe that any Israeli leader would deliberately engage in such a reckless course.

Q. Given the Arab oil weapon and how it affects Western support of Israel, can Israel expect to survive?

Secretary Kissinger: I think the survival of Israel is essential. The United States—and finally, in the last analysis, Europe—will not negotiate over the survival of Israel. This would be an act of such extraordinary cynicism that the world would be morally mortgaged if it ever happened. But it won't happen.

Q. In your list of pluses and minuses for the year, we have not touched on energy yet.

Secretary Kissinger: I think next to SALT, I would consider the most lasting achievement to be the energy policy that we developed. I think the Washington Energy Conference, the International Energy Agency, the emergency sharing program, and the measures which we are currently pursuing may be the beginning of a restructuring of relationships among the advanced industrial countries and eventually serve as a bridge to the producing countries.

Q. What sorts of structure are you referring to?

Secretary Kissinger: The structure that emerged in the immediate postwar period was essentially geared to military defense. Some of the difficulties that emerged in the sixties and early seventies, as a result of the growth of European unity and the emergence of Japan, were that the military organization and the political and economic organization had grown out of phase with each other. It has proved difficult to bring them back into phase by purely military arrangements. This is what I attempted to say in my "Year of Europe" speech,[7] which was a little premature, but many of whose
[7]*AFR, 1973*: 181-9.

basic principles are now being accepted. Now the problem of how the advanced industrialized nations can give effect to the realities of interdependence is one of the most serious problems of our time—in the fields of energy, of food, and of the whole nature of economic policies.

* * *

Q. Are French President Valéry Giscard d'Estaing and West German Chancellor Helmut Schmidt going to be more cooperative in these international structures? Are they really frightened of what is going on in Europe and the world?

Secretary Kissinger: Both countries are convinced that without a greater interaction of economic policies, an economic disaster for everybody is probable. And everybody realizes that they cannot deal with the economic policies on a purely national basis.

Secondly, there is a growing realization that the political demoralization of the industrialized countries must be arrested. This presupposes that governments can be seen to be coping with the problems that confront them. And that again will drive some more in the direction of interdependence. Right now it is really irrelevant to discuss what formula of consultation would be adequate, because the necessities that are imposed on us by the energy crisis would produce their own formula.

Q. Do you think the American public is prepared for the consequences of such a program?

Secretary Kissinger: All I can say is that it is the absolute duty of leaders to tell the people what they believe is necessary. You can make your life easier by not putting tough choices to the public. But then when the inevitable catastrophe occurs, you have lost not only credibility but legitimacy. So I don't think we really have any choice. I think the administration will have to tell the public what is needed, and I know that the President intends to do this. I think this is basically a healthy society, and I think there will be support.

Q. If all else should fail, would the United States consider military intervention in the Middle East to secure oil at prices that we can afford?

Secretary Kissinger: I don't think that would be a cause for military action.

Q. You don't think that the financial bankruptcy of the West would be a casus belli?

Secretary Kissinger: The financial bankruptcy of the West is avoidable by other means. We will find other solutions.

Q. That doesn't answer the question, with all due respect.

Secretary Kissinger: What we would do if there were no other way of avoiding financial bankruptcy and the whole collapse of the Western structure, I cannot now speculate. But I am convinced that we won't reach that point.

Q. What concrete steps might the United States take to induce the Third World countries to pursue a more realistic course in the United Nations?

Secretary Kissinger: I think the Third World countries have to accept the fact that they, too, live in an interdependent world. They cannot both insist on cooperation from the advanced industrial countries and conduct constant warfare—economic or political— against the advanced industrial countries. The spirit of cooperation must be mutual. There will be disagreement, of course. That is unavoidable. But if you have a group of 77 nations that automatically vote as a group, regardless of the merits of the issue, then the United Nations becomes a test of strength and the web of cooperation on which the development of all countries ultimately depends will be severely strained. In future sessions of the United Nations we will look more carefully at the degree of mutuality in the positions of the countries with which we are dealing.

Q. Can you conceive of a situation in which the United States might decide to temporarily suspend itself from the United Nations to protest the tyranny of the majority?

Secretary Kissinger: I can conceive that if an issue is too outrageously decided, that we would suspend our activities in relation to that issue. But it is hard to answer this question in the abstract.

Q. Our détente with China seems to have been stalled.

Secretary Kissinger: Well, this is the constant position of Newsweek magazine. But it is not our position. I believe that on the level of bilateral relations between the two countries we are essentially on course. I found that essentially confirmed by my last visit to the People's Republic of China. It is a relationship of practical necessity, in which two countries have made a decision to cooperate for limited objectives with each other. I don't accept the proposition that our policy is stalled.

Q. Do you think within the next year we might move toward a normalization of relations with Cuba?

Secretary Kissinger: We were prepared to accept a two-thirds vote of the Organization of American States at its recent meeting in Quito, and we were led to believe that this two-thirds vote had been assured. Suddenly we found ourselves in the position of being asked to produce votes for a resolution which we could not possibly sponsor, given the history of our involvement in the sanctions. There will be another occasion next year in a less structured meeting in Buenos Aires to discuss the Cuban issue, where the necessity of producing votes is less intense, and where one can then chart a course on a hemisphere basis more effectively.[8] I think there will be some evolution during the next year.

Q. How do you evaluate your own situation now at the end of the year?

Secretary Kissinger: During the period of President Nixon's crisis, I may have been overprotected from congressional criticism because many of the Senators and Congressmen instinctively were fearful of doing damage to our foreign policy and believed that they had to preserve one area of our national policy from partisan controversy. So it was inevitable that after that restraint was removed I would rejoin the human race and be exposed to the normal criticisms of Secretaries of State.

I have spent a great deal of time with Congress in the last few weeks, and I have the impression that there is a solid relationship. We worked out the Greek-Turkish aid problem, I think, in a cooperative spirit.[9] I really feel passionately that if we don't maintain our foreign policy on a bipartisan basis, we will be in the deepest trouble. Of course fundamental issues ought to be discussed, including fundamental foreign policy issues. But there are various areas in which there is or ought to be substantial agreement. And as far as I am concerned, I am going to go the absolute limit of maintaining it on a bipartisan basis.

Q. Do you think the pendulum has swung too far from one direction, from talk of "Super K," to an overwillingness now to criticize you?

Secretary Kissinger: There is no magic and there are no supermen in foreign policy. The difference between a good and a mediocre foreign policy is the accumulation of nuances. It is meticulousness; it is careful preparation. If a Secretary of State or anybody concerned with foreign policy goes out to hit a home run every time he goes up there, he is putting a burden on himself and a strain on the system.

[8]Cf. Chapter 28 at note 19.
[9]Cf. Chapter 35 at note 25.

Q. You have been quoted as saying that Americans like the lone cowboy, walking into town with his six-guns blazing.

Secretary Kissinger: I think any society needs individuals that symbolize what it stands for. It is difficult to run countries without great figures.

Q. Have we great figures today?

Secretary Kissinger: One of the problems of the modern age is that great figures are not so easy to come by.

Q. Why?

Secretary Kissinger: It may be that the process of reaching high office is so consuming that it leaves little occasion for reflection about what one does. Moreover, modern man doesn't like to stand alone. This is due largely to the impact of the media, in which everybody wants to check tomorrow morning's editorials.

Q. What role do you think the media plays in your conduct of foreign policy?

Secretary Kissinger: The negative aspect is that there is almost a daily pulling up of the trees to see whether the roots are still there. There is almost a daily necessity to explain each day's actions. And in the process there is a danger of losing the essence of a substantial foreign policy, which is the relationship of moves to each other and the overall design. In order to conduct a foreign policy you must be prepared to act alone for some period. You cannot get universal approbation at every step of the way. And so the media have a tendency to produce a congenital insecurity on the part of the top people.

On the positive side, the need of public explanation forces an awareness that would not otherwise exist. The more sophisticated of the journalists often have a reservoir of knowledge and continuity that is better than that of many of the top officials. I could name individuals who, on arms control, on Viet-Nam negotiations, could spot subtleties that many of the officials could not see.

So I think that the interplay is on the whole useful. But as one looks ahead, there are several dangers. There is a danger of a Caesaristic democracy in which the media are manipulated by the government. There is a danger of the media trying to substitute themselves for the government. And you know yourselves that there are fads, that sometimes there is excessive praise and then it swings back to excessive criticism.

Q. You are about to begin your seventh year in Washington. Is there a seven-year itch? Are you thinking of turning to something else?

Secretary Kissinger: I would like to think that the best time to leave is when you are not under pressure. I have been here long enough now so I don't have to continue being here to prove something to myself.

On the other hand, I am also engaged in a number of things from which it would be either difficult to dissociate or painful to dissociate. I would like to think that I will know when to get out. But very few people have mastered this. And most people are carried out instead of walking out. I have no itch to leave. But I also have no compulsion to stay.[10]

---

[10]Dr. Kissinger was relieved as Assistant to the President for National Security Affairs on Nov. 3, 1975, but continued as Secretary of State until the end of the Ford administration on Jan. 20, 1977.

APPENDIX:
PRINCIPAL SOURCES

(The abbreviation GPO refers to the U.S. Government Printing Office.)

"AFR": American Foreign Relations: A Documentary Record (New York: New York University Press, for the Council on Foreign Relations; annual vols., 1971-).

"Bulletin": The Department of State Bulletin (Washington: GPO, weekly). The official source for material of State Department origin appearing in this volume; contains also numerous documents originated by the White House and other governmental and international bodies. Most references are to vols. 70 (Jan.-June 1974), 71 (July-Dec. 1974), and 72 (Jan.-June 1975).

Digest of United States Practice in International Law, 1974, by Arthur W. Rovine (Department of State Publication 8809; Washington: GPO, 1975). The second volume of this new series documents U.S. foreign relations from a legal standpoint.

"Documents": Documents on American Foreign Relations (annual vols., 1939-70). Volumes prior to 1952 published by Princeton University Press (Princeton, N.J.) for the World Peace Foundation; subsequent volumes published for the Council on Foreign Relations by Harper & Brothers/Harper & Row (New York and Evanston) for 1952-66 and by Simon and Schuster (New York) for 1967-70. For continuation volumes see *"AFR"* above.

Documents on Disarmament (Washington: GPO; annual vols. for 1960-74). The most comprehensive collection of documents on disarmament and related topics, published annually by the U.S. Arms Control and Disarmament Agency.

Golan, Matti, *The Secret Conversations of Henry Kissinger: Step-by-Step Diplomacy in the Middle East* (New York: Quadrangle/The New York Times Book Co., 1976). Based largely on unpublished Israeli records.

IMF Survey (Washington: International Monetary Fund, semi-monthly). The official bulletin of the International Monetary Fund. Most references are to vol. 3 (1974).

International Economic Report of the President, Together with the Annual Report of the Council on International Economic

589

Policy, Transmitted to the Congress March 1975 (Washington: GPO, 1975). A detailed analysis of international economic developments involving the United States in 1974.

International Legal Materials: Current Documents (Washington: American Society of International Law, bimonthly). Includes numerous documents of non-U.S. origin.

Kalb, Marvin and Bernard, *Kissinger* (Boston: Little, Brown and Company, 1974). A detailed account of the diplomacy of the Nixon administration from 1969 until early 1974.

"Keesing's": Keesing's Contemporary Archives (Bristol: Keesing's Publications, Ltd., weekly). A detailed review of current developments throughout the world. Most references are to pp. 26261-26876 (1974).

NATO Review (Brussels: NATO Information Service, bimonthly). Contains documents and articles on NATO activities. Most references are to vols. 22 (1974) and 23 (1975).

The New York Times (New York: The New York Times Co., daily). Contains unofficial texts of numerous documents of international interest.

"'Nixon Report, 1973'": U.S. Foreign Policy for the 1970's: Shaping a Durable Peace—A Report to the Congress by Richard Nixon, President of the United States, May 3, 1973 (Washington: GPO, 1973, 234 p.). Text appears also in *Presidential Documents,* 9: 455-653 (1973); *Public Papers, 1973:* 348-518; and *Bulletin,* 68: 717-834 (1973).

OECD Observer (Paris: OECD Information Service, bimonthly). The official review of the Organization for Economic Cooperation and Development.

"Presidential Documents": Weekly Compilation of Presidential Documents (Washington: GPO, weekly). The official source for White House materials reproduced in this volume. Much of the contents is republished in *Public Papers,* and many texts relating to foreign affairs appear also in the Department of State *Bulletin* and/or *Documents on Disarmament.* Most references are to vol. 10 (1974).

Public Laws of the United States, cited in this volume by serial number and date of approval (e.g., Public Law 92-156, Nov. 17, 1971), are issued by the GPO in leaflet form (slip laws) and subsequently collected in the *United States Statutes at Large (Stat.).*

"Public Papers": Public Papers of the Presidents of the United States (Washington: GPO, annual). Contains definitive texts of most presidential statements and some other material of White House origin, most of it previously published in *Presidential Documents.* Separate volumes are devoted to the 1974 papers of Presidents Nixon and Ford.

"Senate Foreign Relations Committee History, 1973-4": U.S. Senate, 94th Cong., *Legislative History of the Committee on Foreign Relations . . . January 3, 1973-December 20, 1974* (S. Rept. 94-37; Washington: GPO, 1975, 196 p.). Records congressional action on treaties and legislation considered by the Foreign Relations Committee during the 93d Congress in 1973-4.

Sheehan, Edward R.F., *The Arabs, Israelis, and Kissinger: A Secret History of American Diplomacy in the Middle East* (New York: Reader's Digest Press/Thomas Y. Crowell Co., 1976). An expanded version of the author's article, "How Kissinger Did It: Step by Step in the Middle East," *Foreign Policy,* No. 22: 3-70 (Spring 1976).

Soviet News (London: Press Department of the Soviet Embassy, weekly). Includes unofficial texts or condensations of numerous Soviet documents.

Stern, Laurence, "Bitter Lessons: How We Failed in Cyprus," *Foreign Policy,* No. 19: 34-78 (Summer 1975).

"TIAS": U.S. Department of State, *Treaties and Other International Acts Series* (Washington: GPO, published irregularly). This series presents the definitive texts of treaties and agreements to which the United States is a party, as authenticated by the Department of State. Issued in leaflet form under their individual serial numbers, items in this series are later republished with consecutive pagination in the official *United States Treaties and Other International Agreements* (UST) series, likewise published by the GPO on behalf of the Department of State.

United Nations General Assembly, *Official Records* (New York: United Nations). Includes official texts of all resolutions adopted by the Assembly, as well as much related material.

United Nations Security Council, *Official Records* (New York: United Nations). Includes official texts of all resolutions adopted by the Security Council, with much related material.

The United States in World Affairs (annual vols., 1931-40, 1945-67, and 1970). The annual survey of U.S. foreign policy developments, published for the Council on Foreign Relations by Harper & Brothers/Harper and Row (New York and Evanston) from 1931 through 1966 and by Simon and Schuster (New York) for 1967 and 1970. Continued by the present series.

UN Monthly Chronicle (New York: United Nations Office of Public Information, monthly). The official account of current U.N. activities, with texts of major resolutions and other documents. Most references are to vols. 11 (1974) and 12 (1975).

U.S. Department of State, Bureau of Public Affairs, Office of Media Services, *Selected Documents: 3. U.S. International Energy Policy, October 1973-November 1975; 4. U.S. Policy in the Middle East, November 1974-February 1976* (Department of

State Publications 8842 and 8878; Washington: GPO, 1975-76). Selected reprints from the Department of State *Bulletin*.

U.S. House of Representatives, 94th Cong., 1st sess., Committee on International Relations, *Congress and Foreign Policy: 1974*, prepared by the Foreign Affairs Division, Congressional Research Service, Library of Congress (Committee print; Washington : GPO, 1975).

"U.S. Participation, 1974": *U.S. Participation in the UN: Report by the President to the Congress for the Year 1974* (Department of State Publication 8827; Washington: GPO, 1975, 478 p.). Published also as House Document 94-293, 94th Congress.

"USUN Press Releases": Press releases of the U.S. Mission to the United Nations, as reprinted in the Department of State *Bulletin*.

White, Theodore H., *Breach of Faith: The Fall of Richard Nixon* (New York: Atheneum Publishers, 1975).

Woodward, Bob, and Bernstein, Carl, *The Final Days* (New York: Simon and Schuster, 1976). A day-by-day account of events preceding the resignation of President Nixon.

Yearbook of the United Nations (New York: United Nations Office of Public Information). A comprehensive review of U.N. activities, issued annually.

INDEX

A

ABM Treaty (Treaty Between the United States of America and the Union of Soviet Socialist Republics on the Limitation of Anti-Ballistic Missile Systems, signed Moscow May 26, 1972), 209; Protocol to the Treaty (signed Moscow July 3, 1974), 226-8; Kissinger statement (same), 235-41; Nixon report (July 3), 242-8

Africa, 8, 391-407; and oil embargo, 6; famine in, 427

Agency for International Development (AID), 78

Algeria, 91, 402

Allende Gossens, Salvador, 4, 10, 49, 131, 447

Allon, Yigal, 164

Amerasinghe, H.S., 316

American Legion, Kissinger address (Miami, Aug. 20), 286-94

Andom, Aman, 390

Angola, 8, 390, 391

ANZUS Pact, 72-5; Council meeting (Wellington, Feb. 26-27), communiqué, 73-5

Arab Heads-of-State meeting (Rabat, Oct. 26-29), 410, 414-15

Arab-Israeli conflict, 1-2, 4, 7, 13-20, 34, 143, 153-64, 210, 340, 409-26, 542-3; Egypt-Israel Disengagement Agreement (signed Jan. 18): Nixon announcement (Jan. 17), 15-16; text, 17-18; Israeli-Syria Disengagement Agreement (signed Geneva May 31): Nixon remarks (May 29), 155-6; text, 157-61; Scali on U.N. Disengagement Observer Force (May 31), 161-3; U.N. Security Council resolution (same), 163-4; U.N. General Assembly resolution on PLO (Oct. 14), 409; Scali statement (same), 410; U.N. Security Council resolution extending UNEF (Oct. 23), 411-12; Scali statement (same), 412-14; Scali statement on Palestine (Nov. 21), 416-19; U.N. General Assembly resolution

B

C

D

E

F

G

L

M

N

R

DATE DUE

GAYLORD

PRINTED IN U.S.A.